D0938086

third edition

California
Criminal Codes

Cliff Roberson, LL.M., Ph.D.
Retired Professor
Department of Criminology
California State University–Fresno

WEST HILLS COLLEGE
LEMOORE LIBRARY/RC

THOMSON
✳
WADSWORTH

Australia • Canada • Mexico • Singapore • Spain • United Kingdom • United States

ISBN: 1-928916-24-4
Library of Congress Catalog Number: 2002113477

© 2004 Thomson Wadsworth, a part of The Thomson Corporation.
Thomson, the Star logo, and Wadsworth are trademarks used herein
under license.

ALL RIGHTS RESERVED. No part of this work covered by the
copyright hereon may be reproduced or used in any form or by any
means — graphic, electronic, or mechanical, including photocopying,
recording, taping, Web distribution, or information storage or retrieval
systems — without the written permission of the publisher.

Thomson Higher Education
10 Davis Drive
Belmont, CA 94002-3098
USA

For information about our products, contact us:
Thomson Learning Academic Resource Center
1-800-423-0563
http://www.wadsworth.com

For permission to use material from this text or product,
submit a request online at http://www.thomsonrights.com

Any additional questions about permissions can be
submitted by email to thomsonrights@thomson.com

Printed in the United States of America
10 9 8 7 6 5 4 3 2

WEST HILLS COLLEGE
LEMOORE LIBRARY/LRC

Brief Contents

Contents

Chapter 3

Capacity to Commit Crimes   55

Chapter 4

Inchoate Offenses   79

Chapter 5

Crimes against Property: Theft, Embezzlement, Forgery, and Check Offenses   91

Chapter 6

Crimes against Property: Burglary, Arson, and Vandalism   121

Chapter 7

Crimes against Persons: Assault, Battery, Mayhem, Robbery, Carjacking, and Extortion   151

Chapter 8

Crimes against Persons: Kidnapping, Homicide, Elder Abuse, and Stalking 177

Chapter 9

Sex Crimes 215

Chapter 10

Juvenile Law and Procedure 239

Chapter 11

Crimes against Children 259

Chapter 12

ABC Law and Controlled Substances 279

Chapter 13

General Criminal Statutes 297

Chapter 14

Crimes against the Justice System and Counterfeiting 321

Chapter 15

Weapons Violations 337

Chapter 16

Regulatory Crimes and Other Misconduct 361

Chapter 17

Computer Crimes 383

Preface

Preface

Whatever views one holds about the penal law, no one will question its importance in society. This is the law on which men place their ultimate reliance for protection against all the deepest injuries that human conduct can inflict on individuals and institutions.
Wechlser "The Challenge of a Model Penal Code"
65 Harvard Law Review, 1097

The study of criminal law should not be considered as the memorization of a set of rules, but as an examination of a cluster of ideas, principles, concepts, and questions about human conduct and the control of human behavior. Criminal law should be viewed as a flexible system of values and principles about which reasonable people can and do disagree (Katkin, *The Nature of Criminal Law*).

This text has several goals: (1) to provide a comprehensive review of California criminal law, (2) to aid students in understanding what conduct constitutes criminal behavior, and (3) to provide a reference for the administration of justice personnel. All texts are biased to some degree. In many cases, the biases are unintentional and are caused by the author's background and frame of reference. This text may have a "conviction" bias, in that it is written from a law enforcement viewpoint based on the author's background. Despite this bias, there is still included a deep respect for the individual rights of all persons.

Acknowledgements

Although I am listed as the sole author of this text and the prior editions, it would not have been possible without the help and assistance of many persons, including Cathy Anderson, Professors Max Futrell, John Burge, Ramond Hill, Robert Perez, Harvey Wallace, and Lance Parr.

In addition, a special thanks to Lynne Shoecraft and Laurie McGee for their assistance on the manuscript.

Cliff Roberson, LL.M., Ph.D.

1

Introduction to Criminal Law

No one is entirely useless. Even the worst of us can serve as horrible examples.
Anonymous

The first prison I ever saw had inscribed on it: "Cease to do evil: learn to do well." The inscription, however, was on the outside of the wall, and the prisoners could not read it.
George Bernard Shaw—On Imprisonment

1

1-1 Historical Development of Criminal Law

In primitive societies, the remedy for wrongs done to one's person or property was personal retaliation against the wrongdoer. Unlike modern society, early primitive societies encouraged personal retaliation. *Blood feuds* developed from the concept of personal retaliation. A blood feud occurred when the victim's family or tribe took revenge on the offender's family or tribe. Often, blood feuds escalated and resulted in continuing vendettas between families or tribes. In many cases, particularly for religious reasons, individuals were expected to avenge the death of a kinsman. The duty of retaliation was imposed universally on the victim or, in case of death, the nearest male relative.

To lessen costly and damaging vendettas, the custom of accepting money or property in place of blood vengeance developed. At first, the acceptance of payments instead of blood vengeance was not compulsory. The victim's family was still free to choose whatever form of vengeance they wished. Often the relative power of families or tribes decided whether payments or blood vengeance was used.

The acceptance of money or property as atonement for wrongs became known as "les salica" or "wergeld." This practice is still used in some Middle Eastern countries. The amount of payment was based on the victim's rank or position. The tradition of accepting money for property damage marked the beginning of the development of a system of criminal law.

One problem with the acceptance of payment as complete satisfaction for the wrong was the concept that punishment of an individual wrongdoer should also include some religious aspects. To many, crime was also a sin against the church and the state. Accordingly, the concept developed that punishment in the form of wergeld (payment to the victim) should also be supplemented with friedensgeld (payment to the church or later to the crown).

Fines and other forms of punishment replaced personal retaliation as tribal leaders began to exert their authority during the negotiations or proceedings concerning the damages caused and the wrongs committed. The wrongdoers were not required to attend the proceedings. If, however, they failed to follow the recommendations of the tribal leaders, they were banished or exiled, and thus considered "outlaws."

Since criminal law requires an element of public action against a wrongdoer, the banishment or pronouncement of outlawry was the first criminal punishment imposed by society. Many researchers today consider the development of this custom as the beginning of criminal law. Subsequent legal codes and punishments for different crimes have either stressed or refined the vengeance principle. The concept that a society expresses its vengeance within a system of rules was present in the ethics of primitive societies.

The two earliest codes involving criminal punishments were the Sumerian and Hammurabic Codes. The punishment phases of these codes contained the concept of personal vengeance. The listed punishments in the codes were harsh, and, in many cases, the victim or nearest relative was allowed personally to inflict punishment. Permitted punishments included mutilation, whipping, or forced labor. At first, the punishments were applied almost exclusively to slaves and bond servants and indicated a base or servile mentality toward those being punished. Later they were extended to all offenders.

The Code of Hammurabi was created under the rule of King Hammurabi, who was the ruler of the ancient city of Babylon about the year 2000 B.C. The Code was engraved on stone tablets and established property and other rights for the citizens of Babylon. The Code dealt with the problems involved with ownership of property, theft of property, sexual relationships, and violent personal crimes. It provided for a variety of corporal punishments and even death as punishment for a number of crimes.

When the Roman legions under Emperor Claudius conquered England, Roman law, customs, and language were forced upon the English people. The Roman law at that time was derived from the *Twelve Tables*, which were developed about 450 B.C. The tables were a collection of basic rules to govern family, religious, and economic life. Later the tables were replaced by the Justinian Code. The Justinian Code was developed under the rule of Emperor Justinian I between 527 and 565 B.C. The Code was actually three lengthy documents: (1) the Institutes, (2) the Digest, and (3) the Code.

Common law was the source of our criminal laws. It originated during the period of time that William the Conqueror was the King of England. At the time of the Norman conquest (1066), there was no uniform criminal law in England. Individual courts were dominated by sheriffs who enforced the village rules as they saw fit. To reduce the arbitrary aspects of the law, William decreed that all prosecutions would be conducted in the name of the king. At that time in England, very few people could read or write. The king, the judges, and the church authorities determined the elements and the scope of criminal offenses. In some cases, they even created new crimes. As William unified England as a nation, rather than isolated villages, the judges developed familiarity with the general customs, usages, and moral concepts of the people. Judicial decisions began to be based on these general customs, usages, and moral concepts. A similar practice exists in California today, where all cases are prosecuted in the name of the people of the state of California.

1-1a In the United States

By the 1600s, the primary criminal law of England was based on the mandatory rules of conduct that the judges laid down. These rules became the common law of England. Prior decisions were accepted as authoritative precepts and were applied to future cases. When the English settlers came to America in the 1600s, they brought with them the English common law. Except for a few modifications, English common law became the common law of the colonies. During the American Revolution, there was a great deal of hostility toward the English in America. This hostility extended to the common law system. Accordingly, most of the new states enacted new statutes defining criminal acts and establishing criminal procedures. The statutes, however, basically enacted into statutory law what was formerly English common law. All states, except Louisiana, can trace their legal systems to the English common law system. Louisiana, whose system was originally based on the French and Spanish code law concept, officially adopted the common law of England as the basis for their system in 1805.

1-1b In California

The California Penal Code (PC) was enacted in 1872. It took effect at noon on the first day of January 1873. Although the Code has been modified many times, it is still the basic criminal law for the state. Many aspects of California's current criminal law system are based on English common law. While the basic concepts and premises of common law were adopted by the state in 1873, several notable exceptions were made. Of particular note, PC 6 provides that no act or omission is criminal or punishable except as prescribed or authorized by code or statute. Accordingly, there are no common law crimes in California. In addition, as discussed later, PC 4 provides that the rule of common law that penal statutes are to be strictly construed does not apply.

1-1c Doctrine of Judicial Review

The doctrine of Judicial Review is an established principle of law in the United States. This doctrine provides the courts with the authority to review all statutory enactments, judicial decisions of lower courts, and administrative determinations within their jurisdiction. The principle, based on common law, was adopted by the U.S. Supreme Court in the famous case of *Marbury v. Madison*, 2 L. Ed. 60 (1803). In this case, Chief Justice John Marshall stated that it is the duty of the courts to say what the law is and that when the courts apply the rule to particular cases, they must of necessity expound and interpret that rule. The Chief Justice then stated that if two laws conflict, the courts must decide on the operation of each. Every state supreme court has accepted the principles set forth by the Chief Justice in *Marbury v. Madison.*

At the time that the decision was issued, Thomas Jefferson objected to the concept of judicial review. In a letter in 1820, Jefferson stated ". . . to consider the judges as the ultimate arbiters of all constitutional questions; a dangerous doctrine indeed, and one which would place us under the despotism of an oligarchy." He correctly pointed out that the concept of judicial review is not contained in our federal Constitution.

1-2 Function of Criminal Law in a Democratic Society

- What is a crime?
- Why do we need criminal laws?
- What purposes do criminal laws serve in our society?

Laws are principles that are created by our government for the orderly functioning of our society. Criminal law is an attempt by society to eliminate or control human behavior. It establishes standards of conduct and punishes those who are convicted of violating those standards. The greatest freedom for all is only possible through an organized society with a system of criminal law that protects our basic rights. A crime is an act committed or omitted in violation of a law forbidding or commanding it, and to which is annexed, upon conviction, a criminal punishment. Note: For the criminal law to work, the great majority of people must have confidence that it is fair and just. Does our system have that confidence?

Crime is specific conduct that is prohibited on the grounds that the conduct is against public policy and is injurious to the public. The injury to the public may involve injury or death to human life, destruction to property, or interference with governmental functions, private property, or other valued interests. At the very least, criminal conduct is a violation of the peace and dignity of the people of the state. The primary purpose of criminal law is to protect society. It performs this purpose by defining certain conduct as socially intolerable and defining other conduct as within limits of what is at least legally acceptable. Some conduct that is legally acceptable may not be socially acceptable.

A U.S. district court expressed the objective and purpose of criminal law in *U.S. v. Watson* (146 F. Supp. 258) as follows:

> The object of the criminal law is to protect the public against depredations of a criminal. On the other hand, its purpose is also to prevent the conviction of the innocent, or the conviction of a person whose guilt is not established beyond a reasonable doubt. The court must balance all these aims at the trial.

One of the functions of criminal law is to punish persons who have committed criminal offenses. The chief justice of the Pennsylvania Supreme Court discussed why punishment is considered necessary in 1930 (*Commonwealth v. Ritter*, 13 D & C 285). He stated:

> Generally speaking, there have been advanced four theories as the basis upon which society should act in imposing penalties upon those who violate its laws. These are: (1) To bring about the reformation of the evildoer; (2) to effect retribution or revenge upon him; (3) to restrain him physically, so as to make it impossible for him to commit further crimes; and (4) to deter others from similarly violating the law.

U.S. Criminal Code Reform Act of 1973 (93d Cong., 1st Sess., March 27, 1973)

The general purposes of this title are:

(a) to define conduct which indefensibly causes or threatens harm to those individuals or public interests for which federal protection is appropriate
(b) to prescribe sanctions for engaging in such conduct which will: (1) assure just punishment for such conduct; (2) deter such conduct; (3) protect the public from persons who engage in such conduct; and (4) promote the correction and rehabilitation of persons who would engage in such conduct . . .

Many scholarly works examine the purpose of criminal law. The most basic reasons attributed by most of the works are to:

1. Provide a framework of behavior that can be repeatedly applied with sufficient uniformity that the desired end will be continuously reproduced within tolerated limits (B. E. Witkin, *California Crimes and Criminal Procedure* [St. Paul, MN: West Group, 1985], Sec. 1)
2. Deter criminal behavior
3. Award good behavior

Criminal behavior is deterred and good behavior is awarded when bad behavior is punished. Persons who have not committed offenses for which they could be punished are awarded by not being punished (passive rewards). If no behavior was punished, then nonpunishment would not be a reward.

California Penal Code 15—Definition of Crime or Public Offense

A crime or public offense is an act committed or omitted in violation of a law forbidding or commanding it, and to which is annexed, upon conviction, either of the following punishments:

- Death
- Imprisonment
- Fine

- Removal from office
- Disqualification to hold and enjoy any office of honor, trust, or profit in this state

California Penal Code 16

Crimes and public offenses include:

- Felonies
- Misdemeanors
- Infractions

Discussion

While the word *crime* may mean every violation of a public law, the statutory definition is much narrower (17 Cal. Jr. 3d [Rev.]1). To set forth a crime, a statute must first describe the conduct that is prohibited and, second, provide a punishment for violation of the act. The Penal Code includes two types of statutes: (1) enabling statutes and (2) criminal statutes. If the statute does not attach a punishment for the violation of it, it is an enabling statute. The enabling statutes are considered explanatory in nature.

A prohibited act is not a crime unless the statute provides a punishment (*People v. McNulty,* 93 Cal. 427). If the statute, however, states that the prohibited act shall be punished as a felony, misdemeanor, or infraction, but does not include a specific penalty provision for its violation, then the general punishment section of the Penal Code applies *(Re Application of Gohike,* 72 Cal. App. 536). In California, the words *crime* and *public offense* are considered synonymous (*Burks v. United States,* 287 F. 2d 117).

If the statute prohibits a certain act or omission and provides a punishment for the violation, it is a crime. There is no requirement that the statute expressly declare the act or omission of a crime. The infliction of harm to someone or damage to property is not required unless expressly declared to be an element by the legislation (*People v. Morrison,* 54 Cal. App. 469).

All crimes are prosecuted in the state courts in the name of "The People of the State of California" and by written complaint (PC 740). Crimes are considered as crimes against the people of the state of California, in general, and not against persons individually. Accordingly, individual persons (except officials in the performance of their duties) have no official voice in making decisions on whether or not to prosecute for the violation of a criminal offense (*People v. Weber,* 84 Cal. App. 2d 126).

1-4 Classification of Crimes

Crimes are classified as *mala in se* or *mala prohibita* crimes. Other classifications include crimes involving moral turpitude, infamous crimes, and high crimes.

1-4a Mala in Se and Mala Prohibita Crimes

An act is said to be *malum in se* when it is inherently and essentially evil, that is, immoral in its nature and injurious in its consequences, without regard to the fact that it violates the law (*State v. Shedoudy,* 45 N.M. 516).

> In contrast, the following definition describes mala prohibitum: A wrong prohibited; a thing which is wrong because it is prohibited; an act which is not inherently immoral, but becomes so because its commission is expressly forbidden by positive law.
> (*Black's Law Dictionary*)

At common law, crimes were classified as either *mala in se* or *mala prohibita. Mala in se* crimes involve conduct that is inherently and essentially wrong and injurious. Crimes such as murder, rape, incest, arson, and so on are considered *mala in se* crimes. *Mala prohibita* crimes are wrong only because they violate legislative acts, not because they are inherently and essentially wrong. Most *mala prohibita* crimes involve traffic, social, and economic behavior. Criminal violation of a rent control statute is an example of a *mala prohibita* crime.

Moral turpitude is a classification used to describe acts that are contrary to justice, honesty, modesty, or good morals (*Marsh v. State Bar of California,* 210 Cal. 303). It has also been defined as an act of baseless, vileness, or depravity in the private and social duties that one person owes to others or to society in general (*Traders & General Ins. Co. v. Russell,* 221 S.W. 2d 1079). Crimes that suggest a lack of honesty or that imply immoral conduct are considered as crimes involving moral turpitude. For example, perjury, theft, and rape are considered as crimes involving moral turpitude. Crimes involving moral turpitude may also be considered as mala in se crimes.

1-4b Moral Turpitude

Conviction of a crime involving moral turpitude may disqualify a person from holding a professional qualification such as attorney-at-law (*Re Application of Westenberg,* 167 Cal. 309). The conviction of an attempt to commit a crime involving moral turpitude has the same disqualifications attached to it as a conviction of the actual offense (*Re O'Connell,* 184 Cal. 584).

Although various crimes are referred to as *infamous crimes* in the California Constitution and statutes, there is no statutory definition of an infamous crime. An infamous crime is one that entails infamy upon the one who committed the crime (*Butler v. Wentworth,* 24 Atlantic 456). At common law, the term *infamous* was applied to those crimes upon the conviction of which the person became incompetent to testify as a witness on the theory that they were so depraved as to be unworthy of credit (*Black's Law Dictionary*). The character of the crime did not determine whether or not it was an infamous crime, but the punishment that may be imposed for conviction of it (*Brede v. Powers,* 263 U.S. 4).

1-4c Infamous Crimes

Crimen falsi is a phrase used to describe those crimes that involve the element of falsehood and includes everything that has a tendency to injuriously affect the administration of justice by the introduction of falsehood and fraud (*Black's Law Dictionary*). The phrase is also used as a general designation of a class of offenses involving fraud and deceit. *Crimen falsi* crimes include forgery, perjury, using false weights or measurements, and counterfeiting.

1-4d Crimen Falsi

High crimes is a phrase used to describe those crimes that, if a person is convicted of them, will disqualify the offender from holding public office or make the person incompetent to act as a juror (Cal. Code of Civ. Pro. 199[b]). High crimes include bribery, perjury, forgery, and malfeasance in office by a public official.

1-4e High Crimes

Penal Code 17—Felony and Misdemeanor Defined

(a) A felony is a crime which is punishable with death or by imprisonment in the state prison. Every other crime or public offense is a misdemeanor except those offenses that are classified as infractions.
(b) When a crime is punishable, in the discretion of the court, by imprisonment in the state prison or by fine or imprisonment in the county jail, it is a misdemeanor for all purposes under the following circumstances:

(1) After a judgment imposing a punishment other than imprisonment in the state prison.

(2) When the court, upon committing the defendant to the Youth Authority, designates the offense to be a misdemeanor.

(3) When the court grants probation to a defendant without imposition of sentence and at the time of granting probation, or on application of the defendant or probation officer thereafter, the court declares the offense to be a misdemeanor.

(4) When the prosecuting attorney files in a court having jurisdiction over misdemeanor offenses a complaint specifying that the offense is a misdemeanor, unless the defendant at the time of his or her arraignment or plea objects to the offense being made a misdemeanor, in which event the complaint shall be amended to charge the felony and the case shall proceed on the felony complaint.

(5) When, at or before the preliminary examination or prior to filing an order pursuant to Section 872, the magistrate determines that the offense is a misdemeanor, in which event the case shall proceed as if the defendant had been arraigned on a misdemeanor complaint.

(c) When a defendant is committed to the Youth Authority for a crime punishable, in the discretion of the court, by imprisonment in the state prison or by fine or imprisonment in the county jail, the offense shall, upon the discharge of the defendant from the Youth Authority, thereafter be deemed a misdemeanor for all purposes.

(d) A violation of any code section listed in Section 19.8 is an infraction subject to the procedures described in Sections 19.6 and 19.7 when:

(1) The prosecutor files a complaint charging the offense as an infraction unless the defendant, at the time he or she is arraigned, after being informed of his or her rights, elects to have the case proceed as a misdemeanor, or;

(2) The court, with the consent of the defendant, determines that the offense is an infraction in which event the case shall proceed as if the defendant had been arraigned on an infraction complaint.

Discussion

Crimes and public offenses are classified as felonies, misdemeanors, or infractions. The highest and most serious crime in California is a felony. A *felony* is any crime that is punishable by death or imprisonment in a state prison. Next, in terms of seriousness, is a misdemeanor. A *misdemeanor* is a crime that is punishable by fine and/or imprisonment in a county jail for not more than one year. The lowest type of crime is an infraction. An *infraction* is a crime that is punishable only by a fine. (Note: A person charged only with an infraction is not entitled to a jury trial.) If a statute provides for imprisonment but does not specify the place of confinement, the crime is a misdemeanor (*Union Ice Co. v. Rose,* 11 Cal. App. 357).

The label that the legislature affixes to a crime does not determine its classification. The classification is based on the nature of the offense and its authorized punishment. In one case, the statute deemed the act a felony, but only authorized punishment in the county jail and/or a fine. The court held that the offense was a misdemeanor, not a felony (*People v. Sacramento Brothers' Butchers' Protective Assoc.,* 12 Cal. App. 471).

When determining whether the accused has been convicted of a felony, PC 17, defining felonies and misdemeanors, is not applicable to crimes committed in other jurisdictions (other states or in federal court), but determination of whether crime committed outside the state is a felony or misdemeanor depends on the law of jurisdiction in which the offense was committed (*People v. Theodore,* 121 Cal. App. 2d 17).

1-4f Wobblers

In most cases, it is not the punishment awarded by a court that determines whether or not a crime is a felony, misdemeanor, or infraction but the punishment that could have been imposed. Some offenses, however, are considered wobblers. *Wobblers* are offenses that are either felonies or misdemeanors depending on the sentences awarded at court or action by the court after conviction. Wobblers are treated as felonies until sentencing time, unless the crimes are formally charged as misdemeanors.

For example, PC 524 provides that an attempted extortion may be punished by imprisonment in the county jail or in a state prison. Accordingly, it is a wobbler. If the accused on conviction receives a jail term, it is a misdemeanor conviction. If he or she receives a prison term, it is a felony conviction. Under California law, a crime that is alternatively a felony or a misdemeanor is regarded as a felony for every purpose until the judgment (*U.S. v. Robinson,* 967 F. 2d 287). Note: The district attorney can charge it as a felony or misdemeanor. If the DA charges the offense as a felony offense, the judge may reduce it to a misdemeanor offense at the preliminary hearing.

1-5 Punishment of Crimes

Penal Code 12—Duty of Court to Pass Sentence and Determine and Impose Punishment

The several sections of this Code which declare certain crimes to be punishable as therein mentioned devolve a duty upon the Court authorized to pass sentence, to determine and impose the punishment prescribed.

Penal Code 13—Punishment to Be Determined by Authorized Court

Whenever the punishment for a crime is left undetermined between certain limits, the punishment to be inflicted in a particular case must be determined by the court authorized to pass sentence, within such limits as may be prescribed by this Code.

Penal Code 18—Punishment for Felony

Except in cases where a different punishment is prescribed by any law of this state, every offense declared to be a felony, or to be punishable by imprisonment in a state prison, is punishable by imprisonment in any of the state's prisons for 16 months, or two or three years; provided, however, every offense which is prescribed by any law of the state to be a felony punishable by imprisonment in any of the state prisons or by a fine, but without an alternate sentence to the county jail, may be punishable by imprisonment in the county jail not exceeding one year or by a fine, or by both.

Penal Code 19—Punishment for Misdemeanor

Except in cases where a different punishment is prescribed by any law of this state, every offense declared to be a misdemeanor is punishable by imprisonment in the county jail not exceeding six months, or by fine not exceeding one thousand dollars ($1,000), or by both.

Penal Code 19.2—Confinement in County Jail Not to Exceed One Year

In no case shall any person sentenced to confinement in a county or city jail, or in a county or joint county penal farm, road camp, work camp, or other county adult detention facility, or committed to the sheriff for placement in any county adult detention facility, on conviction of a misdemeanor, or as a condition of probation upon conviction of either a felony or a misdemeanor, or upon commitment for civil contempt, or upon default in the payment of a fine upon conviction of either a felony or a misdemeanor, or for any reason except upon conviction of more than one offense when consecutive sentences have been imposed, be committed for a period in excess of one year; provided, however, that the time allowed on parole shall not be considered as a part of the period of confinement.

Penal Code 19.4—Public Offense with No Prescribed Penalty Is Misdemeanor

When an act or omission is declared by a statute to be a public offense and no penalty for the offense is prescribed in any statute, the act or omission is punishable as a misdemeanor.

Penal Code 19.6—Infractions Not Punishable by Imprisonment

An infraction is not punishable by imprisonment. A person charged with an infraction shall not be entitled to a trial by jury. A person charged with an infraction shall not be entitled to have the public defender or other counsel appointed at public expense to represent him or her unless he or she is arrested and not released on his or her written promise to appear, his or her own recognizance, or a deposit of bail.

Discussion

When an act or omission is declared by a statute to be a crime and punishment is provided for, but no specific penalty is prescribed in the statute, then the general punishment statutes prevail. In California, even in jury trials, the judge has the duty to impose sentences.

In capital cases with a jury, however, before the death penalty can be imposed, the jury must find whether special circumstances exist, and, if so, whether they outweigh the mitigating circumstances. There are 19 special circumstances listed in PC 190.2 that permit the imposition of the death penalty. They are discussed in Chapter 8. For example, if the accused with no prior criminal record intentionally kills his girlfriend by administering poison, the jury must decide that the special circumstances (death by poisoning) outweigh the mitigating circumstances (no prior criminal record) before the death penalty may be imposed.

1-5a Concurrent or Consecutive Sentences

When the accused is convicted of two or more crimes, the judge is required to determine whether the sentences will be served concurrently or consecutively. Sentences that are served concurrently are served at the same time. Consecutive sentences are served one at a time, one following the other. For example, the defendant is convicted of two crimes: arson and robbery. If he received two years for each offense and the sentences are served concurrently, he will serve a maximum of two years. If the sentences run consecutively, he will first serve one sentence, then the other (e.g., two years plus two years for a maximum of four years). If the accused has pending confinement from a previous court, the court should also indicate whether the present sentence will be served concurrently or consecutively with the sentence given in the prior court.

The maximum time that an accused may serve in a county jail on the conviction of one offense is one year. If, however, the accused is convicted of more than one offense and the sentences are not served concurrently, the one-year maximum time does not apply, and he or she may serve one year for each offense.

1-5b Maximum Jail Term

Indeterminate sentencing refers to those situations where the court does not fix a term of imprisonment as punishment. The sentence of imprisonment that the court awards, therefore, is an indeterminate one. In 1917, California adopted the Indeterminate Sentencing Act. The act divested the trial judge of the authority to fix the term of imprisonment for offenses punishable by imprisonment in a state prison. The power to fix the length of sentence was given to the Adult Authority, an administrative agency. The Indeterminate Sentencing Act was repealed in 1977 and applies now only to persons serving sentences for crimes committed prior to July 1, 1977.

1-5c Indeterminate Sentencing

For offenses committed on or after July 1, 1977, the Determinate Sentencing Act (PC 1170-1170.95) applies. Under this act, if the court gives a sentence that includes confinement in a state prison, the court must specify the term of imprisonment. The act also requires the judge, under most circumstances, to pronounce sentence within 28 days after a guilty verdict or the acceptance of a guilty plea (PC 1191). (The accused may, and often does, waive this 28-day requirement.)

1-5d Determinate Sentencing

If the statute specifies three possible terms of punishment, the court shall order imposition of the middle term (often referred to as midterm), unless there are circumstances in aggravation or mitigation of the crime (PC 1170). For example, the state penalty for extortion is imprisonment in a state prison for two, three, or four years (PC 520). The midterm is three years. If this is the first offense, the court will probably impose only the two-year term (the mitigated term). If the offense is an aggravated one, the court may impose the four-year term (the aggravated term). Aggravated factors include harm or hardship imposed on the victim, prior record of the accused, and so on.

The general objectives of punishment in California under the Determinate Sentencing Act are set forth in California Rules of Court, Rule 410.

Rule 410—General Objectives in Sentencing

General objectives of sentencing include:

a) Protecting society
b) Punishing the defendant
c) Encouraging the defendant to lead a law abiding life in the future and deterring him from future offenses
d) Deterring others from criminal conduct by demonstrating its consequences
e) Preventing the defendant from committing new crimes by isolating him for the period of incarceration
f) Securing restitution for the victims of crime
g) Achieving uniformity in sentencing

Because, in some instances, these objectives may suggest inconsistent dispositions, the sentencing judge shall consider which objectives are of primary importance in the particular case.

The sentencing judge should be guided by statutory statements of policy, the criteria in these rules, and the facts and circumstances of the case.

1-5e Prior Convictions

Penal Code 666—Petit Theft with Prior Theft Conviction

Every person who, having been convicted of petit theft, grand theft, auto theft under Section 10851 of the Vehicle Code, burglary, carjacking, robbery, or a felony violation of Section 496 and having served a term therefor in any penal institution or having been imprisoned therein as a condition of probation for that offense, is subsequently convicted of petit theft, then the person convicted of that subsequent offense is punishable by imprisonment in the county jail not exceeding one year, or in the state prison.

Penal Code 666.5—Grand Theft or Felony Vehicle Theft; Penalty Enhancements for Certain Prior Offenses

(a) Every person who, having been previously convicted of a felony violation of Section 10851 of the Vehicle Code, or felony grand theft involving an automobile in violation of subdivision (d) of Section 487 or former subdivision (3) of Section 487, as that section read prior to being amended by Section 4 of Chapter 1125 of the Statutes of 1993, or felony grand theft involving a motor vehicle, as defined in Section 415 of the Vehicle Code, any trailer, as defined in Section 630 of the Vehicle Code, any special construction equipment, as defined in Section 565 of the Vehicle Code, or any vessel, as defined in Section 21 of the Harbors and Navigation Code in violation of former Section 487h, or a felony violation of Section 496d regardless of whether or not the person actually served a prior prison term for those offenses, is subsequently convicted of any of these offenses shall be punished by imprisonment in the state prison for two, three, or four years, or a fine of ten thousand dollars ($10,000), or both the fine and the imprisonment.

(b) For the purposes of this section, the terms "special construction equipment" and "vessel" are limited to motorized vehicles and vessels.

(c) [Omitted.]

Penal Code 667—Habitual Criminals Defined; Penalty Enhancements

(a) (1) In compliance with subdivision (b) of Section 1385, any person convicted of a serious felony who previously has been convicted of a serious felony in this state or of any offense committed in another jurisdiction which includes all of the elements of any serious felony, shall receive, in addition to the sentence imposed by the court for the present offense, a five-year enhancement for each such prior conviction on charges brought and tried separately. The terms of the present offense and each enhancement shall run consecutively.

(2) This subdivision shall not be applied when the punishment imposed under other provisions of law would result in a longer term of imprisonment. There is no requirement of prior incarceration or commitment for this subdivision to apply.

(3) The Legislature may increase the length of the enhancement of sentence

provided in this subdivision by a statute passed by majority vote of each house thereof.

(4) As used in this subdivision, "serious felony" means a serious felony listed in subdivision (c) of Section 1192.7.

(5) This subdivision shall not apply to a person convicted of selling, furnishing, administering, or giving, or offering to sell, furnish, administer, or give to a minor any methamphetamine-related drug or any precursors of methamphetamine unless the prior conviction was for a serious felony described in subparagraph (24) of subdivision (c) of Section 1192.7.

(b) It is the intent of the Legislature in enacting subdivisions (b) to (i), inclusive, to ensure longer prison sentences and greater punishment for those who commit a felony and have been previously convicted of serious and/or violent felony offenses.

(c) Notwithstanding any other law, if a defendant has been convicted of a felony and it has been pled and proved that the defendant has one or more prior felony convictions as defined in subdivision (d), the court shall adhere to each of the following:

(1) There shall not be an aggregate term limitation for purposes of consecutive sentencing for any subsequent felony conviction.

(2) Probation for the current offense shall not be granted, nor shall execution or imposition of the sentence be suspended for any prior offense.

(3) The length of time between the prior felony conviction and the current felony conviction shall not affect the imposition of sentence.

(4) There shall not be a commitment to any other facility other than the state prison. Diversion shall not be granted nor shall the defendant be eligible for commitment to the California Rehabilitation Center as provided in Article 2 (commencing with Section 3050) of Chapter 1 of Division 3 of the Welfare and Institutions Code.

(5) The total amount of credits awarded pursuant to Article 2.5 (commencing with Section 2930) of Chapter 7 of Title 1 of Part 3 shall not exceed one-fifth of the total term of imprisonment imposed and shall not accrue until the defendant is physically placed in the state prison.

(6) If there is a current conviction for more than one felony count not committed on the same occasion, and not arising from the same set of operative facts, the court shall sentence the defendant consecutively on each count pursuant to subdivision (e).

(7) If there is a current conviction for more than one serious or violent felony as described in paragraph (6), the court shall impose the sentence for each conviction consecutive to the sentence for any other conviction for which the defendant may be consecutively sentenced in the manner prescribed by law.

(8) Any sentence imposed pursuant to subdivision (e) will be imposed consecutive to any other sentence which the defendant is already serving, unless otherwise provided by law.

(d) Notwithstanding any other law and for the purposes of subdivisions (b) to (i), inclusive, a prior conviction of a felony shall be defined as:

(1) Any offense defined in subdivision (c) of Section 667.5 as a violent

felony or any offense defined in subdivision (c) of Section 1192.7 as a serious felony in this state. The determination of whether a prior conviction is a prior felony conviction for purposes of subdivisions (b) to (i), inclusive, shall be made upon the date of that prior conviction and is not affected by the sentence imposed unless the sentence automatically, upon the initial sentencing, converts the felony to a misdemeanor. None of the following dispositions shall affect the determination that a prior conviction is a prior felony for purposes of subdivisions (b) to (i), inclusive:

(A) The suspension of imposition of judgment or sentence.
(B) The stay of execution of sentence.
(C) The commitment to the State Department of Health Services as a mentally disordered sex offender following a conviction of a felony.
(D) The commitment to the California Rehabilitation Center or any other facility whose function is rehabilitative diversion from the state prison.

(2) A conviction in another jurisdiction for an offense that, if committed in California, is punishable by imprisonment in the state prison. A prior conviction of a particular felony shall include a conviction in another jurisdiction for an offense that includes all of the elements of the particular felony as defined in subdivision (c) of Section 667.5 or subdivision (c) of Section 1192.7.

(3) A prior juvenile adjudication shall constitute a prior felony conviction for purposes of sentence enhancement if:

(A) The juvenile was 16 years of age or older at the time he or she committed the prior offense.
(B) The prior offense is listed in subdivision (b) of Section 707 of the Welfare and Institutions Code or described in paragraph (1) or (2) as a felony.
(C) The juvenile was found to be a fit and proper subject to be dealt with under the juvenile court law.
(D) The juvenile was adjudged a ward of the juvenile court within the meaning of Section 602 of the Welfare and Institutions Code because the person committed an offense listed in subdivision (b) of Section 707 of the Welfare and Institutions Code.
(E) For purposes of subdivisions (b) to (i), inclusive, and in addition to any other enhancement or punishment provisions which may apply, the following shall apply where a defendant has a prior felony conviction:

(e) (1) If a defendant has one prior felony conviction that has been pled and proved, the determinate term or minimum term for an indeterminate term shall be twice the term otherwise provided as punishment for the current felony conviction.

(2) (A) If a defendant has two or more prior felony convictions as defined in subdivision (d) that have been pled and proved, the term for the current felony conviction shall be an indeterminate term of life imprisonment with a minimum term of the indeterminate sentence calculated as the greater of:

(i) Three times the term otherwise provided as punishment for each current felony conviction subsequent to the two or more prior felony convictions.

       (ii) Imprisonment in the state prison for 25 years.

       (iii) The term determined by the court pursuant to Section 1170 for the underlying conviction, including any enhancement applicable under Chapter 4.5 (commencing with Section 1170) of Title 7 of Part 2, or any period prescribed by Section 190 or 3046.

   (B) The indeterminate term described in subparagraph (A) shall be served consecutive to any other term of imprisonment for which a consecutive term may be imposed by law. Any other term imposed subsequent to any indeterminate term described in subparagraph (A) shall not be merged therein but shall commence at the time the person would otherwise have been released from prison.

(f)

   (1) Notwithstanding any other law, subdivisions (b) to (i), inclusive, shall be applied in every case in which a defendant has a prior felony conviction as defined in subdivision (d). The prosecuting attorney shall plead and prove each prior felony conviction except as provided in paragraph (2).

   (2) The prosecuting attorney may move to dismiss or strike a prior felony conviction allegation in the furtherance of justice pursuant to Section 1385, or if there is insufficient evidence to prove the prior conviction. If upon the satisfaction of the court that there is insufficient evidence to prove the prior felony conviction, the court may dismiss or strike the allegation.

(g) Prior felony convictions shall not be used in plea bargaining as defined in subdivision (b) of Section 1192.7. The prosecution shall plead and prove all known prior felony convictions and shall not enter into any agreement to strike or seek the dismissal of any prior felony conviction allegation except as provided in paragraph (2) of subdivision (f).

(h) All references to existing statutes in subdivisions (c) to (g), inclusive, are to statutes as they existed on June 30, 1993.

(i) If any provision of subdivisions (b) to (h), inclusive, or the application thereof to any person or circumstance is held invalid, that invalidity shall not affect other provisions or applications of those subdivisions which can be given effect without the invalid provision or application, and to this end the provisions of those subdivisions are severable.

(j) The provisions of this section shall not be amended by the Legislature except by statute passed in each house by rollcall vote entered in the journal, two-thirds of the membership concurring, or by a statute that becomes effective only when approved by the electors.

Penal Code 667.5

Enhancement of prison terms for new offenses because of prior prison terms shall be imposed as follows:

(a) Where one of the new offenses is one of the violent felonies specified in subdivision (c), in addition and consecutive to any other prison terms therefor, the court shall impose a three-year term for each prior separate prison term served by the defendant where the prior offense was one of the violent felonies specified in subdivision (c). However, no additional term shall be imposed under this subdivision for any prison term served prior to a period of 10 years in which the defendant remained free of both prison custody and the commission of an offense which results in a felony conviction.

(b) Except where subdivision (a) applies, where the new offense is any felony for which a prison sentence is imposed, in addition and consecutive to any other prison terms therefor, the court shall impose a one-year term for each prior separate prison term served for any felony; provided that no additional term shall be imposed under this subdivision for any prison term served prior to a period of five years in which the defendant remained free of both prison custody and the commission of an offense which results in a felony conviction.

(c) For the purpose of this section, "violent felony" shall mean any of the following:

    (1) Murder or voluntary manslaughter.

    (2) Mayhem.

    (3) Rape as defined in paragraph (2) or (6) of subdivision (a) of Section 261 or paragraph (1) or (4) of subdivision (a) of Section 262.

    (4) Sodomy by force, violence, duress, menace, or fear of immediate and unlawful bodily injury on the victim or another person.

    (5) Oral copulation by force, violence, duress, menace, or fear of immediate and unlawful bodily injury on the victim or another person.

    (6) Lewd acts on a child under the age of 14 years as defined in Section 288.

    (7) Any felony punishable by death or imprisonment in the state prison for life.

    (8) Any felony in which the defendant inflicts great bodily injury on any person other than an accomplice which has been charged and proved as provided for in Section 12022.7 or 12022.9 on or after July 1, 1977, or as specified prior to July 1, 1977, in Sections 213, 264, and 461, or any felony in which the defendant uses a firearm which use has been charged and proved as provided in Section 12022.5 or 12022.55.

    (9) Any robbery perpetrated in an inhabited dwelling house, vessel, as defined in Section 21 of the Harbors and Navigation Code, which is inhabited and designed for habitation, an inhabited floating home as defined in subdivision (d) of Section 18075.55 of the Health and Safety Code, an inhabited trailer coach, as defined in the Vehicle Code, or in the inhabited portion of any other building, wherein it is charged and proved that the defendant personally used a deadly or dangerous weapon, as provided in subdivision (b) of Section 12022, in the commission of that robbery.

    (10) Arson, in violation of subdivision (a) of Section 451.

    (11) The offense defined in subdivision (a) of Section 289 where the act is accomplished against the victim's will by force, violence, duress, menace, or fear of immediate and unlawful bodily injury on the victim or another person.

    (12) Attempted murder.

    (13) A violation of Section 12308.

    (14) Kidnapping.

    (15) Assault with the intent to commit mayhem, rape, sodomy, or oral copulation in violation of Section 220.

    (16) Continuous sexual abuse of a child, in violation of Section 288.5.

    (17) Carjacking, as defined in subdivision (a) of Section 215, if it is charged and proved that the defendant personally used a dangerous or deadly weapon as provided in subdivision (b) of Section 12022 in the commission of the carjacking.

The Legislature finds and declares that these specified crimes merit special consideration when imposing a sentence to display society's condemnation for these extraordinary crimes of violence against the person.

(d) For the purposes of this section, the defendant shall be deemed to remain in prison custody for an offense until the official discharge from custody or until release on parole, whichever first occurs, including any time during which the defendant remains subject to reimprisonment for escape from custody or is reimprisoned on revocation of parole. The additional penalties provided for prior prison terms shall not be imposed unless they are charged and admitted or found true in the action for the new offense.

(e) The additional penalties provided for prior prison terms shall not be imposed for any felony for which the defendant did not serve a prior separate term in state prison.

(f) A prior conviction of a felony shall include a conviction in another jurisdiction for an offense which, if committed in California, is punishable by imprisonment in the state prison if the defendant served one year or more in prison for the offense in the other jurisdiction. A prior conviction of a particular felony shall include a conviction in another jurisdiction for an offense which includes all of the elements of the particular felony as defined under California law if the defendant served one year or more in prison for the offense in the other jurisdiction.

(g) A prior separate prison term for the purposes of this section shall mean a continuous completed period of prison incarceration imposed for the particular offense alone or in combination with concurrent or consecutive sentences for other crimes, including any reimprisonment on revocation of parole which is not accompanied by a new commitment to prison, and including any reimprisonment after an escape from incarceration.

(h) Serving a prison term includes any confinement time in any state prison or federal penal institution as punishment for commission of an offense, including confinement in a hospital or other institution or facility credited as service of prison time in the jurisdiction of the confinement.

(i) For the purposes of this section, a commitment to the State Department of Mental Health as a mentally disordered sex offender following a conviction of a felony, which commitment exceeds one year in duration, shall be deemed a prior prison term.

(j) For the purposes of this section, when a person subject to the custody, control, and discipline of the Director of Corrections is incarcerated at a facility operated by the Department of the Youth Authority, that incarceration shall be deemed to be a term served in state prison.

(k) Notwithstanding subdivisions (d) and (g) or any other provision of law, where one of the new offenses is committed while the defendant is temporarily removed from prison pursuant to Section 2690 or while the defendant is transferred to a community facility pursuant to Section 3416, 6253, or 6263, or while the defendant is on furlough pursuant to Section 6254, the defendant shall be subject to the full enhancements provided for in this section.

This subdivision shall not apply when a full, separate, and consecutive term is imposed pursuant to any other provision of law.

Three Strikes' Highlights

Increases Sentences for Repeat Offenders

- If an offender has one previous serious or violent felony conviction (first strike), the mandatory sentence for any new felony conviction (second strike) is twice the term otherwise required under the law for the new conviction.

- If an offender has two or more previous serious or violent felony convictions, the mandatory sentence for any new felony conviction (third strike) is life imprisonment with the minimum term being the greater of (1) three times the term otherwise required under the law for the new felony conviction, (2) 25 years, or (3) the term determined by the court for the new conviction.

Counts Previous Convictions of a Minor

- Crimes committed by a minor, who is at least age 16 at the time of the crime, count as strikes.

Restricts Prison Credits

- Offenders who have been convicted previously of one or more serious or violent felonies may not earn credits to reduce the time they spend in prison by more than one-fifth of their sentence (rather than the previous maximum of one-half).

Eliminates Alternatives to Prison

- Requires that persons convicted of any felony who have been previously convicted of a serious or violent felony will be sentenced to state prison (they would not be granted probation or be placed in an alternative punishment or treatment program).

Discussion

Prior convictions have three main effects on the sentences given by the courts:

1. Establish certain minimum penalties
2. Provide for increased sentences
3. May provide for the adjudication of the accused as a habitual criminal

Prior convictions are considered punishment enhancements, referring to their effects on the punishments given by the courts. (Note: Other enhancements are contained in the Penal Code such as the use of a gun in committing a crime.) The enhancements based on prior convictions are found in PC 666 through PC 668. The general provisions of PC 668 permit the use of convictions in other states subject to certain limitations as a sentence enhancement. Penal Code 667 is known as the "Three Strikes and You're Out" law based on the enhancements that include life imprisonment.

1-6 Spirit of the Law versus Letter of the Law

Penal Code 4—Construction According to Fair Import

The rule of common law, that penal statutes are to be strictly construed, has no application to this code. All its provisions are to be construed according to the fair import of their terms, with a view to effect its objects and to promote justice.

Penal Code 5—Construction As to Existing Laws

The provisions of this code, so far as they are substantially the same as existing statutes, must be construed as continuations thereof, and not as new enactments.

Penal Code 7—Words and Phrases

Words used in this code in the present tense include the future as well as the present; words used in the masculine gender include the feminine and neuter;

Is "Three Strikes" a Pyrrhic Victory?

The habitual offender statute known nationwide as "Three Strikes and You're Out" was approved by California in March 1994. The first year it was in effect, there was a 6.3 percent drop in violent crime. Attorney General Dan Lungren said that the data show the benefit of tough sentencing laws. A spokesperson for the attorney general said that the possibility of life in prison has put career felons on notice. In addition, since the law was passed, for the first year in the last two decades fewer parolees came into California from other states than left the state. This fact indicates that people would rather leave than pay the potential sentencing costs.

Officials from Los Angeles County, however, state that the law has caused a logjam in criminal courts as defendants opt for trials in hope of avoiding mandatory life sentences. Others contend that the cost is too high to pay for a criminal justice system that is already underfunded.

California's habitual offender statute is probably the toughest in the nation because it provides for sentences of 25 years to life for two-time "serious or violent" felons upon conviction of any third felon. In addition, a defendant previously convicted of any other felon must serve time in state prison (*Law Enforcement News,* October 15, 1995).

People v. Superior Court (Romero) (31 Cal. App. 4th 653)

"Three Strikes" recidivist statute mandating at least 25 years imprisonment upon proof of prior serious felony convictions did not violate separation of powers doctrine by requiring prosecutional approval of court's exercise of asserted power to strike prior conviction allegations in furtherance of justice; statute had limited or nonexistent impact on asserted judicial power in light of prior statutory amendment that already had eliminated court's authority to strike prior conviction allegations in furtherance of justice.

People v. Rojas (206 Cal. App. 3d 795)

Offense underlying defendant's prior serious felony conviction had to have occurred before commission of present offense to subject defendant to five-year enhancement pursuant to this section; thus, defendant's residential burglary sentence could not be enhanced as result of defendant's prior conviction for rape which had been committed after burglary.

---

the singular number includes the plural, and the plural the singular; the word person includes a corporation as well as an individual; the word county includes city and county; writing includes printing and typewriting; oath includes affirmation or declaration; and every mode of oral statement, under oath or affirmation, is embraced by the term testify, and every written one in the term depose; signature or subscription includes mark, when the person cannot write, his or her name being written near it, by a person who writes his or her own name as a witness; provided, that when a signature is made by mark it must, in order that the same may be acknowledged or serve as the signature to any sworn statement, be witnessed by two persons who must subscribe their own names as witnesses thereto.

Discussion

As stated in the preceding, the common law rule that penal statutes are to be strictly construed has been modified in California. Instead, penal statutes are construed according to their normal usage with a view toward the objectives of the statute in question. Despite this rule, giving the defendant the benefit of any reasonable doubt is still required (*Carlos v. Superior Court,* 35 Cal. 3d 35). Accordingly, when a statute is capable of two reasonable constructions, the one most favorable to the defendant should be used (*People v. Ralph,* 24 Cal. 2d 575).

1-6a Rules of Construction

The general rules of construction for criminal statutes are as follows:

- The codes of the state are to be read as a single unified whole, as if they were a single statute (*Re Porterfield*, 28 Cal. 2d 91).
- Words used in a statute will be construed in accordance with their commonly understood meanings (*Re Newbern*, 53 Cal. 2d 786).
- If a statute is capable of being reasonably construed in more ways than one, the most restricted meaning will normally be used (*People v. Kelly*, 27 Cal. App. 2d Supp. 771).
- A statute should be construed with reference to its purpose (*People v. King*, 115 Cal. App. 2d Supp. 875).
- If special and general statutes both proscribe the same criminal act, the presumption is that the special statute will prevail (17 Cal. Jur. 3d [Rev.] 14).
- Where the constitutional right or privilege of an individual is concerned, there should be a liberal, but reasonable, construction in favor of the individual (*Ex parte Cohen*, 104 Cal. 524).
- If the common law meaning is not repugnant to due process, it shall be used, unless the terms are defined by constitutional or statutory provisions or prior judicial decisions (*Re Application of Lockett*, 179 Cal. 581).
- Words and phrases must be construed according to the context and approved usage of the language; but technical words and phrases, and such other as may have acquired a peculiar and appropriate meaning in law, must be construed according to such peculiar and appropriate meaning (PC 7).

1-7 Torts versus Crimes

In general, the courts say that if an act is merely a threat to private interest or offends it, then the act is only a civil wrong, not a crime. Because of our ideas of dual responsibility (liability both for civil and criminal), the wrongdoer may be made to answer in both a criminal prosecution and in a civil lawsuit for damages (Allen Z. Gammage and Charles F. Hemphill, *Basic Criminal Law*, 4th ed. [New York: McGraw-Hill, 1989]).

The basic difference between a *civil law wrong* and a *crime* is that the civil law wrong is a wrong against an individual, whereas a crime is considered a wrong against all of society. While the crime of assault may be directed toward an individual victim, the wrong is still considered against all of society. Civil cases are prosecuted by a plaintiff who is the person or persons allegedly injured by the alleged wrongful acts of the defendant(s). In the state of California, all crimes are prosecuted in the name of "The People of the State" and are alleged to be violations "against the peace and dignity of the state."

Torts, a French word meaning wrong, is used to describe civil wrongs. Most torts involve either negligent conduct or intentional wrongs. Some conduct is both a civil tort and a criminal act. For example, if an individual assaults a victim, the individual has committed both the tortuous act of assault and the criminal act of assault. The individual may be prosecuted for the criminal act and, at the same time in a separate court case, sued by the victim in civil court for the tortuous conduct.

In a civil case, the standard of proof required to establish a right to recovery is preponderance of proof, whereas in a criminal case, in order to convict an accused, the proof must be beyond a reasonable doubt. Preponderance of proof is a much lessor standard or requirement. This difference in standards can produce different results when the same issue is tried in both civil and criminal courts. For example, if a suspect is tried and acquitted of rape in a criminal court, he can still be sued by the victim in civil court for the tort of sexual assault. The fact that he was acquitted in criminal court is immaterial. If Gary pleads guilty to rape and admits that he committed the crime, however, his statement that he committed the acts necessary to establish the crime of rape could be used against him in civil court to help establish the tort.

One major difference between civil and criminal trials is that in civil trials the defendant does not have the right to refuse to testify. Protection against unreasonable searches and seizures also do not apply in civil cases. In addition, civil defendants are not provided with an attorney if they cannot afford one.

In California, state civil cases are started by the plaintiff filing a complaint or petition in municipal (justice court in rural areas) or superior court. If the amount in controversy is small, the complaint may be filed in the small claims division of municipal or justice court.

Penal Code 20—Unity of Act and Intent or Negligence

1-8 Elements of a Crime

1-8a Act and Intent

To constitute crime, there must be unity of act and intent. In every crime or public offense there must exist a union, joint operation of act and intent, or criminal negligence.

Discussion

To constitute criminal conduct, there must be a unity in time of the act and the intent or criminal negligence. A frequently used equation to illustrate this is

Crime = Criminal Act (actus reus) + Criminal Intent (mens rea)

Both the act and the intent must be joined together in time for at least a brief period. For example, burglary requires the entering of a building with the intent to commit larceny or a felony. To be burglary, the accused must have had the intent to commit either larceny or a felony at the time of the entry. Accordingly, if the accused enters a room and after entry forms the intent to steal, he or she may be guilty of larceny but not burglary since the intent (to steal) and the act (entry) were not connected in time.

Jerry Malcoln, intending to kill his wife, stole a boat. He talked his wife into going out in the boat with him. At the time they left the dock, he intended to turn the boat over in the middle of the lake. He knew that his wife could not swim. Once he got out into the lake, he changed his mind and started back to the dock. A sudden storm came up and the boat capsized. His wife drowned. While he may have committed other crimes, his intent to kill his wife and the act causing her death did not have a unity of time. Accordingly, he is not guilty of premeditated murder. Suppose, however, he intended to take his wife for a boat ride. In the middle of the lake, he decided that this would be a good time to kill his wife. So he turned the boat over, and she drowned. This is premeditated murder. There was a unity of the act and the intent. It does not matter that the unity was for only the briefest of time.

1-8b Criminal Act

Criminal acts are usually affirmative and voluntary acts of the defendants. Criminal acts, however, may include the following:

- Verbal acts or words as in perjury
- A failure to act when there is a duty to act
- The act of agreement in a conspiracy
- The act of possession in crimes involving illegal possession

The act necessary to constitute a crime varies with each crime. Except in absolute liability crimes, involuntary movement is normally not sufficient to constitute the act. For example, Joe shoves Harold into Paul. Harold has not committed any act because his act was involuntary. In one old English case, the court held that a muscle spasm that caused a pistol to discharge was not an act sufficient to establish murder when a bystander was killed. Generally, the following are not considered as voluntary acts necessary to constitute a crime: a reflex or convulsion; a bodily movement during unconsciousness or sleep; conduct during hypnosis or resulting from hypnotic suggestion; or a bodily movement that otherwise is not a product of the effort or determination of the actor, either conscious or habitual.

1-8c Passive Participation

Passive participation or omission is where a person allows an act to occur, but no active act is involved. In cases where the passive individual has a duty to act, passive participation is sufficient to constitute a criminal act. For example, a mother who fails to feed her infant, resulting in death to the infant, has committed a criminal act. The security guard who deliberately allows company materials to be stolen may be a passive participant in the crime. The mere presence at the scene of a crime and failure to take steps to prevent it is not normally criminal conduct (*People v. Vernon*, 89 Cal. App. 3d 853).

Criminal liability can be based on a failure to act only when the individual has a legal duty to act. A moral duty is insufficient to establish criminal liability. For example, a bystander has only a moral duty to aid an injured person. If however, the bystander has a legal duty created by statute or relationship (e.g., a parent), then the failure to aid the child is a crime. The failure to act arises in most cases from statutory sources. For example, an individual involved in an automobile accident has a statutory duty to render aid to persons injured in that accident. Under the tax code, the failure to file a state income tax return is a crime.

1-8d Role of Corpus Delicti

Corpus delicti literally means "the body of the crime." The *corpus delicti* of a criminal offense is the required elements of the crime. A person, therefore, cannot be convicted of a crime unless the prosecution establishes the *corpus delicti*, that is, that a crime has been committed. An exception to this rule is where the accused pleads guilty or nolo contendre. For example, the *corpus delicti* of the crime of murder in violation of PC 187 is (1) the death of a human being and (2) the death was caused by an unlawful act, omission, or other criminal agency. It is not necessary to produce a physical body, only that there was the death of a human being. In addition, the prosecution must establish that the death was caused by an unlawful act, omission, or other criminal agency. Note: PC 194 requires that the prosecution also establish that the death occurred within three years and a day after the injury or cause of death was administered.

Identity of the offender is not an essential element of *corpus delicti*. To successfully prosecute, however, the prosecution must establish that the accused was the one who committed all the elements of the crime. *Corpus delicti* cannot be established solely from the confessions of the accused. Other independent evidence must establish that the crime did occur (*In re Robert P.*, 121 Cal. App. 3d 36). The latter requirement exists to ensure that individuals are not punished unless an actual crime has occurred.

1-9 Concepts of Criminal Intent

Penal Code 21—Intent Manifested by Circumstances

(a) The intent or intention is manifested by the circumstances connected with the offense.

(b) In the guilt phase of a criminal action or a juvenile adjudication hearing, evidence that the accused lacked the capacity or ability to control his conduct for any reason shall not be admissible on the issue of whether the accused actually had any mental state with respect to the commission of any crime. This subdivision is not applicable to Section 26. [Section 26 deals with persons incapable of committing a crime.]

Discussion

Two different kinds of intent are used in criminal law—specific intent and general criminal intent. The legislature determines the type of intent required for the commission of a particular crime. If the language of the statute is unclear as to the type of intent required for conviction, often the courts look to common law for guidance. In the trial of the case, the presence or absence of the required intent is a question of fact. The trial court's determination as to the presence or absence of the required intent, if based on substantial evidence, will not be disturbed on appeal (*People v. Armstrong,* 100 Cal. App. 2d Supp. 852).

The Penal Code provides that intent is manifested by the circumstances connected with the offense. Note: Certain persons are considered incapable of committing certain crimes because of a lack of requisite mental state (e.g., very young children and insane persons). The lack of capacity to commit a crime is discussed later in this chapter.

1-9a General Intent

General intent is the intent that is inferred by the doing of an act or the failure to act. To constitute general criminal intent, it is not necessary that an intent to violate the law exists (*People v. Williams,* 102 Cal. App. 3d 1018). In general intent crimes, there is no requirement to establish that the accused knew his/her act was wrongful. All that is necessary is that the act was done volitionally or willfully. For example, driving 55 mph in a school zone is a crime. It does not matter that the accused was unaware that he was in a school zone or the fact that his speedometer was broken, which prevented him from knowing that he was driving over the speed limit. To successfully prosecute, the state would need only to establish that the accused was willfully driving, and his speed was in excess of the legal limit.

1-9b Specific Intent

Some crimes require more than a general criminal intent. To commit a *specific intent* crime, the accused must have contemplated the ultimate act (*People v. Armentrout,* 118 Cal. App. Supp. 761). For example, larceny is a specific intent crime. Before an accused can be convicted of larceny, the state must establish that he/she had a specific intent to steal at the time that the property was taken. For example, while leaving a restaurant Jerry sees a coat that looks like his. Thinking that the coat is his, he takes it. Even though the taking of the coat was wrong, he is not guilty of larceny (a specific intent crime) since there was no specific intent to steal the coat.

The California Supreme Court discussed the differences between general and specific intent in *People v. Hood* (1 Cal. 3d 857). The Court stated: "When the definition of a crime consists of only the description of a particular act, without reference to intent to do a further act or achieve a future consequence, we ask whether the defendant intended to do the proscribed act. This intention is deemed to be a general criminal intent. When the definition refers to defendant's intent to do some further act or achieve some additional consequence, the crime is deemed to be one of specific intent. There is no real difference, however, only a linguistic one, between an intent to do an act already performed and intent to do that same act in the future."

1-9c Transferred Intent

Transferred intent, also referred to as *constructive intent,* applies where there is a difference between the criminal act intended and the act actually committed. For example, a person intending to kill one person kills another by mistake. In this case, the doctrine of transferred intent would be used to imply a willful killing of the actual victim (*People v. Buenaflore,* 40 Cal. App. 2d 713). The doctrine of transferred intent is most often applied to murder and assault with the intent to kill cases.

As one judge stated (*Gladden v. State,* 273 Md. 383), "The fact that the person actually killed was killed instead of the intended victim is immaterial, and the only question is what would have been the degree of guilt if the result intended had actually been accomplished. The intent is transferred to the person whose death has been caused."

1-9d Criminal Negligence

Negligent conduct in some situations constitutes criminal behavior. In those cases, the negligent conduct is a substitute for criminal intent. To determine whether or not the negligent conduct is sufficient to replace criminal intent, the following rules apply:

- Negligence is not a substitute for specific intent (*People v. Becker,* 94 Cal. App. 2d 434). (Note: Specific intent is also discussed in this chapter.)
- Negligence must amount to a gross or culpable departure from the standard of due care. Mere simple negligence is not sufficient (*People v. Penny,* 44 Cal. 2d 861). To be criminal, the negligent conduct must show an indifference to the consequences and require knowledge, actual or implied, that the conduct tends to endanger another's life (*People v. Peabody,* 46 Cal. App. 3d 43).
- Whether or not the negligent conduct is criminal must be determined from the conduct itself and not from the resultant harm (*People v. Brain,* 110 Cal. App. 3d Supp. 1).
- What obligation or responsibility does the defendant have toward proper conduct?
- What is the standard of proper conduct expected of an ordinary, reasonable, prudent person under the same conditions?
- What standard of conduct was violated?
- There must be a direct connection between the negligent conduct and the injury or harm.
- There must be injury or harm resulting from the negligent conduct.

1-9e Proximate Cause

Causation problems normally arise in criminal law only in those offenses involving homicide. As in tort law, to be legally responsible for the injury, death, or other harm that constitutes the crime, the defendant's act must be the proximate cause of it. *Proximate cause* (also called "legally responsible cause") is established where the act is directly connected with the resulting injury, and there are not intervening independent forces (Witkin, *California Crimes,* Sections 78–80). If there are no other concurrent or contributing causes, normally it is immaterial that the results were not reasonably foreseeable.

1-9f Concurrent or Contributing Cause

In some cases, the defendant is criminally liable for the results of his/her act, even though there is another contributing cause (*People v. Lewis,* 124 Cal. 551). For example, the accused shoots the victim. The victim dies as the results of negligent medical treatment. The accused may be guilty of criminal homicide. In this case, the accused could reasonably foresee that a victim may receive less than adequate medical treatment.

If the intervening cause is so disconnected and unforeseeable, the defendant's act will not be considered as the proximate cause. For example, the defendant steals a car. The victim then borrows his son's car. The victim is killed in a car wreck because of faulty brakes on the son's car. In this case, the defendant cannot be convicted of criminal homicide because the results are disconnected and unforeseeable.

1-9g Strict Liability/Crimes Without Intent

Under many statutes enacted for the protection of the public's health and safety (e.g., traffic, food and drug regulations), criminal sanctions are relied upon even if there is no wrongful intent. These offenses usually involve light penalties and no moral obloquy or damage to reputation. Although criminal sanctions are relied upon, the primary purpose of the statutes is regulation rather than punishment or correction. The offenses are not crimes in the orthodox sense, and wrongful intent is not required in the interest of enforcement (*People v. Vogel*, 46 Cal. 2d 798).

For certain criminal acts, the defendant may be punished without proof of any criminal intent. These offenses normally are public welfare offenses and generally deal with sales of food, beverages, and drugs. The following are the most common of the absolute liability crimes:

- Illegal sale of liquor
- Sale of impure or adulterated food
- Violation of vehicle registration requirements
- Sale of misbranded merchandise
- Violation of sanitary regulations
- Sale of adulterated drugs
- Sale of illegally subdivided land
- Failure to file state income tax return

1-10 Crimes of Accessories or Principals

Penal Code 30—Classification

The parties to crimes are classified as:

- Principals
- Accessories

Penal Code 31—Principals

All persons concerned in the commission of a crime, whether it be felony or misdemeanor, and whether they directly commit the act constituting the offense, or aid and abet in its commission, or not being present, have advised and encouraged its commission; and all persons counseling, advising, or encouraging children under the age of fourteen, lunatics or idiots, to commit any crime, or who, by fraud, contrivance, or force, occasion the drunkenness of another for the purpose of causing him to commit any crime, or who, by threats, menaces, command, or coercion, compel another to commit any crime, are principals in any crime so committed.

Penal Code 32—Accessories

Every person who, after a felony has been committed, harbors, conceals, or aids a principal in such felony, with the intent that said principal may avoid or escape from arrest, trial, conviction, or punishment, having knowledge that said principal has committed such felony or has been charged with such felony or convicted thereof, is an accessory to such felony.

Discussion

In California, there are only two parties to a crime—principals and accessories. The common law classifications of accessory before the fact and principal are merged into "principals," and the common law classification of accessory after the fact is an accessory. To be a principal, one must be involved in either the planning or commission of the offense. Unlike common law, a principal does not need to be present at the scene of the crime. All principals are equally guilty and, thus, are subject to the same punishment.

To be a principal, one must do any of the following:

- Commit the crime
- Aid in the commission of the crime
- Advise or encourage another to commit the crime
- Command, threaten, or force another to commit a crime
- Get another person drunk so that person will commit a crime

An accessory is one who, after a felony has been committed, harbors, conceals, or helps the principal evade punishment or detection. The punishment for an accessory can include imprisonment in a state prison or a county jail.

To be guilty as an accessory

- A felony must have been committed;
- One must have aided, concealed, or harbored the principal; and
- One must have intent that the principal avoid or escape arrest, prosecution, or punishment.

Assume that A, B, and C rob a bank. C takes part in the planning of the robbery and plans to receive a portion of the loot. C is not present at the scene of the crime. A and B actually go into the bank and commit the robbery. After the robbery, D hides A, B, and C. D did not know prior to the robbery that one was being planned. In this example, A, B, and C are all principals. (Note: At the common law, since C was not present at the scene of the crime, he would be an accessory before the fact.) D, not taking part in the robbery nor the planning of it, is an accessory.

1-10a Accomplice

An accomplice may be prosecuted for the identical offense charged against the defendant on trial in the cause in which the accomplice's testimony is given. Penal Code, Section 1111, provides that one may not be convicted upon the testimony of an accomplice unless there is other corroborating evidence that connects the defendant with the commission of the offense.

1-11 Definition of Terms

1-11a Statutory Meanings of Various Words

The following words have in the Penal Code the meaning attached to them in this section, unless otherwise apparent from the context (PC 7):

1. The word *willfully*, when applied to the intent with which an act is done or omitted, implies simply a purpose or willingness to commit the act, or make the omission referred to. It does not require any intent to violate law, or to injure another, or to acquire any advantage.
2. The words *neglect, negligence, negligent,* and *negligently* import a want of such attention to the nature or probable consequences of the act or omission as a prudent man ordinarily bestows in acting in his own concerns.
3. The word *corruptly* imports a wrongful design to acquire or cause some pecuniary or other advantage to the person guilty of the act or omission referred to, or to some other person.

4. The words *malice* and *maliciously* import a wish to vex, annoy, or injure another person, or an intent to do a wrongful act, established either by proof or presumption of law.

5. The word *knowingly* imports only a knowledge that the facts exist which bring the act or omission within the provisions of this code. It does not require any knowledge of the unlawfulness of such act or omission.

6. The word *bribe* signifies anything of value or advantage, present or prospective, or any promise or undertaking to give any, asked, given, or accepted, with a corrupt intent to influence, unlawfully, the person to whom it is given, in his or her action, vote, or opinion, in any public or official capacity.

7. The word *vessel,* when used with reference to shipping, includes ships of all kinds, steamboats, canal boats, barges, and every structure adapted to be navigated from place to place for the transportation of merchandise or persons.

8. The words *peace officer* signify any one of the officers mentioned in Penal Code, Chapter 4.5 (commencing with Section 830) of Title 3 of Part 2.

9. The word *magistrate* signifies any one of the officers mentioned in the Penal Code Section 808.

10. The word *property* includes both real and personal property.

11. The words *real property* are coextensive with lands, tenements, and hereditaments.

12. The words *personal property* include money, goods, chattels, things in action, and evidences of debt.

13. The word *month* means a calendar month, unless otherwise expressed; the word *daytime* means the period between sunrise and sunset, and the word *nighttime* means the period between sunset and sunrise.

14. The word *will* includes codicil.

15. The word *writ* signifies an order or precept in writing, issued in the name of the people, or of a court or judicial officer, and the word *process* a writ or summons issued in the course of judicial proceedings.

16. Words and phrases must be construed according to the context and the approved usage of the language; but technical words and phrases, and such others as may have acquired a peculiar and appropriate meaning in law, must be construed according to such peculiar and appropriate meaning.

17. Words giving a joint authority to three or more public officers or other persons are construed as giving such authority to a majority of them, unless it is otherwise expressed in the act giving the authority.

18. When the seal of a court or public officer is required by law to be affixed to any paper, the word *seal* includes an impression of such seal upon the paper alone, or upon any substance attached to the paper capable of receiving a visible impression. The seal of a private person may be made in like manner, or by the scroll of a pen, or by writing the word *seal* against his or her name.

19. The word *state,* when applied to the different parts of the United States, includes the District of Columbia and the territories, and the words *United States* may include the district and territories.

20. The word *section,* whenever hereinafter employed, refers to a section of this code, unless some other code or statute is expressly mentioned.

21. To *book* signifies the recordation of an arrest in official police records, and the taking by the police of fingerprints and photographs of the person arrested, or any of these acts following an arrest.

1-12 Legal Research and Methodology

Researching legal issues and cases is different from standard literature research. Once the student has mastered the concepts and methodology, legal issues, case law, and statutes can be located quickly and efficiently. In recent years, legal research has changed dramatically. No longer will law offices contain huge law libraries. The use of electronic retrieval methods with on-line legal searches and CD-ROMs enables attorneys to carry their legal libraries with them into court. For example, the entire set of California codes (over 80 volumes) with annotations needs only two CD-ROMs. The *California Reporter,* which consists of California cases, can be fitted on several CD-ROMs. In addition, the update of legal books occurs by obtaining replacement CD-ROMs. Until recently, keeping statutes updated required almost one full-time person. Now, the prosecutor's office receives a monthly replacement disk that is updated.

The addition of on-line computer databases has also changed the concept of legal research. The most popular of these on-line databases is *WestLaw. WestLaw* contains nearly 6,900 databases, including federal and state court cases, the U.S. Code, state statutes, federal and state regulations, state attorney general opinions, administrative law decisions, topical databases, legal periodicals, citation checking services, and restatements of the law.

In conducting legal research, the researcher should do the following:

- Research the subject systematically, going sequentially from one source to the next (e.g., statutes, court decisions, or law reviews).
- Check to ensure that the latest available information has been consulted (i.e., use only the latest copy of the Penal Code). Using only the latest references is essential because legal information and points of authority change frequently as the results of statutory modifications and new court decisions.
- Be patient and thorough. The law frequently does not yield easy yes or no answers to many questions. At times, the answers will be considered ambiguous and conflicting.

1-12a Legal Citations

Legal citations are a form of shorthand to assist in locating the legal sources. Appellate court decisions are published in case law books, more popularly known as reporters. The basic rules of legal citation are as follows:

1. The volume or title number is presented first in most citation formats.
2. Following is the standardized abbreviation for the legal reference source.
3. Next, in the case of court cases, is the page number of the first page of the decision. In the case of statutory references, it is the section number of the statute.

   For example, the citation, 107 Cal. 468, refers to the case starting on page 468 of volume 107 of the California Reports.

The standard abbreviations used in citing federal and state authorities are as follows:

Court Decisions
- U.S. (United States Reports) [Contains U.S. Supreme Court decisions.]
- C or Cal. (California Reports) [Contains California Supreme Court decisions.]
- C2d or C3d; or Cal. 2d and Cal. 3d (California Reports second or third series) [A continuation of California Supreme Court decisions.]

- CA or Cal. App. (California Appellate Reports) [Contains California Courts of Appeal decisions.]
- CA 2d or CA 3d; or Cal. App. 2d and Cal. App. 3d (California Appellate Reports, second or third series) [A continuation of California Courts of Appeal decisions.]
- CA 3d Supp.; or Cal. App. 3d Supp. (California Appellate Reports, third series, supplement edition) [A continuation of California Courts of Appeal decisions.]
- P (Pacific Reporter)
- P2d or P. 2d (Pacific Reporter, second series)
- Cal. Rptr. (West's California Reporter)

Statutes

- USC or U.S.C. (United States Code)
- Ev C. (California Evidence Code)
- PC (California Penal Code)
- Veh C (California Vehicle Code)
- H & S C (California Health and Safety Code)
- B & P C (California Business and Professions Code)
- W & I C (California Welfare and Institutions Code)

United States Reports (US) reports only decisions of the U.S. Supreme Court. California Reports (C, C2d, or C3d) reports only decisions of the California Supreme Court. California Courts of Appeal decisions are reported in California Appellate Reports (CA, Cal. App. 2d, or Cal. App. 3d).

1-12b Legal Digests

Legal digests are not legal authorities. They are used as research tools. Legal digests identify and consolidate similar issues by topical arrangement. The most popular legal digest for California, *West's California Digest*, is published by West Publishing Company. It divides the entire body of law into seven main divisions, 32 subheadings, and approximately 400 topics. A digest is published for each series of case reporters. Each topic is assigned a digest key number. For example, Crim Law 625 is the key number for the legal issue of "exclusion from criminal trial."

The key number is the same for each digest published. Legal points from court decisions are published with a brief statement of the legal point involved and the case citation for the court decision being digested. If, for example, a point being researched is located in a digest under Crim Law 625, then reference to other digests using the same key number (Crim Law 625) will help locate other court decisions on the same or similar issues.

1-12c Shepard's Citations

Shepard's Citations, started in 1873 by Frank Shepard, are widely used to ascertain the current status of a statute or court decision. *Shepard's Citations*, more popularly known as citators, analyze each appellate court decision as to the history of the case, other decisions where that decision has been cited, and whether or not the rule of the case has been modified, overruled, or approved by other cases. A similar analysis is used for statutes. For a detailed explanation of how to use *Shepard's Citations*, read the first pages of any citator volume. Note: *Shepard's Citations* are available on CD-ROMs.

1-12d Legal Dictionaries and Encyclopedias

Like *Shepard's Citations* and legal digests, legal dictionaries and encyclopedias are not legal authorities but research tools. The most popular legal dictionary is *Black's Law Dictionary*.

Legal encyclopedias provide discussions on various legal points in encyclopedic form based on court decisions and statutes. They are arranged by broad legal topics and subdivided by individual areas. The most popular encyclopedia used in California is *California Jurisprudence*, Third Edition (Revised). It provides a detailed discussion on state legal issues. It is cited as Cal. Jur. 3d (Rev.). For example, the citation 17 Cal. Jur. 3d (Rev.) 125 refers to volume 17 of *California Jurisprudence*, Third Edition (Revised), section 125. The cited section deals with robbery and provides a detailed discussion on it.

1-12e Witkin's California Law

A popular series on California law is Witkin's. In the criminal law area, there is the *California Crimes* (two volumes) and *California Criminal Procedure* (two volumes), which contain a critical textbook treatment of the entire field of California criminal law, and which do the same for California criminal procedural law. Witkin also has a multivolume series on California civil law and civil procedure.

1-12f Law Reviews

The major law schools in California publish law reviews. In general, the law reviews contain scholarly articles of various aspects of California law. They are not legal authority but are often cited as persuasive authorities. Law reviews are cited in similar fashion to court cases. For example, an article in volume 50 of the *Stanford Law Review* that begins on page 192 would be cited as (50 Stan. L. Rev. 192). The following are the five most popular law reviews in California:

1. University of California Law Review (Cal. L. Rev.)
2. Hastings Law Journal (Hast. L. J.)
3. Stanford Law Review (Stan. L. Rev.)
4. University of California, Los Angeles Law Review (U.C.L.A. Rev.)
5. University of Southern California Law Review (So. Cal. L. Rev.)

1-12g CALJIC

California Jury Instructions—Criminal (CALJIC) is a series of volumes containing standard jury instructions that a judge may use to instruct the jury regarding elements of crimes, defenses, and other matters relating to the trial.

1-12h LARMAC

LARMAC is a consolidated alphabetized index to the constitution and laws of California. It includes all 28 codes and the general laws of California. It is the most complete index available on California law.

1-13 Attorney General Opinions

Government Code 12510—Department of Justice

The Attorney General is head of the Department of Justice.

Government Code 12511—State Legal Matters

The Attorney General has charge, as attorney, of all legal matters in which the State is interested, except the business of The Regents of the University of California and such other boards or officers as are by law authorized to employ an attorney.

Government Code 12519—Opinions on Questions of Law

The Attorney General shall give his/her opinion in writing to the Legislature or either house thereof, and to the Governor, the Secretary of State, Controller, Treasurer, State Lands Commission, Superintendent of Public Instruction, any state agency prohibited by law from employing legal counsel other than the Attorney General, and any district attorney when required, upon any question of law relating to their respective offices.

Discussion

As required, the attorney general provides written conclusions on the legal questions submitted by the governor, State Senate, Assembly, or any of the other state officials. The opinions are generally of two types—formal and informal. Formal opinions concern legal questions that are of general statewide concern. They are published in *Opinions of the Attorney General.* Informal opinions normally concern problems that are of local interest only. Informal opinions are not usually published, but many are available to the public from the attorney general's office. Informal opinions are generally issued in letter format.

Attorney general opinions are considered as quasi-judicial in character. While they do not have the force and effect of statutes or court decisions, they are entitled to great weight and are persuasive to the courts (*D'Amico v. Medical Examiners,* 6 Cal. App. 3d 716 and *People v. Berry,* 147 Cal. App. 2d 33).

1-14 Police Power of the State

Police power is the power and responsibility of a political unit, such as a county or city, to promote and provide for public health, safety, and morals within its jurisdictional limits. The U.S. Supreme Court noted that police power includes the duty, within constitutional limitations, to protect the well-being and tranquility of a community (*Kovacs v. Cooper,* 336 U.S. 77).

The California constitution provides that counties and cities may establish ordinances that regulate local, police, and sanitary procedures and conduct within their respective geographic limits. The ordinances may not conflict with general laws (Cal. Const. Art. XI, Sec. 7). Any ordinance that penalizes conduct already covered by a general law is void (*Arfsten v. Superior Court,* 20 Cal. App. 269). The police power also may not be used by municipalities to legislate subject matter that is of such statewide concern that it can no longer be considered as only a local concern.

A state or political subdivision of a state cannot act arbitrarily in the use of police power. In addition, the state or municipality must be able to show that there is a compelling public need to regulate the conduct in question. The statute must also not infringe on any individual right secured by the constitution. Cases where the courts have struck down statutes based on police power include:

- A statute that required all persons to attend the church of their choice every Sunday. (This statute violates the First Amendment and is not within the police power of a state.)
- A statute forbidding unmarried persons of the opposite sex from living together in the same house or apartment. (No legitimate state concern.)

Cases where the use of the police power has been upheld include:

- Requiring motorcycle riders to wear protective headgear. (Note: Several state supreme courts have struck down similar statutes. For example, the Ohio Supreme Court stated that liberty included the right to be foolish as long as others would not be injured.) (*State v. Betts* 252 N.E. 2d 866).
- Gun control legislation.
- Requiring the use of seat belts in automobiles.

Cases on Point

Jones v. United States (308 F. 2d 307)

The failure to act may constitute a breach of a legal duty in at least four situations. One can be held criminally liable, first, where a statute imposes a duty to care for another; second, where one stands in certain status relationship to another; third, where one has assumed a contractual duty to care for another; and fourth, where one has so secluded the helpless person as to prevent others from rendering aid.

People v. Battin (77 Cal. App. 3d 635)

"Specific intent" crimes are those wherein defendant is aware of and desires consequences of his actions while "general intent" crimes occur when an act is knowingly or willfully done, with the defendant presumed to have intended all he did and all consequences thereof; "strict liability" crimes are those that, unlike general intent and specific intent crimes, do not require union of criminal acts and criminal intent.

People v. Driggs (111 Cal. App. 42)

To constitute "criminal negligence," some measure of wantonness or flagrant or reckless disregard of the safety of others, or willful indifference, must enter into the act.

Somers v. Superior Court (32 Cal. App. 3d 961)

California law recognizes that one person may cause another's death by conduct that is not criminally culpable, for it absolves those who commit an act under a mistake of fact that disproves any criminal intent and those who commit the acts through misfortune or by accident when there is no evil intention or culpable negligence.

People v. Lewis (9 Cal. App. 279)

In view of Code sections that abrogate the distinction between an accessory before the fact and a principal, and that provide that all persons concerned in a felony, whether they directly commit the act or aid or abet, though not present, shall hereafter be prosecuted as principals, and no other facts need be alleged against such an accessory before the fact than are alleged against his principal, one charged with rape need not be shown to have been present to justify a conviction on evidence that otherwise shows that he aided and abetted in the perpetration of the crime by another as effectually as if he had witnessed it.

People v. Bond (13 Cal. App. 175)

To "aid" does not imply guilty knowledge or felonious intent but means to assist and supplement the efforts of another; to "abet" includes knowledge of the wrongful purpose of the perpetrator, and counsel and encouragement of the crime.

People v. Nguyen (Cal. App. 4th 518)

Being an accessory is not a lesser included offense within aiding and abetting.

People v. Wayne (41 Cal. 2d 814)

Liability for being an accessory, like liability for solicitation, cannot be incurred by one person acting alone; to constitute a violation of Section 32 there must be a principal and an aider, acting in concert.

People v. Nguyen (21 Cal. App. 4th 518)

While a person "concerned" in the commission of crime may be guilty as the principal if that person commits or intentionally encourages or assists another to commit offense before or during commission of crime, the accessory must lend assistance to the principal after commission of offense with the intent of helping him escape capture, trial, or punishment.

People v. Olguin (31 Cal. App. 4th 1355)

No specific intent is required for liability as an aider and abettor other than the intent to aid, encourage, facilitate, or promote a criminal act.

Pinell v. Superior Court (232 Cal. App. 2d 284)

No probable cause existed for rape, robbery, oral copulation, and sodomy prosecution of the accused on the theory of aiding and abetting in absence of showing that the defendant in any way assisted the other defendants or encouraged them by word or gesture. The fact that he knew that the others were going to kidnap the girl and bring her to his home, or that he was aware of her predicament until he actually saw her in his bedroom after the complained-of acts had taken place, does not make him an aider or abettor.

People v. Calban (65 Cal. App. 3d 578)

In every crime there must exist a union or joint operation of act or conduct and criminal intent or criminal negligence, and normally persons who commit an act through misfortune or by accident with no evil design, intention, or culpable negligence are not criminally responsible for the act; the only exceptions to this general rule are the so-called public welfare or malum prohibitum crimes.

McComb v. Superior Court (68 Cal. App. 3d 89)

Under PC 15, defining crime as an act committed or omitted in violation of law and to which is annexed specified punishments, all of the conditions set forth in the section must be satisfied before the act will constitute a crime.

People v. Costello (138 Cal. App. 2d Supp. 894)

A crime is not to be built up by giving an unusual or seldom-used meaning to the words that create it.

People v. Hallner (43 Cal. 2d 715)

The maxim that penal statutes are to be strictly construed is not an inexorable command to override common sense and evident statutory purpose, and it does not require magnified emphasis on a single ambiguous word in order to give it a meaning contradictory to fair import of the whole remaining language.

People v. Blake (179 Cal. App. 2d 246)

Where a statute contains a reasonably adequate disclosure of intent regarding an evil to be combated in language giving fair notice of practices to be avoided, the court will be slow to say that such statute is too indefinite to be enforced.

People v. Jones (155 Cal. App. 3d 153)

When the statutory language in the Penal Code is reasonably susceptible of two constructions, courts are required to adopt that construction which is more favorable to the offender.

Practicum

A simple definition of crime is that a crime is any act that has been designated as a crime by the lawmakers. For our purposes, we will define crime as conduct that has been prohibited by law and that subjects the offender to punishment. To understand our criminal law, it is necessary to focus on the one characteristic that differentiates it from civil law. That characteristic is punishment.

(Arnold H. Loewy, *Criminal Law* [St. Paul: West, 1987])

Question: One problem with Loewy's definition is that in some civil cases, the plaintiff may be awarded punitive damages as a form of punishment against the defendant. Is punishment the one characteristic that differentiates it from civil law? Are there any others?

Discussion Questions

1. What is the function of procedural law? Substantive law?

2. Since common law crimes have been abolished in California, why is it important to understand common law concepts?

3. What do the following legal citations refer to:

   a. 210 Cal. 366   b. 10 USC 43

   c. 177 US 1020   d. PC 285

4. Why is it important to use the latest available information on the subject that you are researching?

5. Distinguish between crimen falsi and high crimes.

6. Define police power of the state.

7. Discuss the role of proximate cause in criminal cases.

8. Explain the differences between general and specific intent crimes.

9. Explain the doctrine of transferred intent.

10. What is the rationale for punishing strict liability crimes?

Self-Study Quiz

Self-Study Quiz

True/False

1. In legal research, it is not important to check the latest available information since statutes are rarely modified.
2. In legal citation formats, the name of the volume being referred to always precedes the volume number.
3. The page number contained in a case citation is the page on which the court opinion starts.
4. In the citation, 18 USC 431, the statute in question can be found in title 18, U.S. Code, page 431.
5. United States Reports (US) reports only decisions issued by the U.S. Supreme Court.
6. Legal digests are legal authorities and may be cited in court.
7. The attorney general issues two types of opinion: formal and informal.
8. Informal attorney general opinions are generally issued in letter format.
9. The phrase case law refers to the body of appellate court decisions that interpret the meanings of constitutions and statutes.
10. Procedural law defines crimes and establishes punishments.
11. Most of the California criminal law principles are traceable to the common law of England.

Chapter Exhibits

Chapter Exhibits

California Constitution, Article IV, Section 24

All official writings and judicial proceedings shall be conducted in the English language. Accordingly, any criminal statute to be constitutional must be enacted in the English language. The statutes may also, however, be translated into other languages.

General Rules Regarding Criminal Prosecution

1. Burden of Proof. All persons are presumed to be innocent until proven guilty.
2. Proof Requirements. In order to convict a person of a criminal offense, the state must prove beyond a reasonable doubt that the accused committed each and every essential element of the crime (except in those cases where the accused pleads either guilty or nolo contendere).
3. Law-finder. In all cases, the judge is responsible for legal rulings and the interpretations of the applicable laws.
4. Fact-finders. In jury cases, the jury is responsible for finding any issues of fact.
5. Crimes Against the State. A criminal case is prosecuted by the state with the state or the people considered as the victim of the criminal act.
6. Unanimous Verdicts. In the state of California, jury verdicts in criminal cases must be unanimous. Failure to obtain a unanimous verdict results in a hung jury.

Endnote

Endnote

1. Material taken from "Three Strikes, You're Out: Impact on California's Criminal Justice System and Options for Ongoing Monitoring," *California Board of Corrections*, September, 1996.

Introduction—Continued

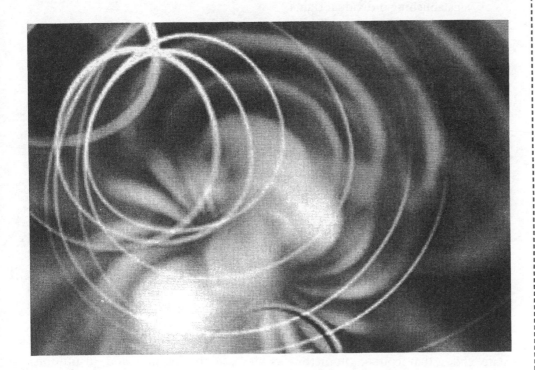

He who does not prevent a crime when he can, encourages it.
William Seneca

2-1 General and Specific Sources of Law

The criminal law in California comes from three primary sources:

1. Federal and state constitutions
2. Statutes
3. Case law

Generally, *constitutions* provide rights and protections for individuals and restrict the power of the government to prosecute or punish. *Statutes* contain the substantive acts and procedural requirements for prosecution. *Case law* (appellate court decisions) contains interpretations of constitutional and statutory provisions.

2-1a Constitutional Law

Both the U.S. Constitution and the constitution of the state of California are sources of criminal law for the courts in California. Constitutions provide the framework for criminal law by:

- Limiting the power of the government
- Establishing individual rights
- Providing for the establishment of a judicial system

As noted earlier, constitutions generally leave the creation and definition of crimes to statutory enactments. The U.S. Constitution, for example, defines criminal acts in only two sections, Article III, Section 3, on treason and Amendment 13, which forbids involuntary servitude except as punishment for a crime. The state constitution defines criminal acts in a few more areas. But, for the most part, the state constitution, like the federal, focuses on individual rights and limitations of government power.

2-1b Statutory Law

In California, there are two types of statutory law: statutes that are passed by the legislature; and initiatives that are passed by the voters.

Under most circumstances, the power to designate state criminal offenses and provide for the punishment of prohibited acts is reserved to the state legislature and cannot be delegated to other governmental bodies (*People v. Knowles*, 35 Cal. 2d 175). In establishing the elements of a crime, the legislature may depart from the norm or common law concepts as long as the elements do not conflict with federal or state constitutions or federal law restrictions (*People v. Perini*, 94 Cal. 573).

Most of the state crimes are set forth in codes that are codifications of statutes on particular subjects (i.e., Penal, Health and Safety, and Vehicle Codes). Other state codes that contain numerous crimes are the Welfare and Institutions, Business and Professions, Fish and Game, and Government Codes.

The legislative bodies of cities and counties have limited authority to create minor crimes. In California, ordinances can only create misdemeanors or infractions. For example, infractions may be created by municipal ordinances. The ordinances are valid only for the municipalities (city or county) for which they were enacted, and they may not regulate conduct that is regulated by state statutes.

In California, the voters have the power via the initiative petition process to propose and approve statutes and amendments to the state constitution. An initiative measure is started by presenting a petition to the secretary of state that has been signed by the number of voters that is equal to at least 5 percent of the number of voters who voted in the last gubernatorial election. The secretary of state is then required to submit the measure at the next general election held at least 131 days after the petition is certified, or a special election may be called (Cal. Const.

Art. II, Sec. 8). A simple majority of votes is sufficient to pass the measure, and it takes effect the day after the election unless the measure provides otherwise. The courts have held that initiative measures should be interpreted liberally to give full effect to its objective and the needs of the people (*Mills v. Trinity County,* 108 Cal. App. 3d 656).

All laws of a general nature have uniform operation within the state. A local or special statute is invalid in any case if a general statute can be made applicable (Cal. Const. Art. IV, Sec.16). A statute or initiative must embrace only one subject, which shall be expressed in its title. If a statute or initiative embraces more than one subject or the subject is not embraced in its title, the provision is void (Cal. Const. Art. IV, Sec. 9). The one subject limitation must, however, be interpreted liberally to uphold legislation whose various parts are reasonably germane to the subject contained in its title *(Fair Political Practices Com. v. Superior Court,* 25 Cal. 3d 33).

Substantive and Procedural Laws

Laws relating to criminal conduct may be divided into two general areas: substantive and procedural. *Substantive law* defines crimes and establishes punishments. *Procedural law* sets forth the rules and requirements that must be followed during the investigation, apprehension, and trial of individual defendants. Procedural law is also referred to as adjective law. Procedural, or adjective, law is also concerned with the carrying out of court orders and redress (compensation) of injuries. That portion of the Penal Code that prohibits theft of another's property (larceny) is substantive in nature, whereas, the Evidence Code is a procedural code.

2-1c Case Law

Case law is the term used to indicate appellate court interpretations of the law. A substantial majority of law is case law (i.e., court opinions that interpret the meaning of constitutions and statutes). Case law also helps clarify and narrow statutory law. For example, the U.S. Constitution (Amendment 14) provides that no state shall deprive any person of life, liberty, or property without due process of law. What constitutes due process of law is decided almost daily in the courts. Hundreds of published opinions are issued by federal and state appellate and supreme courts each year.

Court decisions interpret the relationship of one code provision to another, the meaning of words used in the code provision, the legislative intent in enacting the code provision, the scope and effect of the code provision, and whether or not the provision violates any constitutional restrictions.

Precedent

Precedent is used when a legal principle has been decided by a court. The court decision is then the precedent (guide) for similar situations. There are two basic types of precedent: mandatory and persuasive.

Under *mandatory precedent,* when a higher appellate court renders a decision on an issue, the lower courts under that court's supervision must follow the ruling or face reversal on appeal. For example, if the California Supreme Court decides an issue, then state appellate courts in California must follow that precedent. *Persuasive precedent* indicates a court decision that is not binding on a second court but is persuasive to the second court. For example, a court in California is faced with an issue that has never been decided by a California court. However, a court in Nevada has considered the same issue. The Nevada court decision is not binding on the California court but is of some persuasive authority. Precedent is based on the principle of *stare decisis,* which is discussed next.

Stare Decisis

Stare decisis is a Latin word meaning "to abide by, or adhere to, decided cases." The doctrine provides that when a court has once laid down a principle of law as applicable to a certain state of facts, it will adhere to that principle and apply it to all future cases where the facts are substantially the same (*Moore v. City of Albany*, 98 N.Y. 396). *Stare decisis* is a policy founded on the theory that security and certainty require that accepted and established legal principles, under which rights may accrue, be recognized and followed (*Otter Tail Power Co. v. Von Bank*, 72 N.D. 497).

Common Law

Common law comprises the body of those principles and rules of action, relating to the government and security of persons and property, that derive their authority solely from usages and customs of immemorial antiquity or from the judgments and decrees of the courts recognizing, affirming, and enforcing such usages and customs; and, in this sense, particularly the ancient unwritten laws of England. In general, a body of law develops and derives from judicial decisions, as distinguished from legislative enactments *(Black's Law Dictionary)*.

2-2 Repeal/Amendment

Government Code 9606—Repeal of Statute

Any statute may be repealed at any time, except when vested rights would be impaired. Persons acting under any statute act in contemplation of this power.

Government Code 9608—Termination or Suspension of Law Creating Criminal Offense

This section provides that the termination or suspension (by whatsoever means effected) of any law creating a criminal offense does not prevent the conviction and punishment of a prior act committed in violation of the law before it was terminated or suspended. An exception to this general rule is when there is clearly expressed intent by the legislation to prevent the punishment of the act.

2-2a Discussion

Criminal statutes are repealed or amended by other legislation either directly or by implication (*People v. Dobbins*, 73 Cal. 257). A statute is repealed directly by legislation expressly repealing the statute in question.

Repeal by Implication

Repeal by implication is not favored by the courts (*People v. Armstrong*, 100 Cal. App. 2d Supp. 821). A statute is repealed or amended by implication when a later statute is enacted that is inconsistent with it. Normally, a general statute will not be considered as repealed by a special statute of limited applicability unless the intent of the legislature is clear (*People v. Deibert*, 117 Cal. App. 2d 410).

It is assumed that the legislature did not intend to repeal a former statute by a later statute if, by a fair and reasonable construction, effect can be given to both statutes (*People v. Armstrong*, 100 Cal. App. 2d Supp. 852). If two general statutes clearly conflict with each other, the presumption is that the latest enacted statute prevails (Gov. Code 9605).

Effect of Repeal

The repeal of a statute under which a person has been convicted does not affect the conviction if the conviction is final. Gov. Code 9608 is the "general saving clause" for repealed criminal statutes. It modifies common law by allowing for the prosecution of acts that were criminal at the time of commission even though the statute that made them criminal has since been repealed. Its purpose is to authorize prosecution under a former statute in order to avoid a situation where the defendant could not be prosecuted under any law, simply because the legislature has modified the statute in question between the time that the act was committed and the time of trial (*Re Estrada,* 63 Cal. App. 2d 740). The California Supreme Court decided in 1893 that a person should be punished under the state law as it existed at the time the offense was committed rather than as it existed after amendment. This principle has since been upheld by the U.S. Supreme Court (*McNulty v. California,* 149 US 645). For example, Tom is cited for killing a deer during a prohibited time period. The next day a statute is passed and signed by the governor allowing hunters to kill deer at that time. Tom could be convicted of violating the statute in effect when the act was committed unless the new law clearly expressed an intention not to punish persons who had violated the prior law.

The preceding rules apply even when the act is no longer a criminal offense. For example, if California were to repeal its traffic laws as of January 1, 19XX, an accused could be convicted and punished on January 3, 19XX, on a traffic violation that occurred prior to January 1.

2-3 Vague and Indefinite Statutes

Criminal statutes must clearly describe the conduct that is prohibited. A statute that is vague and uncertain violates the due process clause of the Fourteenth Amendment, U.S. Constitution. To be valid, a criminal statute must give fair notice of what is prohibited or required so that a person of common intelligence can understand its meaning and its application (*Connally v. General Construction Co.,* 269 U.S. 385).

2-4 Conflict between Laws

As already noted, a local ordinance will be invalidated if it directly conflicts with state law. In some cases, however, even where there are no conflicts between state law and local ordinances, the local ordinance will be void if it appears that the legislative purpose of the state law was to fully regulate the field (50 Cal. L. Rev. 740). This is based on the Doctrine of Preemption. Accordingly, the doctrine provides that in those areas where the state sees fit to adopt a general scheme of laws for the regulation of a particular area, those aspects covered by state law cease to be matters that may be controlled by local legislation (*In re Lane,* 58 Cal. 2d 99).

The following factors are used to determine if state law preempts the local regulations:

1. Has the subject matter been fully covered by state law so as to indicate that it has become exclusively a matter of state concern?
2. Are the state statutes couched in terms to indicate that clearly a paramount state concern will not tolerate further or additional local concern?
3. Is the subject matter such that the adverse effects of a local ordinance on transient citizens of the state outweigh any benefits of local control? (53 Cal. L. Rev. 902)

U.S. Constitution, Article VI [second paragraph only]

This Constitution, and the Laws of the United States which shall be made in Pursuance thereof; and all Treaties made, or which shall be made, under the Authority of the United States, shall be the supreme Law of the Land; and the

Judges in every State shall be bound thereby, any Thing in the Constitution or Laws of any State to the Contrary notwithstanding. [This clause is commonly known as the Supremacy Clause.]

2-4a The Supreme Law of the Land

As just stated, the U.S. Constitution is the supreme law of the land. Any state constitution, statute, or court ruling that conflicts with it is unconstitutional. The U.S. Constitution guarantees 23 individual rights to U.S. residents. Of these, 12 pertain to criminal law and procedure. Most of the rights are contained in the amendments to the Constitution. Only two sections of the federal Constitution forbid or define conduct as criminal: Article III, Section 3, which defines treason; and Amendment 13, Section 1, which forbids slavery or involuntary servitude.

Each criminal law enacted in California must be tested to ensure that it does not violate the rights contained in the federal Constitution. The U.S. Supreme Court makes the final decision on whether or not a state constitution or enactment conflicts with the federal Constitution and is thus unconstitutional.

The federal Constitution also provides that federal laws and treaties are part of the supreme law of the land. Accordingly, in case of conflicts, first in supremacy is the U.S. Constitution followed by federal statutes and U.S. treaties. If any part of the California Constitution or a California Code is in conflict with any of those three laws, the California enactment is unconstitutional.

2-4b The California Constitution

The first part of the California Constitution is the Declaration of Rights. The declaration reflects many of the same rights as set forth in the U.S. Constitution. Any state statute that conflicts with the safeguards contained in the California Constitution is unconstitutional. The California Supreme Court makes the final decision on whether or not a state criminal law is in conflict with the state constitution.

2-4c Independent State Grounds

Most of the safeguards in the state constitution are also contained in the U.S. Constitution. The U.S. Supreme Court makes the final determination on federal constitutional issues. If, however, the issue is not a federal one and is decided on independent state grounds, the California courts make the final decision on the question. For example, since 1974 the prosecution under federal law has been allowed to impeach an accused's in-court testimony by use of the accused's prior out-of-court statement obtained without proper warnings. Until 1988, however, the statements could not be used in California state courts on the theory that their use violated the California Constitution, and thus the state courts decided the admissibility on independent state grounds.

2-4d Statutory Conflicts

If the conflict is between a local ordinance and a state statute, then the local ordinance is void and without effect. For example, if a municipal ordinance and a state statute penalize the same conduct, the ordinance is void to the extent that it is not in harmony with the statute (*Ex parte Solomon,* 91 Cal. 440). Even if the ordinance is in harmony with the statute, it may be void based on the concept that the state has preempted the subject.

If two general state statutes are in direct conflict with each other, the last statute enacted will be controlling based on the principle of repeal by implication. Repeal by implication is not a favored principle with the courts. If by reasonable construction both statutes can be given effect, then the courts will presume that the legislature intended that construction. As the court stated in *People v. Armstrong* (100 Cal. App. 2d Supp. 852), it will be presumed that the legislature did not intend by a later act to repeal a former one if, by a fair and reasonable construction, effect can be given to both. In situations involving repeal by implication, only that portion of the earlier statute which is in direct conflict with the latter statute is considered repealed.

Dual federalism refers to the fact that in California, two separate criminal law systems (state and federal) are operating together and, in many situations, overlapping each other. The federal government is restricted by the U.S. Constitution to only those powers set forth or implied by the Constitution. It is, therefore, a limited criminal law system. The majority of criminal cases involve the violation of state penal codes and are tried in state criminal cases. For example, Los Angeles County courts try more criminal cases each year than are tried in the entire federal system. (Despite this fact, there are currently more than 2,800 federal crimes.)

Federal crimes fall within three broad classifications:

2-5 Dual Federalism

- Crimes affecting interstate commerce. The Constitution gives Congress the exclusive power to regulate interstate commerce. Such crimes include taking a female across state lines for immoral purposes (the Mann Act), transporting stolen automobiles across state lines (the Dyer Act), kidnapping where the victim is taken across state lines or the presumption that the victim has been taken across state lines (the Lindbergh Act) and the Fugitive Felon Act.
- Crimes committed beyond the jurisdiction of any state. This includes crimes committed on American ships on the high seas or at overseas military bases.
- Crimes that interfere with the activities of the federal government. This broad category includes the robbery of a federally insured bank, federal income tax fraud, attempts to overthrow the U.S. government, or robbery of a post office.

The conduct of a person may result in the violations of both a federal and a state law, and thus they may be convicted in both federal and state courts.

For a federal court to become involved in the trial of a state court, there must be a federal issue. Accordingly, if a person commits murder under a state penal code, the case will be decided by state courts unless a federal issue is involved. In this situation, however, the accused, by claiming that his or her conviction violates one of the rights protected by the U.S. Constitution, induces a federal issue (violation of federal Constitution). If this occurs, then a federal court would have jurisdiction to decide the federal issues involved.

U.S. Constitution, Amendment 6

In all criminal prosecutions, the accused shall enjoy the right to a speedy and public trial, by an impartial jury of the state and district wherein the crime shall have been committed. . . .

U.S. Constitution, Amendment 14, Section 1

No State shall make or enforce any law which shall abridge the privileges or immunities of citizens of the United States; nor shall any State deprive any person of the life, liberty, or property, without due process of law. . . .

2-6 Federal Constitutional Provisions

2-6a Discussion

The U.S. Constitution provides certain rights and protections for individuals and restricts the power of the states to criminally punish individuals. The due process clause of the Fourteenth Amendment has been interpreted by the U.S. Supreme Court to place certain limitations on the power of states to prosecute individuals. Since the limitations are placed on the states by the U.S. Constitution, the U.S. Supreme Court makes the final decision on whether or not state actions violate those limitations. The California State Constitution contains similar protections. The general limitations on state action imposed by the federal Constitution are included in the following.

Ex Post Facto Laws

An *ex post facto* law does one of the following:

- Makes an act occurring before the enactment of the law a crime
- Aggravates a crime or makes it greater than it was when committed
- Increases the punishment after the offense was committed
- Changes the rules of evidence or procedure to require less or different evidence than was required at the time the offense was committed

Ex post facto laws are prohibited by both the U.S. Constitution and the state constitution. An example of an *ex post facto* law would be the enactment of a statute on January 1, making an act committed three weeks earlier a crime. A more likely case is where the punishment for the crime is increased after the commission of the offense. For example, an individual is arrested in 1995 for driving under the influence. He is prosecuted in 1996. If on January 1, 1996, the punishment for driving under the influence was increased, the accused in this case is subject only to the punishment that was in effect in 1995, the time the offense was committed.

Bill of Attainder

Neither the U.S. Constitution nor the state constitution defines the term "bill of attainder," even though both prohibit it. The judicial interpretation of bill of attainder includes those cases where the punishment is legislatively inflicted on a particular person or class. For example, passing a law punishing a certain person by name would be a bill of attainder. Different punishments can be inflicted on a class of persons if there is a legitimate reason for doing so. For example, persons who have prior convictions can by legislative mandate be punished more severely than those who have not been convicted of any prior offenses. The state, however, may not pass a statute declaring any individual a criminal.

Certainty

Criminal statutes must be certain and definite in order that a person will know what conduct is prohibited and what is not. The certainty must be such that a person of ordinary intelligence would recognize what conduct is prohibited by reading the statute (*People v. Pace*, 73 Cal. App. 548). This requirement is intended to prevent the accidental commission of prohibited conduct. In one case, the court held that a criminal statute that prohibited picketing was too vague and therefore unconstitutional (*Re Application of Harder*, 9 Cal. App. 2d 153).

Equal Protection

The U.S. Constitution prohibits any state from denying to any person within its jurisdiction the equal protection of the laws (U.S. Const. Amend. 14). In addition, the state constitution prohibits the legislature from enacting any special statute if a general statute can be made applicable (Cal. Const. Art. IV, Sec. 16). The state constitution requires, also, that all laws of a general nature must have a uniform operation. The equal protection clauses, however, do not prohibit the legislature from fixing different penalties for different offenses or from permitting courts to impose variations in punishment for the conviction of the same offense by different individuals (*People v. Dawson*, 210 Cal. 366).

When the U.S. Constitution was written, the judicial branch was not expected to be involved in the modification of laws. Under the separation of powers doctrine, this duty was delegated to the legislative branch. Appellate courts do, however, make laws and modify existing laws through court decisions interpreting the constitution and statutes. The judicial legislation is indirect and a spin-off of the judicial duties of the appellate courts. If the actions of the legislature are within its scope of power and do not violate any constitutional protections, the courts do not pass on the reasonableness, wisdom, and propriety of the law (*People v. Ferguson*, 129 Cal. App. 300).

2-7 Appellate Court Decisions

The U.S. Supreme Court has been a leader in modifying criminal law and procedure. As the result of the "criminal justice revolution" started by the Warren Court (the Court during Chief Justice Earl Warren's tenure: 1953–69), every major stage of the criminal justice process has been substantially modified since 1962. Every Supreme Court term since 1962 has resulted in judicial decisions by the Court that have changed the criminal justice system. Changes in the Court membership in the past eight years have, however, created a new Court. The new Court will probably continue to modify or fine-tune the criminal justice system. For the U.S. Supreme Court to modify California criminal law, however, the decisions must be based on the U.S. Constitution or federal law.

   Clear examples of the U.S. Supreme Court modifying the law are the *Miranda* and *Mapp v. Ohio* cases. In both of these cases, the court modified the existing law. Note: The modifications were accomplished even though the Court has only the power to approve or reverse a lower court conviction.

2-7a United States Supreme Court Decisions

The California Supreme Court makes the final decision on those issues involving the Penal Code that do not involve federal constitutional rights or federal law. The court's authority, like that of the U.S. Supreme Court, is limited only to approvals or disapprovals of lower court decisions. With the 1986 changes in court personnel, this court is also a "new court."

2-7b California Supreme Court Decisions

Article IV, Section 1, of the California Constitution

The legislative power of this state is vested in the California legislature which consists of Senate and Assembly, but the people reserve to themselves the powers of initiative and referendum.

In California, as in other states and the federal government, all statutory laws must be initiated by the state legislature or by referendum or initiative as discussed in Chapter 1.

   The California legislature is made up of two houses—the senate and the assembly. Each house can initiate a new statute or modify an existing one. The new law or modification, however, must be approved by both houses before it is sent to

2-8 Development of California Statutory Law

2-8a Discussion

the governor for final action. If the governor signs the bill, it becomes law. If the governor vetoes the bill, it goes back to the legislature. If both houses of the legislature override the governor's veto by a two-thirds vote in each house, the bill becomes law. Unless the enactment is an emergency measure, there will be a "cooling off" period before it becomes effective. The effects of repeal and amendment of statutes are discussed in Chapter 1.

When a new law or modification is introduced by a house member, it is called a *bill*. If and when the bill becomes law, it is then considered a *statute*. If it is a general statute, it will be integrated into one of the state's 27 codes.

The 27 different codes in California are as follows:

1. Business and Professions Code (B & PC)
2. Civil Code (CC)
3. Code of Civil Procedure (CCP)
4. Commercial Code (Com. C)
5. Corporations Code (Corp. C)
6. Education Code (Educ. C)
7. Elections Code (Elec. C)
8. Evidence Code (Evid. C)
9. Financial Code (Fin. C)
10. Fish and Game Code (Fish & Game C)
11. Food and Agricultural Code (F & Agri. C)
12. Government Code (Govt. C)
13. Harbors & Navigation Code (Harb. & Nav. C)
14. Health and Safety Code (H & SC)
15. Insurance Code (Ins. C)
16. Labor Code (Lab. C)
17. Military & Veterans Code (Mil. & Vet. C)
18. Penal Code (PC)
19. Probate Code (Prob.C)
20. Public Resources Code (Pub. Res. C)
21. Public Utilities Code (Pub. Ut. C)
22. Revenue and Taxation Code (Rev. C)
23. Streets and Highways Code (Sts. & HC)
24. Unemployment Insurance Code (Unemp. Ins. C)
25. Vehicle Code (VC)
26. Water Code (Water C)
27. Welfare & Institutions Code (Welf. C)

2-9 City and County Ordinances

City and county ordinances are enacted to fit the special needs of local cities and counties. Since cities and counties derive their powers from state charters, they have only the power to enact ordinances as granted by the state. Local ordinances are normally modified by action of local boards of supervisors and city and town councils.

2-10 United States Code

The basic statutory law of the United States (federal law) is contained in the United States Code (U.S.C.). The code is divided into 50 general subject areas called *titles*. The titles are numbered from 1 to 50. Title 18 is the federal criminal code. In citing the U.S.C., the title number is cited first, then U.S.C., then the section number.

For example 18 U.S.C. 302 defines the federal crime of arson. Changes to the U.S.C. are made by statutes that originate in one of the houses of Congress. Note: Appropriations bills may originate only in the House of Representatives.

Often the citation is to the "annotated" code. In the preceding example, the cite for arson under the federal code would be 18 U.S.C.A. 302. Annotated codes contain, in addition to the official text of the code, historical information on the text, cross-references to legal sources, and notes on court decisions regarding the text.

2-11 Crimes Without Victims

Crimes without victims (or victimless crimes) are those crimes that have no adverse impact on persons other than the actor. They can also be considered consensual crimes. Gambling, prostitution, and drug abuse have traditionally been considered by some as victimless crimes. One problem with the enforcement of victimless crimes is that the police will often not have an aggrieved victim to testify against the offender. Criminologists have traditionally debated about whether acts between consensual adults should be considered criminal. The justification for imposing criminal sanctions for the violation of those statutes on victimless crimes is that there are at least moral victims to those crimes and that society in general is a victim in those situations.

2-12 Victims' Bill of Rights

California Constitution, Article 1, Section 28 (Proposition 8)

(a) The People of the State of California find and declare that the enactment of comprehensive provisions and laws ensuring a bill of rights for victims of crime, including safeguards in the criminal justice system to fully protect those rights, is a matter of grave statewide concern. The rights of victims pervade the criminal justice system, encompassing not only the right to restitution from the wrongdoers for financial losses suffered as a result of criminal acts, but also the more basic expectation that persons who commit felonious acts causing injury to innocent victims will be appropriately detained in custody, tried by the courts, and sufficiently punished so that the public safety is protected and encouraged as a goal of highest importance. Such public safety extends to public primary, elementary, junior high, and senior high school campuses, where students and staff have the right to be safe and secure in their persons.

To accomplish these goals, broad reforms in the procedural treatment of accused persons and the disposition and sentencing of convicted persons are necessary and proper as deterrents to criminal behavior and to serious disruption of people's lives.

(b) Restitution. It is the unequivocal intention of the People of the State of California that all persons who suffer losses as a result of criminal activity shall have the right to restitution from the persons convicted of the crimes for losses they suffer.

Restitution shall be ordered from the convicted persons in every case, regardless of the sentence or disposition imposed, in which a crime victim suffers a loss, unless compelling and extraordinary reasons exist to the contrary. The Legislature shall adopt provisions to implement this section during the calendar year following adoption of this section.

(c) Right to Safe Schools. All students and staff of public primary, elementary, junior high, and senior high schools have the inalienable right to attend campuses which are safe, secure, and peaceful.

(d) Right to Truth-in-Evidence. Except as provided by statute hereafter enacted by a two-thirds vote of the membership in each house of the legislature, relevant evidence shall not be excluded in any criminal proceeding, including pretrial and post conviction motions and hearings, or in any trial or hearing of a juvenile for a criminal offense, whether heard in juvenile or adult court. Nothing in this section shall affect any existing statutory rule of evidence relating to privilege or hearsay, or Evidence Code, Sections 352, 782, or 1103. Nothing in this section shall affect any existing statutory or constitutional right of the press.

(e) Public Safety Bail. A person may be released on bail by sufficient sureties, except for capital crimes when the facts are evident or the presumption great. Excessive bail may not be required. In setting bail, reducing or denying bail, the judge or magistrate shall take into consideration the protection of the public, the seriousness of the offense charged, the previous criminal record of the defendant, and the probability of his or her appearing at the trial or hearing of the case. Public safety shall be the primary consideration.

A person may be released on his or her own recognizance in the court's discretion, subject to the same factors considered in setting the bail. However, no person charged with the commission of any serious felony shall be released on his or her own recognizance.

Before any person arrested for a serious felony may be released on bail, a hearing may be held before the magistrate or judge, and the prosecuting attorney shall be given notice and reasonable opportunity to be heard on the matter. When a judge or magistrate grants or denies bail or release on a person's own recognizance, the reasons for that decision shall be stated in the record and included in the court's minutes.

(f) Use of Prior Convictions. Any prior felony conviction of any person in any criminal proceeding, whether adult or juvenile, shall subsequently be used without limitation for purposes of impeachment or enhancement of sentence in any criminal proceeding. When a prior felony conviction is an element of any felony offense, it shall be proven to the trier of fact in open court.

(g) As used in this article, the term *serious felony* is any crime defined in Penal Code, Section 1192.7(c).

2-12a Discussion

Proposition 8, better known as the *Victims' Bill of Rights,* was passed by the California voters on June 9, 1982. The proposition changed the law regarding diminished capacity, right to bail, standing, restitution, plea bargaining, the use of prior felony convictions for impeachment, and the use of the exclusionary rule for violations of the state constitution. Proposition 8 is applicable only to prosecutions for crimes committed on or after its effective date of June 9, 1982 (*People v. Smith,* 34 Cal. 3d 251). The "Three Strikes and You're Out" proposition also made similar changes in California's statutory law. It is discussed in Chapter 1.

Truth in Evidence

The primary purpose of the "Truth in Evidence" portion of Proposition 8 was to eliminate the "independent state grounds" as a basis for the exclusionary rule. The cases of *In re Lance W.* (37 Cal. 3d 873) and *People v. May* (44 Cal. 3d 309) indicate that Proposition 8 has achieved this purpose.

In the case of *In re Lance W.* (37 Cal. 3d 873), the state supreme court ruled that Proposition 8 changed the remedy for a violation of the substantial rights of citizens under the state constitution. "Independent state grounds" is no longer a basis for excluding evidence from a trial. *In re Lance W.* addressed unreasonable searches and seizures (Fourth Amendment problems). *People v. May* (44 Cal. 3d 309) held that Proposition 8 had the same effect with regard to the Fifth and Sixth Amendments (i.e., confessions, *Miranda* problems, and right to counsel). [Note: Now only a violation of a federal constitutional right will be the basis for excluding evidence under the exclusionary rule.]

Bail Provisions

Proposition 8 provided that a judge or magistrate may consider the protection of the public in setting, reducing, or denying bail. PC 1275 now provides that public safety is the primary consideration in setting bail.

In upholding the constitutionality of this section, a California court of appeals held in the case of *In re Nordin* (143 Cal. App. 3d 538) that since pretrial detention is a regulatory matter, not penal, the denial of bail does not deprive the defendants of their constitutional right to trial by jury. The Eighth Amendment's prohibition against excessive bail is a limitation on the amount of bail that a judge may impose, but it is not a limitation of a state's right to regulate eligibility for bail.

Restitution

Proposition 8 provided that a convicted person shall provide restitution to the victim unless the court finds compelling and extraordinary reasons for not ordering restitution. The requirement is now contained in PC 1202.4.

Prior Convictions

The proposition provides that any prior felony conviction of any person in any criminal proceeding may be used without limitation for purposes of impeachment or enhancement in any criminal proceedings.

The Evidence Code, Section 788, provides that the judge in a criminal trial has discretion to exclude impeachment evidence of prior felony convictions of the accused, if the judge determined that the probative value and credibility of the prior convictions are outweighed by the risk of undue prejudice. In *People v. Olmedo* (167 Cal. App. 3d 1085), a California court of appeals held that Proposition 8 did not change that section in that the judge still had the discretion to exclude the prior conviction if the risk of undue prejudice outweighed the probative value of evidence.

The California Supreme Court, in *People v. Castro* (38 Cal. 3d 301), held that the drafters of the initiative did not merely intend to abolish a trial court's power to exclude certain evidence, but intended to revert to the rule that, subject to the trial court's discretion, priors are admissible to impeach.

Diminished Capacity

The proposition abolished the defense of diminished capacity in all criminal proceedings. Accordingly, evidence of an accused's intoxication, trauma, mental illness, disease, or defect is not admissible to negate the capacity to form a particular intent or motive (PC 25[a]). The court may consider evidence of diminished capacity at the time of sentencing or other disposition.

Insanity

Proposition 8 restored the M'Naghten Test as the test for legal insanity. This test is discussed in Chapter 3.

Prior Conviction When an Element of the Offense

The proposition provides that when a prior conviction is an element of the offense, it shall be proven to the jury (or judge in a court trial) in open court. This section was enacted to stop the defense practice of stipulating as to the prior conviction and thereby keeping from the jury the facts of the prior conviction. In *People v. Callegri* (154 Cal. App. 3d 856), a California court of appeals held that the trial court did not err in refusing to allow the defendant to stipulate to his prior conviction where the prior conviction was an element of the offense with which the defendant was charged.

Victims' Rights

The victim or the next of kin of the victim, if the victim is dead, has a right to amend all sentencing proceedings and shall be given adequate notice by the probation officer of all the proceedings. The victim or next of kin also has the right to make a statement at the sentencing proceedings regarding the crime, the person responsible, and the need for restitution. The trial court shall consider the statements of the victims or next of kin prior to imposing any sentence and shall make a statement on the record of the court's conclusion as to whether or not the defendant would pose a threat to public safety (PC 1191). The failure of the probation officer to comply with the notification requirements set forth in Proposition 8, however, does not deprive a superior court of its jurisdiction to proceed *(People v. Superior Court (Thompson)* 154 Cal. App. 3d 319).

Sentence Enhancement

The proposition modified PC 667(a) to provide that any person convicted of a serious felony who has previously been convicted of a serious felony shall receive, in addition to the sentence imposed by the court for the present offense, a five-year enhancement for each such prior conviction. The terms for the present offense and each enhancement shall run consecutively. In *People v. Fritz* (40 Cal. 3d 227), the California Supreme Court held that a judge had discretionary power to strike a prior felony conviction and thereby forgo the additional five-year serious felony enhancement.

Serious felonies for the purposes of this enhancement are those felonies listed in PC 1192.7 and include the following:

1. Murder or voluntary manslaughter
2. Rape
3. Mayhem
4. Sodomy by force, violence, duress, or fear of immediate and unlawful bodily injury on the victim, or another
5. Lewd or lascivious acts on a child under the age of 14 years
6. Any felony punishable by death or imprisonment for life
7. Oral copulation by force, threat, duress, and so on
8. Robbery
9. Kidnapping
10. Burglary of a residence
11. Selling, furnishing, and so on, of heroin, cocaine, or PCP
12. Any felony where great bodily injury is inflicted on any person
13. Any felony in which the defendant uses a firearm
14. Arson
15. Assault by a life prisoner or with intent to commit rape or robbery

16. Assault with a deadly weapon or instrument on a peace officer
17. Assault with a deadly weapon by an inmate

Plea Bargaining

Proposition 8 prohibits plea bargaining in cases involving any serious felony and DUI/DWI offenses, except in the following circumstances:

1. There is insufficient evidence to prove the people's case.
2. The testimony of a material witness cannot be obtained.
3. The reduction or dismissal would not result in a substantial change in sentence (PC 1192.7).

Cases on Point

People v. Superior Court (31 Cal. App. 4th 653)

The court held that the "three strikes" recidivist statute mandating at least 25 years imprisonment upon proof of prior serious felony convictions did not violate the separation of powers doctrine by requiring prosecutorial approval of the court's exercise of asserted power to strike prior conviction allegations in furtherance of justice; the statute had limited or nonexistent impact on asserted judicial power in light of a prior statutory amendment that already had eliminated the court's authority to strike prior conviction allegations in furtherance of justice.

People v. Jameson (177 Cal. App. 3d 658)

The classification of all arsons as serious felonies by PC 667, which provides for five-year enhancement for each prior conviction of serious felony, did not result in imposition of unconstitutionally cruel and unusual punishment on the defendant, who was sentenced to 16-month concurrent terms on each of two counts of arson, with two consecutive five-year enhancements for prior serious felony convictions, resulting in a total sentence of 11 years and four months, even though the act for which the defendant was convicted, which was the burning of his own property with intent to defraud insurer, did not involve violence.

People v. Smith (33 Cal. App. 4th 1586)

When multiple statutory enhancement provisions are available for the same prior offense, only the greatest enhancement will apply.

People v. Lispier (4 Cal. App. 4th 1317)

A suspect's statement can only be excluded if it was obtained in violation of federal constitutional guidelines; the only exception to this is when the issue involves substantive state privilege against self-incrimination, for which the state judicial law preceding passage of the "Truth-in-Evidence" provision of the state constitution controls.

Toomey v. Bunnell (898 F. 2d 741)

The defendant was arrested before the effective date of Proposition 8, which required admission of relevant evidence not barred by the federal exclusionary rule had no due process right to application of pre-Proposition 8 state case law to his case, even if California courts generally chose not to apply Proposition 8 retroactively.

Creative Legal Defense

During July 1992, six U.S. Army Intelligence analysts went on unauthorized leave from their army unit in Augsburg, Germany. The six soldiers, all of whom had top-secret security clearances, were arrested five days later in Gulf Breeze, Florida. They refused to explain why they left their post and were discharged from the army. Later, one of the six, Vance Davis, revealed that the six had been visited by a spirit through a Ouija board, and the spirit told them to leave and assume their role of preparing people for an impending world cataclysm (*California Bar Journal*, December, 1995).

Practicum

You feel that several provisions in the Evidence Code are unfair to the public. What methods/approaches could you use in an attempt to have them modified?

Explain the processes involved in each method or approach.

Discussion Questions

1. How does an appellate court modify existing law?
2. Who makes the final decision on state criminal law issues that don't involve federal issues?
3. What are the restrictions on plea bargaining in cases involving serious felonies?
4. Why would the defense be willing to stipulate as to a prior conviction?
5. To which branch of the state government is the legislative function delegated?
6. What rights does a victim have at a sentencing proceeding?
7. What is the primary concern of the judge in setting bail in a case involving a serious felony?
8. When does a bill become a statute?
9. Explain the meaning of the Supremacy Clause.
10. What is the meaning of the phrase independent state grounds?
11. If a federal law conflicts with a state constitution, which will prevail?
12. If two state statutes are in direct conflict with each other, which one will prevail?

Self-Study Quiz

True/False

1. Proposition 8 eliminated plea bargaining in California.
2. The primary concern of the judge in all bail decisions is public safety.
3. Proposition 8 eliminated the insanity defense.
4. The U.S. Supreme Court is not involved in reviewing state criminal convictions.
5. Proposition 8 eliminated the discretion of trial judges regarding the admissibility of prior convictions.
6. Judicial legislation is direct and a spin-off of legislative power.
7. The California Supreme Court makes the final decision on state issues.
8. In the state of California, only the assembly can initiate a new criminal statute.
9. If one of the two houses of the legislature and the governor agree, a bill becomes a law.
10. Local ordinances are normally modified by legislative action of the state legislature.
11. Most state crimes are contained in the Penal and Motor Vehicle Codes.
12. General laws have uniform operation within the state.
13. Constitutions generally leave the creation and definition of crimes to statutory enactments.
14. There are two basic types of precedent—mandatory and persuasive.

Chapter Exhibits
Chapter Exhibits

California Constitution, Article II, Section 8

(a) The initiative is the power of the electors to propose statutes and amendments to the Constitution and to adopt or reject them.

(b) An initiative measure may be proposed by presenting to the Secretary of State a petition that sets forth the text of the proposed statute or amendment to the Constitution and is certified to have been signed by electors equal in number to 5 percent in the case of a statute, and 8 percent in the case of an amendment to the Constitution, of the votes for all candidates for Governor at the last gubernatorial election.

(c) The Secretary of State shall then submit the measure at the next general election held at least 131 days after it qualifies or at any special statewide election held prior to that general election. The Governor may call a special statewide election for the measure.

(d) An initiative measure embracing more than one subject may not be submitted to the electors or have any effect.

Capacity to Commit Crimes

Justice is the right to the maximum of individual independence compatible with the same liberty for others.
Henri-Frederic Amiel, 1870

3-1 Persons Incapable of Committing Crimes

Penal Code 26—Persons Capable of Committing Crime; Exceptions

All persons are capable of committing crimes except those belonging to the following classes:

- Children under the age of 14, in the absence of clear proof that at the time of committing the act charged against them, they knew its wrongfulness
- Idiots
- Persons who committed the act or made the omission charged under an ignorance or mistake of fact, which disproves any criminal intent
- Persons who committed the act charged without being conscious thereof
- Persons who committed the act or made the omission charged through misfortune or by accident, when it appears that there was no evil design, intention, or culpable negligence
- Persons (unless the crime be punishable with death) who committed the act or made the omission charged under threats or menaces sufficient to show that they had reasonable cause to and did believe their lives would be endangered if they refused

3-1a Discussion

All persons are presumed to have the ability to commit crimes except those just listed in Section 26 of the Code.

Children

The age referred to in PC 26 is chronological age, not mental or moral age. This section creates a rebuttable presumption that a child under the age of 14 is incapable of committing a criminal offense (*In re Gladys R.*, 1 Cal. 3d 855). The "clear proof" standard is the same as "clear and convincing evidence" (*In re Michael B.*, 149 Cal. App. 3d 1073). Juvenile court has primary jurisdiction over youths under the age of 18 who commit criminal offenses. If appropriate, the juvenile court may refer the case to adult criminal court (W & I Code 707). The following criteria are used to determine if the case would be referred to adult criminal court:

1. The degree of criminal sophistication exhibited by the minor
2. Whether the minor can be rehabilitated prior to the expiration of the juvenile court's jurisdiction
3. The minor's previous delinquent history
4. Success of previous attempts by the juvenile court to rehabilitate the minor
5. The circumstances and gravity of the offense alleged in the petition to have been committed by the minor

Idiots

An idiot is a person who is totally without understanding or mentality. An idiot does not know right from wrong and, therefore, does not realize the nature of his or her wrongful act. (Note: Insanity is discussed later in Section 3-10 of this chapter.)

Mistake of Fact

The mistake referred to in PC 26 is a mistake of fact, not of law. A mistake of law (ignorance) is not normally an excuse for committing a criminal act. For example, an accused who takes someone else's coat by mistake is not guilty of larceny (mistake of fact). But the accused who, thinking that the speed limit is 55 mph, drives 50 mph in a 40 mph zone is not excused, since this is not a mistake of fact. In the latter situation, the accused is mistaken as to the legal speed limit (i.e., the law). Likewise, ignorance was not a defense in the case involving a nurse in charge of a private hospital who thought she had the authority to possess narcotics (*People v. Marschalk*, 206 Cal. App. 2d 346). A mistake of law is no excuse even when based on an attorney's advice (*People v. Flumerfelt*, 35 Cal. App. 2d 495).

For specific intent crimes and those crimes that require a special mental element, normally an "honest" mistake of fact is sufficient, if the mistake negates the specific intent or special mental element (*People v. Navarro*, 99 Cal. App. 2d Supp. 1). For general intent crimes, in most cases an "honest and reasonable" mistake of fact is required to excuse criminal liability (*Re Application of Ahart*, 172 Cal. 762). For example, theft is a specific intent crime. Accordingly, if you mistakenly take someone else's coat, it is not theft.

Accident/Misfortune

If the act causing the injury or harm was committed by accident or misfortune not involving criminal negligence, the injury or harm is considered to be "an act of God," and the actor is not criminally responsible for the resultant harm. Strict liability crimes, discussed in Section 1-9g, are an exception to these general rules. An example of an accident would be where an automobile driver is driving with normal caution and not speeding when a young child darts out from between two parked cars. If the driver, without being at fault, hits the child, the resulting injury would be considered as "an act of God." The driver would not be criminally at fault for the injury.

Unconsciousness

Subdivision 5 of PC 26 refers to persons who would otherwise have sufficient capacity but are incapable of committing criminal acts because they are somnambulists, or persons suffering with delirium from fever or drugs (*People v. Methever*, 132 Cal. 326). For example, a person may defend a murder accusation based on unconsciousness following a blow to the head by the assailant (*People v. Cox*, 67 Cal. App. 2d 166). A criminal act committed while a person is "sleepwalking" (somnambulism) is covered by this subdivision. Unconsciousness is a complete defense to the crime. It does not, however, include mental illness.

The subdivision dealing with exceptions to those held accountable for their criminal conduct does not cover insanity or voluntary intoxication (*People v. Taylor*, 31 Cal. App. 2d 723). If the voluntary intoxication, over a period of time, causes permanent brain damage, the issue of insanity may be present. (See discussion on insanity later in Section 3-10a of this chapter.)

Involuntary intoxication, however, appears to be covered by this subdivision. Involuntary intoxication exists when a person becomes intoxicated by taking a substance or drink without realizing that the substance or drink contains alcohol or drugs. The defendant in *People v. Velez* (175 Cal. App. 3d 785) could not use the defense of unconsciousness as the result of involuntary intoxication based on the fact that he did not know the marijuana he was smoking was laced with PCP. The court stated that the defendant's act of smoking the marijuana, an intoxicating substance, prevented him from raising the unconsciousness defense.

If the defendant committed the criminal act under duress, the duress may be a complete defense.

3-2 Duress

3-2a Elements of Duress

For duress under Subdivision 6 to constitute a defense, there must be

- A reasonable and
- Actual belief
- That a life is in danger or serious bodily injury is threatened, and
- That the danger is present and immediate (*People v. Coleman*, 53 Cal. App. 2d 18).

The following threats of duress are not sufficient:

- Threats of future harm
- Threats to damage reputation or profession
- Unreasonable beliefs

Duress is not a defense to a capital crime. In cases involving aggravated assault or battery, if the duress is not sufficient to constitute a defense, it may still reduce the crime to a simple assault or battery.

3-3 Entrapment

The entrapment defense is intended to prevent the government from "manufacturing" crime (Loewy, *Criminal Law* 2d ed. 187). Therefore, the defense of entrapment is available only in those cases where the crime was not contemplated by the defendant but was actually planned and instigated by the police (*People v. Benford*, 53 Cal. 2d 1). The entrapment defense does not prevent the police from setting a trap for the unwary criminal (*Sherman v. U.S.*, 356 U.S. 369). The police may provide a person who is predisposed to commit a crime with the opportunity to commit the crime. For example, it is not entrapment to set up a drug buy from a person who is predisposed to sell drugs. Note: The entrapment defense is aimed at governmental misconduct. Thus, the entrapment defense is not available if the entrapment is accomplished by a private person not associated with the government (*People v. Wirth*, 186 Cal. App. 2d 68).

The one test for entrapment is the "innocence" test (*People v. Benford*, 53 Cal. 2d 1). Was the crime the result of "creative activity" by the police or did the police merely offer an opportunity for a willing criminal to commit a criminal offense? The test currently being used in state cases is set forth in *People v. Barranza* (23 Cal. 3d 675). The test is: "Was the conduct of the law enforcement agent likely to induce a normally law-abiding person to commit a criminal offense?"

3-4 Battered Person Syndrome

Evidence Code 1107

(a) In a criminal action, expert testimony is admissible by either the prosecution or the defense regarding battered women's syndrome, including the physical, emotional, or mental effects upon the beliefs, perceptions, or behavior of victims of domestic violence, except when offered against a criminal defendant to prove the occurrence of the act or acts of abuse which form the basis of the criminal charge.

(b) The foundation shall be sufficient for admission of this expert testimony if the proponent of the evidence establishes its relevancy and the proper qualifications of the expert witness. Expert opinion testimony on battered women's syndrome shall not be considered a new scientific technique whose reliability is unproven.

(c) For purposes of this section, "abuse" is defined in Section 6203 of the Family Code and "domestic violence" is defined in Section 6211 of the Family Code.

(d) This section is intended as a rule of evidence only and no substantive change affecting the Penal Code is intended.

Penal Code 4801—Prisoners Deserving Pardons, etc.; Report by Board of Prison Terms

The Board of Prison Terms may report to the Governor, from time to time, the names of any and all persons imprisoned in any state prison who, in its judgment, ought to have a commutation of sentence or be pardoned and set at liberty on account of good conduct, or unusual term of sentence, or any other cause, including evidence of battered woman syndrome. For purposes of this section, "evidence of battered woman syndrome" may include evidence of the effects of physical, emotional, or mental abuse upon the beliefs, perceptions, or behavior of victims of domestic violence where it appears the criminal behavior was the result of that victimization.

3-5 Alibi

An accused relying on an alibi must prove the alibi to such a degree of certainty as will, upon a consideration of all the evidence, leave a reasonable doubt of the accused's guilt in the minds of the jury (*People v. Alexander*, 78 Cal. App. 2d 954). The defendant need not prove the alibi beyond a reasonable doubt or by a preponderance of evidence, but he or she has the burden to prove the alibi to such degree of certainty as will leave a reasonable doubt of guilt in the minds of the jury, and if he or she carries such burden, he is entitled to acquittal (*People v. Lewis*, 81 Cal. App. 2d 119). Note, an alibi needs be proven only so as to raise a reasonable doubt whether the defendant was present when the crime was committed (*People v. Roberts*, 122 Cal. 377).

Penal Code 1054.3 requires that the defense disclose the names and addresses of persons other than the defendant whom the defense intends to call as witnesses at trial. Thus, the defense must notify the prosecution when the defense intends to call any alibi witnesses. The courts have held that the requirement of the defense to provide discovery regarding its witnesses in support of an alibi defense does not constitute compelled self-incrimination, and therefore, does not implicate Fifth Amendment privilege, where discovery merely forces defendant to divulge at earlier date information that defendant from beginning planned to divulge at trial. (*Izazaga v. Superior Court [People]*, 54 Cal. 3d 356).

3-6 Consent

Consent of the victim is not a defense to criminal prosecution, except in those cases where lack of consent of the victim is an element of the crime (Witkin, *California Crimes*, 163). Listed in the following are some of the common situations involving the question of consent:

1. Assault and battery—Consent is not a defense to assault and battery. It is a consent to ordinary physical contact involved in sporting events.
2. Rape—In most cases, sexual intercourse is not rape if the victim consents. However, the victim must be legally capable of giving consent. This aspect is discussed in Chapter 9.
3. Theft and robbery—Valid consent to taking of the property is a defense to theft and robbery crimes. Failure to take action to prevent the taking of the property (passive conduct) is not considered as consent.
4. To constitute consent on the part of the victim, the consent must be freely and voluntarily given and not under the influence of fraud, threats, force, or duress.

3-7 Necessity

The defense of necessity is very similar to that of duress discussed earlier in Section 3-2. In the necessity defense, however, the coercive force that is used to justify the criminal act is one of nature rather than human forces. For example, breaking and entering into a cabin in the mountains to keep from freezing may constitute a defense to the crime of breaking and entering. Unlike duress, however, the necessity defense need not be based on the avoidance of death or injury to humans. It may be used to avoid a greater harm. The necessity defense is not available if another alternative is available and is legal. For example, it is not permissible to steal clothes for needy children because other legal alternatives are available. The defense is also not available to defendants who created the necessity to choose between two evils. For example, the hunter who decided not to take warm clothing because if he needs them but doesn't have them he could break into a cabin, will not be able to use this defense.

3-8 Multiple-Personality Disorder

Multiple-personality disorder has been used in many cases in an attempt to establish the defendant's inability to form the necessary mental state or as a factor in mitigation. The condition known as multiple-personality disorder (MPD) was first discussed in 1908 by Morton Prince. It is surrounded by controversy, and actual scientific evidence on the disorder is limited. Most researchers contend that multiple personalities are diagnosed because of an interaction between the patient's needs and the therapist's goals. According to one line of thought, transference creates a situation in which the therapist has the power to encourage some character tendencies and discourage others, allowing what was merely a tendency to blossom into an apparent personality. For example, a defendant feeling guilty about committing a rape, but not guilty enough to admit guilt, develops two personalities and blames the other personality for the horrible crime. This line of thought continues with the theory that self-dramatizing, hysterical persons are most likely to be affected with MPD, and many want to use it to attract attention or avoid responsibility for some of their behavior.

3-9 Cultural Disorientation

Cultural disorientation has been presented in some cases to mitigate the seriousness of the offense or to lower the degree of the offense. The defense is based on the concept that the defendant failed to adapt to the culturalization process. The culturalization process is that process whereby an individual learns the proper rules of society and how to act. The gist of this defense is to blame society for the defendant's failure to learn how to act properly.

3-10 Insanity

Penal Code 25—Diminished Capacity; Insanity; Evidence

(a) The defense of diminished capacity is hereby abolished. In a criminal action, as well as any juvenile court proceeding, evidence concerning an accused person's intoxication, trauma, mental illness, disease, or defect shall not be admissible to show or negate capacity to form the particular purpose, intent, motive, malice aforethought, knowledge, or other mental state required for the commission of the crime charged.

(b) In any criminal proceeding, including any juvenile court proceeding, in which a plea of not guilty by reason of insanity is entered, this defense shall be found by the trier of fact only when the accused person proves by a preponderance of the evidence that he or she was incapable of knowing or understanding the nature and quality of his or her act and of distinguishing right from wrong at the time of the commission of the offense.

(c) Notwithstanding the foregoing, evidence of diminished capacity or of a mental disorder may be considered by the court only at the time of sentencing or other disposition or commitment.

(d) The provisions of this section shall not be amended by the legislature except by statute passed in each house by roll call vote entered in the journal, two-thirds of the membership concurring, or by a statute that becomes effective only when approved by the electors.

Penal Code 25.5—Insanity Plea—Limitations

In any criminal proceeding in which a plea of not guilty by reason of insanity is entered, this defense shall not be found by the trier of fact solely on the basis of a personality or adjustment disorder, a seizure disorder, or an addiction to, or abuse of, intoxicating substances.

The doctrine of partial insanity is not recognized in California (*People v. Troche,* 206 Cal. 35). Insanity is either a complete defense or no defense at all. There is no middle ground in California criminal law (*People v. Perry,* 195 Cal. 623). Prior to 1978, California used the M'Naghten Test (a person is insane if, when the offense was committed, the person was laboring under such a mental disease or defect that he or she did not know the nature and quality of the act, or, if the accused did know it, the accused did not know that what he or she was doing was wrong) as the test for insanity. In 1978, the California Supreme Court in *People v. Drew* (22 Cal. 3d 333) adopted the American Law Institute Test as the standard for California. Proposition 8 (June 1982), however, reinstated the M'Naghten Test (*People v. Horn,* 158 Cal. App. 3d 1014). Note: The M'Naghten Test is also referred to as the "right from wrong" test.

3-10a Discussion

The leading case in California on insanity is *People v. Skinner* (39 Cal. 3d 765). In that case, the court held that if mental illness is manifested in delusions that render individuals incapable either of knowing the nature and character of their act, or of understanding that it is wrong, in the moral rather than legal sense, they are legally insane.

In California state trials, the issue of insanity must be specially pled. This is accomplished by pleading "not guilty by reason of insanity." Note: To raise the issue of not guilty of the crime and the issue of insanity, the accused must plead both "not guilty" and "not guilty by reason of insanity." The law presumes that an individual is sane, and the burden of proof to establish the insanity defense by a preponderance of evidence is on the accused (*People v. Loomis,* 170 Cal. 347). The hearing on the issue of insanity will be conducted after a finding that the accused committed the offense.

Temporary Insanity

Temporary insanity existing at the time of the act may be sufficient to meet the legal test of insanity (*People v. Donegan,* 32 Cal. App. 2d 716). If the defendant is insane at the time that the act is committed, it is immaterial whether the insanity lasted several months or merely a number of hours (*People v. McCarthy,* 110 Cal. App. 3d 296).

Diminished Capacity

Proposition 8 (passed June 1982) abolished the diminished capacity defense in California. This defense was used in the past to negate the necessary intent in specific intent crimes. For example, in many cases, the accused would enter evidence to establish that he or she was too intoxicated to form the necessary intent to commit murder in the first degree. Currently, the court may consider evidence of diminished capacity only at the time of sentencing or other disposition or commitment of the defendant (PC 25). As discussed later, evidence of mental disorder may be used to establish that the defendant is not guilty by reason of insanity.

3-11 Intoxication

Penal Code 22—Voluntary Intoxication

(a) No act committed by a person while in a state of voluntary intoxication is less criminal by reason of his having been in such condition. Evidence of voluntary intoxication shall not be admitted to negate the capacity to form any mental states for the crimes charged, including, but not limited to, purpose, intent, knowledge, premeditation, deliberation, or malice aforethought, with which the accused committed the act.
(b) Evidence of voluntary intoxication is admissible solely on the issue of whether or not the defendant actually formed a required specific intent, or, when charged with murder, whether the defendant premeditated, deliberated, or harbored malice aforethought, when a specific intent crime is charged.
(c) Voluntary intoxication includes the voluntary ingestion, injection, or taking by any other means of any intoxicating liquor, drug, or other substance.

3-11a Discussion

In most cases, voluntary intoxication is not a defense to or an excuse for criminal conduct. An exception to the preceding general rule is where the voluntary intoxication causes insanity. Insanity caused by voluntary intoxication is a defense (*People v. Kelly,* 10 Cal. 3d 565).

Evidence of voluntary intoxication may not be admitted to negate the capacity to form the criminal intent regarding:

- Knowledge
- Premeditation
- Deliberation
- Purpose
- Intent
- Malice aforethought

Specific Intent Crimes

With crimes involving specific intent, evidence that the accused was too intoxicated and therefore did not form the required specific intent is admissible to establish that the crime was not committed. For example, an accused may establish that he or she did not have the necessary criminal intent to commit the crime of burglary because of voluntary intoxication. In this situation, the accused is not entering evidence to negate the capacity to commit the crime, but to establish that the crime was not committed. Note: Voluntary intoxication is not a defense to, nor a legal excuse for, general intent crimes.

3-12 Urban Survival Syndrome

Urban survival syndrome is based on the concept that an individual growing up in an urban environment learns to react to events (socialization process) in an aggressive manner. Accordingly, the defendant reacted violently in a situation not because he or she was bad or mean, but because that was the natural reaction as the result of poor socialization. The syndrome is derived from Marven Wolfgang's subculture of violence theory. Wolfgang contends that certain youth in our inner cities learn to react with violence as a normal course of conduct.

Post-traumatic stress syndrome is used to either show that the defendant was not mentally capable to commit the crime or to mitigate the seriousness of the crime. It is based on the fact that the defendant has been exposed to a traumatic event in which he or she experienced, witnessed, or was confronted with an event or events that involved actual or threatened death or serious injury, or a threat to the physical integrity of self or others. The defendant's normal responses involve intense fear, helplessness, or horror. The disturbance is considered to cause impairment in social, occupational, or other important areas of functioning. The reactions may be delayed for years after the traumatic event. According to researchers, the traumatic event is persistently reexperienced in one or more of the following ways:

3-13 Post-Traumatic Stress Syndrome

- Recurrent and intrusive distressing recollection of the event, including images, thoughts, or perceptions
- Recurrent distressing dreams of the event
- Acting or feeling as if the traumatic event were recurring (including a sense of reliving the experience, illusions, hallucinations, and dissociative flashbacks, including those that occur on awaking or when intoxicated)
- Intense psychological distress at exposure to internal or external cues that symbolize or resemble an aspect of the traumatic event
- Physiological reactivity on exposure to internal or external cues that symbolize or resemble an aspect of the traumatic event
- Persistent avoidance of stimuli associated with the trauma and numbing of general responsiveness
- Efforts to avoid thought, feelings, or conversations associated with the trauma
- Feelings of detachment or estrangement from others

During the first set of symptoms, the victims are generally edgy, irritable, easily startled, and constantly on guard. For example, the Vietnam veteran always sits with his back to a wall; the rape victim watches for potential rapists everywhere. Victims sleep poorly, and they are agitated and find it difficult to concentrate. This group of symptoms is often described as hyperalertness or hyperarousal.

The second set of symptoms is called intrusion. Victims involuntarily reexperience the traumatic event in the form of memories, nightmares, and flashbacks during which they may feel or even act as though the event were recurring. Often they recall these episodes poorly or not at all. They also suffer when they are exposed to anything that resembles, recalls, or symbolizes some aspect of the trauma: an anniversary, the sight of a uniformed guard, the sound of fire or gunfire. For example, a woman who was raped in an elevator may begin to sweat and breathe rapidly whenever she enters one. A man whose comrade died from a grenade thrown at his chest develops these symptoms of pain after open-heart surgery.

The third set of symptoms occurs when victims no longer suffer these involuntary reminders of trauma. These symptoms are often described as emotional constriction or numbing (i.e., a need to avoid feelings, thoughts, and situations reminiscent of the trauma, a loss of normal emotional responses, or both). Most of their feelings seem unreal to them, and the ordinary business of life no longer matters.

They feel cut off from the concerns of others and unable to trust them. It seems to them that the future holds nothing. At the same time, they may feel anger at those responsible for the traumatic experience, ashamed of their own helplessness, or guilt about what they thought or did or failed to do. They become demoralized and isolated because of their anger, guilt, shame, avoidance, and emotional numbness.

3-14 Malice

Penal Code 7(4)—Malice Defined

The words *malice* and *maliciously* import a wish to vex, annoy, or injure another person, or an intent to do a wrongful act, established either by proof or presumption of law.

3-14a Discussion

Malice, as used in PC 7(4), has a different meaning from the general usage definition. Malice under this statute can be classified as "malice in fact" and "malice in law." Malice in fact (or actual malice), similar to the general usage definition, is referred to in the first part of the statute by the words "import a wish to vex, annoy, or injure another person." Malice in law is set forth by the words "an intent to do a wrongful act."

Malice in law may exist in addition to or independent of malice in fact. Malice in fact has been described as the intentional doing of a wrongful act without just reason or excuse for the conduct (*Davis v. Hearst*, 160 Cal. 143).

The Penal Code refers to a third type of malice—malice aforethought. The definition of malice aforethought is contained in PC 188 immediately after the crime of murder. It has no general application and is limited only to those crimes that have malice aforethought as an element of the crime. Malice aforethought is discussed in Chapter 8, which covers homicide.

3-15 Motive

Motive is the cause or reason that an act is committed (*People v. Lane*, 100 Cal. 379). It is the moving cause or the ulterior purpose of the offender (*People v. Durrant*, 116 Cal. 179). Except for crimes involving the heat of passion or sudden and sufficient provocation, motive is not normally an element of the crime and need not be proven by the prosecution (*People v. Woo*, 181 Cal. 315). Often evidence of motive is used to establish or rebut malice when malice is an element of the crime.

There is a difference between motive and intention. Intention to commit a crime may exist with or without a motive for doing it. In most cases, motive precedes intent. The classical example of the difference between motive and intent is when A kills B to get B's money. A's intent was to commit murder; A's motive was to get the money.

3-16 Statute of Limitations

Penal Code 799—No Limitation for Commencement of Prosecution

Prosecution for an offense punishable by death or imprisonment in the state prison for life or for life without the possibility of parole, or for the embezzlement of public money, may be commenced at any time.

Penal Code 800—Six-Year Limitation

Except as provided in Section 799, prosecution for an offense punishable by imprisonment in the state prison for eight years or more shall be commenced within six years after the commission of the offense.

Penal Code 801—Three-Year Limitation

Except as provided in Sections 799 and 800, prosecution for an offense punishable by imprisonment in the state prison shall be commenced within three years after commission of the offense. [A felony]

The statute of limitations sets forth the period of time after the commission of the crime within which prosecution against the accused must be started. Failure to start the prosecution within the required time period acts as a bar to prosecution. As indicated in PC 799, some crimes, like murder, have no statute of limitations.

3-16a Definition

Section 801 provides a limitation period of three years applicable to all felonies not otherwise dealt with expressly. Section 801 does not apply to capital crimes or crimes punishable by life imprisonment, or to embezzlement of public money, for which there is no limitation period (Section 799), or to felonies punishable by eight years or more imprisonment, for which there is a six-year limitation period (Section 800). In addition, the three-year limitation period of Section 801 is tolled until discovery of crimes involving fraud or public officials (Section 803).

3-16b Discussion

Penal Code 803.6—Three-Year Limitation; Fraudulent Insurance Claims

Notwithstanding Section 801 or any other provision of the law, prosecution for a violation of Section 556 of the Insurance Code shall be commenced within four years after discovery of the commission of the offense, or within four years after the completion of the offense, whichever is later.

Penal Code 802—One-Year Limitation; Exceptions

(a) Except as provided in subdivision (b), prosecution of an offense not punishable by death or imprisonment in the state prison shall be commenced within one year after commission of the offense. [A misdemeanor]
(b) Prosecution for a misdemeanor violation of Section 647.6 or former Section 647.6 [Note: Those sections pertain to misdemeanor child molesters, i.e., annoying or molesting a child under circumstances not amounting to a felony], committed with or upon a minor under the age of 14, shall be commenced within two years after the commission of the offense.

Penal Code 804—When Prosecution for an Offense Is Commenced

For the purpose of this chapter, prosecution for an offense is commenced when any of the following occurs:

- An indictment or information is filed.
- A complaint is filed with an inferior court charging a public offense of which the inferior court has original trial jurisdiction.
- A case is certified to the superior court.
- An arrest warrant or bench warrant is issued, providing the warrant names or describes the defendant with the same degree of particularity required for an indictment, information, or complaint.

Time Requirements

The statute of limitations requires that criminal prosecutions commence within a certain period of time after the crime occurred. There are time periods, however, that are excluded in determining whether or not prosecution was started within the required time. The excluded time periods are noted in the following discussion. The statute of limitations is a jurisdictional requirement.

Accordingly, failure to begin prosecution within the required time bars the state from prosecuting the accused (*People v. Doctor*, 257 Cal. App. 2d 105). In addition, the accused may assert the bar of limitations at any time during the trial (*People v. Witt*, 53 Cal. App. 3d 154).

Offenses with a six-year statute of limitations include:

- Rape (PC 261)
- Child molesting (PC 288)
- Sodomy by force or fear (PC 286d)
- Oral copulation by force or fear (PC 288a)

Offenses with a three-year statute of limitations include:

- Grand theft (PC 487)
- Felony welfare fraud (W & I 11483)
- Forgery (PC 470)
- Manslaughter (PC 192.1 or .2)
- Perjury (PC 118)

There is no statute of limitations for murder, embezzlement of public money, and kidnapping for ransom.

Prosecution, for statute of limitations purposes, is normally started with an arrest of the defendant on a warrant or the filing of a sworn information, complaint, or indictment. The information, complaint, or indictment must indicate on its "face" that the statute has not expired (run out). This requirement is normally accomplished by pleading the date on which the offense occurred. By looking at that date and the date on which the information or indictment was filed is normally sufficient to indicate that the statute of limitations does not bar prosecution. When the pleadings are sufficient, then the question as to whether the statute of limitations bars prosecution is an evidentiary question for the courts to decide (*People v. Padfield*, 136 Cal. App. 3d 218).

Time is computed by excluding the first day (date the crime was committed) and including the last (when prosecution starts) (*People v. Twedt*, 1 Cal. 2d 392). In the case of a continuing offense, the last day that the offense was committed or continued is the date used as the first day.

Certain periods of time (tolled) are excluded in computing the statute of limitations. The following is a list of the most common events that either toll or delay the running of the statute of limitations:

1. During the period of time that the accused is absent from the jurisdiction of the state (for a maximum of three years) (PC 803[e]). The absence may be established by circumstantial evidence such as a fruitless search for the defendant (*People v. McGill*, 10 Cal. App. 2d 159).
2. In many cases, the statute of limitations does not start until the discovery of the offense or the date when it should have been discovered (PC 803).
3. During the period of time that the accused is being prosecuted or prosecution is pending for the same conduct in any California state court (PC 803[b]). For example, the defendant is charged with the commission of an offense within the time period. If all charges are later dismissed, the period of time that the charges were pending is excluded in computing the time period.

If the defendant is accused of an offense for which the statute does not bar prosecution, he or she cannot be convicted of a lesser included offense for which the state does bar prosecution. For example, in *People v. Rose* (28 Cal. App. 3d 415), the defendant was indicted for murder many years after the crime was committed. (Note: There is no limitation period for this offense.) The court held that he could not be convicted of manslaughter (a lesser included offense) because the statute of limitations barred prosecution for the manslaughter charge. A court, however, held in one case that an accused could be convicted of conspiracy to commit a misdemeanor (a felony) even though the statute of limitations barred prosecution on the subject misdemeanor (*People v. Lilliock,* 265 Cal. App. 2d 419).

Modification of Statute of Limitations

If the statute of limitations bars the prosecution of a crime, the later modification of the statute does not extend the period of time to prosecution. If, however, the statute of limitations does not currently bar prosecution, the legislature may extend it for previously committed crimes (*Sobiek v. Superior Court,* 28 Cal. App. 3d 846). In that case, the accused was charged with forgery committed before the legislature extended the statute of limitations. The court stated that the legislature could extend a still operative period of limitations but could not revive a period that had already expired.

U.S. Constitution, Amendment V [partial]

[N]or shall any person be subject for the same offense to be twice put in jeopardy of life or limb. . . .

Persons may not be twice put in jeopardy for the same offense.

3-17 Double Jeopardy

3-17a Definition

The constitutional guarantee against double jeopardy involves three separate protections:

1. Protecting an accused from being prosecuted for the same offense after acquittal
2. Protecting an accused from being prosecuted for the same offense after conviction
3. Protecting an accused from multiple punishments for the same criminal conduct (*United States v. DiFrancesco,* 449 U.S. 117)

3-17b Discussion

The doctrine is intended to protect an accused from the harassment of multiple trials. Accordingly, to be placed in jeopardy for a second time, the accused must be placed on trial for a second time (*People v. Thomas,* 121 Cal. App. 2d 754). Double jeopardy does not apply where the trial is bifurcated (separated into two proceedings) by the defendant who enters both "not guilty" and "not guilty by reason of insanity" pleas (*People v. Coen,* 205 Cal. 596).

Identity of Offenses

For double jeopardy to apply, the prosecution must be for the same offense as that involved in the earlier proceedings. For purposes of double jeopardy, offenses are considered the same if one is necessarily included in the other.

Waiver

Since double jeopardy is not a jurisdictional issue, the accused must assert the bar against prosecution. The double jeopardy bar is regarded as waived unless the defense raises it during pleading. If the defense is asserted, the defense has the burden to establish the validity of the former jeopardy claim (*People v. Eggleston*, 255 Cal. App. 2d 337).

Double jeopardy as a bar to prosecution must be specifically pleaded in the form prescribed by the Penal Code. The pleas must indicate the time, place, and court of the alleged former jeopardy. A general plea of not guilty does not raise the issue (*People v. Barry*, 153 Cal. App. 2d 193).

Different Crimes

If the same act is made punishable by different provisions of the California statutes, it may be punished under any of them. In no case, however, may the accused be punished under more than one, and an acquittal or conviction and sentence under one bars (prevents) the prosecution under another provision (*People v. Manago*, 230 Cal. App. 2d 645). If either crime requires the proof of a different fact additional to those involved in the other, there is no double jeopardy (*People v. Coltrin*, 5 Cal. 2d 649). For example, the accused may be charged with the possession of an illegal firearm and robbery involving the use of a firearm. This is based on the fact that to establish robbery, additional facts are needed other than the possession of a firearm. In addition, to establish illegal possession of a firearm, the prosecution must establish that possession of the weapon was illegal; a fact that is not required for the robbery charge. In one case, a defendant's conviction for reckless driving did not prevent the state from trying him for manslaughter committed by the same conduct since different elements were required to be established for each crime (*People v. Herbert*, 6 Cal. 2d 541).

Res Judicata

Double jeopardy is not the same as *res judicata*. *Res judicata*, a Latin phrase meaning "stands decided," is based on a final adjudication of the same issue involving the same parties to the trial. In most cases, double jeopardy attaches prior to final adjudication and, unlike *res judicata*, it is a constitutionally protected right. In addition, *res judicata* applies to civil proceedings, whereas double jeopardy applies only to criminal cases.

Protection against double jeopardy does not apply to civil or administrative proceedings. Accordingly, in *U.S. v. One Assortment of Firearms* (79 L. Ed. 2d 361), a gun owner's acquittal on criminal charges involving firearms did not bar a subsequent prosecution in forfeiture proceedings (civil action) against the firearms. Note: *Res judicata* did not apply because there are different parties involved. In the criminal case, the accused was the principal party; in the civil case, being "in rem" the case was against the guns. ("In rem" proceedings refer to the fact that the action in the case is against an object, not a person.)

Attachment of Jeopardy

As noted, double jeopardy does not apply unless the accused has previously been put in jeopardy. The following are some of the cases involving the question of whether or not the accused was placed in jeopardy.

1. The accused is acquitted based on a variance between the pleading and the evidence entered at trial. No double jeopardy if the acquittal is based on mere variance rather than on an entire want of evidence. This is based on the concept that since he could not be convicted on the pleadings, he never was in jeopardy. If the variance, however, is immaterial and the accused could have been convicted, the double jeopardy bar would apply (*People v. Webb*, 38 Cal. 467).

2. Jeopardy attaches in a jury case, when the jury has been impaneled and sworn (*People v. Hinshaw,* 194 Cal. 1).

3. Jeopardy attaches in a judge alone case when the trial has been "entered upon" (*People v. Beasley,* 5 Cal. App. 3d 617). A trial has been "entered upon" when either the first witness is sworn or evidence is entered against the accused.

4. Jeopardy does not attach if the pleadings are invalid (*People v. Webb,* 38 Cal. 467).

After Jeopardy Attaches

In certain situations, the accused may be tried again even if jeopardy has attached. The following list includes some common situations involving the question of whether or not the accused may be tried a second time.

1. A double jeopardy bar prevents prosecution when the first case is dismissed after the jury is sworn without the consent of the accused and when not authorized by law (*Cardenas v. Superior Court,* 56 Cal. 2d 273).

2. Discharge of the jury prior to the jury rendering a verdict without the consent of the accused and not required by law is tantamount to an acquittal and bars a retrial (*People v. Webb,* 38 Cal. 467).

3. A mistrial granted on motion of the defense is not a bar to a second trial. A mistrial, however, granted by the court to protect the rights of the accused is a bar to a second trial unless the accused consents to the mistrial or a mistrial is required by the law (*People v. McNeer,* 8 Cal. App. 2d 676).

4. A mistrial granted when the jury is unable to reach a verdict is within the discretion of the judge and absent abuse of discretion by the judge, it is not a bar to a second trial (*Curry v. Superior Court,* 2 Cal. 3d 707) and (PC 1140).

5. A mistrial granted where because of sickness of a jury member or an accident prevents the jury from reaching a verdict is not a bar to a second trial (PC 1141).

6. A mistrial granted on motion of the defendant is no bar to a second prosecution (*Oregon v. Kennedy,* 456 U.S. 667). When an accused requests a mistrial or appeals a court judgment, the motion or appeal is considered a waiver of the double jeopardy bar. The one exception to this rule is when the conviction is reversed on appeal based on insufficient evidence to support the conviction as a matter of law. In this latter case, double jeopardy protection is a bar to retrial (*Burks v. U.S.,* 437 U.S. 1).

7. The double jeopardy protection prevents the state from appealing an acquittal. If, however, the state successfully appeals a court order dismissing an indictment or information prior to jeopardy attaching, the accused may be retried (*People v. Petti,* 149 Cal. App. 3d 1).

Dual Sovereignty Doctrine

Dual sovereignty doctrine applies when the same conduct constitutes crimes against more than one state or the federal government. In these situations, the accused has violated the criminal statutes of two different sovereigns (normally state and federal), and therefore he or she may be tried by both governments. For example, robbing a federally insured bank in the state is a violation of both state and federal law, and the accused may be prosecuted by both. Note: See restrictions imposed in California by PC 794 (discussed in following "Statutory Bar" section).

Statutory Bar

"Statutory bar" is a term sometimes used by the courts if the bar to prosecution is created by statute and not by constitution. The Penal Code includes several provisions that bar prosecution in cases where the constitutional protection of double jeopardy does not. For example, PC 794 provides that when an act is also a criminal act in another state or country, the acquittal by a court in the other state or country will bar prosecution in the state of California.

3-18 Lesser and Included Offenses

Penal Code 1159—Conviction of Offense Included in Charge

The jury, or the judge if a jury trial is waived, may find the defendant guilty of any offense, the commission of which is necessarily included in that with which he is charged, or of an attempt to commit the offense.

3-18a Discussion

As stated in the PC 1159, the defendant may be convicted of any offense, the commission of which is necessarily included in the crime with which he or she was charged. A defendant, however, cannot be convicted of an included offense that is barred by the statute of limitations, even if the statute has not expired for the greater offense charged (*People v. Miller,* 12 Cal. 291). If the defendant is charged with two offenses in separate courts and one is necessarily included in the other, he or she cannot be sentenced for both (*People v. Sutton,* 35 Cal. App. 3d 264). For example, assault is a necessarily included offense to battery. Accordingly, for one act that amounts to a battery, the accused may not be sentenced for both the assault (which is included in the battery) and the battery.

Test for Lesser and Included Offense

The test to determine if one offense is a necessarily included offense of another is that when one offense cannot be committed without committing the other offense, then the latter offense is a necessarily included offense. For example, an accused could not be convicted of both an assault and a battery for the same act of striking a victim in the face with his or her fist. The assault is a necessarily included offense of the battery. It is not an included offense if additional evidence is required to convict the accused of the lesser offense. For example, speeding is not a necessarily included offense of driving under the influence, because an individual may be driving under the influence without exceeding the speed limit. A single act may violate two separate statutes and therefore constitute two separate crimes. For example, the accused may be speeding and also driving under the influence. The act of driving, therefore, constitutes two separate crimes.

3-19 Jurisdiction and Venue

Penal Code 681—Legal Conviction Prerequisite to Punishment

No person can be punished for a public offense, except upon a legal conviction in a court having jurisdiction thereof.

Penal Code 777—Crimes in General

Every person is liable to punishment by the laws of this State, for a public offense committed by him therein, except where it is by law cognizable exclusively in the courts of the United States; and except as otherwise provided by law the jurisdiction of every public offense is in any competent court within the jurisdictional territory of which it is committed.

U.S. Constitution, Amendment VI

In all criminal prosecutions, the accused shall enjoy the right to a speedy and public trial, by an impartial jury of the state and district wherein the crime shall have been committed. . . .

Jurisdiction is the authority by which courts and judicial officers take cognizance of and decide cases. There are two types of jurisdiction: (1) of the subject matter and (2) of the person. Venue refers to the physical or geographical location of the court in which trial will be or has been tried. In the Penal Code, the term *territory jurisdiction* is used in place of the common law word *venue*. In most cases, the two are considered interchangeable.

Jurisdiction is the power of a court to try a case and to issue an order. Jurisdiction cannot be conferred by consent (*Griggs v. Superior Court,* 16 Cal. 3d 341). Jurisdiction must be alleged in the accusatory pleadings (*People v. Smith,* 231 Cal. App. 2d 140). Jurisdiction may, however, be established by a preponderance of the evidence, and circumstantial evidence is sufficient to establish jurisdiction (*People v. Cavanaugh,* 44 Cal. 2d 252). The two important types of jurisdiction are *subject matter jurisdiction* and *jurisdiction over the person.*

Subject Matter Jurisdiction

Subject matter jurisdiction refers to the power of a court to try the offense. There are three basic aspects to subject matter jurisdiction.

1. The offense in question must be one that the state has the power to prosecute. The power of a state to prosecute is restricted to the crimes that occur wholly within the state, partially within the state, or has an effect within the state.
2. The court must be competent to try the crime. For example, a superior court has no jurisdiction over the case, charging only misdemeanors in a county with a municipal court (*People v. Smith,* 231 Cal. App. 2d 140).
3. If exclusive federal jurisdiction exists or the offense is only a federal crime, then a state court in California has no subject matter jurisdiction.

Jurisdiction of Person

Jurisdiction of the person is also a basic requirement in criminal proceedings. Presence in court usually establishes jurisdiction over the person. In most cases, the defendant must be present at the start of his or her felony criminal trial. In misdemeanor cases, if the state takes personal jurisdiction over an accused by arresting or citing him or her to appear at a certain time and date, the failure of the accused to appear at the time set for trial can be considered as a waiver by the defendant of his or her right to appear.

Venue

Normal venue of a criminal case is in the county and the district within which the crime was alleged to have been committed. A change of venue from a court of one county to the same court in another county does not affect the latter court's jurisdiction over the subject matter of the case (*People v. Richardson,* 138 Cal. App. 404).

Unlike subject matter jurisdiction, the parties to a trial can consent to venue. For example, by pleading guilty to the sale of a controlled substance, the accused admits every essential element of the crime charged except subject matter jurisdiction (*People v. Tabucchi,* 64 Cal. App. 3d 133). In this case, the accused pled guilty to a crime that was alleged to have occurred in Stanislaus County. Later, he

3-19a Discussion

attempted to get the conviction reversed because the offense did not occur in Stanislaus County; therefore, he could not be tried by the Superior Court in that county. The California Supreme Court upheld his conviction.

The general rules regarding the proper court for venue are as follows:

1. For crimes in general, in the county where the crime was committed (PC 777).
2. For nonsupport of child, in the county where the child is cared for or in the county where the parent is apprehended (PC 777a).
3. For perjury committed outside of the state that is punishable in California, in the county where the proceeding was being conducted (PC 777b). This situation would normally occur when a false document is made outside of the state to be used in court proceedings within the state.
4. For offenses planned outside the state and committed within the state, in the county in which the offense is completed (PC 778).
5. For offenses planned within the state and committed outside the state, in the county in which the offense was planned (PC 778a).
6. For offenses committed in more than one venue, in any county in which any of the acts were committed or effects of the crime were felt (PC 781).
7. For offenses committed within 500 yards of any county boundary or on the boundary line, in either county (PC 782).
8. For offenses committed on trains, airplanes, ships, motor vehicles in transit, in any county over which the vehicle traveled in the course of a trip (PC 782).
9. Abduction, kidnapping, and seduction, in any county in which the offense occurred or to which the victim was taken (PC 784).
10. For child concealment, in any county in which the child was taken, detained, concealed, found, or where the victimized person resides or agency deprived of custody is located (PC 279.1).
11. For bringing or receiving stolen goods, in any county in which the goods were taken or received or in the county in which they were stolen (PC 786).
12. For criminal homicide, in any county where the crime was committed or in the county in which the body was found (PC 790).

Establishing Venue

Venue represents a question of fact, and therefore must be alleged in the pleadings. This is normally accomplished by alleging that the offense occurred in X county. The burden of proof is on the prosecution to establish proper venue of the court. Failure of the prosecution to enter any evidence of venue in a "not guilty" case will cause the conviction to be overturned on appeal (*People v. Pollock,* 26 Cal. App. 2d 602). The courts, however, can make reasonable inferences from the evidence to establish venue. For example, the accused was charged with robbing a service station in Fresno. The names of the streets where the station was located were entered into evidence, but not the name of the city. The victim testified that he lived in Fresno, and the Fresno Police Department investigated the robbery. The court, in upholding the conviction, stated that a reasonable inference was that the crime had occurred in the city of Fresno and that venue, unlike elements of the offense, is not required to be proven beyond a reasonable doubt (*People v. Arline,* 13 Cal. App. 3d 200).

Change of Venue

Although the accused has a right to be tried in the county where the crime occurred, often it is to the accused's advantage to be tried elsewhere. The most common reasons are that the accused will be unable to receive a fair trial in the local county or that trial in a different county will be more convenient (i.e., family and witnesses are located in a different county). The defense must request by motion prior to trial for a change of venue.

Penal Code 27—Persons Liable to Punishment

(a) The following persons are liable to punishment under the laws of this state:

 1. All persons who commit, in whole or in part, any crime with this state
 2. All who commit any offense without this state which, if committed within this state, would be larceny, carjacking, robbery, or embezzlement under the laws of this state, and bring the property stolen or embezzled, or any part of it, or are found with it, or any part of it, within this state
 3. All who, being without this state, cause or aid, advise or encourage, another person to commit a crime within this state, and are afterwards found therein.

(b) Perjury, in violation of Section 118, is punishable also when committed outside of California to the extent provided in Section 118.

Cases on Point

People v. Guiterrez (137 Cal. App. 3d 542)

An offense is "lesser included" if all its elements must necessarily be included in elements of greater offense as each is defined by statute or by the charging language of information.

In re Marven C. (33 Cal. App. 4th 482)

To defeat a presumption that a minor under age 14 is incapable of committing crime, the state must show by clear proof that when a minor committed the charged act, he or she knew of its wrongfulness.

In re Manuel L. (7 Cal. 4th 229)

The term "clear proof"—as used in the statute requiring people, in order to rebut presumption of incapacity, to prove clearly that at the time a minor committed the charged act, he or she knew of its wrongfulness—refers to the burden of persuasion akin to clear and convincing evidence, rather than proof beyond reasonable doubt; such standard comports fully with due process requirements of state and federal constitutions, since criminal capacity is not an element of offense.

People v. Fisher (49 Cal. App. 3d 174)

Imbecility is no defense against a crime unless its existence deprived the individual of the power to distinguish between right and wrong.

People v. Goodrum (31 Cal. App. 430)

If a person, by long-continued indulgence in intoxicants, has become so permanently diseased mentally that he or she cannot distinguish right from wrong and is generally insane, the individual is no more legally responsible for his or her acts than a person congenitally insane or insane from violent injury to the brain.

In re Saul S. (167 Cal. App. 3d 1061); Green v. United States (355 U.S. 184)

The protection against second prosecution is intended to prevent the state from making repeated attempts to convict an individual for an alleged offense, thereby subjecting the person to embarrassment, expense, and ordeal and compelling him or her to live in continuing state of anxiety and insecurity, as well as enhancing the possibility that, even though innocent, he or she may be found guilty.

The underlying idea, one that is deeply ingrained in at least the Anglo-American system of jurisprudence, is that the state with all of its resources and power should not be allowed to make rcpeated attempts to convict an individual for an alleged offense, thereby subjecting him to embarrassment, expense, and ordeal and compelling him to live in a continuing state of anxiety and insecurity, as well as enhancing the possibility that even though innocent he may be found guilty.

Provigo Corp. v. Alcoholic Beverage Control Appeals Bd. (7 Cal. 4th 561)

The use of underage decoys to enforce liquor laws prohibiting sale to minors was not held to be "outrageous conduct," giving rise to a due process violation barring prosecution, even though the officers failed to follow Department of Alcoholic Beverage Control's suggested decoy program guidelines and instead used more mature-appearing persons as decoys; liquor licensees had ready means of protecting themselves from liability by simply asking any purchasers who could possibly be minors to produce bona fide evidence of their age and identity.

People v. Cordova (14 Cal. 2d 308)

Insanity is either a complete defense or none at all, and alleged insanity may not be used as a basis for extending leniency, or to reduce the degree of the crime.

People v. Leever (173 Cal. App. 3d 853)

The test for an insanity defense is whether at the time of the offense, mental disease or defect rendered the defendant incapable of either knowing or understanding the nature and quality of his or her act or distinguishing right from wrong, in the disjunctive rather than the conjunctive, despite literal statutory language.

People v. Kimball (5 Cal. 2d 608)

The defendant's "responsibility" for an act depends on whether the defendant knows the nature and quality of the act when it is committed, and, if the defendant does, he or she is legally accountable for the act, notwithstanding that the defendant may be mentally abnormal or defective or may suffer from some nervous disorder.

People v. Norton (138 Cal. App. 70)

Low mentality is not "insanity" and does not excuse one who otherwise is able to distinguish between right and wrong.

U.S. v. Schneiderman (106 F. Supp. 906)

"Motive" is that which prompts a person to act, while "intent" refers only to state of mind with which the act is done.

People v. Monroe (168 Cal. App. 3d 1205)

A conviction under PC 647.6, which proscribes annoying or molesting a child under age of 18 years, requires a motivation of unnatural or abnormal sexual interest in children.

People v. Thompson (206 Cal. App. 3d 459)

The offense of annoying or molesting a child under 18 does not require the specific act of annoying to be lewd or obscene, but only requires proof of articulable objective acts that would cause a normal person to be unhesitatingly irritated, provided the acts are motivated by abnormal or unnatural sexual interest in the child victim.

Although the act of viewing for sexual pleasure may not, in itself, be criminal under PC 647.6, when the viewing is associated with an activity that ordinarily causes annoyance to the subject of the attention, it may constitute a crime under this section.

People v. Moore (185 Cal. App. 3d 1005)

The defendant's repeated sexual exposure to minor females constituted conduct that might in a single instance be accidental and unintentional and be insufficient to violate the child annoyance and molestation statute, but the cumulative effect of the conduct clearly violated the statute; therefore, no instruction—that the jury must unanimously agree beyond reasonable doubt that the defendant committed the same specific criminal act—was required.

People v. La Fontaine (79 Cal. App. 3d 176)

Unmistakably lewd and obscene words that a defendant used toward a 13-year-old victim constituted conduct that would "annoy or molest" victim and, hence, fell within provisions of PC 647.6 proscribing offense of annoying or molesting a minor under the age of 18 years.

In re R. (1 Cal. 3d 855)

The words "every person" within PC 647.6 mean that every person who annoys or molests any child under the age of 18 is a vagrant to include a minor as well as an adult.

People v. Romero (48 Cal. App. 3d 752)

A charge of contributing to the delinquency of a minor is not a lesser included offense within the charge of annoying and molesting a child under 18 years of age.

People v. Greene (34 Cal. App. 3d 622)

Simple assault is not a lesser included offense of the crime of annoying or molesting a child, nor can the latter offense be an included offense of simple assault.

Creative Legal Defenses

During May 1979, Sandie Craddock (aka Sandie Smith), while working as a barmaid in a London pub, stabbed another barmaid to death. She had previously been convicted of more than 30 lesser crimes of violence and had attempted suicide at least 18 times. A review of her background established that her outbursts of erratic behavior always occurred several days prior to her menstrual period. Her attorney was successful in getting the British Court to accept premenstrual syndrome

(PMS) as a mitigating factor. She was released on probation with the stipulation that she receive progesterone treatment (Ruth Masters and Cliff Roberson, *Inside Criminology* (Englewood Cliffs, NJ: Prentic-Hall, 1990).

In 1897, a member of a local tribe of Indians in Canada by the name of Machekequonable killed his foster father. The defendant contended that he believed in the existence of an evil spirit form called a Wendigo clothed in human being form, which would eat a human being. The defendant stated that he saw what appeared to him to be a Wendigo. After calling to the "object" to stop, he killed it. The "object" later was determined to be his foster father. The court refused to accept this as a defense.

Practicum

Practicum I
Problem One—Elements of an Offense and Capacity to Commit a Crime

As noted in Chapter 1, to convict a person of a crime, the state must prove beyond a reasonable doubt each and every element of the crime charged. For example, Barney Fife is charged with a violation of Section 647.6 of the Penal Code, Annoying or Molesting a child Under 18.

PC 647.6—Annoying or Molesting Child Under 18; Punishment

Every person who annoys or molests any child under the age of 18 is punishable by a fine not exceeding one thousand dollars ($1,000) or by imprisonment in the county jail for not exceeding one year or by both the fine and imprisonment. . . .

1.   What are the elements of this offense?
2.   Do we need to look at case decisions to help ascertain the elements?
3.   Does it make any difference if Barney is only 16 years of age and the female victim is 15 years of age? What if Barney is only 14 years old?

4.   What constitutes annoyance sufficient to commit the crime?
5.   Are there any lesser included offenses to this crime?
6.   If the victim consented to his conduct, would that be a defense?
7.   Does it make any difference that Barney cannot resist the urge to commit the crime?
8.   What would be necessary to establish that Barney is not legally sane?

Practicum II

Jerry plans the crime of kidnapping in Arizona. He then goes to California and kidnaps a child in Fresno. He takes the child to Los Angeles and then to Hawaii. Explain your answers to the following questions.

1.   In what state(s) may Jerry be prosecuted?
2.   What state(s) have jurisdiction over the offense (assuming Hawaii and Arizona have the same jurisdictional laws as California)?
3.   In what county(ies) in California may the case be tried?
4.   How can the defendant get the case moved to a different county?

Discussion Questions

Discussion Questions

1. Explain the test for lesser included offenses.
2. Under what circumstances may an accused be placed in jeopardy twice for the same conduct?
3. What are the purposes of the protection against double jeopardy?
4. What periods of time are excluded in determining whether or not the statute of limitations bars prosecution in a case?
5. An accused commits the crime of murder on September 1, 1996. He leaves the state the next day. When does the statute of limitations start to run?
6. When may a 13-year-old be held accountable for a criminal act?
7. Jerry wants you to defend him in a criminal case. He seems very dull and may have been intoxicated at the time of the crime. What factors should you consider regarding the issues of intoxication and insanity?

8. Explain the differences between motive and malice.
9. Why is a mistake of law not a defense to most criminal conduct?
10. Explain the present test for insanity in California.
11. Is a defendant who killed his wife, who clearly could not distinguish right and wrong with regard to his act, who believed that the marriage vow "till death do us part" bestows on a marital partner the godgiven right to kill the other partner if he or she violates those marital vows, entitled to judgment of not guilty by reason of insanity? Why or why not?

Self-Study Quiz

Self-Study Quiz

True/False

1. The purpose of the statute of limitations is to protect an accused from harassment of multiple trials.
2. The protection against double jeopardy also applies to civil proceedings.
3. A second trial may not be held when the first trial ends in a mistrial because of a jury member's sickness.
4. Some crimes, such as murder, have no statute of limitations.
5. The statute of limitations sets forth the time in which the accused must be convicted.
6. In some cases, the statute of limitations does not start to run until the offense has been discovered.
7. In computing the period of time to determine if the statute of limitations has run, the day that the offense was committed is excluded.
8. The period that an accused is absent from the state (up to a maximum of three years) is excluded for the time period for statute of limitations purposes.
9. Certain persons are incapable of some crimes because of the lack of requisite mental state.
10. Children under the age of 14 may never be punished for committing a criminal offense.
11. All persons are presumed to have the ability to commit crimes.

12. An idiot is a person who is almost totally without understanding or mentality.
13. A mistake of law is an excuse for criminal conduct.
14. California has abolished the defense of diminished capacity.
15. Consent of the victim is a defense in most criminal cases.
16. Temporary insanity is not a defense to criminal conduct in California.
17. Malice means only an ill will.
18. Motive and malice are the same.
19. Voluntary intoxication is a defense to certain crimes in California.
20. Venue refers to the geographical or physical location of the court in which a trial will be or has been tried.
21. Subject matter jurisdiction requirement may be waived by the accused.
22. The normal venue of a criminal case is in the county where the crime occurred.
23. For offenses committed in more than one county, the correct venue is in the county where most of the acts occurred.

Chapter

4

Inchoate Offenses

Intent to commit a crime is not itself criminal. There is no law against a man's intending to commit a murder the day after tomorrow. The law only deals with conduct.
Oliver Wendell Holmes, The Common Law, 1881

The act is not criminal unless the mind is criminal.
Old legal maxim

4-1 Inchoate Offenses

nchoate means imperfect or unfinished. Inchoate offenses are crimes that generally lead to other crimes. Traditionally, attempts to commit a crime, solicitation to commit a criminal offense, and conspiracies are considered inchoate offenses. These offenses are also referred to as *anticipatory offenses*. Other crimes, though considered complete crimes, are also hidden inchoate offenses. Examples include burglary, which is the entering of a building with the intent to commit a crime, and possession of burglary tools. The crime of *stalking* also fits this category. From a historical point of view, most inchoate crimes were not recognized until the late eighteenth century. Prior to then, the adage of "a miss is as good as a mile" was the general rule.

4-2 Attempt to Commit Crime

Penal Code 21a—Attempt to Commit Crime; Specific Intent and Ineffectual Act

An attempt to commit a crime consists of two elements: a specific intent to commit the crime, and a direct but ineffectual act done toward its commission.

Penal Code 663—Attempts to Commit Crimes When Punishable

Any person may be convicted of an attempt to commit a crime, although it appears on the trial that the crime intended or attempted was perpetrated by such person in pursuance of such attempt, unless the Court, in its discretion, discharges the jury and directs that such person be tried for such crime.

Penal Code 664

Every person who attempts to commit any crime, but fails, or is prevented, or intercepted in the perpetration thereof, is punishable. . . .

Penal Code 665

Sections 663 and 664 do not protect a person who, in attempting unsuccessfully to commit a crime, accomplishes the commission of another and different crime, whether greater or lesser in guilt, from suffering the punishment prescribed by law for the crime committed.

4-2a Elements

The elements of an attempt include:

1. A specific intent to commit a particular crime. Even if the attempted crime is a general intent crime, the accused must have the specific intent to commit that particular crime (*People v. Rupp*, 41 Cal. 2d 527).
2. A direct but unsuccessful act toward completion of the intended crime. To be an attempt, the act or acts committed must go further than mere preparation (*People v. Werner*, 16 Cal. 2d 216).
3. An apparent ability to commit the intended crime.
4. The crime must be legally possible to commit.

In some cases, a person may in an unsuccessful attempt to commit one crime commit another crime. In this case, he or she may be punished for the attempt to commit the intended crime or the other crime (PC 665). For example, a husband attempts to kill his wife. He actually kills someone else. He can be prosecuted for attempted murder of the wife and the murder of the other person.

An attempt to commit a crime is also a crime (PC 664). A person may be convicted of an attempt to commit a crime, although it appears by the evidence that the crime intended or attempted was actually not completed (PC 663).

4-2b Discussion

Beyond Preparation

It takes six steps or stages for a person to intentionally commit a crime.

1. The person must conceive the idea.
2. The person must evaluate the idea.
3. The person must make the decision to go forward with the idea.
4. The person must make preparations to commit the act.
5. The person starts the acts necessary to commit the crime.
6. The person finishes the necessary actions to complete the crime.

In the first two stages, there is no criminal misconduct because the person lacks the intent to commit the crime. In the third stage, there is no criminal misconduct because there is no act (*actus reus*). We don't punish people for their thoughts. In the sixth step, a crime has been committed. In the fifth stage, there is at least an attempt. It is in the fourth stage that it is difficult to determine whether criminal misconduct has occurred.

As noted earlier, to constitute an attempt a direct act or acts must be committed leading up to the intended crime. Mere preparation for committing the intended crime is not sufficient to constitute an attempt. A difficult question to answer in many cases is whether the act or acts committed go beyond mere preparation and thus constitute an attempt. The act or acts are sufficient to constitute an attempt if the overt act or acts reach far enough toward the accomplishment of the intended offense to amount to the commencement of its consummation (*People v. Lanzit*, 70 Cal. App. 498). As Judge Oliver Wendall Holmes once stated: "Preparation is not an attempt. But some preparations may amount to an attempt. It is a question of degree" (*Commonwealth v. Peaslee*, 59 N.E. 55 [1901]).

The following acts were held sufficient to constitute an attempt:

1. Intending to kill his wife, the accused allowed his accomplice to enter the house for the purposes of choking her (*People v. Parrish*, 87 Cal. App. 2d 853).
2. The defendant, planning to commit a burglary, was found outside of a bedroom with hands upraised to a bedroom window (*People v. Gibson*, 94 Cal. App. 2d 468).
3. The defendant, intending to bomb a railroad track, noticed officers observing him while he was a block away from the track and fled (*People v. Davis*, 24 Cal. App. 2d 408).
4. The defendant was found crouched outside a public telephone booth with lock picks and his car equipped with coin box burglary tools (*People v. Charles*, 218 Cal. App. 2d 812).

The fact of purchasing a gun is only preparation and not a direct act toward robbery (i.e., no attempt). A similar holding resulted in a case where the defendant, several days before the planned robbery, drove by the bank in question to look it over.

Once a direct act leading toward the commission of the intended offense is completed, the crime of attempt is completed, and a later abandonment of the plan to commit the intended offense is not a defense for the attempt.

There can be no attempt if it is legally impossible to commit the intended offense. For example, the accused tries to kill a person who is already dead. This is considered no attempt; it is legally impossible to kill a dead person. That other conditions make the crime impossible to complete is not normally a defense. For example, the accused, intending to steal money from a person, reaches into the victim's pocket and finds it empty. The accused may be convicted of an attempt to steal.

The test regarding the possibility of completion of the intended crime is as follows:

> If there is an apparent ability to commit the crime in the way attempted, the attempt is indictable, although, unknown to the person making the attempt, the crime cannot be committed because the means employed are unsuitable or because of extrinsic facts, such as the nonexistence of some essential object, or an obstruction by the intended victim, or by a third person. (*People v. Siu,* 126 Cal. App. 2d 41)

4-3 Conspiracies to Commit Crime

Penal Code 182—Conspiracy Defined

If two or more persons conspire:

1. To commit any crime
2. Falsely and maliciously to indict another for any crime, or to procure another to be charged or arrested for any crime
3. Falsely to move or maintain any suit, action, or proceeding
4. To cheat and defraud any person of any property, by any means which are in themselves criminal, or to obtain money or property by false pretenses or by false promises with fraudulent intent not to perform such promises
5. To commit any act injurious to the public health, to public morals, or to pervert or obstruct justice, or the due administration of the laws
6. To commit any crime against the person of the president or vice president of the United States, the governor of any state or territory, any United States justice or judge, or the secretary of any of the executive departments of the United States. [The last portion of this section on punishment is omitted.]

Penal Code 182.5

Penal Code 182.5 provides, in part, that any person who actively participates in any criminal street gang with knowledge that its members engage in or have engaged in a pattern of criminal gang activity and who willfully promotes, furthers, assists, or benefits from any felonious criminal conduct by members of that gang is guilty of conspiracy to commit that felony.

Penal Code 183 Non-Criminal Conspiracies; No Criminal Punishment

No conspiracies, other than those enumerated in the preceding section, are punishable criminally.

4-3a Definition

Conspiracy is an agreement by two or more persons to commit any crime, and one of them does an overt act in furtherance of the conspiracy. The essence of the crime of conspiracy is the agreement to commit a crime. Penal Code 182(b) requires that where an overt act in furtherance of the agreement is necessary to constitute the offense, one or more overt acts must be expressly alleged in the information or indictment and at least one alleged overt act is proved.

The basic elements of the crime of conspiracy are found in PC 182:

1. Two or more persons conspire to commit any crime.
2. An overt act is done in furtherance of the agreement.

Cases involving criminal conspiracy generally involve many defendants, complex evidentiary issues, and many complicated charges. For example, one recent federal case involving criminal conspiracy had 21 defendants, 275 witnesses, and over 40,000 pages of transcripts (*United States v. Casamento*, 887 F. 2d 1141). Conspiracy was first formulated by the English Star Chamber in 1611. While at common law it was a misdemeanor, in most states today, it is a felony. Conspiracy is also a controversial crime. Many judges and scholars have advocated for its abolition. The critics contend that it provides an aggressive prosecutor with a dangerous and potent weapon, that the very nature of the crime gives the prosecutor extraordinary latitude in prosecuting criminal behavior, and the crime is so vague that it defies definition. Justice Learned Hand once described the crime of conspiracy as the "darling of the modern prosecutor's nursery."

Penal Code 184 Overt Act; Venue

No agreement amounts to a conspiracy, unless some act besides such agreement be done within *this state* to effect the object thereof, by one or more of the parties to such agreement and the trial of cases of conspiracy may be had in any county in which any such act be done.

Conspiracy As an Overt Act

For conspiracy to be a crime, it is not necessary that the conspired crime to be completed or even attempted. The overt act required must go beyond the agreement or planning stage. The act must be more than planning, but need not amount to an attempt. The act, however, must be in furtherance of the conspiracy and must take place within California. The overt act may be a lawful act as long as it is in furtherance of the conspiracy (*People v. Jones,* 228 Cal. App. 2d 74 and *People v. Smith,* 63 Cal. 2d 779).

Conspiracy is a specific intent crime, since it must be established that the accused entered into the agreement with the intent to do an unlawful act or do a lawful act by unlawful means (*People v. Jones,* 228 Cal. App. 2d 74). All persons involved in the conspiracy are equally responsible for the actions of all other parties taken in furtherance of the conspiracy. It includes crimes committed in preparation for, during commission of, and during escape and arrest. This liability does not, however, include independent and unrelated crimes. Crimes committed prior to entry by the accused into the conspiracy, also, are not charged against him or her.

Conspiracy requires the agreement of two or more persons. This requirement is considered as the *plurality* requirement. At least two of the persons must be legally capable of committing a crime. Accordingly, if only two people are involved and one is an idiot, then no conspiracy exists. The two required persons may be husband and wife. If one of the two is an undercover police officer who enters into the agreement as part of his or her official duties, there is no conspiracy. This is based on the concept that the undercover police officer did not in fact agree to commit a crime, therefore there is no agreement. If there are two otherwise qualified persons who agree to commit a crime in addition to the undercover police officer, then a conspiracy may exist.

It is not necessary that all members agree with all other members of the conspiracy, only that each must know of the agreement and must make an agreement with at least one other member of the conspiracy. In complex conspiracies, especially those involving organized crime, the parties may not know each other. Complex conspiracies are generally either the "wheel" type or the "chain" type. In the wheel type, the conspirators deal only with the leader and not with each other. The leader is the "hub," and the conspirators who deal with the leader are considered the "spokes." To constitute the wheel type, each spoke must know that other spokes exist. It is not necessary that they know each other's identity. In addition, there must be a community of interests between the spokes. For example, a woman who referred pregnant women to a doctor who performed illegal abortions was convicted of conspiracy based on the theory that she was aware that others were also referring pregnant women to the doctor for illegal abortions.

The "chain" conspiracy exists where there is a sequence of individuals involved in the conspiracy. For example, the illegal distribution of drugs from importer to wholesaler, to retailer, to customer, is a chain-type conspiracy. Under both types of conspiracies, the precise identity of the other conspirators is not important as long as there is knowledge that others are involved in the scheme. For example, the drug importer does not need to know the precise identity of local distributors as long as he or she is aware that such people exist.

In one federal case, *U.S. v. James* (528 F2d 999), certain defendants were convicted of conspiracy to assault a federal officer based on the fact that they were part of a group and attended drills designed to train for an anticipated attack by law enforcement personnel. Defendants who were present for some of the drills, but were not present when the shoot-out occurred, were convicted on the theory that attendance at the drills established that there must have been an agreement to assault a federal officer.

It is often difficult to determine the duration of the conspiracy. This is often a critical issue since the statute of limitations does not begin to run until the conspiracy is over. Second, declarations of co-conspirators are admissible against the other conspirators if the declarations are made while the conspiracy continues.

Withdrawal from Conspiracy

Prior to the commission of the conspired offense, one may withdraw, and the withdrawal will avoid criminal liability if the below requirements are present.

- A complete withdrawal from all aspects of the conspiracy.
- Must remain away from the scene of the crime at time of crime.
- Must communicate abandonment to all known confederates prior to the commission of intended offense.

As a practical matter, to prove an abandonment, the accused should have communicated to authorities information regarding the conspiracy. (While communication to proper authorities is not required, it is almost impossible to prove abandonment without the communication.)

4-4 Solicitation to Commit a Crime

Unlike most states, California has no general solicitation law. The Penal Code has at least 18 different sections dealing with the solicitation of specific crimes. The more common offenses are found in PC 653(f). Note: The crime of solicitation applies only to those offenses listed in the Code. In California, under Section 653(f) of the Penal Code, it is a crime to solicit another person to commit carjacking, bribery, murder, robbery, burglary, felony theft, arson, receive stolen property, forcible rape, extortion, perjury, forgery, kidnapping, felony assault, sodomy by force, and oral copulation by force. Other sections of the Code prohibit the solicitation for prostitution, lewd acts, and so on.

The elements of the crime of solicitation are as follows:

4-4a Elements

- Act of solicitation.
- With the specific intent to induce the commission of one of the listed offenses.

Completion of Solicitation

4-4b Discussion

No overt act or agreement by the person solicited is required. The crime is completed with the solicitation. In most cases, conviction requires testimony of two witnesses or one witness and other corroborating evidence.

Solicitation is a lesser and included offense of conspiracy. To constitute the crime of conspiracy, there must be an agreement and an act committed in furtherance of agreement; however, to constitute solicitation, all that is required is the solicitation to commit the offense (*People v. Bottger*, 142 Cal. App. 3d 974). As noted earlier, the essence of the offense of conspiracy is the agreement, whereas in the offense of solicitation it is the "offer or request." The crime of solicitation is a distinct crime from the crime solicited. For example, soliciting one to offer a bribe is a crime that is distinct from the crimes of attempted bribery or bribery (*People v. Litt*, 221 Cal. App. 2d 543).

Penal Code 653(f) requires that, except for those solicitation crimes involving welfare fraud and controlled substance violations, solicitation must be proved by the corroboration of the testimony of two witnesses or of one witness and corroborating circumstances.

Penal Code 153

4-5 Compounding a Crime

Every person who, having knowledge of the actual commission of a crime, takes money or property of another, or any gratuity or reward, or any engagement, or promise thereof upon the agreement or understanding to compound or conceal such crime, or to abstain from any prosecution thereof, or to withhold any evidence thereof, except in the cases provided for by law, in which crimes may be compromised by leave of the court, is punishable as follows:

- By imprisonment in the state prison, or in a county jail not exceeding one year, where the crime was punishable by death or imprisonment in the state prison for life
- By imprisonment in the state prison, or in the county jail not exceeding six months, where the crime was punishable by imprisonment in the state prison for any term other than life
- By imprisonment in the county jail not exceeding six months, or by fine not exceeding one thousand dollars ($1,000), where the crime was a misdemeanor

4-5a Elements

The elements of this offense are as follows:

- The knowledge that a crime has been committed
- Receiving or agreeing to receive something of value
  In return for:

  - Concealing that a crime has occurred
  - Refraining from prosecution of the crime
  - Withholding or concealing evidence of the crime

4-5b Discussion

Like the crime of solicitation, all that is needed for the overt act of compounding is an agreement to conceal the crime. For practical purposes, the courts have defined "compounding" as the act of concealing the crime or evidence.

An affirmative defense to the crime of compounding is that the actions taken were provided for by law. For example, while defending a person charged with murder, an attorney finds out that her client has committed two other murders. The attorney may not take active steps to conceal the other crimes or to tamper with the evidence. The attorney, however, has a duty not to disclose the existence of the other murders. A victim of a crime has a legal right to sue the offender in civil court for the injuries or damages received. Accordingly, as long as the victim of a crime does not agree to compound the crime, the victim may accept compensation from the offender for any injuries or damages that the victim has suffered.

Penal Code Sections 1377, 1378, and 1379 provide that a misdemeanor may be legally compounded or compromised under the following conditions:

- The crime is a misdemeanor.
- The victim is entitled to civil reimbursement.
- A court agrees to the compromise.
- The offender pays court costs.
- The action is recorded in the official minutes of the court.

Penal Code 1177 provides that a misdemeanor may not legally be compromised if the victim was a police officer on duty, the act was done riotously, or the act was done with intent to commit a felony.

Cases on Point

U.S. v. Baker (129 F. Supp. 684)

Legal elements of an "attempt" are intent to commit a crime, execution of some overt act in pursuance of the intention, and failure to consummate the crime.

People v. Seach (215 Cal. App. 2d 779)

To justify a conviction for the attempt to commit a crime, it is not necessary that the overt act proved should be the ultimate step toward commission of a crime; it is sufficient if it was the first or some subsequent step in direct movement toward such consummation.

People v. MacEwing (216 Cal. App. 2d 33)

To establish the attempt to commit a crime, it must appear that the defendant had a specific intent to commit a crime and did directly and unequivocally act toward that end; preparation alone is not enough, and some appreciable fragment of crime must have been accomplished.

Young v. Superior Court (253 Cal. App. 2d 848)

Law considers "attempt" to be a specific intent to commit a substantive crime plus a direct, equivocal act toward that end; intent alone is not enough.

People v. Michaels (193 Cal. App. 2d 194)

Where a crime remains unfinished and the participant is charged with attempt, there must be a direct ineffectual act done toward the commission of the crime, and a specific intent to commit that crime.

People v. Franquelin (241 P. 2d 651)

"Preparation" is devising or arranging the means or measures necessary to commit a criminal offense, whereas "attempt" is the direct movement toward commission after preparations are made.

People v. Grant (233 P. 2d 660)

An unforeseen circumstance that prevents the commission of a crime attempted is not a matter of defense when the defendant is charged with the crime of attempt.

People v. Claborn (224 Cal. App. 2d 38)

Abandonment of intent is only a defense if the attempt to commit a crime is freely and voluntarily abandoned before the act is put into the process of final execution.

People v. Walker (33 Cal. 2d 250)

Failure to complete a crime because of threatened arrest or appearance of police is not such a free and voluntary act as to constitute abandonment of the attempt to commit a crime.

People v. Cuellar (222 Cal. App. 2d 752)

Evidence of breaking a window in a food store after closing, identification of the defendant as the person squatting on the ledge of window, and his apprehension about a block from the scene sustained conviction of attempted burglary.

People v. Martone (101 P. 2d 537)

Evidence that at 2:16 A.M. an officer saw the defendant leaning against the glass door of a store with the defendant's arm extended through broken glass, that upon officer's approach the defendant stepped away from door and placed hand in pocket, that the defendant had a wrench in hand when withdrawn from pocket, and that the lock on the door had been scratched by a hard substance, warranted conviction of "attempted burglary of the second degree."

Lorenson v. Superior Court (216 P. 2d 859)

Defining acts committed to pervert or obstruct justice or the due administration of the laws as criminal conspiracy is not so vague and uncertain as to violate constitutional requirements of due process of law.

People v. Malotte (292 P. 2d 517)

"Conspiracy" is not synonymous with "aiding and abetting" or participating; whereas conspiracy implies an agreement to commit a crime, to aid and abet requires actual participation in the act constituting the offense.

People v. Louie Gem Hang (131 Cal. App. 2d 69)

Unlawful agreement, which is the gist of conspiracy, need not be explicit or expressed in words but may consist of any tacit mutual understanding to commit crime.

Hutchins v. Municipal Court (61 Cal. App. 3d 77)

The rule that agreement by two persons to commit a particular crime cannot be prosecuted as a conspiracy when the crime is of such a nature that it requires two persons for its commission is inapplicable where completion of the substantive offense necessarily involves a third person.

People v. Saugstad (203 Cal. App. 2d 536)

The essential element of conspiracy is unlawful agreement between two or more persons to commit an offense prohibited by statute, accompanied by some overt act in furtherance of such agreement, and the unlawful agreement may be established by circumstantial evidence.

People v. Sanchez (197 Cal. App. 2d 617)

Conspiracy may be by express agreement or by tacit mutual understanding.

People v. Buckman (186 Cal. App. 2d 38)

It need not be shown, to establish a conspiracy, that the parties entered into a definite agreement, but it is sufficient that they tacitly came to an understanding to accomplish the act and unlawful design, and such agreement may be inferred from the acts and conduct of the parties in mutually carrying out a common purpose in violation of law.

People v. Bishop (220 Cal. App. 2d 148)

Only one overt act must be proved to support conspiracy conviction.

People v. McKinney (218 Cal. App. 2d 174)

Conspiracy is a distinct and separate offense from crime that is the substantive object of the conspiracy, so that an overt act required by law as evidence of conspiracy need not amount to an attempt to commit the offense.

People v. Sconce (228 Cal. App. 3d 693)

An "overt act," for conspiracy purposes, need not be criminal in nature and need not amount to an attempt to commit an offense or to aiding and abetting.

People v. Von Villas (11 Cal. App. 4th 175)

Because conspiracy is a continuous crime, an overt act does not have to be committed only after complete agreement is formed in order to be punishable.

Practicum

Tracy and Molly are both 12 years of age and students in the sixth grade. They were angry at their teacher, Mrs. Geiger. They agreed to kill their teacher. The next day, Molly placed a packet of rat poison in her purse and went to school. On the school bus, Tracy informed another student about the plan. The other student informed the teacher. When Molly arrived at school and was searched, the rat poison was found in her purse.

1. Did Molly and Tracy's conduct constitute an attempt?
2. Could Tracy's statement to the other student be used against Molly?
3. What other crimes did Tracy and Molly commit?

Discussion Questions

1. Explain the meaning of inchoate offenses.
2. At what point does conduct no longer involve mere preparation and constitutes a criminal attempt?
3. Explain the differences between the crimes of conspiracy and solicitation.
4. Explain the differences between compounding a felony and conspiracy.
5. What evidence is required to convict a person of soliciting the crime of carjacking?

Self-Study Quiz

True/False

1. Murder is an anticipatory offense.
2. Inchoate means imperfect or unfinished.
3. There are four elements to the crime of attempt.
5. Generally, preparation to commit a crime is sufficient to constitute an attempt.
6. The essence of the crime of conspiracy is the request to commit a crime.
7. Conspiracy must always be proven by at least two witnesses.
8. An element of the crime of compounding a felony is the knowledge that a crime has occurred.
9. Compounding a crime is always a felony.
10. Conspiracy, unlike solicitation, does not require an overt act in furtherance of the agreement.

Crimes against Property: Theft, Embezzlement, Forgery, and Check Offenses

The thief is sorry that he is to be hanged, but not that he is a thief.
Thomas Fuller, 1732

5-1 Theft

Penal Code 484—Theft Defined

(a) Every person who shall feloniously steal, take, carry, lead, or drive away the personal property of another, or who shall fraudulently appropriate property which has been entrusted to him, or who shall knowingly and designedly, by any false or fraudulent representation or pretense, defraud any other person of money, labor, or real or personal property, or who causes or procures others to report falsely of his wealth or mercantile character and by thus imposing upon any person, obtains credit and thereby fraudulently gets or obtains possession of money, or property, or obtains the labor or service of another, is guilty of theft. In determining the value of the property obtained, for the purposes of this section, the reasonable and fair market value shall be the test, and in determining the value of services received the contract price shall be the test. If there be no contract price, the reasonable and going wage for the service rendered shall govern. For the purposes of this section, any false or fraudulent representation or pretense made shall be treated as continuing, so as to cover any money, property, or service received as a result thereof, and the complaint, information, or indictment may charge that the crime was committed on any date during the particular period in question. The hiring of any additional employee or employees without advising each of them of every labor claim due and unpaid and every judgment that the employer has been unable to meet shall be prima facie evidence of intent to defraud.

Penal Code 490a—Larceny, Embezzlement, or Stealing Renamed

Wherever any law or statute of this state refers to or mentions larceny, embezzlement, or stealing, said law or statute shall hereinafter be read and interpreted as if the word "theft" was substituted therefor.

5-1a Theft-Related Crimes

The following is a list of theft-related crimes, as defined by Penal Code statutes:

- Theft by Larceny (PC 484)
- Grand Theft (PC 487)
- Petty Theft (PC 488)
- Theft by False Pretense or Fraud (PC 532)
- Theft by Trick or Device (PC 332 and 484)
- Theft by Credit Card (PC 484d, e, and f)
- Defrauding Proprietors of Hotels, Inns, etc. (PC 537)
- Theft of Utility Services (PC 498a)
- Theft of Trade Secrets (PC 499c)

- Theft by Embezzlement (PC 484 and 503)
- Vehicle Theft (PC 499b and VC 10581)
- Diversion of Construction Funds (PC 484b)
- Receiving Stolen Property (PC 496)
- Receiving Property Stolen in Another State (PC 497)
- Alteration of Serial Numbers (PC 537e)

The current California theft statutes have merged the common law crimes of larceny, embezzlement, and obtaining property by false pretenses into the crime of theft (Witkin, *California Crimes* 341 and *People v. Otterman*, 154 Cal. App. 2d 193). Larceny consisted of the unlawful taking of property. Embezzlement consisted of the taking of property that had been previously entrusted to the individual taking the property (*People v. Ailanjian,* 114 Cal. App. 260). Obtaining property by false pretenses consisted of using false pretenses or trick to get possession of the property.

In merging the offenses into the crime of theft, California eliminated the fine distinctions and technical niceties that formerly existed between the common law crimes (William L. Clark and William L. Marshall, *Crimes* (New York: William S. Hein, 1996), 764 and *People v. Carter*, 131 Cal. App. 177). The consolidation of the common law offenses in PC 484 did not create new crimes or enlarge the scope of the old crimes (*People v. Kassab,* 219 Cal. App. 2d 687).

Common Law Theft Defined

Common law theft (larceny) consists of the taking and carrying away of the property of another person, without the consent of the owner, with the specific intent to permanently deprive the owner of the use and benefit of the property (*People v. Pace,* 2 Cal. App. 2d 464).

The four elements of theft are as follows:

1. Taking possession of property from the owner
2. Without the consent of the owner or the person with the right of possession, and
3. With the specific intent to permanently deprive the owner of use or title to the property
4. Asportation (movement) of the property

One cannot commit theft by looking at, longing for, or even wanting to steal property (*People v. Johnson,* 136 Cal. App. 2d 665).

Distinctions still exist between the various types of theft crimes (see 5 Cal. L. Rev. 73). Except for cases involving theft by false pretense and embezzlement, the property must be personal property. To be considered personal property, the property must not be real property (land or substances attached to the land; see 25 Santa Clara L. Rev. 367). It also must have some value and be subject to ownership (*People v. Quiet,* 68 Cal. App. 2d 674).

Real property was not subject to common law larceny since there could be no taking and carrying away (*People v. Folcey,* 78 Cal. App. 62). If a substance is severed from real property, it then becomes personal property and is subject to the theft statutes. For example, gravel on the ground is a part of the real estate and is not subject to theft by larceny until it is severed from the ground. If an individual, however, severs the gravel from the ground by loading it into a truck, then the property changes its nature from real to personal property. Accordingly, the

5-1b Discussion

5-2 The Act of Taking in Theft

5-2a Elements

5-2b Discussion

individual is subject to the theft statutes when he takes possession of the gravel and transports it. A similar situation would exist had the individual picked fruit from trees belonging to others. Real property can be the subject of theft by false pretenses or embezzlement.

The definition of *personal property* under the theft statutes is very broad. For example, a list of subscribers to a telephone service has been considered by one court as personal property and thus subject to the theft statute. Utility services are considered personal property and, therefore, subject to the theft statutes.

Property that is unlawful to possess may still be the subject of a theft. For example, a thief could be convicted of stealing marijuana from a drug dealer.

Asportation

To complete the crime of theft, the individual must take possession of the property *and* carry it away (*People v. Meyer*, 75 Cal. 383). The term *asportation* is used to describe the act of taking possession and carrying away of property (*People v. Edwards*, 72 Cal. App. 102). In one case, a thief who attempted to remove an overcoat from a store dummy was not convicted of theft because the overcoat was chained to the dummy (*People v. Meyer*, 75 Cal. 383). The court held that there was no taking possession and carrying away of the property. He was, however, guilty of attempted theft.

A person who takes property and hides it in a box containing other products has sufficiently taken possession and carried away the property even if the property is not removed from the premises.

It is not necessary that the taking be from the immediate physical presence of the owner or possessor. It is assumed that the property is in possession of the person who has a right to possess it. It is grand theft, however, if the property is taken from the person's physical presence.

Once the individual takes possession, the slightest movement is sufficient to establish the carrying away requirement. For example, a thief who takes a purse from an automobile and then immediately drops it beside the car when he sees the owner approaching the car can be convicted of theft. The fact that the property was quickly abandoned in an attempt to prevent detection is immaterial.

Once possession and carrying away has occurred, the crime is complete. The fact that the property is returned to its original owner before the owner notices that it is missing does not erase the fact that a theft has occurred.

Property That Belongs to Another

A person cannot be convicted of stealing his or her own property unless someone else has a greater right of possession (*People v. Cleary*, 1 Cal. App. 50). The victim of the crime need not be the owner, as long as the victim has a right of possession of the property. For most purposes, ownership and right of possession are treated as the same under this requirement (*People v. Brunwin*, 2 Cal. App. 2d 287). The actual status of ownership of the property is immaterial to the thief. Theft is actually a crime against possession rather than ownership (*People v. Beach*, 62 Cal. App. 2d 803).

"Thief A" steals a car and drives it for two weeks. Then, "Thief B" steals the car from "A." In this case, "B" can be convicted of stealing from "A" on the theory that the first thief has a greater right of possession. (When two claims to the right of possession are equal, the first in time prevails.) "B" cannot successfully defend on the theory that "A" does not own the property. The general rule is that the thief cannot use the unlawful acts of the victim in obtaining the property to erase the crime.

Without the Consent of the Owner

At common law, to be larceny, the property must be taken without the consent of the owner or the person with the right of possession of the property. That is, the taking must have been against the will of the owner or possessor (*People v. Re Estrada,* 63 Cal. 2d 740). Under the current theft statutes, the taking may be (a) against the will, (b) by trick or fraud, or (c) by converting property that has been entrusted to a person.

The taking against the will is the common law crime of larceny. The taking by trick or fraud is the common law crime of theft by false pretense. In the common law crime of embezzlement, the "taking without the consent of the owner" is the converting of property that has been entrusted to a person. A classic example of embezzlement is where the cashier of a store lawfully takes money from customers, but instead of depositing the money, he wrongly keeps it for his own use.

Except for those cases involving embezzlement, theft by trick or device, and theft by false pretense, to constitute theft the taking and carrying away of property must be without the consent of the owner or possessor. If a person has a suspicion that someone is planning to steal his or her property, the person is under no duty to take steps to prevent the crime. This nonaction is not considered as consent to the taking and carrying away. The setting of a trap and thereby providing an opportunity for a thief to steal property is also not considered as consent.

With the Specific Intent to Permanently Deprive

Except as noted in the following, theft requires that the taking be with the specific intent to permanently deprive the owner of the property, money, and so on (*People v. Kunkin,* 9 Cal. 3d 245).

Specific Intent

Theft is a specific intent crime. The person taking the property must know that his or her taking of the property was wrong. Accordingly, if one mistakenly takes the property, he or she has not committed a theft crime.

If a person takes another person's property believing that he or she has a legal right to take the property, he is not guilty of theft. For example, mistakenly taking another person's book does not constitute theft.

Permanently Deprive

The crime of theft requires the specific intent to permanently deprive the owner or possessor of the property. Accordingly, one who takes another's property with the intent to use it only temporarily is not guilty of theft. Unauthorized borrowing may be another crime, but it is not stealing. Embezzlement, thefts by false pretenses, and vehicle thefts are exceptions to the requirement of "the intent to permanently deprive." With embezzlement crimes, thefts by false pretenses, and vehicle thefts, the legislature has eliminated "the intent to permanently deprive" requirement.

The intent to permanently deprive is normally established by proof that the taker acted to convert the property to his or her own use. For example, picking up the personal property of another and walking away would create a presumption that the taker of the property intended to steal it.

Joe walks into the local grocery store, picks up a package of gum, and puts it in his pocket. He leaves the store without paying for the gum. Joe is arrested for theft. He claims that he forgot to pay for the gum. If he did in fact forget, then he has not committed the crime of theft. To establish his guilt, the prosecution would only be required to prove that Joe put the gum in his pocket and walked out without paying for it. It would be up to Joe to establish that the failure to pay was a mistake.

The intent to take the property must exist at the time of the taking. There is no requirement that the taking be for gain. All that is needed is the specific intent to deprive the owner or possessor of his or her property permanently. Taking a typewriter without the consent of the owner, but without the intention of depriving him of it permanently, is not a violation of the theft statutes. It may be a violation of another code section.

Value

Before an item is subject to the theft statutes, it must have some value. The value may only be slight. Intrinsic value is considered sufficient to support a theft charge (*People v. Franco*, 4 Cal. App. 3d 535).

Penal Code 484(b), (c), (d), and (e)—Rental or Lease Fraud

(b) Except as provided in Section 10855 of the Vehicle Code, intent to commit theft by fraud is presumed if one who has leased or rented the personal property of another pursuant to a written contract fails to return the personal property to its owner within 20 days after the owner has made written demand by certified or registered mail following the expiration of the lease or rental agreement for return of the property so leased or rented.

(c) Notwithstanding the provisions of subdivision (b), if one presents with criminal intent identification which bears a false or fictitious name or address for the purpose of obtaining the lease or rental of the personal property of another, the presumption created herein shall apply upon the failure of the lessee to return the rental property at the expiration of the lease or rental agreement, and no written demand for the return of the leased or rented property shall be required.

(d) The presumptions created by subdivisions (b) and (c) are presumptions affecting the burden of producing evidence.

(e) Within 30 days after the lease or rental agreement has expired, the owner shall make written demand for return of the property so leased or rented. Notice addressed and mailed to the lessee or renter at the address given at the time of the making of the lease or rental agreement and to any other known address shall constitute proper demand. Where the owner fails to make such written demand the presumption created by subdivision (b) shall not apply.

Rental and Lease Fraud

Rental or lease fraud presumptions set forth in PC 484(b), (c), (d), and (e) are designed to reduce some of the problems encountered when trying to establish in court fraudulent intent. The subdivisions provide that when a person leases personal property from another by a written contract, the failure to return the property within 20 days after the owner has made a written demand by certified or registered mail following the expiration of the lease or rental agreement gives rise to a presumption that the property was taken with the intent to commit theft by fraud. To use this presumption, there must be a proper written demand for its return. If the owner fails to make proper demand, the presumption does not apply (PC 484[e]).

Theft crimes are classified and punished as either petty theft or grand theft. Petty theft is a misdemeanor (PC 488) and grand theft is a felony (PC 487).

5-3 Classifications of Theft

Penal Code 488—Petty Theft

Theft in other cases [not grand theft] is petty theft.

Penal Code 666—Conviction of Crime after Serving Term for Theft

Every person who, having been convicted of petty theft, grand theft, auto theft under Section 10851 of the Vehicle Code, burglary, carjacking, robbery, felony receiving of stolen property, or a felony violation of Section 496 and having served a term therefore in a penal institution or having been imprisoned therein … is subsequently convicted of petty theft, then the person convicted of such subsequent offense is punishable by imprisonment in the county jail not exceeding one year, or in the state prison.

5-3a Definition

Petty theft is defined in PC 488 as those thefts that are not classified as grand theft. Except as noted in PC 666, petty theft is punishable by fine or by imprisonment in the county jail.

Grand theft is difficult to define because of the many considerations and conditions under which theft is classified as "grand theft." The definition of grand theft is set forth in PC 487. The punishment for grand theft is imprisonment in the county jail or in the state prison (wobbler) and/or a fine. Grand theft is theft committed under any of the circumstances under PC 487.

Penal Code 487—Grand Theft Is Theft Committed in Any of the Following Cases

(a) When the money, labor, or real or personal property taken is of a value exceeding four hundred dollars ($400), except as provided in subdivision (b).
(b) Notwithstanding subdivision (a), grand theft is committed in any of the following cases:

  (1) (A) When domestic fowls, avocados, olives, citrus or deciduous fruits, other fruits, vegetables, nuts, artichokes, or other farm crops are taken of a value exceeding one hundred dollars ($100).

    (B) For the purposes of establishing that the value of avocados or citrus fruit under this paragraph exceeds one hundred dollars ($100), that value may be shown by the presentation of credible evidence which establishes that on the day of the theft avocados or citrus fruit of the same variety and weight exceeded one hundred dollars ($100) in wholesale value.

  (2) When fish, shellfish, mollusks, crustaceans, kelp, algae, or other aquacultural products are taken from a commercial or research operation which is producing that product, of a value exceeding one hundred dollars ($100).

  (3) Where the money, labor, or real or personal property is taken by a servant, agent, or employee from his or her principal or employer and aggregates four hundred dollars ($400) or more in any 12 consecutive-month period.

(c) When the property is taken from the person of another.

(d) When the property taken is an automobile, firearm, horse, mare, gelding, any bovine animal, any caprine animal, mule, jack, jenny, sheep, lamb, hog, sow, boar, gilt, barrow, or pig.

(e) This section shall become operative on January 1, 1997.

5-3b Value Used

To determine the value of the property for the purposes of establishing grand theft, *the reasonable and fair market value at the time that the item is stolen* is used. If the item is stolen from a retail store, then the retail price is used. If services are stolen, the reasonable and going wage for those services is used. The value used is the general market value of the property, not any special value it may have to the victim (*People v. Lizarraga,* 122 Cal. App. 2d 436; *People v. Brown,* 138 Cal. App. 3d 832).

In one case the defendant stole jewelry from a store. The cost of the jewelry to the store was $54,000 and the retail value was $130,000. The appellate court held that the trial court was correct in valuing the property at its retail value of $130,000 for the purposes of sentence enhancement (*People v. Swanson,* 142 Cal. App. 3d 104).

In the case of *People v. Ross* (25 Cal. App. 3d 190), the accused, an automobile dealer, was charged with theft for selling automobiles on which mileage shown by the odometers had been reduced. The court held that the value for the purposes of punishment and classification of the crime was the amount of money received for the cars by the accused, not the damages suffered by the victims.

In another case, the accused received $550 from the victims to buy a horse that was represented as a full-blooded Arabian mare. The horse was only half-Arabian. The defendant contended that for purposes of sentence enhancement that only the difference in value between a full-blooded Arabian and the one received should be considered. The court held that the total amount of money received by the accused ($550) should be the amount used in determining the type of theft involved (*People v. Hess,* 10 Cal. App. 3d 1071).

5-4 Embezzlement

Penal Code 503—Embezzlement Defined

Embezzlement is the fraudulent appropriating of property by a person to whom it has been entrusted.

5-4a Elements

The following are elements of embezzlement:

1. The property embezzled belongs to another.
2. The property was legally entrusted to the accused as agent, employee, bailee, trustee, or servant (a fiduciary relationship exists).
3. The necessary taking and carrying away occurred.
4. At the time of the taking and carrying away, the accused had the intent to permanently or temporarily deprive the owner of the property.

5-4b Discussion

Theft by embezzlement is theft of property that has been entrusted to the taker. In embezzlement cases, the thief steals property that has legally been entrusted to him or her. It is a violation of the relationship of trust and confidence (fiduciary relationship) (*People v. Fox,* 43 Cal. App. 399; *People v. Whitney,* 121 Cal. App. 2d 515).

If a bank teller receives money from a bank's customer for deposit, and the bank teller steals the money rather than deposits it, the teller has committed the crime of theft by embezzlement. If an attorney receives money on behalf of his client, and rather than forwarding the money to the client, the attorney deposits it to his own account and fails to tell his client of the payment, the attorney has committed the crime of embezzlement.

The two key distinctions between embezzlement and theft by larceny are as follows:

1. In embezzlement, the original taking of the property is legal (*People v. Burchers*, 199 Cal. 52).
2. In embezzlement, the intent may be to only temporarily deprive the owner of the property (*People v. Braiker*, 61 Cal. App. 2d 406).

There is no requirement that the property belong wholly to another. For example, a partner may be convicted of embezzling property belonging to a partnership. It is necessary that at the time of the embezzlement the accused have actual control of the property (entrusted to the accused). If the property has not been entrusted to the accused, he or she is not guilty of embezzlement but may be guilty of another type of theft.

Property subject to embezzlement may be money, goods, chattels, things in evidence of debt, right of action, and real property. If the amount taken by a servant, agent, or employee from his or her employer or principal totals $400 or more in any 12-month period, the crime is grand theft.

Embezzlement is a modern-day statutory crime. At common law, there was no crime of theft by embezzlement.

A special embezzlement statute, Penal Code 504, which pertains to public employees, applies to any state, county, or city employee who fraudulently appropriates for his own use, or for any purpose not authorized, any public property in his possession or under his control.

5-5 Theft of Public Funds and Embezzlement

Penal Code 514—Embezzlement of Public Fund; Punishment

Every person guilty of embezzlement is punishable in the manner prescribed for theft of property of the value or kind of embezzlement; and where the property embezzled is an evidence of debt or right of action, the sum due upon it or secured to be paid by it must be taken as its value; if the embezzlement or defalcation is of the public funds of the United States, or of this state, or of any county or municipality within this state, the offense is a felony, and is punishable by imprisonment in the state prison; and the person so convicted is ineligible thereafter to any office of honor, trust, or profit in this state.

5-6 Theft by Larceny

Larceny is the wrongful taking and carrying away of personal property belonging to another with the intent to permanently deprive the owner of it. In larceny-type thefts, the taking is unlawful. In cases involving a wrongful taking, the intent to permanently deprive the owner of the property may be during the taking of the property or at any time while the property is in the possession of the thief. Theft by larceny is contained in PC 484(a), set forth earlier in this chapter.

5-6a Elements

The elements of theft by larceny are as follows:

1. An unlawful taking
2. Of personal property belonging to another
3. With the intent to permanently deprive the owner of the use or enjoyment of the property

5-7 Theft by False Pretense

Penal Code 532—False Pretense—Obtaining Property, Labor, or Services

(a) Every person who knowingly and designedly, by any false or fraudulent representation or pretense, defrauds any other person of money, labor, or property, whether real or personal, or who causes or procures others to report falsely of his or her wealth or mercantile character, and by thus imposing upon any person obtains credit, and thereby fraudulently gets possession of money or property, or obtains the labor or service of another, is punishable in the same manner and to the same extent as for larceny of the money or property so obtained.

(b) Upon a trial for having, with an intent to cheat or defraud another designedly, by any false pretense, obtained the signature of any person to a written instrument, or having obtained from any person any labor, money, or property, whether real or personal, or valuable thing, the defendant cannot be convicted if the false pretense was expressed in language unaccompanied by a false token or writing, unless the pretense, or some note or memorandum thereof is in writing, subscribed by or in the handwriting of the defendant, or unless the pretense is proven by the testimony of two witnesses, or that of one witness and corroborating circumstances. This section does not apply to a prosecution for falsely representing or personating another, and, in that assumed character, marrying, or receiving any money or property.

5-7a Elements

The elements of the offense of theft by false pretenses are as follows:

1. The defendant made false pretense or representation.
2. The pretense or representation was made with the intent to defraud owner of property.
3. The owner was in fact defrauded in that he or she parted with the property in reliance on the pretense or representation.

5-7b Discussion

Theft by false pretense occurs when the victim is induced to part with the property by false pretenses of the thief. The victim relying on false representations parts with the title to the property. The accused must know that the representations are false at the time they are made. The majority of the time this crime occurs during the transfer or exchange of property. For example, the selling of an automobile with the mileage on the odometer rolled back is theft by false pretense, in that the seller is selling an automobile that is represented to have lower mileage and thus a higher value.

The false representations must be representations of fact, not opinion. The statements in selling a car, that this is a "good buy" or "this is the best buy in town" are statements of opinion, not fact. The statement that this car has "never been in a wreck," however, is a false statement.

Although a false promise may be the basis for theft by false pretense, the prosecution must establish that the failure to keep the promise was not "merely a commercial default"(*People v. Kiperman*, 64 Cal. App. 3d Supp. 25).

The false statement must be of a past, not future, event. To be theft by false pretenses, the victim must rely on the false representation. It is not necessary, however, that the false representation be the sole inducement, but it must be a substantial part of the inducement. The suspect may be convicted of an attempted theft without establishing that the victim relied on the false representation. Theft by false pretense applies to both real and personal property.

WEST HILLS COLLEGE
LEMOORE LIBRARY/LRC

To be theft by false pretense, the false pretense or representation must have materially influenced the owner to part with the property. It, however, need not be the sole inducing cause (*People v. Taylor*, 30 Cal. App. 3d 117). The accused in Taylor, to obtain property from its owner, made a false statement regarding his financial character. The owner of the property who wanted to get rid of the property knew that the statement was false but still turned the property over to the accused. This is not theft by false pretense, since the owner of the property was not materially influenced by the false statement in parting with the property.

In the case of *People v. Lorenzo* (64 Cal. App. 3d Supp. 25), the defendant switched price tags on merchandise to buy the goods for less than the correct price. The store owner was aware that the tags had been switched, but allowed the defendant to complete the purchase at the incorrect price in order to arrest the accused for theft by false pretense. When the accused left the store, he was arrested in the parking lot. The court held that the defendant could not be convicted of theft by false pretense since the owner of the merchandise was not misled by the defendant's conduct.

In another case, the accused was convicted of theft by false pretense when he took money from a farmer by a false promise that the money would be used to bribe a county supervisor to obtain favorable consideration of a lease of county-owned property (*People v. Fujita*, 43 Cal. App. 3d 454).

5-8 Theft by Trick or Device

Penal Code 332—Winning by Fraudulent Means, Trick, or Cheating

(a) Every person who by the game of "three card monte," so-called, or any other game, device, sleight of hand, pretensions to fortune telling, trick, or other means whatever, by use of cards or other implements or instruments, or while betting on sides or hands of any play or game, fraudulently obtains from another person money or property of any description, shall be punished as in case of larceny of property of like value.

(b) For the purposes of this section, "fraudulently obtains" includes, but is not limited to, cheating, including, for example, gaining an unfair advantage for any player in any game through a technique or device not sanctioned by the rules of the game.

(c) For the purposes of establishing the value of property under this section, poker chips, tokens, or markers have the monetary value assigned to them by the players in any game.

5-8a Definition

This crime is committed when the possession of personal property is obtained by fraud. The owner intends to depart with the possession of the property but not the title to it. The intent to steal must exist at the time that the property is taken (*People v. Maggart*, 194 Cal. App. 2d 84).

5-8b Discussion

The crime is different from theft by false pretenses in that in the case of theft by false pretenses, the owner intends to part with title to the property. In theft by trick or device, the owner may intend to temporarily part with custody, but does not intend to part with the title to the property. Larceny by trick or device requires that the intent to steal be present at the time of the taking of the property (*People v. Mason*, 86 Cal. App. 2d 445).

A thief intending to steal a typewriter obtains custody of it from the victim after convincing the victim that he only wants to borrow it. If the thief does not intend to return the typewriter at the time of the taking, he has committed the crime of theft by trick or device.

Obtaining a loan of money based on a false statement that the money will be used for a special purpose and with the intent to deprive the owner of it is also theft by trick or device. Pigeon drops and switches are thefts by trick and device. In cases involving theft by trick or device, unlike larceny, the intent to permanently deprive must exist at the time of the taking or the transfer of possession.

The crime is completed when the thief has obtained possession of the property.

5-9 Theft by Access (Credit) Card

The Penal Code sets forth the following five different types of theft by access card crimes:

1. Acquiring access cards without the cardholder's or issuer's consent (PC 484[e])
2. Forgery of access card (PC 484[f])
3. Use of forged access card or the misrepresentation as to the identity of the cardholder (PC 484[g])
4. Fraud by a merchant in accepting forged access cards; knowingly honoring illegally obtained access cards; or receiving payment for access card vouchers for items not furnished (PC 484[h])
5. Counterfeiting or illegally completing incomplete access cards (PC 484[i])

An accused who uses another person's credit card and signs the other person's name to the access card may be guilty of both theft and forgery (*People v. Cobb*, 15 Cal. App. 3d 1).

5-10 Defrauding Proprietors of Hotels, Inns, and So On

Any person who obtains any food, fuel, services, lodging, or accommodations at a hotel, inn, restaurant, boarding house, apartment house, motel, and so on, without paying for it and with the intent to defraud is guilty of this crime (PC 547). In addition, leaving any of the preceding places after obtaining credit without the intent to pay for the services provided is a crime under this statute. The use of false pretenses to obtain services, and so on, is also a crime under this provision.

Leaving a restaurant without paying for the meals or filling up the car with gas and driving off without paying creates a presumptive violation of this statute.

5-11 Theft of Utility Services

Penal Code 498—Theft of Utility Services; Definitions; Presumptions; Penalties

(a) The following definitions govern the construction of this section:

   (1) *Person* means any individual, or any partnership, firm, association, corporation, limited liability company, or other legal entity.

   (2) *Utility* means any electrical, gas, or water corporation as those terms are defined in the Public Utilities Code, and electrical, gas, or water systems operated by any political subdivision.

   (3) *Customer* means the person in whose name utility service is provided.

   (4) *Utility service* means the provision of electricity, gas, water, or any other service provided by the utility for compensation.

   (5) *Divert* means to change the intended course or path of electricity, gas, or water without the authorization or consent of the utility.

   (6) *Tamper* means to rearrange, injure, alter, interfere with, or otherwise prevent from performing a normal or customary function.

(7) *Reconnection* means the reconnection of utility service by a customer or other person after service has been lawfully disconnected by the utility.

(b) Any person who, with intent to obtain for himself or herself utility services without paying the full lawful charge therefor, or with intent to enable another person to do so, or with intent to deprive any utility of any part of the full lawful charge for utility services it provides, commits, authorizes, solicits, aids, or abets any of the following shall be guilty of a misdemeanor:

(1) Diverts or causes to be diverted utility services, by any means whatsoever.

(2) Prevents any utility meter, or other device used in determining the charge for utility services, from accurately performing its measuring function by tampering or by any other means.

(3) Tampers with any property owned by or used by the utility to provide utility services.

(4) Makes or causes to be made any connection with or reconnection with property owned or used by the utility to provide utility services without the authorization or consent of the utility.

(5) Uses or receives the direct benefit of all or a portion of utility services with knowledge or reason to believe that the diversion, tampering, or unauthorized connection existed at the time of that use, or that the use or receipt was otherwise without the authorization or consent of the utility.

(c) In any prosecution under this section, the presence of any of the following objects, circumstances, or conditions on premises controlled by the customer or by the person using or receiving the direct benefit of all or a portion of utility services obtained in violation of this section shall permit an inference that the customer or person intended to and did violate this section:

(1) Any instrument, apparatus, or device primarily designed to be used to obtain utility services without paying the full lawful charge therefor.

(2) Any meter that has been altered, tampered with, or bypassed so as to cause no measurement or inaccurate measurement of utility services.

(d) If the value of all utility services obtained in violation of this section totals more than four hundred dollars ($400) or if the defendant has previously been convicted of an offense under this section or any former section which would be an offense under this section, or of an offense under the laws of another state or of the United States which would have been an offense under this section if committed in this state, then the violation is punishable by imprisonment in the county jail for not more than one year, or in the state prison.

(e) This section shall not be construed to preclude the applicability of any other provision of the criminal law of this state.

5-11a Discussion

Any person who obtains utility services with the intent to avoid payment for the services is guilty of the theft of utility services. Utility services are defined as any electrical, gas, or water, or any other service provided by a public utility for compensation. This crime includes the act of reconnecting utility service that has been lawfully disconnected by the utility and the use of devices to prevent the meter from accurately measuring the services provided.

5-12 Appropriation of Lost Property

Penal Code 485—Lost Property

One who finds lost property under circumstances which gives him knowledge of or means of inquiry as to the true owner, and who appropriates such property to his own use, or to the use of another person not entitled thereto, without first making a reasonable and just effort to find the owner is guilty of theft.

5-12a Discussion

Civil Code Section 2080 provides that any person who finds lost property is not bound to take charge of it, but if he or she does, he or she has the obligation to take care of the property and inform the owner, if known, within a reasonable time of the location of the property. The finder may legally charge the owner only a reasonable charge for saving and taking care of the property.

A person who steals lost or mislaid property is guilty of theft under the following conditions:

1. The property is lost or mislaid under circumstance that by inquiry the true owner can be identified and located
2. No reasonable inquiry is made to find the owner and restore the property to him
3. The finder appropriates the property for his own use or the use of another (PC 485).

The preceding conditions only apply to property that has been lost or mislaid. It does not apply to property that has been abandoned. The crime is completed when, having possession of the property, the finder forms the intent to appropriate the property for his own use (*In re Greg F.,* 159 Cal. App. 3d 466).

5-13 Vehicle Theft

California has two vehicle theft statutes. In both statutes, only temporary taking is required to constitute the theft. The two crimes are described in the codes.

Penal Code 499b

Vehicle theft is the wrongful taking of any automobile, motorcycle, motorboat, vessel, or vehicle for the purposes of temporarily using or operating. This offense is also known as the "joy-ride" crime. It is designed to prevent the unauthorized "joy-riding" in other people's autos. This crime is a misdemeanor.

Vehicle Code Sec. 10851

Theft and unlawful driving or taking of a vehicle (a) Any person who drives or takes a vehicle not his or her own, without the consent of the owner thereof, and with intent either to permanently or temporarily deprive the owner thereof of his or her title to or possession of the vehicle, whether with or without intent to steal the vehicle, or any person who is a party or an accessory to or an accomplice in the driving or unauthorized taking or stealing, is guilty of a public offense and, upon conviction thereof, shall be punished by imprisonment in the state prison for 16 months or two or three years or a fine of not more than ten thousand dollars ($10,000), or both, or by imprisonment in the county jail not to exceed one year or a fine of not more than one thousand dollars ($1,000), or both. (b) Any person who, having been convicted of two previous misdemeanor violations of this section, subdivision (d) of Section 487 of the Penal Code, involving an automobile, or any combination of these offenses as misdemeanors, is subsequently convicted of a violation of subdivision (a) shall be punished for the subsequent conviction by imprisonment in the state prison for two, three, or four years.

Penal Code 484b provides that any person who receives money for construction purposes and willfully fails to apply the funds for the intended purposes is guilty of a felony if the amount applied is in excess of $1,000.00. If the amount misapplied is $1,000.00 or less, the crime is a misdemeanor.

Penal Code 484c provides that any person who submits a false voucher to obtain construction funds and does not use the funds for the intended purposes is guilty of embezzlement.

5-14 Diversion of Construction Funds

Penal Code 499c(b)

Every person is guilty of theft who, with intent to deprive or withhold from the owner thereof control of a trade secret, or with an intent to appropriate a trade secret to his or her own use or to the use of another, does any of the following:

1. Steals, takes, carries away, or uses without authorization a trade secret
2. Fraudulently appropriates any article representing a trade secret entrusted to him
3. Having unlawfully obtained access to the article, without authority makes or causes to be made a copy of any article representing a trade secret
4. Having obtained access to the article through a relationship of trust and confidence, without authority and in breach of the obligations created by such relationship makes or causes to be made, directly from and in the presence of the article, a copy of any article representing a trade secret

5-15 Trade Secrets

Penal Code 496—Receiving Stolen Property

(a) Receiving; knowledge; concealment; punishment. Every person who buys or receives any property that has been stolen or that has been obtained in any manner constituting theft or extortion, knowing the property to be so stolen or obtained, or who conceals, sells, withholds, or aids in concealing, selling, or withholding any property from the owner, knowing the property to be so stolen or obtained, is punishable by imprisonment in a state prison, or in a county jail for not more than one year . However, if the district attorney or the grand jury determines that this action would be in the interests of justice, the district attorney or the grand jury, as the case may be, may, if the value of the property does not exceed four hundred dollars ($400), specify in the accusatory pleading that the offense shall be a misdemeanor, punishable only by imprisonment in a county jail not exceeding one year.

    A principal in the actual theft of the property may be convicted pursuant to this section. However, no person may be convicted both pursuant to this section and of the theft of the same property.

(b) Swap meet vendors; secondhand dealers and collectors; inquiry; presumption. Every swap meet vendor, as defined in Section 21661 of the Business and Professions Code, and every person whose principal business is dealing in, or collecting, used or secondhand merchandise or personal property, and every agent, employee, or representative of that person, who buys or receives any property that has been stolen or obtained in any manner constituting theft or extortion, under circumstances that should cause the person, agent, employee, or representative to make reasonable inquiry to ascertain that the person from whom the property was bought or received had the legal right to sell or deliver it, without making a reasonable inquiry, shall be presumed to have bought or received the property knowing it to have been so stolen or

5-16 Receiving Stolen Property

obtained. This presumption may, however, be rebutted by proof.

(c) Swap meet vendors; secondhand dealers and collectors; inquiry; burden of proof. When in a prosecution under this section it shall appear from the evidence that the defendant was a swap meet vendor or that the defendant's principal business was as set forth in subdivision (b), that the defendant bought, received, or otherwise obtained, or concealed, withheld, or aided in concealing or withholding, from the owner, any property that had been stolen or obtained in any manner constituting theft or extortion, and that the defendant bought, received, obtained, concealed, or withheld that property under circumstances that should have caused him or her to make reasonable inquiry to ascertain that the person from whom he or she bought, received, or obtained the property had the legal right to sell or deliver it to him or her, then the burden shall be upon the defendant to show that before buying, receiving, or otherwise obtaining the property, he or she made a reasonable inquiry to ascertain that the person selling or delivering the same to him or her had the legal right to sell or deliver it.

5-16a Elements

The required elements of receiving stolen property are as follows:

1. A person who *knowingly*
2. Buys, receives, conceals, or withholds
3. Property that has been obtained by theft or extortion

5-16b Discussion

PC 496 provides that any person who knowingly buys or receives any property that has been stolen is guilty of this crime. If a person buys or receives stolen property under such circumstances that he should suspect that the property is stolen, there is an inference that he was aware that it was stolen.

To be convicted of this offense, the property must be stolen property. If the police use their own property or property borrowed from someone as a setup, the accused may be guilty of only an attempt to receive stolen property. This is based on the concept that the property that the accused is receiving is not, in fact, stolen property.

Receiving stolen property is distinct from the crime of stealing the property. A person cannot be convicted of both stealing and receiving the same stolen property. In *People v. Stewart* (185 Cal. App. 3d 197), the defendant's conviction of receiving stolen property was overturned. The defendant had been convicted of both burglary and receiving stolen property. The court held that a person could not be convicted of both stealing the property and receiving stolen property where the evidence shows that the property received was the same as the property taken in the theft and that a burglar could not be convicted of receiving stolen property from himself. However, if the burglar or thief disposes of the property and then receives it back, he or she may be guilty of both theft or burglary and receiving stolen property.

Mere possession of stolen property alone is insufficient to establish the offense of receiving stolen property. A person in the business of buying, dealing with, or collecting used property, however, has a duty to conduct an inquiry into the legal right of a seller to sell or deliver the property being offered. Failure to do so under such circumstances that would indicate that the property may be stolen creates an inference that the person receiving the property knew that it was stolen property.

Possession accompanied by suspicious circumstances may be sufficient to establish the inference that the property was received with knowledge that it was stolen. Factors used to indicate knowledge that the property was stolen include:

1. False statements regarding how the property came into the accused's possession
2. Hiding the property
3. Failure to identify the person from whom the accused received the property
4. Flight from location of the property when the police arrived
5. Attempting to destroy the property
6. Possession of the property with identifying marks removed
7. Extremely low price on high-value items

In one case, the court held that while the unexplained possession of stolen property, standing alone, is not sufficient to support a conviction for receiving stolen property, the circumstances could lead reasonable persons to believe that the possessor either stole it or received it with the knowledge that it was stolen (*People v. Edwards*, 14 Cal. App. 3d 57). Possession of recently stolen property raises such a strong inference that only slight additional evidence is needed to support a conviction (*People v. Britz*, 17 Cal. App. 3d 743).

Possession under this statute is defined as the exercise of dominion and control over the property. The property does not need to be under the immediate control of the accused, as long as he or she has control of it and knows of its location. The property can be in the possession of more than one person.

A person who receives stolen property is not guilty of being an accomplice to the crime of theft, unless the person makes an arrangement with the thief before the theft is committed. If an arrangement is made between the thief and the receiver prior to the theft, then the thief is an accomplice of the receiving of stolen property, and the receiver is an accomplice to the theft.

Penal Code 497

5-17 Goods Stolen in Another State

Every person who, in another state or country steals or embezzles the property of another, or receives such property knowing it to have been stolen or embezzled, and brings the same into this state, may be convicted and punished in the same manner as if such larceny, or embezzlement, or receiving, had been committed in this state.

5-18 Single or Multiple Thefts

It is sometimes necessary to determine if one single theft or separate smaller thefts have occurred. The general rule is if there is one general intent to steal and one general plan, it is all one theft (*People v. Fleming*, 220 Cal. 601). In this case, the values may be added to determine if a grand theft has occurred. If the takings do not meet those requirements, then each one is considered a separate crime and may be punished separately.

The taking of several articles at one time normally is considered one crime. In *People v. Sullivan* (80 Cal. App. 3d 16), the defendant stole several items of property belonging to different owners. In determining if the accused committed grand theft or several petty thefts, the court instructed the jury that the value of the articles should be aggregated if the defendant had one general overall plan and should be considered separate offenses if the accused had no overall plan to steal them.

A series of thefts from one person as a part of one general plan is also considered one crime. A mother who obtained monthly welfare checks for a period of six months based on one false representation was guilty of only one theft. An angry employee who sold his employer's goods during a two-week period and kept the proceeds was considered guilty of only one crime since he had only one general plan.

5-19 Alteration of Serial Numbers

Penal Code 537e—Possession of Articles from Which Name Plates Removed; Misdemeanor

(a) Any person who knowingly buys, sells, receives, disposes of, conceals, or has in his possession a radio, piano, phonograph, sewing machine, washing machine, typewriter, adding machine, comptometer, bicycle, a safe, vacuum cleaner, dictaphone, watch, watch movement, watch case, or any mechanical or electrical device, appliance, . . . from which the manufacturer's nameplate, serial number, or any other distinguishing number or identification mark has been removed, defaced, covered, altered, or destroyed, is guilty of a misdemeanor. If the value of any integrated chip from which the name plate, serial number, or other distinguishing mark is removed, defaced, covered, altered, or destroyed exceeds four hundred dollars ($400), the offense is a felony punishable by imprisonment in the county jail not to exceed one year or in the state prison.

5-20 Forgery and Check-Related Crimes

Penal Code 470—Forgery, Intent; Documents of Value; Counterfeiting Seal; Uttering; Falsification of Records; Elements of Proof

(a) Every person who, with intent to defraud, signs the name of another person, or a fictitious person, knowing that he or she has no authority to do so, or falsely makes, alters, forges, or counterfeits, any charter, letters patent, deed, lease, indenture, writing obligatory, will, testament, codicil, bond, covenant, bank bill or note, post note, check, draft, bill of exchange, contract, promissory note, due bill for the payment of money or property, receipt for money or property, passage ticket, lottery ticket or share purporting to be issued under the California State Lottery Act of 1984, trading stamp, power of attorney, certificate of ownership or other document evidencing ownership of a vehicle or undocumented vessel, or any certificate of any share, right, or interest in the stock of any corporation or association, or any controller's warrant for the payment of money at the treasury, county order or warrant, or request for the payment of money, or the delivery of goods or chattels of any kind, or for the delivery of any instrument of writing, or acquittance, release, or receipt for money or goods, or any acquittance, release, or discharge of any debt, account, suit, action, demand, or other thing, real or personal, or any transfer or assurance of money, certificate of shares of stock, goods, chattels, or other property whatever, or any letter of attorney, or other power to receive money, or to receive or transfer certificates of shares of stock or annuities, or to let, lease, dispose of, lien, or convey any goods, chattels, lands, or tenements, or other estate, real or personal, or any acceptance or endorsement of any bill of exchange, promissory note, draft, order, or any assignment of any bond, writing obligatory, promissory note, or other contract for money or other property; or counterfeits or forges the seal or handwriting of another; or utters, publishes, passes, or attempts to pass, as true and genuine, any of the above-named false, altered, forged, or counterfeited matters, as above specified and described, knowing the same to be false, altered, forged, or counterfeited, with intent to prejudice, damage, or defraud any person; or who, with intent to defraud, alters, corrupts, or falsifies any record of any will, codicil, conveyance, or other instrument, the record of which is by law evidence, or any record of any judgment of a court or the return of any officer to any process of any court, is guilty of forgery.

(b) Upon a trial for forging any bill or note purporting to be the bill or note of an incorporated company or bank, or for passing, or attempting to pass, or having in possession with intent to pass, any forged bill or note, it is not necessary to prove the incorporation of the bank or company by the charter or act of incorporation, but it may be proved by general reputation; and persons of skill are competent witnesses to prove that the bill or note is forged or counterfeited.

Penal Code 470a—Forging Driver's License; Identification Card

Every person who alters, falsifies, forges, duplicates, or in any manner reproduces or counterfeits any driver's license or identification card issued by a governmental agency with the intent that such driver's license or identification card be used to facilitate the commission of any forgery, is punishable by imprisonment in the state prison, or by imprisonment in the county jail. . . .

Penal Code 470b—Possessing Forged Driver's License; Identification Card

Every person who displays or causes or permits to be displayed or in his possession any driver's license or identification card of the type enumerated in Section 470a with the intent that such driver's license or identification card be used to facilitate the commission of any forgery, is punishable by imprisonment in the state prison, or by imprisonment in the county jail for not more than one year.

The forgery and check-related crimes are as follows:

- Forgery-Acts Constituting (PC 470)
- Forging Driver's License-Identification Card (PC 470a)
- Possessing Forged Driver's License-Identification Card (PC 470b)
- Altering Entries in Books and Records (PC 471)
- Possessing, Receiving or Uttering Forged Paper (PC 475)
- Forging or Counterfeiting State, Corporate and Official Seals (PC 472)
- Sending False Message by Phone or Telegraph (PC 474)
- Uttering or Passing Check, Money Order, or Warrant to Defraud (PC 475a)
- Making, Drawing or Possessing Fictitious Bill, Note or Check (PC 476)
- Making, Drawing or Passing Worthless Check, Draft or Order (PC 476a)
- Offering False or Forged Instrument to be File of Record (PC 115)
- Altering Certified Copies of Official Records (PC 115.3)
- Filing False or Forged Documents or Instruments (PC 115.5)
- Forgery of Initiative Signatures (Elections Code 29733)
- Forgery of Trademark (B & P 14322)

5-20a Definition

At both common law and by statute, forgery is the making of a false instrument or the material alteration of an existing genuine instrument. The common law crime of uttering a forged document is also included in the statutory crime of forgery under PC 470. Uttering is the offering, passing, or attempted passing of a false instrument with knowledge thereof and with the intent to defraud. Forgery is complete when one either makes or passes a false instrument with the intent to defraud (*People v. Ross*, 198 Cal. App. 2d 723). The gist of forgery offenses is the intent to defraud. Actual defrauding is not required (*People v. Garin*, 174 Cal. App. 2d 654).

5-20b Elements

The following are the elements of the crime of forgery (making a false document or alteration of a genuine instrument):

1. A false signature or material alteration
2. Signed or altered without authority
3. A writing or other instrument that if genuine would have legal significance
4. An intent to defraud

The elements necessary to establish forgery of endorsement are as follows:

1. The person whose name was alleged to have been forged was a real person.
2. The person's name was signed to the check without his or her authority.
3. The check was signed with intent to defraud (*People v. Epperson*, 134 Cal. App. 2d 413).

The elements of the crime of forgery (uttering, passing, publishing, or attempting to pass) are as follows:

1. A forged document that if genuine would have legal significance
2. Uttering, passing, publishing, or attempting to pass the forged document with the intent to defraud

5-20c Discussion

The forgery statute is intended to protect society against fabrication, falsification, and uttering, publishing, and passing of forged instruments, which, if genuine, would establish or defeat some claim, impose duty, create liability, or work prejudice to another in his rights of person or property (*People v. Tomlinson*, 35 Cal. 503). In prosecution for forgery, it is immaterial whether forgery is of the name of an existing or a fictitious person (*People v. McDonald*, 16 Cal. App. 2d 687).

The alleged fact that no person was actually injured by forgeries is no defense to forgery charges. Crime of forgery is complete when one makes or passes an incorrectly named instrument with intent to defraud, prejudice, or damage, and proof of loss or detriment is immaterial (*People v. Parker*, 255 Cal. App. 2d 664).

Forgery is a *specific intent* crime, in that a specific intent to defraud is a necessary element of the offense. The term *writing* includes printed or typewritten material. In one case, the accused was convicted of forgery where he signed his own name to a check. In this case, the defendant wrongly received a check that was made payable to another person with the same name as the defendant. The defendant knew that the check was not his and thus, by signing his name with the intention of having it accepted as the other person's signature, committed forgery. The crime of forgery is complete when one either makes or passes a false instrument with intent to defraud (*People v. Parker*, 255 Cal. App. 2d 664).

Fraud in Inception

Forgery may be committed by obtaining a genuine signature to an instrument by fraudulent representations regarding the nature of the document. For example, a blank check signed by a victim, who was promised that it was to be used only as an example, was later filled in without authority. The court held that this was a forgery (*People v. Bartges* 126 Cal. App. 2d 763).

Authority to Sign

The prosecution must establish that there was a lack of authority to sign the other person's name. Accordingly, the implied authority to sign the other person's name is a defense.

Instruments Subject to Forgery

To be subject to forgery the instrument, if genuine, must create some legal right or obligation (have apparent legal significance). If the instrument has no legal significance on its face, then it is not subject to forgery. If it has no legal significance, but this is not apparent on its face, then the instrument is subject to forgery statutes. For example, in one case, the conviction for the forgery of a will was upheld on review even though the deceased had no estate (property) to pass under the will (*People v. Bibby*, 91 C 470).

Instruments that the courts have found to have apparent legal significance include:

1. Transcript of college record or college diploma (*People v. Russel*, 214 Cal. App. 2d 445)
2. Letter of credit (*People v. Kagan*, 264 Cal. App. 2d 656)
3. Insurance form of proof of loss (*People v. Di Ryana*, 8 Cal. App. 333)
4. Divorce decree (*Ex parte Finley*, 66 C 262)
5. Signing false name to a charge slip while using a stolen credit card (*People v. Searcy*, 199 Cal. App. 2d 740).

Alteration

The alteration of a document is expressly included in PC 470. The general theory is that when a genuine document is altered, it becomes a false document. To be forgery, however, alteration must be of a material part. For example, changing the date on a check from April 4 to April 14 will not be a forgery unless the change in date has some legal significance. The alteration must result in some material change in the rights and obligations of the parties involved. For example, the material alteration of a check already made, with the intent to defraud another, is forgery (*People v. Brotherton*, 47 Cal. 388).

Intent

An intent to defraud is a necessary element. The intent, however, may be inferred from circumstances (*People v. Cullen*, 99 Cal. App. 2d 468). A general intent to defraud members of the public is sufficient. There is no requirement to establish that the defendant intended to defraud any particular person, as long as a general intent to defraud another is established (*People v. Brown*, 113 Cal. App. 492).

Drawing of a check payable to cash under an assumed name, if done in good faith, and not for purposes of defrauding, is not the use of a fictitious name within the meaning of PC 470 providing that one, who with intent to defraud signs the name of a fictitious person, shall be guilty of forgery (*People v. Ryan*, 74 Cal. App. 125, 239 P. 419).

Multiplicity

Unlike most other crimes, each document involved constitutes a separate offense. As one court noted: "Although defendant's theft of four warrants from the city of Los Angeles gave rise to only one offense of attempted grand theft, his forgery of signatures on each of the documents gave rise to four separate forgery offenses" (*People v. Richardson*, 83 Cal. App. 3d 853).

As explained by another court: "The doctrine that theft by larceny, false pretenses or embezzlement, where several takings are motivated by one intention, one general impulse and one plan, as a single crime does not extend to forgery; thus, a defendant who was present with codefendant when she used another's credit card to forge three separate sales slips for purchase of different goods from different sales clerks was guilty of three separate offenses even though forgeries were probably motivated by preconceived plan to obtain merchandise from one store" (*People v. Neder*, 16 Cal. App. 3d 846).

Uttering

The crime of "uttering a forgery" is the offense of trying to pass a forged document as genuine. To be guilty of this offense, the accused need not complete the passing or uttering of it. Attempting to pass is sufficient to constitute the offense (*People v. Clark*, 233 Cal. App. 2d 725). A conviction of uttering a forgery was upheld where one defendant was caught attempting to cash a forged payroll check by representing to a cashier that he was the individual whose name was on the check (*People v. Ford*, 233 Cal. App. 2d 725). Possession of a forged instrument with the intent to pass it is not forgery under PC 470. There must be at least an attempt to pass the false document. (Note: Possession of a forged document may be a violation of the "possession" statutes.)

5-21 Making False Entries in Records or Returns

Penal Code 471—Making False Entries in Records or Returns

Every person who, with intent to defraud another, makes, forges, or alters any entry in any book of records, any instrument purporting to be any record or return specified in the preceding section, is guilty of forgery.

Penal Code 471.5—Falsifying Medical Records

Any person who alters or modifies the medical record of any person, with fraudulent intent, or who, with fraudulent intent, creates any false medical records, is guilty of a misdemeanor.

5-22 Forgery of Corporate and Public Seals

Penal Code 472—Forgery of Corporate and Public Seals

Any person who, with intent to defraud another, forges, or counterfeits the seal of this state, the seal of any public officer authorized by law, the seal of any court of record, or the seal of any corporation, or any other public seal authorized or recognized by the laws of this state, or of any other state, government, or country, or who falsely makes, forges, or counterfeits any impression purporting to be an impression of any such seal, or who has in his possession any such counterfeited seal or impression thereof, knowing it to be counterfeited, and willfully conceals the same, is guilty of forgery.

5-23 Sending False Messages

Penal Code 474—False Messages

Every person who knowingly and willfully sends by telegraph or telephone to any person a false or forged message, purporting to be from a telegraph or telephone office, or from any other person, or who willfully delivers or causes to be delivered to any other person any such message falsely purporting to have been received by telegraph or telephone, or who furnished to any agent, operator, or employee, to be sent by telegraph or telephone, or to be delivered, any such message, knowing the same to be false or forged, with the intent to deceive, injure, or defraud another, is punishable by imprisonment in the state prison . . . or in the county jail. . . .

In *People v. Tolstoy* (250 Cal. App. 2d 22), the defendant was convicted of this offense for sending a telegraph message to her former husband stating that their 14-year-old son had been killed and his remains cremated. Apparently, she was trying to defraud her ex-husband of his visitation rights awarded by the court.

5-23a Discussion

PC 538(a) makes it a misdemeanor to sign another person's name to a letter and send it to a newspaper with the intent to cause the newspaper to believe that the letter was written by the person whose name is signed to the letter.

5-24 False Signature on Letter to Newspaper

Penal Code 115—Offering False or Forged Instruments to Be Filed

5-25 Filing Forged Instruments

(a) Every person who knowingly procures or offers any false or forged instrument to be filed, registered, or recorded in any public office within this state, which instrument, if genuine, might be filed, registered, or recorded under any law of this state or of the United States, is guilty of a felony.

(b) Each instrument which is procured or offered to be filed, registered, or recorded in violation of subdivision (a) shall constitute a separate violation of this section.

[Subsections (c) and (d) referring to punishments are omitted.]

Penal Code 115.5—Filing False or Forged Documents or Instruments

(a) Every person who files any false or forged document or instrument with the county recorder which affects title to, places an encumbrance on, or places an interest secured by a mortgage or deed or trust on, real property consisting of a single-family residence containing not more than four dwelling units, with knowledge that the document is false or forged is punishable. . . .

(b) Every person who makes a false sworn statement to a notary public, with knowledge that the statement is false, to induce the notary public to perform an improper notarial act on an instrument or document affecting title to, or placing an encumbrance on, real property containing not more than four dwelling units is guilty of a felony.

The preceding offenses required that the filing or offering for filing or the making of a false sworn statement to a notary public be "with the knowledge" that the documents or statements are forged or false. There is no requirement, however, to establish an "intent to defraud."

5-25a Discussion

Penal Code 115.3—Altering Certified Copies of Official Records

5-26 Altering Certified Copies of Official Records

Any person who alters a certified copy of an official record, or knowingly furnishes an altered certified copy of an official record, of this state, including the executive, legislative, and judicial branches thereof, or of any city, county, city and county, district, or political subdivision thereof, is guilty of a misdemeanor.

5-26a Discussion

The offense of altering certified copies of official records does not require an "intent to defraud." The mere altering of certified copies is sufficient to constitute the offense.

5-27 Possession of Forged Bills

Penal Code 475—Forged or Unfinished Bills or Notes, Possession

Every person who has in his possession, or receives from another person, any forged promissory note or bank bill, or bills, or any counterfeited trading stamp, or stamps, or lottery ticket or share purporting to be issued under the California State Lottery Act of 1984, or tickets or shares, for the payment of money or property, with the intention to pass the same, or to permit, cause, or procure the person, knowing the same to be forged or counterfeited, or has or keeps in his or her possession any blank or unfinished note or bank bill made to be issued by an incorporated bank or banking company, or any blank or unfinished check, money order, or traveler's check, whether the parties thereto are real or fictitious, with intention to fill up and complete the blank and unfinished note or bill, check, money order, or traveler's check, or to permit, or cause, or procure the same, or to permit, or cause, or procure the same to be uttered or passed, to defraud any person, is punishable by imprisonment in the state prison, or by imprisonment in the county jail. . . .

Penal Code 475a—Fraudulent Possession of Money Order, Warrant, or Completed Check

Every person who has in his possession a completed check, money order, traveler's check, controller's warrant for the payment of money at the treasury, or county order or warrant, whether the parties thereto are real or fictitious, with intention to utter or pass the same, or to permit, cause, or procure the same to be uttered or passed, to defraud any person, is punishable by imprisonment in the state prison, or by imprisonment in the county jail. . . .

Penal Code 476—Possessing Fictitious Bill, Note, or Check

Every person who makes, passes, utters, or publishes, with intention to defraud any other person, or who, with the like intention, attempts to pass, utter, or publish, or who has in his possession, with like intent to utter, pass, or publish, any fictitious bill, note, or check, purporting to be the bill, note, or check, or other instrument in writing for the payment of money or property of some bank, corporation, copartnership, or individual, when, in fact, there is no such bank, corporation, copartnership, or individual in existence knowing the bill, note, check, or instrument in writing to be fictitious, is punishable by imprisonment in the county jail . . . or . . . in the state prison.

5-27a Discussion

For the possession to be a crime, the possession must be with the knowledge that the instrument was false or was not genuine. Each instrument possessed constitutes a separate crime.

5-28 Check Offenses

Penal Code 476a—Delivering or Making Check with Insufficient Funds

(a) Any person, who for himself or as the agent or representative of another or as an officer of a corporation, willfully, with intent to defraud, makes or draws or utters or delivers any check, draft, or order upon any bank or depository, of person, or firm, or corporation, for the payment of money, knowing at the time of such making, drawing, uttering, or delivering that the maker or drawer or the corporation has not sufficient funds in, or credit with said bank or depository, or person, or firm, or corporation, for the payment of such check, draft, or order and all other checks, drafts, or orders upon such funds then outstanding, in full upon its presentation, although no express representation is made with reference thereto, is punishable by imprisonment in the county jail. . . .

(b) However, if the total amount of all such checks, drafts, or orders that the defendant is charged with and convicted of making, drawing, or uttering does not exceed two hundred dollars ($200), the offense is punishable only by imprisonment in the county jail for not more than one year, except that this subdivision shall not be applicable if the defendant . . . [has a previous conviction of this Section or Sections 470, 475, or 476].

(c) Where such check, draft, or order is protested, on the ground of insufficiency of funds or credit, the notice of protest thereof shall be admissible as proof of presentation, nonpayment and protest and shall be presumptive evidence or knowledge of insufficiency of funds or credit with such bank or depository, or person, or firm, or corporation.

(d) In any prosecution under this section involving two or more checks, drafts, or orders, it shall constitute prima facie evidence of the identity of the drawer of a check, draft, or order if:

   (1) At the time of the acceptance of such check, draft, or order from the drawer by the payee there is obtained from the drawer the following information: name and residence of the drawer, business or mailing address, either a valid driver's license number or Department of Motor Vehicles identification card number, and the drawer's home or work phone number or place of employment. Such information may be recorded on the check, draft, or order itself or may be retained on file by the payee and referred to on the check, draft, or order by identifying number or other similar means; and

   (2) The person receiving the check, draft, or order witnesses the drawer's signature or endorsement, and, as evidence of that, initials the check, draft, or order at the time of the receipt.

(e) The word *credit* as used herein shall be construed to mean an arrangement or understanding with the bank or depository or person or firm or corporation for the payment of such check, draft, or order.

(f) [Omitted.]

The following are the elements of the offense of delivering or making a check with insufficient funds:

5-28a Elements

1. The making of, uttering, or the delivery of
2. A check, draft, or order
3. With the intent to defraud
4. For the payment of money or property
5. With knowledge that at the time of the making, delivering, or uttering, there were insufficient funds or credit to cover the check, draft, or order

5-28b Discussion

In most cases, the conduct required to establish a violation of this offense, also, is sufficient to constitute theft. A critical problem with the prosecution of most theft by check offenses is in establishing the identity of the maker or presenter of the check. This problem is made easier by the presumptions contained in (d)(1) above. The evidentiary presumptions, therefore, make it easier in most cases to establish a violation of this statute rather than the theft statute.

Although this section requires an intent to defraud, it is not necessary to establish that any person was actually defrauded. It does require proof that at the time of the making, uttering, or delivery that the defendant knew that he or she had neither sufficient funds or credit with the bank, and so on, to cover the check, draft, or order.

Cases on Point

People v. Darling (230 Cal. App. 2d 615)

The statutory redefinition of theft consolidates various criminal acquisitive techniques that were subjects of different common-law-defined larcenous offenses, but it does not change elements of several types of theft so that conviction must be supported by evidence establishing elements of one of the consolidated offenses.

People v. Ashley (42 Cal. 2d 246)

The purpose of PC 484 in consolidating crimes of larceny by trick and device, and of obtaining property by false pretenses, into a single crime of theft was to remove technicalities that existed in pleading and proof of the consolidated crimes at common law.

People v. Dunn (164 Cal. App. 2d 335)

In prosecution for petty theft, the prosecution must prove an unlawful taking and asportation of property of some intrinsic value with intent to deprive the owner thereof.

People v. Butler (65 Cal. 2d 569)

Taking of property is not theft in absence of an intent to steal.

People v. Arriola (164 Cal. App. 2d 430)

To complete the crime of grand theft, the intent to steal or take property is necessary in addition to the actual stealing or taking.

People v. Rath (196 Cal. App. 2d 638)

To constitute theft by trick or device, there must be a taking, there must be an asportation of the thing taken, the thing taken must be property of another, and the taking and carrying away must be with an intent, without claim or pretense of right or justification, to deprive the owner of his or her property wholly and permanently.

People v. Quiel (68 Cal. App. 2d 674)

"Asportation" within the meaning of the statute penalizing theft may be fulfilled by wrongfully and unlawfully removing property from the possession or control of the owner against his or her will with the intent to steal it, though property may be retained by a thief but a moment.

People v. Hanselman (76 Cal. 460)

An officer, to detect the author of certain thefts, feigned a drunken slumber, with intent to allow any thief to rob him in order to make a case against him, having no suspicion that the defendant would be the one, and while in this condition, perfectly conscious and making no resistance, the defendant took money from the officer. In this case, the failure to resist was not such consent as to take away a material element of the crime.

People v. Green (27 Cal. 3d 1)

If the defendant intends to permanently deprive an owner of his or her property, taking is larceny or robbery even if the defendant's sole intent is to destroy property.

People v. Mills Sing (42 Cal. App. 385)

In embezzlement there is no intent at the time of taking to steal or wrongfully appropriate the property, but the accused, having rightfully come into possession thereafter, forms the intent fraudulently to convert the property to his or her own use.

People v. Weitz (42 Cal. 2d 338)

To convict for grand theft consisting of obtaining property by false pretense, the false pretense or representation must have materially influenced the owner to part with his or her property, but false pretense need not be the sole inducing cause, and the defendant need not have been benefited personally from the fraudulent acquisition.

People v. Hodges (153 Cal. App. 2d 788)

"Larceny by trick and device" is the appropriation of fraudulently acquired property; "obtaining property by false pretenses" is the fraudulent or deceitful acquisition of both title and possession.

People v. Green (34 Cal. App. 4th)

The language of the statute prohibiting unlawful driving of a vehicle is to be applied under circumstances where a person either (1) obtains lawful possession of the vehicle and thereafter forms specific intent to deprive the owner of possession or (2) obtains the vehicle under circumstances that indicate the perpetrator has the knowledge, absent his or her taking of the vehicle, that use or operation of the vehicle is depriving the owner of possession of vehicle.

People v. Hutchings (242 Cal. App. 2d 294)

An automobile was being driven "without consent of the owner" where accused had received consent from a used car dealer only for a taking for 30 or 40 minutes so the accused's wife could inspect the vehicle, and the accused was arrested some four hours after the limited consent time had expired and was alone in the car at a substantial distance from the home to which he had asked to drive it.

People v. Rhinehart (137 Cal. App. 2d 497)

The defendant, who was trying to start a stolen automobile, was in possession of such automobile under suspicious circumstances, and the mere possession of a stolen automobile under suspicious circumstances is sufficient to sustain conviction for taking a vehicle without the owner's consent.

People v. Stuart (272 Cal. App. 2d 653)

Essential elements of receiving stolen property are as follows: property must be stolen property; defendant must receive, conceal, or withhold it or aid in receiving, concealing, or withholding it from its owner; and defendant must have knowledge that property is stolen property.

Creative Legal Defense

When former First Lady Imelda Marcos returned to the Philippines in November 1991, she and her late husband were accused of stealing five billion dollars from the national treasury. Mrs. Marcos claimed that it was all a misunderstanding, that she and her husband had not robbed and looted the treasury. She contended that the source of her family's wealth was actually the fabled Yamashita treasure, which her husband had found while he was a guerrilla fighting the Japanese. The Filipino authorities were not convinced and refused to drop the charges.

Practicum

Practicum I

A group of apparently unrelated theft crimes has occurred in your city. The police chief assigns you as an investigator. Prepare notes establishing the essential elements of each theft crime and other information that is necessary for you to brief rookies on the problems and issues involving theft crimes.

Practicum II

Donald was unhappy with the grade he received in his Substantive Criminal Law course. Afraid that it would affect his chances of going to law school, he altered his transcript before including it with his application package. He also sent a copy of the transcript to the local police department with his application for the police academy. A third copy was framed and hung in his den. What and how many crimes has Donald committed? Explain your answer.

Discussion Questions

1. On a rainy day, Jerry goes to the local restaurant for lunch. As he was leaving the restaurant, he picks up what he thinks is his umbrella. The umbrella does not belong to him. What crime, if any, has he committed? Explain your answer.
2. Same as the facts in number 1, however, Jerry knows that the umbrella does not belong to him. What crime, if any, has he committed?
3. Same as number 1, except Jerry takes the umbrella that he thinks does not belong to him. He, however, actually picked up one that belonged to him that he had left there last week and forgot about. What crime, if any, has he committed?

4. Judy buys a new car on credit. The seller retains title to the car until the payments are completed. After she had made three payments, she sold the car to Ralph. Can she be convicted of stealing the car?
5. Kathy was a checker at a Kmart Store in Los Angeles. The defendant, her brother, was observed with a shopping cart containing several items approaching and stopping at her register. Kathy took the items out of the cart and put them on the counter. Next, she placed the items in a shopping bag and handed the bag to her brother. He walked out of the store with the items without paying for them. What crime, if any, has he committed? What crime, if any, has she committed?

6. The victim received a watch as a gift in 1949 from her father shortly before his disappearance. The victim, having no need for the watch, stored it in a chest. The defendant stole the watch from the chest. The watch originally cost $295. A similar watch would cost about $500 on today's market. Should the defendant be charged with petty theft or grand theft?

7. Explain the differences between theft by trick or device and theft by false pretenses.

8. How does common law theft compare with statutory larceny?

9. Why was real property not subject to common law theft?

10. What are the key distinctions between embezzlement and theft by larceny?

11. Explain the difference between the crimes of possession of forged instruments and uttering a forged document.

12. Bob writes a check to pay his rent. At the time of writing his check, he thinks that he has sufficient credit with the bank to cover the check. Two days prior, however, he had received a letter from his bank indicating that his line of credit was canceled. Bob had misread the letter and thought that it had increased his line of credit. Has he committed a check offense under PC 476a?

13. Joe finds four tickets to the UCLA/USC football game. He needs money to pay his tuition to UC. He attempts to sell the tickets. What crime(s), if any, has he committed?

14. Jim White has the same name as a famous football player. He writes a letter to the newspaper regarding football. The newspaper, thinking the letter is from the famous Jim White, publishes it. What crime(s), if any, has Jim committed?

15. Mike asks Jerry to cash his check for him (Mike) at the local bank. Mike forgets to endorse the check. Jerry, realizing this, signs Mike's name to the check, cashes it, and gives the money to Mike. Is Jerry guilty of forgery?

16. Susan finds a check with the name of the payee blank. She fills in her name and cashes the check. What crimes has she committed?

Self-Study Quiz

True/False

1. Theft by larceny requires the intent to permanently deprive the owner of the property.

2. Both petty and grand thefts may be felonies.

3. Embezzlement requires that the accused use false pretenses to obtain possession of the property.

4. Real property may be subject to theft by false pretense.

5. California has eliminated most of the fine distinctions and technical niceties that formerly existed between the common law theft crimes.

6. If fruit is picked from a tree, it is then subject to the theft by larceny statutes.

7. For the crime to be theft, it is necessary that the taking be from the immediate physical presence of the owner of the property.

8. The value of the property is determined by the original cost of it.

9. Theft by trick or device is committed when the possession of the property is obtained by fraud.

10. To be guilty of theft, a person must steal property that has some value.

11. A pawn shop owner cannot be convicted of receiving stolen property unless he or she knew for certain that the property was stolen.

12. Jerry devises a plan to steal $5 per day from his employer. He stole a total of $550 in this manner. He has committed the crime of petty theft only.

13. Caren picks up a package of gum and hides it in her purse. She is stopped prior to leaving the store. She cannot be convicted of theft, since she is still in the store.

14. Stealing from the physical presence of a person is a petty theft.

15. Grand theft may be punished by jail, a fine, or by prison term.

16. Forgery requires an intent to defraud.

17. Implied authority is a defense to forgery.

18. Making a false lottery ticket is not forgery.

19. Altering a lottery ticket to make it a winning ticket is not forgery.

20. Trading stamps are not subject to be forged.

21. The crime of uttering a forged document requires that the transfer of the document be completed.

22. A material alteration of a bank check is a forgery.

23. Forgery may be committed by obtaining a genuine signature by fraud.

24. The offense of sending false messages under PC 474 requires an intent to injure, deceive, or defraud.

25. A person may be convicted of possession of a forged check without establishing that the person was aware of its falsity.

26. To be guilty of the crime of altering certified copies of official records, it must be proven that the individual did the altering with an intent to defraud.

27. Passing a forged driver's license is always a felony.

28. Uttering a forged document is the offense of offering, passing, or attempting to pass a forged document with the knowledge of its falsity and with the intent to defraud.

Crimes against Property: Burglary, Arson, and Vandalism

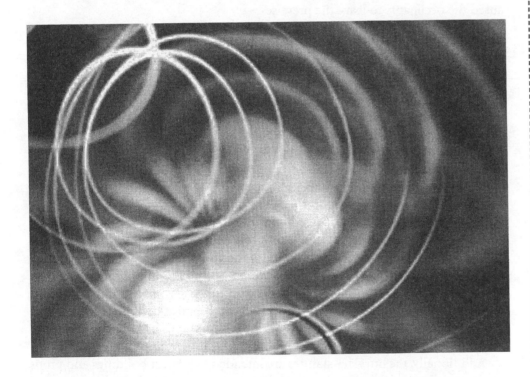

We inflict atrocious injuries on the burglars we catch in order to make the rest take effectual precautions against detection.

George Bernard Shaw

6-1 Burglary

Penal Code 459—Acts Constituting Burglary; Inhabited Defined

Every person who enters any house, room, apartment, tenement, shop, warehouse, store, mill, barn, stable, outhouse or other building, tent, vessel, . . . floating home, . . . railroad car, locked or sealed cargo container, whether or not mounted on a vehicle, trailer coach, . . . any house car, . . . inhabited camper, . . . vehicle . . . when the doors are locked, aircraft . . . or mine or any underground portion thereof, with intent to commit grand or petit larceny or any felony is guilty of burglary. As used in this chapter, *inhabited* means currently being used for dwelling purposes, whether occupied or not. A house, trailer, vessel designed for habitation, or portion of a building is currently being used for dwelling purposes if, at the time of the burglary, it was not occupied solely because a natural or other disaster caused the occupants to leave the premises.

6-1a Burglary-Related Crimes

The following is a list of crimes related to burglary and the relevant Penal Code sections that apply to them.

- Burglary (PC 459)
- Unauthorized Entry (PC 602.5)
- Burglary by Use of Acetylene Torch or Explosive (PC 464)
- Possession of Burglary Tools (PC 466)
- Sale of Burglary Tools (PC 466.1)
- Forced Entry (PC 603)
- Vending Machine Theft (PC 466.3)

6-1b Definition

The entering of a building or place listed in PC 459, with the intent to commit grand or petit larceny (theft) or any felony, constitutes burglary.

The essence of the crime of burglary is the unlawful entry with a felonious intent and the dangers associated with such an entry (*People v. Lamica*, 249 Cal. App. 2d 640). The crime is completed with the entry (*People v. Clifton*, 148 Cal. App. 2d 276). Burglary statutes are based on the premise that the intruder may harm the occupants in the process of attempting to commit the crime (*People v. Lewis*, 274 Cal. App. 2d 912).

Additionally, the burglary statutes are intended to protect buildings and property, especially residences. At common law, burglary required the breaking and entering of a dwelling house during the time of darkness. California burglary statutes have eliminated the requirements of "breaking" and "entry during the hours of darkness" (*People v. Scofield*, 149 Cal. App. 3d 536).

The statutes have also included structures other than dwellings and vehicles to the places subject to burglary.

To constitute burglary, the entering of the building or vehicle must be with the intent to commit grand or petty theft or any felony (*People v. Lamica*, 274 Cal. App. 2d 640). Burglary is a specific intent crime (*People v. Green*, 228 Cal. App. 2d 437). The intended offense is separate from the burglary crime (*People v. Garnett*, 29 Cal. 622). Accordingly, one entering a building to commit a theft therein is guilty of both the crime of burglary and, at least, an attempted theft. In many cases, the crime of burglary is a more serious offense than the crime contemplated after entry. For example, petty theft is a misdemeanor, but entering an inhabited dwelling with the intent to commit a petty theft is first-degree burglary *(People v. Wolfe,* 257 Cal. App. 2d 420).

The following are the elements of statutory burglary in California:

1. An entry
2. Into a building, structure, or vehicle
3. With the intent to commit grand or petty larceny (theft) or a felony

6-1c Elements

The Entry Requirement

6-1d Discussion

There is no requirement that the entry be a forcible entry *(People v. Talbot,* 64 Cal. 2d 691). The entry may either be actual or constructive. A constructive entry occurs when an agent, confederate, accessory, or aider and abettor enters the structure, instead of the defendant *(People v. Bonilla,* 124 Cal. App. 2120). For example, in one case, the accused was convicted of burglary based on his confederate's entry into a railroad car. In this case, the confederate passed stolen hams outside the railroad car to the defendant *(People v. Failla,* 64 Cal. 2d 560).

If more than one entry is made into the building, the crime is completed when the first entry is made *(People v. Jones,* 225 Cal. App. 2d 434). There is also no requirement that the entry be illegal *(People v. Edwards,* 22 Cal. App. 3d 598 and *People v. Barry,* 94 Cal. 481). That is, a person may be convicted of burglary even though he or she had permission to enter the building from the owner. For example, the entering of a store that is open for business is a sufficient entry provided that at the time of the entry, the accused had the intent to commit a crime *(People v. Brittian,* 142 Cal. 8). This is based on the concept that any permission to enter is canceled by the criminal intent of the accused.

In one case, the accused was invited into a house by the resident and asked to wait for a few moments. The accused instead stole some jewelry and left. The court instructed the jury that the accused could be convicted of burglary if the jury determined that he had the intent to steal at the time he entered the house *(People v. Lowen,* 42 P. 32).

Although an entry, either actual or constructive, is an essential element of the crime, an accused may not be convicted of burglary if the accused has an absolute right to enter the building. Thus, if the accused who leases a building for a legal purpose and later during the period of the lease enters it to steal its fixtures, there has been no entry for purposes of the burglary statutes. This is based on the theory that the accused had an unconditional right to enter the building and therefore did not violate any possessory right *(People v. Gauze,* 15 Cal. 3d 709).

Entering the building is an essential requirement. The body of the accused, however, does not have to physically enter the structure *(People v. Allison,* 200 Cal. 407). Constructive entering is sufficient. For example, using a drill bit to bore a hole into the building has been held to be an entry where a portion of the bit entered into the building. In another case, entry was considered complete when the accused used a crowbar to open a window and then reached into the building with a hook and removed an item of personal property *(People v. Pettinger,* 94 Cal. App. 297). Sending a trained animal into the building to fetch an item of property would also be an entry. Reaching an arm through a broken window into a building to steal a ham hanging in the building constitutes a sufficient entry.

The entry of an agent, accessory, and so on is imputed to the accused (*People v. Walters*, 249 Cal. App. 2d 547).

The required entry may be to an interior room of a building. An accused, for example, enters a building without the necessary intent. After entering the building and finding it empty, he decides to steal and enters another room to find something to steal. The entering of the interior room with the intent to steal is sufficient to constitute the crime of burglary. In *People v. Garcia* (214 Cal. App. 2d 681), where the accused entered one building to facilitate the commission of theft in an adjoining area, the entry was sufficient to constitute burglary.

In one case, the accused stole an automatic teller machine (ATM) card and attempted to use it to withdraw money from an ATM built into the wall of a bank. He was convicted of burglary. The question on appeal was whether or not inserting a bank card into the ATM was sufficient entry of the building to constitute the crime of burglary. The California Court of Appeals, Second Circuit, in affirming the conviction, held that where the ATMs are firmly affixed to and attached to the inside of a bank building and covered by the bank roofs, they are buildings within the meaning of the burglary statutes. Thus, inserting a stolen card into them to withdraw money is sufficient entry of the building to constitute burglary (*People v. Ravenscroft*, 198 Cal. App. 3d 639).

In one case, the accused, on appeal, contended that he was not guilty of burglary where the evidence established that he had penetrated the window screen but not the window. The court held that the penetration of the screen was a sufficient entry to uphold a burglary conviction. The California Court of Appeals, Third Appellate District, stated:

> Burglary laws are based primarily upon a recognition of the dangers to personal safety created by the usual burglary situation. . . . The laws are designed not to deter trespass . . . so much as to forestall the germination of a situation dangerous to personal safety.

At common law, the entry was required to be during the hours of darkness. Since a 1982 amendment to the Penal Code, time of entry is immaterial.

The Building

A building, structure, or vehicle includes:

- Structure with enclosed walls and a roof
- An open pit mine
- Enclosed telephone booth
- Railroad cars
- Aircraft
- Cargo container of at least 1,000 cubic feet, permanent character, strong enough for repeated use, designed to facilitate the carriage of goods and designed to be easy to fill and empty (PC 458)
- Locked vehicle
- Locked trunk of a locked or unlocked vehicle
- Locked or unlocked inhabited camper

To be a building, the structure must have four walls and a roof. A bin with a roof and three walls was not a building for purposes of burglary in *People v. Gibbons* (206 Cal. 112). A telephone booth with three walls, a roof, and a folding door on the fourth side was a building for purposes of burglary in *People v. Miller* (95 Cal. App. 2d 631).

Required Intent

The intent to commit grand theft, petty theft, or any felony must be a specific intent (*People v. Falls,* 64 Cal. 2d 560 and *People v. Earl,* 29 Cal. App. 3d 894). The accused must have the specific intent at the time of the entry. It does not need be a completed intention. The fact that outside factors frustrate the intention or a voluntary cessation of effort occurs after entry does not eliminate an otherwise sufficient intent (*People v. Markus,* 82 Cal. App. 3d 477).

It is not necessary that the accused intended to commit the crime in the building (*People v. Wright,* 206 Cal. App. 2d 1840), only that the intended entry was to help commit the crime. For example, the accused has committed the crime of burglary when he enters the house to hide while waiting for an opportunity to steal from people passing by.

If the entry is made without the specific intent, the crime of burglary has not been committed (*People v. Collins,* 53 Cal. 185). An accused who is too intoxicated to form an intent to steal or to commit a felony does not commit the crime of burglary when he or she enters the building (*People v. Yoder,* 100 Cal. App. 3d 333).

If the accused makes only one entry into a building with the intent to commit two or more felonies, he or she is guilty of only one burglary since the entry is the primary focus of the offense (*People v. Failla,* 64 Cal. 2d 560). Accordingly, in *People v. Clifton* (148 Cal. App. 2d 276), the accused was convicted of only one burglary when he entered a home with the intent to both assault and rob the woman resident.

The required intent may be established in court by circumstantial evidence and by reasonable inferences (*People v. Martin,* 275 Cal. App. 2d 769). For example, if it is proven that an accused entered a home and attempted to rape a woman therein, the court or jury may reasonably infer that the accused intended to commit rape at the time he entered.

Completed Crime

The crime of burglary is completed when the accused enters the building. It does not matter that the accused could not complete the intended offense. For example, if an accused intending to steal a briefcase breaks open the door of a locked vehicle, and if he is stopped after opening the door, but before stealing the briefcase, he has committed the crimes of burglary and attempted theft. In one case, the court held that the crime of burglary was completed when the defendant entered his ex-wife's apartment with the intent to commit an assault and a theft therein. It was immaterial that he did not assault the ex-wife or commit theft after the entry (*People v. Clifton,* 148 Cal. App. 2d 276). In another case, the defendant, intending to enter the house by the window, cut the window screen. The court held that cutting the screen was sufficient entry for purposes of burglary and, thus, the crime was completed.

Locked Vehicle

As noted earlier, automobiles are subject to burglary if they are locked. A trailer was considered a locked vehicle where the doors were sealed by a locked metal clip (*People v. Massie,* 241 Cal. App. 2d 812).

In *People v. Woods* (112 Cal. App. 3d 226), the court held that a vehicle was not a "locked" vehicle where the doors were locked, but one window was deliberately rolled down approximately five inches. In *People v. Malcolm* (47 Cal. App. 3d 217), however, the court held that a vehicle was locked where all the doors were locked and the windows rolled up. The wing lock on the left front window, however, was broken. The broken wing lock enabled the accused to push open the window and thus open the door. In *People v. Burns* (114 Cal. App. 2d 566), a burglary conviction was reversed where no proof was entered that the motor vehicle was locked at the time of the entry.

6-2 Degrees of Burglary

Penal Code 460—Degrees; Construction of Section

(a) Every burglary of an inhabited dwelling house, vessel, as defined in the Harbors and Navigation Code, which is inhabited and designed for habitation, floating home . . . , or trailer coach, as defined by the Vehicle Code, or the inhabited portion of any other building, is burglary of the first degree.

(b) All other kinds of burglary are of the second degree.

6-2a Discussion

Burglary is classified as either first or second degree (PC 460). First-degree burglary is every burglary of an inhabited dwelling house or trailer coach as defined by the Vehicle Code, or the inhabited portion of any other building. An inhabited camper, railroad car, and a vehicle when its doors are locked are omitted from the list of places subject to first-degree burglary. One appellate court held that such an omission raised an inference that the legislature did not intend to include such places in the classification of first-degree burglary even if they were inhabited (*People v. Moreland*, 146 Cal. Rptr. 118).

The statement in the code: "All other kinds of burglary are of the second degree" is subject to an important exception to the classification of burglaries, in that burglary by use of acetylene torch or explosive (PC 464) has its own punishment schedule.

Inhabited Dwelling

For the purposes of the burglary statutes, inhabited means that the structure is currently being used for dwelling purposes. Dwelling purposes refers to a place where a person with possessory rights uses the place as sleeping quarters and intends to do so in the future. There can be more than one dwelling under a common roof as in an apartment house or hotel. For example, in one case, a furniture store where a night watchman regularly slept was an inhabited dwelling (*People v. Marquez*, 143 Cal. App. 3d 797).

In those cases where the residents are absent, the house is considered as inhabited as long as the residents intend to return. For example, a house was considered as inhabited where the sole resident was confined to a hospital for an indefinite time. In this case, the resident still intended to return to the house and considered it her home at the time (*People v. Marquez*, 143 Cal. App. 3d 797).

Whether burglary is of first or second degree does not depend on the burglar's belief that the residence is actually occupied at the time of entry, but rather on whether dwelling is the usual abode of the person irrespective of whether he or she happens to be home at the time of illegal entry (*People v. Wilson*, 208 Cal. App. 3d 611).

The entry into an attached garage of an inhabited house was considered in one case as burglary of an inhabited dwelling. The court stated that where the garage is an integral part of the structure, it is simply one room of several. Burglary of a storeroom connected to the home by a breezeway was also considered as burglary of an inhabited dwelling (*People v. Cook*, 135 Cal. App. 3d 785).

There is no requirement for the accused to know that the building was inhabited. In one case, the accused entered a building to steal items. He was under the impression that the house was no longer occupied as a residence. Nevertheless, he was convicted of first-degree burglary. The appellate court stated that the knowledge of the accused as to whether or not the house was inhabited is not an element of first-degree burglary (*People v. Guthrie*, 144 Cal. App. 3d 832).

In a similar case, the defendant broke into the first floor of a three-story warehouse. The accused was unaware that the third floor was being used as a residence by a couple who worked in the building. He appealed his conviction of first-degree burglary on the basis that his mistake as to the nature of the building (as an inhabited building) was reasonable. The court upheld the conviction and stated that the belief of the accused as to whether or not the building was inhabited had no bearing on the case (*People v. Parker*, 175 Cal. App. 3d 818).

A house, trailer, or portion of the building that is currently being used for dwelling purposes is still inhabited if the occupants are not occupying it solely because of a natural or other disaster that caused the occupants to leave the premises.

6-3 Punishment

The punishments for burglary are as follows:

1. First-degree burglary is punished by imprisonment in the state prison.
2. Second-degree burglary is punished by imprisonment in the county jail not exceeding one year or in the state prison.
3. Burglary by use of acetylene torch or explosive is punished by imprisonment in the state prison.

Penal Code 1170.95 provides that the total of the terms for consecutive residential burglaries that are not "violent felonies" shall not exceed 10 years. Residential burglary is defined as burglary of an inhabited house, trailer coach, or the inhabited portion of any other building.

Penal Code 462—Probation; Conviction of Burglary; Specification of Reasons for Granting Probation

(a) Except in unusual cases where the interests of justice would best be served if the person is granted probation, probation shall not be granted to any person who is convicted of a burglary of an inhabited dwelling house or trailer coach as defined in Section 635 of the Vehicle Code, an inhabited floating home as defined in subdivision (d) of Section 18075.55 of the Health and Safety Code, or the inhabited portion of any other building.
(b) If the court grants probation under subdivision (a), it shall specify the reason or reasons for that order on the court record.

6-3a Discussion

PC 462 provides that, except in unusual cases where the interests of justice would best be served if the person is granted probation, probation shall not be granted to any person convicted of a burglary of an inhabited dwelling house or trailer or the inhabited portion of any other building.

If the court grants probation as an unusual case, the court must specify the reason or reasons for granting probation.

6-4 Burglary by Use of Acetylene Torch or Explosive

Penal Code 464

Any person who, with intent to commit a crime, enters either by day or night, any building, whether inhabited or not, and opens or attempts to open any vault, safe, or other secure place by use of acetylene torch or electric arc, burning bar, thermal lance, oxygen lance, or any other similar device capable of burning through steel, concrete, or any other solid substance, or by use of nitroglycerine, dynamite, gunpowder, or any other explosive, is guilty of a felony and, upon conviction, shall be punished by imprisonment in the state prison. . . .

6-4a Elements

The following are elements of burglary by use of torch or explosives:

1. Entry to any building
2. With the specific intent to commit a crime
3. By use of torch, explosive, etc.
4. Opening or an attempt to open a safe, vault, or other secure place

6-4b Discussion

Burglary by use of a torch or by explosives is an aggravated form of burglary, since using a torch or explosives increases the danger that someone will be injured or killed. The increased penalty also is intended to discourage an accused from using a torch or explosives when confronted with a secure depository (*People v. Chastain*, 262 Cal. App. 2d 433).

A "secure place" is a storage place that has most of the attributes of a safe or vault and is designed to keep valuables. "Safe" and "vault" are used in their ordinary and popular meaning (*People v. Cook,* 135 Cal. App. 3d 785).

6-5 Unlawful Entry

Penal Code 602.5—Unauthorized Entry of Dwelling

Every person other than a public officer or employee acting within the course and scope of his employment in performance of a duty imposed by law, who enters or remains in any noncommercial dwelling house, apartment, or other such place without consent of the owner, his agent, or the person in lawful possession thereof, is guilty of a misdemeanor.

Penal Code 603—Forcible Entry; Vandalism

Every person other than a peace officer engaged in the performance of his duties as such who forcibly and without the consent of the owner, representative of the owner, lessee or representative of the lessee thereof, enters a dwelling house, cabin, or other building occupied or constructed for occupation by humans, and who damages, injures, or destroys any property of value in, around, or appertaining to such dwelling house, cabin, or other building, is guilty of a misdemeanor.

6-5a Discussion

The unauthorized entering or remaining in a noncommercial dwelling is not a necessarily included lesser offense of the crime of burglary. In *People v. Muis* (102 Cal. App. 3d 206), an accused was convicted of unlawful entry under PC 602.5 when evidence established that the accused had entered a dwelling to steal but was too drunk to form the specific intent necessary for a burglary conviction. Unlawful entry under this statute does not apply to nonresidential structures (*In Re D.C.L.*, 147 Cal. Rptr. 54).

Unauthorized entering or remaining in a building may be a lesser included offense of burglary. One defendant was convicted of unauthorized entry as a lesser included offense of burglary where whatever variance existed between the burglary offense charged and the lesser included offense of unlawful entry was not material, where the defendant's opportunity to prepare and defend against such a charge was not impaired by the fact that the offense was not charged in the information, and where the omission of such an offense from the information did not result in a miscarriage of justice (*People v. Muis*, 102 Cal. App. 3d 206).

Penal Code 466—Burglars' Tools; Possession; Intent; Making or Altering Key; Making, Altering, or Repairing Things for Use in Committing Offense; Building Defined

6-6 Possession of Burglary Tools

Every person having upon him or her in his or her possession a picklock, crow, keybit, crowbar, screwdriver, vice grip pliers, water-pump pliers, slidehammer, slim jim, tension bar, lock pick gun, tubular lock pick, floor-safe door puller, master key, or other instrument or tool with intent feloniously to break or enter into any building, railroad car, aircraft, or vessel, trailer coach, or vehicle as defined in the Vehicle Code, or who shall knowingly make or alter, or shall attempt to make or alter, any key or other instrument above named so that the same will fit or open the lock of a building, railroad car, aircraft, vessel, trailer coach, or vehicle as defined in the Vehicle Code, without being requested so to do by some person having the right to open the same, or who shall make, alter, or repair any instrument or thing, knowing or having reason to believe that it is intended to be used in committing a misdemeanor or felony, is guilty of misdemeanor. Any of the structures mentioned in Section 459 shall be deemed to be a building within the meaning of this section.

Any person who violates any provision of this section is guilty of a misdemeanor.

The following are elements of possession of burglary tools:

6-6a Elements

1. The possession of certain tools
2. Required intent

   a. With the intent to break or enter any building or structure mentioned in PC 459 (Burglary);
   b. Knowingly make or attempt to make a key or other instrument to fit another building without legal request;
   c. The failure by a maker to ascertain the right to open or make or alter, or repair any instrument or thing; or
   d. Knowing or having reason to believe that the tool(s) is (are) intended to be used in committing a misdemeanor or felony.

Possession of burglary tools is a criminal offense if one of the four types of intent listed in the Elements section is present. Subparagraphs (a) and (b) require a specific intent, whereas (c) and (d) require only a general intent.

6-6b Discussion

Penal Code 466.1—Sale or Provision of Lock Pick, Tension Bar, Lock Pick Gun, Tubular Lock Pick, or Floor-Safe Door Puller; Information on Purchaser or Person to Whom Provided on Bill of Sale or Receipt; Inspection; Violation

6-7 Sale of Burglar Tools

Any person who knowingly and willfully sells or provides a lock pick, a tension bar, a lock pick gun, a tubular lock pick, or a floor-safe door puller, to another, whether or not for compensation, shall obtain the name, address, telephone number, if any, date of birth, and driver's license number or identification number, if any, of the person to whom the device is sold or provided. This information, together with the date the device was sold or provided and the signature of the person to whom the device was sold or provided, shall be set forth on a bill of sale or receipt. A copy of each bill of sale or receipt shall be retained for one year and shall be open to inspection by any peace officer during business hours.

6-8 Vending Machine Theft

Penal Code 466.3—Vending Machine Theft—Possession of Tool, Device, etc., Designed to Open, Break into, Tamper with, or Damage Coin-Operated Machine with Intent to Commit Theft; Punishment

(a) Whoever possesses a key, tool, instrument, explosive, or device, or a drawing, print, or mold of a key, tool, instrument, explosive, or device, designed to open, break into, tamper with, or damage a coin-operated machine as defined in subdivision (b), with intent to commit a theft from such machine, is punishable by imprisonment in the county jail for not more than one year, or by fine of not more than one thousand dollars ($1,000), or by both.

(b) As used in this section, the term "coin-operated machine" shall include any automatic vending machine or any part thereof, parking meter, coin telephone, coin laundry machine, coin dry cleaning machine, amusement machine, music machine, vending machine dispensing goods or services, or moneychanger.

6-9 Other Related Crimes

Related crimes involving the possession, use of, or making of duplicate keys are listed next. The crimes discussed are misdemeanors.

Penal Code 466.6—Keys Capable of Operating Motor Vehicle or Personal Property Registered under Vehicle Code; Making Other Than by Duplication of Existing Key; Work Orders; Information; Misdemeanor

(a) Any person who makes a key capable of operating the ignition of a motor vehicle or personal property registered under the Vehicle Code for another by any method other than by the duplication of an existing key, whether or not for compensation, shall obtain the name, address, telephone number, if any, date of birth, and driver's license number or identification number of the person requesting or purchasing the key; and the registration or identification number, license number, year, make, model, color, and vehicle identification number of the vehicle or personal property registered under the Vehicle Code for which the key is to be made. Such information, together with the date the key was made and the signature of the person for whom the key was made, shall be set forth on a work order. A copy of each such work order shall be retained for two years, shall include the name and permit number of the locksmith performing the service, and shall be open to inspection by any peace officer or by the Bureau of Collection and Investigative Services during business hours or submitted to the bureau upon request. Any person who violates any provision of this subdivision is guilty of a misdemeanor.

(b) The provisions of this section shall include, but are not limited to, the making of a key from key codes or impressions.

(c) Nothing contained in this section shall be construed to prohibit the duplication of any key for a motor vehicle from another key.

Penal Code 466.8—Keys Capable of Opening Entrance to Residence or Commercial Establishment; Work Orders; Information; Misdemeanor

(a) Any person who knowingly and willfully makes a key capable of opening any door or other means of entrance to any residence or commercial establishment for another by any method involving an onsite inspection of such door or entrance, whether or not for compensation, shall obtain, together with the date the key was made, the street address of the residence or commercial establishment, and the signature of the person for whom the key was made, on a work order form, the following information regarding the person requesting or purchasing the key:

(1) Name
(2) Address
(3) Telephone number, if any
(4) Date of birth
(5) Driver's license number or identification number, if any

A copy of each such work order shall be retained for two years and shall be open to inspection by any peace officer or by the Bureau of Collection and Investigative Services during business hours or submitted to the bureau upon request.

Any person who violates any provision of this subdivision is guilty of a misdemeanor.

(b) Nothing contained in this section shall be construed to prohibit the duplication of any key for a residence or commercial establishment from another such key.
(c) Locksmiths licensed by the Bureau of Collection and Investigative Services are subject to the provisions set forth in Chapter 8.5 (commencing with Section 6980) of Division 3 of the Business and Professions Code.
(d) The provisions of this section shall include, but are not limited to, the making of a key from key codes or impressions.

6-9a Discussion

Penal Code 466.7 makes it unlawful to possess a key made other than by duplication with the intent to use it in the commission of an unlawful act.

Penal Code 469 makes it a crime to duplicate any key to a building or other area owned, operated, or controlled by the state of California without proper authorization.

6-10 Arson

Penal Code 450—Definition of Terms

In this chapter, the following terms have the following meanings:

(a) *Structure* means any building, or commercial or public tent, bridge, tunnel, or power plant.
(b) *Forest land* means any brush covered land, cut-over land, forest, grasslands, or woods.
(c) *Property* means real property or personal property, other than a structure or forest land.
(d) *Inhabited* means currently being used for dwelling purposes whether occupied or not. "Inhabited structure" and "inhabited property" do not include the real property on which an inhabited structure or an inhabited property is located.
(e) *Maliciously* imports a wish to vex, defraud, annoy, or injure another person, or an intent to do a wrongful act, established either by proof or presumption of law.
(f) *Recklessly* means a person is aware of and consciously disregards a substantial and unjustifiable risk that his or her act will set fire to, burn, or cause to burn a structure, forest land, or property. The risk shall be of such nature and degree that disregard thereof constitutes a gross deviation from the standard of conduct that a reasonable person would observe in the situation. A person who creates such a risk but is unaware thereof by reason of voluntary intoxication also acts recklessly with respect thereto.

Penal Code 451—Arson of Structure, Forest Land or Property; Great Bodily Injury; Inhabited Structure or Property; Owned Property; Punishment

A person is guilty of arson when he or she willfully and maliciously sets fire to or burns or causes to be burned or who aids, counsels, or procures the burning of, any structure, forest land, or property.

(a) Arson that causes great bodily injury is a felony punishable by imprisonment in the state prison for five, seven, or nine years.

(b) Arson that causes an inhabited structure or inhabited property to burn is a felony punishable by imprisonment in the state prison for three, five, or eight years.

(c) Arson of a structure or forest land is a felony punishable by imprisonment in the state prison for two, four, or six years.

(d) Arson of property is a felony punishable by imprisonment in the state prison for 16 months, two, or three years. For purposes of this paragraph, arson of property does not include one burning or causing to be burned his or her own personal property unless there is an intent to defraud or there is injury to another person or another person's structure, forest land, or property.

(e) In the case of any person convicted of violating this section while confined in a state prison, prison road camp, prison forestry camp, or other prison camp or prison farm, or while confined in a county jail while serving a term of imprisonment for a felony or misdemeanor conviction, any sentence imposed shall be consecutive to the sentence for which the person was then confined.

6-10a Arson-Related Crimes

The following is a list of arson-related crimes and the relevant Penal Section that refers to them:

- Arson (PC 451)
- Unlawfully Causing a Fire (PC 452)
- Possession of Flammable Explosive or Combustible Material or Substance or Device With Intent to Set Fire to or Burn (PC 453)
- Attempt to Set Fire to, Burn, and, Counsel or Procure the Burning of Structure, Forest Land, or Property (PC 455)

6-10b Definition

Under early common law, arson was a crime against the home. It consisted of the willful and malicious burning of another person's dwelling and/or surrounding buildings. The burning could be either during the day or at night, but a burning at night was the more serious crime. Arson was considered as a crime against the security of the home. Arson was a common law felony. Similar to present-day arson, the word *malicious* did not require ill will or hate. California, like most other states, has expanded the definition of arson to include the burning of other structures, forest land, and other types of property.

6-10c Elements

The following are the elements of arson:

1. Setting fire to, or burns, or causes to be burned, or who aids, counsels, or procures the burning of
2. Any structure, forest land, or property
3. By the intentional act of the accused

For the purposes of arson-related crimes, *willful* means an intentional act. *Maliciousness* means only that the setting of the fire was intentional and deliberate. A fire is started willfully and maliciously when the accused intentionally and deliberately sets fire to the building (*People v. Green*, 146 Cal. App. 3d 369).

A fire that is started accidentally or unintentionally is not considered the result of willful and malicious conduct. Arson is not established unless it is shown that the fire was of incendiary rather than accidental origin. To "intend to cause a structure to burn," within the meaning of the statute defining the offense of arson, means to intend that structure to burn by whatever act initiated fire (*People v. Fabris*, 31 Cal. App. 4th 685).

The malicious intent of the defendant must be malicious only in the sense that his or her mind-set is one of doing an intentional wrong. In the *Green* case (cited in the first paragraph of this section), the defendant set fire to his wife's apartment, and the fire spread to the carport and destroyed a car parked in the carport. The defendant contended that he should not be convicted of arson of the car, since he did not intend to burn it. The court held that the fire was set willfully and maliciously, and the fact that some of the results of the fire were unintentional was irrelevant.

In the majority of cases, the willful and malicious intent is established by circumstantial evidence. For example, in a case where the firefighters found the windows closed, shades drawn, doors locked, a smell of kerosene, and fire starting in three different rooms, the jury's finding that the fire was intentionally set was upheld on appeal (*People v. Patello*, 13 P. 2d 1068).

In another case, the court considered the fact that the accused had financial problems, most of his personal effects had been removed from the house shortly before the fire, and the house was overinsured as evidence that the owner of the house had willfully set fire to the house (*People v. Freeman*, 135 Cal. App. 2d 11).

In *People v. Nance* (25 Cal. App. 3d 925), the court held that the defense of diminished capacity was not a defense to the charge of arson. In this decision, the court stated that arson does not require a specific mental state as long as the burning involved is intentional. In another case, the police were notified of the accused's plan to burn a building. The police hid nearby until the accused started the fire and then arrested him for arson. The court stated that the actions of the police did not excuse the accused nor did the facts negate the accused's malicious intent (*People v. Greening*, 102 Cal. 384).

In *People v. Hiltel* (131 Cal. 577), an accused was found guilty of willfully and maliciously causing a dwelling to burn where he intentionally set fire to a nearby building, which then spread to the dwelling. His conviction was upheld even though there was evidence that the burning of the dwelling was not intended. In another case, the defendant was found guilty of arson of structure (i.e., carport) despite the trial court's finding that he did not intend to burn carport, but rather only to burn the car in the carport, in light of trial court's implicit finding that defendant willfully and maliciously set fire to car (*People v. Fry*, 19 Cal. App. 4th 1334).

Intent

Arson requires an intent to burn or set fire to a structure or cause a structure to be burned; there is no reference to intent to do further acts or achieve consequences beyond acts therein defined. Arson is categorized as a general intent crime (*People v. Fabris*, 31 Cal. App. 4th 685). Arson of an inhabited structure or property is a general intent crime (*People v. Lee*, 28 Cal. App. 4th 659). That is, to convict a defendant

6-10d Discussion

of arson, the jury is only required to find that the person willfully and maliciously set fire to or burned a structure, forest land, or property—or caused the preceding to be burned; the trier of fact need not find specific intent to burn a particular piece of property (*People v. Fry*, 19 Cal. App. 4th 1334).

Motive

Motive is not an essential element of the offense of arson. The presence of motive may, however, be important in proving the presence of a wrongful intent. The defendant may use lack of motive to dispute the presence of the required intent.

Malice

One court held that for purposes of conviction of arson of property requiring a "willful and malicious" burning, "willful" means intentional, and "malice" denotes nothing more than a deliberate and intentional firing of a building or other defined structure as contrasted with an accidental or unintentional ignition thereof; therefore, where fire is set willfully and maliciously, conviction under this section is proper, notwithstanding that some of the resulting damage may be unintentional (*People v. Green*, 146 Cal. App. 3d 369). A fire set on a spur of the moment impulse is no less willful and malicious than one set with motive (*In re Stephen P.*, 145 Cal. App. 3d 123).

Burning

To constitute a burning, no outbreak of flame is necessary, but some part of the building, and so on, must be at least charred. A burning, however slight, is sufficient to meet this requirement. For example, the floor of a building that is charred in a single place is considered as a "burning" (*People v. Haggerty*, 46 Cal. 354). Some fibers, however, must be destroyed to constitute a burning. For example, mere blacking of the wood was held to be insufficient to establish a burning in *People v. Simpson* (50 Cal. 304). As one court stated: "If an attempt is made to burn a house by lighting a fire, and the wood of the house was charred in a single place so as to destroy its fiber, the crime of arson was complete, even if the fire was then extinguished" (*People v. Haggerty*, 46 Cal. 354).

In *People v. Mentzer* (163 Cal. App. 3d 482), the accused was convicted of arson of a building made of marble, plaster, and concrete. The defendant had contended that the building, a mausoleum, was incapable of burning. However, the court held that since part of the marble floor was destroyed by "spawling," a conviction of arson was proper. Note: "Spawling" is the disintegration of marble by heat.

Burning Own Property

Individuals who burn their own property may be convicted of arson under PC 451, if the burning was with the intent to defraud or when it results in injury to property of others. The intent-to-defraud situation often involves the burning of insured property with the intent to collect an insurance recovery. In cases involving protected forest lands, an individual may also be guilty of arson when he or she deliberately burns his or her own protective forest land.

The restrictions and limitations placed on an owner's right to dispose of his or her own property is a valid exercise of a state's "police power" (*People v. George*, 42 Cal. App. 2d 568).

Structures, Forest Land, and Property

The arson statute covers structures of any type, forest land, and any other type of property. The term *property* includes both real and personal property. Apparently, *personal property* does not include intangible personal property. *Intangible personal property* includes items such as stocks, bonds, deeds, and so on.

Inhabited

As discussed later, the burning of an inhabited structure is considered a more serious offense and incurs greater maximum punishment than the burning of an uninhabited one. The increased punishment schedule is based on the theory that there is a greater danger of injury or death when an inhabited structure is burned.

In one case, the defendant was convicted of arson of an inhabited structure based on the fact that the apartment that he set fire to had been vacated several days earlier. The court stated that for the purposes of arson, PC 450 defines "inhabited" as "currently being used for dwelling purposes whether occupied or not." Therefore, the legislative intent was to cover structures likely to be inhabited because of the danger to human life (*People v. Green*, 146 Cal. 3d 369). The term *inhabited* has a slightly different meaning for arson than for burglary.

For purposes of the offense of setting fire to an inhabited structure, a current intent to use a house as a dwelling determines whether the house was inhabited. Thus, the offense of setting fire to an inhabited structure requires that someone be using the structure as a dwelling at the time of the fire and not merely that the structure's purpose is to serve as a dwelling. For example, in one case, a house was not being used for dwelling purposes at the time of the defendant's offense of setting fire to inhabited structure where tenants were physically evicted from the premises the day before fire, tenants were allowed to remove their possessions at time of eviction, no one was seen reentering house day of eviction except for defendant, and no one had slept in house after eviction; the fact that some clothing and furniture remained in the premises was not determinative (*People v. Jones*, 199 Cal. App. 3d 543).

Penal Code 452—Unlawfully Causing a Fire of Any Structure, Forest Land, or Property; Great Bodily Injury; Inhabited Structure or Property; Punishment

6-11 Unlawfully Causing a Fire

A person is guilty of unlawfully causing a fire when he recklessly sets fire to or burns or causes to be burned, any structure, forest land, or property.

(a) Unlawfully causing a fire that causes great bodily injury is a felony punishable by imprisonment in the state prison for two, four, or six years, or by imprisonment in the county jail for not more than one year, or by a fine, or by both such imprisonment and fine.

(b) Unlawfully causing a fire that causes an inhabited structure or inhabited property to burn is a felony punishable by imprisonment in the state prison for two, three, or four years, or by imprisonment in the county jail for not more than one year, or by a fine, or by both such imprisonment and fine.

(c) Unlawfully causing a fire of a structure or forest land is a felony punishable by imprisonment in the state prison for 16 months, two or three years, or by imprisonment in the county jail for not more than six months, or by a fine, or by both such imprisonment and fine.

(d) Unlawfully causing a fire of property is a misdemeanor. For purposes of this paragraph, unlawfully causing a fire of property does not include one burning or causing to be burned his own personal property unless there is injury to another person or to another person's structure, forest land, or property.

(e) In the case of any person convicted of violating this section while confined in a state prison, prison road camp, prison forestry camp, or other prison camp or prison farm, or while confined in a county jail while serving a term of imprisonment for a felony or misdemeanor conviction, any sentence imposed shall be consecutive to the sentence for which the person was then confined.

6-11a Discussion

The only difference between PC 451 and 452 is that under PC 451, the fire is the result of a "willful and malicious" act, whereas under PC 452, the fire is the result of recklessness. To be guilty of this offense, the accused must recklessly set fire to or burn or cause to be burned any structure, and so on. In *People v. Budish* (131 Cal. App. 3d 1043), the accused's conduct was not considered reckless when he negligently built a small campfire that was the source of a large fire after an unprecedented wind force developed. To be guilty of this offense, the court ruled that the accused must consciously disregard the risk involved so as to characterize his conduct as reckless.

Unlawfully causing a fire is a lesser included offense of arson; a defendant may be charged with unlawfully causing fire when he or she did not specifically intend to burn structure but was aware of and consciously disregarded the substantial and unjustifiable risk that his or her act would cause a structure to burn (*People v. Schwartz*, 2 Cal. App. 4th 1319).

Since unlawfully causing a fire is considered an unintentional crime, a person may not be convicted of an attempt to commit this offense (*In re Kent W.*, 181 Cal. App. 3d 721). The court in *In re Kent W.* held that since an attempt requires the specific intent to commit the target offense, it was logically impossible to specifically intend an unintentional result. Accordingly, there could be no such crime as attempting to recklessly start an unlawful fire.

6-12 Possession of Firebomb

Penal Code 453—Possession of Flammable, Explosive or Combustible Material or Substance, or Device; Intent; Possession, Manufacture, or Disposal of Firebomb

(a) Every person who possesses any flammable, explosive, or combustible material or substance, or any device in an arrangement or preparation, with intent to willfully and maliciously use such material, substance, or device to set fire to or burn any structure, forest land, or property, is punishable by imprisonment in the state prison, or in the county jail, not exceeding one year.

(b) Every person who possesses, manufactures, or disposes of a firebomb is guilty of a felony.

For the purposes of this subdivision, "disposes of" means to give, give away, loan, offer, offer for sale, sell, or transfer.

For the purposes of this subdivision, a "firebomb" is a breakable container containing a flammable liquid with a flashpoint of 150 degrees Fahrenheit or less, having a wick or similar device capable of being ignited, but no device commercially manufactured primarily for the purpose of illumination shall be deemed to be a firebomb for the purposes of this subdivision.

(c) Subdivisions (a) and (b) of this section shall not prohibit the authorized use or possession of any material, substance, or device described therein by a member of the armed forces of the United States or by firemen, police officers, peace officers, or law enforcement officers authorized by the properly constituted authorities; nor shall those subdivisions prohibit the use or possession of any material, substance, or device described therein when used solely for scientific research or educational purposes, or for disposal of brush under permit as provided for in Section 4494 of the Public Resources Code, or for any other lawful burning. Subdivision (b) of this section shall not prohibit the manufacture or disposal of a firebomb for the parties or purposes described in this subdivision.

In *People v. Diamond* (2 Cal. App. 3d 860), the defendant was convicted of the possession of a combustible substance when three firebombs were found in his automobile near a downtown mall during a period of racial unrest.

6-12a Discussion

Penal Code 455—Attempts; Acts Preliminary or in Furtherance; Punishment; Attempt to Burn Defined

6-13 Attempted Arson

Any person who willfully and maliciously attempts to set fire to or attempts to burn or to aid, counsel, or procure the burning of any structure, forest land, or property, or who commits any act preliminary thereto, or in furtherance thereof, is punishable by imprisonment in the state prison for 16 months, two, or three years.

The placing or distributing of any flammable, explosive, or combustible material or substance, or any device in or about any structure, forest land, or property in an arrangement or preparation with intent to eventually willfully and maliciously set fire to or burn same, or to procure the setting fire to or burning of the same shall, for the purposes of this act constitute an attempt to burn such structure, forest land, or property.

(a) Any person who willfully and maliciously attempts to set fire or attempts to burn or to aid, counsel, or procure the burning of any structure, forest land, or who commits any act preliminary thereto, or in furtherance thereof, is punishable by imprisonment in the state prison. . . .

The placing or distribution of any flammable, explosive, or combustible material or substance, or any device in or about any structure, forest land, or property in an arrangement or preparation with intent to eventually willfully and maliciously set fire to or burn the same or to procure the setting fire to or burning of the same shall, for the purposes of this act, constitute an attempt to burn such structure, forest land, or property.

6-13a Discussion

Frequently, persons with emotional disorders frequently commit arson-related offenses. Accordingly, Penal Code 457 permits the court to order a psychiatric examination of anyone convicted of an arson-related offense. In addition, Penal Code 457.1 requires that persons convicted of arson or attempted arson may be required by the court to register with the chief of police or sheriff.

6-14 Psychiatric Examination

6-15 Notice of Release of Arsonist

PC 11150 requires that prior to the release of a person convicted of arson, the director of corrections shall notify in writing the state fire marshall and all police departments and the sheriff in the county in which the person was convicted and, if known, the county to which he or she is released. PC 11151 requires similar notification by the director of mental hygiene within five days of the release from a state mental institution or hospital of a person convicted of arson.

6-16 Vandalism

Penal Code 594—Vandalism; Penalty

(a) Every person who maliciously commits any of the following acts with respect to any real or personal property not his or her own, in cases other than those specified by state law, is guilty of vandalism:

(1) Defaces with graffiti or other inscribed material.
(2) Damages.
(3) Destroys.

Whenever a person violates this subdivision with respect to real property, vehicles, signs, fixtures, or furnishings belonging to any public entity, as defined by Section 811.2 of the Government Code, or the federal government, it shall be a permissive inference that the person neither owned the property nor had the permission of the owner to deface, damage, or destroy the property.

(b)

(1) If the amount of defacement, damage, or destruction is fifty thousand dollars ($50,000) or more, vandalism is punishable by imprisonment in the state prison or in a county jail not exceeding one year, or by a fine of not more than fifty thousand dollars ($50,000), or by both that fine and imprisonment.

(2) If the amount of defacement, damage, or destruction is five thousand dollars ($5,000) or more but less than fifty thousand dollars ($50,000), vandalism is punishable by imprisonment in the state prison, or in a county jail not exceeding one year, or by a fine of not more than ten thousand dollars ($10,000), or by both that fine and imprisonment.

(3) If the amount of defacement, damage, or destruction is four hundred dollars ($400) or more but less than five thousand dollars ($5,000), vandalism is punishable by imprisonment in a county jail not exceeding one year, or by a fine of five thousand dollars ($5,000), or by both that fine and imprisonment.

(4)

(A) If the amount of defacement, damage, or destruction is less than four hundred dollars ($400), vandalism is punishable by imprisonment in a county jail for not more than six months, or by a fine of not more than one thousand dollars ($1,000), or by both that fine and imprisonment.

(B) If the amount of defacement, damage, or destruction is less than four hundred dollars ($400), and the defendant has been previously convicted of vandalism or affixing graffiti or other inscribed material under Sections 594, 594.3, 594.4, 640.5, 640.6, or 640.7, vandalism is punishable by imprisonment in a county jail for not more than one year, or by a fine of not more than five thousand dollars ($5,000), or by both that fine and imprisonment.

(c)

    (1) Upon conviction of any person under this section for acts of vandalism consisting of defacing property with graffiti or other inscribed materials, the court may, in addition to any punishment imposed under subdivision (b), order the defendant to clean up, repair, or replace the damaged property himself or herself, or, if the jurisdiction has adopted a graffiti abatement program, order the defendant, and his or her parents or guardians if the defendant is a minor, to keep the damaged property or another specified property in the community free of graffiti for up to one year. Participation of a parent or guardian is not required under this subdivision if the court deems this participation to be detrimental to the defendant, or if the parent or guardian is a single parent who must care for young children.

    (2) Any city, county, or city and county may enact an ordinance that provides for all of the following:

        (A) That upon conviction of any person pursuant to this section for acts of vandalism, the court may, in addition to any punishment imposed under subdivision (b), provided that the court determines that the defendant has the ability to pay any law enforcement costs not exceeding two hundred fifty dollars ($250), order the defendant to pay all or part of the costs not to exceed two hundred fifty dollars ($250) incurred by a law enforcement agency in identifying and apprehending the defendant. The law enforcement agency shall provide evidence of, and bear the burden of establishing, the reasonable costs that it incurred in identifying and apprehending the defendant.

        (B) The law enforcement costs authorized to be paid pursuant to this subdivision are in addition to any other costs incurred or recovered by the law enforcement agency, and payment of these costs does not in any way limit, preclude, or restrict any other right, remedy, or action otherwise available to the law enforcement agency.

(d) If a minor is personally unable to pay a fine levied for acts prohibited by this section, the parent of that minor shall be liable for payment of the fine. A court may waive payment of the fine, or any part thereof, by the parent upon a finding of good cause.

(e) As used in this section, the term "graffiti or other inscribed material" includes any unauthorized inscription, word, figure, mark, or design that is written, marked, etched, scratched, drawn, or painted on real or personal property.

(f) As used in this section, "graffiti abatement program" means a program adopted by a city, county, or city and county by resolution or ordinance that provides for the administration and financing of graffiti removal, community education on the prevention of graffiti, and enforcement of graffiti laws.

(g) The court may order any person ordered to perform community service or graffiti removal pursuant to paragraph (1) of subdivision (c) to undergo counseling.

(h) No amount paid by a defendant in satisfaction of a criminal matter shall be applied in satisfaction of the law enforcement costs that may be imposed pursuant to this section until all outstanding base fines, state and local penalty assessments, restitution orders, and restitution fines have been paid.

(i) This section shall remain in effect until January 1, 2002, and as of that date is repealed, unless a later enacted statute that is enacted before January 1, 2002, deletes or extends that date.

6-16a Discussion

Penal Code 594.3 provides that any person who knowingly commits any act of vandalism to a church, synagogue, building owned and occupied by a religious education institution, or other place primarily used as a place of worship where religious services are regularly conducted is guilty of vandalism of a church and is punishable by confinement in the county jail or state prison (a wobbler).

Education Code Section 48905 deals with vandalism of school property. Its provisions are similar to those already noted. In addition, Education Code Section 48904 and Civil Code Section 1714.1 impose civil liability on parents or guardians for the vandalism of the child.

6-17 Aid, Counsel, or Procure to Burn Property or Land

Penal Code 455—Attempts to Burn

Any person who willfully and maliciously attempts to set fire to or attempts to burn or to aid, counsel, or procure the burning of any structure, forest land, or property, or who commits any act preliminary thereto, or in furtherance thereof, is punishable by imprisonment in the state prison for 16 months, two or three years.

The placing or distributing of any flammable, explosive, or combustible material or substance, or any device in or about any structure, forest land, or property in an arrangement or preparation with intent to eventually willfully and maliciously set fire to or burn same, or to procure the setting fire to or burning of the same shall, for the purposes of this act constitute an attempt to burn such structure, forest land, or property.

6-17a Discussion

In addition to establishing the punishment for attempted arson, PC 455 also makes it a crime to aid, counsel, or procure the burning of any structure, forest land, or property. Generally the conduct of aiding, counseling, or procuring anyone to commit any offense is punishable under the law of principles discussed in Chapter 1, but the legislators felt it was necessary to have a specific statute regarding aiding, counseling, or procuring anyone to commit arson.

6-18 Repossession Laws

Penal Code 419—Repossession of Land after Legal Ouster

Every person who has been removed from any lands by process of law, or who has removed from any lands pursuant to the lawful adjudication or direction of any Court, tribunal, or officer, and who afterwards unlawfully returns to settle, reside upon, or take possession of such lands, is guilty of a misdemeanor.

Vehicle Code 28—Notification of Repossession

(a) Whenever possession is taken of any vehicle by or on behalf of any legal owner thereof under the terms of a security agreement or lease agreement, the person taking possession shall notify, within one hour after taking possession of the vehicle, and by the most expeditious means available, the city police department where the taking of possession occurred, if within an incorporated city, or the sheriff's department of the county where the taking of possession occurred, if outside an incorporated city, or the police department of a campus of the University of California or the California State University, if the taking of possession occurred on that campus, and shall within one business day forward a written notice to the city police or sheriff's department.

(b) Any person failing to notify the city police department, sheriff's department, or campus police department as required by this section is guilty of an infraction, and shall be fined a minimum of three hundred dollars ($300), and up to five hundred dollars ($500). The district attorney, city attorney, or city prosecutor shall promptly notify the Bureau of Security and Investigative Services of any conviction resulting from a violation of this section.

Vehicle Code 4022—Repossessed Vehicle: Exempt from Registration

A vehicle repossessed pursuant to the terms of a security agreement is exempt from registration solely for the purpose of transporting the vehicle from the point of repossession to the storage facilities of the repossessor, and from the storage facilities to the legal owner or a licensed motor vehicle auction, provided that the repossessor transports with the vehicle the appropriate documents authorizing the repossession and makes them available to a law enforcement officer on request.

Vehicle Code 22852.5—Loss of Possessory Lien

(a) Whenever the possessory lien upon any vehicle is lost through trick, fraud, or device, the repossession of the vehicle by the lienholder revives the possessory lien, but any lien so revived is subordinate to any right, title, or interest of any person under any sale, transfer, encumbrance, lien, or other interest acquired or secured in good faith and for value between the time of the loss of possession and the time of repossession.

(b) It is a misdemeanor for any person to obtain possession of any vehicle or any part thereof subject to a lien pursuant to the provisions of this chapter by trick, fraud, or device.

(c) It is a misdemeanor for any person claiming a lien on a vehicle to knowingly violate any provision of this chapter.

Civil Code 3073—Proceeds of Sale; Disposition; Claims; Limitation of Actions

The proceeds of a vehicle lien sale under this article shall be disposed of as follows:

(a) The amount necessary to discharge the lien and the cost of processing the vehicle shall be paid to the lienholder. The cost of processing shall not exceed seventy dollars ($70) for each vehicle valued at two thousand five hundred dollars ($2,500) or less, or one hundred dollars ($100) for each vehicle valued over two thousand five hundred dollars ($2,500).

(b) The balance, if any, shall be forwarded to the Department of Motor Vehicles within 15 days of any sale conducted pursuant to Section 3071 or within five days of any sale conducted pursuant to Section 3072 and deposited in the Motor Vehicle Account in the State Transportation Fund, unless federal law requires these funds to be disposed in a different manner.

(c) Any person claiming an interest in the vehicle may file a claim with the Department of Motor Vehicles for any portion of the funds from the lien sale that were forwarded to the department pursuant to subdivision (b). Upon a determination of the Department of Motor Vehicles that the claimant is entitled to an amount from the balance deposited with the department, the department shall pay that amount determined by the department, which amount shall not exceed the amount forwarded to the department pursuant to subdivision (b) in connection with the sale of the vehicle in which the claimant claims an interest. The department shall not honor any claim unless the claim has been filed within three years of the date the funds were deposited in the Motor Vehicle Account.

6-19 Landlord/Tenant Laws

Civil Code 1954—Entry of Dwelling by Landlord; Conditions

A landlord may enter the dwelling unit only in the following cases:

(a) In case of emergency.
(b) To make necessary or agreed repairs, decorations, alterations or improvements, supply necessary or agreed services, or exhibit the dwelling unit to prospective or actual purchasers, mortgagees, tenants, workmen, or contractors.
(c) When the tenant has abandoned or surrendered the premises.
(d) Pursuant to court order.

Except in cases of emergency or when the tenant has abandoned or surrendered the premises, entry may not be made during other than normal business hours unless the tenant consents at the time of entry.

The landlord shall not abuse the right of access or use it to harass the tenant. Except in cases of emergency, when the tenant has abandoned or surrendered the premises, or if it is impracticable to do so, the landlord shall give the tenant reasonable notice of his intent to enter and enter only during normal business hours. Twenty-four hours shall be presumed to be reasonable notice in absence of evidence to the contrary.

Civil Code 1980 Definitions

As used in this chapter:

(a) *Landlord* means any operator, keeper, lessor, or sublessor of any furnished or unfurnished premises for hire, or his agent or successor in interest.
(b) *Owner* means any person other than the landlord who has any right, title, or interest in personal property.
(c) *Premises* includes any common areas associated therewith.
(d) *Reasonable belief* means the actual knowledge or belief a prudent person would have without making an investigation (including any investigation of public records) except that, where the landlord has specific information indicating that such an investigation would more probably than not reveal pertinent information and the cost of such an investigation would be reasonable in relation to the probable value of the personal property involved, "reasonable belief" includes the actual knowledge or belief a prudent person would have if such an investigation were made.
(e) *Tenant* includes any paying guest, lessee, or sublessee of any premises for hire.

Civil Code 1950.5—Security for Rental Agreement for Dwelling Property of Tenant

(a) This section applies to security for a rental agreement for residential property that is used as the dwelling of the tenant.
(b) As used in this section, "security" means any payment, fee, deposit, or charge, including, but not limited to, an advance payment of rent, used or to be used for any purpose, including, but not limited to, any of the following:

(1) The compensation of a landlord for a tenant's default in the payment of rent.
(2) The repair of damages to the premises, exclusive of ordinary wear and tear, caused by the tenant or by a guest or licensee of the tenant.
(3) The cleaning of the premises upon termination of the tenancy.

Civil Code 789.3

(a) A landlord shall not with intent to terminate the occupancy under any lease or other tenancy or estate at will, however created, of property used by a tenant as his residence willfully cause, directly or indirectly, the interruption or termination of any utility service furnished the tenant, including, but not limited to, water, heat, light, electricity, gas, telephone, elevator, or refrigeration, whether or not the utility service is under the control of the landlord.

(b) In addition, a landlord shall not, with intent to terminate the occupancy under any lease or other tenancy or estate at will, however created, of property used by a tenant as his or her residence, willfully:

(1) Prevent the tenant from gaining reasonable access to the property by changing the locks or using a bootlock or by any other similar method or device;
(2) Remove outside doors or windows; or
(3) Remove from the premises the tenant's personal property, the furnishings, or any other items without the prior written consent of the tenant, except when done pursuant to the procedure set forth in Chapter 5 (commencing with Section 1980) of Title 5 of Part 4 of Division 3.

Nothing in this subdivision shall be construed to prevent the lawful eviction of a tenant by appropriate legal authorities, nor shall anything in this subdivision apply to occupancies defined by subdivision (b) of Section 1940.

(c) Any landlord who violates this section shall be liable to the tenant in a civil action for all of the following:

(1) Actual damages of the tenant.
(2) An amount not to exceed one hundred dollars ($100) for each day or part thereof the landlord remains in violation of this section. In determining the amount of such award, the court shall consider proof of such matters as justice may require; however, in no event shall less than two hundred fifty dollars ($250) be awarded for each separate cause of action. Subsequent or repeated violations, which are not committed contemporaneously with the initial violation, shall be treated as separate causes of action and shall be subject to a separate award of damages.

(d) In any action under subdivision (c) the court shall award reasonable attorney's fees to the prevailing party. In any such action the tenant may seek appropriate injunctive relief to prevent continuing or further violation of the provisions of this section during the pendency of the action. The remedy provided by this section is not exclusive and shall not preclude the tenant from pursuing any other remedy which the tenant may have under any other provision of law.

Civil Code 1951.2—Termination of Lease

Termination of lease; remedy of lessor

(a) Except as otherwise provided in Section 1951.4, if a lessee of real property breaches the lease and abandons the property before the end of the term or if his right to possession is terminated by the lessor because of a breach of the lease, the lease terminates. Upon such termination, the lessor may recover from the lessee:

(1) The worth at the time of award of the unpaid rent which had been earned at the time of termination;

(2) The worth at the time of award of the amount by which the unpaid rent which would have been earned after termination until the time of award exceeds the amount of such rental loss that the lessee proves could have been reasonably avoided;

(3) Subject to subdivision (c), the worth at the time of award of the amount by which the unpaid rent for the balance of the term after the time of award exceeds the amount of such rental loss that the lessee proves could be reasonably avoided; and

(4) Any other amount necessary to compensate the lessor for all the detriment proximately caused by the lessee's failure to perform his obligations under the lease or which in the ordinary course of things would be likely to result therefrom.

(b) The "worth at the time of award" of the amounts referred to in paragraphs (1) and (2) of subdivision (a) is computed by allowing interest at such lawful rate as may be specified in the lease or, if no such rate is specified in the lease, at the legal rate. The worth at the time of award of the amount referred to in paragraph (3) of subdivision (a) is computed by discounting such amount at the discount rate of the Federal Reserve Bank of San Francisco at the time of award plus 1 percent.

(c) The lessor may recover damages under paragraph (3) of subdivision (a) only if:

(1) The lease provides that the damages he may recover include the worth at the time of award of the amount by which the unpaid rent for the balance of the term after the time of award, or for any shorter period of time specified in the lease, exceeds the amount of such rental loss for the same period that the lessee proves could be reasonably avoided; or

(2) The lessor relet the property prior to the time of award and proves that in reletting the property he acted reasonably and in a good-faith effort to mitigate the damages, but the recovery of damages under this paragraph is subject to any limitations specified in the lease.

(d) Efforts by the lessor to mitigate the damages caused by the lessee's breach of the lease do not waive the lessor's right to recover damages under this section.

(e) Nothing in this section affects the right of the lessor under a lease of real property to indemnification for liability arising prior to the termination of the lease for personal injuries or property damage where the lease provides for such indemnification.

Civil Code 890—Rent Skimming

(a) "Rent skimming" means using revenue received from the rental of a parcel of residential real property at any time during the first year period after acquiring that property without first applying the revenue or an equivalent amount to the payments due on all mortgages and deeds of trust encumbering that property.

(b) "Multiple acts of rent skimming" means knowingly and willfully rent skimming with respect to each of five or more parcels of residential real property acquired within any two-year period.

(c) "Person" means any natural person, any form of business organization, its officers and directors, and any natural person who authorizes rent skimming or who, being in a position of control, fails to prevent another from rent skimming.

Civil Code 892—Criminal Penalties

(a) Any person who engages in multiple acts of rent skimming is subject to criminal prosecution. Each act of rent skimming comprising the multiple acts of rent skimming shall be separately alleged. A person found guilty of five acts shall be punished by imprisonment in the state prison or by imprisonment in the county jail for not more than one year, by a fine of not more than ten thousand dollars ($10,000), or by both that fine and imprisonment. A person found guilty of additional acts shall be separately punished for each additional act by imprisonment in the state prison or by imprisonment in the county jail for not more than one year, by a fine of not more than ten thousand dollars ($10,000), or by both that fine and imprisonment.

(b) If a defendant has been once previously convicted of a violation of subdivision (a), any subsequent knowing and willful act of rent skimming shall be punishable by imprisonment in the state prison or by imprisonment in the county jail for not more than one year, or by a fine of not more than ten thousand dollars ($10,000), or by both that fine and imprisonment.

[subparagraphs (c) and (d) omitted.]

Civil Code 1942.5—Retaliation

(a) If the lessor retaliates against the lessee because of the exercise by the lessee of his rights under this chapter or because of his complaint to an appropriate agency as to tenantability of a dwelling, and if the lessee of a dwelling is not in default as to the payment of his rent, the lessor may not recover possession of a dwelling in any action or proceeding, cause the lessee to quit involuntarily, increase the rent, or decrease any services within 180 days:

(1) After the date upon which the lessee, in good faith, has given notice pursuant to Section 1942, or has made an oral complaint to the lessor regarding tenantability; or

(2) After the date upon which the lessee, in good faith, has filed a written complaint, or an oral complaint which is registered or otherwise recorded in writing, with an appropriate agency, of which the lessor has notice, for the purpose of obtaining correction of a condition relating to tenantability; or

(3) After the date of an inspection or issuance of a citation, resulting from a complaint described in paragraph (2) of which the lessor did not have notice; or

(4) After the filing of appropriate documents commencing a judicial or arbitration proceeding involving the issue of tenantability; or

(5) After entry of judgment or the signing of an arbitration award, if any, when in the judicial proceeding or arbitration the issue of tenantability is determined adversely to the lessor.

In each instance, the 180-day period shall run from the latest applicable date referred to in paragraphs (1) to (5), inclusive.

(b) A lessee may not invoke the provisions of subdivision (a) more than once in any 12-month period.

(c) It shall be unlawful for a lessor to increase rent, decrease services, cause a lessee to quit involuntarily, bring an action to recover possession, or threaten to do any of such acts, for the purpose of retaliating against the lessee because he or she has lawfully organized or participated in a lessees' association or an organization advocating lessees' rights or has lawfully and peaceably exercised any rights under the law. In an action brought by or against the lessee pursuant to this subdivision, the lessee shall bear the burden of producing evidence that the lessor's conduct was, in fact, retaliatory.

(d) Nothing in this section shall be construed as limiting in any way the exercise by the lessor of his rights under any lease or agreement or any law pertaining to the hiring of property or his right to do any of the acts described in subdivision (a) or (c) for any lawful cause. Any waiver by a lessee of his rights under this section shall be void as contrary to public policy.

(e) Notwithstanding the provisions of subdivisions (a) to (d), inclusive, a lessor may recover possession of a dwelling and do any of the other acts described in subdivision (a) within the period or periods prescribed therein, or within subdivision (c), if the notice of termination, rent increase, or other act, and any pleading or statement of issues in an arbitration, if any, states the ground upon which the lessor, in good faith, seeks to recover possession, increase rent, or do any of the other acts described in subdivision (a) or (c). If such statement be controverted, the lessor shall establish its truth at the trial or other hearing.

(f) Any lessor or agent of a lessor who violates this section shall be liable to the lessee in a civil action for all of the following:

(1) The actual damages sustained by the lessee.
(2) Punitive damages in an amount of not less than one hundred dollars ($100) nor more than one thousand dollars ($1,000) for each retaliatory act where the lessor or agent has been guilty of fraud, oppression, or malice with respect to such act.

(g) In any action brought for damages for retaliatory eviction, the court shall award reasonable attorney's fees to the prevailing party if either party requests attorney's fees upon the initiation of the action.

(h) The remedies provided by this section shall be in addition to any other remedies provided by statutory or decisional law.

6-19a Discussion

Civil Code 1954 allows a landlord to enter the dwelling unit of a tenant only in the cases provided for. All other entries are an offense. Civil Code 1950.5 provides that security deposits can be used for only the uses listed in that section. Civil Code 789.3 prevents the landlord from interrupting or cutting off utilities and other services with the intent to force the tenant to vacate the property. Civil Code 1951.2 provides for landlord remedies where the tenant breaches the terms of the lease. Civil Code sections 890 and 892 deal with rent skimming. Multiple acts of rent skimming are misdemeanor offenses under the code. Civil Code 1942.5 prevents the landlord from retaliating against any tenant who complains to an appropriate agency regarding the tenantability of the dwelling unit. Tenants who are not in default of payment of rent may invoke a defense of retaliatory eviction in unlawful detainer action, upon proof that they made an oral complaint to the landlord regarding the tenantability of premises, without making a valid claim to a government entity. Rights protected to a lessee because of his or her complaint to governmental agency as to suitability of a dwelling relate to the fitness of the building for human occupancy and the lessor's duty to repair. For example, in one case, an eviction by a landlord of a tenant in retaliation for the tenant's complaint to the police that the landlord had committed a crime in sexually molesting her nine-year-old daughter violated the prohibition against evictions in retaliation for the exercise of any rights under the law, and also the common-law defense of retaliatory eviction. Tenants who assert the defense of retaliatory eviction in unlawful detainer action have the burden of proving by preponderance of evidence that the landlord evicted them in retaliation for their complaints to county health department and their filing of a lawsuit against the landlord (*Western Land Office, Inc. v. Cervantes*, 220 Cal. Rptr. 784).

Cases on Point

People v. Carter (130 Cal. App. 95)

Burglary is entry of a building with the intent to commit grand or petit larceny or any felony.

People v. Salemme (2 Cal. App. 4th 775)

The primary purpose of the burglary statute is to protect possessory rights in property.

People v. Lewis (274 Cal. App. 2d 912)

Laws against burglary are primarily designed not so much to deter trespass and intended crime, which are prohibited by other laws, as to forestall the germination of a situation dangerous to personal safety; thus, the higher degree of burglary law is intended to prevent those situations that are most dangerous, that are the most likely to cause personal injury.

People v. Brown (6 Cal. App. 4th 1489)

California's statutory definition of burglary is broader than common law definition; under California law, breaking is no longer required.

People v. Nance (25 Cal. App. 3d 925)

Within the purview of the section defining burglary, intent to commit larceny or any felony is not confined to an intent to commit the crime in the building that is entered, if intent at the time of injury is to commit the offense in the immediate vicinity of the place entered by defendant, if entry is made as a means of facilitating the theft or felony, and if the two places are so closely connected that intent and consummation of the crime would constitute a single and practically continuous transaction.

People v. Gauze (15 Cal. 3d 709)

The defendant could not be convicted of burglarizing his own home, as long as he had the right to enter the home. If the home was leased to someone else and the defendant did not have the right to enter the home, then he could be convicted of burglarizing his own home. To constitute burglary, there must be an unlawful entry.

In re Amber S. (33 Cal. App. 4th 185)

"Building" under California's burglary statute is any structure that has walls on all sides and is covered by a roof; "walls" can take various forms and need not reach the roof, but they must act as a significant barrier to entrance without cutting or breaking.

People v. Coutu (171 Cal. App. 3d 192)

Burglary of storeroom connected to an inhabited dwelling by a breezeway constitutes first-degree burglary.

People v. Brooks (133 Cal. App. 3d 200)

The loading dock at the rear of the market was a "building" within the meaning of this section, even though two sides of it were chainlink fence that did not connect with the roof and left a gap of 6 to 12 inches between the top of the fence and the roof, where the loading dock was completely enclosed and all doors were closed and locked at time of the theft, and the other two walls were made of concrete block and attached to the building in which the market was located.

People v. Hines (210 Cal. App. 3d 945)

The second house on the property, which was 200 yards from the primary family residence, and which was used as a guest house and as a rental unit, was an "inhabited dwelling house" within the meaning of PC 460 even though no one was using the house as sleeping quarters at the time of the burglary.

In re Christopher J. (102 Cal. App. 3d 76)

With respect to a carport appurtenant to the dwelling house, the requirement of a structure with four walls is satisfied by the dwelling house itself; it is unnecessary to find that the carport alone satisfies the definition of a separate "building." An entry into such portion of a dwelling house is a sufficient entry to constitute the offense of burglary.

People v. O'Keefe (222 Cal. App. 3d 517)

Individual student dormitory rooms constituted separate inhabited "dwellings" within the meaning of PC 460 supporting multiple convictions for entry of each individual room.

People v. Nunez (7 Cal. App. 3d 655)

A telephone booth with three walls, a door, a roof, and a floor was a "building" within the meaning of PC 459.

People v. Wilson (160 Cal. App. 2d 606)

One who enters a store with the intent of committing larceny is guilty of burglary, even though entry was made through the public entrance during business hours.

People v. Woods (112 Cal. App. 3d 226)

The defendant could not be convicted of burglary of a vehicle, where, as part of decoy operation, a police officer placed a coin purse and camera on the passenger seat of his private automobile, parked the vehicle in a parking lot, locked the doors and rolled up all windows except for passenger window, which was rolled down approximately five and one-half inches, and then observed the defendant reach in through the passenger window of the vehicle and remove the purse and camera. The partially open window prevented the car from being "locked" within meaning of PC 459 defining offense.

In re Charles G. (95 Cal. App. 3d 62)

Although an essential element of burglary of an automobile is that vehicle must be locked, neither forced entry in the usual sense of the word nor use of burglary tools are essential elements.

Creative Legal Defense

In 1992, Kenneth Solomon, a state employee, confessed to submitting 154 fake expense reports between 1982 and 1990. His excuse, supported by a psychologist's report, was that his behavior was caused by a "deep-seated resentment" at having to make frequent business trips to Philadelphia.

Practicum

Practicum I

Joe, a 17-year-old student, goes to the home of his stepmother and requests that she give him money to find a place to live. She refuses. He then goes to a new house that she is moving into. All of her possessions are in the house, but she has not slept there. He reaches into the guest home by use of a doggie door and attempts to reach the keys. He is unsuccessful. The guest house is detached from the home and is located about 100 yards behind the new house.

1. Has he committed burglary? Is so, what degree?
2. Is the guest house considered an inhabited dwelling?
3. Would it make any difference if the guest house belonged to his recently deceased father and that when the will is probated, the guest house will belong to him?
4. Would it make any difference if Joe thought he had the right to enter the house?
5. Would your answers be any different if Joe broke into the stepmother's car? Her store?

Practicum II

Don Johnson is unhappy with his employer. He decides to burn the company shop. He purchases a firebomb from his friend Jim. On the way back to the company area, Don is involved in an automobile accident. The company car that he is driving is destroyed when the firebomb explodes. After this incident, Don is fired from his job. He has no place to live, so he moves into the attic of the company shop.

1. Has Don committed arson?
2. What other crimes has Don committed?
3. What crimes, if any, has Jim committed?

Discussion Questions

Discussion Questions

1. Chandler entered a hotel in the city of Los Angeles to obtain a room for the evening. No one was present at the reception desk. He noticed a valuable watch on the counter. Unobserved, he picked up the watch and walked out of the hotel. Chandler is charged with the crime of burglary. Is he guilty? Explain your answer.

2. The Bradley family moved from their home on the first of the month leaving most of their furniture. The next day, the house was burglarized. The crime was discovered when the family returned to remove their belongings. Was this first- or second-degree burglary? Explain your answer. (To look at the court decision in this case see: *People v. Cardona,* 142 Cal. App. 3d 481, 191 Cal. Rptr. 109.)

3. What purposes are served by requiring a vehicle to be locked before it is protected by PC 459?

4. When is a building considered inhabited under PC 460?

5. At what point is the crime of burglary completed?

6. Which burglaries are classified as first degree?

7. If the accused does not know that the house is inhabited, can he or she still be convicted of first-degree burglary? Explain.

8. What are the restrictions on the granting of probation for a defendant convicted of burglary?

9. What importance does the fact that the burglary was committed during day or night have in burglary statutes?

10. What information is required to be kept by a person who sells a lock pick gun?

11. Paul starts a fire in his garage to destroy his automobile. The fire spreads to his neighbor's house. What crimes can Paul be convicted of?

12 Karl attempts to burn his home to collect insurance on it. He is unaware at the time that he started the fire that his insurance policy had expired, and the house was uninsured. After he starts the fire, he changes his mind and puts it out. The house suffered only minor damage from the fire. What crimes has Karl committed?

13. Explain the differences between PC 451 and 452.

14. What part does motive play in the crime of arson?

15. Why does the court have the authority to order a psychiatric examination of a person convicted of arson?

16. Define recklessness for the purposes of PC 452.

17. When is vandalism a wobbler?

Self-Study Quiz

Self-Study Quiz

True/False

1. John enters a dwelling with the intent to steal valuables. After entry, he could not find any valuables to steal. He cannot be convicted of burglary under these circumstances.

2. Joe entered a residence to commit the crimes of rape and theft. He may be convicted of two burglaries since he entered with the intent to commit two separate crimes in the building.

3. It is not burglary unless the breaking occurred during the hours of darkness.

4. The accused must physically enter the building to commit the crime of burglary.

5. The entry of the building under the burglary statute requires a breaking.

6. An automobile is not covered by the statutory burglary laws.

7. The entry into the building must be with the intent to commit a crime, but there is no requirement that the crime be committed in the building.

8. It is not a crime to possess burglary tools unless one plans to use them.

9. Sending a dog into a house to fetch property may, in some cases, be burglary.

10. Burglary of an inhabited dwelling is only a misdemeanor.

11. The crime of arson is a misdemeanor.

12. Motive is an essential element of arson.

13. To be convicted of arson, the burning must be during the hours of darkness.

14. Forest land, for the purposes of the arson statutes, does not include grassland.

15. A person may be convicted of an attempt to unlawfully set a fire under Penal Code 452.

16. A judge may order the defendant to undergo psychiatric examination if the defendant is convicted of arson.

17. Arson requires that the burning be accomplished with a malicious and willful intent.

18. To constitute the crime of arson, there must be some burning or charring of the structure, forest land, or property.

19. A person may be convicted of arson if the individual recklessly starts a fire.

20. To establish the crime of arson, it must be shown that the fire was of incendiary rather than accidental origin.

Crimes against Persons: Assault, Battery, Mayhem, Robbery, Carjacking, and Extortion

Nobody ever commits a crime without doing something stupid.
Oscar Wilde, The Picture of Dorian Grey

A code of laws is like a vast forest; the more it is divided, the better it is known.
Jeremy Bentham, A General View on a Complete Code of Laws

151

7-1 Definition of Assault and Battery

An assault is an attempt to inflict violent injury (i.e., battery) upon another person by some form of contact. If the violent injury is actually inflicted or contact is made upon the person of another, then the crime is a battery. Accordingly, one may be convicted of an assault even if the evidence establishes that a battery was committed (*People v. Whalen,* 124 Cal. App. 2d 713). To constitute assault, there must be specific intent to commit battery and an act that is close to accomplishment and not mere preparation (*People v. Corson,* 221 Cal. App. 2d 579).

7-1a Assault/Battery-Related Crimes

The following is a list of assault and battery-related crimes and the relevant Penal Codes that apply to them.

- Assault (PC 240)
- Battery (PC 242)
- Assault Against a Peace Officer (PC 241.4)
- Sexual Battery (PC 243.4)
- Assault With Deadly Weapon (PC 245)
- Assault With Intent to Commit Mayhem, Rape, Sodomy, Oral Copulation (PC 220)
- Motor Vehicle Assaults (PC 417.3)
- Assault With Caustic Chemicals (PC 244)
- Mayhem (PC 205)
- Aggravated Mayhem (PC 205)
- Spousal or Cohabitant Battery (PC 273.5)

7-2 Assault

Penal Code 240—Assault Defined

An *assault* is an unlawful attempt, coupled with a present ability, to commit a violent injury on the person of another.

7-2a Elements

The following are the elements of the crime of assault:

1. An unlawful attempt
2. With the (apparent) present ability
3. To commit an injury to the person of another

7-3 Battery

Penal Code 242—Battery Defined

A *battery* is any willful and unlawful use of force or violence upon the person of another.

7-3a Elements

The following are elements of the crime of battery:

1. The willful and unlawful
2. Use of force or violence
3. Against the person of another

To constitute an assault, the attempt to commit a violent injury must be unlawful. For example, an attempt to commit a violent injury in a prize fight or in self-defense is not normally unlawful and, thus, not an assault. In many cases, it is not an assault if the act is made with the consent of the victim (*People v. Gordon*, 70 Cal. 467).

Required Intent

To constitute the offense of an assault under California statutes, there must be an intent to inflict violent injury against another and a direct act toward carrying out that intent. Accordingly, an individual cannot "accidentally" commit an assault. Reckless conduct, but without the intent to commit violent injury, on the part of an accused is not an assault (*People v. Barnes*, 101 Cal. App. 3d 341). In *People v. Barnes*, the court held that the intent necessary to commit an assault is the intent to commit a battery. The intent to commit a battery, however, may be implied from the act. The general rule is that it is enough that the act be intentional and unlawful. There is no requirement to prove an intent to injure.

Present Ability

The direct act also depends on the present ability of the offender to carry out the intended injury. If the individual does not have the present ability to commit a violent injury, then there is no assault. The victim's belief as to the ability of the defendant to commit the assault is immaterial (*People v. Mosqueda*, 5 Cal. App. 3d 540).

Pointing an unloaded gun at a person in a threatening manner is not an assault under California law since there is no present ability to commit a battery. However, this may be a violation of PC 417, threatening with a weapon, and it does constitute an assault in most other states and under federal criminal law.

In *People v. Ranson* (40 Cal. App. 3d 317), the accused pointed a loaded weapon at the victim. The top cartridge was improperly loaded causing the weapon to jam. The court held that the defendant had "present ability" to commit a violent injury since he could have quickly cleared the jam and fired the weapon. In a similar case, the present ability was present when an automatic weapon without a round in the firing chamber, but with a loaded magazine, was pointed at the victim.

In another case, the defendant's firing of a handgun at a victim standing less than 10 feet away satisfied the "present ability" element of assault, even if bullet-proof glass, unknown to defendant, made it physically impossible for the defendant to succeed, because the defendant had reached point where he could strike immediately at the intended victim; the fact that the victim's form of seeking to avoid injury was more effective than most other actions taken by those threatened with battery did not immunize the attacker (*People v. Valdez*, 175 Cal. App. 3d 103).

Violent Injury

The phrase *violent injury* is misleading. For purposes of the assault and battery crimes, violent injury has a special meaning. It is not the same as bodily harm. Actual bodily harm is not required. The term *violent injury* includes any wrongful act committed by means of physical force against the person of another. Thus, an offensive touching is sufficient. The violent injury referred to may be only to the dignity of the person, and the kind of physical force used is immaterial. The act of spitting at another or attempting to touch someone in an offensive manner is considered sufficient.

In one case, a conviction of battery was upheld on evidence that the accused pushed on the door of an office to prevent the victim from closing the door. The

7-3b Discussion of Assault and Battery Crimes

court stated that the closing of the door while it was touching the victim could be deemed an offensive touching (*People v. Puckett,* 44 Cal. App. 3d 607). As one court stated: "The word violent is not synonymous with bodily harm, but includes any wrongful act committed by means of physical force against person of another, and is synonymous with physical force, the degree of physical force being immaterial (*People v. Whalen,* 124 Cal. App. 2d 713).

It is not important that the victim fear the violent injury. If, for example, you were to take a swing at close range with your fist at a heavyweight boxing champion, that conduct would constitute an assault. It does not matter that the boxer did not fear your assault.

Battery on Peace Officers

It is a felony (wobbler) to commit a battery:

1. On the person of a:

   a. Peace officer
   b. Firefighter
   c. Emergency medical technician
   d. Custodial officer
   e. Process server
   f. Operator of passenger of transportation for hire vehicle (PC 243.3)

2. When the victim is engaged in the performance of his/her official duties
3. The offender knows or should reasonably know that the victim is one of the above persons

7-4 Attempted Assault

As noted earlier, an assault is an attempted battery. An attempted assault, however, is not a crime (*In re James,* 9 Cal. App. 3d 517). For example, threat of injury without the present ability to commit a battery is not an assault—nor is leering at a woman. One court stated: "Where legislature defined criminal assault as attempt to commit a battery by one having present ability to do so and no offense known as attempt to assault was recognized in state at time that the statutory definition of assault was adopted, there was clear manifestation of legislative intent that attempt to commit battery without present ability was to go unpunished" (*In re M.,* 9 C. 3d 517). Another court explained: "Offense of attempted assault would mean, in substance, an attempt to commit a battery without present ability to do so, but there has been no legislative enactment that would manifest a legislative intent to create a crime of an attempt to commit a battery without present ability" (*People v. Duens,* 64 Cal. App. 3d 310).

7-5 Simple and Felonious Assaults

7-5a Simple Assault

Simple assault is the popular term used to denote a misdemeanor assault (*People v. Egan,* 91 Cal. App. 44). To constitute a simple assault, there must be an ability and an attempt to commit a battery. Basically, it is an assault without any aggravating factors such as a completed battery or assault with a dangerous weapon. It is also a lesser included offense to other types of assault. For example, if the accused is tried for assault with the intent to commit rape and the state proves an assault but cannot establish the intent to commit the rape, the accused may be convicted of at least simple assault.

Felonious assault describes those assaults that are committed with the intent to commit a felony. For example, the following are some of the more common felonious assaults:

- Assault with a deadly weapon
- Battery with serious bodily injury
- Sexual battery
- Assault with intent to commit mayhem, rape, sodomy, or oral copulation
- Assault on a peace officer in the performance of duty

7-5b Felonious Assault

Penal Code 273.5—Willful Infliction of Corporal Injury; Violation; Punishment

(a) Any person who willfully inflicts upon a person who is his or her spouse, former spouse, cohabitant, former cohabitant, or the mother or father of his or her child, corporal injury resulting in a traumatic condition, is guilty of a felony, and upon conviction thereof shall be punished by imprisonment in the state prison for two, three, or four years, or in a county jail for not more than one year, or by a fine of up to six thousand dollars ($6,000) or by both that fine and imprisonment.

(b) Holding oneself out to be the husband or wife of the person with whom one is cohabiting is not necessary to constitute cohabitation as the term is used in this section.

(c) As used in this section, "traumatic condition" means a condition of the body, such as a wound or external or internal injury, whether of a minor or serious nature, caused by a physical force.

(d) For the purpose of this section, a person shall be considered the father or mother of another person's child if the alleged male parent is presumed the natural father under Sections 7611 and 7612 of the Family Code.

(e) Any person convicted of violating this section for acts occurring within seven years of a previous conviction under subdivision (a), or subdivision (d) of Section 243, or Section 243.4, 244, 244.5, or 245, shall be punished by imprisonment in a county jail for not more than one year, or by imprisonment in the state prison for two, four, or five years, or by both imprisonment and a fine of up to ten thousand dollars ($10,000).

(f) If probation is granted to any person convicted under subdivision (a), the court shall impose probation consistent with the provisions of Section 1203.097.

(g) If probation is granted, or the execution or imposition of a sentence is suspended, for any defendant convicted under subdivision (a) who has been convicted of any prior offense specified in subdivision (e), the court shall impose one of the following conditions of probation:

  (1) If the defendant has suffered one prior conviction within the previous seven years for a violation of any offense specified in subdivision (e), it shall be a condition thereof, in addition to the provisions contained in Section 1203.097, that he or she be imprisoned in a county jail for not less than 15 days.

  (2) If the defendant has suffered two or more prior convictions within the previous seven years for a violation of any offense specified in subdivision (e), it shall be a condition of probation, in addition to the provisions contained in Section 1203.097, that he or she be imprisoned in a county jail for not less than 60 days.

7-6 Inflicting Corporal Injury on Spouse or Cohabitant or Noncohabiting Former Spouse

(3) The court, upon a showing of good cause, may find that the mandatory imprisonment required by this subdivision shall not be imposed and shall state on the record its reasons for finding good cause.

(h) If probation is granted upon conviction of a violation of subdivision (a), the conditions of probation may include, consistent with the terms of probation imposed pursuant to Section 1203.97, in lieu of a fine, one or both of the following requirements:

(1) That the defendant make payments to a battered women's shelter, up to a maximum of five thousand dollars ($5,000), pursuant to Section 1203.097.

(2) That the defendant reimburse the victim for reasonable costs of counseling and other reasonable expenses that the court finds are the direct result of the defendant's offense. For any order to pay a fine, make payments to a battered women's shelter, or pay restitution as a condition of probation under this subdivision, the court shall make a determination of the defendant's ability to pay. In no event shall any order to make payments to a battered women's shelter be made if it would impair the ability of the defendant to pay direct restitution to the victim or court-ordered child support. Where the injury to a married person is caused in whole or in part by the criminal acts of his or her spouse in violation of this section, the community property may not be used to discharge the liability of the offending spouse for restitution to the injured spouse, required by Section 1203.04, as operative on or before August 2, 1995, or Section 1202.4, or to a shelter for costs with regard to the injured spouse and dependents, required by this section, until all separate property of the offending spouse is exhausted.

For any order to pay a fine, make payments to a battered women's shelter, or pay restitution as a condition of probation under this subdivision, the court shall make a determination of the defendant's ability to pay. In no event shall any order to make payments to a battered women's shelter be made if it would impair the ability of the defendant to pay direct restitution to the victim or court-ordered child support. Where the injury to a married person is caused in whole or in part by the criminal acts of his or her spouse in violation of this section, the community property may not be used to discharge the liability of the offending spouse for restitution to the injured spouse, required by Section 1203.04, as operative on or before August 2, 1995, or Section 1202.4, or to a shelter for costs with regard to the injured spouse and dependents, required by this section, until all separate property of the offending spouse is exhausted.

7-6a Discussion

Penal Code 12028.5 permits law enforcement personnel to take possession of any firearms at the scene of a domestic violence incident. The Domestic Violence Prevention Act (Code of Civil Procedure, Sections 533-540) allows any family member who can show that he or she has been abused in the past by a spouse or other member of the household to obtain a temporary restraining order (TRO) to prevent further violence. Violation of a TRO is a misdemeanor under PC 273.6.

The statute stating that any person who willfully inflicts corporal injury upon spouse or person with whom he or she is cohabiting or mother or father of his or her child is guilty of a felony expands its predecessor section, a wife-beating statute, to protect the large numbers of couples who live in intimate and significant relationships, but without marriage (*People v. Vega*, 33 Cal. App. 4th 706). A finding of sexual relationship between defendant and victim was not required to sustain conviction of felony infliction of corporal injury on cohabitant (*People v. Ballard,* 203 Cal. App. 3d 311).

Penal Code 220—Assault with Intent to Commit Mayhem, Rape, Sodomy, Oral Copulation, Rape in Concert with Another, Lascivious Acts upon a Child, or Penetration of Genitals or Anus with Foreign Object

7-7 Felonious Assault

Every person who assaults another with intent to commit mayhem, rape, sodomy, oral copulation, or any violation of Section 264.1, 288, or 289 is punishable by imprisonment in the state prison for two, four, or six years.
[Note: Sections 264.1, 288, and 289 pertain to rape and other sexual offenses.]

The following are elements of the crime of felonious assault:

7-7a Elements

1. An unlawful attempt to commit a violent injury upon the person of another
2. With the present ability
3. With the *specific intent* to commit mayhem, rape, sodomy, oral copulation, or any of the sexual offenses listed in Sections 264.1, 288, or 289 of the Penal Code.

The crime of assault with intent to commit rape is complete if at any moment during the assault, the defendant intends to have carnal knowledge of victim and to use for that purpose whatever force may be required, and, hence, the fact that the defendant desists is immaterial (*People v. Lutes,* 79 Cal. App. 2d 233). The crime of assault with intent to commit rape requires proof that an assault was committed, and that at some time during the assault it was the defendant's intention to have sexual intercourse with his victim by force (*People v. Clifton,* 248 Cal. App. 2d 126).

That the defendant may have been intoxicated at the time of assault, and that he was impotent when intoxicated, are not of themselves defenses to assault with intent to commit rape (*People v. Peckham,* 232 Cal. App. 2d 163). Sexual capacity is not a matter for consideration in a prosecution for assault with intent to rape (*People v. Meichtry,* 37 Cal. 2d 385).

Penal Code 243.4—Sexual Battery

7-8 Sexual Battery

(a) Any person who touches an intimate part of another person while that person is unlawfully restrained by the accused or an accomplice, and if the touching is against the will of the person touched and is for the purpose of sexual arousal, sexual gratification, or sexual abuse, is guilty of sexual battery. . . .
(b) Any person who touches an intimate part of another person who is institutionalized for medical treatment and who is seriously disabled or medically incapacitated, if the touching is against the will of the person touched, and if the touching is for the purpose of sexual arousal, sexual gratification, or sexual abuse, is guilty of sexual battery. . . .
(c) Any person who, for the purpose of sexual arousal, sexual gratification, or sexual abuse, causes another, against that person's will while that person is unlawfully restrained either by the accused or an accomplice, or is institutionalized for medical treatment and is seriously disabled or medically incapacitated, to masturbate or touch an intimate part of either of those persons or a third person, is guilty of sexual battery. . . .

(d)

    (1) Any person who touches an intimate part of another person, if the touching is against the will of the person touched, and is for the specific purpose of sexual arousal, sexual gratification, or sexual abuse, is guilty of misdemeanor sexual battery. . . . However, if the defendant was an employer and the victim was an employee of the defendant, the misdemeanor sexual battery shall be punishable by a fine not exceeding three thousand dollars ($3,000), by imprisonment in a county jail not exceeding six months, or by both that fine and imprisonment. . . .

    (2) As used in this subdivision, *touches* means physical contact with another person, whether accomplished directly, through the clothing of the person committing the offense, or through the clothing of the victim.

(e) As used in subdivisions (a), (b), and (c), *touches* means physical contact with the skin of another person whether accomplished directly or through the clothing of the person committing the offense.

(f) As used in this section, the following terms have the following meanings:

    (1) *Intimate part* means the sexual organ, anus, groin, or buttocks of any person, and the breast of a female.

    (2) *Sexual battery* does not include the crimes defined in Section 261 or 289. [rape offenses]

    (3) *Seriously disabled* means a person with severe physical or sensory disabilities.

    (4) *Medically incapacitated* means a person who is incapacitated as a result of prescribed sedatives, anesthesia, or other medication.

    (5) *Institutionalized* means a person who is located voluntarily or involuntarily in a hospital, medical treatment facility, nursing home, acute care facility, or mental hospital.

    (6) *Minor* means a person under 18 years of age.

(g) This section shall not be construed to limit or prevent prosecution under any other law which also proscribes a course of conduct that also is proscribed by this section.

(h) In the case of a felony conviction for a violation of this section, the fact that the defendant was an employer and the victim was an employee of the defendant shall be a factor in aggravation in sentencing.

(i) A person who commits a violation of subdivision (a), (b), or (c) against a minor when the person has a prior felony conviction for a violation of this section shall be guilty of a felony, punishable by imprisonment in the state prison for two, three, or four years and a fine not exceeding ten thousand dollars ($10,000).

(j) Upon conviction of a felony for a violation or attempted violation of this section committed on or after January 1, 1993, the court may enter an order requiring that the defendant register pursuant to Section 290 [as a sex offender].

7-8a Discussion

Touching Required

One court held that the touching of the outside of victim's clothing at the vaginal area was not a touching of the skin and thus did not constitute the crime of sexual battery. The victim's testimony, however, that the juvenile touched her breasts and chest area while attempting to pull down her leotard sufficiently supported finding that juvenile touched the victim's skin as required for commission of sexual battery (*In re Gustavo M.*, 214 Cal. App. 3d 1485).

In another case, evidence that a juvenile grabbed the victim by the crotch for a brief period but did not touch her skin was insufficient basis for adjudging juvenile to be a ward of the court for committing sexual battery *(In re Keith T.*, 156 Cal. App. 3d 983).

Unlawful Restraint

For purposes of conviction of sexual battery, "unlawful restraint" does not require showing that physical restraint occurred. In *People v. Grant* (8 Cal. App. 4th 1105), the defendant "unlawfully restrained" the victim within the meaning of the sexual battery statute, even though he did not use physical force against her where he presented himself as an authority figure, removed victim from car, ordered her boyfriend to remain in car, and threatened victim and her boyfriend that they could be taken away by police if they did not cooperate. The court held that the defendant's conduct forced the victim to remain in location in which she did not voluntarily wish to be and that the restraint was not accomplished by lawful authority.

In another case, the "unlawful restraint" necessary to hold the defendant teacher guilty of sexual battery was not shown by his conduct in grabbing a student's buttocks and putting his hands down her top where the student had voluntarily accompanied the defendant on a nonschool-related function knowing she would be alone with him and thinking something might happen, and student was successful in escaping restraints imposed by defendant; there was no evidence that initial activity by the defendant in restraining student by grabbing her by the buttocks was against her will and without her consent *(People v. Arnold*, 6 Cal. App. 4th 18).

Penal Code 245—Assault with Deadly Weapon or Force Likely to Produce Great Bodily Injury; Punishment

7-9 Assault with Deadly Weapon

(a)

(1) Any person who commits an assault upon the person of another with a deadly weapon or instrument other than a firearm or by any means of force likely to produce great bodily injury shall be punished by imprisonment in the state prison for two, three, or four years, or in a county jail for not exceeding one year, or by a fine not exceeding ten thousand dollars ($10,000), or by both the fine and imprisonment.

(2) Any person who commits an assault upon the person of another with a firearm shall be punished by imprisonment in the state prison for two, three, or four years, or in a county jail for not less than six months and not exceeding one year, or by both a fine not exceeding ten thousand dollars ($10,000) and imprisonment.

(3) Any person who commits an assault upon the person of another with a machine gun . . . , or an assault weapon . . . shall be punished by imprisonment in the state prison for 4, 8, or 12 years.

(b) Any person who commits an assault upon the person of another with a semi-automatic firearm shall be punished by imprisonment in the state prison for three, six, or nine years.

(c) Any person who commits an assault with a deadly weapon or instrument, other than a firearm, or by any means likely to produce great bodily injury upon the person of a peace officer or firefighter, and who knows or reasonably should know that the victim is a peace officer or firefighter engaged in the performance of his or her duties, when the peace officer or firefighter is engaged in the performance of his or her duties, shall be punished by imprisonment in the state prison for three, four, or five years.

(d)
   (1) Any person who commits an assault with a firearm upon the person of a peace officer or firefighter, and who knows or reasonably should know that the victim is a peace officer or firefighter engaged in the performance of his or her duties, when the peace officer or firefighter is engaged in the performance of his or her duties, shall be punished by imprisonment in the state prison for four, six, or eight years.

   (2) Any person who commits an assault upon the person of a peace officer or firefighter with a semiautomatic firearm and who knows or reasonably should know that the victim is a peace officer or firefighter engaged in the performance of his or her duties, when the peace officer or firefighter is engaged in the performance of his or her duties, shall be punished by imprisonment in the state prison for five, seven, or nine years.

   (3) Any person who commits an assault with a machine gun . . . or an assault weapon . . . , upon the person of a peace officer or firefighter, and who knows or reasonably should know that the victim is a peace officer or firefighter engaged in the performance of his or her duties, shall be punished by imprisonment in the state prison for 6, 9, or 12 years.

(e) When a person is convicted of a violation of this section in a case involving use of a deadly weapon or instrument or firearm, and the weapon or instrument or firearm is owned by that person, the court shall order that the weapon or instrument or firearm be deemed a nuisance, and it shall be confiscated and disposed of in the manner provided by . . . [law].

[Section (f) omitted].

7-9a Elements

The following are the elements of an assault with a deadly weapon:

1. An unlawful attempt to commit a violent injury
2. Upon the person of another
3. With the present ability
4. Using a deadly weapon or a force likely to produce great bodily injury

7-9b Discussion

There are two different crimes. The first involves the use of a deadly weapon, and the second involves the use of force (with or without a weapon) in a means likely to produce great bodily injury.

Deadly Weapon

A deadly weapon can be any object capable of causing death or great bodily injury. For example, hitting the person over the head with an unloaded pistol could cause great bodily injury and, therefore, the unloaded pistol is a deadly weapon, whereas the pointing of an unloaded rifle at a person would not. To be guilty of assault with a deadly weapon, it is not necessary for an actual injury to result from the assault.

To determine if the weapon used is a deadly weapon, the nature of the weapon, the manner of its use, the location of the person at which the weapon was directed, and the injury inflicted, if any, will be considered. Any physical force that is capable of producing great bodily injury is sufficient for purposes of the deadly force requirement. If the victim is injured and no weapon is found, the nature of the victim's injury may justify an inference that a dangerous weapon was used.

Where an assault is committed with a deadly weapon, or with force likely to produce great bodily injury, the aggravated assault is complete on the attempted use of the force; if halted at such point, no battery has been committed; since assault with force likely to produce great bodily injury may be committed without committing battery, battery is not an offense necessarily included within assault by means of force likely to produce great bodily injury.

In determining whether use of deadly weapon other than a firearm is an element of assault with a deadly weapon other than a firearm or by means of force likely to produce great bodily injury, the means by which the defendant committed the offense must be considered, rather than as an abstract question of whether the statute could be violated without using a deadly weapon; the offense of assault by means of force likely to produce great bodily injury is not an offense separate from the offense of assault with a deadly weapon other than a firearm (*People v. McGee*, 15 Cal. App. 4th 107).

In one case, the court held that hypodermic needles in the possession of a suspected drug user presented a "threatening possibility," and were considered "deadly weapons," and thus an officer who felt two objects that were similar to hypodermic needles and syringes in a patdown search of a suspected drug dealer could remove the objects from the suspect's jacket (*People v. Autry*, 232 C.A. 3d 365). In another case, a juvenile's conduct in knowingly offering to the potential victim an apple with straight pin embedded in it constituted an assault with a deadly weapon (*In re Jose D.R.*, 137 Cal. App. 3d 269). In *People v. Claborn* (224 Cal. App. 2d 38), an automobile that was aimed at the victim's automobile and that struck the victim's car head-on was held to be a "deadly weapon" or "instrument or force likely to produce great bodily injury."

Injury

It is unnecessary for prosecution that a victim actually receive injuries in order to support conviction for assault by means of force that is likely to produce great bodily injury, but the absence of serious injuries is a factor that a jury may consider in determining what kind of force was used (*People v. Roth*, 228 Cal. App. 2d 522). A victim's fear, lack of fear, injury, or lack of injury are not elements that need to be proved or disproved to convict a defendant of assault with a deadly weapon (*People v. Griggs*, 216 Cal. App. 3d 734).

A jury finding that a 13-year-old minor had committed assault by means of force likely to produce great bodily injury was sufficiently supported by evidence that the minor struck the victim in the face with sufficient force to knock her down, resulting in the victim's treatment at the hospital for four to five hours (*In re Nirran W.*, 207 Cal. App. 3d 1157).

Actual bodily injury is not a necessary element of the crime of assault with means likely to produce great bodily injury, but if such injury is inflicted, its nature and extent may be considered in connection with all the evidence in determining whether the means used and the manner in which it was used were such that they were likely to produce great bodily injury (*People v. Richardson*, 23 Cal. App. 3d 403). In one case, the defendant's use of force in grabbing both sides of the assault victim's face, pinching both sides of her mouth, ripping her clothing, holding her jaw tightly, and shoving his whole hand down her throat so that she would not scream while he was on top of her was found to be likely to produce great bodily injury (*People v. Armstrong*, 8 Cal. App. 4th 1060).

Intent

Assault with a deadly weapon is not a special intent crime. For example, one accused was convicted of an assault with a deadly weapon for pointing a loaded pistol at the victim. There is no requirement to establish that the accused intended to use the weapon. Also, the firing of a pistol in the direction of the victim without an intent to hit the victim, but to only "scare him" is an assault with a deadly weapon (*People v. McCoy*, 25 Cal. App. 2d 518).

The court held in *People v. Walker* (99 Cal. App. 2d 238) that since specific intent is not an element of the crime of assault with a deadly weapon, and where evidence is sufficient to establish character of instrument as charged, it is not necessary for the prosecution to prove specifically that a defendant intends to injure a complaining witness, as such intent may then be implied from performing an unlawful act. In another case, it was not a defense to the charge of assault with a deadly weapon that a defendant, while engaged in killing another person, did not intend to shoot a bystander, who was wounded at the time (*People v. Carr*, 72 Cal. App. 2d 191). A defendant's knowledge of the probability of success of his or her intended action is not relevant to the determination of whether the defendant committed assault with a deadly weapon (*People v. Craig*, 227 Cal. App. 3d 644).

A defendant's voluntary unconsciousness due to intoxication would not constitute complete defense to charges of assault with intent to commit murder and assault with a deadly weapon (*People v. Flowers*, 38 Cal. App. 3d 813).

Victim

The naming of the particular victim is not an element of assault with a deadly weapon (*People v. Griggs*, 216 Cal. App. 3d 734). In one case, the defendant could be convicted of assault upon the "person of another" with a firearm, even though the intended victim was unknown, where the defendant was clearly aware that a crowd was assembled in the direction in which he fired gun (*People v. Griggs*, 216 Cal. App. 3d 734).

7-10 Mayhem

Penal Code 203—Mayhem Defined

Every person who unlawfully and maliciously deprives a human being of a member of his body, or disables, disfigures, or renders it useless, or cuts or disables the tongue, or puts out an eye, or slits the nose, ear, or lip is guilty of mayhem.

Penal Code 205—Aggravated Mayhem

A person is guilty of aggravated mayhem when he or she unlawfully, under circumstances manifesting extreme indifference to the physical or psychological well-being of another person, intentionally causes permanent disability or disfigurement of another human being or deprives a human being of a limb, organ, or member of his or her body.

For purposes of this section, it is not necessary to prove an intent to kill. Aggravated mayhem is a felony punishable by imprisonment in the state prison for life with the possibility of parole.

The following are the elements of mayhem:

1. An unlawful battery
2. Maliciously inflicting or attempting to inflict violent injury
3. One or more described injuries as a result of above action

Mayhem is a form of aggravated battery (*People v. DeFoor*, 100 Cal. 150). Unlike assault with the intent to commit mayhem, there is no requirement of a specific intent to inflict the resulting injury. For example, one defendant was convicted of mayhem when he hit the victim in the head, breaking his glasses and destroying the sight in one eye. No evidence, however, was presented regarding an intent to destroy the eyesight (*People v. Wright*, 93 Cal. 564 and *People v. Vigil*, 242 Cal. App. 2d 862).

Mayhem is a general intent rather than a specific intent crime, despite use of the term "maliciously" in statutory definition (*People v. Sekona*, 27 Cal. App. 4th 443). The crime of mayhem does not require specific intent to vex, annoy, or injure (*People v. Pitts*, 223 Cal. App. 3d 1547).

The nature of the injuries involved in mayhem convictions includes:

- Biting off the nose, or portions thereof
- Cutting off a piece of an ear or a portion of a lip
- Rendering an eye useless for practical purposes
- Disabling the tongue by biting it
- Biting through the lip ("slit")

Involuntarily tattooing a woman's abdomen and breast could constitute mayhem (*People v. Page*, 104 Cal. App. 3d 569). In one case, the intentional disfigurement of the complainant's face permitted prosecution for the crime of mayhem where although the five-inch wound, which left a scar running from above the eyebrow to below the eye, resulted in no functional impairment, it was probably a permanent disfigurement, with attendant emotional and economic disabilities (*Goodman v. Superior Court of Alameda County*, 84 Cal. App. 3d 621). An injury may be considered legally permanent, for purposes of mayhem, despite the fact that cosmetic repair may be medically feasible (*People v. Hill*, 23 Cal. App. 4th 1566).

Aggravated mayhem was created by the legislature for punishing those who permanently disable or disfigure victims. Offenders convicted of this offense may be sentenced to life imprisonment.

Penal Code 244—Assault with Caustic Chemicals

Any person who willfully and maliciously places or throws, or causes to be placed or thrown, upon the person of another, any vitriol, corrosive acid, flammable substance, or caustic chemical of any nature, with the intent to injure the flesh or disfigure the body of such person, is punishable by imprisonment in the state prison for two, three, or four years.

As used in this section, "flammable substance" means gasoline, petroleum products, or flammable liquids with a flashpoint of 150 degrees Fahrenheit or less.

For this crime, willfully and maliciously has the same meaning as that set forth for other assaultive crimes. This form of aggravated assault requires the specific intent to injure or disfigure. Disfigure has the same meaning as set forth in the discussion under mayhem, presented earlier in Section 7-11a. Violation of PC 244, denouncing assault with caustic chemical, does not require that great bodily harm be or may have been caused (*People v. Day*, 248 P. 250).

An assault is a necessary element of the offense of throwing vitriol upon another with intent to injure him or her (*People v. Stanton,* 106 Cal. 139). The crime of assault by means of force likely to produce great bodily injury, however, is not an offense necessarily included within offense of assault with a caustic chemical (*People v. Warren,* 223 Cal. App. 2d 798).

7-12 Robbery

Penal Code 211—Robbery Defined

Robbery is the felonious taking of personal property in the possession of another, from his person or immediate presence, and against his will, accomplished by means of force or fear.

7-12a Definition

As defined in PC 211, robbery is an aggravated form of theft with the additional element of the taking from the immediate presence and will of the victim. In California, robbery is considered as both a crime against the person and the property (*People v. Jones,* 53 Cal. 58). Robbery is a combination of assault and larceny (*People v. Blue,* 161 Cal. App. 2d 1).

7-12b Robbery and Extortion-Related Crimes

The following is a list of robbery and extortion-related crimes and the Penal Code section that applies to them.

- Robbery (PC 211)
- Extortion (PC 518)
- Kidnapping for Ransom or Robbery (PC 209) [discussed in Chapter 8]
- Simulating Court Process (PC 526)

7-12c Elements

The following are the elements of the crime of robbery:

1. The wrongful taking of personal property (including asportation)
2. From the possession of another, or
3. From his or her person, or
4. From immediate presence
5. Against the will of the person
6. Accomplished by means of force or fear

Penal Code 212—Fear Defined

The fear mentioned in Section 211 may be either:
1. The fear of an unlawful injury to the person or property of the person robbed, or of any relative of his or member of his family; or
2. The fear of an immediate and unlawful injury to the person or property of anyone in the company of the person robbed at the time of the robbery.

Penal Code 212.5—Robbery; Degrees

(a) Every robbery of any person who is performing his or her duties as an operator of any bus, taxicab, cable car, streetcar, trackless trolley, or other vehicle, including a vehicle operated on stationary rails or on a track or rail suspended in the air, and used for the transportation of persons for hire, every robbery of any passenger which is perpetrated on any of these vehicles, and every robbery which is perpetrated in an inhabited dwelling house, a vessel . . . (that) is inhabited and designed for habitation, an inhabited floating home . . . , a trailer coach as defined in the Vehicle Code which is inhabited, or the inhabited portion of any other building is robbery of the first degree.

(b) Every robbery of any person while using an automated teller machine or immediately after the person has used an automated teller machine and is in the vicinity of the automated teller machine is robbery of the first degree.

(c) All kinds of robbery other than those listed in subdivisions (a) and (b) are of the second degree.

[Note: Section 212.5 was passed by the legislature to overrule in part the decision in *People v. Beller* (172 Cal. App. 3d 904), which held that robbery and residential robbery were separate substantive crimes. The legislature indicated that there was only one crime of robbery, which is set forth in Section 211, and that some forms of robbery are more aggravated and deserving of greater punishment (Stats. 186 ch. 1428, Section 6).]

7-12d Discussion

To be robbery, the property taken must have at least some intrinsic (real or true) value that is subject to larceny (*People v. Stevens*, 141 Cal. 2d 699). Property that is the subject of larceny is also the subject of robbery, since robbery contains the elements of larceny, with the additional element of either force or fear (*People v. Leyvas*, 73 Cal. App. 2d 863). One defendant was convicted of robbery based on the severance of a standing crop of marijuana from land where the other required elements were present. The court stated that since the severance and taking of a growing crop is now subject to larceny, the same property is also now subject to robbery (*People v. Dillon*, 34 Cal. 3d 441).

Neither the value of the property or the amount of money taken is material to the robbery offense as long as the property has some value or some money was taken (*People v. Coleman*, 8 Cal. App. 3d 722). The fact that the victim from whose possession the money is taken is not the true owner of the money is not a defense to the crime of robbery. In one case, the victim had earlier stolen the money from someone else. The court held that even a thief could be robbed (*People v. Moore*, 4 Cal. App. 3d 668).

Immediate Presence or Possession

The term "immediate presence" is broadly interpreted to include any place within sight or hearing of the person (*People v. Lavender*, 137 Cal. App. 582). In determining whether or not the property is in the immediate presence of the victim, all sensory perceptions are used. Immediate presence, for purposes of robbery conviction, has to do with dominion and control over property as well as receipt by the victim of some threat or assault *(People v. Dominguez*, 11 Cal. App. 4th 1342). As one court observed, the term "immediate presence" in the section involving robbery is to be liberally construed, and any and all sensory perceptions are included in determining presence but actual corporeal presence of victim is not required (*People v. Hays*, 147 Cal. App. 3d 534).

In *People v. Arline* (13 Cal. App. 3d 200), a robbery was held to have been committed in the immediate presence of a victim (an employee), even though the employee was not in charge nor had immediate control of the items stolen. A security guard or night watchman had constructive possession of the merchandise to the same degree as a salesperson (*People v. Estes*, 147 Cal. App. 3d 23). In one case, an employee's mother entered the store during the robbery. The accused handed her a bag and ordered her to take the money from the cash register. A conviction of robbery by taking the money from the possession of the mother was upheld on appeal (*People v. Moore*, 4 Cal. App. 3d 668).

In one case, the court held that money was taken from the "immediate possession" of the victim when the defendant removed the victim's pants and allowed his brother to look through the pockets while the defendant had sex with the victim (*People v. Moore*, 4 Cal. App. 3d 668). In another case (*People v. Davis*, 100 Cal. App. 179), the defendant pointed a weapon at the cashier in a movie theater. When she ran out the back door, the defendant entered the ticket booth and took the money. His conviction for robbery was upheld by the appellate court.

To establish the element of presence necessary for robbery conviction, a victim need not perceive the actual taking as long as he perceives any overt act in the commission of the robbery and is subjected to the requisite force or fear (*People v. Martinez*, 150 Cal. App. 3d 579).

One court held that robbery could be found to have been committed in the immediate presence of the victim, although when the victim surprised the defendant in the victim's apartment he did not observe defendant taking any property but only saw him stand over a stereo, at which time the defendant pulled a knife and the victim immediately fled. The defendant was apprehended minutes later in possession of jewelry and a knife belonging to the victim (*People v. Miramon*, 140 Cal. App. 3d 118). Presence depends on the circumstances of each case and implies area with no metes and bounds, while immediate may be defined as being near at hand, not far apart, or distant (*People v. Risenhoover*, 70 Cal. 2d 39).

Force or Fear

The property must be taken by either force or fear. Unless one or the other is used, the crime is not robbery. The particular means, however, by which force is used or fear imposed is not an element of robbery (*In re Michael*, 39 Cal. 3d 81). Something more, however, than the amount of force necessary to lift or seize the property is necessary to change the offense from "theft from a person" to robbery (*People v. Morales*, 49 Cal. App. 3d 134). The hasty snatching of a purse without resistance may be only larceny if no force was used nor fear imposed (*People v. Church*, 115 Cal. 300).

In a prosecution for armed robbery, evidence that the defendant entered a liquor store with his hand in his jacket pocket and with the handle of a gun visible to attendant of liquor store and demanded money established that the attendant did not voluntarily part with the money and that the money was taken by means of force or fear (*People v. Thomas*, 145 Cal. App. 2d 401).

The force or fear must have been used to take the property, not some other reason. Thus, an accused who used force to commit rape and after the rape took a cigarette from the victim was not guilty of robbery. This result was based on the lack of evidence establishing that the victim was afraid to resist the taking and that no additional force was used in taking the cigarette (*People v. Welsh*, 7 Cal. 2d 209).

In one case, during the robbery, two victims were in joint possession of the property. The court stated that since the central element of robbery is the force or fear applied to the individual victim, two convictions for robbery were appropriate where both victims were in joint possession of the property (*People v. Ramos*, 30 Cal. 3d 553).

The degree of fear necessary must be sufficient to cause the victim to comply with the unlawful demand for his or her property. It is not necessary that terror exists (*People v. Borra*, 123 Cal. App. 482). Fear may be inferred from the circumstances surrounding the demand. In one case, the victim testified that he did not fear the accused even though the accused pointed a weapon at him. The court, in upholding the robbery conviction, stated that the element of fear could be inferred from the fact that a pistol was pointed at the victim (*People v. Renteria*, 61 Cal. 2d 497). In another case, the conviction for robbery was upheld despite the testimony of the victim that she was not afraid of the defendant because she did not think he was serious when he pointed a weapon at her (*People v. Harris*, 65 Cal. App. 3d 978). The general rule is that the degree of fear needed to establish robbery by fear is:

> An amount of fear that would cause a reasonable person under the same set of circumstances to be in fear of his or her life, fear or danger of injury or fear that his or her property may be injured or damaged.

In one case, even though the checker in a market did not affirmatively testify that she handed over money from a cash register because she was afraid, testimony that the defendant pointed a gun at her and said, "This is a holdup, give me all the money," was sufficient to show that the taking was accomplished by means of force or fear (*People v. Franklin*, 200 Cal. App. 2d 797).

It is not necessary that robbery be accomplished by means of both force *and* fear. Either by force or fear is sufficient (*People v. Winters*, 163 Cal. App. 2d 619). One court held that a defendant committed robbery, not grand theft, when he pointed a loaded gun at a motorist's face, demanded money and gold, caused the motorist to flee, and then took the motorist's vehicle; the force the defendant applied caused the motorist to flee and enabled the defendant to take vehicle, and the defendant's intent to steal did not need to be directed toward vehicle when he applied the force (*People v. Brito*, 232 Cal. App. 3d 316).

The threat to inflict injury required for a robbery need not be accompanied by present ability to carry it out; thus, the use of an unloaded gun or a simulated gun is sufficient if it causes a victim to part with his or her property (*People v. Wolcott*, 34 Cal. 3d 92). Evidence of assault, verbal threats, or use of a weapon is not requisite for a finding of robbery, where intimidation is relied upon (*People v. Brew*, 2 Cal. App. 4th 99).

Inhabited Building

For purposes of first-degree robbery, *inhabited* means a building currently being used as a dwelling or living quarters. For example, a jail cell in which seven or eight inmates live is an "inhabited portion of any other building" for the purpose of first-degree burglary (*People v. McDade*, 230 Cal. App. 3d 118). In *People v. Alvarado* (274 Cal. Rptr. 452), evidence that the defendant robbed two victims in a motel room was sufficient to support convictions for first-degree robbery; robbery that occurs in inhabited dwelling house is robbery of the first degree, and the legislature did not exempt motel rooms from that category.

Can a person commit first-degree robbery by robbing someone in his or her own house? The question was answered in the affirmative by one court. The court stated that the policy purpose underlying the imposition of the enhanced penalty under the residential robbery statute, in the case of robbery committed by person in own dwelling, is the heightened vulnerability created by the dwelling environment, and the guest is just as vulnerable as the resident (*People v. McCullough*, 9 Cal. App. 4th 1298). In another case, the court held that the defendant could be found guilty of residential robbery even if robbery occurred in the defendant's own dwelling (*People v. McCullough*, 9 Cal. App. 4th 1298). Residential burglary is not a necessary predicate for residential robbery; from the victim's psychological standpoint, robbery in a defendant's residence to which a victim is invited is no different from robbery committed by some unknown third person inside the friend's house because in either case, the victim assumes an enhanced level of security and privacy that is violated by the crime (*People v. Jackson*, 6 Cal. App. 4th 1185).

Asportation

The requirement of asportation (movement) is similar to the same element required in theft crimes. Only slight movement is required. It is not necessary that the property be taken out of the physical presence of the victim. As one court stated, "Whether the appellant conveyed the money one yard or one mile from the presence of the victim is immaterial insofar as the requirement of asportation is concerned" (*People v. Beal*, 3 Cal. App. 2d 252). In one case, a robbery conviction was upheld where the accused was apprehended by police officers while leaving the store with the money. He never got out of the store (*People v. LeBlanc*, 25 Cal. App. 3d 576).

It is not necessary that the accused take actual physical possession of the property. In one case, the accused pointed a weapon at the victim and ordered the victim to drop his wallet on the ground. The victim did as ordered. When the victim stated that there was no money in the wallet, the accused ordered him to pick it up and allowed the victim to leave. The court held that the acts were sufficient to constitute the crime of robbery since all that was required was the "taking of possession away from the victim and into the control of the taker . . ." (*People v. Quinn*, 77 Cal. App. 2d 734).

Intent to Steal

Robbery is a specific intent crime since an intent to steal is an essential element of the crime (*People v. Ford*, 60 Cal. 2d 772). The intent to steal requirement is the same as that for larceny. The necessary intent to steal was missing in one case where the money was taken under a good faith claim of the right to possession of it (*People v. Sheasbey*, 82 Cal. App. 459). The good faith claim of the right to possession need not be reasonable. For example, in one case, the defendant was charged with attempted robbery for taking money from a bar that operated an illegal gambling game. The defendant stated that he was only trying to regain money that he had illegally lost in the game. The court said that if the defendant in "good faith" believed that he had a right to retake his money, that was a defense to the crime of robbery. He was, however, convicted of assault (*People v. Littleton*, 25 Cal. App. 3d 96).

It is not the original intent but the intent at the time of taking that determines whether or not the crime is robbery. If in the preceding gambling case, the accused, while at first intending to retake only his money, decides at the time of taking to take more than he lost, the crime is robbery.

In *People v. Alvardo* (133 Cal. App. 3d 1003), a robbery conviction was upheld (approved) where the evidence established that the defendants robbed the victim, not to recover property that they had given him in exchange for inferior drugs, but to settle the score. The specific intent to steal can be inferred from the circumstances surrounding the taking of the property.

Completed Crime of Robbery

Robbery is completed when the robber has taken possession of the property and the element of asportation is fulfilled. The intervention of the police before the property has been taken off the premises is immaterial as long as the essential elements are satisfied (*People v. Johnson*, 219 Cal. App. 2d 631).

Lesser and Necessarily Included Offenses

Theft is a lesser and necessarily included offense of robbery, which latter offense includes element of force or fear (*People v. Smith*, 29 Cal. App. 4th 739). Crime of false imprisonment is not, however, a lesser necessarily included offense within crime of robbery, because robbery can occur without a violation of freedom to stand still or be mobile (*People v. Von Villas*, 10 Cal. App. 4th 201).

One defendant could not be convicted of both robbery and grand theft of automobile, merely because he took more than one item of property from the victim when, after forcing his way into the victim's car, he ordered her to give him her money and purse and to exit from vehicle, in which he then drove away; the defendant's theft of the car was a lesser and necessarily included offense of one act of robbery perpetrated on a single victim over a limited period of time (*People v. Irvin*, 230 Cal. App. 3d 180).

Defenses to Robbery

As noted earlier in Section 7-13d it is no defense to a charge of robbery or theft that the victim is not the true owner of property taken; a theft can be committed against one who is himself or herself a thief (*People v. Moore*, 4 Cal. App. 3d 668). A defendant who received facial cuts from broken beer bottle in a fight at a bar and allegedly took money from the cash register because he felt that barmaid who was in charge of the tavern was at fault and that his doctor bills should be paid had no defense to charge of robbery (*People v. Poindexter*, 255 Cal. App. 2d 566). Self-defense is not a defense to a charge of robbery (*People v. Costa*, 218 Cal. App. 2d 310). The return of stolen money to robbery victim does not absolve the thief from guilt (*People v. Tipton*, 96 Cal. App. 2d 840).

The fact that defendant was intoxicated was not a defense in a prosecution for robbery in the absence of evidence that the intoxication was involuntary (*People v. Stephens*, 66 Cal. App. 2d 755).

Penal Code 215—Carjacking

7-13 Carjacking

(a) "Carjacking" is the felonious taking of a motor vehicle in the possession of another, from his or her person or immediate presence, or from the person or immediate presence of a passenger of the motor vehicle, against his or her will and with the intent to either permanently or temporarily deprive the person in possession of the motor vehicle of his or her possession, accomplished by means of force or fear.
(b) Carjacking is punishable by imprisonment in the state prison for a term of three, five, or nine years.
(c) This section shall not be construed to supersede or affect Section 211. A person may be charged with a violation of this section and Section 211. However, no defendant may be punished under this section and Section 211 for the same act which constitutes a violation of both this section and Section 211.

Penal Code 209.5—Kidnapping Pursuant to Carjacking

(a) Any person who, during the commission of a carjacking and in order to facilitate the commission of the carjacking, kidnaps another person who is not a principal in the commission of the carjacking shall be punished by imprisonment in the state prison for life with the possibility of parole.
(b) This section shall only apply if the movement of the victim is beyond that merely incidental to the commission of the carjacking, the victim is moved a substantial distance from the vicinity of the carjacking, and the movement of the victim increases the risk of harm to the victim over and above that necessarily present in the crime of carjacking itself.

(c) In all cases in which probation is granted, the court shall, except in unusual cases where the interests of justice would best be served by a lesser penalty, require as a condition of the probation that the person be confined in the county jail for 12 months. If the court grants probation without requiring the defendant to be confined in the county jail for 12 months, it shall specify its reason or reasons for imposing a lesser penalty.

7-14 Extortion

Penal Code 518—Extortion Defined

Extortion is the obtaining of property from another, with his consent, or the obtaining of an official act of a public officer, induced by wrongful use of force or fear, or under the color of official right.

Penal Code 519—Fear Induced by Threat

Fear, such as will constitute extortion, may be induced by a threat, either

1. To do an unlawful injury to the person or property of the individual threatened or of a third person; or
2. To accuse the individual threatened, or any relative of his, or member of his family, of any crime; or
3. To expose, or to impute to him or them any deformity, disgrace, or crime; or
4. To expose any secret affecting him or them.

Penal Code 521—When under Color of Office

Every person who commits any extortion under color of official right, in cases for which a different punishment is not prescribed in this code, is guilty of a misdemeanor.

Penal Code 522—Extorting Signature to Transfer of Property

Every person who, by any extortionate means, obtains from another his signature to any paper or instrument, whereby, if such signature were freely given, any property would be transferred, or any debt, demand, charge, or right of action created, is punishable in the same manner as if the actual delivery of such debt, demand, charge, or right of action were obtained.

Penal Code 523—Written Threat Made to Extort

Every person who, with intent to extort any money or other property from another, sends or delivers to any person any letter or other writing, whether subscribed or not, expressing or implying, or adapted to imply, any threat such as is specified in Section 519, is punishable in the same manner as if such money or property were actually obtained by means of such threat.

7-14a Definition

Common law extortion is defined as taking money or other valuable thing either by compulsion, by actual force, or by force or motives applied to the will and often more overpowering and irresistible than physical force (*Commonwealth v. O'Brien*, 12 Cush. Mass. 90). Extortion is popularly known as blackmail. Both extortion and robbery are aggravated forms of theft. Extortion, however, is broader than robbery in the following ways.

- Extortion does not require a taking of the property from the presence or possession of the victim.

- Extortion does not require that the threat be of immediate harm as in robbery.
- The types of harms that constitute extortion are much broader than those covered in the robbery statute.
- Robbery pertains only to personal property, whereas extortion can involve real property.
- With extortion, the victim "consents" to the turning over of the property or money.

The following are elements of the crime of extortion:

1. The act of obtaining property or money from another
2. With the consent of the other, or
3. Obtaining an official act of a public officer,
4. By inducement through wrongful use of force or fear
5. Under color of official right.

7-14b Elements

Extortion may be committed to obtain property or an official act of a public officer. The property requirement is broadly interpreted. A threat to expose the victim unless the victim withdrew an appeal in a pending civil law suit was considered property in one case (*People v. Cadman*, 57 Cal. 562). Extortion is a crime that involves moral turpitude (*In re Coffey*, 123 Cal. 522). To be extortion, the threat must imply or express one of the statutory threats listed in Section 519 (*People v. Choynski*, 95 Cal. 640).

At common law, "extortion" was confined to the unlawful taking by any officer, by color of his office, of any money or thing of value not due him, or more than his due, or before it was due, but under this section, the crime may be committed by any person (*People v. Peck*, 43 Cal. App. 638).

As one court explained: Extortion is the obtaining of property from another, with his consent, induced by a wrongful use of force or fear, or under a color of official right, and "fear" such as will constitute extortion may be induced by threat to do an unlawful injury to person threatened, to accuse him of any crime, or to expose or to impute to him any disgrace or crime (*People v. Goodman*, 159 Cal. App. 2d 54).

It is a necessary ingredient of the crime of extortion, or the attempt to commit extortion, that a threat be used (*Mitchell v. Sharon*, 59 F. 980). By definition, extortion punishes conditional threats, specifically those in which victim complies with mandated condition (*People v. Stanfield*, 32 Cal. App. 4th 1152).

To constitute extortion, the wrongful use of fear must be the operating cause producing consent (*People v. Beggs*, 178 Cal. 79). The threat to imprison another, or to detain another in prison without any ground, constitutes the offense of extortion as a threat to do unlawful injury to that person (*People v. Phillips*, 10 Cal. App. 2d 457).

Although robbery and extortion both have roots in common law larceny and share the element of acquisition by means of force or fear, property is taken from another against his will in robbery, whereas in extortion, property is taken from another with his or her consent. Robbery requires felonious taking, which means a specific intent to permanently deprive the victim of property, and also requires property to be taken from the victim's person or immediate presence, whereas extortion does not require proof of either of these elements; however, extortion requires a specific intent of inducing the victim to consent to part with his or her property (*People v. Torres*, 33 Cal. App. 4th 37).

7-14c Discussion

Consent

The crime of extortion is committed only when the property is obtained with the consent of the owner, and this consent must be induced by an unlawful use of force or fear; PC 518 can only mean that the unlawful use of force or fear must be the operating or controlling cause that produces the consent, and if some other cause were the primary and controlling one in inducing the consent, then there would be no extortion (*People v. Williams,* 127 Cal. 212).

Threats Inducing Fear

The threats inducing fear may include the following:

- Threat to injure person or property
- To accuse one of a crime
- To defame or expose
- To expose a secret

No precise or particular form of words is necessary to constitute a threat within PC 518; rather, threats can be made by innuendo and the circumstances under which the threat is uttered and relations between parties may be considered when determining the question involved (*People v. Massengale,* 261 Cal. App. 2d 758).

The "threat to accuse one of a crime" is extortion, "if other elements are present," even if the person is in fact guilty of the crime. The motives of the person making the threat make no difference. Accordingly, a just motive for making the threat is normally not a defense to extortion. For example, it is extortion for a person from whom property was stolen to threaten the thief with prosecution unless the thief pays for the property (*People v. Beggs,* 178 Cal. 79).

The threat to expose a secret must be such that it is unfavorable to the reputation of the person exposed or defamed. The secret normally must be unknown to the general public, or some particular part thereof, that others might be interested in obtaining. The damage of the exposure must be such that it would likely induce a person through fear to pay out money or give up property to avoid the exposure (*People v. Lavine,* 115 Cal. App. 289).

Intent Required

To commit the offense of extortion, there must be *specific intent* to commit the crime, and direct ineffectual act done toward its commission, but the effect produced on the person at whom the act is directed is immaterial (*People v. Franquelin,* 9 Cal. App. 2d 777). Whether the person making the threat is guilty of an attempt to commit extortion depends on his or her conduct and intent, regardless of the effect on the person threatened (*People v. Robinson,* 130 Cal. App. 664).

One defendant did not commit, or intend to commit, crime of extortion as defined by PC 518 when, after obtaining a gun, he ordered police officers who held him in custody to drive him to a safe haven and release him (*People v. Norris,* 40 Cal. 3d 51).

There is no good-faith exception based on rightfulness of claim to money, for extortion or kidnapping for ransom (*People v. Serrano,* 11 Cal. App. 4th 1672).

Sending Threatening Letters

The offense of sending threatening letters does not require that the threat be apparent on the face of the writing. The prosecution may produce evidence of the facts surrounding the writings to establish the nature of the threat. It is enough if the writings use language that implies any of the threats specified in PC 519. This offense is completed at the time that the letter is deposited in the mail or the writing is delivered. The offense is punishable in the same manner as if the property were actually obtained (*People v. Choynski,* 95 Cal. 640). Extortion is not committed by a creditor sending a letter to a debtor threatening to take legal action if the debt is not paid (*Murray Showcase & Fixture Co. v. Sullivan,* 15 Cal. App. 475).

Any transfers of property or right of action transferred under threat of extortion is void. In addition, the threat of extortion is punishable as extortion, that is, as if the actual delivery of the property or right of action were obtained (*People v. Peppercorn,* 34 Cal. App. 2d 603). This crime is complete when a signature is obtained (*People v. Massengale,* 10 Cal. App. 3d 689). The obtaining of a written confession regarding a crime is not a violation of this offense, since a confession is neither property nor an instrument that creates a right of action (*People v. Kohn,* 258 Cal. App. 2d 368).

Cases on Point

People v. Daniels (18 Cal. App. 4th 1046)

Evidence that the defendant pointed a gun at everyone in living room and told them to get down was sufficient to support the inference that the defendant's conduct was a conditional threat constituting an assault.

People v. Pena (25 Cal. App. 3d 414)

To constitute assault, there must be physical means to accomplish an injury.

People v. Corson (221 Cal. App. 2d 579)

To constitute assault there must be specific intent to commit battery and an act that is close to accomplishment and not mere preparation.

People v. Yslas (27 Cal. 630)

An intent to commit violence, accompanied by acts that, if not interrupted, will be followed by personal injury, is sufficient to constitute an assault, although the assailant may not be at any time within striking distance.

People v. McMakin (8 Cal. 547)

The drawing of a pistol on another, accompanied by a threat to use it, unless the other immediately leaves the spot, is an assault, even if the pistol is not pointed at the person threatened.

People v. Stanfield (32 Cal. App. 4th 1152)

A conditional threat can be punished as an assault when the condition imposed must be performed immediately, the defendant has no right to impose the condition, the intent is to immediately enforce performance by violence, and the defendant places himself or herself in a position to do so and proceeds as far as is then necessary.

People v. Vaiza (244 Cal. App. 2d 121)

Threatening to shoot another with a toy gun does not constitute assault because there is no ability to commit violence or any injury with it on the person of another.

People v. Herrera (6 Cal. App. 3d 846)

The term "violent injury" used in defining an assault is not synonymous with the term "bodily harm" but includes any wrongful act committed by means of physical force against the person of another.

People v. Grant (8 Cal. App. 4th 1105)

For purposes of conviction of sexual battery, "unlawful restraint" does not require showing that physical restraint occurred.

A defendant "unlawfully restrained" a victim within the meaning of the sexual battery statute, even though he did not use physical force against her, when he presented himself as an authority figure, removed the victim from car, ordered her boyfriend to remain in car, and threatened the victim and her boyfriend that they could be taken away by police if they did not cooperate; the defendant's conduct forced the victim to remain in a location in which she did not voluntarily wish to be and that restraint was not accomplished by lawful authority.

People v. Ferrell (218 Cal. App. 3d 828)

A defendant may at the same time intend to both kill his victim and to disable or disfigure that victim (mayhem) if the attempt to kill is unsuccessful.

Practicum

Practicum I

Joe needs money. He takes his mother's purse from her hands. She resists, but he overpowers her. To keep her from reporting the crime, he requires her to accompany him to his cabin. He then agrees to let her go if she will sign a statement indicating that she had given him the money taken from the purse as a Christmas present. He then sends his creditors a copy of a document that looks like a court order. The letter appears to be a court order directing them to stop bothering him. What crimes has he committed?

Practicum II

Jerry Lopez lost a prize fight when his opponent hit him in the head. Jerry then stormed into his dressing room, obtained some chemicals that are used to stop bleeding, and threw them in the direction of his opponent. The chemicals hit a person sitting at ringside. Jerry then brandished a weapon and demanded a rematch. What crimes, if any, did Jerry commit?

Discussion Questions

1. The owner of a store put a bag of money down beside his car and went back into his store to get the car keys. When the owner returned, he encountered the defendant who had the money in one hand and a gun in the other. The defendant ordered the store owner to move away, got into the car, and left. Do the above facts support the offense of robbery or only theft? (Facts taken from the case of *People v. Perhab,* 92 Cal. App. 2d 430)

2. The defendants forced a bank manager at gunpoint to take money from the vault. The manager then carried the money to the rear of the bank in order to give it to the defendants. The defendants were apprehended before receiving the money from the manager. Has the crime of robbery been completed? (Facts taken from the case of *People v. Price,* 25 Cal. App. 3d 576)

3. What degree of force is necessary to constitute robbery by force?
4. Define *asportation*.
5. Is robbery a specific intent crime?
6. Differentiate between robbery and extortion?
7. Define *immediate presence* for purposes of the robbery statutes.
8. Explain the differences between an assault and a battery.
9. What is meant by the term *apparent present ability*?

10. What constitutes a violent injury for purposes of the assault and battery crimes?
11. Define *offensive touching*.
12. What is the gist of the crime of mayhem?
13. Under what circumstances is consent a defense to battery?
14. Distinguish between the types of intent required to establish simple assault and assault with an intent to commit mayhem.

Self-Study Quiz

True/False

1. Robbery is the felonious taking of real property from the possession of another.
2. Robbery requires that the taking of the property be by means of force or fear.
3. Robbery of a train conductor is first-degree robbery.
4. Robbery of an elderly person is first-degree robbery.
5. Robbery in California is both a crime against the person and the property.
6. To be robbery, the property taken must be worth at least $50.
7. The property must be in the immediate possession of the owner to be subject to the crime of robbery.
8. To be robbery, force or fear must be used to take the property.
9. The requirement of asportation is very similar to the same requirement in theft cases.
10. It is necessary that the accused take actual physical custody of the property before the crime of robbery is completed.
11. Robbery is not a specific intent crime.
12. Extortion is the obtaining of property from another by use of force or fear and without the consent of the possessor of the property.
13. Extortion does not require a taking of property from the immediate presence of the victim.

14. Robbery pertains only to personal property, whereas extortion may also pertain to real property.
15. To be extortion, the threat must be of immediate harm to the victim.
16. An assault is an attempt to inflict violent injury upon another person by some form of contact.
17. An assault is an attempt to commit a battery.
18. To be an assault, the attempt to commit a violent injury must be unlawful.
19. Consent is a defense to battery.
20. Pointing an unloaded weapon at a person is not an assault.
21. Violent injury has a special meaning in assault and battery cases.
22. Simple assault is normally used to denote a felony assault.
23. Assault with a deadly weapon is a specific intent crime.
24. Battery is a general intent crime.
25. Mayhem is a form of aggravated battery.
26. To be mayhem, the injury must disfigure the victim.
27. Threatening a person with an unloaded weapon is not a crime in California.

Crimes against Persons: Kidnapping, Homicide, Elder Abuse, and Stalking

If you can't do time, don't do the crime.
John Morgan, *after being sentenced to seven years imprisonment*

Truth will come to light; murder cannot be hid long.
Shakespeare, Merchant of Venice

8-1 Kidnapping

Penal Code 207—Definition of Kidnapping

(a) Every person who forcibly, or by any other means of instilling fear, steals or takes, or holds, detains, or arrests any person in this state, and carries the person into another country, state, or county, or into another part of the same county, is guilty of kidnapping.

(b) Every person, who for the purpose of committing any act defined in Section 288, hires, persuades, entices, decoys, or seduces by false promises, misrepresentations, or the like, any child under the age of 14 years to go out of this country, state, or county, or into another part of the same county, is guilty of kidnapping.

(c) Every person who forcibly, or by any other means of instilling fear, takes or holds, detains, or arrests any person, with a design to take the person out of this state, without having established a claim, according to the laws of the United States, or of this state, or who hires, persuades, entices, decoys, or seduces by false promises, misrepresentations, or the like, any person to go out of this state, or to be taken or removed therefrom, for the purpose and with the intent to sell that person into slavery or involuntary servitude, or otherwise to employ that person for his or her own use, or to the use of another, without the free will and consent of that persuaded person, is guilty of kidnapping.

(d) Every person who, being out of this state, abducts or takes by force or fraud any person contrary to the law of the place where that act is committed, and brings, sends, or conveys that person within the limits of this state, and is afterwards found within the limits thereof, is guilty of kidnapping.

(e) Subdivisions (a) to (d), inclusive, do not apply to any of the following:

(1) To any person who steals, takes, entices away, detains, conceals, or harbors any child under the age of 14 years, if that act is taken to protect the child from danger of imminent harm.

(2) To any person acting under Section 834 or 837 [lawful arrests].

8-1a Kidnapping and False-Imprisonment-Related Crimes

The following are crimes related to kidnapping and false imprisonment and the Penal Code sections that apply to them.

- Kidnapping (PC 207)
- False Imprisonment (PC 236)
- Posing as a Kidnapper (PC 210)
- Kidnapping Child Under 14 (PC 667.85)
- Kidnapping for Purposes of Sexual Offense (PC 667.8)
- Kidnapping for Ransom or Reward (PC 209)
- Taking Hostages (PC 210.5)

- Malicious Taking of a Child (PC 277)
- Unlawful Detention (PC 278)
- Violation of Custody Decree (PC 278.5)

At common law, kidnapping involved the forcible asportation (carrying away) of a person from his or her own county to another. In California, the statutory crime of kidnapping requires only the movement of a person from one part of a county to another part. Accordingly, kidnapping by force is the unlawful, forcible taking of a person against his or her will from one place to another.

8-1b Definition

Under Penal Code 207, there are four different crimes of kidnapping in California. The elements of each are set forth in the following:

8-1c Elements

1. Forcible Kidnapping [PC 207(a)] elements:

    a. The unlawful movement by force
    b. Of a person by another
    c. Against the person's will
    d. From one place to another

2. Kidnap with Intent to Commit PC 288 Felony (crimes against children, lewd and lascivious acts) [PC 207(b)] elements:

    a. Hiring, persuading, decoying, enticing, seducing, by false promises, mis-representations, or the like of
    b. A child under the age of 14 years
    c. To go from one place to another
    d. With the intent to commit a violation of PC 288 [crimes against children, lewd and lascivious acts]

3. Kidnapping with Intent to Take Out of State [PC 207(c)] elements:

    a. A forcible taking or arresting of another
    b. With the specific intent to remove the person from the state
    c. Without legal authority

4. Bringing Kidnapped Victim Into State [PC 207(d)] elements:

    a. The unlawful abduction or taking of a victim in another state
    b. Bringing the victim into this state

The movement required to constitute the offense of kidnapping must be unlawful. Movement is *not* unlawful if accomplished pursuant to a legal arrest or with the valid consent of the victim. The term *unlawful* means only that the victim has not given consent and the movement is not pursuant to a valid legal order or court process.

8-1d Discussion

Force

The force required to constitute the offense is sufficient as long as the victim feels compelled to obey and reasonably fears some kind of harm will occur if the force is used. No physical force or express threats are needed to effectuate the movement (*People v. Caudillo*, 21 Cal. 3d 562). If the kidnapping starts in a vehicle, the victim's initial consent to enter the vehicle is immaterial as long as the victim is subsequently restrained during movement of the automobile (*People v. Galvin*, 187 Cal. App. 3d 1205).

If the victim consents to the movement, even if the consent was obtained by fraud, the crime is not kidnapping under PC 207 (a), (c), and (d). Only movements accomplished by force are material to the offense of forcible kidnapping under PC 207 (*People v. Stephenson*, 10 Cal. 3d 652). In one case, the defendant's tricking a victim into believing she was simply being taken on a quick trip to her sister's house and back constituted asportation by fraud and was insufficient to support conviction for kidnapping (*People v. Green*, 27 Cal. 3d 1). A taking is forcible within the meaning of this section where it is accomplished by giving orders that the victim feels compelled to obey because he or she fears harm or injury from defendant, and victim's apprehension is not unreasonable under the circumstances (*People v. Dagampat*, 167 Cal. App. 2d 492).

Where a victim of an alleged kidnapping has at first willingly accompanied the accused, the accused might nevertheless be guilty of kidnapping if he or she subsequently restrains the victim's liberty by force and compels the victim to accompany him further (*People v. Gallagher*, 164 Cal. App. 2d 414).

Movement

The statute does not define the distance required to constitute the offense of kidnapping. The courts have had difficulty with this element, caused by the common law requirement that the victim be taken to another county. PC 207 requires only that the movement be to a different county or "another part of the county." Based on this phrase, the courts have required that the "movement" necessary to complete the offense of kidnapping must be substantial as opposed to slight or trivial.

Substantial movement was defined by one court as the movement that subjects the victim to a substantial increase in the risk of harm. A movement of one city block was considered sufficient, whereas the movement of the victim across a room or from a vehicle to a storefront was not (*People v. Maxwell*, 94 Cal. App. 3d 562). In one case, forcing a victim at gunpoint to walk one-quarter mile was considered as substantial movement (*People v. Stanworth*, 11 Cal. 3rd 601). In another case, dragging a victim from the front of a laundromat to the rear to sexually assault her was considered insufficient movement to constitute kidnapping (*People v. Thornton*, 11 Cal. 3d 738).

In *People v. Bradley* (15 Cal. App. 4th 1144), however, the court held that the defendant's movement of the victim was sufficiently substantial to support conviction for kidnapping with intent to commit rape; the victim was moved 50 to 60 feet from an open street and was forcibly led around building to the inside of enclosed dumpster area that was separate structure. Distance, in and of itself, is not the only factor probative of asportation for purposes of kidnapping with the intent to commit rape; consideration must be given to the change in surroundings between the point of capture and the destination. Arbitrary boundaries established by buildings or other enclosures, ownership of property, fences, and other points of reference vary in size and distance and, thus, movement cannot be determined simply by reference to those boundaries for purposes of kidnapping with intent to commit rape. If all the elements are present except substantial movement, the offense may be an "attempted kidnapping."

A two-prong test is used to establish forcible kidnapping (*People v. Caudillo*, 21 Cal. 3d 562):

- Was the movement by compulsion?
- Was the movement substantial?

It is the forcible removal of one person by another that constitutes the essence of kidnapping, and the harm contemplated by PC 207 occurs at least as much when the victim is forced to do the driving as when the defendant does it (*People v. Salazar*, 108 Cal. App. 3d 992).

For the offense of kidnapping to be committed, only forcible movement of victim is necessary, and there need be no actual movement beyond the area in which the victim intended to travel voluntarily prior to his or her forcible transportation (*People v. Rich*, 177 Cal. App. 2d 617).

Intent to Take Victim out of State

The offense of kidnapping with the intent to take the victim out of the state (PC 207[c]) is designed, in part, to prevent law enforcement officers from unlawfully taking suspects out of the state to avoid extradition laws. For example, if the police from another state locate a person wanted in that state living in California, they cannot cross state lines and forcibly take the person out of California without going through the required legal process.

Intent

Simple kidnapping is a general intent crime. As one court noted, the legislature did not intend to change simple kidnapping from a general intent crime to a specific intent crime by adding the phrase taking person "by any other means of instilling fear" (*People v. Moya*, 4 Cal. App. 4th 912). In one case, evidence showing, *inter alia*, that the defendant seized a 13-year-old girl by the hair and head, ordered her into an automobile whose motor was running, and threatened to strike her if she refused was sufficient to establish the requisite intent and affirmative act required to constitute the crime of attempted kidnapping (*People v. Fields*, 56 Cal. App. 3d 954).

Lesser Included Crimes

False imprisonment is necessarily a lesser included offense of kidnapping so that the defendant cannot be convicted of both offenses (*People v. Magana*, 230 Cal. App. 3d 1117). Simple kidnapping also is a lesser offense included within the crime of kidnapping with the intent to commit robbery (*People v. Bailey*, 38 Cal. App. 3d 693).

Penal Code 236—False Imprisonment Defined

False imprisonment is the unlawful violation of the personal liberty of another.

The following are the elements of false imprisonment:

1. The unlawful violation
2. Of the personal liberty of another

The essential element in false imprisonment is the restraint of the person (*Hanna v. Raphael Weill & Co.*, 90 Cal. App. 2d 461). Some restraint of the person is essential to false imprisonment, but depriving another of his or her liberty by any exercise of force or express or implied threat of force, or thereby compelling the person to remain where he or she does not wish to remain or to go constitutes false imprisonment (*People v. Zilbauer*, 44 Cal. 2d 43).

8-2 False Imprisonment

8-2a Elements

8-2b Discussion

False imprisonment is always a lesser and included offense of the offense of kidnapping (*People v. Maxwell*, 94 Cal. App. 3d 562). False imprisonment is a misdemeanor unless it is committed by violence, menace, fraud, or deceit. If so committed, it is a felony (PC 237). False imprisonment, unlike forcible kidnapping, is not considered an inherently dangerous felony by the courts. Accordingly, the felony-murder rule does not apply (*People v. Henderson,* 19 Cal. 3d 86).

Any exercise of force, express or implied, by which another person is deprived of liberty or freedom of movement, or is compelled to remain where he or she does not wish to remain or does not wish to go, is imprisonment, the within meaning of crime of false imprisonment; confinement in some type of enclosed space is not required (*People v. Fernandez,* 26 Cal. App. 4th 710).

Misdemeanor false imprisonment is a lesser included offense of felony false imprisonment, since all elements of misdemeanor are also elements of felony, and felony cannot be committed without necessarily committing misdemeanor (*People v. Babich,* 14 Cal. App. 4th 801).

Although it is not essential that a motive on the part of defendant be established to show the crime of false imprisonment, a motive on his or her part is an important circumstance to be considered in determining the facts (*People v. Hernon,* 106 Cal. App. 2d 638).

Intent

False imprisonment is a general intent crime. False imprisonment requires only general criminal intent, that the defendant intended to commit an act, the natural probable and foreseeable consequence of which was the nonconsensual confinement of another (*People v. Olivencia,* 204 Cal. App. 3d 1391).

8-3 False Imprisonment for Purposes of Shield

Penal Code 210.5—False Imprisonment for Purposes of Protection from Arrest or Use As Shield

Every person who commits the offense of false imprisonment, as defined in Section 236, against a person for purposes of protection from arrest, which substantially increases the risk of harm to the victim, or for purposes of using the person as a shield is punishable by imprisonment in the state prison for three, five, or eight years.

8-3a Discussion

PC 210.5 is designed to discourage criminals from using others as shields or to prevent being arrested. To constitute the crime, however, there must be a threat or risk of imminent arrest. As one court stated, "A robbery defendant who tied victim to fence could not be convicted under statute proscribing false imprisonment for purpose of protection from arrest or use as a shield, absent evidence of threat or risk of imminent arrest" (*People v. Gomez,* 2 Cal. App. 4th 819).

8-4 Posing As Kidnapper

Penal Code 210—Extortion by Posing as Kidnapper or by Claiming Ability to Obtain Release of Victim; Punishment; Exception

Every person who for the purpose of obtaining any ransom or reward, or to extort or exact from any person any money or thing of value, poses as, or in any manner represents himself to be a person who has seized, confined, inveigled, enticed, decoyed, abducted, concealed, kidnapped, or carried away any person, or who poses as, or in any manner represents himself to be a person who holds or detains such person, or who poses as or in any manner represents himself to be a person who has aided or abetted any such act, or who poses as or in any manner represents himself to be a person who has the influence, power, or ability, to obtain the release of such person so seized, confined, inveigled, enticed, decoyed, abducted, concealed, kidnapped, or carried away, is guilty of a felony and upon conviction thereof shall be punished by imprisonment for two, three, or four years.

Nothing in this section prohibits any person who, in good faith, believes that he can rescue any person who has been seized, confined, inveigled, enticed, decoyed, abducted, concealed, kidnapped, or carried away, and who has had no part in, or connection with, such confinement, inveigling, decoying, abducting, concealing, kidnapping, or carrying away, from offering to rescue or obtain the release of such person for a monetary consideration or other thing of value.

8-4a Discussion

PC 210 is designed to prevent persons trying to profit from a kidnapping. It does not require that the purported kidnap victim have been actually kidnapped (*People v. Alday,* 10 Cal. 3d 392).

8-5 Kidnapping for Purposes of Committing Sexual Offense

Penal Code 667.8 provides for a sentence enhancement if convicted of kidnapping for the purposes of committing sexual offense. PC 667.8(a) provides, in part, that any person convicted of kidnapping in violation of PC 207 or 209 shall be punished by an additional (prison) term of nine years.

Penal Code 667.85—Prison Term for Kidnapping Child under 14 Years

8-6 Kidnapping Child under 14

Any person convicted of a violation of Section 207, who kidnapped or carried away any child under the age of 14 years with the intent to permanently deprive the parent or legal guardian custody of that child, shall be punished by an additional term of five years.

Penal Code 209—Kidnapping for Ransom, Reward, Extortion, or Robbery; Punishment

8-7 Kidnapping for Ransom, Reward, Extortion, or Robbery

(a) Any person who seizes, confines, inveigles, entices, decoys, abducts, conceals, kidnaps, or carries away another person by any means whatsoever with intent to hold or detain, or who holds or detains, that person for ransom, reward or to commit extortion or to exact from another person any money or valuable thing, or any person who aids or abets any such act, is guilty of a felony, and upon conviction thereof, shall be punished by imprisonment in the state prison for life without possibility of parole in cases in which any person subjected to any such act suffers death or bodily harm, or is intentionally confined in a manner which exposes such person to a substantial likelihood of death, or shall be punished by imprisonment in the state prison for life with the possibility of parole in cases where no such person suffers death or bodily harm.

(b) Any person who kidnaps or carries away any individual to commit robbery shall be punished by imprisonment in the state prison for life with possibility of parole.

(c) In all cases in which probation is granted, the court shall, except in unusual cases where the interests of justice would best be served by a lesser penalty, require as a condition of the probation that the person be confined in the county jail for 12 months. If the court grants probation without requiring the defendant to be confined in the county jail for 12 months, it shall specify its reason or reasons for imposing a lesser penalty.

8-7a Discussion

Unlike forcible kidnapping (which is a general intent crime), kidnapping for ransom, reward, or extortion is a specific intent crime. To be an offense under PC 209, at the time of the kidnapping, the offender must commit the offense with the specific intent to either rob, extort, or obtain a ransom or reward.

To constitute kidnap for robbery, asportation of victim must be accomplished by force or threat of force and use of fraud or deceit to induce movement is insufficient (*People v. Isitt*, 55 Cal. App. 3d 23).

Specific intent to commit robbery, required to support conviction of kidnapping in furtherance of robbery, must be formed before asportation is undertaken (*In re Gregory S.*, 85 Cal. App. 3d 206). To convict one of kidnapping with intent to commit robbery, the intent must have been formed before the commencement of kidnapping; if the intent to rob was formed after victim was seized, the offense as it relates to kidnapping is simple kidnapping and not kidnapping for the purpose of robbery even though robbery is carried out during the kidnapping (*People v. Bailey*, 38 Cal. App. 3d 693).

Movement

Movements of a victim can constitute kidnapping for the purpose of robbery only if the movements (1) are not merely incidental to the robbery and (2) substantially increase the risk of harm beyond that inherent in the crime of robbery; both prongs of this test must be satisfied (*In re Earley*, 14 Cal. 3d 122). In one case, where two men and a woman were enticed to get voluntarily into the defendant's automobile by deceit or fraud and, though the defendant's intent to commit crimes of robbery against each could reasonably be inferred from evidence, the defendant did not forcibly require any of them to enter his vehicle initially (though the defendant later forcibly required the woman to reenter vehicle against her will and transported her several blocks to commit robbery), the offense of kidnapping for the purpose of robbery was established as to the woman but was not established as to the men (*People v. Stephenson*, 10 Cal. 3d 652).

There is no minimum number of feet defendant must move a victim to satisfy the requirement for movement of victim that is not merely incidental to commission of robbery so as to support conviction of kidnapping for robbery. Forced movement of victim is not a required element of kidnapping for ransom, extortion, or reward (*People v. Rayford*, 9 Cal. 4th 1). Aggravated kidnapping, whether for ransom, extortion, or robbery, warrants use of a two-prong analysis directing the trier of fact to assess whether movement was substantial distance and whether movement substantially increased the risk of injury over and beyond those risks inherent in committing the underlying crime (*People v. Bradley*, 15 Cal. App. 4th 1144).

In *People v. Martin* (250 Cal. App. 2d 263), the defendant who, after robbery, led victims at gunpoint into storeroom about 30 feet away and instructed them to stay put and who in another robbery led a victim at gunpoint to an office about 30 to 35 yards away was properly charged with kidnapping to commit robbery.

In another case, movement of the robbery victim approximately 465 feet was insufficient to support conviction of kidnapping for purposes of robbery where the victim was never forced to move outside of interconnected living quarters shared by him and his parents, and where, although victim was initially confronted with an armed assailant, his subsequent treatment was not violent, he was not injured, and he was moved only on foot from place to place on the grounds and within his home while the crime was continued (*People v. John*, 149 Cal. App. 3d 798).

A defendant was found guilty of "kidnapping for purpose of robbery" in *People v. Norman* (177 Cal. App. 2d 59). In this case, the defendant had forced his way into apartment where he was told by the occupant that her purse was in the bedroom; he had a gun in hand at all times as he ordered the woman to go into bedroom, followed her through a hall about 40 feet, where she found the purse, and took her engagement and wedding rings, which he forced her to remove from her finger, and the woman gave him $8. In another case, movement of the victim from a market for one-half block to a residential area so that the defendant could search victim more fully was brief movement to facilitate robbery, was incidental to robbery, and was not kidnapping for robbery (*People v. Daniels*, 202 Cal. App. 3d 671).

Bodily Harm

In a trial for kidnapping to rob, evidence that victims were blindfolded and bound with copper wire and one of them struck over head showed that they suffered bodily harm, as required by PC 209 to warrant sentence of life imprisonment without possibility of parole (*People v. Britton*, 6 Cal. 2d 1). In prosecution for the kidnapping occupants of a school bus, evidence that several of the kidnapped children suffered nose bleeds, fainting, and stomachaches was insufficient to constitute "bodily harm" within the meaning of this section providing enhanced penalty of life imprisonment without possibility of parole for conviction of kidnapping in which victims suffer bodily harm (*People v. Schoenfeld*, 111 Cal. App. 3d 671).

Bodily harm sufficient to sustain conviction of kidnapping for robbery with bodily harm must either be directly inflicted by kidnapper, or must be the proximate result, the reasonably foreseeable consequence, of the kidnapper's intentional acts (*People v. Isitt*, 55 Cal. App. 3d 23). The phrase *bodily harm* within PC 209 was not intended to include as aggravation self-inflicted injuries suffered by a victim as a consequence of escape or attempt to escape (*People v. Baker*, 231 Cal. App. 2d 301).

Defenses

In *People v. Isitt* (55 Cal. App. 3d 23), the defendant's reasonable good-faith belief that victim had voluntarily consented to accompany him constituted the complete defense to the charge of kidnapping.

To be guilty of kidnapping for the purposes of robbery, there must be substantial movement similar to that required for forcible kidnapping under PC 207. The movement need not, however, be related to the same victim as is the robbery victim, as long as the kidnapping was done to commit robbery. For example, if the accused robs a store owner, then kidnaps a customer to assist in his escape, he is guilty of kidnapping for the purposes of committing robbery.

The offense of kidnapping for the purposes of ransom or extortion, unlike forcible robbery, does not require any movement. Merely holding the person with the specific intent to obtain payment of a ransom or reward or to commit extortion is sufficient to constitute the offense.

Penal Code 401—Suicide; Aiding, Advising, or Encouraging

8-8 Aiding or Encouraging a Suicide

Every person who deliberately aids, or advises, or encourages another to commit suicide, is guilty of a felony.

8-8a Discussion

Suicide is not considered a criminal homicide in California. Attempted suicide is also not a crime in the state. Encouraging another to commit suicide is, however, a felony under PC 401. In a suicide pact where one party survives, the surviving party normally may be tried for encouraging a suicide. Note: This is not the case in murder/suicide situations where the dead party did not intend to commit suicide. In this latter situation, it is probably murder. Also, if the survivor actually commits the death-causing act on the other person, then it is murder even if the act was done at the request of the victim.

8-9 Homicide

Penal Code 187—Murder Defined; Death of Fetus

(a) Murder is the unlawful killing of a human being, or a fetus, with malice aforethought.

(b) This section shall not apply to any person who commits an act which results in the death of a fetus if any of the following apply:

   (1) The act complied with the Therapeutic Abortion Act. . . .
   (2) The act was committed by a holder of a physician's and surgeon's certificate, as defined in the Business and Professions Code, in a case where, to a medical certainty, the result of childbirth would be death of the mother of the fetus or where her death from childbirth, although not medically certain, would be substantially certain or more likely than not.
   (3) The act was solicited, aided, abetted, or consented to by the mother of the fetus.

(c) Subdivision(b) shall not be construed to prohibit the prosecution of any person under any other provision of law.

8-9a Homicide-Related Crimes

The following are crimes related to homicide and the relevant Penal Codes that apply to them.

   • Murder in the First Degree (PC 189)
   • Murder in the Second Degree (PC 189)
   • Voluntary Manslaughter (PC 192a)
   • Involuntary Manslaughter (PC 192b)
   • Vehicular Manslaughter (PC 192c)
   • Aiding Another to Commit Suicide (PC 401)

8-9b Discussion

Homicide is the killing of a human being by another human. Not all homicides are crimes. For example, excusable homicides and justifiable homicides are not crimes. These are discussed later in this chapter. Criminal homicides are those homicides that are crimes (i.e., murder and manslaughter).

8-10 Criminal Homicide

The following crimes are classified as criminal homicides:

   • Murder
      • First-degree murder
      • Second-degree murder

   • Manslaughter
      • Voluntary
      • Involuntary
      • Vehicular

The circumstances surrounding the killing and the mental state of the actor determines, in most cases, the type of criminal homicide involved (*People v. Mar Gin Suie*, 11 Cal. App. 42). All criminal homicides are considered *mala in se* (evil in itself) crimes (*People v. Herbert*, 6 Cal. 2d 541).

The following are elements of criminal homicide:

8-10a Elements

1. A criminal activity (either act or omission)
2. Resulting in the killing of another human being or a fetus

Corpus Delicti

8-10b Discussion

The literal meaning of the term *corpus delicti* is "body of the crime." In criminal homicide, the *corpus delicti* is the death of a human being under criminal circumstances. *Corpus delicti* is the required elements of a particular crime. As one court stated: "The *corpus delicti* of murder consists of death of alleged victim and existence of some criminal agency as cause of death; proof of *corpus delicti* does not, however, require proof of identity of perpetrator of crime" (*People v. Wetzel*, 198 Cal. App. 2d 541). In a murder prosecution it is not necessary for conviction that the body of the victim actually be found (*People v. Cullen*, 37 Cal. 2d 614).

The Killing of a Live Person

The elements of a criminal homicide include the requirement that the human being was "alive" at the time of the act (*People v. Smith*, 215 Cal. 749). An exception to this requirement exists in the case of the killing of a fetus, which is discussed later. A person who has suffered a mortal wound and will die shortly may still be the victim of a criminal homicide by the infliction of a new injury that hastens his death. For example, if the deceased attempts to kill himself and inflicts grave injuries on himself, the act of another in putting the deceased out of his misery is considered a criminal homicide (*People v. Lewis*, 124 Cal. 551).

Under prior statutes, whether the killing of a fetus in a woman's body was a homicide depended on the viability of the fetus. A fetus is "viable" if it is capable of surviving the trauma of birth and living outside of the womb. Viability is no longer an element of crime of fetal homicide; third-party killing of a fetus with malice aforethought is "murder" under PC 187, as long as the state can show that the fetus has progressed beyond the embryonic stage of seven to eight weeks (*People v. Davis*, 7 Cal. 4th 797). The killing of a fetus is not criminal homicide if an abortion is conducted under the Therapeutic Abortion Act or is required for the mother's safety.

Where parties, by mutual understanding, engage in a conflict with deadly weapons, and death ensues to either, the slayer is guilty of murder (*People v. Bush*, 65 Cal. 129). In absence of factors of excuse or justification, the use of fatal physical force or violence against another person is unlawful. As used in various homicide instructions, the word "unlawful" does not signify an affirmative element of offenses; it is instead a negative element, which simply means there is an absence of excuse or justification (*People v. Frye*, 7 Cal. App. 4th 1148).

Time Requirement

At common law, the death must occur within one year and a day after the cause of the death. This has been modified by PC 194, which requires that the death occur within three years and one day after the cause. In those cases where there is a delay between the act or omission causing the death and the death, the date of the act is used for legal purposes. For example, in the case of *People v. Gill* (6 Cal. 63), the death occurred after the enactment of a new statute on criminal homicide, but the act causing the death was prior to the new law. The court held that since it was the date of the act, not the date of death that controlled, the new law did not apply.

Penal Code 194 has been modified—"To make the killing either murder or manslaughter it is *not* requisite that the party die within three years and a day after the stroke received or the cause of death administered. *If death occurs beyond the time of three years and a day, there shall be a rebuttable presumption that the killing was not criminal. The prosecution shall bear the burden of overcoming this presumption.*"

Definition of Death

Inflicting an injury that would otherwise be a fatal injury is not a criminal homicide if the victim is already "brain dead" (*People v. Lewis,* 124 Cal. 551). In California, the brain death concept is used as the definition of death. Health and Safety Code, Section 7180, describes death as "the total and irreversible cessation of brain functions." Accordingly, once the determination of brain death has been made, the person is no longer alive, even if the body is still breathing.

Proximate Cause

Criminal homicide must be the result of an affirmative act, an omission to act, or criminal negligence. The act causing the death, however, need not be the only cause of death (*People v. Fowler,* 178 Cal. 657 and *People v. Lewis,* 124 Cal. 551). For homicide liability to be found, the cause of harm not only must be direct, but also must not be so remote as to fail to constitute natural and probable consequence of the defendant's act (*People v. Roberts,* 2 Cal. 4th 271). Murder is never more than a shortening of life; if a defendant's culpable act has decreased the span of human life, the law will not hear him or her say that the victim would have died in any event (*People v. Phillips,* 64 Cal. 2d 574).

The death must be the proximate result of a human act. It need not, however, be the direct result. Proximate cause means that the death was a natural and probable consequence of the act. The test is "if the original act had not occurred, would the victim have died?" For example, if the victim is shot by the accused resulting in a nonfatal wound, but the victim dies on the operating table as the result of shock, the shooting is the "proximate cause" of the death (*People v. Freudenberg,* 121 Cal. App. 2d 564). In *People v. Moan* (65 Cal. 532), the victim, being quite ill, suffered an injury that accelerated his death. The injury was considered the proximate cause of his death.

In another case, a murder defendant was not entitled to the instruction that the finding of proximate cause required proof that the conduct in question produced a significant decrease in the span of the victim's life where there was no issue of intervening and/or superseding causes independent of the defendant's conduct (*People v. Ainsworth,* 45 Cal. 3d 984).

Concurring and Intervening Causes of Death

Where concurring causes contribute to a victim's death, one may be criminally liable by reason of his or her own conduct that directly contributes to the fatal result (*People v. Ross,* 92 Cal. App. 3d 391). When the conduct of two or more persons contributes concurrently as the proximate cause of death, the conduct of each person is a proximate cause regardless of the extent to which each contributes to the death (*People v. Vernon,* 89 Cal. App. 3d 853).

In one case, the court held that the removal of artificial life-support systems from a homicide victim after all electrical activity in the brain had ceased was not an independent, intervening cause of death that relieved the defendant of criminal responsibility (*People v. Saldana*, 47 Cal. App. 3d 954). A delay in treatment of deceased is not in fact an intervening force and is not in law a supervening cause of death that would relieve a defendant from criminal responsibility for shooting the deceased (*People v. McGee*, 187 P. 2d 706). An accused is not guilty of murder, however, in a case where death is caused by grossly erroneous medical or surgical treatment rather than by the wound itself.

Penal Code 189—Murder; Degrees

8-11 Murder

All murder which is perpetrated by means of a destructive device or explosive, knowing use of ammunition designed primarily to penetrate metal or armor, poison, lying in wait, torture, or by any other kind of willful, deliberate, and premeditated killing, or which is committed in the perpetration of, or attempt to perpetrate, arson, rape, carjacking, robbery, burglary, mayhem, kidnapping, train wrecking, or any act punishable under Section 206, 286, 288, 288a, or 289, or any murder which is perpetrated by means of discharging a firearm from a motor vehicle, intentionally at another person outside of the vehicle with the intent to inflict death, is murder of the first degree. All other kinds of murders are of the second degree.

As used in this section, *destructive device* means any destructive device as defined in Section 12301, and *explosive* means any explosive as defined in Section 12000 of the Health and Safety Code.

To prove the killing was deliberate and premeditated, it shall not be necessary to prove the defendant maturely and meaningfully reflected upon the gravity of his or her act.

The manner and means employed to accomplish the killing are important considerations in determining the degree of murder (*People v. Mulqueen*, 9 Cal. App. 3d 532). The difference between first- and second-degree murder is basically one of the amount of the offender's personal turpitude, but this amount is measured by the character of the particular homicide involved (*People v. Caylor*, 259 Cal. App. 2d 191). Second-degree murder is a lesser included offense of first-degree murder (*People v. Cooper*, 53 Cal. 3d 771). A specific intent to kill is not a necessary element of second-degree murder, nor is it necessary to establish malice (*People v. Alvarado*, 232 Cal. App. 3d 501).

8-11a Discussion

Defense of Necessity and Duress

Necessity is not a defense to any crime that involves taking the life of an innocent person (*People v. Fields*, 30 Cal. App. 4th 1731). Duress may be used, however, to reduce first-degree murder to a lesser offense (e.g., second-degree murder). In one case, in absence of substantial evidence of the immediacy of threatened harm, the defendant was not entitled to the instruction that the duress could negate the mental states necessary for first-degree murder; that is, the defendant's vague and unsubstantiated assertion that the Columbian Mafia had threatened to kill him and members of his family if he did not kill his victims did not constitute substantial evidence that the threat of death to defendant and his family was imminent (*People v. Bacigalupo*, 1 Cal. 4th 103).

Penal Code 188—Malice, Express Malice, and Implied Malice Defined

Such malice may be express or implied. It is *express* when there is manifested a deliberate intention unlawfully to take away the life of a fellow creature. It is *implied*, when no considerable provocation appears, or when the circumstances attending the killing show an abandoned and malignant heart.

When it is shown that the killing resulted from the intentional doing of an act with express or implied malice as defined above, no other mental state need be shown to establish the mental state of malice aforethought. Neither an awareness of the obligation to act within the general body of laws regulating society nor acting despite such awareness is included within the definition of malice.

8-11b Discussion

As noted in PC 188, malice may be expressed or implied. It is expressed when there is manifested a deliberate unlawful intention to take away the life of another. It is implied when no considerable provocation appears or when the circumstances attending the killing show an "abandoned and malignant heart." In one case, malice needed to support murder conviction was evidenced by circumstances indicating that the killing was proximately caused by the act, the natural consequences of which are dangerous to life, which act was deliberately performed by a person who knew that his conduct endangered the life of another and who acted with conscious disregard for life (*People v. Mills*, 1 Cal. App. 4th 898).

When it is shown that the killing results from the intentional doing of an act with expressed implied malice as defined at the beginning of this section, no other mental state needs to be shown to establish malice aforethought (*People v. Semone*, 140 Cal. App. 318).

Intent

The concept of specific intent relates to murder in two ways: (1) a specific intent to kill is a necessary element to first-degree murder based on willful, deliberate and premeditated killing, and (2) a specific intent to kill is necessary to establish express malice (*People v. Alvarado*, 232 Cal. App. 3d 501). Under the statutory definition of *malice*, the word *unlawfully* modifies the word *intend* so that the statute requires the intent to act unlawfully or that defendant must have wrongful intent (*In re Christian S.*, 7 Cal. 4th 768). Although murder is a "specific intent" crime, specific intent to kill is not an independent element of crime (*People v. Alvarado*, 232 Cal. App. 3d 501).

The intent that is required for first-degree murder, as well as voluntary manslaughter, is to kill, not to murder (*People v. Fusselman*, 46 Cal. App. 3d 289). Deliberate intent is not an essential element of murder as such but is an essential element only of first-degree murder, and not at all an element of second-degree murder (*People v. Goodman*, 8 Cal. App. 3d 705). One can commit murder even when he or she has no intent to kill or injure (*People v. Laws*, 12 Cal. App. 4th 786). Intent to kill may be inferred from the circumstances of an unlawful act resulting in killing (*People v. Garcia*, 2 Cal. 2d 573).

Malice Aforethought

Malice aforethought is an essential element of the crime of murder (*People v. Holt*, 25 Cal. 2d 59). The difference between murder and manslaughter is the presence or absence of malice aforethought. The malice may be either expressed or implied. Except for those cases involving implied malice, there must either be an intent to kill or an intent to commit acts likely to kill with a conscious disregard for human life (*People v. Washington*, 62 Cal. 2d 777). As stated by one court: "Malice aforethought, which is ordinarily used to distinguish between murder and manslaughter, denotes purpose and design in contradistinction to accident or mischance, but does not imply deliberation or lapse of considerable time between the malicious intent to take life and its actual execution" (*People v. Wells*, 33 Cal. 2d 330). Where there is nothing showing provocation or justification for homicide, malice will be implied (*People v. Cole*, 47 Cal. 2d 99).

Implied malice, for purposes of a murder charge, requires proof that the accused acted deliberately with conscious disregard for life and contemplates subjective awareness of a higher degree of risk than does gross negligence and involves an element of wantonness that is absent in gross negligence (*People v. Contreras*, 26 Cal. App. 4th 944).

Malice aforethought as required in second-degree murder is not synonymous with the term "deliberate" as used in defining first-degree murder (*People v. Washington*, 58 Cal. App. 3d 620. The mental state comprising malice is independent of that encompassed within the willful, deliberate, and premeditated concepts that are elements of first-degree murder (*People v. Sedeno*, 10 Cal. 3d 703).

For express malice, all that is required is the intent to kill. It does not require any ill will or hatred toward the victim (*People v. Bender*, 27 Cal. 2d 164). The intent to kill may be formed at any time prior to or at the time of the act. Accordingly, the intent to kill may be formed at the time that the death-causing act is administered (*People v. Jamarillo*, 57 Cal. 111). A trial court is not required to find that a defendant acted with a wanton disregard for human life or with some antisocial motivation in order to find the requisite malice aforethought (*People v. Stress*, 205 Cal. App. 3d 1259). Malice aforethought is found where one acts with wanton disregard for human life by doing an act that more than likely will result in death (*People v. Matta*, 57 Cal. App. 3d 472).

Premeditation

Under California law, premeditation is not established by a reference to time as much as it focuses on the level of reflection; a calculated judgment may be arrived at very quickly (*Bloom v. Vasquez*, 840 F. Supp. 1362). For purposes of committing first-degree murder, premeditation can occur in a short period of time (*People v. Francisco*, 22 Cal. App. 4th 1180).

Transferred Intent

Under the transferred intent doctrine, if the accused intends to kill one person, but in attempting to do so kills another, the intent to kill is transferred to the actual victim. Accordingly, the accused may be convicted of murder of the other person (*People v. Henderson*, 34 Cal. 2d 340). In one case, the accused shot at his wife but missed her and killed a bystander. He was guilty of assault with the intent to murder (on the wife) and murder of the other person (*People v. Brannon*, 70 Cal. 225). As explained by one court: "Under the doctrine of transferred intent, where person purposefully attempts to kill one person but by mistake or inadvertence kills another instead, the law transfers the felonious intent from object of the assault to the actual victim" (*People v. Carlson*, 37 Cal. App. 3d 349).

Implied malice occurs when:

- No considerable provocation is present.
- The circumstances indicate an abandoned and malignant heart.
- The killing resulted from the intentional doing of an act likely to cause death or serious bodily injury.

Malice aforethought actually refers to the accused's state of mind. It manifests itself in one of the following situations:

- The result of an act done with the specific intent to kill (expressed malice)
- The result of an act done with the intent to produce serious bodily harm (expressed malice)
- The result of an act done during the perpetration of or the attempt to commit one of the felonies listed in PC 188 (implied malice) (See discussion of felony-murder later in Section 8-12 of this chapter.)
- The result of an act done in conscious disregard of the consequences, where death or serious injury is likely to occur, and which indicates an "abandoned and malignant heart" such as the tossing of a firebomb into a crowd (implied malice)
- The result of an act of resisting a lawful arrest and done in a manner that demonstrates a conscious disregard for human life (implied malice)

Motive

Although motive is not a necessary element of murder under California law, it is material evidence that a jury may properly consider in deciding whether a defendant was the perpetrator of a crime (*Brown v. Borg*, 951 F. 2d 1011). In one first-degree murder prosecution, evidence was sufficient to justify instructing the jury on premeditated murder as well as first-degree felony-murder in that there was strong evidence of the defendant's relationship with the victim prior to shooting from which the jury could reasonably infer a motive to kill the victim; the jury could infer from the manner of killing that the defendant must have intentionally killed according to a preconceived design to take victim's life in a particular way for a reason that the jury could reasonably infer from prior relationship evidence (*People v. Salazar*, 74 Cal. App. 3d 875).

One court observed that although motive is often valuable, it is not an indispensable element of proof in a murder prosecution (*People v. Beasley*, 328 P. 2d 834). In another case, the absence of a motive of killing of the accused's child did not require a reduction in the degree of murder since the presence or absence of a motive is only one factor to be considered by a jury in connection with other factors (*People v. Steward*, 156 Cal. App. 2d 177).

One court instructed the jury as follows, "If you are satisfied to a moral certainty, and beyond a reasonable doubt, that the crime of murder has been committed, and there is evidence sufficient to satisfy you to a moral certainty and beyond a reasonable doubt that defendant is guilty thereof, then the motive for its commission is unimportant and not material." The appellate courts held that the instruction was erroneous, being simply equivalent to a direction that the jury might convict defendant of murder if they were satisfied of his guilt, though no motive for the crime was disclosed (*People v. Petruzo*, 13 Cal. App. 569).

8-12 Felony-Murder Rule

At common law, under the felony-murder rule, a murder committed during the perpetration of or an attempt to commit a serious felony was considered premeditated murder. In California, the rule is incorporated into PC 189. Accordingly, murders committed during the perpetration of, or an attempt to commit, one of the listed felonies is first-degree murder. (Note: For the felony-murder rule to apply, there must be a murder, not merely a homicide [*People v. Coefield*, 37 Cal. 2d 865]).

The felony-murder rule is intended to deter felons from killing negligently or accidentally in commission of an underlying crime. The felony-murder doctrine is disfavored and should not be extended beyond any rational function that it is designed to serve (*People v. Esquivel,* 28 Cal. App. 4th 1386).

The effect of the felony-murder rule is that it is a substitute for "malice aforethought" in homicides when there is a direct causal connection between the commission or attempted commission of a listed felony and the death (*People v. Ireland,* 70 Cal. 2d 522).

Specific intent required for murder in the first degree is still required, but under the felony-murder rule, it is a transferred intent. Accordingly, in *People v. Dillon* (34 Cal. 3d 441), the accused had a specific intent to commit a felony and that intent was transferred to the killing.

A criminal is accountable for all killings committed by him or her and his or her associates in the course of the felonious conduct. This liability is not limited to foreseeable deaths. It also includes accidental deaths. For example, in one case the accused, intending to commit arson, set fire to a building that he thought was unoccupied. During the fire, a person sleeping in the building was killed. The accused was convicted of first-degree murder under the felony-murder rule (*People v. Milton,* 145 Cal. 169).

The felony-murder rule contained in the Penal Code requires that the killing occur in the perpetration of one of the listed felonies. A coincidental death is not a killing within the meaning of the statute (*People v. Gunnerson,* 74 Cal. App. 3d 370). The death, however, need not be a direct cause of the felony; a concurrent cause is sufficient. A killing to escape the scene of a felony or to prevent discovery or apprehension is a killing within the meaning of the felony-murder rule.

The felony-murder rule does not apply to crimes not listed. There is also a corresponding misdemeanor-manslaughter rule. Murder committed during the perpetration of or an attempt to commit a felony not listed, or a misdemeanor, may be second-degree murder or manslaughter.

If two or more persons conspire to commit one of the felonies listed in PC 189, and during the commission of the felony a murder is committed, then each may be tried for the murder as if each had conspired to commit the murder.

In one case, the defendants had conspired to take money from a victim. One of the defendants struck the victim in the head causing his death. The other defendants stated that they had conspired to roll a drunk and that striking the victim was not part of the plan. The court instructed the jury that the degree of murder depended on whether the defendants conspired to rob the victim (murder in the first degree) or merely "drunk rolling" (murder in the second degree) (*People v. Bauman,* 39 Cal. App. 2d 587).

8-13 Multiplicity

The general rule is that each victim is considered a separate crime. Accordingly, if an individual causes the death of five people by a single criminal act, the individual may be tried for five murders. In one case, the accused killed two people with a single criminal act. The court held that the acquittal of the accused in one case did not bar prosecution for the other death (*People v. Carson,* 37 Cal. App. 3d 349).

8-14 Punishment for Murder

The punishment for murder is set forth in PC 190. The punishment schedule is as follows:

- Murder in the first degree—death, life imprisonment, or a term of 25 years to life.
- Murder in the second degree—term of 15 years to life.
- Murder in the second degree involving either the death of a peace officer who was killed in the performance of his or her duties, or the defendant knew, or reasonably should have known, the victim was a police officer engaged in the performance of his or her duties, may be punished by life imprisonment without the possibility of parole.
- The punishment for murder in the second degree perpetrated by means of shooting a firearm from a motor vehicle intentionally at another person outside the vehicle is 20 years confinement.

(Note: In both of the preceding situations, the offender may be convicted of murder in the first degree.)

The penalty for murder with special circumstances is death or confinement for life without the possibility of parole. Special circumstances are set forth in PC 190.2. Some of them are as follows:

- Intentional murder was committed for financial gain.
- Murder was committed by means of a destructive device, bomb, or explosive planted, hidden, or concealed in any place, area, dwelling, and so on, and the defendant knew or reasonably should have known that his or her act or acts would create a great risk of death to a human being or human beings.
- Murder was committed to avoid or prevent a lawful arrest or to perfect or attempt to perfect an escape from lawful custody.
- The victim was a peace officer in the performance of his or her duties, and the defendant knew or should have known of the victim's status as a peace officer.
- The victim was a witness to a crime who was killed to prevent his or her testimony.
- The defendant was lying in wait.
- The victim was killed because of his or her race, color, religion, nationality, or country of origin.
- The defendant intentionally killed the victim while the defendant was an active participant in a criminal street gang and the murder was carried out to further the activities of the criminal street gang.

Penal Code 189 has been modified to include as *murder in the first degree* ". . . any murder which is perpetrated by means of discharging a firearm from a motor vehicle, intentionally at another person outside the vehicle with the intent to inflict death . . ."

The penalty for certain types of murder was significantly changed by S.B. 310 (Stats. 1993, c. 609). When the governor signed that bill, he issued the following message, dated September 29, 1993:

To the Members of the California Senate:

I have signed this date Senate Bill No. 310 which I have sponsored.
This bill adds intentional drive-by killing to the first degree murder statute and increases the penalty for second degree drive-by murder by five years to twenty years to

life. Additionally, this bill imposes a sentence enhancement of up to five years for the use of the firearm.

This bill represents substantial progress in the effort to curb and punish senseless acts of violence perpetrated on innocent, and often random, victims.

The codification of drive-by killing in the first degree murder statute allows prosecutors to convict drive-by assassins upon proof of a specific intent to kill. The penalty for this act of cowardice in the first degree can be as high as 30 years to life with the application of the penalty enhancement provided in this bill.

For second degree drive-by murder, this bill increases the penalty from 15 years to life to as high as 25 years to life with the application of the penalty enhancement provided in this bill.

While these provisions are important policy achievements, they are still not enough. As introduced, this bill would have made drive-by killers eligible for the death penalty or life without the possibility of parole. However, the Assembly Committee on Public Safety removed these critical provisions much to the detriment of the public safety.

I firmly believe that there should only be two penalties for drive-by killers: death or life imprisonment. Only after this is done will justice be fully served.

Penal Code 192—Manslaughter; Voluntary, Involuntary, and Vehicular; Construction of Section

8-15 Manslaughter

Manslaughter is the unlawful killing of a human being without malice. It is of three kinds:

(a) Voluntary—upon a sudden quarrel or heat of passion.
(b) Involuntary—in the commission of an unlawful act, not amounting to felony; or in the commission of a lawful act which might produce death, in an unlawful manner, or without due caution and circumspection. This subdivision shall not apply to acts committed in the driving of a vehicle.
(c) Vehicular—

(1) Except as provided in Section 191.5, driving a vehicle in the commission of an unlawful act, not amounting to felony, and with gross negligence; or driving a vehicle in the commission of a lawful act which might produce death, in an unlawful manner, and with gross negligence.
(2) Except as provided in paragraph (3), driving a vehicle in the commission of an unlawful act, not amounting to felony, but without gross negligence; or driving a vehicle in the commission of a lawful act which might produce death, in an unlawful manner, but without gross negligence.
(3) Driving a vehicle in violation of Section 23140, 23152, or 23153 of the Vehicle Code and in the commission of an unlawful act, not amounting to felony, but without gross negligence; or driving a vehicle in violation of Section 23140, 23152, or 23153 of the Vehicle Code (driving under the influence) and in the commission of a lawful act which might produce death, in an unlawful manner, but without gross negligence.

This section shall not be construed as making any homicide in the driving of a vehicle punishable which is not a proximate result of the commission of an unlawful act, not amounting to felony, or of the commission of a lawful act which might produce death, in an unlawful manner.

Gross negligence, as used in this section, shall not be construed as prohibiting or precluding a charge of murder under Section 188 upon facts exhibiting wantonness and a conscious disregard for life to support a finding of implied malice, or upon facts showing malice, consistent with the holding of the California Supreme Court in *People v. Watson*, 30 Cal. 3d 290.

8-15a Discussion

Voluntary manslaughter is the unlawful killing of a human being without malice upon a sudden quarrel or in the heat of passion. The distinguishing characteristic between murder and manslaughter is malice, rather than the presence or absence of an intent to kill (*People v. Mears*, 298 P. 2d 40).

Heat of Passion

To reduce the unlawful killing of a human being from murder to manslaughter, the killing must be done without malice and as the result of a sudden quarrel or done in the heat of passion. Sudden quarrel refers to an unplanned mutual combat such as a fistfight in a bar caused by a quarrel. To constitute adequate heat of passion, the accused must be in a state of blinding rage that is sufficient to cloud the judgment and common sense of a reasonable person and prompts the person to act rashly and without deliberation.

The heat of passion must exist at the time of the killing. If the provocation is adequate, but there is a cooling-off period between the provocation and the killing, the crime is murder not manslaughter. (Note: The amount of provocation may affect the length of the cooling-off period.)

One court observed that before homicide may be classified as voluntary manslaughter, it must appear that there was no "cooling" period (*People v. Taylor*, 197 Cal. App. 2d 372). "Cooling time," as respects manslaughter, is not the time it would take an ideal man or the defendant, but the time it would take the average man, or the ordinarily reasonable person, under like circumstances, to cool, and does not, as stated in one court's requested instruction, "differ with different persons according to the constitution of their nature" (*People v. Golsh*, 63 Cal. App. 609).

As stated in another court case: "To be sufficient to reduce a homicide to manslaughter the heat of passion must be such as would naturally be aroused in the mind of an ordinary, reasonable person, under the given facts and circumstances, or in the mind of a person of ordinary self-control" (*People v. Brunk*, 258 Cal. App. 2d 453). In determining whether a homicide is voluntary manslaughter, the fundamental inquiry is whether a defendant's reason was, at time of his act, so disturbed or obscured by some passion, not necessarily fear and never the passion for revenge, to such an extent as would render ordinary men of average disposition liable to act rashly or without due deliberation and reflection, and from such passion rather than from judgment (*People v. Domingo*, 210 Cal. App. 2d 120).

Words or gestures, however grievous or insulting, are not sufficient provocation to reduce an intentional homicide with a deadly weapon from murder to manslaughter (*People v. Dixon*, 192 Cal. App. 2d 88).

8-16 Involuntary Manslaughter

Involuntary manslaughter is the unlawful and unintentional killing of a human being without malice during the commission of an unlawful nonfelony act or the commission of a lawful act that might produce death in an unlawful manner and without due caution. (Note: PC 192[b] regarding involuntary manslaughter does not apply to deaths involving driving a vehicle.)

Involuntary manslaughter is the commission of an act that involves a high degree of risk of death or great bodily injury, committed with criminal negligence; that is, conduct that is such a departure from the conduct of an ordinarily prudent person under the same circumstances as to be incompatible with proper regard for human life (*People v. Cleaves*, 229 Cal. App. 3d 367).

There are two basic types of involuntary manslaughter in California. The first involves the unintentional killing of another during the commission of an unlawful act that does not amount to a felony. For example, the accused hits the victim in the head with his fist without just cause. The victim falls and strikes his head on a boulder causing his death. The accused has committed involuntary manslaughter. If the assault was with a dangerous weapon rather than with fists, the crime is murder. This is based on the fact that assault with a dangerous weapon is a felony, whereas simple battery is only a misdemeanor. To be an unlawful act within the manslaughter statute, the act in question must be dangerous to human life or safety, and there must exist a union or joint operation of act and intent, or criminal negligence (*People v. Wong*, 35 Cal. App. 3d 812).

The second type of involuntary manslaughter involves those situations where the accidental killing results from the commission of a lawful act but in a criminally negligent manner. For example, taking target practice in a rural area without checking out the impact area and thus causing the death of a person camping in the vicinity.

Criminal negligence, such as will support involuntary manslaughter charge, is of higher order of culpability than ordinary civil negligence and is measured objectively: If a reasonable person would have been aware of risk, then the defendant is presumed to have had that awareness (*Sea Horse Ranch, Inc. v. Superior Court*, 24 Cal. App. 4th 446).

An essential distinction between second-degree murder based on implied malice and involuntary manslaughter is subjective versus objective criteria to evaluate the defendant's state of mind; if the defendant commits an act that endangers human life without realizing the risk involved, he or she is guilty of manslaughter, whereas if the defendant realized risk and acted in total disregard of danger, he or she is guilty of murder based on implied malice (*People v. Cleaves*, 229 Cal. App. 3d 367).

8-17 Vehicular Manslaughter

Vehicular manslaughter is the unlawful killing of a human being, without malice and unintentional, while driving a vehicle.

The types of vehicular manslaughter include the following:

- Death caused by the gross negligence of the driver (felony)
- Death caused by the negligence, but not gross negligence, of the driver (misdemeanor)
- Death caused by a negligent and unlawful act of the driver (felony)
- Death caused by the gross negligence of the driver while under the influence of drugs or alcohol (felony)

8-17a Discussion

A homicide involving the driving of a vehicle is not manslaughter if the death is not the proximate result (cause) of the unlawful act or negligence. For purposes of vehicular manslaughter statute, to determine whether an unlawful act is inherently dangerous, its elements are viewed in the abstract, and not from the point of view of the particular facts of the case (*People v. Wells*, 31 Cal. App. 4th 1272). Viewed in the abstract, violation of the maximum speed law is not an inherently dangerous act for purposes of vehicular manslaughter prosecution; numerous circumstances can be conjured under which the maximum speed law could be violated with little or no danger to human life, much less a high probability of death (*People v. Wells*, 31 Cal. App. 4th 1272).

The words *without due caution and circumspection*, in the statute providing that involuntary manslaughter is an unlawful killing of a human being without malice in commission of lawful act that might produce death, in an unlawful manner, or *without due caution and circumspection*, refer to criminal negligence; in other words, unintentional conduct that is gross or reckless, amounting to disregard of human life or an indifference to consequences (*People v. Evers,* 10 Cal. App. 4th 588).

Violation of vehicular manslaughter need not be based on any intent to harm the victim or victims, the only intent required for conviction under this section is intent to drive a vehicle in an unlawful manner (*People v. Jones,* 164 Cal. App. 3d 1173).

8-18 Gross Negligence

Gross negligence is defined as follows:

- Such a degree of negligence or carelessness that shows a willful and wanton disregard for the life and safety of others
- Amounts to the want of even slight diligence
- A failure to exercise care of so slight a degree as to justify the belief that there is an indifference to the safety of others and a conscious indifference to the consequences

8-19 Punishment for Manslaughter

Penal Code 193—Voluntary Manslaughter, Involuntary Manslaughter and Vehicular Manslaughter; Punishment

(a) Voluntary manslaughter is punishable by imprisonment in the state prison for three, six, or eleven years.
(b) Involuntary manslaughter is punishable by imprisonment in the state prison for two, three, or four years.
(c) Vehicular manslaughter is punishable as follows:

    (1) A violation of paragraph (1) of subdivision (c) of Section 192 is punishable either by imprisonment in the county jail for not more than one year or by imprisonment in the state prison for two, four, or six years.
    (2) A violation of paragraph (2) of subdivision (c) of Section 192 is punishable by imprisonment in the county jail for not more than one year.
    (3) A violation of paragraph (3) of subdivision (c) of Section 192 is punishable either by imprisonment in the county jail for not more than one year or by imprisonment in the state prison for 16 months or two or four years.

8-20 Noncriminal Homicides

As stated earlier, not all homicides are criminal. The following are classified as noncriminal homicides:

- Excusable Homicide
- Justifiable Homicide
  - By a police officer
  - By others

Penal Code 195—Excusable Homicide

Homicide is excusable in the following cases:

- When committed by accident and misfortune, or in doing any other lawful act by lawful means, with usual and ordinary caution, and without any unlawful intent
- When committed by accident and misfortune, in the heat of passion, upon any sudden and sufficient provocation, or upon a sudden combat, when no undue advantage is taken, nor any dangerous weapon used, and when the killing is not done in a cruel or unusual manner

Penal Code 196—Justifiable Homicide; Public Officers

Homicide is justifiable when committed by public officers and those acting by their command in their aid and assistance, either:

1. In obedience to any judgment of a competent Court
2. When necessarily committed in overcoming actual resistance to the execution of some legal process, or in the discharge of any other legal duty
3. When necessarily committed in retaking felons who have been rescued or have escaped, or when necessarily committed in arresting persons charged with felony, and who are fleeing from justice or resisting such arrest

Penal Code 199—Justifiable and Excusable Homicide; Discharge of Defendant

The homicide appearing to be justifiable or excusable, the person indicted must, upon his trial, be fully acquitted and discharged.

Excusable homicide is a homicide caused by an accident or other misfortune while doing a lawful act by lawful means and using usual and ordinary caution. There must be no unlawful intent involved with the act causing the death. For example, an automobile accident not involving an unlawful act or negligence that causes the death of a person would be excusable homicide (PC 195).

8-20a Discussion

A justifiable homicide is one that was committed for the protection of society or a part of society. Under California law, the defendant must raise the issue of justification, but he or she does not bear any burden of proof or persuasion in the murder prosecution (*People v. Frye*, 7 Cal. App. 4th 1148). A homicide is considered justifiable when committed by a public officer as set forth in PC 196 or in any of the following circumstances:

1. When resisting any attempt by the deceased to murder any person, or to commit a felony, or to do some great bodily injury to any person
2. When committed in defense of home, person, or property, against one who manifestly intends or endeavors, by violence or surprise, to commit a felony
3. When committed against one who manifestly intends and endeavors, in a violent, riotous, or tumultuous manner, to enter the home of another to offer violence to any person therein
4. When reasonably committed in the lawful defense of one's self or others
5. When necessarily committed in attempting by lawful ways and means to apprehend any person for a felony committed or in lawfully suppressing any riot, or in lawfully keeping and preserving the peace

In the situations just listed, a "bare fear" of the commission of a felony is not sufficient to justify the homicide. The circumstances must be sufficient to excite the fears of a reasonable person, and the party doing the killing must have acted under the influence of such fears alone (PC 198).

Use of Deadly Force by a Police Officer

The U.S. Supreme Court held in *Tennessee v. Garner* (471 U.S. 1) that a statute which permitted the police to use deadly force to prevent the escape of an unarmed and nondangerous felon was unconstitutional. This case limited the use of deadly force to only those situations where the use is necessary to prevent serious bodily harm or death to the police officer or others. The *Garner* case modifies the provisions of

PC 196 (in civil liability cases), which indicates that homicide is justifiable in overcoming actual resistance to the execution of some legal process, or in the discharge of any other legal duty.

8-21 Home Protection

Penal Code 198.5—Home Protection; Use of Deadly Force; Presumption of Fear of Death or Great Bodily Injury

Any person using force intended or likely to cause death or great bodily injury within his or her residence shall be presumed to have held a reasonable fear of imminent peril of death or great bodily injury to self, family, or a member of the household when that force is used against another person, not a member of the family or household, who unlawfully and forcibly enters or has unlawfully and forcibly entered the residence and the person using the force knew or had reason to believe that an unlawful and forcible entry occurred.

As used in this section, great bodily injury means a significant or substantial physical injury.

8-22 Self-Defense

The right of self-defense involves the right of an individual to repel force with similar force to protect his or her life, members of the family, the home, and other property. Deadly force may be used only to prevent great bodily harm or to prevent the perpetration of a felony by surprise or violence against one's person or home.

Deadly force is not normally justified for the protection of property. A person may, however, use deadly force to prevent anyone from entering his or her home to commit a felony or to inflict serious bodily harm on people living in the home. In determining whether or not excessive force has been used, the courts look to what action appeared to be reasonable under the circumstances as they appeared to the defender at the time of the attack.

8-22a Discussion

Imperfect Self-Defense

The concept of imperfect self-defense, which applies when a defendant has an honest, but unreasonable, belief that it is necessary to defend himself or herself from imminent peril, is not an element of either first- or second-degree murder, but rather is a mitigating factor, which, when raised by sufficient evidence, negates the element of malice, so that the charge may be reduced to manslaughter (*People v. Martinez*, 230 Cal. App. 3d 197). Imperfect self-defense is a term used to denote those situations that fail to qualify as self-defense; for example, where the defendant wrongly uses deadly force in response to nondeadly force. Although an imperfect self-defense is not a complete defense to homicide, it may negate malice aforethought and thereby reduce homicide that would otherwise be murder to voluntary manslaughter (*People v. Curtis*, 30 Cal. App. 4th 1337). For purposes of murder, imperfect self-defense rebuts malice only when all its prerequisites are met; the defendant's belief in the need for self-defense is not enough (*People v. Curtis*, 30 Cal. App. 4th 1337).

Instigator

In most cases, the individual who starts a fight cannot rely on self-defense to justify the killing. An exception to this general rule is where the original instigator gives up the fight and attempts to retreat. Under these circumstances, the original instigator may regain the right to self-defense (*People v. Hoover*, 107 Cal. App. 635). Note: A police officer making an arrest is not an instigator (PC 835a).

Duty to Retreat

In some states, a person has a duty to retreat before using deadly force when the individual can safely retreat. In California, an individual who is attacked may stand his or her ground and defend himself or herself (*People v. Zuckerman*, 56 Cal. App. 2d 366).

Defense of Habitation

Defense of habitation applies when a defendant uses reasonable force to exclude someone he or she reasonably believes is trespassing in, or about to trespass in, his or her home. For purposes of the defense of habitation in a homicide prosecution, the intentional use of deadly force merely to protect property is never reasonable. Homicide involving the intentional use of deadly force can never be justified by defense of habitation alone; the defendant must also show either self-defense or defense of others; that is, that he or she reasonably believed the intruder intended to kill or inflict serious injury on someone in the home (*People v. Curtis,* 30 Cal. App. 4th 1337).

Penal Code 422.6—Civil Rights; Interfere with, Property Damage or Speech

8-23 Conspiracy against the Rights of Citizens

(a) No person, whether or not acting under color of law, shall by force or threat of force, willfully injure, intimidate, interfere with, oppress, or threaten any other person in the free exercise or enjoyment of any right or privilege secured to him or her by the Constitution or laws of this state or by the Constitution or laws of the United States because of the other person's race, color, religion, ancestry, national origin, disability, gender, or sexual orientation, or because he or she perceives that the other person has one or more of those characteristics.

(b) No person, whether or not acting under color of law, shall knowingly deface, damage, or destroy the real or personal property of any other person for the purpose of intimidating or interfering with the free exercise or enjoyment of any right or privilege secured to the other person by the Constitution or laws of this state or by the Constitution or laws of the United States, because of the other person's race, color, religion, ancestry, national origin, disability, gender, or sexual orientation, or because he or she perceives that the other person has one or more of those characteristics.

(c) Any person convicted of violating subdivision (a) or (b) shall be punished by imprisonment in a county jail not to exceed one year, or by a fine not to exceed five thousand dollars ($5,000), or by both that imprisonment and fine. However, no person shall be convicted of violating subdivision (a) based upon speech alone, except upon a showing that the speech itself threatened violence against a specific person or group of persons and that the defendant had the apparent ability to carry out the threat.

Penal Code 422.7—Civil Rights Violations, Punishments

Except in the case of a person punished under Section 422.6, any crime which is not made punishable by imprisonment in the state prison shall be punishable by imprisonment in the state prison or in a county jail not to exceed one year, by a fine not to exceed ten thousand dollars ($10,000), or by both that imprisonment and fine, if the crime is committed against the person or property of another for the purpose of intimidating or interfering with that other person's free exercise or enjoyment of any right secured to him or her by the Constitution or laws of this state or by the Constitution or laws of the United States and because of the other person's race, color, religion, ancestry, national origin, disability, gender, or sexual orientation, or because the defendant perceives that the other person has one or more of those characteristics, under any of the following circumstances, which shall be charged in the accusatory pleading:

- The crime against the person of another either includes the present ability to commit a violent injury or causes actual physical injury.
- The crime against property causes damage in excess of five hundred dollars ($500).
- The person charged with a crime under this section has been convicted previously of a violation of subdivision (a) or (b) of Section 422.6, or has been convicted previously of a conspiracy to commit a crime described in subdivision (a) or (b) of Section 422.6.

Penal Code 422.75—Commission of Felony because of Race, Color, Religion, etc.; Punishments

(a) Except in the case of a person punished under Section 422.7, a person who commits a felony or attempts to commit a felony because of the victim's race, color, religion, nationality, country of origin, ancestry, disability, or sexual orientation, or because he or she perceives that the victim has one or more of those characteristics, shall receive an additional term of one, two, or three years in the state prison, at the court's discretion.

(b) Except in the case of a person punished under Section 422.7 or subdivision (a) of this section, any person who commits a felony or attempts to commit a felony against the property of a public agency or private institution, including a school, educational facility, library or community center, meeting hall, or offices of an advocacy group, or the grounds adjacent to, owned, or rented by the public agency or private institution, because the property of the public agency or private institution is identified or associated with a person or group of an identifiable race, color, religion, nationality, country of origin, ancestry, gender, disability, or sexual orientation, shall receive an additional term of one, two, or three years in the state prison, at the court's discretion.

(c) Except in the case of a person punished under Section 422.7 or subdivision (a) or (b) of this section, any person who commits a felony, or attempts to commit a felony, because of the victim's race, color, religion, nationality, country of origin, ancestry, gender, disability, or sexual orientation, or because he or she perceives that the victim has one or more of those characteristics, and who voluntarily acted in concert with another person, either personally or by aiding and abetting another person, shall receive an additional two, three, or four years in the state prison, at the court's discretion.

(d) For the purpose of imposing an additional term under subdivision (a) or (c), it shall be a factor in aggravation that the defendant personally used a firearm in the commission of the offense. Nothing in this subdivision shall preclude a court from also imposing a sentence enhancement pursuant to Section 12022.5 or 12022.55, or any other law.

(e) A person who is punished pursuant to this section also shall receive an additional term of one year in the state prison for each prior felony conviction on charges brought and tried separately in which it was found by the trier of fact or admitted by the defendant that the crime was committed because of the victim's race, color, religion, nationality, country of origin, ancestry, disability, or sexual orientation, or that the crime was committed because the defendant perceived that the victim had one or more of those characteristics. This additional term shall only apply where a sentence enhancement is not imposed pursuant to Section 667 or 667.5.

(f) Any additional term authorized by this section shall not be imposed unless the allegation is charged in the accusatory pleading and admitted by the defendant or found to be true by the trier of fact.

(g) Any additional term imposed pursuant to this section shall be in addition to any other punishment provided by law.

(h) Notwithstanding any other law, the court may strike any additional term imposed by this section if the court determines that there are mitigating circumstances and states on the record the reasons for striking the additional punishment.

Penal Code 422.8—Prosecution Permitted

Except as otherwise required by law, nothing in this title shall be construed to prevent or limit the prosecution of any person pursuant to any provision of law.

Penal Code 422.6 makes it a crime to interfere, intimidate, and so on, with the civil rights of another person. The following are elements of this offense:

1. By use of force or threat of force
2. Willfully injure, intimidate, interfere with, oppress, or threaten another person
3. To prevent the other person from the enjoyment of any right or privilege
4. Secured by law or constitution
5. Because of the other person's race, color, religion, ancestry, national origin, disability, gender, or sexual orientation, or because he or she perceives that the other person has one or more of those characteristics.

8-23a Discussion

Since the statute requires that the acts be intentional and done because of actual or preceived membership in a protected class (race, religion, ancestry, etc.), the crime is a specific intent crime and cannot be committed by mistake or negligence. The violation of a person's civil rights under PC 422.6 is a misdemeanor. PC 422.7, however, elevates the offense to a felony if one of three conditions described in PC 422.7 is present. PC 422.75 allows additional punishments to be imposed for any felony that was committed because of a person's race, color, religion, and so on. This section of the code was designed to combat "hate crimes."

Penal Codes 422.6, 422.7, and 422.75 also punish persons who violate the civil rights of another person under "color of law." *Under color of law* means that the official is using his or her office or position, and the action is taken under the guise of that office. The official is acting beyond the permissible scope of the office. Accordingly, to deprive a person of his or her civil rights under the color of law, the offender must be a public official or one acting in that capacity. A law enforcement officer is considered a public official. For example, a police officer who without probable cause stops an individual and searches the individual may be depriving

8-24 Deprivation of Rights under Color of Law

that person of his or her civil rights under color of law. A police brutality case would constitute the deprivation of an individual's civil rights under color of law. The brutality case would probably also be an assault and battery.

8-25 Elder and Dependent Adult Abuse

Penal Code 270c—Neglect of Indigent Parent

Except as provided in Chapter 2 (commencing with Section 4410) of Part 4 of Division 9 of the Family Code, every adult child who, having the ability to do so, fails to provide necessary food, clothing, shelter, or medical attendance for an indigent parent, is guilty of a misdemeanor.

Penal Code 368—Person Causing Pain, Suffering, or Injury to Elder or Dependent Adult; Theft or Embezzlement by Caretaker

(a) Any person who, under circumstances or conditions likely to produce great bodily harm or death, willfully causes or permits any elder or dependent adult, with knowledge that he or she is an elder or a dependent adult, to suffer, or inflicts thereon unjustifiable physical pain or mental suffering, or having the care or custody of any elder or dependent adult, willfully causes or permits the person or health of the elder or dependent adult to be injured, or willfully causes or permits the elder or dependent adult to be placed in a situation such that his or her person or health is endangered, is punishable by imprisonment in the county jail not exceeding one year, or in the state prison for two, three, or four years.

(b) Any person who, under circumstances or conditions other than those likely to produce great bodily harm or death, willfully causes or permits any elder or dependent adult, with knowledge that he or she is an elder or a dependent adult, to suffer, or inflicts thereon unjustifiable physical pain or mental suffering, or having the care or custody of any elder or dependent adult, willfully causes or permits the person or health of the elder or dependent adult to be injured or willfully causes or permits the elder or dependent adult to be placed in a situation such that his or her person or health may be endangered, is guilty of a misdemeanor.

(c) Any caretaker of an elder or a dependent adult who violates any provision of law proscribing theft or embezzlement, with respect to the property of that elder or dependent adult, is punishable by imprisonment in the county jail not exceeding one year, or in the state prison for two, three, or four years when the money, labor, or real or personal property taken is of a value exceeding four hundred dollars ($400), and by fine not exceeding one thousand dollars($1,000) or by imprisonment in the county jail not exceeding one year, or both, when the money, labor, or real or personal property taken is of a value not exceeding four hundred dollars ($400).

(d) As used in this section, *elder* means any person who is 65 years of age or older.

(e) As used in this section, *dependent adult* means any person who is between the ages of 18 and 64, who has physical or mental limitations which restrict his or her ability to carry out normal activities or to protect his or her rights, including, but not limited to, persons who have physical or developmental disabilities or whose physical or mental abilities have diminished because of age. *Dependent adult* includes any person between the ages of 18 and 64 who is admitted as an inpatient to a 24-hour health facility, as defined in Sections 1250, 1250.2, and 1250.3 of the Health and Safety Code.

(f) As used in this section, *caretaker* means any person who has the care, custody, or control of or who stands in a position of trust with an elder or a dependent adult.

Civil Code 206 establishes a reciprocal duty of support for parent and child. Accordingly, the parent or child has a duty to support the other if the other is unable to maintain himself or herself. PC 270c provides that the failure of an adult child to support an indigent parent is a misdemeanor. Similar to those statutes involving child abuse, PC 368 makes it an offense for a person to abuse an elder or dependant adult.

8-25a Discussion

The following statutes involve the state of California's Domestic Violence Program. They are to be considered in conjunction with the statutes on spousal abuse that are discussed earlier in this chapter.

8-26 Domestic Violence

Penal Code 13700—Definitions

As used in this title:

(a) *Abuse* means intentionally or recklessly causing or attempting to cause bodily injury, or placing another person in reasonable apprehension of imminent serious bodily injury to himself or herself, or another.
(b) *Domestic violence* means abuse committed against an adult or a fully emancipated minor who is a spouse, former spouse, cohabitant, former cohabitant, or person with whom the suspect has had a child or is having or has had a dating or engagement relationship. For purposes of this subdivision, "cohabitant" means two unrelated adult persons living together for a substantial period of time, resulting in some permanency of relationship. Factors that may determine whether persons are cohabiting include, but are not limited to: (1) sexual relations between the parties while sharing the same living quarters, (2) sharing of income or expenses, (3) joint use or ownership of property, (4) whether the parties hold themselves out as husband and wife, (5) the continuity of the relationship, and (6) the length of the relationship.
(c) *Officer* means any officer or employee of a local police department or sheriff's office, and any peace officer of the Department of the California Highway Patrol, the Department of Parks and Recreation, the University of California Police Department, or the California State University and College Police Departments, as defined in Section 830.2, a housing authority patrol officer, as defined in subdivision (d) of Section 830.31, or a peace officer as defined in subdivisions (a) and (b) of Section 830.32.
(d) *Victim* means a person who is a victim of domestic violence.

Penal Code 13701—Domestic Violence Call Response—Policies and Standards for Officers

(a) Every law enforcement agency in this state shall develop, adopt, and implement written policies and standards for officers' responses to domestic violence calls by January 1, 1986. These policies shall reflect that domestic violence is alleged criminal conduct. Further, they shall reflect existing policy that a request for assistance in a situation involving domestic violence is the same as any other request for assistance where violence has occurred.

(b) The written policies shall encourage the arrest of domestic violence offenders if there is probable cause that an offense has been committed. These policies also shall require the arrest of an offender, absent exigent circumstances, if there is probable cause that a protective order issued under Chapter 4 (commencing with Section 2040) of Part 1 of Division 6, Division 10 (commencing with Section 6200), or Chapter 6 (commencing with Section 7700) of Part 3 of Division 12, of the Family Code, or Section 136.2 of this code, or by a court of any other state, a commonwealth, territory, or insular possession subject to the jurisdiction of the United States, a military tribunal, or a tribe has been violated. These policies shall discourage, when appropriate, but not prohibit, dual arrests. Peace officers shall make reasonable efforts to identify the primary aggressor in any incident. The primary aggressor is the person determined to be the most significant, rather than the first, aggressor. In identifying the primary aggressor, an officer shall consider the intent of the law to protect victims of domestic violence from continuing abuse, the threats creating fear of physical injury, the history of domestic violence between the persons involved, and whether either person acted in self-defense. These arrest policies shall be developed, adopted, and implemented by July 1, 1996. Notwithstanding subdivision (d), law enforcement agencies shall develop these policies with the input of local domestic violence agencies.

(c) These existing local policies and those developed shall be in writing and shall be available to the public upon request and shall include specific standards for the following:

  (1) Felony arrests
  (2) Misdemeanor arrests
  (3) Use of citizen arrests
  (4) Verification and enforcement of temporary restraining orders when (A) the suspect is present and (B) the suspect has fled
  (5) Verification and enforcement of stay-away orders
  (6) Cite and release policies
  (7) Emergency assistance to victims, such as medical care, transportation to a shelter, and police standbys for removing personal property
  (8) Assisting victims in pursuing criminal options, such as giving the victim the report number and directing the victim to the proper investigation unit
  (9) Furnishing written notice to victims at the scene, including, but not limited to, all of the following information:

    (A) A statement informing the victim that despite official restraint of the person alleged to have committed domestic violence, the restrained person may be released at any time.
    (B) A statement that, "For further information about a shelter you may contact ____."
    (C) A statement that, "For information about other services in the community, where available, you may contact ____."
    (D) A statement informing the victim of domestic violence that he or she may ask the district attorney to file a criminal complaint.
    (E) A statement informing the victim of the right to go to the superior court and file a petition requesting any of the following orders for relief:

(i) An order restraining the attacker from abusing the victim and other family members.

(ii) An order directing the attacker to leave the household.

(iii) An order preventing the attacker from entering the residence, school, business, or place of employment of the victim.

(iv) An order awarding the victim or the other parent custody of or visitation with a minor child or children.

(v) An order restraining the attacker from molesting or interfering with minor children in the custody of the victim.

(vi) An order directing the party not granted custody to pay support of minor children, if that party has a legal obligation to do so.

(vii) An order directing the defendant to make specified debit payments coming due while the order is in effect.

(viii) An order directing that either or both parties participate in counseling.

(F) A statement informing the victim of the right to file a civil suit for losses suffered as a result of the abuse, including medical expenses, loss of earnings, and other expenses for injuries sustained and damage to property, and any other related expenses incurred by the victim or any agency that shelters the victim.

(G) In the case of an alleged violation of Section 261, 261.5, 262, 286, 288a, or 289, a "Victims of Domestic Violence" card which shall include, but is not limited to, the following information:

(i) The names and locations of rape victim counseling centers within the county, including those centers specified in Section 13837, and their 24-hour counseling service telephone numbers.

(ii) A simple statement on the proper procedures for a victim to follow after a sexual assault.

(iii) A statement that sexual assault by a person who is known to the victim, including sexual assault by a person who is the spouse of the victim, is a crime.

(10) Writing of reports

(d) In the development of these policies and standards, each local department is encouraged to consult with domestic violence experts, such as the staff of the local shelter for battered women and their children. Departments may utilize the response guidelines developed by the commission in developing local policies.

Penal Code 13702—Domestic Violence Call Response—Policies and Standards for Dispatchers

Every law enforcement agency in this state shall develop, adopt, and implement written policies and standards for dispatchers' response to domestic violence calls by July 1, 1991. These policies shall reflect that calls reporting threatened, imminent, or ongoing domestic violence, and the violation of any protection order, including orders issued pursuant to Section 136.2, and restraining orders, shall be ranked among the highest priority calls. Dispatchers are not required to verify the validity of the protective order before responding to the request for assistance.

Penal Code 13710—Domestic Violence Protective Orders—Records to Be Maintained by Agencies

(a)

> (1) Law enforcement agencies shall maintain a complete and systematic record of all protection orders with respect to domestic violence incidents, including orders which have not yet been served, issued pursuant to Section 136.2, restraining orders, and proofs of service in effect. This shall be used to inform law enforcement officers responding to domestic violence calls of the existence, terms, and effective dates of protection orders in effect.
>
> (2) The police department of a community college or school district described in subdivision (a) or (b) of Section 830.32 shall notify the sheriff or police chief of the city in whose jurisdiction the department is located of any protection order served by the department pursuant to this section.

(b) The terms and conditions of the protection order remain enforceable, notwithstanding the acts of the parties, and may be changed only by order of the court.

(c) Upon request, law enforcement agencies shall serve the party to be restrained at the scene of a domestic violence incident or at any time the party is in custody.

Penal Code 13711—Protection Order; Application for an Issuance; Pamphlet to Person to Be Protected; Contents

Whenever a protection order with respect to domestic violence incidents, including orders issued pursuant to Section 136.2 and restraining orders, is applied for or issued, it shall be the responsibility of the clerk of the superior court to distribute a pamphlet to the person who is to be protected by the order that includes the following:

(a) Information as specified in subdivision (i) of Section 13701.

(b) Notice that it is the responsibility of the victim to request notification of an inmate's release.

(c) Notice that the terms and conditions of the protection order remain enforceable, notwithstanding any acts of the parties, and may be changed only by order of the court.

(d) Notice that the protection order is enforceable in any state, in a commonwealth, territory, or insular possession subject to the jurisdiction of the United States, or on a reservation, and general information about agencies in other jurisdictions that may be contacted regarding enforcement of a protective order issued by a court of this state.

8-27 Stalking

Penal Code 646.9—Stalking and Threatening Death or Great Bodily Injury

(a) Any person who willfully, maliciously, and repeatedly follows or harasses another person and who makes a credible threat with the intent to place that person in reasonable fear for his or her safety, or the safety of his or her immediate family, is guilty of the crime of stalking, punishable by imprisonment in a county jail for not more than one year or by a fine of not more than one thousand dollars ($1,000), or by both that fine and imprisonment, or by imprisonment in the state prison.

(b) Any person who violates subdivision (a) when there is a temporary restraining order, injunction, or any other court order in effect prohibiting the behavior described in subdivision (a) against the same party, shall be punished by imprisonment in the state prison for two, three, or four years.

(c) Every person who, having been convicted of a felony under this section, commits a second or subsequent violation of this section shall be punished by imprisonment in the state prison for two, three, or four years.

(d) In addition to the penalties provided in this section, the sentencing court may order a person convicted of a felony under this section to register as a sex offender pursuant to subparagraph (E) of paragraph (2) of subdivision (a) of Section 290.

(e) For the purposes of this section, *harasses* means a knowing and willful course of conduct directed at a specific person that seriously alarms, annoys, torments, or terrorizes the person, and that serves no legitimate purpose. This course of conduct must be such as would cause a reasonable person to suffer substantial emotional distress, and must actually cause substantial emotional distress to the person.

(f) For purposes of this section, *course of conduct* means a pattern of conduct composed of a series of acts over a period of time, however short, evidencing a continuity of purpose. Constitutionally protected activity is not included within the meaning of "course of conduct."

(g) For the purposes of this section, *credible threat* means a verbal or written threat or a threat implied by a pattern of conduct or a combination of verbal or written statements and conduct made with the intent to place the person that is the target of the threat in reasonable fear for his or her safety or the safety of his or her family and made with the apparent ability to carry out the threat so as to cause the person who is the target of the threat to reasonably fear for his or her safety or the safety of his or her family. It is not necessary to prove that the defendant had the intent to actually carry out the threat. The present incarceration of a person making the threat shall not be a bar to prosecution under this section.

(h) This section shall not apply to conduct that occurs during labor picketing.

(i) If probation is granted, or the execution or imposition of a sentence is suspended, for any person convicted under this section, it shall be a condition of probation that the person participate in counseling, as designated by the court. However, the court, upon a showing of good cause, may find that the counseling requirement shall not be imposed.

(j) The sentencing court also shall consider issuing an order restraining the defendant from any contact with the victim, that may be valid for up to 10 years, as determined by the court. It is the intent of the Legislature that the length of any restraining order be based upon the seriousness of the facts before the court, the probability of future violations, and the safety of the victim and his or her immediate family.

(k) For purposes of this section, "immediate family" means any spouse, parent, child, any person related by consanguinity or affinity within the second degree, or any other person who regularly resides in the household, or who, within the prior six months, regularly resided in the household.

(l) The court shall consider whether the defendant would benefit from treatment pursuant to Section 2684. If it is determined to be appropriate, the court shall recommend that the Department of Corrections make a certification as provided in Section 2684. Upon the certification, the defendant shall be evaluated and transferred to the appropriate hospital for treatment pursuant to Section 2684.

8-27a Discussion

Stalking is a relatively new crime in most states, including California. It became a crime in California in 1990. The offense was created because many people believed that traditional criminal laws were not adequate to control the conduct of "stalkers." California was the first state to enact a "stalking" statute. A problem with stalking statutes is that they are subject to attack for being unconstitutional because of the prohibition against vagueness and overbreadth.

Cases on Point

People v. Fields (56 Cal. App. 3d 954)

Evidence showing, *inter alia*, that the defendant seized a 13-year-old girl by the hair and head, ordered her into automobile whose motor was running, and threatened to strike her if she refused was sufficient to establish the requisite intent and affirmative act required to constitute crime of attempted kidnapping.

People v. Bruno (49 Cal. App. 372)

Where defendant forcibly placed the complaining witness in an automobile and carried her away, he was guilty of kidnapping, though he did so with no intent of injuring her or her feelings, but solely for the purpose of conversing with her, and under the belief, based on probable ground therefore, that such action would not be offensive to her or hurt her feelings.

People v. Bradley (15 Cal. App. 4th 1144)

The defendant's movement of the victim was sufficiently substantial to support conviction for kidnapping with the intent to commit rape; the victim was moved 50 to 60 feet from the open street and was forcibly led around the building to the inside of an enclosed dumpster area, which was separate structure. Distance, in and of itself, is not only the factor necessary to prove asportation for purposes of kidnapping with intent to commit rape; consideration must be given to change in surroundings between the point of capture and destination.

People v. Daly (8 Cal. App. 4th 47)

Moving the victim approximately 40 feet across parking structure in unsuccessful effort to get her into van was insufficient asportation to support a kidnapping conviction; the risk of harm was not increased by the movement.

People v. Galvan (187 Cal. App. 3d 1205)

Asportation of victim was sufficient to constitute kidnapping where the victim accepted a ride expecting that she would be taken home; the driver, however, continued driving toward the freeway, and the victim could not get out of the moving vehicle when she indicated that she wanted to go home.

McMillan v. Gomez (19 F. 3d 465)

California's felony-murder rule is not unconstitutional, notwithstanding the contention that it creates a mandatory presumption of malice; the rule is not an evidentiary shortcut to malice, but a rule of substantive law establishing a first-degree murder penalty for murders that occur in the course of committing another felony, and the defendant's intent, which prosecution must still prove, relates to the other felony, rather than murder.

People v. Apodaca (76 Cal. App. 3d 479)

Defining murder to include an unborn child gives all persons of common intelligence ample warning that assault on a pregnant woman without her consent for the purpose of unlawfully killing her unborn child can constitute the crime of murder and, therefore, this section does not contravene constitutional due process requirement that persons be given fair notice as to what the state commands or forbids.

People v. Bush (65 Cal. 129)

Where parties, by mutual understanding, engage in a conflict with deadly weapons, and death ensues to either, the slayer is guilty of murder.

People v. Hall (212 Cal. App. 2d 480)

The effect of Sections 187 to 189 and 1105 construed together is that every killing is a murder unless the defendant proves the contrary and he has burden of raising reasonable doubt as to his being guilty of murder as distinguished from manslaughter or justifiable homicide, though, to do so, he may take advantage of any evidence as well as that which he himself produces.

People v. Olivas (172 Cal. App. 3d 984)

Any impropriety in the conduct of the police, who allegedly violated their own departmental regulations by pursuing defendant at high speeds and attempting to disable his car, causing him to panic, did not mitigate the conduct of defendant, who chose to continue a demonstrably life-threatening course of conduct, and did not affect conviction of second-degree murder arising from vehicular homicide committed under the influence of phencyclidine.

People v. Saldana (47 Cal. App. 3d 954)

Removal of artificial life-support systems from homicide victim after all electrical activity in brain had ceased was not independent, intervening cause of death so as to relieve defendant of criminal responsibility.

People v. Phillips (64 Cal. 2d 574)

"Murder" is never more than a shortening of life; if the defendant's culpable act has significantly decreased the span of human life, the law will not hear him or her say that the victim would have died in any event.

People v. Moan (65 Cal. 532)

A person is liable for a homicide in accelerating the death of another whose death would necessarily have soon occurred from an incurable disease.

People v. Roberts (2 Cal. 4th 271)

If a person inflicted a dangerous wound on another, it is ordinarily no defense that inadequate medical treatment contributed to the victim's death. However, when medical treatment to a victim is grossly improper, it may discharge liability for homicide if maltreatment is the sole cause of death and, hence, an unforeseeable intervening cause.

People v. Fields (30 Cal. App. 4th 1731)

Necessity is not a defense to any crime that involves taking the life of an innocent person.

People v. Roberts (51 Cal. App. 3d 125)

A crucial distinction between murder and manslaughter is that malice aforethought is an element of the former.

People v. Conley (411 P. 2d 911)

One who commits euthanasia bears no ill will toward his victim and believes his act is morally justified, but he nonetheless acts with malice if he is able to comprehend that society prohibits his act regardless of his personal belief.

People v. Cleaves (229 Cal. App. 3d 367)

The defendant was not entitled to jury instructions on lesser included offenses of aiding and abetting suicide or manslaughter during the murder trial resulting from the victim's strangulation suicide, even though the victim asked the defendant to assist in suicide and the victim applied pressure to the ligature that was the immediate cause of death, where the defendant tied the sash between the victim's neck and wrists, and the defendant held the victim to keep him from falling off bed while accomplishing strangulation and, thus, the defendant actively assisted in the overt act of strangulation.

People v. Mitchell (132 Cal. App. 3d 389)

Evidence was sufficient to show beyond a reasonable doubt that the victim was "brain dead" when taken off life support, notwithstanding the pathologist's testimony that, although hospital records showed the victim had classic symptoms of brain death, he personally was vague on the brain death standard in state.

Kortum v. Alkire (69 Cal. App. 3d 325)

The Penal Code, as construed by the courts, prohibits the use of deadly force by anyone, including a police officer, against a fleeing felony suspect unless the felony is of the violent variety, that is, a forcible and atrocious felony that threatens death or serious bodily harm or unless there are other circumstances that reasonably create a fear of death or serious bodily harm to the officer or to another.

People v. Orr (22 Cal. App. 4th 780)

A killing is not "justifiable" if it does not constitute a lawful defense of self, others, or property; prevention of a felony; or preservation of the peace. Killing is not "excusable" if it does not result from a lawful act done by lawful means with ordinary caution and lawful intent, and does not result from accident and misfortune under very specific circumstances.

People v. Danielly (33 Cal. 2d 362)

Mere unrestrained and unprovoked rage, or a heat of passion to wreak vengeance, of a legally sane though emotionally unstable or nervous person, is no defense to homicide.

People v. Valentine (169 P. 2d 1)

Defining the "heat of passion" as a passion that would naturally be aroused in the mind of an ordinarily reasonable person under the given facts, and that consequently no defendant may set up his own standard of conduct and justify or excuse himself because of the fact his passions were aroused, unless the jury believed that the facts were sufficient to arouse passion of an ordinarily reasonable man, was proper.

Practicum

Practicum I

Four persons were on a lifeboat in high seas during a storm. After the storm, they floated in the ocean with no food or water. For the first three days, they had nothing to eat or drink. On the fourth day, they caught a sea turtle, on which they subsisted for several days. They had no fresh water except for an occasional rain. On the 18th day, after several discussions, three of the four sailors decided to kill the fourth sailor, who was very weak, and eat his remains. Four days later, the three were rescued. It appears that had the three not killed the other sailor, all of them would have died. Should the survivors be convicted of murder? Would the defense of necessity be available for the three? If all had agreed to a plan to draw lots and kill the unlucky person, would the survivors still be guilty of murder?

Practicum II

The defendant claimed she was attempting to shoot over the head of her boyfriend to scare him. She hit him in the head, killing him. Is she guilty of murder or manslaughter?

Practicum III

Three weeks prior to the killing, the defendant discovered that the victim was involved in a sexual relationship with the defendant's wife. On the afternoon of the killing, the defendant decided to put an end to this activity. He purchased a gun and hunted the victim. After killing the victim, he turned himself in to the police and claimed that the killing was in the heat of a sudden passion. Is he guilty of manslaughter or murder?

Discussion Questions

1. Explain the differences between false imprisonment and kidnapping for the purposes of ransom.
2. In which kidnapping offenses is movement required?
3. What is meant by the terms *consent* and *without free will*?
4. What constitutes sufficient movement for kidnapping crimes?
5. List the essential differences between murder and manslaughter.
6. What is meant by *heat of passion*?
7. When is a homicide not a criminal one?
8. What are the elements of murder in the first degree?
9. When is the killing of a fetus a criminal homicide?
10. Name the types of criminal homicide in California.
11. What are the two types of noncriminal homicides in California?
12. Define *death* as used in murder cases.
13. What is the difference between *expressed* and *implied* *malice*?
14. Define *malice aforethought*.

Self-Study Quiz

True/False

1. All homicides are criminal.
2. To be a criminal homicide, the death must occur within one year and a day after the act causing the death.
3. The *corpus delicti* of a criminal homicide does not contain the elements of the crime.
4. California uses *brain death* as the definition of death.
5. *Malice aforethought* requires a feeling of ill will toward the victim.
6. Malice may be either expressed or implied.
7. A killing to make an escape from a robbery scene is within the felony-murder rule.
8. The felony-murder rule does not apply to those felonies not listed by the statute.
9. The accused killed two people with one rifle shot. He has committed only one murder.
10. The heat of passion may reduce an unlawful killing from murder to manslaughter.
11. Forcible kidnapping in California requires that the victim be moved to at least another county.
12. To be kidnapping in California, the victim must be taken in California.
13. Consent is a valid defense to forcible kidnapping.
14. The movement necessary to constitute forcible kidnapping must be unlawful.
15. If consent is obtained by fraud, the offense may be forcible kidnapping.
16. A two-prong test is often used to determine if forcible kidnapping has been committed.
17. False imprisonment is always a felony in California.
18. False imprisonment involves the unlawful violation of the personal liberty of another.
19. False imprisonment is a lesser and included offense of forcible kidnapping.
20. Posing as a kidnapper is a crime in California.
21. Kidnapping for a ransom, like forcible kidnapping, requires movement to establish the offense.
22. Kidnapping for purposes of robbery is a specific intent crime.
23. A person may conceal a child from the person with legal rights to custody without committing a crime if there is "good cause" for the concealment.

Sex Crimes

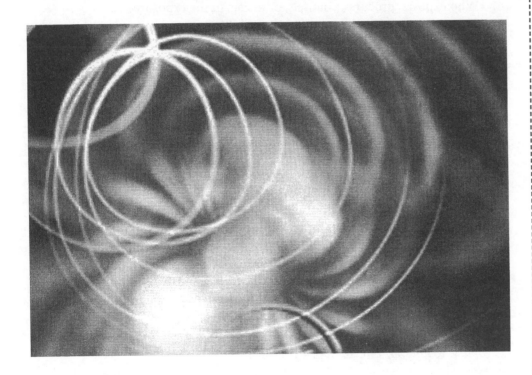

Unnatural deeds do breed unnatural problems.
Shakespeare, MacBeth

9-1 Indecent Exposure

Penal Code 314—Lewd or Obscene Conduct; Indecent Exposure; Obscene Exhibitions; Punishment

Every person who willfully and lewdly, either:

1. Exposes his person, or the private parts thereof, in any public place, or in any place where there are present other persons to be offended or annoyed thereby; or,
2. Procures, counsels, or assists any person so to expose himself or take part in any model artist exhibition, or to make any other exhibition of himself to public view, or the view of any number of persons, such as is offensive to decency, or is adapted to excite to vicious or lewd thoughts or acts, is guilty of a misdemeanor. . . .

9-1a Elements

The following are elements of indecent exposure:

1. Willful exposure of person or private parts
2. At a place where other persons are present who may be annoyed or
3. In public view
4. Who exposes, procures, counsels, or assists in the exposure
5. The act is offensive to decency or designed to incite vicious or lewd thoughts or acts

9-1b Discussion

Sexual motivation for public exposure of a person's privates is an essential requirement of the felony offense of indecent exposure (*People v. Swearington,* 71 Cal. App. 3d 935). In one case, evidence was sufficient to sustain the defendant's conviction of attempted indecent exposure, even though the victim did not see the defendant's genitals, where the defendant appeared nude in the victim's apartment (*People v. Rehmeyer,* 19 Cal. App. 4th 1758). Nudity in and of itself is not within the proscription of this section relating to exposure of person or the private parts thereof (*Eckl v. Davis,* 51 Cal. App. 3d 831).

Nude sunbathing on Black's Beach in San Diego (a beach where nude sunbathing is popular), while located in an area open to the public was not considered as lewd conduct under Section 647(a) in *In re Smith* (7 Cal. 3d 362). The court in this case stated that nudity of this type is not of itself lewd conduct.

Felony indecent exposure may be an underlying felony for a burglary charge. As one court noted, in elevating residential indecent exposure to felony status, the legislature did not intend to preclude burglary prosecutions of persons who enter residential structures with the specific felonious intent to expose themselves (*People v. Rehmeyer,* 19 Cal. App. 4th 1758).

9-2 Sex-Related Crimes

The following is a list of sex-related crimes and the Penal Code section that applies to them.

- Rape (PC 261)
- Rape of Spouse (PC 292b)
- Penetration of Genitals or Anus with Foreign Object (PC 289)
- Sexual Battery (PC 243.4)
- Indecent Exposure (PC 314)
- Oral Copulation (PC 288a)
- Sodomy (PC 286)
- Sexually Assaulting Animal (PC 286.5)
- Unlawful Sexual Intercourse (PC 261.5)
- Incest (PC 285)

- Pimping (PC 266h) [Discussed in Chapter 13]
- Selling Person for Illicit Use (PC 266f) [Discussed in Chapter 13]
- Pandering (PC 266i) [Discussed in Chapter 13]
- Prostitution (PC 647b) [Discussed in Chapter 13]

Penal Code 261—Rape; Acts Constituting

9-3 Rape

(a) Rape is an act of sexual intercourse accomplished with a person not the spouse of the perpetrator, under any of the following circumstances:

  (1) Where a person is incapable, because of a mental disorder or developmental or physical disability, of giving legal consent, and this is known or reasonably should be known to the person committing the act . . .

  (2) Where it is accomplished against a person's will by means of force, violence, duress, menace, or fear of immediate and unlawful bodily injury on the person or another.

  (3) Where a person is prevented from resisting by any intoxicating or anesthetic substance, or any controlled substance, and this condition was known, or reasonably should have been known by the accused.

  (4) Where a person is at the time unconscious of the nature of the act, and this is known to the accused. As used in this paragraph, *unconscious of the nature of the act* means incapable of resisting because the victim meets one of the following conditions:

  (A) Was unconscious or asleep
  (B) Was not aware, knowing, perceiving, or cognizant that the act occurred
  (C) Was not aware, knowing, perceiving, or cognizant of the essential characteristics of the act due to the perpetrator's fraud in fact

  (5) Where a person submits under the belief that the person committing the act is the victim's spouse, and this belief is induced by any artifice, pretense, or concealment practiced by the accused, with intent to induce the belief.

  (6) Where the act is accomplished against the victim's will by threatening to retaliate in the future against the victim or any other person, and there is a reasonable possibility that the perpetrator will execute the threat. As used in this paragraph, *threatening to retaliate* means a threat to kidnap or falsely imprison, or to inflict extreme pain, serious bodily injury, or death.

  (7) Where the act is accomplished against the victim's will by threatening to use the authority of a public official to incarcerate, arrest, or deport the victim or another, and the victim has a reasonable belief that the perpetrator is a public official. As used in this paragraph, *public official* means a person employed by a governmental agency who has the authority, as part of that position, to incarcerate, arrest, or deport another. The perpetrator does not actually have to be a public official.

(b) As used in this section, *duress* means a direct or implied threat of force, violence, danger, or retribution sufficient to coerce a reasonable person of ordinary susceptibilities to perform an act which otherwise would not have been performed, or acquiesce in an act to which one otherwise would not have submitted. The total circumstances, including the age of the victim, and his or her relationship to the defendant, are factors to consider in appraising the existence of duress.

(c) As used in this section, *menace* means any threat, declaration, or act which shows an intention to inflict an injury upon another.

Penal Code 263—Essential Elements; Penetration

The essential guilt of rape consists in the outrage to the person and feelings of the victim of the rape. Any sexual penetration, however slight, is sufficient to complete the crime.

9-3a Elements

The following are the elements of rape:

1. Sexual intercourse with a person not the spouse of the perpetrator
2. Without the lawful consent of the victim

9-3b Discussion

The fundamental wrong at which the law of rape is aimed is not an application of physical force that causes physical harm, but, rather, the violation of a woman's will and sexuality; thus, the law of rape does not require that the force used cause physical harm (*People v. Cicero,* 157 Cal. App. 3d 465).

In California, a conviction of rape may be had solely on the testimony of the victim. There is no requirement for corroboration of the victim's testimony (*People v. Frye,* 117 Cal. App. 3d 101). Note: Since the elements of rape involve sexual intercourse with a person, a female may be convicted of raping a male in California.

As noted, to be convicted of rape under PC 261, the victim must not be the spouse of the perpetrator. (Spousal rape is discussed later in Section 9-16 in this chapter.) Only one punishable offense of rape results from a single act of intercourse, even though that act may be accomplished under more than one set of conditions or circumstances specified in subdivisions of PC 261. The subdivisions merely define the circumstances under which acts of intercourse may be deemed an act of rape and are not to be construed as creating several offenses of rape based upon that single act (*People v. Blankenship,* 103 Cal. App. 2d 60).

Live Victim

For purposes of rape conviction, an act of sexual intercourse must involve a live victim who does not effectively consent (*People v. Rowland,* 4 Cal. 4th 238). A person who attempts to rape a live victim, kills the victim in attempt, and then has intercourse with the body has committed only attempted rape, not actual rape, but the person is guilty of felony-murder and is subject to rape special circumstance (*People v. Kelly,* 1 Cal. 4th 495).

Attempted Rape and Lesser Offenses

Attempted rape requires the intent and attempt to make penetration (*People v. Ray,* 187 Cal. App. 2d 182). An assault with intent to commit rape and simple assault are lesser and included offenses of rape (*People v. Chavez,* 103 Cal. 407).

Rape Trauma Syndrome

Although in a rape prosecution expert testimony on the aftereffects of rape may be admitted for a variety of purposes, expert testimony that a complaining witness suffers from rape trauma syndrome is not admissible to prove that the witness was raped, and even where the expert stops short of expressing an opinion on the ultimate issue but merely states that the witness is suffering from rape trauma syndrome, use of that terminology is likely to mislead the jury into inferring that such a classification reflects the scientific judgment that the witness was, in fact, raped (*People v. Bledsoe,* 36 Cal. 3d 236).

Intoxication

That the defendant may have been intoxicated at the time of assault and that he was impotent when intoxicated are not of themselves defenses to assault with intent to commit rape (*People v. Peckham*, 232 Cal. App. 2d 163). In one case, the inability by reason of intoxication to form specific intent was not a defense to the charge of rape (*People v. Potter*, 77 Cal. App. 3d 45). Sterility is also not a defense (*People v. Langdon*, 192 Cal. App. 3d 1419).

Intent

A defendant does not possess the wrongful intent that is necessary for a conviction of either kidnapping or rape by means of force or threat if he entertains a reasonable and bona fide belief that the victim voluntarily consented to accompany him and to engage in sexual intercourse. The burden is on the defendant, to establish his mistake of fact defense, to prove that he had a bona fide and reasonable belief that the prosecutrix consented to movement and to sexual intercourse and, as to that issue, the defendant is only required to raise a reasonable doubt as to whether he had such a belief (*People v. Mayberry*, 15 Cal. 3d 143).

Penetration

Penetration is an essential element of the crime of rape. Sexual intercourse for the purposes of Section 261 is completed with a sexual penetration, however slight (*People v. Karsai*, 131 Cal. App. 3d 224).

Lack of Consent

Penal Code 261.6—Consent Defined

In prosecutions under Section 261, 262, 286, 288a, or 289, in which consent is at issue, "consent" shall be defined to mean positive cooperation in act or attitude pursuant to an exercise of free will. The person must act freely and voluntarily and have knowledge of the nature of the act or transaction involved.

A current or previous dating or marital relationship shall not be sufficient to constitute consent where consent is at issue in a prosecution under Section 261, 262, 286, 288a, or 289.

Nothing in this section shall affect the admissibility of evidence or the burden of proof on the issue of consent.

Penal Code 261.7—Sex Crime Victim; Request for Condom, Other Birth Control Device Not Sufficient to Constitute Consent

In prosecutions under Section 261, 262, 286, 288a, or 289, in which consent is at issue, evidence that the victim suggested, requested, or otherwise communicated to the defendant that the defendant use a condom or other birth control device, without additional evidence of consent, is not sufficient to constitute consent.

Valid consent to the sexual intercourse is a defense to the crime of rape (*People v. Alfrand*, 61 Cal. App. 3d 414). A good faith belief by the accused that the woman had consented to the sexual intercourse was a defense to the crime of rape by force or fear in *People v. Anderson* (144 Cal. App. 3d 55).

If a woman initially gives consent, but later withdraws her consent, any sexual penetration after she withdraws her consent is rape. If consent is, however, withdrawn after penetration has occurred, that act of intercourse is not rape (*People v. Vela*, 172 Cal. App. 3d 237).

Consent Obtained by Fraud

Fraudulent statements or misrepresentations that induce sexual intercourse is material only for rape under subsection (5) of PC 261 (regarding misrepresentation of status as a spouse). Lack of the consent of the victim is an essential element of rape under subsections (2) and (3). "Consent" even though induced by fraud is still a defense to subsections (2) and (3) (*People v. Harris*, 93 Cal. App. 3d 103). Note: PC 266(c) makes it a crime (unlawful intercourse) to induce sexual intercourse by the use of false representation made with the intent to create fear.

A conviction was upheld under subsection (5) where the female, in good faith, entered into a "mock marriage" that was arranged by the accused. She then engaged in sexual intercourse with him on the mistaken belief that she was married to him (*People v. McCoy*, 58 Cal. App. 534).

Unconscious Victim

To constitute rape under subsection (4) (unconscious victim), it is not necessary that the victim be totally and physically unconscious. A victim is considered unconscious when the victim is unaware of the nature of the act being committed on her, and the accused is aware of her state (*People v. Ogunmola*, 193 Cal. App. 3d 274). In one case, a conviction was upheld under PC 261(4), where the victim went to the defendant's office for an abortion. During one of the follow-up visits, the defendant had intercourse with her after giving her an injection that made her lightheaded and carefree (*People v. Ing*, 65 Cal. 2d 603).

In another case prosecuted under subsection (4), the conviction was reversed where the accused identified himself as a doctor and induced the victim to engage in sexual intercourse based on his false statement to her that she was suffering from a dangerous, highly infectious and fatal disease and would die unless she had sexual intercourse with an anonymous donor who had been injected with a serum that would cure the disease. The court held that based on the preceding facts, there was no rape of a victim who was unconscious as to the nature of the act, that the woman understood the nature of the act, and there was no evidence indicating that she lacked the capacity to appreciate the nature of the sex act (*Boro v. Superior Court*, 163 Cal. App. 3d 1224).

A victim need not be totally and physically unconscious in order that the statute defining rape as an act of sexual intercourse where person is at the time unconscious of nature of act, and this is known to the accused, apply (*Boro v. Superior Court*, 163 Cal. App. 3d 1224).

Rape by Force or Fear

The crime of forcible rape is committed if at any time during the struggle, the accused intends to use force or threatens to use force to gratify his lustful concupiscence against the victim's will (*People v. Royal*, 53 Cal. 62). The actual use of physical force is not necessary. The threat of great and immediate bodily harm is sufficient to constitute force. The threat, however, must be sufficient to put the victim in actual fear of bodily injury (*People v. Benavidez*, 255 Cal. App. 2d 563).

The amount of force or threats of force required for conviction of forcible rape is that amount of physical force required under the circumstances to overcome the victim's resistance (*People v. Wheeler*, 71 Cal. App. 3d 902). To convict an accused of forcible rape, actual physical resistance by the victim is not required (*People v.*

Barnes, 42 Cal. 3d 284). The necessary threats need not be verbally expressed. Acts, conduct, or the exhibition of a weapon may imply the necessary threats (*People v. Benadivez,* 255 Cal. App. 2d 563).

Sexual molestation can be accomplished by duress, even if the molester does not know why the victim is submitting (*People v. Senior,* 3 Cal. App. 4th 765). The particular means by which fear is imparted is not an element of rape (*People v. Iniguez,* 7 Cal. 4th 847).

In one case, there was sufficient evidence of "force, violence, duress, menace, or fear of immediate and unlawful bodily injury on the victim or another person" to support the defendant's convictions for sexual offenses, despite his claim that he had, at most, fraudulently obtained the consent of victims, who believed he was a holy man; the victims' initial consent was only to submit to "treatment" of illnesses, not to specific acts he performed on them and, moreover, he imposed psychological and physical deprivations upon victims to coerce them to submit to treatments against their will, trading upon their strongly held religious beliefs (*People v. Cardenas,* 21 Cal. App. 4th 927).

9-4 Penetration by Foreign Object

Penal Code 289

(a) (1) Any person who commits an act of sexual penetration when the act is accomplished against the victim's will by means of force, violence, duress, menace, or fear of immediate and unlawful bodily injury on the victim or another person shall be punished by imprisonment in the state prison for three, six, or eight years.

(2) Any person who commits an act of sexual penetration when the act is accomplished against the victim's will by threatening to retaliate in the future against the victim or any other person, and there is a reasonable possibility that the perpetrator will execute the threat, shall be punished by imprisonment in the state prison for three, six, or eight years.

[Subsections (b) and (c) prohibit such conduct on a person incapable of giving consent.]

[Subsection (d) prohibits similar conduct on an unconscious person.]

[Subsection (e) prohibits such conduct on an intoxicated person.]

[Subsection (f) prohibits such conduct where the person submits under the belief that the person committing the act is the spouse of the victim.]

[Subsection (g) prohibits such conduct where consent is obtained by threat to use the authority of a public official.]

[Subsection (h) prohibits such conduct on a person under the age of 18.]

[Subsection (i) prohibits such conduct by a person over the age of 21 years against a person under the age of 16. Note: This offense has a greater maximum punishment than the offense under subsection (h) above.]

[Subsection (j) prohibits such conduct by a person under the age of 14 where the offender is more than 10 years older than the victim. Note: This offense has a greater maximum punishment that the offenses under subsections (h) and (i).]

(k) As used in this section, "foreign object, substance, instrument, or device" shall include any part of the body, except a sexual organ.

(l) As used in Subsection (a) "threatening to retaliate" means a threat to kidnap or falsely imprison, or inflict extreme pain, serious bodily injury or death.

9-4a Elements

The elements of the crime of anal or genital penetration are as follows:

1. The intentional anal or genital penetration of another
2. With any object except a "sexual organ"
3. Without the lawful consent of the other person

9-4b Discussion

In cases where the victim is a child, lack of consent is automatically assumed. There is no requirement that the accused make the penetration for sexually motivated reasons as long as the acts are intentionally committed (*People v. White*, 179 Cal. App. 3d 193). A finger is a "foreign object" within meaning of statute prohibiting penetration of genital or anal openings by foreign object (*People v. Adams*, 19 Cal. App. 4th 412).

9-5 Gang Rape

Penal Code 264.1 prohibits conduct when the defendant, voluntarily acting in concert with another person, by force or violence and against the will of the victim, commits rape or anal or genital penetration by a foreign object. These acts are more commonly known as "gang rape," which is a separate crime from the crime of rape. To be guilty of this offense, the accused need only aid or abet in some manner. He or she does not need to personally participate in the act (*People v. Best*, 143 Cal. App. 3d 232).

9-6 Unlawful Sexual Intercourse

Penal Code 261.5—Unlawful Sexual Intercourse with Person under Age 18; Age of Perpetrator

(a) Unlawful sexual intercourse is an act of sexual intercourse accomplished with a person who is not the spouse of the perpetrator, if the person is a minor. For the purposes of this section, a *minor* is a person under the age of 18 years and an *adult* is a person who is at least 18 years of age.

(b) Any person who engages in an act of unlawful sexual intercourse with a minor who is not more than three years older or three years younger than the perpetrator, is guilty of a misdemeanor.

(c) Any person who engages in an act of unlawful sexual intercourse with a minor who is more than three years younger than the perpetrator is guilty of either a misdemeanor or a felony, and shall be punished by imprisonment in a county jail not exceeding one year, or by imprisonment in the state prison.

(d) Any person over the age of 21 years who engages in an act of unlawful sexual intercourse with a minor who is under 16 years of age is guilty of either a misdemeanor or a felony, and shall be punished by imprisonment in a county jail not exceeding one year, or by imprisonment in the state prison for two, three, or four years.

(e)

(1) Notwithstanding any other provision of this section, an adult who engages in an act of sexual intercourse with a minor in violation of this section may be liable for civil penalties in the following amounts:

(A) An adult who engages in an act of unlawful sexual intercourse with a minor less than two years younger than the adult is liable for a civil penalty not to exceed two thousand dollars ($2,000).

(B) An adult who engages in an act of unlawful sexual intercourse with a minor at least two years younger than the adult is liable for a civil penalty not to exceed five thousand dollars ($5,000).

(C) An adult who engages in an act of unlawful sexual intercourse with a minor at least three years younger than the adult is liable for a civil penalty not to exceed ten thousand dollars ($10,000).

(D) An adult over the age of 21 years who engages in an act of unlawful sexual intercourse with a minor under 16 years of age is liable for a civil penalty not to exceed twenty-five thousand dollars ($25,000).

(2) The district attorney may bring actions to recover civil penalties pursuant to this subdivision. From the amounts collected for each case, an amount equal to the costs of pursuing the action shall be deposited with the treasurer of the county in which the judgment was entered, and the remainder shall be deposited in the Underage Pregnancy Prevention Fund, which is hereby created in the State Treasury. Amounts deposited in the Underage Pregnancy Prevention Fund may be used only for the purpose of preventing underage pregnancy upon appropriation by the Legislature.

(3) [Omitted.]

9-6a Discussion

Consent is not an issue in this crime, since sexual intercourse with a female under the age of 18 years is prohibited (*Michael M. v. Superior Court*, 25 Cal. 3d 608). The section defining unlawful sexual intercourse as an act of intercourse with a female under age of 18 is not unconstitutional as making a classification of minor females to exclusion of minor males and hence denying the male equal protection of the law (*People v. Mackey*, 46 Cal. App. 3d 755). In *People v. Courtney* (180 Cal. App. 2d 61), sexual intercourse with a female who was under age 18 and who was not the defendant's wife constituted the crime of rape even though the female was a married woman.

A defendant who exploits women in the field of prostitution and has women perform sex acts for money in making pornographic movies, which is a form of prostitution, has the burden of making sure that his victims are of the age of consent (*People v. Zeihm*, 40 Cal. App. 3d 1085).

The defendant's reasonable belief (referred to in some cases as a "good faith and reasonable" belief) that the victim was over the age of 18 years is a defense to statutory rape. The burden, however, to establish this defense is on the defense (*People v. Zeihm*, 40 Cal. App. 3d 1085 and *People v. Hernandez*, 61 Cal. 2d 519). Note: The belief as to the age of the victim must not only be in good faith but also reasonable.

9-7 Spousal Rape

Penal Code 262—Rape of Person Who Is Spouse of Perpetrator

(a) Rape of a person who is the spouse of the perpetrator is an act of sexual intercourse accomplished under any of the following circumstances:

(1) Where it is accomplished against a person's will by means of force, violence, duress, menace, or fear of immediate and unlawful bodily injury on the person or another.

(2) Where a person is prevented from resisting by any intoxicating or anesthetic substance, or any controlled substance, and this condition was known, or reasonably should have been known, by the accused.

(3) Where a person is at the time unconscious of the nature of the act, and this is known to the accused. As used in this paragraph, "unconscious of the nature of the act" means incapable of resisting because the victim meets one of the following conditions:

(A) Was unconscious or asleep.

(B) Was not aware, knowing, perceiving, or cognizant that the act occurred.

(C) Was not aware, knowing, perceiving, or cognizant of the essential characteristics of the act due to the perpetrator's fraud in fact.

(4) Where the act is accomplished against the victim's will by threatening to retaliate in the future against the victim or any other person, and there is a reasonable possibility that the perpetrator will execute the threat. As used in this paragraph, "threatening to retaliate" means a threat to kidnap or falsely imprison, or to inflict extreme pain, serious bodily injury, or death.

(5) Where the act is accomplished against the victim's will by threatening to use the authority of a public official to incarcerate, arrest, or deport the victim or another, and the victim has a reasonable belief that the perpetrator is a public official. As used in this paragraph, "public official" means a person employed by a governmental agency who has the authority, as part of that position, to incarcerate, arrest, or deport another. The perpetrator does not actually have to be a public official.

(b) Section 800 shall apply to this section. However, no prosecution shall be commenced under this section unless the violation was reported to medical personnel, a member of the clergy, an attorney, a shelter representative, a counselor, a judicial officer, a rape crisis agency, a prosecuting agency, a law enforcement officer, or a firefighter within one year after the date of the violation. This reporting requirement shall not apply if the victim's allegation of the offense is corroborated by independent evidence that would otherwise be admissible during trial.

(c) As used in this section, *duress* means a direct or implied threat of force, violence, danger, or retribution sufficient to coerce a reasonable person of ordinary susceptibilities to perform an act which otherwise would not have been performed, or acquiesce in an act to which one otherwise would not have submitted. The total circumstances, including the age of the victim, and his or her relationship to the defendant, are factors to consider in apprising the existence of duress.

(d) As used in this section, *menace* means any threat, declaration, or act that shows an intention to inflict an injury upon another.

(e) If probation is granted upon conviction of a violation of this section, the conditions of probation may include, in lieu of a fine, one or both of the following requirements:

(1) That the defendant make payments to a battered women's shelter, up to a maximum of one thousand dollars ($1,000)

(2) That the defendant reimburse the victim for reasonable costs of counseling and other reasonable expenses that the court finds are the direct result of the defendant's offense

For any order to pay a fine, make payments to a battered women's shelter, or pay restitution as a condition of probation under this subdivision, the court shall make a determination of the defendant's ability to pay. In no event shall any order to make payments to a battered women's shelter be made if it would impair the ability of the defendant to pay direct restitution to the victim or court-ordered child support. Where the injury to a married person is caused in whole or in part by the criminal acts of his or her spouse in violation of this section, the community property may not be used to discharge the liability of the offending spouse for restitution to the injured spouse, required by Section 1203.04, as operative on or before August 2, 1995, or Section 1202.4, or to a shelter for costs with regard to the injured spouse and dependents, required by this section, until all separate property of the offending spouse is exhausted.

Penal Code 286—Sodomy [Partial]

9-8 Sodomy

(a) Sodomy is sexual contact consisting of contact between the penis of one person and the anus of another person. Any sexual penetration, however slight, is sufficient to complete the crime of sodomy.
[Subsections (b) through (k) are similar to those for oral copulation noted below.]

The following are the elements of sodomy:

9-8a Elements

1. Sexual contact by penetration
2. Of the penis of one person and the anus of another person
3. Under one of the prohibited situations or circumstances

No specific intent, purpose, or motive is required to commit sodomy. Sodomy requires "penetration" not merely "contact" (*People v. Martinez*, 188 Cal. App. 3d 19 and *People v. McElrath*, 220 Cal. App. 4).

9-8b Discussion

Oral copulation is the act of copulating the mouth of one person with the sexual organ or anus of another person.

9-9 Oral Copulation

Penal Code 288a—Oral Copulation

9-9a Definition

(a) Oral copulation is the act of copulating the mouth of one person with the sexual organ or anus of another person.
[Subsection (b)(1) prohibits oral copulation with another person who is under the age of 18.]
[Subsection (b)(2) prohibits oral copulation by a person over the age of 21 with another person under the age of 16. This offense has a greater maximum punishment than the offense under subsection (b)(1).]
[Subsection (c) prohibits oral copulation with a person under the age of 14 by a person who is 10 years older. This offense has a greater maximum punishment than the offenses under subsections (b)(1) and (2).]
[Subsection (d) prohibits oral copulation by force or fear.]
[Subsection (e) prohibits oral copulation by any person confined in a state or local confinement facility.]
[Subsection (f) prohibits oral copulation where the other party is unconscious of the nature of the act.]
[Subsections (g) and (h) prohibit oral copulation with a person who is incapable of giving lawful consent.]
[Subsection (i) prohibits oral copulation with an intoxicated person.]
[Subsection (j) prohibits oral copulation where consent is obtained under the false belief that the person committing the act is the spouse of the other person.]
[Subsection (k) prohibits oral copulation where consent is obtained under the threat to use the authority of a public official.]

9-9b Discussion

No specific intent, purpose, or motive is necessary to commit this offense. Oral copulation is not illegal if engaged in private by consenting persons over the age of 18. It is a crime, however, if committed by someone confined in a state or local confinement facility or on a victim who is unconscious, insane, or otherwise unable to give consent, and this condition is known or should have been known by the perpetrator.

9-10 Sexually Assaulting Animals

Penal Code 286.5

Any person who sexually assaults any animal protected by Section 597(f) for the purpose of arousing or gratifying the sexual desire of the person is guilty of a misdemeanor.

[Section 597(f) refers to animal neglect and protects pets and other domestic animals.]

9-11 Incest

Penal Code 285—Incest Defined

Persons being within the degrees of consanguinity within which marriages are declared by law to be incestuous and void, who intermarry with each other, or who commit fornication or adultery with each other, are punishable by imprisonment in the state prison.

Evidence Code 621(a)

Except as provided in subdivision (b), the issue of a wife cohabiting with her husband, who is not impotent or sterile, is conclusively presumed to be the child of the marriage. [Subdivision (b) refers to those cases where a blood test establishes that the husband cannot be the father of the child.]

9-11a Elements

The following are the elements of the crime of incest:

1. The marriage or sexual intercourse between
2. Parties who are related by blood to each other by certain degrees of relationship

9-11b Discussion

Only marriage and sexual intercourse between persons closely related by blood are prohibited under PC 285. It does not prohibit oral copulation. Lack of knowledge of the relationship is a defense to incest (*People v. Koller*, 142 Cal. 621). To be incestuous, there must be a blood relationship. Accordingly, where a father has sexual intercourse with his adopted daughter, while he is guilty of other crimes, he is not guilty of incest (*People v. Russell*, 22 Cal. App. 3d 330).

If both parties are over the age of 14, and both consent to the sexual acts, then both are guilty of incest (*People v. Pettis*, 95 Cal. App. 2d 790).

Consanguineous

Civil Code 4400 lists the following relationships as consanguineous (such close blood relatives as to make marriage and/or intercourse illegal):

- Natural parents, or any degree of grandparents and their children grandchildren, etc.
- Uncles or aunts and their nieces and nephews
- Brothers and sisters and other siblings, whether whole-blood or half-blood

Penal Code 266c—Inducing Commission of Sexual Act through False Representations Creating Fear

Every person who induces any other person to engage in sexual intercourse, penetration of the genital or anal openings by a foreign object, substance, instrument, or device, oral copulation, or sodomy when his or her consent is procured by false or fraudulent representation or pretense that is made with the intent to create fear, and which does induce fear, and that would cause a reasonable person in like circumstances to act contrary to the person's free will, and does cause the victim to so act, is punishable by imprisonment in either the county jail ... or in the state prison. ... As used in this section, *fear* means the fear of unlawful physical injury or death to the person or to any relative of the person or member of the person's family.

The following are the elements of the crime of inducing the commission of a sexual act through false representation:

1. Inducing a person, not the spouse of the perpetrator
2. To engage in sexual intercourse or
3. Penetration of the genital or anal openings by a foreign object or
4. Oral copulation or
5. Sodomy
6. By consent procured by
7. False or fraudulent representation or
8. Pretense made with the intent to and actually creating reasonable fear in the victim
9. By such conduct that would deprive a reasonable person of their free will

Penal Code 647—Disorderly Conduct

Every person who commits any of the following acts is guilty of disorderly conduct, a misdemeanor:

(a) Who solicits anyone to engage in or who engages in lewd or dissolute conduct in any public place or in any place open to the public or exposed to public view.

(b) Who solicits or who agrees to engage in or who engages in any act of prostitution. A person agrees to engage in an act of prostitution when, with specific intent to so engage, he or she manifests an acceptance of an offer or solicitation to so engage, regardless of whether the offer or solicitation was made by a person who also possessed the specific intent to engage in prostitution. No agreement to engage in an act of prostitution shall constitute a violation of this subdivision unless some act, in addition to the agreement, is done within this state in furtherance of the commission of an act of prostitution by the person agreeing to engage in that act. As used in this subdivision, *prostitution* includes any lewd act between persons for money or other consideration.

(c) Who accosts other persons in any public place or in any place open to the public for the purpose of begging or soliciting alms.

(d) Who loiters in or about any toilet open to the public for the purpose of engaging in or soliciting any lewd or lascivious or any unlawful act.

(e) Who loiters or wanders upon the streets or from place to place without apparent reason or business and who refuses to identify himself or herself and to account for his or her presence when requested by any peace officer so to do, if the surrounding circumstances would indicate to a reasonable person that the public safety demands this identification.

(f) Who is found in any public place under the influence of intoxicating liquor, any drug, controlled substance, toluene, or any combination of any intoxicating liquor, drug, controlled substance, or toluene, in such a condition that he or she is unable to exercise care for his or her own safety or the safety of others, or by reason of his or her being under the influence of intoxicating liquor, any drug, controlled substance, toluene, or any combination of any intoxicating liquor, drug, or toluene, interferes with or obstructs or prevents the free use of any street, sidewalk, or other public way.

(g) When a person has violated subdivision (f) of this section, a peace officer, if he or she is reasonably able to do so, shall place the person, or cause him or her to be placed, in civil protective custody. The person shall be taken to a facility, designated pursuant to Section 5170 of the Welfare and Institutions Code, for the 72-hour treatment and evaluation of inebriates. A peace officer may place a person in civil protective custody with that kind and degree of force which would be lawful were he or she effecting an arrest for a misdemeanor without a warrant. No person who has been placed in civil protective custody shall thereafter be subject to any criminal prosecution or juvenile court proceeding based on the facts giving rise to this placement. This subdivision shall not apply to the following persons:

(1) Any person who is under the influence of any drug, or under the combined influence of intoxicating liquor and any drug

(2) Any person who a peace officer has probable cause to believe has committed any felony, or who has committed any misdemeanor in addition to subdivision (f) of this section

(3) Any person who a peace officer in good faith believes will attempt escape or will be unreasonably difficult for medical personnel to control

(h) Who loiters, prowls, or wanders upon the private property of another, at any time, without visible or lawful business with the owner or occupant. As used in this subdivision, *loiter* means to delay or linger without a lawful purpose for being on the property and for the purpose of committing a crime as opportunity may be discovered

(i) Who, while loitering, prowling, or wandering upon the private property of another, at any time, peeks in the door or window of any inhabited building or structure, without visible or lawful business with the owner or occupant

(j) Who lodges in any building, structure, vehicle, or place, whether public or private, without the permission of the owner or person entitled to the possession or in control of it

(k) (1) Any person who looks through a hole or opening, into, or otherwise views, by means of any instrumentality, including, but not limited to, a periscope, telescope, binoculars, camera, motion picture camera, or camcorder, the interior of a bathroom, changing room, fitting room, dressing room, or tanning booth, or the interior of any other area in which the occupant has a reasonable expectation of privacy, with the intent to invade the privacy of a person or persons inside. This subdivision shall not apply to those areas of a private business used to count currency or other negotiable instruments.

(2) Any person who uses a concealed camcorder, motion picture camera, or photographic camera of any type, to secretly videotape, film, photograph, or record by electronic means, another, identifiable person under or through the clothing being worn by that other person, for the purpose of viewing the body of, or the undergarments worn by, that other person, without the consent or knowledge of that other person, with the intent to arouse, appeal to, or gratify the lust, passions, or sexual desires of that person and invade the privacy of that other person, under circumstances in which the other person has a reasonable expectation of privacy.

In any accusatory pleading charging a violation of subdivision (b), if the defendant has been once previously convicted of a violation of that subdivision, the previous conviction shall be charged in the accusatory pleading. If the previous conviction is found to be true by the jury, upon a jury trial, or by the court, upon a court trial, or is admitted by the defendant, the defendant shall be imprisoned in a county jail for a period of not less than 45 days and shall not be eligible for release upon completion of sentence, on probation, on parole, on work furlough or work release, or on any other basis until he or she has served a period of not less than 45 days in a county jail. In all cases in which probation is granted, the court shall require as a condition thereof that the person be confined in a county jail for at least 45 days. In no event does the court have the power to absolve a person who violates this subdivision from the obligation of spending at least 45 days in confinement in a county jail.

In any accusatory pleading charging a violation of subdivision (b), if the defendant has been previously convicted two or more times of a violation of that subdivision, each such previous conviction shall be charged in the accusatory pleading. If two or more of these previous convictions are found to be true by the jury, upon a jury trial, or by the court, upon a court trial, or are admitted by the defendant, the defendant shall be imprisoned in a county jail for a period of not less than 90 days and shall not be eligible for release upon completion of sentence, on probation, on parole, on work furlough or work release, or on any other basis until he or she has served a period of not less than 90 days in a county jail. In all cases in which probation is granted, the court shall require as a condition thereof that the person be confined in a county jail for at least 90 days. In no event does the court have the power to absolve a person who violates this subdivision from the obligation of spending at least 90 days in confinement in a county jail.

In addition to any punishment prescribed by this section, a court may suspend, for not more than 30 days, the privilege of the person to operate a motor vehicle pursuant to Section 13201.5 of the Vehicle Code for any violation of subdivision (b) that was committed within 1,000 feet of a private residence and with the use of a vehicle.

Penal Code 288—Lewd or Lascivious Acts with Child under Age 14; Punishment; Prevention of Psychological Harm to Victim; Additional Fine

(a) Any person who willfully and lewdly commits any lewd or lascivious act, including any of the acts constituting other crimes provided for in Part 1, upon or with the body, or any part or member thereof, of a child who is under the age of 14 years, with the intent of arousing, appealing to, or gratifying the lust, passions, or sexual desires of that person or the child, is guilty of a felony and shall be punished by imprisonment in the state prison for three, six, or eight years.

(b)

    (1) Any person who commits an act described in subdivision (a) by use of force, violence, duress, menace, or fear of immediate and unlawful bodily injury on the victim or another person, is guilty of a felony and shall be punished by imprisonment in the state prison for three, six, or eight years.

    (2) Any person who is a caretaker and commits an act described in subdivision (a) upon a dependent adult by use of force, violence, duress, menace, or fear of immediate and unlawful bodily injury on the victim or another person, with the intent described in subdivision (a), is guilty of a felony and shall be punished by imprisonment in the state prison for three, six, or eight years.

(c)

    (1) Any person who commits an act described in subdivision (a) with the intent described in that subdivision, and the victim is a child of 14 or 15 years, and the defendant is at least 10 years older than the child, is guilty of a public offense and shall be punished by imprisonment in the state prison for one, two, or three years, or by imprisonment in a county jail for not more than one year.

    (2) Any person who is a caretaker and commits an act described in subdivision (a) upon a dependent adult, with the intent described in subdivision (a), is guilty of a public offense and shall be punished by imprisonment in the state prison for one, two, or three years, or by imprisonment in a county jail for not more than one year.

(d) In any arrest or prosecution under this section or Section 288.5, the peace officer, district attorney, and the court shall consider the needs of the child victim and shall do whatever is necessary, within existing budgetary resources, and constitutionally permissible to prevent psychological harm to the child victim or to prevent psychological harm to the dependent adult victim resulting from participation in the court process.

(e) Upon the conviction of any person for a violation of subdivision (a) or (b), the court may, in addition to any other penalty or fine imposed, order the defendant to pay an additional fine not to exceed ten thousand dollars ($10,000). In setting the amount of the fine, the court shall consider any relevant factors, including, but not limited to, the seriousness and gravity of the offense, the circumstances of its commission, whether the defendant derived any economic gain as a result of the crime, and the extent to which the victim suffered economic losses as a result of the crime. Every fine imposed and collected under this section shall be deposited in the Victim-Witness Assistance Fund to be available for appropriation to fund child sexual exploitation and child sexual abuse victim counseling centers and prevention programs pursuant to Section 13837.

If the court orders a fine imposed pursuant to this subdivision, the actual administrative cost of collecting that fine, not to exceed 2 percent of the total amount paid, may be paid into the general fund of the county treasury for the use and benefit of the county.

(f) For purposes of paragraph (2) of subdivision (b) and paragraph (2) of subdivision (c), the following definitions apply:

(1) *Caretaker* means an owner, operator, administrator, employee, independent contractor, agent, or volunteer of any of the following public or private facilities when the facilities provide care for elder or dependent adults:

(A) Twenty-four-hour health facilities, as defined in Sections 1250, 1250.2, and 1250.3 of the Health and Safety Code

(B) Clinics

(C) Home health agencies

(D) Adult day health care centers

(E) Secondary schools that serve dependent adults ages 18 to 22 years and postsecondary educational institutions that serve dependent adults or elders

(F) Sheltered workshops

(G) Camps

(H) Community care facilities, as defined by Section 1402 of the Health and Safety Code, and residential care facilities for the elderly, as defined in Section 1569.2 of the Health and Safety Code

(I) Respite care facilities

(J) Foster homes

(K) Regional centers for persons with developmental disabilities

(L) A home health agency licensed in accordance with Chapter 8 (commencing with Section 1725) of Division 2 of the Health and Safety Code

(M) An agency that supplies in-home supportive services

(N) Board and care facilities

(O) Any other protective or public assistance agency that provides health services or social services to elder or dependent adults, including, but not limited to, in-home supportive services, as defined in Section 14005.14 of the Welfare and Institutions Code

(P) Private residences

(2) *Board and care facilities* means licensed or unlicensed facilities that provide assistance with one or more of the following activities:

(A) Bathing

(B) Dressing

(C) Grooming

(D) Medication storage

(E) Medical dispensation

(F) Money management.

(3) *Dependent adult* means any person 18 years of age or older who has a mental disability or disorder that restricts his or her ability to carry out normal activities or to protect his or her rights, including, but not limited to, persons who have developmental disabilities, persons whose mental abilities have significantly diminished because of age.

(g) Paragraph (2) of subdivision (b) and paragraph (2) of subdivision (c) apply to the owners, operators, administrators, employees, independent contractors, agents, or volunteers working at these public or private facilities and only to the extent that the individuals personally commit, conspire, aid, abet, or facilitate any act prohibited by paragraph (2) of subdivision (b) and paragraph (2) of subdivision (c).

(h) Paragraph (2) of subdivision (b) and paragraph (2) of subdivision (c) do not apply to a caretaker who is a spouse of, or who is in an equivalent domestic relationship with, the dependent adult under care.

Penal Code 288.1—Persons Convicted of Lewd Acts upon Minor—Psychiatric Report Required

Any person convicted of committing any lewd or lascivious act including any of the acts constituting other crimes provided for in Part 1 of this code upon or with the body, or any part or member thereof, of a child under the age of 14 years shall not have his or her sentence suspended until the court obtains a report from a reputable psychiatrist, from a reputable psychologist who meets the standards set forth in Section 1027, or from a recognized treatment program pursuant to Section 1000.12 or 1203.066, as to the mental condition of that person.

9-13a Elements of Lewd or Dissolute Conduct

The following are the elements of lewd and dissolute conduct:

1. Soliciting, or engaging in lewd or dissolute conduct
2. In any public place, or in any place open to the public or
3. Exposed to public view

9-13b Discussion

Lewd conduct refers to conduct that disregards socially accepted constraints. Lascivious refers to wanton, lustful conduct. Dissolute refers to conduct that is unashamed, lawless, loose in morals and conduct. For example, dancing in the nude at a party open to the public was considered dissolute conduct in *People v. Scott* (113 Cal. App. 778).

A *lewd and lascivious act* has been defined as an act that has a tendency to excite lust, committed with a disregard for sexual constraints. It is not necessary that the act be sexual in nature (*People v. Dontanville*, 172 Cal. App. 3d 783). The preceding elements require willful and lewd conduct on the part of the participant. There is, however, no requirement for any movement or manipulation of the body or parts thereof. A person convicted under this section is required to register as a sex offender under PC 290.

In one case, the fact that the defendant secretly expected that his allegedly lewd conduct would not be discovered because of a curtain on the booth in a movie arcade did not demonstrate objectively reasonable expectation of privacy (*People v. Freeman*, 66 Cal. App. 3d 424).

9-13c Elements of Lewd Act on Child under 14

The following are elements of a lewd act on a child under 14:

1. A lewd or lascivious act upon any part of the body of
2. A child under the age of 14
3. With the specific intent to arouse, appeal or to gratify the lust or passions or sexual desires of either party

9-13d Discussion

This crime was enacted to protect children from lustful advances and tamperings of callous and unscrupulous persons as well as from the assaults of depraved unfortunates (*People v. Hobbs*, 109 Cal. App. 2d 189). Any touching of any part of body of child under the age of 14 can be a lewd or lascivious act within the meaning of the criminal statute if, under the totality of circumstances in which the act occurred, including any secretive or predatory conduct by the defendant, a reasonable person could conclude that it was sexual in nature. Inadvertent or casual, nonoffensive touching, which is unaccompanied by other direct or circumstantial evidence of intent to arouse, appeal to, or gratify lust, passion, or sexual desire of the defendant or child, will not qualify as a lewd or lascivious act within the meaning of the criminal statute proscribing lewd or lascivious acts with children (*People v. Sharp*, 29 Cal. App. 4th 1772).

One court stated that the defendant's "lewd or lascivious act" and his specific intent of arousing, appealing to, or gratifying passions or sexual desires are separate elements, both of which must be proven to support conviction for lewd and lascivious conduct with a child (*People v. Sharp*, 29 Cal. App. 4th 1772). Conduct that may be innocuous given one intent may be lewd or lascivious within the meaning of the statute prohibiting lewd or lascivious acts with a child under age 14, given sexual intent (*People v. Carson*, 30 Cal. App. 4th 1810). In a prosecution for lewd and lascivious conduct with a child, under this section, providing that the offense may be committed by "any person," a child under the age of 14 years is such a person (*People v. Love*, 29 Cal. App. 521).

In one case, the acts of the defendant of placing his hand under a 12-year-old victim's shirt and bra and touching her breasts, kissing her, and placing her hand on his exposed penis should not have been fragmented into three separate counts of lewd and lascivious acts upon a 12-year-old, and thus, conviction and punishment for two duplicate crimes had to fall; the acts were all committed during one incident (*People v. Bevan*, 208 Cal. App. 3d 393).

The court found in *People v. Sharp* (29 Cal. App. 4th 1772) that a defendant's lewd or lascivious act and his specific intent of arousing, appealing to, or gratifying passions or sexual desires are separate elements, both of which must be proven in order to support conviction for lewd and lascivious conduct with child.

A minor under 14 years of age may be adjudged responsible for committing lewd or lascivious act with another child under 14 years old, or for participating in oral copulation with a person under age of 18, upon clear proof of the minor's knowledge of wrongfulness of acts along with evidence of criminal intent under the charged offenses (*In re Paul C.*, 221 Cal. App. 3d 43).

A reasonable mistake as to the victim's age is not a defense to a charge of lewd or lascivious conduct with a child under the age of 14 years (*People v. Olsen*, 36 Cal. 3d 638). The statute prohibiting lewd and lascivious acts with a child under the age of 14 is violated by a person who directs children to take off their clothing, even if they do not initially remove their underwear (*People v. O'Connor*, 8 Cal. App. 4th 941).

Penal Code 290—Person Convicted of Certain Lewd Crimes Must Register with Sheriff (partial)	**9-14 Registration As Sex Offender**

(a)

   (1) (A) Every person described in paragraph (2), for the rest of his or her life while residing in, or, if he or she has no residence, while located within California, or while attending school or working in California, as described in subparagraph (G), shall be required to register with the chief of police of the city in which he or she is residing, or if he or she has no residence, is located, or the sheriff of the county if he or she is residing, or if he or she has no residence, is located, in an unincorporated area or city that has no police department, and, additionally, with the chief of police of a campus of the University of California, the California State University, or community college if he or she is residing, or if he or she has no residence, is located upon the campus or in any of its facilities, within five working days of coming into, or changing his or her residence or location within, any city, county, or city and county, or

campus in which he or she temporarily resides, or, if he or she has no residence, is located.

(B) If the person who is registering has more than one residence address or location at which he or she regularly resides or is located, he or she shall register in accordance with subparagraph (A) in each of the jurisdictions in which he or she regularly resides or is located. If all of the addresses or locations are within the same jurisdiction, the person shall provide the registering authority with all of the addresses or locations where he or she regularly resides or is located.

(C) If the person who is registering has no residence address, he or she shall update his or her registration no less than once every 90 days in addition to the requirement in subparagraph (A), on a form as may be required by the Department of Justice, with the entity or entities described in subparagraph (A) in whose jurisdiction he or she is located at the time he or she is updating the registration.

(D) Beginning on his or her first birthday following registration or change of address, the person shall be required to register annually, within five working days of his or her birthday, to update his or her registration with the entities described in subparagraph (A), including, verifying his or her name and address, or temporary location, and place of employment including the name and address of the employer, on a form as may be required by the Department of Justice.

(E) In addition, every person who has ever been adjudicated a sexually violent predator, as defined in Section 6600 of the Welfare and Institutions Code, shall, after his or her release from custody, verify his or her address no less than once every 90 days and place of employment, including the name and address of the employer, in a manner established by the Department of Justice.

(F) No entity shall require a person to pay a fee to register or update his or her registration pursuant to this section. The registering agency shall submit registrations, including annual updates or changes of address, directly into the Department of Justice Violent Crime Information Network (VCIN).

(G) Persons required to register in their state of residence who are out-of-state residents employed in California on a full-time or part-time basis, with or without compensation, for more than 14 days, or for an aggregate period exceeding 30 days in a calendar year, shall register in accordance with subparagraph (A). Persons described in paragraph (2) who are out-of-state residents enrolled in any educational institution in California, as defined in Section 22129 of the Education Code, on a full-time or part-time basis, shall register in accordance with subparagraph (A). The place where the out-of-state resident is located, for purposes of registration, shall be the place where the person is employed or attending school. The out-of-state resident subject to this subparagraph shall, in addition to the information required pursuant to subdivision (e), provide the registering authority with the name of his or her place of employment or the name of the school attended in California, and his or her address or location in his or her state of residence. The registration requirement for persons subject to this subparagraph shall become operative on November 25, 2000.

(2) The following persons shall be required to register pursuant to paragraph (1):

(A) Any person who, since July 1, 1944, has been or is hereafter convicted in any court in this state or in any federal or military court of a violation of Section 207 or 209 committed with intent to violate Section 261, 286, 288, 288a, or 289, Section 220, except assault to commit mayhem, Section 243.4, paragraph (1), (2), (3), (4), or (6) of subdivision (a) of Section 261, or paragraph (1) of subdivision (a) of Section 262 involving the use of force or violence for which the person is sentenced to the state prison, Section 264.1, 266, 266c, subdivision (b) of Section 266h, subdivision (b) of Section 266i, 266j, 267, 269, 285, 286, 288, 288a, 288.5, or 289, subdivision (b), (c), or (d) of Section 311.2, Section 311.3, 311.4, 311.10, 311.11, or 647.6, former Section 647a, subdivision (c) of Section 653f, subdivision 1 or 2 of Section 314, any offense involving lewd or lascivious conduct under Section 272, or any felony violation of Section 288.2; or any person who since that date has been or is hereafter convicted of the attempt to commit any of the above-mentioned offenses.

(B) Any person who, since July 1, 1944, has been or hereafter is released, discharged, or paroled from a penal institution where he or she was confined because of the commission or attempted commission of one of the offenses described in subparagraph (A).

(C) Any person who, since July 1, 1944, has been or hereafter is determined to be a mentally disordered sex offender under Article 1 (commencing with Section 6300) of Chapter 2 of Part 2 of Division 6 of the Welfare and Institutions Code or any person who has been found guilty in the guilt phase of a trial for an offense for which registration is required by this section but who has been found not guilty by reason of insanity in the sanity phase of the trial.

(D) Any person who, since July 1, 1944, has been, or is hereafter convicted in any other court, including any state, federal, or military court, of any offense which, if committed or attempted in this state, would have been punishable as one or more of the offenses described in subparagraph (A) or any person ordered by any other court, including any state, federal, or military court, to register as a sex offender for any offense, if the court found at the time of conviction or sentencing that the person committed the offense as a result of sexual compulsion or for purposes of sexual gratification.

[Penal Code Section 290 lists additional individuals who are required to register in subsequent subparagraphs. Those subparagraphs are omitted. Listed next is the information that may be disclosed regarding the individuals who are required to be registered.]

(m)(4) The information that may be disclosed pursuant to this section includes the following:

(A) The offender's full name.
(B) The offender's known aliases.
(C) The offender's gender.
(D) The offender's race.
(E) The offender's physical description.
(F) The offender's photograph.

(G) The offender's date of birth.
(H) Crimes resulting in registration under this section.
(I) The offender's address, which must be verified prior to publication.
(J) Description and license plate number of offender's vehicles or vehicles the offender is known to drive.
(K) Type of victim targeted by the offender.
(L) Relevant parole or probation conditions, such as one prohibiting contact with children.
(M) Dates of crimes resulting in classification under this section.
(N) Date of release from confinement.

However, information disclosed pursuant to this subdivision shall not include information that would identify the victim.

(5) If a law enforcement agency discloses information pursuant to this subdivision, it shall include, with the disclosure, a statement that the purpose of the release of the information is to allow members of the public to protect themselves and their children from sex offenders.

[Remainder of section omitted.]

9-14a Discussion

Penal Code 290 requires persons convicted of sex offenses or sex-related crimes to register within five working days of coming into any county or city in which he or she will reside for any period of time with the chief of police or the sheriff of the county. The registration laws set forth in PC 290 are called the "Megan's Law" based on a child in New Jersey who was sexually abused and killed by a sex offender.

Cases on Point

People v. Blankenship (103 Cal. App. 2d 60)

Only one punishable offense of rape results from single act of intercourse, even though that act may be accomplished under more than one of conditions or circumstances specified in subdivisions of that Penal Code section, and those subdivisions merely define circumstances under which acts of intercourse may be deemed an act of rape and are not to be construed as creating several offenses of rape based on that single act.

People v. Mummert (57 Cal. App. 2d 849)

The statute defining rape is divided into six subdivisions to put beyond doubt the rule that if the things mentioned in the subdivisions are proved, they would establish the crime, and it is not thereby intended to create six different kinds of crime.

People v. Sheffield (9 Cal. App. 130)

Section 263, making sexual penetration, however slight, sufficient to complete rape, is applicable to all the subdivisions of this section, defining the offense.

People v. Kelly (3 Cal. Rptr. 2d 677)

For purposes of rape conviction, an act of sexual intercourse must involve a live victim who does not effectively consent. A person who attempts to rape a live victim, kills the victim in the attempt, then has intercourse with the body, has committed only "attempted rape," not actual "rape," but the person is guilty of felony-murder and is subject to rape special circumstance.

In re Alberto S. (277 Cal. Rptr. 475)

Sexual battery, a specific intent crime, is not a lesser included offense of rape, a general intent crime.

People v. Ramirez (82 Cal. Rptr. 665)

Any rape committed by force and violence necessarily includes the crime of assault with the intent to commit rape, and an attempt to commit rape is necessarily included in every rape.

People v. Thomas (164 Cal. App. 2d 571)

To constitute an attempt to commit rape, it is not necessary that the act done should be the last proximate one for the completion of the offense or that there be any penetration whatever.

People v. Peckham (232 Cal. App. 2d 163)

That a defendant may have been intoxicated at the time of an assault, and that he was impotent when intoxicated, are not of themselves defenses to assault with intent to commit rape.

People v. Battles (49 Cal. Rptr. 367)

In this prosecution for statutory rape, the defendant had the burden of proving that he entertained a good faith belief, based on reasonable grounds, that the prosecutrix was of an age to give legal consent.

People v. Hernandez (61 Cal. 2d 529)

The lack of a female's consent is not, in one sense, an element of the offense of statutory rape, but in a broader sense, the lack of consent remains an element but the law makes a conclusive presumption of lack thereof because the female is presumed too innocent and naive to understand the implications and nature of her act.

People v. Williams (4 Cal. 4th 354)

Regardless of how strongly a rape defendant may subjectively believe a person has consented to sexual intercourse, that belief must be formed under circumstances that society will tolerate as reasonable in order for defendant to have adduced substantial evidence giving rise to the *Mayberry* instruction.

Practicum

David is mad at his girlfriend who is a prostitute. He forces her to have sex with him. She is under 18 years of age. After having sex with her and while he is still nude, he runs out in the front yard and gets the morning paper. At the time, he thought that nobody was home next door. He was mistaken and was seen by Ms. Busybody. He then makes an obscene gesture toward her. What crimes has he committed?

Discussion Questions

Discussion Questions

1. What is the nature of the crime of rape?
2. Who is incapable of giving legal consent to sexual intercourse?
3. What are the essential differences between the various types of rape?
4. Why is the inability by reason of intoxication to form a specific intent to rape not a defense to the charge of rape?

5. What act completes the crime of rape?
6. Explain the differences between statutory rape and unlawful sexual intercourse.
7. What acts constitute incest?
8. What constitutes lewd conduct?
9. What constitutes indecent exposure?
10. Distinguish between sexual battery and rape.

Self-Study Quiz

Self-Study Quiz

True/False

1. Rape is an act of sexual intercourse involving consent of all parties.
2. Some persons are incapable of giving consent to sexual intercourse.
3. To be considered unconscious for purposes of prosecution under PC 261(4), the victim must be completely unaware of the nature of the act and in a state of total unconsciousness.
4. The essential guilt of rape is the outrage to the person and the feelings to the victim.
5. For rape, the penetration is not an essential element.
6. Sexual intercourse under PC 261 is considered complete with *any* sexual penetration.
7. Consent, even though obtained by fraud, is a defense to rape by force or fear.
8. An assault is a lesser and included offense of rape.

9. Statutory rape is the sexual intercourse with a female under the age of 18 and who is not the wife of the perpetrator.
10. To be prosecuted for spousal rape, the rape must be reported to the proper authorities within 90 days after the violation.
11. The statute of limitations for spousal rape is six years.
12. Incest can be committed only by marriage or sexual intercourse between two people who are closely related by blood.
13. Lewd conduct refers to conduct that disregards socially accepted constraints.
14. To be lewd, the act must be sexual in nature.
15. Indecent exposure is not a crime in California unless the exposure is committed in a public place.

Juvenile Law and Procedure

The philosophical underpinnings of the juvenile court have always been problematic. American society has been schizophrenic in its attitudes toward the juvenile offender, as well as toward the juvenile court. Feelings of compassion and humanitarianism for juveniles in trouble (particularly those who have caused trouble) have been tinged with fear and vengeance.

Martin L. Forst, 1995

10-1 Purpose of the Juvenile Court Law

When asked about the philosophy or purpose behind juvenile justice, many people will state that it is based on the concept of rehabilitation. Clearly that was the philosophy behind the now "old" juvenile court system. As discussed in this chapter, the "new" court's philosophy is focused on crime control.

Traditionally, the purpose of juvenile court was to "save the children." As noted in *Commonwealth v. Fisher,* a 1905 court decision, juvenile court "is not for the punishment of offenders but for the salvation of children . . . whose salvation may become the duty of the state." During the early years, the juvenile courts acted in an informal manner in an attempt to rehabilitate children. A series of U.S. Supreme Court decisions between 1965 and 1975, however, changed the court from an informal proceeding to a more formal legalistic court.

One of the impetuses for the creation of juvenile court was the dissatisfaction with the treatment of juveniles and the penal system. Reformers viewed the prior methods of treating juveniles as cruel and inhumane. The reformers were also interested in developing more effective means of controlling urban lower-class youths. Based on these concerns, juvenile court developed with a dual orientation of more humane treatment of the youth and control of the youth. The dual orientation, however, gave rise to a set of procedures and a legal framework that was entirely different from those of adult criminal courts.

Using the doctrine of *parens patriae,* juvenile courts were considered a special class of civil courts rather than criminal courts. Whereas the essence of criminal court was in determining guilt and assessing punishment, the juvenile courts originally were tasked with the responsibility of saving the youth. As one juvenile court judge wrote in 1909:

> The problem for determination . . . is not, has this boy or girl committed a specific wrong, but what is he, how has he become what he is, and what had best be done in his interest and in the interest of the state to save him from a downward career? *In re Michael D.* 188 Cal. App. 2d 1392 (1987)

In the case cited in the preceding quote, the minor contended that the juvenile court judge abused his discretion by committing the minor to the California Youth Authority (CYA) for reasons based on punishment and public safety. The minor also contended that his commitment to CYA was an abuse of discretion by the juvenile court in that (1) the minor was improperly committed to CYA for purposes of retribution rather than rehabilitation; (2) the juvenile court did not properly consider less restrictive alternatives; and (3) the minor could not benefit from the commitment. The minor had admitted to one count of sexual battery. He was caught in the act of rape. Evidence indicated that during the rape, the youth had choked the victim. After the incident, the minor showed no remorse or concern for the victim. The probation officer in her report to the court stated: "The magnitude and outrageousness of the conduct alone warrants a commitment to the California Youth Authority." The judge stated in his findings that he found the youth to be a threat and a danger to society. The appellate court noted that at the core of the dispute was a fundamental disagreement over the purposes of the juvenile court law; that is, that prior to a 1984 amendment to the Welfare and Institutions Code (WIC), Section 202, California courts had consistently held that juvenile commitment proceedings were designed for rehabilitation and treatment, not for punishment. In 1984, that section was amended to emphasize different priorities for the juvenile justice system. The current provisions recognize punishment as a rehabilitative tool. The amendment also resulted in greater emphasis on protecting public safety. Commitment to CYA, however, cannot be based solely on retribution grounds, and there must be some evidence to demonstrate probable benefits to the youth. In *In re Michael D.*, the appeals court upheld the commitment to CYA and stated that the minor would benefit from an environment providing firm, strict discipline for his "out of control" behavior.

For dependency cases, the stated intent of the state legislatures has been to provide maximum protection for children who are currently being physically, sexually, or emotionally abused, being neglected, or being exploited, and to protect children who are at risk of that harm. This protection includes provision of a full array of social and health services to help the child and family and to prevent reabuse of children. That protection shall focus on the preservation of the family whenever possible. Nothing is intended to permit the state to disrupt the family unnecessarily or to intrude inappropriately into family life, to prohibit the use of reasonable methods of parental discipline, or to prescribe a particular method of parenting. Further, nothing is intended to limit the offering of voluntary services to those families in need of assistance.

10-2 Scope and Authority of the Juvenile Court

Delinquency and status offenses represent only a fraction of the work of juvenile court. Juvenile courts also decide matters involving abuse, neglect, and other matters pertaining to the welfare of children. The jurisdiction of juvenile court depends in part on whether the juvenile is before the court on a delinquency or dependency matter. *Delinquency cases* are those cases where the juvenile is alleged to have committed a criminal act. *Dependency cases* are those cases where the child is in need of supervision or protection. In determining the age of the child for jurisdiction purposes, the courts look at the age of the child at the time of the proceedings, not at the time that the act occurred.

In California, superior courts exercise the jurisdiction for juvenile courts, and while sitting in the exercise of such jurisdiction are known and referred to as the juvenile courts (WIC 245). In counties having more than one superior court judge, the presiding judge of such court or the senior judge, if there is no presiding judge, shall annually, in the month of January, designate one or more judges of the superior court to hear all juvenile cases during the ensuing year. He or she shall, from time to time, designate such additional judges as may be necessary for the prompt disposition of the judicial business before the juvenile court. In all counties where more than one judge is designated as a judge of the juvenile court, the presiding judge of the superior court shall also designate one such judge as presiding judge of the juvenile court (WIC 246).

10-2a Delinquency (Criminal Misconduct)

In delinquency cases, juvenile courts have jurisdiction over any person who is under the age of 18 years and the person has violated any law of the state or any ordinance of any city or county of the state defining crime other than an ordinance establishing a curfew based solely on age. In these cases, the juvenile is within the jurisdiction of the juvenile court, which may adjudge the juvenile to be a ward of the court.

The juvenile court has primary jurisdiction over juveniles. Accordingly, other courts generally do not have jurisdiction to conduct a preliminary examination or to try the case of any person charged with the commission of a crime when the person was under the age of 18 years at the time of the proceedings, unless the matter has first been submitted to the juvenile court, and juvenile court has made a finding that the juvenile is over the age of 16 and that the minor is not a fit subject for juvenile jurisdiction.

WIC 602 provides that when any person who is under the age of 18 years violates any law of California or of the United States or any ordinance of any city or county of California defining crime other than an ordinance establishing a curfew based solely on age, that person is within the jurisdiction of the juvenile court. That section provides that the court may adjudge such an individual to be a ward of the court. WIC 603 provides that only juvenile courts have jurisdiction to conduct a preliminary examination or to try the case of a juvenile (person under 18 years of age) upon an accusatory pleading charging, unless the matter has first been submitted to the juvenile court by petition and the juvenile court has made an order directing that the juvenile be prosecuted under the general law or in any case involving a minor against whom a complaint may be filed directly in a court of criminal jurisdiction pursuant to Section 707.01. WIC 707.1 and 707.01 define those juveniles who are considered unfit for juvenile court and juvenile corrections.

WIC 707.1—Filing of Accusatory Pleading in Criminal Court for Minor

(a) If the minor is declared not a fit and proper subject to be dealt with under the juvenile court law, or as to a minor for whom charges in a petition or petitions in the juvenile court have been transferred to a court of criminal jurisdiction pursuant to Section 707.01, the district attorney, or other appropriate prosecuting officer may file an accusatory pleading against the minor in a court of criminal jurisdiction. The case shall proceed from that point according to the laws applicable to a criminal case. If a prosecution has been commenced in another court but has been suspended while juvenile court proceedings are being held, it shall be ordered that the proceedings upon that prosecution shall resume.

(b) [omitted]

WIC 707.01—Minor Unfit for Juvenile Court Law

(a) If a minor is found an unfit subject to be dealt with under the juvenile court law pursuant to Section 707, then the following shall apply:

   (1) The jurisdiction of the juvenile court with respect to any previous adjudication resulting in the minor being made a ward of the juvenile court that did not result in the minor's commitment to the Youth Authority shall not terminate, unless a hearing is held pursuant to Section 785 and the jurisdiction of the juvenile court over the minor is terminated.

   (2) The jurisdiction of the juvenile court and the Youth Authority with respect to any previous adjudication resulting in the minor being made a ward of the juvenile court that resulted in the minor's commitment to the Youth Authority shall not terminate.

   (3) All petitions pending against the minor shall be transferred to the court of criminal jurisdiction where one of the following applies:

      (A) Jeopardy has not attached and the minor was 16 years of age or older at the time he or she is alleged to have violated the criminal statute or ordinance.

      (B) Jeopardy has not attached and the minor is alleged to have violated a criminal statute for which he or she may be presumed or may be found to be not a fit and proper subject to be dealt with under the juvenile court law.

(4) All petitions pending against the minor shall be disposed of in the juvenile court pursuant to the juvenile court law, where one of the following applies:

(A) Jeopardy has attached.

(B) The minor was under 16 years of age at the time he or she is alleged to have violated a criminal statute for which he or she may not be presumed or may not be found to be not a fit and proper subject to be dealt with under the juvenile court law.

(5) If, subsequent to a finding that a minor is an unfit subject to be dealt with under the juvenile court law, the minor is convicted of the violations which were the subject of the proceeding that resulted in a finding of unfitness, a new petition or petitions alleging the violation of any law or ordinance defining crime which would otherwise cause the minor to be a person described in Section 602 committed by the minor prior to or after the finding of unfitness need not be filed in the juvenile court if one of the following applies:

(A) The minor was 16 years of age or older at the time he or she is alleged to have violated a criminal statute or ordinance.

(B) The minor is alleged to have violated a criminal statute for which he or she may be presumed or may be found to be not a fit and proper subject to be dealt with under the juvenile court law.

(6)and (7) [omitted.]

WIC 300—Jurisdiction of Juvenile Court

10-2b Dependency

Any minor who comes within any of the following descriptions is within the jurisdiction of the juvenile court which may adjudge that person to be a dependent child of the court:

(a) The minor has suffered, or there is a substantial risk that the minor will suffer, serious physical harm inflicted nonaccidentally upon the minor by the minor's parent or guardian. For the purposes of this subdivision, a court may find there is a substantial risk of serious future injury based on the manner in which a less serious injury was inflicted, a history of repeated inflictions of injuries on the minor or the minor's siblings, or a combination of these and other actions by the parent or guardian which indicate the child is at risk of serious physical harm. For purposes of this subdivision, "serious physical harm" does not include reasonable and age-appropriate spanking to the buttocks where there is no evidence of serious physical injury.

(b) The minor has suffered, or there is a substantial risk that the minor will suffer, serious physical harm or illness, as a result of the failure or inability of his or her parent or guardian to adequately supervise or protect the minor, or the willful or negligent failure of the minor's parent or guardian to adequately supervise or protect the minor from the conduct of the custodian with whom the minor has been left, or by the willful or negligent failure of the parent or guardian to provide the minor with adequate food, clothing, shelter, or medical treatment, or by the inability of the parent or guardian to provide regular care for the minor due to the parent's or guardian's mental illness, developmental disability, or substance abuse. . . .

(c) The minor is suffering serious emotional damage, or is at substantial risk of suffering serious emotional damage, evidenced by severe anxiety, depression, withdrawal, or untoward aggressive behavior toward self or others, as a result of the conduct of the parent or guardian or who has no parent or guardian capable of providing appropriate care. No minor shall be found to be a person described by this subdivision if the willful failure of the parent or guardian to provide adequate mental health treatment is based on a sincerely held religious belief and if a less intrusive judicial intervention is available.

(d) The minor has been sexually abused, or there is a substantial risk that the minor will be sexually abused . . . by his or her parent or guardian or a member of his or her household, or the parent or guardian has failed to adequately protect the minor from sexual abuse when the parent or guardian knew or reasonably should have known that the minor was in danger of sexual abuse.

(e) The minor is under the age of five and has suffered severe physical abuse by a parent, or by any person known by the parent, if the parent knew or reasonably should have known that the person was physically abusing the minor. For the purposes of this subdivision, "severe physical abuse" means any of the following: any single act of abuse which causes physical trauma of sufficient severity that, if left untreated, would cause permanent physical disfigurement, permanent physical disability, or death; any single act of sexual abuse which causes significant bleeding, deep bruising, or significant external or internal swelling; or more than one act of physical abuse, each of which causes bleeding, deep bruising, significant external or internal swelling, bone fracture, or unconsciousness; or the willful, prolonged failure to provide adequate food. . . .

(f) The minor's parent or guardian has been convicted of causing the death of another child.

The juvenile court may retain jurisdiction over any person who is found to be a dependent child of the juvenile court until the ward or dependent child attains the age of 21 years in most states. A juvenile court may assume jurisdiction over a child under the conditions noted above regardless of whether the child was in the physical custody of both parents or was in the sole legal or physical custody of only one parent at the time that the events or conditions occurred that brought the child within the jurisdiction of the court.

10-3 Taking a Juvenile into Temporary Custody

WIC 270.1 provides, in part, the following:

A minor, 14 years of age or older, who is taken into temporary custody by a peace officer on the basis of being a person, and who, in the reasonable belief of the peace officer, presents a serious security risk of harm to self or others, may be securely detained in a law enforcement facility that contains a lockup for adults, if all of the following conditions are met:

(1) The minor is held in temporary custody for the purpose of investigating the case, facilitating release of the minor to a parent or guardian, or arranging transfer of the minor to an appropriate juvenile facility.

(2) The minor is detained in the law enforcement facility for a period that does not exceed six hours except as otherwise provided.

(3) The minor is informed at the time he or she is securely detained of the purpose of the secure detention, of the length of time the secure detention is expected to last, and of the maximum six-hour period the secure detention is authorized to last. In the event an extension is granted pursuant, the minor shall be informed of the length of time the extension is expected to last.

(4) Contact between the minor and adults confined in the facility is restricted.

(5) The minor is adequately supervised.

(6) A log or other written record is maintained by the law enforcement agency showing the offense which is the basis for the secure detention of the minor in the facility, the reasons and circumstances forming the basis for the decision to place the minor in secure detention, and the length of time the minor was securely detained.

10-3a Discussion

Any other minor who is taken into temporary custody by a peace officer on the basis that the minor is a person described by WIC 602 (violation of a criminal statute) may be taken to a law enforcement facility that contains a lockup for adults and may be held in temporary custody in the facility for the purposes of investigating the case, facilitating the release of the minor to a parent or guardian, or arranging for the transfer of the minor to an appropriate juvenile facility. However, while in the law enforcement facility, the minor may not be securely detained and shall be supervised in a manner to ensure that there will be no contact with adults in custody in the facility. If the minor is held in temporary, nonsecure custody within the facility, the peace officer shall exercise one of the dispositional options, without unnecessary delay and, in every case, within six hours. "Law enforcement facility" includes a police station or a sheriff's station but does not include a jail.

Under Vehicle Code 40302.5, whenever any person under the age of 18 is taken into custody in connection with any traffic infraction case, and he or she is not taken directly before a magistrate, the individual shall be delivered to the custody of the probation officer. Unless sooner released, the probation officer shall keep the minor in the juvenile hall pending his or her appearance before a magistrate. When a minor is cited for an offense not involving the driving of a motor vehicle, the minor shall not be taken into custody pursuant solely for failure to present a driver's license.

Under EC 48265, any person arresting or assuming temporary custody of a minor for truancy shall immediately deliver the minor either to the parent, guardian, or other person having control or charge of the minor, or to the school from which the minor is absent, or to a nonsecure youth service or community center designated by the school or district for counseling prior to returning the minor to his or her home or school. Or the minor can be delivered to a school counselor or pupil services and attendance officer located at a police station to obtain immediate counseling from the counselor or officer prior to returning or being returned to his home or school, or if the minor is found to have been declared an habitual truant, the minor shall be brought before the probation officer of the county having jurisdiction over minors.

10-4 Advising Juveniles of Their Rights

WIC 625 provides that whenever a minor is taken into temporary custody on the ground that there is reasonable cause for believing that the minor has violated a criminal statute or that he or she has violated a juvenile court order or has escaped from any commitment ordered by the juvenile court, the officer shall advise of his or her *Miranda* rights.

WIC 627.5 provides that in any case where a minor is taken before a probation officer pursuant and it is alleged that such minor is a person who has committed an act prohibited by a criminal statute, the probation officer shall immediately advise the minor and his parent or guardian of the minor's *Miranda* rights. If the minor or his parent or guardian requests counsel, the probation officer shall notify the judge of the juvenile court of the request, and counsel for the minor shall be appointed.

Under WIC 625.1, any minor who is taken into temporary custody—when the peace officer has reasonable cause for believing the minor has committed criminal misconduct—may be requested to submit to voluntary chemical testing of his or her urine to determine the presence of alcohol or illegal drugs. The peace officer shall inform the minor that the chemical test is voluntary. The court may consider the results of this test in determining the disposition of the minor.

WIC 625.2 requires that before administering the chemical test, the peace officer shall give the following admonition: "I am asking you to take a voluntary urine test to test for the presence of drugs or alcohol in your body. You have the right to refuse to take this test. If you do take the test, it cannot be used as the basis for filing any additional charges against you. It can be used by a court for the purpose of sentencing. You have the right to telephone your parent or guardian before you decide whether or not to take this test."

This admonition is not given, however, when a chemical test is administered pursuant to the Vehicle Code. (The Vehicle Code has the requirement for a different admonishment.)

10-5 Segregation of Juvenile and Adult Prisoners

Under WIC 207.1, no court, judge, referee, peace officer, or employee of a detention facility shall knowingly detain any minor in a jail or lockup, except in the following situations. Any minor who is alleged to have committed an offense and is not a fit and proper subject to be dealt with under the juvenile court law, or any minor who has been charged directly in or transferred to a court of criminal jurisdiction, may be detained in a jail or other secure facility for the confinement of adults, if all of the following conditions are met:

(1) The juvenile court or the court of criminal jurisdiction makes a finding that the minor's further detention in the juvenile hall would endanger the safety of the public or would be detrimental to the other minors in the juvenile hall.
(2) Contact between the minor and adults in the facility is restricted.
(3) The minor is adequately supervised.

A minor who is either found not to be a fit and proper subject to be dealt with under the juvenile court law or who will be transferred to a court of criminal jurisdiction, at the time of transfer to a court of criminal jurisdiction or at the conclusion of the fitness hearing, as the case may be, shall be entitled to be released on bail or on his or her own recognizance upon the same circumstances, terms, and conditions as an adult who is alleged to have committed the same offense.

10-6 Driving under the Influence

VC 23140 makes it unlawful for a person under the age of 21, who has 0.05 percent or more, by weight, of alcohol in his or her blood, to drive a vehicle.

10-7 Truancy

WIC 601 provides that any juvenile (person under the age of 18) who persistently or habitually refuses to obey the reasonable and proper orders or directions of his or her parents, guardian, or custodian, or who is beyond the control of that person, or who is under the age of 18 years when he or she violated any ordinance of any city or county of this state establishing a curfew based solely on age is within the jurisdiction of the juvenile court that may adjudge the minor to be a ward of the court.

The Education Code, Section 48264.5, provides that a minor who is a truant on the first truancy may be personally given a written warning by any peace officer. A record of the written warning may be kept at the school for a period of not less than two years, or until the pupil graduates or transfers from that school. If the pupil transfers, the record may be forwarded to any school receiving the pupil's school records. A record of the written warning may be maintained by the law enforcement agency in accordance with that law enforcement agency's policies and procedures. Upon the second truancy within the same school year, the pupil may be assigned by the school to an after-school or weekend study program located within the same county as the pupil's school. Upon the third truancy within the same school year, the pupil may be referred to, and required to attend, an attendance review board or a truancy mediation program. If the school district does not have a truancy mediation program, the pupil may be required to attend a comparable program deemed acceptable by the school district's attendance supervisor. Upon the fourth truancy within the same school year, the pupil shall be classified a habitual truant and shall be within the jurisdiction of the juvenile court, which may adjudge the pupil to be a ward of the court. If the pupil is adjudged a ward of the court, the pupil shall be required to do one or more of the following:

(1) Performance at court-approved community services sponsored by either a public or private nonprofit agency for not less than 20 hours but not more than 40 hours over a period not to exceed 90 days, during a time other than the pupil's hours of school attendance or employment. The probation officer shall report to the court the failure of the pupil to comply with this paragraph.
(2) Payment of a fine by the pupil of not more than one hundred dollars ($100) for which a parent or guardian of the pupil may be jointly liable.
(3) Attendance of a court-approved truancy prevention program.
(4) Suspension or revocation of driving privileges. This subdivision shall apply only to a pupil who has attended a school attendance review board program, a program operated by a probation department acting as a school attendance review board, or a truancy mediation program.

10-8 Participants in Juvenile Court

The group of courthouse persons who perform key courtroom roles in the juvenile justice system include: defense counsel, the judge, the prosecutor, referees, and the juvenile probation officer. One of the problems in defining the various roles is that often the roles of the prosecutor and the juvenile probation officer are interwoven.

10-8a The Judge

Generally juvenile court judges treat their work as an attempt to balance the efforts to help and rehabilitate the youthful offender with the concerns of society for punishment and deterrence. The judge is both a helper and a punisher. This dual orientation may account for the different judicial attitudes and styles that have developed. Different judges accomplish the two competing roles by emphasizing one role and de-emphasizing the other.

10-8b Referees

To handle the caseload in juvenile courts, the appointment of referees is permitted. The rules regarding the use of referees are very similar in most states. Accordingly, set forth in the following are the California rules, which are representative of most state laws allowing the use of referees.

For example, in California the judge of the juvenile court, or the presiding judge of the juvenile court, or the senior judge if there is no presiding judge, may appoint one or more referees to serve on a full-time or part-time basis. A referee shall serve at the pleasure of the appointing judge. Referees must be licensed to practice law in the state for a period of not less than 5 years or in any other state and the state for a combined period of not less than 10 years.

A referee shall hear such cases as are assigned to him or her by the presiding judge of the juvenile court, with the same powers as a judge of the juvenile court, except that a referee shall not conduct any hearing to which the state or federal constitutional prohibitions against double jeopardy apply unless all of the parties stipulate in writing that the referee may act in the capacity of a temporary judge.

A referee shall promptly furnish to the presiding judge of the juvenile court and the minor, if the minor is 14 or more years of age or if younger has so requested, and shall serve upon the minor's attorney of record and the minor's parent or guardian or adult relative and the attorney of record for the minor's parent or guardian or adult relative, a written copy of his or her findings and order and shall also furnish to the minor, if the minor is 14 or more years of age or if younger has so requested, and to the parent or guardian or adult relative, with the findings and order, a written explanation of the right of such persons to seek review of the order by the juvenile court.

Generally, the orders of a referee are immediately effective, subject also to the right of review, and are in full force until vacated or modified upon rehearing by order of the judge of the juvenile court. In a case in which a referee's order becomes effective without a juvenile court judge's approval, it becomes final when the time allowed for application for rehearing has expired, if the application is not made within that time and if the judge of the juvenile court has not ordered a rehearing within that time.

Where a referee sits as a temporary judge, his or her orders become final in the same manner as orders made by a judge. At any time prior to the expiration of 10 days after service of a written copy of the order and findings of a referee, a minor or his parent or guardian may apply to the juvenile court for a rehearing. Such an application may be directed to all, or to any specified part of the order or findings, and shall contain a statement of why such rehearing is requested. If all of the proceedings before the referee have been recorded by an official reporter, the judge of the juvenile court may, after reading the transcript of the proceedings, grant or deny the application. If the proceedings before the referee have not been recorded by an official reporter, a rehearing shall be granted as a matter of right.

If an application for rehearing is not granted, denied, or extended within 20 days following the date of its receipt, it shall be deemed granted. A juvenile court judge may, on his or her own motion made within 20 judicial days of the hearing before a referee, order a rehearing of any matter heard before a referee.

10-8c The Prosecutor

Under our system of justice, the final decision as to whether or not a criminal case goes to court rests with the prosecutor. This also applies to juvenile court, although in many juvenile cases the decision as to whether the court will conduct a hearing is delegated to the probation officer.

Cases are referred by the police, teachers, social workers, and so on. Frequently, it is stated that these individuals refer cases to the juvenile court; however, that is incorrect, as these cases are referred to the prosecutor's office. After the case is referred to the prosecutor, he or she must then file the case with the juvenile court. Until the prosecutor takes action, nothing happens on the case.

The juvenile justice commission or regional juvenile justice commission of a county shall nominate probation officers in the county as the judge of the juvenile court in that county shall direct, and they are then to be appointed by the judge.

The probation officer may appoint as many deputies or assistant probation officers as he or she desires, but these deputies or assistant probation officers do not have authority to act until the juvenile court judge approves their appointments. Probation officers may at any time be removed by the juvenile court judge for good cause shown.

Except where waived by the probation officer, judge, or referee and the minor, the probation officer must be present in court to represent the interests of each person who is the subject of a petition to declare that person to be a ward or dependent child for all hearings or rehearings of his or her case, and must furnish to the court such information and assistance as the court may require. If so ordered, the probation officer shall take charge of that person before and after any hearing or rehearing.

The probation officer has a duty to prepare for a hearing on the disposition of a case as is appropriate for the specific hearing of a social study of the minor, containing such matters as may be relevant to the case. The social study must include a recommendation for settling the case.

The probation officer shall upon order of any court in any matter involving the custody, status, or welfare of a minor or minors investigate the appropriate facts and circumstances and prepare and file with the court written reports and written recommendations in reference to such matters. The court is authorized to receive and consider the probation officer's reports and recommendations in determining any such matter. In some cases, all or part of the probation officer's duties concerning dependent children may be delegated to the county welfare department.

Probation officers generally have a right to access a state summary of criminal history as is necessary to carry out its duties concerning children. The information shall include any current incarceration, the location of any current probation or parole, any current requirement that the individual register, and any history of offenses involving abuse or neglect of, or violence against, a child, or convictions of any offenses, involving violence, sexual offenses, the abuse or illegal possession, manufacture, or sale of alcohol or controlled substances, and any arrest for which the person is released on bail or on his or her own recognizance.

Generally a probation officer may employ such psychiatrists, psychologists, and other clinical experts as are required to assist in determining and implementing appropriate treatment of minors within the jurisdiction of the juvenile court. If a probation officer decides to recommend to the court that a minor should be removed from the physical custody of his parent or guardian, the probation officer shall give primary consideration to recommending to the court that the minor be placed with a relative of the minor, if such a placement is in the best interests of the minor and will be conducive to reunification of the family.

At any time, the juvenile court judge may require the probation officer to investigate and then report about the qualifications and management of any society, association, or corporation, other than a state institution, that applies for or receives custody of any ward or dependent child of the juvenile court. Probation officers, however, do not have the authority to enter any institution without its consent. If consent is refused, juvenile commitments to that institution are normally not made.

If a probation officer, after investigation of an application for petition or other investigation he or she is authorized to make, determines that a minor is within the jurisdiction of the juvenile court or will probably soon be within that jurisdiction,

10-8d Probation Officer

the probation officer may, in lieu of filing a petition or subsequent to dismissal of a petition already filed, and with the consent of the minor's parent or guardian, undertake a program of supervision of the minor. If a program of supervision is undertaken, the probation officer shall attempt to ameliorate the situation that brings the minor within, or creates the probability that the minor will be within, the jurisdiction by providing or arranging to contract for all appropriate child welfare services.

If a family refuses to cooperate with the services being provided, the probation officer may file a petition with the juvenile court. The program of supervision of the minor undertaken pursuant to PC 654 may call for the minor to obtain care and treatment for the misuse of, or addiction to, controlled substances from a county mental health service or other appropriate community agency.

10-8e Defense Counsel

The American Bar Association outlines the defense counsel's role in juvenile court in its *Standards Relating to Counsel for Private Parties.* According to the ABA, the defense counsel's duties include providing legal representation in all proceedings arising from or related to delinquency; in-need-of supervision actions including mental competency, transfer, and disciplinary or other actions related to any treatment program; postdisposition proceedings; probation revocation; and any other proceedings that may substantially affect a juvenile's custody, status, or course of treatment.

Unlike the early court reformers' concept of juvenile court, juvenile court proceedings are now generally considered adversarial in nature. Currently, most juveniles are represented by counsel in court. In addition, in many cases the parents are also represented by counsel. In many situations both the parents and the juvenile are represented by counsel. In those cases, because of possible conflicts of interest, generally separate counsel must be appointed for the parents and the juvenile.

The two major categories of defense counsel are the retained counsel and the appointed counsel. A *retained counsel* is a private attorney who has been retained or hired by the juvenile or the juvenile's family. In most cases, the juvenile is represented by an appointed counsel. An *appointed counsel* is one appointed by the judge. The appointed counsel may be from the public defender's office or a private counsel who is appointed by the judge and paid a minimal amount by the county to represent the juvenile.

Assistant public defenders are usually young lawyers interested in criminal law who work in the public defenders' office to obtain additional experience before going into private practice. Public defenders' offices have heavy caseloads and limited investigative resources. Accordingly, public defenders spend the majority of their time negotiating pleas and little time investigating the case. Although many public defenders pursue their clients' interests with all possible vigor, frequently public defenders do not use every possible legal strategy to defend their clients. For example, a public defender is generally less likely to object to minor legal errors made by the judge or the prosecutor. On the whole, it appears that juveniles who are represented by private counsel fare better than those represented by appointed counsel. Accordingly, public defenders generally have less favorable image among their clients than do retained attorneys.

The duties of the defense counsel are the same whether they are appointed or retained counsel. The duties include seeing that the client is properly represented at all stages of the systems, that the client's rights are not violated, and that evidence favorable to the defendant is presented to the judge. The defense counsel should ensure that the case is presented in the light most favorable to the juvenile. To accomplish these duties, the defense counsel is at least, in theory, the adversary of the prosecutor.

The court may also appoint a *guardian ad litem* to promote and protect the interests of the juvenile. The guardian is normally not an attorney. In some cases, the guardian is an employee of the county's child protective services. Generally, a guardian ad litem is appointed in cases involving child abuse, neglect, or other dependency cases where the courts have questions regarding the ability or desire of the parents to protect the child's interests.

10-8f Guardian Ad Litem

Unless their parental rights have been terminated, both parents must be notified of all proceedings involving the child. In any case where the probation officer is required to notify a parent or guardian of a proceeding at which the probation officer intends to present a report, the probation officer must also provide both parents, whether custodial or noncustodial, or any guardian, or the counsel for the parent or guardian a copy of the report prior to the hearing, either personally or by first-class mail.

10-9 Rights of Juveniles and Parents

When a minor is adjudged a dependent of the juvenile court, any issues regarding custodial rights between his or her parents shall be determined solely by the juvenile court so long as the minor remains a dependent of the juvenile court. No minor shall be found to be a dependent of the court, however, if the willful failure of the parent or guardian to provide adequate mental health treatment is based on a sincerely held religious belief and if a less intrusive judicial intervention is available.

When a peace officer or social worker takes a minor into custody pursuant to PC 627, he or she shall immediately notify the minor's parent, guardian, or a responsible relative that the minor is in custody and the place where he or she is being held, except when, upon order of the juvenile court, the parent or guardian shall not be notified of the exact whereabouts of the minor.

Immediately after being taken to a place of confinement pursuant PC 625 and, except where physically impossible, no later than one hour after he or she has been taken into custody, a minor 10 years of age or older shall be advised that he or she has the right to make at least two telephone calls from the place where he or she is being held, one call completed to his or her parent, guardian, or a responsible relative, and another call completed to an attorney. The calls shall be at public expense if the calls are completed to telephone numbers within the local calling area and in the presence of a public officer or employee. Any public officer or employee who willfully deprives a minor taken into custody of his or her right to make these telephone calls is guilty of a misdemeanor.

As a condition for the release of such a minor, the probation officer may require the minor or his parent, guardian, or relative, or both, to sign a written promise that either or both of them will appear before the probation officer at a suitable place designated by the probation officer at a specified time.

Cases on Point

Kent v. United States, 383 U.S. 541 (1966)

Kent v. United States set forth the procedural guidelines to be used in the waiver of a delinquent from juvenile to adult courts. Morris Kent was a 16-year-old with a police record. He was arrested and charged with housebreaking, robbery, and rape. He admitted committing the crimes. After being held in juvenile detention center for about six days, the juvenile court judge transferred jurisdiction to the adult criminal court without holding a hearing.

This case was decided on the narrow issue of whether juveniles have a right to a hearing before being transferred to adult criminal court. The impact of the decision, however, went far beyond its narrow issue. It was a warning to juvenile courts that their traditional laxity toward procedural and evidentiary standards would be subject to scrutiny by the U.S. Supreme Court. The Supreme Court had indicated its concern regarding juveniles as early as 1948 in *Haley v. Ohio*, 322 U.S. 596 (1948). The *Haley* case involved a juvenile tried in adult criminal court for first-degree murder. The Court held that the due process clause barred the use of a confession obtained by force by juvenile authorities. The *Kent* case was the first case directly involving the juvenile court. In an appendix to the Court's decision, the Court set forth the criteria to be used by juvenile courts in determining whether to waive jurisdiction of juveniles.

In re Gault, 387 U.S. 1 (1976)

Any examination of legal rights of juveniles must include a study of the *In re Gault* case. Gerald Francis Gault was 15 years old at the time he was committed to the State Industrial School by the Juvenile Court of Gila County, Arizona.

On June 8, 1964, Gerald and a friend were taken into custody by the sheriff. At the time Gerald was on six months' probation from a February 25, 1964, court order as the result of his having been in the company of another boy who had stolen a wallet from a lady's purse. He was taken into custody on June 8 as the result of a verbal complaint of a neighbor, Mrs. Cook. The neighbor alleged that Gerald had made a telephone call to her that contained lewd and indecent remarks.

When Gerald was taken into custody, his parents were at work. No notice that Gerald was taken into custody was served on his parents or left at their residence. No steps were taken to advise them of their son's location. When Gerald's mother arrived home and Gerald was not present, she sent his oldest brother to look for him. Later that evening they learned that Gerald was in custody at the Children's Detention Home. When his mother contacted the home, a deputy probation officer informed her that Gerald was in custody and that a hearing in his case would be held in Juvenile Court at 3:00 P.M. the following day, June 9.

The arresting officer, Flagg, filed a petition with the court on the day of the hearing, June 9. No copy was served on the parents or Gerald. They did not see the petition until August 17, 1964, at a habeas corpus hearing to set aside the commitment. The petition was stated in formal language with no factual statements regarding the basis for the judicial action. The petition alleged only: ". . . said minor is under the age of eighteen years, and is in need of the protection of this Honorable Court." The petition prayed (requested) that ". . . a hearing be held and that an order be issued regarding the care and custody of the said minor."

Gerald, his mother, his older brother, the probation officer, and Officer Flagg appeared before the juvenile court judge on June 9, 1964. Mrs. Cook, the complainant was not present. No one was sworn. No witnesses were called. No transcript of the proceeding or memorandum of the substance of the hearing was made. At the hearing, there was a conflict over Gerald's role in the telephone call episode. According to Gerald's mother, Gerald admitted dialing the telephone but claimed that he gave the telephone to his friend who made the remarks. Officer Flagg recalled that Gerald admitted making the lewd remarks. After the hearing, Gerald was taken back to the detention home. He was released from custody on either June 11 or 12 with no explanation as to why he was released. When he was released, the mother received a letter signed by Officer Flagg. The entire text of the letter was as follows:

Mrs. Gault:
Judge McGhee has set Monday June 15, 1964 at 11:00 A.M. as the date and time for
further hearing on Gerald's delinquency.
/s/ Flagg

At the June 15 hearing, a probation report was filed with the court. The contents of the report were not disclosed to Gerald or his parents. The report listed the charge against Gerald as "Lewd Phone Calls." Gerald's mother requested that Mrs. Cook be called so that she could identify which youth made the remarks. The judge refused her request. After the hearing, the judge committed Gerald as a delinquent to the State Industrial School for the period of his minority [until he was 21] unless sooner discharged by due process of law. Note: Had Gerald been tried in adult criminal court, the maximum jail term would have been six months. At that time, no appeal was permitted from juvenile court by Arizona law. This case went to the U.S. Supreme Court by writ of habeas corpus.

The Court noted that the state was proceeding as *parens patriae*. The Court stated that this Latin phrase proved to be a great help to those who sought to rationalize the exclusion of juveniles from the constitutional scheme; but its meaning is murky and its historic credentials are of dubious relevance. The Court also noted that there was no trace of the doctrine of *parens patriae* in criminal jurisprudence.

The U.S. Supreme Court in its opinion noted that from the inception of the juvenile court system, wide differences have been tolerated between the procedural rights accorded to adults and those of juveniles. From the start, the idea of crime and punishment was to be abandoned. The child was to be treated and rehabilitated. The right of the state, as parens patriae, to deny to the child procedural rights available to his or her elders was elaborated by the assertion that a child, unlike an adult, has a right not to liberty but to custody. He can be made to attorn to his parents, to go to school, and so on. If his or her parents default in effectively performing their custodial functions—that is, if the child is delinquent—the state may intervene. In doing so, it does not deprive the child of any rights because he or she has none. The state merely provides custody to which the child is entitled. On this basis, proceedings involving juveniles were described as civil not criminal and therefore not subject to the requirements that restrict the state when it seeks to deprive a person of his or her liberty.

The Court reasoned that the initial hearing in the case was a hearing on the merits. Notice at that time was not timely; even if there were a conceivable purpose served by the deferral proposed by the justice court, it would have to yield to the requirements that the child and his parents or guardian be notified, in writing, of the specific charge of factual allegations to be considered at the hearing, and that such written notice be given at the earliest practicable time.

The Court decided that the concept of fundamental fairness must be made applicable to juvenile delinquency proceedings. Accordingly, the Court held that the due process clause of the Fourteenth Amendment required that certain procedural guarantees were essential to the adjudication of delinquency. Juveniles who have violated a criminal statute and who may be committed to an institution in which their freedom may be curtailed are entitled to the following:

1. Fair notice of the charges against them
2. The right to be represented by counsel
3. The right to confrontation and cross-examination of witnesses against them
4. The right to the privilege against self-incrimination

The Court, however, did not hold that juvenile offenders were entitled to all the procedural guarantees applicable to adults charged in criminal cases. In addition, the decision was not clear as to what rights should apply to nondelinquent children before the juvenile court. The practical effects of the *Gault* decision were that juvenile courts could no longer deal with children in a benign and paternalistic fashion and that the courts must process juvenile offenders within the framework of appropriate constitutional procedures. Today, the right to counsel, the privilege against self-incrimination, and the right to fair notice is applied at all stages of the juvenile justice process.

Schall v. Martin, 467 U.S. 253 (1984)

In *Schall v. Martin,* the Supreme Court established the right of juvenile court judges to deny youths pretrial release if they perceive the youths to be dangerous. The case also establishes due process standards for detention hearings that include notice and statement of substantial reasons for continued detention.

The youth, Gregory Martin, was arrested on December 13, 1977, and charged with first-degree robbery, second-degree assault, and criminal possession of a weapon under New York law. He, with two others, allegedly hit a youth on the head with a loaded gun and stole the victim's jacket and sneakers. Martin was 14 years old at the time of the crime and subsequent detention. He was taken into custody about 11:30 at night on December 13 and detained overnight.

On December 14, a petition of delinquency was filed, and he made his initial appearance in Family Court that day. The judge cited the possession of the loaded weapon, the false address given to the police, and the lateness of the hour of the incident as evidence of a lack of supervision and ordered Martin detained. On December 19, a probable-cause hearing was held, and probable cause was found to exist for all the crimes charged. At a fact-finding hearing on December 27–29, Martin was determined to have committed the offenses of robbery and criminal possession charges. He was adjudicated a delinquent and placed on two years probation. At that time, he had been detained a total of 15 days.

On December 21, while still in detention, Martin's attorney had filed a habeas corpus class action on behalf of those persons who are, or during the pendency of the action would be, preventively detained. The Court stated that there was no doubt that the due process clause is applicable to juvenile proceedings. One of the questions before the Court was whether preventive detention of juveniles is compatible with the fundamental fairness required by due process. To answer this question, the Court looked at whether preventive detention under the New York statute serves a legitimate state objective and what procedural safeguards are required regarding pretrial detention of youths.

The Court held that the preventive detention was designed to protect the child and society from the potential consequences of his or her criminal acts and, therefore, was permissible. The Court concluded that the state has a legitimate and compelling interest in protecting the community from crime. The Court then indicated that juveniles and their parents should be provided adequate notice, given a right to a hearing, counsel, and a statement of reasons for the necessity to continue a detention.

Breed v. Jones, 421 U.S. 519 (1975)

In *Breed v. Jones,* the Supreme Court provides answers to several questions involving transfer proceedings. First, the case prohibits trying a juvenile in adult court after there has been a prior adjudicatory juvenile hearing involving the same misconduct. Second, while probable causes to hold a child may be established at the transfer hearing, this does not violate subsequent jeopardy if the child is transferred to the adult criminal court. Third, since the same evidence is often used in both the transfer hearing and the subsequent trial in either adult or juvenile court, a different judge is required at trial from the judge who was involved in the transfer hearing.

This case involved a youth who was alleged to have committed armed robbery with a deadly weapon. An adjudicatory hearing was held. After the hearing, a transfer hearing was then held and he was transferred to adult court. The youth's attorney filed a petition raising the claim of violation of the constitutional protection against double jeopardy.

Prior to this case, many states would hold an adjudicatory hearing to determine if the youth was involved in misconduct and then, if appropriate, hold a transfer hearing to determine if the youth should be tried by adult court or subject to juvenile sanctions. The Court held that a trial on the merits of the charge after the youth has been subjected to an adjudicatory hearing was double jeopardy. As a result of this case, a transfer hearing, if held, must be held prior to a determination as to whether the juvenile committed the misconduct in question.

In re Winship, 397 U.S. 358 (1970)

The Supreme Court in the case of *In re Winship* held that due process requires proof beyond a reasonable doubt as a standard for juvenile adjudication proceedings. The New York Family Act defines a juvenile delinquent as any person over 7 years of age and less than 16 years of age who does any act that, if done by an adult, would constitute a crime. The Family Court in this case found that the youth had entered a locker and stolen $112 from a woman's pocketbook. The Family Court judge noted that proof of guilt might not be established beyond a reasonable doubt, but that the New York Family Act requires that any determination at the conclusion of an adjudicatory hearing must be based on a preponderance of evidence. The New York Court of Appeals affirmed the decision and it was appealed to the U.S. Supreme Court.

The Court noted that the requirement that guilt of a criminal charge be established by proof beyond a reasonable doubt dates at least from our early years as a nation. The Court then stated that the observance of the standard of proof beyond a reasonable doubt will not compel the states to abandon or displace any of the substantive benefits of the juvenile justice process. The Court also held that the constitutional safeguard of proof beyond a reasonable doubt is as much required during the adjudicatory stage of a delinquency proceeding as are those safeguards applied in *Gault*.

McKeiver v. Pennsylvania, 403 U.S. 528 (1971)

McKeiver v. Pennsylvania, decided in 1971, marked a shift in the U.S. Supreme Court's thinking. Not only did this case deny juveniles the constitutional right to a jury trial, but it also retreated from the previously standard practice of judicial equalization of procedure in adult and juvenile courts. The Court, in deciding for the State, recognized that while recent constitutional cases focused on the issue of fundamental fairness in fact-finding procedures, juries are not actually an essential part of the juvenile justice due process.

Joseph McKeiver, then age 16, was charged with robbery, larceny, and receiving stolen goods as acts of delinquency. At the adjudication hearing his counsel requested a jury trial. His request was denied based on Pennsylvania law. This case was consolidated on appeal with the case of *Terry v. Pennsylvania*. Both cases involved the same question—the right of juveniles to a jury. Edward Terry, then age 15, was charged with assault and battery on a police officer and conspiracy. At the adjudication hearing, Terry's counsel also requested a jury trial and was denied. Both youths were adjudged to be delinquents.

The Court noted that the right to an impartial jury in all federal criminal prosecutions is guaranteed by the Sixth Amendment. The Court also noted that it had held that trial by jury in criminal cases is fundamental to the American scheme of justice. The Court concluded that in spite of all the disappointments and shortcomings, trial by jury in juvenile court's adjudicative stage is not a constitutional requirement for state juvenile justice systems. The Court stated that if the formalities of the criminal adjudicative process are to be superimposed upon the juvenile courts, there is little need for its separate existence.

New Jersey v. T.L.O., 469 U.S. 325 (1985)

The *New Jersey v. T.L.O.* case involved the question of whether school officials may search students to determine whether they are in possession of contraband. In 1980, a teacher discovered two girls smoking in a lavatory. One of the two girls was T.L.O., who at the time was a 14-year-old high school freshman. Because smoking in the lavatory was in violation of a school rule, the teacher took the two girls to the principal's office. In response to questioning by the assistant principal, Mr. Choplick, T.L.O. denied that she had been smoking in the lavatory and claimed that she did not smoke at all.

Mr. Choplick asked T.L.O. to come into his private office and demanded to see her purse. Opening the purse, he found a pack of cigarettes, which he removed from the purse and held before T.L.O. as he accused her of having lied to him. He also noticed a package of rolling papers in the purse. He then conducted a full search of the purse and discovered a small amount of marijuana, a pipe, a number of empty plastic bags, a substantial quantity of money in one-dollar bills, an index card that appeared to be a list of students who owed T.L.O. money, and two letters that implicated T.L.O. in marijuana dealing.

The State brought delinquency charges against T.L.O. Her counsel moved to suppress the evidence as a violation of her rights against unreasonable searches and seizures under the Fourth Amendment. The Court first found that the Fourth Amendment's prohibition against unreasonable searches and seizures also applies to searches conducted by public school officials. The Court, however, held that the search in question was not unreasonable nor unlawful. The Court stated that the need to maintain an orderly educational environment modified the usual requirements of warrants and probable cause. The Court declared that the school's right to maintain discipline on school grounds allowed it to search a student and his or her possessions as a safety precaution based only on the lesser standard of "reasonable suspicion."

Thompson v. Oklahoma, 108 S. Ct. 2687 (1988)

The *Thompson v. Oklahoma* case, decided by the U.S. Supreme Court on June 29, 1988, examined the question of whether an individual could be executed for a crime committed while a juvenile. Thompson, in concert with three older persons, committed a brutal murder of his former brother-in-law. The evidence indicated that the victim had been shot twice and that his throat, chest, and abdomen had been cut. The victim also had multiple bruises and a broken leg. His body was chained to a concrete block and dumped into a river. Each of the four participants were tried separately and each was sentenced to death.

At the time of the crime, Thompson was 15 years old. He was tried as an adult. At the penalty phase of the trial, the prosecutor asked for the death penalty based on the fact that the murder was especially heinous, atrocious, or cruel and that there was a high probability that Thompson would commit criminal acts of violence and thus would constitute a continuing threat to society. The Court granted his writ to consider whether a sentence of death is cruel and unusual for a crime committed by a 15-year-old child.

The Court stated that the authors of the Eighth Amendment drafted a categorical prohibition against the infliction of cruel and unusual punishments, but they made no attempt to define the contours of that category. They delegated that task to future generations of judges who have been guided by the "evolving standards of decency that mark the progress of a maturing society." The Court noted that they were reminded of the importance of "the experience of mankind, as well as the long history of our law, recognizing that there are differences which must be accommodated in determining the rights and duties of children as compared with those of adults." The Court also noted that there are distinctions between the treatment of children and adults in contracts, in torts, in criminal law and procedure, in criminal sanctions and rehabilitation, and in the right to vote and hold political office. Oklahoma also recognizes these differences in a number of its statutes. The Court noted that in Oklahoma a person under the age of 18 could not vote or purchase alcohol or cigarettes. The Court stated that it could not find any Oklahoma statutes that treated a person under the age of 16 as anything but a "child" except the certification procedures used to authorize petitioner's trial in this case.

The Court's opinion pointed out that the line between childhood and adulthood is drawn in different ways by various states. There is, however, complete or near unanimity among all 50 states in treating a person under 16 years of age as a minor. All states have enacted legislation designating the maximum age for juvenile court jurisdiction at no less than 16. The Court then concluded that it would offend civilized standards of decency to execute a person who was less than 16 years old at the time of his or her offense. The Court stated that the Eighth and Fourteenth Amendments prohibit the execution of a person who is under the age of 16 years at the time of his or her offense.

Note: The U.S. Supreme Court in *Stanford v. Kentucky,* 109 S. Ct. 2969 (1989) decided by a five to four plurality decision on June 26, 1989, that the imposition of the death penalty on persons who murder at 16 to 17 years of age does not violate the Eighth Amendment.

Practicum

Jerry, a 16-year-old youth, is involved in the robbery of a fast-food mart. During the robbery, one of the other youths shoots and kills the clerk. Jerry did not know that the other youth had a gun.

1. Should Jerry be tried in adult criminal court or in juvenile court?

2. If Jerry is tried in adult criminal court, what is the appropriate punishment for this crime?

3. If Jerry knew that a gun was going to be used and that the clerk was going to be killed, how would this affect the sentence that you would recommend?

Discussion Questions
Discussion Questions

1. Explain the dual orientation of juvenile court.
2. What should be the primary goals of juvenile court?
3. Explain the role that the doctrine of *parens patriae* plays in juvenile justice.
4. What is the importance of the *In re Michael D.* case?
5. Explain the scope and authority of juvenile court.
6. When is a youth considered not a proper subject for juvenile court jurisdiction?
7. In dependency cases, what is the jurisdiction of juvenile court?
8. What steps must be taken when a juvenile is taken into temporary custody?
9. Who are the primary participants in juvenile court?
10. What roles does a probation officer play in juvenile court proceedings?

Self-Study Quiz
Self-Study Quiz

True/False

1. Traditionally the purpose of juvenile court was to punish youths.
2. One of the reasons for the creation of juvenile court was the dissatisfaction with the treatment of juveniles.
3. The *In re Michael D.* case held that commitment to CYA could be based solely on retribution grounds.
4. As a general rule, juvenile courts have jurisdiction of any person under the age of 18 years who commits a criminal offense.
5. For the most part, juvenile courts are only involved in delinquency and status cases.
6. A police officer may not take into custody a minor under the age of 16 years.
7. It is permissible to confine adults and minors together if they are jointly involved in the criminal misconduct.
8. The probation officer may force a juvenile to take a drug test when the juvenile is initially arrested.
9. Juvenile court does not have jurisdiction over truancy cases.
10. Referees are used to assist judges in handling the large caseloads.
11. Parents are not required to be notified of any proceeding involving a delinquent minor.
12. In *Thompson v. Oklahoma*, the court held that the death penalty is never appropriate for an individual under 21 years of age.
13. The *Kent* case established the right of a hearing before being transferred to an adult criminal court.
14. The *In re Gault* case held that juveniles in delinquency cases never have a right to counsel.
15. *Schall v. Martin* established the right of juvenile court judges to deny pretrial release for dangerous youths.

Crimes against Children

11-1 Child Endangerment (Cruelty toward Children)

Under PC 273a, any person who, under circumstances or conditions likely to produce great bodily harm or death, willfully causes or permits any child to suffer, or inflicts on a child unjustifiable physical pain or mental suffering, or having the care or custody of any child, willfully causes or permits the person or health of that child to be injured, or willfully causes or permits that child to be placed in a situation where his or her person or health is endangered, may be punished by imprisonment in a county jail not exceeding one year, or in the state prison for two, four, or six years. If the circumstances or conditions are not likely to produce great bodily harm or death, willfully causes or permits any child to suffer, or inflicts thereon unjustifiable physical pain or mental suffering, the individual is guilty of a misdemeanor.

PC 11165.3 makes it a crime to cause the "willful cruelty or unjustifiable punishment of a child." It is a crime under this section when any person willfully causes or permits any child to suffer, or inflicts thereon, unjustifiable physical pain or mental suffering, or having the care or custody of any child, willfully causes or permits the person or health of the child to be placed in a situation such that his or her person or health is endangered.

PC 11165.4 makes it a crime to inflict unlawful corporal punishment or injury on a child. As used in this article, *unlawful corporal punishment or injury* means a situation where any person willfully inflicts upon any child any cruel or inhuman corporal punishment or injury resulting in a traumatic condition. It does not include an amount of force that is reasonable and necessary for a person employed by or engaged in a public school to quell a disturbance threatening physical injury to person or damage to property, for purposes of self-defense, or to obtain possession of weapons or other dangerous objects within the control of the pupil, as authorized by the Education Code. It also does not include an injury caused by reasonable and necessary force used by a peace officer acting within the course and scope of his or her employment as a peace officer.

11-2 Physical Abuse of a Child

PC 11165.6 defines *child abuse* as a physical injury that another person inflicts on a child by other than accidental means. Child abuse also means the sexual abuse of a child or any act or omission proscribed by PC 273a (willful cruelty or unjustifiable punishment of a child) or PC 273d (unlawful corporal punishment or injury). Child abuse also means the neglect of a child or abuse in out-of-home care, as defined in this article. Child abuse does not mean a mutual affray between minors. Child abuse does not include an injury caused by reasonable and necessary force that a peace officer uses acting within the course and scope of his or her employment as a peace officer. PC 11165 defines a child as a person under the age of 18 years.

PC 11165.2 defines child neglect. *Child neglect* means the negligent treatment or the maltreatment of a child by a person responsible for the child's welfare under circumstances indicating harm or threatened harm to the child's health or welfare. The term includes both acts and omissions on the part of the responsible person. *Severe neglect* means the negligent failure of a person having the care or custody of a child to protect the child from severe malnutrition or medically diagnosed nonorganic failure to thrive. Severe neglect also means those situations of neglect where any person having the care or custody of a child willfully causes or permits the child to be placed in a situation that endangers his or her person or health, including the intentional failure to provide adequate food, clothing, shelter, or medical care. *General neglect* means the negligent failure of a person having the care or custody of a child to provide adequate food, clothing, shelter, medical care, or supervision where no physical injury to the child has occurred. A child receiving treatment by spiritual means or not receiving specified medical treatment for religious reasons shall not for that reason alone be considered a neglected child. An informed and appropriate medical decision made by parent or guardian after consultation with a physician or physicians who have examined the minor does not constitute neglect.

If it appears that the child has been abused and there is a risk of further abuse, law enforcement, child protective services, and so on, may temporarily remove the child from the home. The official removing the child should then petition juvenile court for a judicial determination as to the disposition of the child. Unless the safety of the child is in danger, the agency removing the child must normally notify the parents within a short period of time after taking custody of the child. In most states, the child has a right to establish telephone contact with the parents within a few hours after the child has been taken into custody. In most cases, the child is taken to a hospital for examination. California has a protocol for emergency room persons who examine victims of sexual assault. In addition, many major hospitals have established SCAN (Suspected Child Abuse and Neglect) teams.

If the child is taken into custody, a hearing must be held within 48 hours or the next court day by the juvenile court. At that hearing, an attorney is required to be appointed for parents who cannot afford one. If the minor wants an attorney and the judge believes that there is a conflict between the rights of the parents and the rights of the juvenile, the court will appoint another attorney for the juvenile. An attorney from the district or county attorney's office normally represents child protective services and in some cases the juvenile.

After the filing of a petition and the detention hearing, unless the hearing is waived, an additional hearing is held to determine whether the child has been physically abused. If the court determines that the child is in need of protection, the child becomes a ward of the court. This hearing is frequently referred to as the *jurisdictional hearing* in that the court must find that the child is in need of protection before the court has jurisdiction to proceed in the case. Usually jurisdictional hearings must take place within a few days after detention. For example, in California the jurisdictional hearing must occur within 10 days after the child is placed in detention.

If a child is determined to be a victim of physical or sexual abuse and there is no reasonable method to prevent its reoccurrence, the child is declared to be a ward of the court and will be permanently removed from the home. In most states, family reunification is a stated legislative goal. Accordingly, children are placed with relatives when possible. If this is not a reasonable option, they are generally placed in foster homes. In many cases, children are placed in foster homes with the goal of family reunification within 18 months. If that goal is not possible or not met, generally steps are taken to terminate parental rights over the child. The parent may return to court at a later time to have the court orders modified or set aside and parental control reinstated. The average stays in foster homes are from about six months to two and one-half years. In some cases, the child may be turned over to the nonabusing parent.

Most law enforcement departments have special units to investigate child abuse. Officers assigned to those units will interview the child, the parents, friends, and so on in an attempt to determine if the abuse is of a nature to warrant criminal prosecution.

11-3 Legal Entry Without Warrant: Endangered Child

If there is reason to believe that a child inside a house may be injured or ill and in immediate need of help, a peace officer may enter the house without a warrant (*State v. Tamborino,* 41 Cal. 3d 919). Courts will go fairly far in finding an exigency and permitting a warrantless entry into premises to prevent possible child abuse offenses. For example, late one evening, the brother of a victim personally reported hearsay information to the police that his father was right then having sexual intercourse forcibly with the daughter of the family, who had cerebral palsy and was retarded. The officer had heard other information about prior acts of sexuality in the house from a probation officer who was working with the family. Accompanied by the brother, the officer entered the house and the father's closed bedroom, finding the sex offense in progress. The warrantless entries were upheld (*State v. Brown,* 12 Cal. App. 3d 600).

In another case, an informant reported that the defendant was molesting children in a bedroom in his garage. Police set up surveillance and saw the defendant pick up a male juvenile and drive him to the garage. Thereafter, the defendant failed to respond to repeated knocks on the bedroom door by the investigating officer, plus announcement of his purpose. Despite the lack of any cry for help from the juvenile, the warrantless entry was proper, given the heinous nature of the crime possibly being committed (*Payne* [1977] 65 Cal. App. 3d 679).

WIC 305 provides that when a peace officer has reasonable cause for believing that the minor has an immediate need for medical care, or the minor is in immediate danger of physical or sexual abuse, or the physical environment or the fact that the child is left unattended poses an immediate threat to the child's health or safety, the officer may take temporary custody of the child. In cases in which the child is left unattended, the peace officer shall first attempt to contact the child's parent or guardian to determine if the parent or guardian is able to assume custody of the child. If the parent or guardian cannot be contacted, the peace officer shall notify a social worker in the county welfare department to assume custody of the child.

11-4 Reporting Requirements of Suspected Abuse

Certain professional workers are required to report suspected physical or sexual child abuse. Generally, workers required to report include child-care workers, medical and other health-care persons, and public school employees. Others may report suspected abuse but may not be required to. If the abuse is discovered by a physician or mental health professional, the rule protecting privileged communications does not apply and the professional is required to report the abuse.

In those cases where a person is under a legal duty to report, the reporting person is immune from both criminal and civil liability as long as the report is made in good faith. In those cases where the reporting person was not required to report the child abuse, the reporting person will be immune as long as any false report was not made either knowingly or with reckless disregard for the truth or falsity of the report. All reports filed are confidential and the name of the reporting person may not be released except under court order.

The report must be forwarded immediately to a law enforcement agency, child protective services, county welfare, or probation department. The agency that receives the report is generally under a duty to report the information to other agencies.

The reporting requirements of suspected child abuse are set forth in PC 11166. Any child-care custodian, health practitioner, employee of a child protective agency, child visitation monitor, firefighter, animal control officer, or humane society officer who has knowledge of or observes a child, in his or her professional capacity or within the scope of his or her employment, whom he or she knows or reasonably suspects has been the victim of child abuse, shall report the known or suspected instance of child abuse to a child protective agency immediately or as soon as practically possible by telephone and shall prepare and send a written report thereof within 36 hours of receiving the information concerning the incident. A child protective agency shall be notified and a report shall be prepared and sent even if the child has expired, regardless of whether or not the possible abuse was a factor contributing to the death, and even if suspected child abuse was discovered during an autopsy. *Reasonable suspicion* means that it is objectively reasonable for a person to entertain a suspicion, based on facts that could cause a reasonable person in a like position, drawing, when appropriate, on his or her training and experience, to suspect child abuse. For the purpose of PC 11166(1)(a), the pregnancy of a minor does not, in and of itself, constitute a basis of reasonable suspicion of sexual abuse.

Any clergy member who has knowledge of or observes a child, in his or her professional capacity or within the scope of his or her duties, whom he or she knows or reasonably suspects has been the victim of child abuse, shall report the known or suspected instance of child abuse to a child protective agency immediately or as soon as practically possible by telephone and shall prepare and send a written report thereof within 36 hours of receiving the information concerning the incident. A child protective agency shall be notified and a report shall be prepared and sent even if the child has expired, regardless of whether or not the possible abuse was a factor contributing to the death.

A clergy member who acquires the knowledge or reasonable suspicion of child abuse during a penitential communication, however, is not required to make the report. *Penitential communication* means a communication, intended to be in confidence, including, but not limited to, a sacramental confession, made to a clergy member who, in the course of the discipline or practice of his or her church, denomination, or organization, is authorized or accustomed to hear those communications, and under the discipline, tenets, customs, or practices of his or her church, denomination, or organization, has a duty to keep those communications secret. Nothing in this subdivision shall be construed to modify or limit a clergy member's duty to report known or suspected child abuse when he or she is acting in the capacity of a child-care custodian, health practitioner, employee of a child protective agency, child visitation monitor, firefighter, animal control officer, humane society officer, or commercial film print processor.

Any commercial film and photographic print processor who has knowledge of or observes, within the scope of his or her professional capacity or employment, any film, photograph, videotape, negative, or slide depicting a child under the age of 16 years engaged in an act of sexual conduct, shall report the instance of suspected child abuse to the law enforcement agency having jurisdiction over the case immediately, or as soon as practically possible, by telephone, and shall prepare and send a written report of it with a copy of the film, photograph, videotape, negative, or slide attached within 36 hours of receiving the information concerning the incident.

Sexual conduct means any of the following:

- Sexual intercourse, including genital-genital, oral-genital, anal-genital, or oral-anal, whether between persons of the same or opposite sex or between humans and animals
- Penetration of the vagina or rectum by any object
- Masturbation for the purpose of sexual stimulation of the viewer

- Sadomasochistic abuse for the purpose of sexual stimulation of the viewer
- Exhibition of the genitals, pubic, or rectal areas of any person for the purpose of sexual stimulation of the viewer.

Any other person who has knowledge of or observes a child whom he or she knows or reasonably suspects has been a victim of child abuse may report the known or suspected instance of child abuse to a child protective agency. When two or more persons who are required to report are present and jointly have knowledge of a known or suspected instance of child abuse, and when there is agreement among them, the telephone report may be made by a member of the team selected by mutual agreement and a single report may be made and signed by the selected member of the reporting team. Any member who has knowledge that the member designated to report has failed to do so shall thereafter make the report.

The reporting duties are individual, and no supervisor or administrator may impede or inhibit the reporting duties, and no person making a report shall be subject to any sanction for making the report. However, internal procedures to facilitate reporting and apprize supervisors and administrators of reports may be established provided that they are not inconsistent with this article.

A county probation or welfare department shall immediately, or as soon as practically possible, report by telephone to the law enforcement agency having jurisdiction over the case, to the agency given the responsibility for investigation of child abuse cases, and to the district attorney's office every known or suspected instance of child abuse, based on risk to a child that relates solely to the parent's inability to provide the child with regular care due to the parent's substance abuse, which shall be reported only to the county welfare department. A county probation or welfare department also shall send a written report within 36 hours of receiving the information concerning the incident to any agency to which it is required to make a telephone report under this subdivision.

A law enforcement agency shall immediately, or as soon as practically possible, report by telephone to the agency given responsibility for investigation of child abuse cases and to the district attorney's office every known or suspected instance of child abuse reported to it.

Under PC 11166.1, when a child protective agency receives either of the following reports, it shall, within 24 hours, notify the licensing office with jurisdiction over the facility.

Under PC 11166.2, a child protective agency shall immediately or as soon as practically possible report by telephone to the appropriate licensing agency every known or suspected instance of child abuse when the instance of abuse occurs while the child is being cared for in a child day care facility, involves a child day care licensed staff person, or occurs while the child is under the supervision of a community care facility or involves a community care facility licensee or staff person. A child protective agency shall also send a written report thereof within 36 hours of receiving the information concerning the incident to any agency to which it is required to make a telephone report under this subdivision. A child protective agency shall send the licensing agency a copy of its investigation report and any other pertinent materials.

PC 11172 provides that no child-care custodian, health practitioner, firefighter, clergy member, animal control officer, humane society officer, employee of a child protective agency, child visitation monitor, or commercial film and photographic print processor who reports a known or suspected instance of child abuse shall be civilly or criminally liable for any report required or authorized by that section. Any other person reporting a known or suspected instance of child abuse shall not incur civil or criminal liability as a result of any report authorized by this article unless it can be proven that a false report was made and the person knew that the report was false or was made with reckless disregard of the truth or falsity of the report, and any person who makes a report of child abuse known to be false or with reckless disregard of the truth or falsity of the report is liable for any damages caused. No person required to make a report pursuant to this article, nor any person taking photographs at his or her direction, shall incur any civil or criminal liability for taking photographs of a suspected victim of child abuse, or causing photographs to be taken of a suspected victim of child abuse, without parental consent, or for disseminating the photographs with the reports required by this article. However, this section shall not be construed to grant immunity from this liability with respect to any other use of the photographs.

PC 11172 provides that it is a misdemeanor for any person who fails to report an instance of child abuse that he or she knows to exist, or reasonably should know to exist, as required by this article, punishable by confinement in a county jail for a term not to exceed six months, by a fine of not more than one thousand dollars ($1,000), or by both that imprisonment and fine.

11-5 Failure to Make Report of Suspected Abuse

Penal Code 288—Lewd or Lascivious Acts with Child under Age 14; Punishment; Prevention of Psychological Harm to Victim; Additional Fine

11-6 Lewd Acts upon Child

(a) Any person who willfully and lewdly commits any lewd or lascivious act, including any of the acts constituting other crimes . . . , upon or with the body, or any part or member thereof, of a child who is under the age of 14 years, with the intent of arousing, appealing to, or gratifying the lust, passions, or sexual desires of that person or the child, is guilty of a felony and shall be punished by imprisonment in the state prison for three, six, or eight years.

(b)

    (1) Any person who commits an act . . . by use of force, violence, duress, menace, or fear of immediate and unlawful bodily injury on the victim or another person, is guilty of a felony and shall be punished by imprisonment in the state prison for three, six, or eight years.

    (2) Any person who is a caretaker and commits an act described in subdivision (a) upon a dependent adult by use of force, violence, duress, menace, or fear of immediate and unlawful bodily injury on the victim or another person, with the intent described in subdivision (a), is guilty of a felony and shall be punished by imprisonment in the state prison for three, six, or eight years.

(c)

    (1) Any person who commits an act described in subdivision (a) with the intent described in that subdivision, and the victim is a child of 14 or 15 years, and the defendant is at least 10 years older than the child, is guilty of a public offense and shall be punished by imprisonment in the state prison for one, two, or three years, or by imprisonment in a county jail for not more than one year.

(2) Any person who is a caretaker and commits an act described in subdivision (a) upon a dependent adult, with the intent described in subdivision (a), is guilty of a public offense and shall be punished by imprisonment in the state prison for one, two, or three years, or by imprisonment in a county jail for not more than one year.

(d) In any arrest or prosecution under this section or Section 288.5, the peace officer, district attorney, and the court shall consider the needs of the child victim and shall do whatever is necessary, within existing budgetary resources, and constitutionally permissible to prevent psychological harm to the child victim or to prevent psychological harm to the dependent adult victim resulting from participation in the court process.

(e) Upon the conviction of any person for a violation of subdivision (a) or (b), the court may, in addition to any other penalty or fine imposed, order the defendant to pay an additional fine not to exceed ten thousand dollars ($10,000). In setting the amount of the fine, the court shall consider any relevant factors, including, but not limited to, the seriousness and gravity of the offense, the circumstances of its commission, whether the defendant derived any economic gain as a result of the crime, and the extent to which the victim suffered economic losses as a result of the crime. Every fine imposed and collected under this section shall be deposited in the Victim-Witness Assistance Fund to be available for appropriation to fund child sexual exploitation and child sexual abuse victim counseling centers and prevention programs pursuant to Section 13837.

If the court orders a fine imposed pursuant to this subdivision, the actual administrative cost of collecting that fine, not to exceed 2 percent of the total amount paid, may be paid into the general fund of the county treasury for the use and benefit of the county.

[paragraph (f) omitted.]

Penal Code 288.1—Persons Convicted of Lewd Acts upon Minor— Psychiatric Report Required

Any person convicted of committing any lewd or lascivious act including any of the acts constituting other crimes . . . upon or with the body, or any part or member thereof, of a child under the age of 14 years shall not have his or her sentence suspended until the court obtains a report from a reputable psychiatrist, from a reputable psychologist . . . or from a recognized treatment program . . . , as to the mental condition of that person.

Penal Code 266j—Providing or Transporting Child under 16 for Purpose of Lewd or Lascivious Act

Any person who intentionally gives, transports, provides, or makes available, or who offers to give, transport, provide, or make available to another person, a child under the age of 16 for the purpose of any lewd or lascivious act as defined in Section 288, or who causes, induces, or persuades a child under the age of 16 to engage in such an act with another person, is guilty of a felony and shall be imprisoned in the state prison for a term of three, six, or eight years, and by a fine not to exceed fifteen thousand dollars ($15,000).

Penal Code 273g—Lewdness and Drunkenness in Presence of Child

Any person who in the presence of any child indulges in any degrading, lewd, immoral, or vicious habits or practices, or who is habitually drunk in the presence of any child in his care, custody, or control, is guilty of a misdemeanor.

Penal Code 309—Admitting or Keeping Minor in House of Prostitution

Any proprietor, keeper, manager, conductor, or person having the control of any house of prostitution, or any house or room resorted to for the purpose of prostitution, who shall admit or keep any minor of either sex therein; or any parent or guardian of any such minor, who shall admit or keep such minor, or sanction, or connive at the admission or keeping thereof, into, or in any such house, or room, shall be guilty of a misdemeanor.

The following are the elements of a lewd act on a child under 14:

1. A lewd or lascivious act upon any part of the body of
2. A child under the age of 14
3. With the specific intent to arouse, appeal, or to gratify the lust or passions or sexual desires of either party

11-6a Elements

Lewd conduct refers to conduct that disregards socially accepted constraints. *Lascivious* refers to wanton, lustful conduct. *Dissolute* refers to conduct that is unashamed, lawless, and loose in morals and conduct. For example, dancing in the nude at a party open to the public was considered dissolute conduct (*People v. Scott*, 113 Cal. App. 778).

11-6b Discussion

A lewd and lascivious act has been defined as an act that has a tendency to excite lust, committed with a disregard for sexual constraints. It is not necessary that the act be sexual in nature (*People v. Dontanville*, 172 Cal. App. 3d 783). The preceding elements require willful and lewd conduct on the part of the participant. There is, however, no requirement for any movement or manipulation of the body or parts thereof. In *People v. Freeman*, 66 Cal. App. 3d 424, the fact that the defendant secretly expected that his allegedly lewd conduct would not be discovered because of a curtain on a booth in a movie arcade did not demonstrate objectively reasonable expectation of privacy.

In another case, the court noted that the crime of lewd and lascivious conduct was enacted to protect children from lustful advances and tampering of callous and unscrupulous persons as well as from the assaults of depraved unfortunates (*People v. Hobbs*, 109 Cal. App. 2d 189). Any touching of any part of body of child under the age of 14 can be a lewd or lascivious act within the meaning of the criminal statute if, under the totality of circumstances in which the act occurred, including any secretive or predatory conduct by a defendant, a reasonable person could conclude that it was sexual in nature. Inadvertent or casual, nonoffensive touching, which is unaccompanied by other direct or circumstantial evidence of intent to arouse, appeal to, or gratify lust, passion, or sexual desire of the defendant or child, will not qualify as lewd or lascivious act within the meaning of criminal statute proscribing lewd or lascivious acts with children (*People v. Sharp*, 29 Cal. App. 4th 1772).

One court stated that the defendant's "lewd or lascivious act," and his specific intent of arousing, appealing to, or gratifying passions or sexual desires are separate elements, both of which must be proven in order to support conviction for lewd and lascivious conduct with child (*People v. Sharp*, 29 Cal. App. 4th 1772). Conduct that may be innocuous given one intent may be lewd or lascivious, within the meaning of the statute prohibiting lewd or lascivious acts with a child under age 14, given sexual intent (*People v. Carson*, 30 Cal. App. 4th 1810). In a prosecution for lewd and lascivious conduct with a child, under this section, providing that the offense may be committed by "any person," a child under the age of 14 years is such a person (*People v. Love*, 29 Cal. App. 521).

11-7 Annoying or Molesting Children

PC 273d states that any person who willfully inflicts upon a child any cruel or inhuman corporal punishment or injury resulting in a traumatic condition is guilty of a felony. If a person is convicted of violating PC 273d and probation is granted, the court must require the following minimum conditions of probation:

(1) A mandatory minimum period of probation of 36 months.
(2) A criminal court protective order protecting the victim from further acts of violence or threats, and, if appropriate, residence exclusion or stay-away conditions.
(3) Successful completion of no less than one year of a child abuser's treatment counseling program approved by the probation department. The defendant shall be ordered to begin participation in the program immediately upon the grant of probation.

If the offense was committed while the defendant was under the influence of drugs or alcohol, the defendant must abstain from the use of drugs or alcohol during the period of probation and is subject to random drug testing by his or her probation officer. The court may waive any of the preceding minimum conditions of probation upon a finding that the condition would not be in the best interests of justice. The court must state on the record its reasons for any waiver.

PC 273.1 establishes a child abuser treatment program. Any treatment program to which a child abuser convicted of a violation of Section 273a or 273d is referred as a condition of probation, shall meet the following criteria:

- Staff must have substantial expertise and experience in the treatment of victims of child abuse and the families in which abuse and violence has occurred.
- Staff providing direct service are therapists licensed to practice in California or are under the direct supervision of a therapist licensed to practice in California.
- The treatment regimen must be designed to specifically address the offense, including methods of preventing and breaking the cycle of family violence, anger management, and parenting education that focuses on, among other things, identifying the developmental and emotional needs of the child.
- Group and individual therapy and counseling must be used with groups no larger than 12 persons.
- The program must be capable of identifying substance abuse and either treating the abuse or referring the offender to a substance abuse program to the extent that the court has not already done so.

- Program representatives must enter into a written agreement with the defendant that includes an outline of the components of the program, the attendance requirements, a requirement to attend group session free of chemical influence, and a statement that the defendant may be removed from the program if it is determined that the defendant is not benefiting from the program or is disruptive to the program.
- The program may include, on the recommendation of the treatment counselor, family counseling. However, no child victim shall be compelled or required to participate in the program, including family counseling, and no program may condition a defendant's enrollment on participation by the child victim. The treatment counselor shall privately advise the child victim that his or her participation is voluntary.

If the program finds that the defendant is unsuitable, the program shall immediately contact the probation department or the court. The probation department or court shall either recalendar the case for hearing or refer the defendant to an appropriate alternative child abuser's treatment counseling program. Upon request by the child abuser's treatment counseling program, the court shall provide the defendant's arrest report, prior incidents of violence, and treatment history to the program. The child abuser's treatment counseling program shall provide the probation department and the court with periodic progress reports at least every three months that include attendance, fee payment history, and program compliance. The program shall submit a final evaluation that includes the program's evaluation of the defendant's progress, and recommendation for either successful or unsuccessful termination of the program. The defendant shall pay for the full costs of the treatment program, including any drug testing.

PC 273.4 makes it a crime to mutilate the female genitals. *Female genital mutilation* means the excision or infibulation of the labia majora, labia minora, clitoris, or vulva, performed for nonmedical purposes.

PC 288.5 directs that any person who either resides in the same home with the minor child or has recurring access to the child, who over a period of time, not less than three months in duration, engages in three or more acts of substantial sexual conduct with a child under the age of 14 years at the time of the commission of the offense or three or more acts of lewd or lascivious conduct under Section 288, with a child under the age of 14 years at the time of the commission of the offense, is guilty of the offense of continuous sexual abuse of a child and shall be punished by imprisonment in the state prison for a term of 6, 12, or 16 years. To convict under this section the trier of fact, if a jury, needs to unanimously agree only that the requisite number of acts occurred, not on which acts constitute the requisite number.

PC 288a makes it a crime to engage in oral copulation with another person under 18 years of age. *Oral copulation* is the act of copulating the mouth of one person with the sexual organ or anus of another person. Any person over the age of 21 years who participates in an act of oral copulation with another person who is under 16 years of age is guilty of a felony. Any person who participates in an act of oral copulation with another person who is under 14 years of age and more than 10 years younger than he or she, or when the act is accomplished against the victim's will by means of force, violence, duress, menace, or fear of immediate and unlawful bodily injury on the victim or another person or where the act is accomplished against the victim's will by threatening to retaliate in the future against the victim or any other person, and there is a reasonable possibility that the perpetrator will execute the threat, shall be punished by imprisonment in the state prison for three, six, or eight years.

PC 310.5 provides that any parent or guardian of a child who enters into an agreement on behalf of that child for an unlawful sex act upon that child is guilty of a misdemeanor. *Unlawful sex act* means a felony sex offense committed against a minor.

11-8 Possession of Child Pornography

PC 311.1 states that every person who knowingly sends or causes to be sent, or brings or causes to be brought, into California for sale or distribution, or in California possesses, prepares, publishes, produces, develops, duplicates, or prints any representation of information, data, or image, including, but not limited to, any film, filmstrip, photograph, negative, slide, photocopy, videotape, video laser disc, computer hardware, computer software, computer floppy disc, data storage media, CD-ROM, or computer-generated equipment or any other computer-generated image that contains or incorporates in any manner, any film or filmstrip, with intent to distribute or to exhibit to, or to exchange with, others, or who offers to distribute, distributes, or exhibits to, or exchanges with, others, any obscene matter, knowing that the matter depicts a person under the age of 18 years personally engaging in or personally simulating sexual conduct has committed a crime. This crime is a wobbler. It does not apply to the activities of law enforcement and prosecuting agencies in the investigation and prosecution of criminal offenses or to legitimate medical, scientific, or educational activities, or to lawful conduct between spouses.

The section does not apply to matter that depicts a legally emancipated child under the age of 18, including lawful conduct between spouses when one or both are under the age of 18.

PC 311.3 provides that a person is guilty of sexual exploitation of a child if he or she knowingly develops, duplicates, prints, or exchanges any representation of information, data, or image, including, but not limited to, any film, filmstrip, photograph, negative, slide, photocopy, videotape, video laser disc, computer hardware, computer software, computer floppy disc, data storage media, CD-ROM, or computer-generated equipment or any other computer-generated image that contains or incorporates in any manner, any film or filmstrip that depicts a person under the age of 18 years engaged in an act of sexual conduct.

PC 311.4 makes it a crime to use minors in the distribution of obscene matter or for posing or modeling involving sexual conduct. PC 311.10 prohibits the sale or distribution of any obscene matter if the seller knows that it depicts a person under the age of 18 personally engaging in or personally simulating sexual conduct. It is not necessary to prove that the matter is obscene to establish a violation of this section. This section does not apply to drawings, figurines, statues, or any film rated by the Motion Picture Association of America, nor does it apply to live or recorded telephone messages when transmitted, disseminated, or distributed as part of a commercial transaction.

11-9 Obscenity Laws Related to Juveniles

PC 288.2 prohibits the distribution or exhibition of lewd material to a minor. The section provides that every person who, with knowledge that a person is a minor, or who fails to exercise reasonable care in ascertaining the true age of a minor, knowingly distributes, sends, causes to be sent, exhibits, or offers to distribute or exhibit by any means, including, but not limited to, live or recorded telephone messages, any harmful matter, as defined in Section 313, to a minor with the intent of arousing, appealing to, or gratifying the lust or passions or sexual desires of that person or of the minor, with the intent, or for the purpose of seducing the minor, is guilty of a public offense punishable by imprisonment in the state prison or in the county jail. Upon the second and each subsequent conviction for a violation of this subdivision, the person is guilty of a felony. Under this section, any prosecution may use the defense that a parent or guardian committed the act charged in aid of legitimate sex education or in aid of legitimate scientific or educational purposes.

PC 273e makes it a crime to employ or send a minor a to house of prostitution, variety theater, and so on.

Every telephone, special delivery company or association, and every other corporation or person engaged in the delivery of packages, letters, notes, messages, or other matter, and every manager, superintendent, or other agent of such person, corporation, or association, who sends any minor in the employ or under the control of any such person, corporation, association, or agent, to the keeper of any house of prostitution, variety theater, or other place of questionable repute, or to any person connected with, or any inmate of, such places, or who permits the minor to enter such places, is guilty of a misdemeanor.

PC 273f also provides that any person, whether as parent, guardian, employer, or otherwise, and any firm or corporation, who as employer or otherwise, sends, directs, or causes any minor to be sent or directed to any saloon, gambling house, house of prostitution, or other immoral place is guilty of a misdemeanor.

11-10 Contributing to the Delinquency of a Minor

Penal Code 277—Definitions

11-11 Child Abduction

The following definitions apply for the purposes of this chapter:

(a) *Child* means a person under the age of 18 years.
(b) *Court order* or *custody order* means a custody determination decree, judgment, or order issued by a court of competent jurisdiction, whether permanent or temporary, initial or modified, that affects the custody or visitation of a child, issued in the context of a custody proceeding. An order, once made, shall continue in effect until it expires, is modified, is rescinded, or terminates by operation of law.
(c) *Custody proceeding* means a proceeding in which a custody determination is an issue, including, but not limited to, an action for dissolution or separation, dependency, guardianship, termination of parental rights, adoption, paternity, except actions under Section 11350 or 11350.1 of the Welfare and Institutions Code, or protection from domestic violence proceedings, including an emergency protective order pursuant to Part 3 (commencing with Section 6240) of Division 10 of the Family Code.
(d) *Lawful custodian* means a person, guardian, or public agency having a right to custody of a child.
(e) A *guardian* means the right to the physical care, custody, and control of a child pursuant to a custody order as defined in subdivision (b) or, in the absence of a court order, by operation of law, or pursuant to the Uniform Parentage Act contained in Part 3 (commencing with Section 7600) of Division 12 of the Family Code. Whenever a public agency takes protective custody or jurisdiction of the care, custody, control, or conduct of a child by statutory authority or court order, that agency is a lawful custodian of the child and has a right to physical custody of the child. In any subsequent placement of the child, the public agency continues to be a lawful custodian with a right to physical custody of the child until the public agency's right of custody is terminated by an order of a court of competent jurisdiction or by operation of law.

(f) In the absence of a court order to the contrary, a parent loses his or her right to custody of the child to the other parent if the parent having the right to custody is dead, is unable or refuses to take the custody, or has abandoned his or her family. A natural parent whose parental rights have been terminated by court order is no longer a lawful custodian and no longer has a right to physical custody.

(g) *Keeps* or *withholds* means retains physical possession of a child whether or not the child resists or objects.

(h) *Visitation* means the time for access to the child allotted to any person by court order.

(i) *Person* includes, but is not limited to, a parent or an agent of a parent.

(j) *Domestic violence* means domestic violence as defined in Section 6211 of the Family Code.

(k) *Abduct* means take, entice away, keep, withhold, or conceal.

Penal Code 278—Taking Minor from Parent or Guardian

Every person, not having a right to custody, who maliciously takes, entices away, keeps, withholds, or conceals any child with the intent to detain or conceal that child from a lawful custodian shall be punished by imprisonment in a county jail not exceeding one year, a fine not exceeding one thousand dollars ($1,000), or both that fine and imprisonment, or by imprisonment in the state prison for two, three, or four years, a fine not exceeding ten thousand dollars ($10,000), or both that fine and imprisonment.

Penal Code 278.5—Concealment, Detention, Taking, or Enticement of Child in Violation of Custody Order

(a) Every person who takes, entices away, keeps, withholds, or conceals a child and maliciously deprives a lawful custodian of a right to custody, or a person of a right to visitation, shall be punished by imprisonment in a county jail not exceeding one year, a fine not exceeding one thousand dollars ($1,000), or both that fine and imprisonment, or by imprisonment in the state prison for 16 months, or two or three years, a fine not exceeding ten thousand dollars ($10,000), or both that fine and imprisonment.

(b) Nothing contained in this section limits the court's contempt power.

(c) A custody order obtained after the taking, enticing away, keeping, withholding, or concealing of a child does not constitute a defense to a crime charged under this section.

Penal Code 278.6—Factors and Circumstances in Aggravation

(a) At the sentencing hearing following a conviction for a violation of Section 278 or 278.5, or both, the court shall consider any relevant factors and circumstances in aggravation, including, but not limited to, all of the following:

    (1) The child was exposed to a substantial risk of physical injury or illness.

    (2) The defendant inflicted or threatened to inflict physical harm on a parent or lawful custodian of the child or on the child at the time of or during the abduction.

    (3) The defendant harmed or abandoned the child during the abduction.

    (4) The child was taken, enticed away, kept, withheld, or concealed outside the United States.

    (5) The child has not been returned to the lawful custodian.

(6) The defendant previously abducted or threatened to abduct the child.

(7) The defendant substantially altered the appearance or the name of the child.

(8) The defendant denied the child appropriate education during the abduction.

(9) The length of the abduction.

(10) The age of the child.

(b) At the sentencing hearing following a conviction for a violation of Section 278 or 278.5, or both, the court shall consider any relevant factors and circumstances in mitigation, including, but not limited to, both of the following:

(1) The defendant returned the child unharmed and prior to arrest or issuance of a warrant for arrest, whichever is first.

(2) The defendant provided information and assistance leading to the child's safe return.

(c) In addition to any other penalties provided for a violation of Section 278 or 278.5, a court shall order the defendant to pay restitution to the district attorney for any costs incurred in locating and returning the child as provided in Section 3134 of the Family Code, and to the victim for those expenses and costs reasonably incurred by, or on behalf of, the victim in locating and recovering the child. An award made pursuant to this section shall constitute a final judgment and shall be enforceable as such.

Penal Code 278.7—Exceptions; Requirements

(a) Section 278.5 does not apply to a person with a right to custody of a child who, with a good faith and reasonable belief that the child, if left with the other person, will suffer immediate bodily injury or emotional harm, takes, entices away, keeps, withholds, or conceals that child.

(b) Section 278.5 does not apply to a person with a right to custody of a child who has been a victim of domestic violence who, with a good faith and reasonable belief that the child, if left with the other person, will suffer immediate bodily injury or emotional harm, takes, entices away, keeps, withholds, or conceals that child. *Emotional harm* includes having a parent who has committed domestic violence against the parent who is taking, enticing away, keeping, withholding, or concealing the child.

(c) The person who takes, entices away, keeps, withholds, or conceals a child shall do all of the following:

(1) Within a reasonable time from the taking, enticing away, keeping, withholding, or concealing, make a report to the office of the district attorney of the county where the child resided before the action. The report shall include the name of the person, the current address and telephone number of the child and the person, and the reasons the child was taken, enticed away, kept, withheld, or concealed.

(2) Within a reasonable time from the taking, enticing away, keeping, withholding, or concealing, commence a custody proceeding in a court of competent jurisdiction consistent with the federal Parental Kidnapping Prevention Act (Section 1738A, Title 28, United States Code) or the Uniform Child Custody Jurisdiction Act (Part 3 (commencing with Section 3400) of Division 8 of the Family Code).

(3) Inform the district attorney's office of any change of address or telephone number of the person and the child.

(d) For the purposes of this article, a reasonable time within which to make a report to the district attorney's office is at least 10 days and a reasonable time to commence a custody proceeding is at least 30 days. This section shall not preclude a person from making a report to the district attorney's office or commencing a custody proceeding earlier than those specified times.

(e) The address and telephone number of the person and the child provided pursuant to this section shall remain confidential unless released pursuant to state law or by a court order that contains appropriate safeguards to ensure the safety of the person and the child.

Penal Code 279—Violation by Person Not a Resident; Mitigating Circumstances

A violation of Section 278 or 278.5 by a person who was not a resident of, or present in, this state at the time of the alleged offense is punishable in this state, whether the intent to commit the offense is formed within or outside of this state, if any of the following apply:

(a) The child was a resident of, or present in, this state at the time the child was taken, enticed away, kept, withheld, or concealed.

(b) The child thereafter is found in this state.

(c) A lawful custodian or a person with a right to visitation is a resident of this state at the time the child was taken, enticed away, kept, withheld, or concealed.

Penal Code 279.1—Offenses Continuous

The offenses enumerated in Sections 278 and 278.5 are continuous in nature and continue for as long as the minor child is concealed or detained.

11-11a Discussion

In kidnapping, the victim is forced to go with the offender. Child stealing, however, is a crime against the person with the right to custody, and therefore, the consent of the child is irrelevant. The preceding quoted Penal Code sections make it a crime to maliciously take, detain, conceal, or entice a child away from the person or agency who has the legal right to custody. The right to lawful custody of the other person or agency may exist as the result of a court order or the "natural" right of a parent. It is also a crime under the preceding sections if the person taking the child has some right to custody but violates the visitation periods or rights (terms) of the custody order, judgment, or decree. For example, in one case the father was convicted of a violation of PC 278.5 (felony) even though he had custody 50 percent of the time. In this case, the father took the child and moved to another state where he concealed the location of the child from the child's mother (*People v. Lortz*, 137 Cal. App. 3d 363).

If the taking is for good cause, there is no crime. *Good cause*, for the purposes of these sections, is defined as a good faith belief that the taking, detaining, concealing, or enticing away of the child is necessary to protect the child from *immediate bodily injury or emotional harm*. In some situations, a person may be convicted as a substitute for attempted child molestation charges. For example, if the offender entices the child to another location to sexually molest him or her but does not complete the offense of child molesting, the movement of the child by the enticement of the offender may constitute a crime.

A defendant charged with kidnapping a person under age of 14 years may not rely on the defense of reasonable mistake as to victim's age (*People v. Magpuso*, 23

Cal. App. 4th 112). In *People v. Patrick* (126 Cal. App. 3d 952), the necessity defense was not available in a false imprisonment and kidnapping case that arose out of an abduction of a suspected cult member for the purpose of deprogramming. The defendant, claiming that because the subjective belief of the cult member's parents about the danger to their daughter was objectively justifiable, the defendant as the parents' agent was entitled to the defense; however, the agent pointed to no action that he took to independently assure himself that the daughter was a member of cult or that forcible abduction and deprogramming was the only reasonable alternative available.

A parent entitled to custody cannot be liable for kidnapping his or her own child. This did not apply, however, to a defendant who kidnapped his daughter when he took her into a motel room to molest her; his right to physical custody ended when he exercised it for a physical purpose known to be illegal (*People v. Senior*, 3 Cal. App. 4th 765).

The criminal act of child stealing is committed when a person, with the intent to detain and conceal a child from its parent, regardless of whether detention and concealment actually occur, takes or entices away the child (*People v. Bormann*, 6 Cal. App. 3d 292). When referring to maliciously, forcibly, or fraudulently taking or enticing away a minor child, forcibly does not necessarily imply the use of physical force. Maliciously imports a wish to vex, annoy, or injure another person, or intent to do a wrongful act established either by proof or presumption of law. Fraudulently is very broad in its meaning, and no definite and invariable rule can be laid down as a general proposition defining *fraud*, which includes all surprise, trick, cunning, dissembling, and other unfair ways by which another is deceived (*People v. Casagranda*, 43 Cal. App. 2d 818).

The taking contemplated is a taking with intent to detain and conceal child from person having lawful charge of such child (*People v. Hyatt*, 18 Cal. App. 3d 618). *Takes* is the equivalent of seizes (*People v. Bormann*, 6 Cal. App. 3d 292).

Detention or Concealment

The word *detain* does not necessarily include the idea of force but includes delaying, hindering, retarding, and so on (*People v. Moore*, 67 Cal. App. 2d 789). Actual concealment and detention are not essential to constitute the offense of child stealing. The element of "detaining" does not necessarily include the idea of force (*People v. Smith*, 17 Cal. App. 2d 468).

In a prosecution for child stealing, the length of time during which the defendant intended to detain child from parents was immaterial (*People v. Annunzio*, 120 Cal. App. 89). In another case, a defendant's keeping a 13-year-old girl with him under the claim of marriage over a period of many weeks was sufficient evidence of his intent with respect to detaining child from her mother to support a conviction for child stealing (*People v. Lindsey*, 159 Cal. App. 2d 353). In *People v. Palmer* (50 Cal. App. 2d 697), the fact that the girl was able to escape from defendant, charged with attempted child stealing, had no bearing on the inference of intent to detain and conceal, which might reasonably be drawn from evidence disclosing the defendant's attempt to force the girl into his automobile. The fact that the child might have gone with the accused willingly was also immaterial in another case in determining the accused's guilt of child stealing, since the offense was one against the parent and not against the child (*People v. Moore*, 67 Cal. App. 2d 789).

A mother who was convicted of stealing her child from her husband's custody prior to a child custody hearing was not entitled to necessity defense instruction, where the mother never reported the crime to authorities, failed to appear at a scheduled custody hearing, did not seek to obtain legal custody of child, and deliberately evaded authorities (*People v. Beach*, 194 Cal. App. 3d 955).

Reconciliation

In *People v. Howard* (36 Cal. 3d 852), where the husband and wife reconciled before a final judgment of dissolution was entered, a child custody order that had been granted as part of an interlocutory dissolution decree was canceled; under such circumstances, there was no existing child custody order when the father took the children out of the state without consulting the mother.

Residence of Child

The parent with lawful custody has the right to determine the residence of the child. Whether a father had a right to choose the residence of his child was irrelevant in one case since the issue in the child stealing prosecution was whether the father concealed the baby with the intent to deprive the mother of a right to visitation (*People v. Lortz*, 137 Cal. App. 3d 363).

Cases on Point

People v. Bevan, 208 Cal. App. 3d 393

The acts of the defendant of placing his hand under a 12-year-old victim's shirt and bra and touching her breasts, kissing her, and placing her hand on his exposed penis should not have been fragmented into three separate counts of lewd and lascivious acts upon a 12-year-old, and thus, conviction and punishment for two duplicate crimes had to fall; the acts were all committed during one incident.

In re Paul C., 221 Cal. App. 3d 43

A defendant's lewd or lascivious act, and his specific intent of arousing, appealing to, or gratifying passions or sexual desires are separate elements, both of which must be proven to support conviction for lewd and lascivious conduct with a child (*People v. Sharp*, 29 Cal. App. 4th 1772). A minor under 14 years of age may be adjudged responsible for committing lewd or lascivious act with another child under 14 years of age, or for participating in oral copulation with a person under age of 18, upon clear proof of the minor's knowledge of the wrongfulness of acts along with evidence of criminal intent under charged offenses.

People v. Olsen, 36 Cal. 3d 638

A reasonable mistake as to the victim's age is not a defense to a charge of lewd or lascivious conduct with a child under the age of 14 years.

People v. O'Connor, 8 Cal. App. 4th 941

The statute prohibiting lewd and lascivious acts with a child under the age of 14 is violated by a person who directs children to take off their clothing, even if they do not initially remove their underwear.

Practicum

Your next-door neighbor spanks his kids extremely hard. You are a doctor.

1. What are the reporting requirements if you feel that the neighbor is abusing his children?

2. Would it make any difference if you discovered the suspected abuse as a nosy neighbor or as a healthcare professional treating the children?

Discussion Questions

1. Explain what constitutes child endangerment.
2. Define *child neglect*.
3. What are the reporting requirements for suspected child abuse?
4. What constitutes *lewd acts upon a child*?
5. Define *child abduction*.

Self-Study Quiz

True/False

1. It is a crime to punish a child under PC 11165.3.
2. *Child abuse* refers to any physical injury to a child caused by an adult.
3. *Child neglect* does not include an injury a peace officer causes by reasonable and necessary force within the scope of his or her duties.
4. A peace officer may enter a private residence without a warrant if there is reason to believe that a child is in immediate need of help.
5. Public school officials are not required to report suspected child abuse.
6. A clergy member who acquires the knowledge of child abuse during a penitential communication is required to report this knowledge.
7. It is a felony for any person who is required to report suspected cases of child abuse and fails to do so.
8. *A lewd act upon a child under the age of 14* requires that the act be accomplished with the specific intent to arouse, appeal to, or to gratify the lust or passions or sexual desires of either party.
9. It is a crime to use minors in the distribution of obscene matter.
10. For purposes of the crime of child abduction, a child is defined as a person under the age of 14 years.
11. It may be a felony to maliciously take a child from the lawful custody of his or her parents.
12. The residence of a child is determined by the residence of the parent or parents with lawful custody.

ABC Law and Controlled Substances

There are two ways of being addicted to heroin. One way is to mainline it. The other way is to traffic in it.
Richard Berdin
Code Name Richard

12-1 Sale of Alcoholic Beverages Without a License

BP (Business & Professions Code) 23300 makes it a crime for anyone to sell alcoholic beverages unless the person is authorized to do so by a license. BP 24046 requires that the license shall be posted in a conspicuous place on the premises. Licenses issued for trains, boats. or airplanes may, in lieu of being posted upon the train, boat, or airplane for which they are issued, may be posted in such other place in California as the department shall designate.

BP 25616 provides that any person who knowingly or willfully files a false license fee report with the department, and any person who refuses to permit the department or any of its representatives to make any inspection or examination for which provision is made in this division, or who fails to keep books of account as prescribed by the department, or who fails to preserve such books for the inspection of the department for such time as the department deems necessary, or who alters, cancels, or obliterates entries in such books of account in order to falsify the records of sales of alcoholic beverages made under this division is guilty of a misdemeanor.

12-2 Encouraging the Sale of Alcoholic Beverages

BP 25600 provides that, except as permitted by the Department of Alcohol Beverage Control rules, the giving of premiums or free goods in connection with sale of alcoholic beverages is a crime. The exceptions to this are refunds to, or exchanges of products for, dissatisfied consumers. Winegrowers may advertise or otherwise offer consumers a guarantee of product satisfaction only in newsletters or other publications of the winegrowers or at the winegrowers' premises. A winegrower may refund to a dissatisfied consumer the entire purchase price of wine produced by that winegrower and sold to that consumer, regardless of where the wine was purchased. No rule of the department may permit a licensee to give any premium, gift, or free goods of greater than inconsequential value with the sale or distribution of beer. With respect to beer, premiums, gifts, or free goods, including advertising specialties that have no significant utilitarian value other than advertising, shall be deemed to have greater than inconsequential value if they cost more than twenty-five cents ($0.25) per unit, or cost more than fifteen dollars ($15) in the aggregate for all those items given by a single supplier to a single retail premises per calendar year.

PC 303 makes it unlawful for any person engaged in the sale of alcoholic beverages, other than in the original package, to employ on the premises where the alcoholic beverages are sold any person for the purpose of procuring or encouraging the purchase or sale of such beverages, or to pay any person a percentage or commission on the sale of such beverages for procuring or encouraging such purchase or sale.

PC 303a provides that it is unlawful, in any place of business where alcoholic beverages are sold to be consumed on the premises, for any person to loiter in or about the premises in order to beg or solicit any patron or customer of, or visitor in, the premises to purchase any alcoholic beverage for the person begging or soliciting.

BP 25620 makes the possession of an opened container in a public park or public place illegal.

Any person possessing any can, bottle, or other receptacle containing any alcoholic beverage that has been opened, or had a seal broken, or the contents of which has been partially removed, in any city, county, or city- and county-owned park or other adjacent city, county, or city- and county-owned public place, or any recreation and park district, or any regional park or open-space district, is guilty of an infraction if the city, county, or city and county has enacted an ordinance that prohibits the consumption of alcoholic beverages in such areas. This section does not apply where the possession is within premises located in a park or other public place for which a license has been issued.

BP 25612.5 requires a sign be posted where the store is only licensed for sale of alcoholic beverages to be consumed off the premises. A prominent, permanent sign or signs stating "NO LOITERING IS ALLOWED ON OR IN FRONT OF THESE PREMISES" shall be posted in a place that is clearly visible to patrons of the licensee. The size, format, form, placement, and languages of the sign or signs shall be determined by the department. This paragraph shall apply to a licensee only upon written notice to the licensee from the department. The department shall issue this written notice only upon a request, from the local law enforcement agency in whose jurisdiction the premises are located, that is supported by substantial evidence that there is drinking in public adjacent to the premises.

No alcoholic beverages may be consumed on the premises of an off-sale retail establishment, and no alcoholic beverages shall be consumed outside the edifice of an on-sale retail establishment. The exterior of the premises, including adjacent public sidewalks and all parking lots under the control of the licensee, shall be illuminated during all hours of darkness during which the premises are open for business to ensure that law enforcement personnel can identify persons standing in those areas at night. However, the required illumination must be placed to minimize interference with nearby residents' quiet enjoyment of their property.

The section also requires that litter shall be removed daily from the premises, including adjacent public sidewalks and all parking lots under the control of the licensee. These areas shall be swept or cleaned, either mechanically or manually, on a weekly basis to control debris. Also, graffiti shall be removed from the premises and all parking lots under the control of the licensee within 120 hours of application.

BP 25607 regulates the possession of unauthorized beverages on licensed premises. Generally, it is unlawful for any person or licensee to have on any premises for which a license has been issued any alcoholic beverages other than the alcoholic beverage that the licensee is authorized to sell at the premises under his or her license. It shall be presumed that all alcoholic beverages found or located upon premises for which licenses have been issued belong to the person or persons to whom the licenses were issued. Every person violating the provisions of this section is guilty of a misdemeanor. The department may seize any alcoholic beverages found in violation of the section. A bona fide public eating place for which an on-sale beer and wine license has been issued may have on the premises brandy, rum, or liqueurs for use solely for cooking purposes.

12-4 Furnishing Alcohol to an Intoxicated Person

BP 25602 prohibits the sale of alcohol to an intoxicated person. Thus, every person who sells, furnishes, gives, or causes to be sold, furnished, or given away, any alcoholic beverage to any habitual or common drunkard or to any obviously intoxicated person is guilty of a misdemeanor.

The section also provides that no person who sells, furnishes, gives, or causes to be sold, furnished, or given away, any alcoholic beverage is civilly liable to any injured person or the estate of such person for injuries inflicted on that person as a result of intoxication by the consumer of such alcoholic beverage. The Legislature declared that this section shall be interpreted so that the holdings in cases such as *Vesely v. Sager* (5 Cal. 3d 153), *Bernhard v. Harrah's Club* (16 Cal. 3d 313), and *Coulter v. Superior Court* (21 Cal. 3d 144) be abrogated in favor of prior judicial interpretation finding the consumption of, rather than the serving of, alcoholic beverages as the proximate cause of injuries inflicted upon another by an intoxicated person. This legislative declaration states in essence that the consumer of alcoholic beverages, not the seller, is liable in civil court for damages sustained as the result of the consumption of alcoholic beverages.

BP 25602.1 provides that a civil action may be brought by or on behalf of any person who has suffered injury or death against any person who sells, furnishes, gives, or causes to be sold, furnished, or given away any alcoholic beverage, and any other person who sells, or causes to be sold, any alcoholic beverage, to any obviously intoxicated minor where the furnishing, sale, or giving of that beverage to the minor is the proximate cause of the personal injury or death sustained by that person.

12-5 Sale after Hours

BP 2563 makes it a misdemeanor crime when any on- or off-sale licensee, or agent or employee of such licensee, sells, gives, or delivers to any persons any alcoholic beverage or any person who knowingly purchases any alcoholic beverage between the hours of 2:00 A.M. and 6:00 A.M. of the same day. For the purposes of this section, on the day that a time change occurs from Pacific Standard Time to Pacific Daylight Time, or back again to Pacific Standard Time, "2:00 A.M." means two hours after 12:00 P.M. of the day preceding the day such change occurs.

BP 25633 restricts Sunday deliveries of certain alcoholic beverages. That section states that except as otherwise, no person licensed as a manufacturer, winegrower, distilled spirits manufacturer's agent, rectifier, or wholesaler of any alcoholic beverage shall deliver or cause to be delivered any alcoholic beverage to or for any person holding an on-sale or off-sale license on Sunday or except between the hours of 3 A.M. and 8 A.M. of any day other than Sunday. Any alcoholic beverage may be delivered at the platform of the manufacturing, producing, or distributing plant at any time. Nothing contained in this section prohibits the transportation or the carriage and delivery in transit at any time of any alcoholic beverage between the premises of a manufacturer, winegrower, wholesaler, distiller, importer, or any of them. Every person violating the provisions of this section is guilty of a misdemeanor.

12-6 Sale of an Alcoholic Beverage to a Minor

BP 25659 provides that to prevent the sale of alcoholic beverages to a minor, any licensee, or his or her agent or employee, may refuse to sell or serve alcoholic beverages to any person who cannot produce adequate written evidence that he or she is over the age of 21 years. BP 25660 states that bona fide evidence of majority and identity of the person is a document issued by a federal, state, county, or municipal government, or subdivision or agency thereof, including, but not limited to, a motor vehicle operator's license or an identification card issued to a member of the armed forces, which contains the name, date of birth, description, and picture of the person. Proof that the defendant-licensee, or his or her employee or agent, demanded, was shown, and acted in reliance upon such bona fide evidence in any transaction shall be a defense to any criminal prosecution or to any proceedings for the suspension or revocation of any license based thereon.

BP 25658 makes it a misdemeanor for any person who sells, furnishes, gives, or causes to be sold, furnished, or given away, any alcoholic beverage to any person under the age of 21 years. Also, any person under the age of 21 years who purchases any alcoholic beverage, or any person under the age of 21 years who consumes any alcoholic beverage in any on-sale premises, is guilty of a misdemeanor.

Any on-sale licensee who knowingly permits a person under the age of 21 years to consume any alcoholic beverage in the on-sale premises, whether or not the licensee has knowledge that the person is under the age of 21 years, is guilty of a misdemeanor. Any person who violates the section shall be punished by a fine of not less than two hundred fifty dollars ($250), no part of which shall be suspended, or the person shall be required to perform not less than 24 hours or more than 32 hours of community service during hours when the person is not employed and is not attending school, or a combination of fine and community service as determined by the court. The department may revoke a license for a third violation that occurs within any 36-month period. This provision shall not be construed to limit the department's authority and discretion to revoke a license prior to a third violation when the circumstances warrant that penalty.

Persons under the age of 21 may be used by peace officers in the enforcement of the section to apprehend licensees, or employees or agents of licensees, who sell alcoholic beverages to minors. Any person under the age of 21 who purchases or attempts to purchase any alcoholic beverage while under the direction of a peace officer is immune from prosecution for that purchase or attempt to purchase an alcoholic beverage. Guidelines with respect to the use of persons under the age of 21 as decoys shall be adopted and published by the department in accordance with the rulemaking portion of the Administrative Procedure Act (Chapter 3.5 [commencing with Section 11340] of Part 1 of Division 3 of Title 2 of the Government Code). Law enforcement-initiated minor decoy programs in operation prior to the effective date of regulatory guidelines adopted by the department shall be authorized as long as the minor decoy displays to the seller of alcoholic beverages the appearance of a person under the age of 21. This subdivision shall not be construed to prevent the department from taking disciplinary action against a licensee who sells alcoholic beverages to a minor decoy prior to the department's final adoption of regulatory guidelines.

PC 307 makes it a misdemeanor to sell, give away, or furnish confections containing alcohol to a minor. Every person, firm, or corporation that sells or gives or in any way furnishes to another person who is in fact under the age of 21 any candy, cake, cookie, or chewing gum that contains alcohol in excess of 1/2 of 1 percent by weight is guilty of a misdemeanor.

BP 25658.5 makes it a misdemeanor for any person under the age of 21 years to attempt to purchase or to purchase any alcoholic beverage from a licensee, or the licensee's agent or employee.

BP 25662 allows the seizure of alcohol from a person under the age of 21. Any person under the age of 21 who has any alcoholic beverage in his or her possession on any street or highway or in any public place or in any place open to the public is guilty of a misdemeanor. This section does not apply to possession by a person

12-7 Minor in Possession of an Alcoholic Beverage

under the age of 21 making a delivery of an alcoholic beverage in pursuance of the order of his or her parent, responsible adult relative, or any other adult designated by the parent or legal guardian, or in pursuance of his or her employment. That person shall have a complete defense if he or she was following, in a timely manner, the reasonable instructions of his or her parent, legal guardian, responsible adult relative, or adult designee relating to disposition of the alcoholic beverage.

12-8 Minor Present inside On-Sale Public Premises

BP 25665 makes it a misdemeanor for any licensee under an on-sale license issued for public premises who permits a person under the age of 21 to enter and remain in the licensed premises without lawful business. In addition, any person under the age of 21 who enters and remains in the licensed public premises without lawful business there is guilty of a misdemeanor and shall be punished by a fine of not less than two hundred dollars ($200), no part of which shall be suspended.

BP 25663 makes it a misdemeanor for any person who employs or uses the services of any person under the age of 21 in or on that portion of any premises, during business hours, which are primarily designed and used for the sale and service of alcoholic beverages for consumption on the premises. Any off-sale licensee who employs or uses the services of any person under the age of 18 to sell alcoholic beverages shall be subject to suspension or revocation of his or her license, except that a person under 18 may be employed or used for those purposes if that person is under the continuous supervision of a person 21 years of age or older.

BP 25663.5 allows for the employment of persons under 21 as musicians. Persons 18 to 21 years of age may be employed as musicians, for entertainment purposes only, during business hours on premises that are primarily designed and used for the sale and service of alcoholic beverages for consumption on the premises, if live acts, demonstrations, or exhibitions that involve the exposure of the private parts or buttocks of any participant or the breasts of any female participant are not allowed on such premises. However, the area of such employment is limited to a portion of the premises that is restricted to the use exclusively of musicians or entertainers in the performance of their functions, and no alcoholic beverages shall be sold, served, consumed, or taken into that area.

BP 25664 prohibits the use of advertisements encouraging minors to consume alcoholic beverages. The use in any advertisement of alcoholic beverages of any subject matter, language, or slogan addressed to and intended to encourage minors to drink the alcoholic beverages is prohibited. Nothing in the section is deemed to restrict or prohibit any advertisement of alcoholic beverages to those persons of legal drinking age.

12-9 Possession of Alcohol on School Grounds

BP 25608 prohibits the possession of alcoholic beverage on school property. Accordingly, every person who possesses, consumes, sells, gives, or delivers to any other person, any alcoholic beverage in or on any public schoolhouse or any of the grounds thereof, is guilty of a misdemeanor. This section does not, however, make it unlawful for any person to acquire, possess, or use any alcoholic beverage in or on any public schoolhouse, or on any grounds thereof, if any of the following applies:

(a) The alcoholic beverage is acquired, possessed, or used in connection with a course of instruction given at the school and the person has been authorized to acquire, possess, or use it by the governing body or other administrative head of the school.

(b) The public schoolhouse is surplus school property and the grounds thereof are leased to a lessee that is in a general law city with a population of less than 50,000, or the public schoolhouse is surplus school property and the grounds thereof are located in an unincorporated area and are leased to a lessee that is a civic organization, and the property is to be used for community center purposes and no public school education is to be conducted on it by either the lessor or the lessee, and the property is not being used by persons under the age of 21 years for recreational purposes at any time during which alcoholic beverages are being sold or consumed on the premises.

(c) The alcoholic beverages are acquired, possessed, or used during events at a college-owned or operated veterans stadium with a capacity of over 12,000 people, located in a county with a population of over six million people. As used in this subdivision, "events" mean football games sponsored by a college, other than a public community college, or other events sponsored by noncollege groups.

(d) The alcoholic beverages are acquired, possessed, or used during an event not sponsored by any college at a performing arts facility built on property owned by a community college district and leased to a nonprofit organization that is a public benefit corporation formed under Part 2 (commencing with Section 5110) of Division 2 of Title 1 of the Corporations Code. As used in this subdivision, "performing arts facility" means an auditorium with more than 300 permanent seats.

(e) The alcoholic beverage is wine for sacramental or other religious purposes and is used only during authorized religious services held on or before January 1, 1995.

(f) The alcoholic beverages are acquired, possessed, or used during an event at a community center owned by a community services district and the event is not held at a time when students are attending a public school sponsored activity at the center.

(g) The alcoholic beverage is wine that is acquired, possessed, or used during an event sponsored by a community college district or an organization operated for the benefit of the community college district where the college district maintains both an instructional program in viticulture on no less than five acres of land owned by the district and an instructional program in enology, which includes sales and marketing.

(h) The alcoholic beverage is acquired, possessed, or used at a professional minor league baseball game conducted at the stadium of a community college located in a county with a population of less than 250,000 inhabitants, and the baseball game is conducted pursuant to a contract between the community college district and a professional sports organization.

Any person convicted of a violation of the section shall, in addition to the penalty imposed for the misdemeanor, be barred from having or receiving any privilege of the use of public school property that is accorded by Article 2 (commencing with Section 82530) of Chapter 8 of Part 49 of the Education Code.

12-10 Minor Displaying False Identification

BP 25660.5 makes it a misdemeanor for any person who sells, gives, or furnishes to any person under the age of 21 any false or fraudulent written, printed, or photostatic evidence of the majority and identity of such person under the age of 21 evidence of majority and identification of any other person.

BP 25661 provides that any person under 21 who presents or offers to any licensee, or his or her agent or employee, any written, printed, or photostatic evidence of age and identity that is false, fraudulent, or not actually his or her own to order, purchase, attempt to purchase, or otherwise procure or attempt to procure, the serving of any alcoholic beverage, or who has in his or her possession any false or fraudulent written, printed, or photostatic evidence of age and identity, is guilty of a misdemeanor and shall be punished by a fine of at least two hundred fifty dollars ($250), no part of which shall be suspended; or the person shall be required to perform not less than 24 hours nor more than 32 hours of community service during hours when the person is not employed and is not attending school, or a combination of fine and community service as determined by the court.

12-11 Disorderly Conduct

BP 25601 makes it a misdemeanor to maintain a disorderly house. Any licensee, or agent or employee of a licensee, who keeps, permits to be used, or suffers to be used, in conjunction with a licensed premises, any disorderly house or place in which people abide or to which people resort, to the disturbance of the neighborhood, or in which people abide or to which people resort for purposes that are injurious to the public morals, health, convenience, or safety, is guilty of a misdemeanor.

12-12 Sale of Mislabeled Alcoholic Beverages

BP 25609 prohibits the sale of mislabeled alcoholic beverages. Every person who, in response to an inquiry or request for any brand, type, or character of alcoholic beverages, sells or offers for sale under an on-sale license a different brand, type, or character without first informing the purchaser of the difference is guilty of a misdemeanor.

12-13 Social Gathering/Alcoholic Beverages

A peace officer who has lawfully entered the premises may seize any alcoholic beverage in plain view that is in the possession of, or provided to, a person under the age of 21 at social gatherings, when those gatherings are open to the public, 10 or more persons under the age of 21 are participating, persons under the age of 21 are consuming alcoholic beverages, and there is no supervision of the social gathering by a parent or guardian of one or more of the participants. Where a peace officer has seized alcoholic beverages pursuant to this subdivision, the officer may destroy any alcoholic beverage contained in an opened container and in the possession of, or provided to, a person under the age of 21, and, with respect to alcoholic beverages in unopened containers, the officer shall impound those beverages for a period not to exceed seven working days pending a request for the release of those beverages by a person 21 years of age or older who is the lawful owner or resident of the property upon which the alcoholic beverages were seized. If no one requests release of the seized alcoholic beverages within that period, those beverages may be destroyed.

12-14 Uniform Controlled Substances Act

Most drug offenses in California are contained in the Uniform Controlled Substances Act (referred to as the Act), which is set forth in the Health and Safety Code (H&S), Sections 11000–11853.

12-14a Definition

The following listed definitions are set forth in the Act.

Controlled Substances

A controlled substance is defined as a drug, substance, or immediate precursor that is listed in any section of the Act (H&S 11007).

Drug

(a) A substance recognized as drugs in the official United States Pharmacopoeia of the United States or official National Formulary, or any supplement to any of them

(b) Substances intended for use in the diagnosis, cure, mitigation, treatment, or prevention of disease in man or animals

(c) Substances (other than food) intended to affect the structure or any function of the body of man or animals

(d) Substances intended for use as a component of any article specified in subdivisions (a), (b) and (c).

Drugs do not include devices or their components, parts, or accessories (H&S 11014).

Marijuana

Marijuana means all parts of the plant *Cannabis sativa L.*, whether growing or not; the seeds thereof; the resin extracted from any part of the plant; and every compound, manufacture, salt, derivative, mixture, or preparation of the plant, its seeds or resin. It does not include the mature stalks of the plant, fiber produced from the stalks, oil or cake made from the seeds of the plant, any other compound, manufacture, salt, derivative, mixture, or preparation of the mature stalks (except the resin extracted therefrom), fiber, oil, or cake, or the sterilized seed of the plant that is incapable of germination (H&S 11018).

Since California does not draw distinction among different types of marijuana, the prosecutor, in prosecution for possession or sale of marijuana, does not need to specify and prove the species of the marijuana subject of charge.

Narcotic Drug

Narcotic drug means any of the following whether produced directly or indirectly by extraction from substances of vegetable origin, or independently by means of chemical synthesis, or by a combination of extraction and chemical synthesis:

(a) Opium and opiate, and any salt, compound, derivative, or preparation of opium or opiate

(b) Any salt, compound, isomer, or derivative, whether natural or synthetic, or the substances referred to in subdivision (a), but not including the isoquinoline alkaloids of opium

(c) Opium poppy and poppy straw

(d) Coca leaves and any salt, compound, derivative, or preparation of coca leaves, but not including decocainized coca leaves or extraction of coca leaves that do not contain cocaine or ecgonine

(e) Cocaine, whether natural or synthetic, or any salt, isomer, derivative, or preparation thereof

(f) Ecgonine, whether natural or synthetic, or any salt, isomer, derivative, or preparation thereof

(g) Acetylfentanyl, the thiophene analog thereof, derivatives of either, and any salt, compound, isomer, or preparation of acetylfentanyl or the thiophene analog thereof (H&S 11019).

Opiate

Opiate means any substance having addiction-forming or addiction-sustaining liability similar to morphine or being capable of conversion into a drug having addiction-forming or addiction-sustaining liability (H&S 11020).

Opium Poppy

Opium poppy means the plant of the species *Papaver somniferum L.*, except its seeds (H&S 11021).

12-14b Schedules

The Act divides the controlled substances into five different schedules.

Schedule I

Those drugs classified as Schedule I controlled substances are listed in H&S 11054. Substances classified under Schedule I include:

1. Opiates unless specifically listed in another schedule
2. Heroin
3. LSD (lysergic acid diethylamide)
4. Mescaline
5. Marijuana
6. Hallucinogenic substances unless specifically listed in another section
7. Morphine methylbromide
8. Peyote
9. Cocaine base
10. Methaqualone

Note: This is not a complete list of all Schedule I substances.

Schedule II

H&S 11055 contains a list of those substances classified as Schedule II. The list includes:

1. Opium
2. Codeine
3. Cocaine except that classified as Schedule I
4. Pentobarbital
5. Morphine
6. Methadone
7. Amphetamines
8. Methylphenidate

Note: This is not a complete list of substances under Schedule II.

Schedule III

Schedule III controlled substances are listed in H&S 11056. The list of Schedule III substances includes:

1. Phencyclidine (PCP)
2. Methaqualone
3. Barbiturates
4. Stimulants unless specifically listed under another schedule
5. Depressants unless specifically listed under another schedule
6. Secobarbital

7. Lysergic acid
8. Chorthexadol

Note: This is not a complete list of substances listed under Schedule III.

Schedule IV

Schedule IV substances are listed in H&S 11057 and include the following listed substances:

1. Veronal
2. Luminal
3. Chloral hydrate
4. Valmid
5. Placidyl
6. Barbital
7. Chloral betaine
8. Pipradrol

Note: This is not a complete list of substances under Schedule IV.

Schedule V

The Schedule V controlled substances listed in H&S 11058 include:

1. Not more than 200 milligrams of codeine per 100 milliliters or per 100 grams
2. Not more than 100 milligrams of opium per 100 milliliters or per 100 grams
3. Not more than 100 milligrams of dihydrocodeine per 100 milliliters or per 100 grams

The Act requires certain reports be submitted regarding the manufacture, sale, or delivery of controlled substances. Reports required include:

12-14c Reporting Requirements

1. (H&S 11100) Any manufacturer, wholesaler, retailer, or other person who sells, transfers, or otherwise furnishes certain controlled substances shall submit a monthly report to the State Department of Justice of all of those transactions. Those substances include:

   • Phenyl-2-propanone
   • Methylamine
   • Ethylamine
   • D-lysergic acid
   • Ergotamine tartrate
   • Diethyl malonate
   • Malonic acid
   • Ethyl malonate
   • Barbituric acid
   • Piperidine
   • N-acetylanthranilic acid
   • Pyrrolinine
   • Penylacetic acid
   • Anthranilic acid
   • Morpholine
   • Ephedrine
   • Pseudoephedrine

2. (H&S 11100.1) Any manufacturer, wholesaler, and so on, who receives the controlled substances listed in the preceding from outside the state shall make a report of the transaction to the State Department of Justice.
3. (H&S 11103) Reports are required to be made on the thefts or loss of any of the controlled substances listed under Section 11100.

Forms for Reports

H&S 11101 requires that the monthly reports contain at least the following information on those substances covered by Section 11100:

1. Name of substance
2. Quantity of the substance involved
3. Date of the transaction
4. Name and address of the receiver of the substance
5. Name and address of the person providing the substance

12-14d Felony Offense for Certain Sales

Health & Safety Code 11104

Any manufacturer, wholesaler, retailer, or other person who sells, transfers, or otherwise furnishes any of the substances listed in subdivision (a) of Section 11100 with knowledge or the intent that the recipient will use the substance to unlawfully manufacture a controlled substance is guilty of a felony.

12-14e Permits for Sale, Transfer, and So On

H&S 11106 requires that any manufacturer, wholesaler, and so on, who sells, transfers, and so on any of the controlled substances listed in Section 11100 must obtain a permit prior to the transfer from the State Department of Justice. Permits may be granted for a maximum period of one year.

12-14f Prescriptions

Only physicians, dentists, podiatrists, or veterinarians or pharmacists acting within the provisions of Article 18 of the Health and Safety Code and registered nurses under certain circumstances may write prescriptions. Some of the general rules on writing and filling prescriptions include:

1. No person shall write, issue, fill, compound or dispense a prescription except as authorized by the Act.
2. Prescriptions for a controlled substance shall only be issued for a legitimate medical purpose.
3. Both the prescribing practitioner and the pharmacist filling the prescription have the responsibility to ensure that only legal prescriptions are filled.
4. It is unlawful to solicit, directly or indirectly, any persons to prescribe, fill, and so on, an illegal prescription.
5. No person shall issue a prescription that is false or fictitious in any respect.
6. No person shall issue, prescribe, administer, and so on, a controlled substance to an addict except as permitted under the Act.
7. With minor exceptions, controlled substances classified under Schedules II, III, IV, and V may not be dispensed without a prescription.
8. In most cases, a maximum 72-hour supply of a Schedule II substance may be dispensed pursuant to a valid prescription.
9. Prescription blanks are issued by the State Department of Justice in serially numbered groups of not more than 100 forms each in triplicate.
10. Possession of unauthorized prescription blanks or counterfeit blanks is a criminal offense under the Act.

11. The giving of a false name or address in connection with prescribing, dispensing, and so on of a controlled substance is unlawful.
12. Records of all prescriptions prescribed, dispensed, and so on shall be maintained for a period of at least three years.
13. Records shall contain, at least, the following information:

    a. Name and address of the patient
    b. Date
    c. Character and quantity of controlled substances involved
    d. Pathology and purpose for which the prescription was issued (or in the case of the pharmacist, the name and address of the prescriber of the controlled substance)

12-14g Unlawful Possession

It is unlawful to possess any controlled substance except as permitted by law. In most cases, the unlawful possession is a felony (H&S 11350–11356). The possession of substances under Schedules III, IV, or V may in most cases be treated by the court as a misdemeanor (wobbler). Possession for purposes of sale or distribution is an aggravated form of possession. There are two types of possession—actual and constructive. *Actual possession* is where the individual has the substance in his or her possession. *Constructive possession* is where the substance is possessed by someone else, but the defendant has control of it.

The elements of unlawful possession are:

1. The person had possession or the right to exercise control of a controlled substance.
2. The possession is unlawful.
3. The person had knowledge of the nature of the substance.
4. The amount of substance possessed was a usable quantity. Note: While a usable amount must be possessed, there is no requirement that the amount be sufficient to produce a narcotic effect (*People v. Piper*, 19 Cal. App. 3d 248).

12-14h Unlawful Manufacture, Import, Sale, and So On, of Controlled Substances

H&S 11379 makes it a felony to illegally transport, import, manufacture, sell, and so on, a controlled substance listed under Schedules III, IV, and V.

Marijuana

Possession

The possession of less than 28.5 grams of marijuana (any concentrated cannabis) is normally a misdemeanor (H&S 11357).

Cultivation

Every person who plants, cultivates, harvests, dries, or processes any marijuana or any part thereof, except as otherwise provided by law, shall be punished by imprisonment in the state prison (felony) (H&S 11358).

Possession for Sale

Every person who possesses for sale any marijuana, except as otherwise provided by law, shall be punished by imprisonment in the state prison (felony) (H&S 11359).

Transportation, Distribution, or Importation

Except as provided for by law, every person who transports, imports into the state, sells, furnishes, and so on, marijuana is guilty of a felony (H&S 11360). If the amount is less than 28.5 grams of marijuana, other than concentrated cannabis, the offense is a misdemeanor.

Minors

The employment or using of minors in the unlawful selling, distributing, and so on, of marijuana is a felony. It is also a felony for an adult to distribute, give, sell, and so on, marijuana to a minor (H&S 11361).

Peyote

Health and Safety Code 11363

Every person who plants, cultivates, harvests, dries, or processes any plant of the genus Lophophora, also known as peyote, or any part thereof shall be punished by imprisonment in the county jail. . . . [A misdemeanor offense.]

12-14i Possession of Paraphernalia for Unlawful Use

H&S 11364 makes it unlawful to possess any opium pipe or any device, and so on, used for unlawfully injecting or smoking a controlled substance.

12-14j Presence during Unlawful Use

It is unlawful to visit or to be in any room or place where any controlled substances are being unlawfully used, smoked, and so on (H&S 11365).

12-15 Driving under the Influence

Vehicle Code 23152—Driving While under Influence of Alcohol or Drugs

(a) It is unlawful for any person who is under the influence of an alcoholic beverage or any drug, or under the combined influence of an alcoholic beverage and any drug, to drive a vehicle.
(b) It is unlawful for any person who has 0.08 percent or more, by weight, of alcohol in his/her blood to drive a vehicle.
   For purposes of this subdivision, percent, by weight, of alcohol shall be based upon grams of alcohol per 100 milliliters of blood.
   In any prosecution under this subdivision, it is a rebuttable presumption that the person has 0.08 percent or more, by weight, of alcohol in his/her blood at the time of driving the vehicle if the person had 0.08 percent or more, by weight, of alcohol in his/her blood at the time of the performance of a chemical test within three hours after the driving.
(c) It is unlawful for any person who is addicted to the use of any drug to drive a vehicle. This subdivision shall not apply to a person who is participating in a methadone maintenance treatment program. . . .

12-15a Discussion

There are three offenses under Vehicle Code 23152:

1. Driving under the influence
2. Driving with a blood alcohol content of 0.08 or higher
3. Driving by a person who is addicted to the use of any drug, unless the person is on an approved methadone maintenance treatment program.

   Prior to 1982, the preceding offenses were only committed by driving on a public highway. In 1982, the section was changed to remove the public highway requirement. The section now applies to highways and elsewhere within California. As discussed under the laws of arrest, normally a misdemeanor must be committed in the presence of the officer before an officer has the authority to make a misdemeanor arrest without a warrant. DWI/DUI offenses, however, are exceptions to this rule (PC 836).

Under the Influence

Under the influence means that alcohol or drugs or a combination thereof have so affected the nervous system, the brain, or muscles as to impair to an appreciable degree the ability of the person to operate a motor vehicle in an ordinary and cautious manner (*People v. Byrd*, 125 Cal. App. 3d 1054). Under the influence does not require that the driver be drunk (*People v. Haeussler*, 41 Cal. 2d 252).

The drug involved may be a prescribed drug and need not be illegal. For example, where the accused is stopped for driving under the influence, it is not a defense that the drugs were duly prescribed and were taken according to the doctor's directions (*People v. Keith*, 184 Cal. App. 2d Supp. 884).

For the offense of driving while a drug addict, it is not necessary to establish that the driver was under the influence of drugs at the time he or she was driving. All that is necessary is that the defendant is a drug addict and operated a vehicle during the time he or she was addicted (*People v. Diaz*, 234 Cal. App. 2d 818 and *People v. O'Neil*, 62 Cal. App. 2d 748).

Driver Defined

The driver is the person who drives or is in actual physical control of the vehicle (Vehicle Code, Section 305). The person steering the vehicle is considered the driver, even if the vehicle is being towed or pushed by another vehicle. The identity of the driver may be proven by circumstantial evidence (*People v. Moreno*, 188 Cal. App. 3d 1179).

Driving

To constitute driving for purposes of DWI/DUI statutes, some movement of the vehicle is necessary. It need only be a slight movement. The movement may be coasting downhill or pedaling a moped, as long as the vehicle is capable of moving under its own power. A movement of a few feet is sufficient (*People v. Padilla*, 184 Cal. App. 3d 1022).

Vehicle

A *vehicle* is defined as any device that permits persons or property to be propelled, drawn, or moved upon a public highway, except a device moved exclusively by human power (Vehicle Code, Section 670). The definition includes animal-drawn vehicles, go-carts, forklifts, snowmobiles, bulldozers, mopeds, and mobile cranes (*People v. Jordan*, 75 Cal. App. 3d Supp. 1). Separate code sections apply to operating a bicycle under the influence (Vehicle Code, Sections 21200 and 21200.5).

12-16 Felony Drunk Driving

Vehicle Code 23153—Driving While under the Influence of Alcohol or Drugs—Causing Injury

(a) It is unlawful for any person, while under the influence of an alcoholic beverage or any drug, or under the combined influence of an alcoholic beverage and any drug, to drive a vehicle and, when so driving, do any act forbidden by law or neglect any duty imposed by law in the driving of the vehicle, which act or neglect proximately causes bodily injury to any person other than the driver.

(b) It is unlawful for any person while having 0.08 percent or more, by weight, of alcohol in his/her blood to drive a vehicle and, when so driving, do any act forbidden by law or neglect any duty imposed by law in the driving of the vehicle, which act or neglect proximately causes bodily injury to any person other than the driver. . . .

(c) In proving the person neglected any duty imposed by law in the driving of the vehicle, it is not necessary to prove that any specific section of this code was violated.

12-16a Discussion

The preceding offenses are similar to those set forth under VC 23152 (a) and (b) with the following two additional requirements:

1. Bodily injury to any person other than the defendant
2. The injury was caused by an act or failure to act, which constitutes a violation of the code or of a duty imposed by the code.

12-17 Operating an Aircraft or Boat While under the Influence

Various code provisions make it unlawful to operate an aircraft or boat while under the influence of alcohol or drugs. The restrictions are similar to those for driving a vehicle, except that it is illegal to operate an aircraft (on the ground or in the air) with a blood alcohol level of .04 or more.

12-18 Juveniles

Vehicle Code 23140—Driving While under the Influence of Alcohol— under the Age of 18

(a) It is unlawful for a person under the age of 18 years who has 0.05 percent or more, by weight, of alcohol in his or her blood to drive a vehicle.

(b) A person may be found to be in violation of subdivision (a) if the person was, at the time of driving, under the age of 18 years and under the influence of, or affected by, an alcoholic beverage regardless of whether a chemical test was made to determine that person's blood-alcohol concentration and if the trier of fact finds that the person had consumed an alcoholic beverage and was driving a vehicle while having a concentration of 0.05 percent or more, by weight, of alcohol in his or her blood.

12-18a Discussion

Vehicle Code 23140 makes it unlawful for a juvenile whose blood alcohol level is .05 or more to drive a vehicle. A violation under this section may be established even if no chemical test was taken. This section applies only to driving under the influence of alcohol and does not apply to driving under the influence of drugs. If this section does not apply, the juvenile may still be prosecuted under regular DWI/DUI offenses.

12-19 Chemical Test Advisement

Under the provisions of VC 23157, prior to asking a driver to submit to a chemical test, the driver must be advised of the following items:

1. Refusal to submit to, or failure to complete, a chemical test will result in suspension or revocation of his or her driving license and mandatory imprisonment upon conviction.
2. He or she has a choice of either blood, breath, or urine tests. If taken to a medical facility for treatment, the driver must take whatever tests are available.
3. A refusal to take or a failure to complete a test may be used in court against the driver as evidence that the driver was driving in violation of VC 23152 or 23153.

4. The driver has no right to consult with counsel prior to taking the test or making a choice of which test to take.
5. If he or she is unable to complete one test, he or she must submit to another one.

Note: *Miranda* warnings are not required during field investigations prior to an arrest.

Creative Legal Defense

"Dan Rather made them do it."—James Campbell, a chemist at Virginia Tech University, was caught making methamphetamines (speed) in the university laboratory. In his confession to the police, he stated that he needed money to pay off his debts. While watching TV's *48 Hours*, he saw Dan Rather explain how to make speed and decided to try it. He received probation.

Practicum

The use of criminal law to control drugs and alcohol does not appear to be working. What other alternatives are there to combat the drug problem? Which would you support if you were a state legislator?

Discussion Questions

1. Explain the general rules regarding the transfer of controlled substances.
2. Define the term *drug*.
3. What is a *narcotic*?
4. Explain the differences between Vehicle Code Section 23152 and Section 23153.
5. What are the essential differences between the various schedules under the Uniform Controlled Substances Act?
6. Who may prescribe a controlled substance under the provisions of the Uniform Controlled Substances Act?
7. What records are required to be kept by a person who prescribes controlled substances?
8. What are the elements of unlawful possession of a controlled substance?

Self-Study Quiz

True/False

1. The term *marijuana*, as used in the Act, includes the seeds of the plant.
2. A controlled substance is a substance or drug listed in the Act.
3. Opium is a narcotic drug.
4. Opiates are habit forming.
5. There are six schedules under the Act.
6. Opium and morphine are Schedule II substances.
7. Lysergic acid is a Schedule III substance.
8. Permits are required prior to the manufacture of D-lysergic acid.
9. Possession of minor amounts of marijuana is normally a misdemeanor.
10. Growing marijuana is a misdemeanor.
11. Providing marijuana to a minor may be a felony.
12. It is not unlawful for an addict to drive a vehicle unless he or she is under the influence of a drug or alcohol.
13. The person steering the vehicle is considered the driver.
14. It is not unlawful to drive while under the influence of a duly prescribed drug.

General Criminal Statutes

Justice is always violent to the party offending, for every man is innocent in his own eyes.
Daniel Defoe

T his chapter discusses the general criminal statutes that are not discussed in other chapters and that are designed to protect the peace and tranquility of the community.

13-1 Disturbing the Peace

PC 415 defines three types of disturbing the peace crimes. The three are as follows:

1. Unlawfully fighting or challenging another person to fight in a public place
2. Maliciously and willfully disturbing another person by loud and unreasonable noise
3. Using offensive words in a public place that are likely to produce an immediate violent reaction

PC 415.5 is similar to PC 415, except that it applies only to the building and grounds of any public school, elementary school, community college, state college, and so on. PC 415.5 does not apply to any person who is registered as a student of the school where the disturbance took place. The crime of disturbing the peace is a misdemeanor.

13-1a Discussion

Unlawfully Fighting

To constitute this crime, the involvement must be voluntary. If all the participants are voluntarily fighting, then all are equally guilty of disturbing the peace. If one or more of the participants are not voluntarily involved, then those parties may be victims of an assault or battery and the other parties guilty of assault and/or battery.

Loud and Unreasonable Noise

One of the problems with the sections involving "loud and unreasonable noise" is that generally communications are protected by the First Amendment to the U.S. Constitution. Accordingly, first the court must decide whether the loud and unreasonable noise is a communication. If it is not a communication, then it is not protected by the First Amendment. If it is a communication, then the decision must be made as to whether that particular communication is protected speech. For example, a loud shout done to disrupt is not considered protected speech. The test to determine if the noise is "loud and unreasonable" is whether a reasonable person would be disturbed by it. To determine this, the court looks at the time, place, and manner in which the noise is made, in addition to the volume of the noise.

The Vehicle Code, Section 27007, provides that no driver of a vehicle shall operate any sound amplification system that can be heard outside the vehicle from 50 feet or more when the vehicle is being operated on a public road, unless the system is being used to request assistance or warn of a hazardous situation. Accordingly, it is illegal to use a "boom" system on a highway. Note: The statute does not apply to vehicles being operated in a parade, and so on, if they are being operated with a city or county permit.

Offensive Words

Offensive words are words that by their very utterance inflict injury or tend to incite an immediate breach of peace. The uttering of offensive words or "fighting words" is not protected by the First Amendment. Case law has required that the words be the kind of language that is "inherently likely to provoke an immediate violent reaction" (*People v. Callahan*, 168 Cal. App. 3d 631). Note in the *Callahan* case, the court held that use of the words "fucking asshole" to a police officer was not a use of offensive words because the police officer was neither offended or provoked by the language. In another case, the U.S. Supreme Court held that a person wearing a jacket bearing the words "Fuck the Draft" in a courthouse hallway was not using offensive words, because no reasonable person would regard the words as a direct personal insult (*Cohen v. California*, 403 U.S. 15).

PC 653(m) makes the conduct of harassing by telephone a crime. That section provides that every person who, with intent to annoy, telephones another and addresses to or about the other person any obscene language or addresses to the other person any threat to inflict injury to the person or property of the person addressed or any member of his or her family, is guilty of a misdemeanor. Every person who makes repeated telephone calls with the intent to annoy another person at his or her residence, is, whether or not conversation ensues from making the telephone call, guilty of a misdemeanor. Nothing in PC 653(m) applies to telephone calls made in good faith. The conduct is a crime only if one or both of the following circumstances exist:

13-2 Harassing Telephone Calls

1. There is a temporary restraining order, an injunction, or any other court order, or any combination of these court orders, in effect prohibiting the behavior described in this section.
2. The person makes repeated telephone calls with the intent to annoy another person at his or her place of work, totaling more than 10 times in a 24-hour period, whether or not conversation ensues from making the telephone call, and the repeated telephone calls are made to the workplace of an adult or fully emancipated minor who is a spouse, former spouse, cohabitant, former cohabitant, or person with whom the person has a child or has had a dating or engagement relationship or is having a dating or engagement relationship.

Any offense committed by use of a telephone as provided in this section may be deemed to have been committed at either the place at which the telephone call or calls were made or at the place where the telephone call or calls were received.

Under PC 653(x) any person who telephones the 911 emergency line with the intent to annoy or harass another person is guilty of a misdemeanor punishable by a fine of not more than one thousand dollars ($1,000), by imprisonment in a county jail for not more than six months, or by both the fine and imprisonment. Nothing in this section applies to telephone calls made in good faith. An intent to annoy or harass is established by proof of repeated calls over a period of time, however short, that are unreasonable under the circumstances. Upon conviction of a violation of this section, a person also is liable for all reasonable costs incurred by any unnecessary emergency response.

PC 640 deals with misconduct in facilities or on vehicles of a public transportation system. That section prohibits:

13-3 Misconduct on Public Transportation

(1) Evasion of the payment of any fare of the system.
(2) Misuse of any transfer, pass, ticket, or token with the intent to evade the payment of any fare.
(3) Playing sound equipment on or in any system facility or vehicle.
(4) Smoking, eating, or drinking in or on any system facility or vehicle in those areas where those activities are prohibited by that system.
(5) Expectorating upon any system facility or vehicle.
(6) Willfully disturbing others on or in any system facility or vehicle by engaging in boisterous or unruly behavior.

(7) Carrying any explosive or acid, flammable liquid, or toxic or hazardous material in any public transit facility or vehicle.

(8) Urinating or defecating in any system facility or vehicle, except in a lavatory. However, this paragraph does not apply to any person who cannot comply with this paragraph as a result of a disability, age, or a medical condition.

(9) Willfully blocking the free movement of another person in any system facility or vehicle. This paragraph (9) shall not be interpreted to affect any lawful activities permitted or first amendment rights protected under the laws of this state or applicable federal law, including, but not limited to, laws related to collective bargaining, labor relations, or labor disputes.

(10) Skateboarding, rollerskating, or rollerblading in any system facility, vehicle, or parking structure.

13-4 Disturbing Schools

The Education Code, Section 32210, prohibits disturbing schools. That section provides that any person who willfully disturbs any public school or any public school meeting is guilty of a misdemeanor, and shall be punished by a fine of not more than five hundred dollars ($500).

Education Code 32211—Remaining upon School Grounds after Requested to Leave

(a) Any person who is not a student of the public school, a parent or guardian of a student of the public school, or an officer or employee of the school district maintaining the public school, or who is not required by his or her employment to be in a public school building or on the grounds of the public school, and who has entered any public school building or the grounds of any public school, during school hours, and who is requested either by the principal of the public school or by the designee of the principal to leave a public school building or public school grounds, shall promptly depart therefrom and shall not return thereto for at least 48 hours. A request that a person depart from a public school building or public school grounds shall be made by the principal, or the designee of the principal, exclusively on the basis that it appears reasonable to the principal, or the designee of the principal to conclude that the continued presence of the person requested to depart would be disruptive of, or would interfere with, classes or other activities of the public school program.

(b) Any person who fails to leave a public school building or public school grounds promptly upon request of the principal of the public school or the designee of the principal made pursuant to subdivision (a) or who, after leaving a public school building or public school grounds pursuant to a request of the principal of the public school, or the designee of the principal, made pursuant to subdivision (a), returns thereto, except pursuant to subdivision (d), within 48 hours, is guilty of a misdemeanor and shall be punished pursuant to Section 626.8 of the Penal Code.

(c) Any person who is requested pursuant to subdivision (a) to leave a public school building or school grounds may appeal to the superintendent of the school district in which the public school is located. Such an appeal shall be made not later than the second succeeding school day after the person has departed from the public school building or public school grounds. The superintendent shall, after reviewing the matter with the principal, or the designee of the principal, and the person seeking ingress to the public school during school hours, render his or her decision within 24 hours after the appeal is made, and such decision shall be binding upon both parties. A decision of the superintendent may be appealed by the person seeking ingress to the public school during public school hours to the governing board of the school district in which the public school is located. Such an appeal shall be made not later than the second succeeding school day after the superintendent has rendered his or her decision. The governing board of the school district shall consider and decide the appeal at its next scheduled regular or adjourned regular public meeting, and the decision of the governing board shall be final.

(d) Where the office of the superintendent of the school district or the office of the governing board of the school district is situated in the public school building or on the grounds of the public school from which a person has been requested, pursuant to subdivision (a), to depart, the person may enter the public school building or the grounds of the public school solely for the purpose of, and only to the extent necessary for, personally making at the office of the superintendent or the office of the governing board an appeal pursuant to subdivision (c).

(e) The governing board of every school district shall cause to have posted at every entrance to each school and grounds of the district a notice which shall set forth "school hours," which are hereby defined for the purposes of this section as the period commencing one hour before classes begin and one hour after classes end at any school, or as otherwise defined by the governing board of the school district.

(f) For the purposes of subdivision (a), a representative of a school employee organization engaged in activities related to representation, as defined by Section 7104, shall be deemed to be a person required by his or her employment to be in a school building or on the grounds of a school.

(g) Nothing in this section shall be construed as preempting any ordinance of any city, county, or city and county.

Penal Code 647—Disorderly Conduct

13-5 Disorderly Conduct

Every person who commits any of the following acts is guilty of disorderly conduct, a misdemeanor:

(a) Who solicits anyone to engage in or who engages in lewd or dissolute conduct in any public place or in any place open to the public or exposed to public view.

(b) Who solicits or who agrees to engage in or who engages in any act of prostitution. A person agrees to engage in an act of prostitution when, with specific intent to so engage, he or she manifests an acceptance of an offer or solicitation to so engage, regardless of whether the offer or solicitation was made by a person who also possessed the specific intent to engage in prostitution. No agreement to engage in an act of prostitution shall constitute a violation of this subdivision unless some act, beside the agreement, be done within this state in furtherance of the commission of an act of prostitution by the person agreeing to engage in that act. As used in this subdivision, "prostitution" includes any lewd act between persons for money or other consideration.

(c) Who accosts other persons in any public place or in any place open to the public for the purpose of begging or soliciting alms.

(d) Who loiters in or about any toilet open to the public for the purpose of engaging in or soliciting any lewd or lascivious or any unlawful act.

(e) Who loiters or wanders upon the streets or from place to place without apparent reason or business and who refuses to identify himself or herself and to account for his or her presence when requested by any peace officer so to do, if the surrounding circumstances are such as to indicate to a reasonable person that the public safety demands this identification.

(f) Who is found in any public place under the influence of intoxicating liquor, any drug, controlled substance, toluene, or any combination of any intoxicating liquor, drug, controlled substance, or toluene, in such a condition that he or she is unable to exercise care for his or her own safety or the safety of others, or by reason of his or her being under the influence of intoxicating liquor, any drug, controlled substance, toluene, or any combination of any intoxicating liquor, drug, or toluene, interferes with or obstructs or prevents the free use of any street, sidewalk, or other public way.

(g) When a person has violated subdivision (f) of this section, a peace officer, if he or she is reasonably able to do so, shall place the person, or cause him or her to be placed, in civil protective custody. The person shall be taken to a facility, designated pursuant to Section 5170 of the Welfare and Institutions Code, for the 72-hour treatment and evaluation of inebriates. A peace officer may place a person in civil protective custody with that kind and degree of force which would be lawful were he or she effecting an arrest for a misdemeanor without a warrant. No person who has been placed in civil protective custody shall thereafter be subject to any criminal prosecution or juvenile court proceeding based on the facts giving rise to this placement. This subdivision shall not apply to the following persons:

(1) Any person who is under the influence of any drug, or under the combined influence of intoxicating liquor and any drug.

(2) Any person who a peace officer has probable cause to believe has committed any felony, or who has committed any misdemeanor in addition to subdivision (f) of this section.

(3) Any person who a peace officer in good faith believes will attempt escape or will be unreasonably difficult for medical personnel to control.

(h) Who loiters, prowls, or wanders upon the private property of another, at any time, without visible or lawful business with the owner or occupant thereof. As used in this subdivision, *loiter* means to delay or linger without a lawful purpose for being on the property and for the purpose of committing a crime as opportunity may be discovered.

(i) Who, while loitering, prowling, or wandering upon the private property of another, at any time, peeks in the door or window of any inhabited building or structure located thereon, without visible or lawful business with the owner or occupant thereof.

(j) Who lodges in any building, structure, vehicle, or place, whether public or private, without the permission of the owner or person entitled to the possession or in control thereof.

(k) Anyone who looks through a hole into a bathroom with the intent to invade the privacy of persons therein.

In any accusatory pleading charging a violation of subdivision (b), if the defendant has been once previously convicted of a violation of that subdivision, the previous conviction shall be charged in the accusatory pleading. If the previous conviction is found to be true by the jury, upon a jury trial, or by the court, upon a court trial, or is admitted by the defendant, the defendant shall be imprisoned in the county jail for a period of not less than 45 days and shall not be eligible for release upon completion of sentence, on probation, on parole, on work furlough or work release, or on any other basis until he or she has served a period of not less than 45 days in the county jail. In all cases in which probation is granted the court shall require as a condition thereof that the person be confined in the county jail for at least 45 days. In no event does the court have the power to absolve a person who violates this subdivision from the obligation of spending at least 45 days in confinement in the county jail.

Penal Code 647b—Loitering around Adult Schools

Every person who loiters about any school in which adults are in attendance at courses established pursuant to Chapter 10 (commencing with Section 52500) of Part 28 of the Education Code, and who annoys or molests any person in attendance therein shall be punished by a fine of not exceeding one thousand dollars ($1,000) or by imprisonment in the county jail for not exceeding six months, or by both such fine and imprisonment.

Penal Code 647 provides, in part, that a person is guilty of a misdemeanor who does one of the following listed acts:

13-5a Discussion

- *Lewd or Dissolute Conduct*—Solicits anyone to engage in or who engages in lewd or dissolute conduct in any public place or in any place open to the public or exposed to public view.
- *Prostitution*—Solicits or who agrees to engage in or who engages in any act of prostitution. For purposes of PC 647, prostitution includes any lewd act between persons for money or other consideration.
- *Begging*—Accosts other persons in any public place or in any place open to the public for the purposes of begging or soliciting alms.
- *Loitering*—Who loiters, prowls, or wanders upon the private property of another, at any time, without visible or lawful business with the owner or occupant thereof.
- *Peeping*—Who, while loitering, prowling, or wandering upon the private property of another, at any time, peeks in the door or window of any inhabited building or structure without visible or lawful business with the owner or occupant of the building or structure.
- *Loitering*—Who lodges in any building, structure, vehicle, or place, whether public or private, without the permission of the owner or person entitled to the possession or control thereof.

Lewd and Lascivious Conduct

The terms *lewd* and *lascivious* as used in PC 647(d), prohibiting loitering for the purpose of engaging in or soliciting any lewd or lascivious or unlawful act, are synonymous and refer to sexually motivated conduct, and the term *unlawful act* must necessarily be construed as referring to sexually motivated conduct that could be described as lewd or lascivious; thus, subdivision (d) is violated by a person who loiters in or about a public restroom with the specific intent of violating PC 647(a), which prohibits engaging in or soliciting anyone to engage in lewd or dissolute conduct in any public place (*People v. Soto*, 171 Cal. App. 3d 1158).

In *People v. Fitzgerald* (106 Cal. App. 3d Supp. 1), the definition of lewd or dissolute as the solicitation or commission of conduct in a public place or one open to the public or exposed to the public involving touching of the genitals, buttocks, or female breast, for purposes of sexual arousal, gratification, annoyance, or offense, by a person who knows or should know of the presence of persons who may be offended by the conduct did not apply to subdivision (b) of the section proscribing solicitation or engaging in act of prostitution, which included any lewd act between persons for money or other consideration.

Prostitution

Prostitution is the common lewdness of a woman for gain, the act or practice of engaging in sexual intercourse for money, or any lewd act between persons for money or other consideration (*People v. Fixler*, 56 Cal. App. 3d 321). The completed crime of engaging in an act of prostitution in violation of PC 647 is a general intent crime with both participants being principals in crime and also accomplices of each other (*People v. Norris*, 88 Cal. App. 3d Supp. 32). Sexual intercourse for hire by models whose activity is photographed for pornographic publications is prostitution (*People ex rel. Van De Kamp v. American Art Enterprises, Inc.*, 75 Cal. App. 3d 523). If one person pays a second person to engage in sexual intercourse with a third person, then the second person is engaging in prostitution, and that situation is not changed by the fact that the first person may stand by to observe the act or photograph it, as a criminal act is not made any the less criminal by pictorial recordation of the act (*People v. Fixler*, 56 Cal. App. 3d 321).

Pimping

Pimping is defined in PC 266h, which provides that any person who, knowing another person is a prostitute, lives or derives support or maintenance in whole or in part from the earnings or proceeds of the person's prostitution, or from money loaned or advanced to or charged against that person by any keeper or manager or inmate of a house or other place where prostitution is practiced or allowed, or who solicits or receives compensation for soliciting for the person, is guilty of *pimping*, a felony, and shall be punished by imprisonment in the state prison for three, four, or six years. Under PC 266h(b), if the person engaged in prostitution is a minor over the age of 16 years, the offense is punishable by imprisonment in the state prison for three, four, or six years. If the person engaged in prostitution is under 16 years of age, the offense is punishable by imprisonment in the state prison for three, six, or eight years. In addition, PC 266f provides that every person who sells any person or receives any money or other valuable thing for or on account of his or her placing in custody, for immoral purposes, any person, whether with or without his or her consent, is guilty of a felony. An earlier version of the statute covered only females, but in 1975, the crime was enlarged to include "all persons."

Pandering

The crime of pandering is set forth in PC 266i, which provides that any person who does any of the following is guilty of *pandering*, a felony, and shall be punished by imprisonment in the state prison for three, four, or six years:

(1) Procures another person for the purpose of prostitution.

(2) By promises, threats, violence, or by any device or scheme, causes, induces, persuades, or encourages another person to become a prostitute.

(3) Procures for another person a place as an inmate in a house of prostitution or as an inmate of any place in which prostitution is encouraged or allowed within this state.

(4) By promises, threats, violence, or by any device or scheme, causes, induces, persuades, or encourages an inmate of a house of prostitution, or any other place in which prostitution is encouraged or allowed, to remain therein as an inmate.

(5) By fraud or artifice, or by duress of person or goods, or by abuse of any position of confidence or authority, procures another person for the purpose of prostitution, or to enter any place in which prostitution is encouraged or allowed within this state, or to come into this state or leave this state for the purpose of prostitution.

(6) Receives or gives, or agrees to receive or give, any money or thing of value for procuring, or attempting to procure, another person for the purpose of prostitution, or to come into this state or leave this state for the purpose of prostitution.

Public Place

A public place includes any park, street, or building open to the public, or any public offices. A business open to the public is a *public place* within the meaning of this section (*People v. Blatt*, 23 Cal. App. 3d 148). In one case, the area behind a service counter in a men's clothing store open for business was a "public place" within the meaning of PC 647. The arrest and subsequent search, which revealed contraband, of the person who was found to be sitting behind the service counter and who was intoxicated and unable to care for herself, were proper (*People v. Blatt*, 23 Cal. App. 3d 148). The court held in *People v. Olson* (18 Cal. App. 3d 592) that the area in front of a house, whether it is a driveway, lawn, or front porch is a "public place" within PC 647, providing that anyone who is found in any public place under the influence of intoxicating liquor or any drug in such a condition that he or she is unable to exercise care for his or her own safety or the safety of others is guilty of a misdemeanor. In one case, the emergency room of the hospital where the defendant was taken after being found lying unconscious on roadway was a "public place" within the meaning of PC 647 making it a misdemeanor to be found in any public place under the influence of intoxicating liquor or drug (*People v. Kemick*, 17 Cal. App. 3d 419).

Solicit

Solicit means to strongly urge, to entice or lure, especially into evil, attempt to seduce, or to accost for an immoral purpose (PC 648). The prohibiting of solicitation of anyone to engage in lewd or dissolute conduct in any public place refers to public solicitations of lewd or dissolute conduct regardless of where the solicited acts are to be performed (*Silva v. Municipal Court*, 40 Cal. App. 3d 733). The mere presence at a particular place, without more, does not amount to solicitation; nor, without more, is waving to a passing vehicle, nodding to a passing stranger, or standing on a street corner in a miniskirt (*In re White*, 97 Cal. App. 3d 141). In a prosecution for soliciting an act of prostitution, the uncorroborated testimony of a police officer that he was solicited by the defendant was sufficient, there being no statutory requirement that such testimony be corroborated (*People v. Norris*, 88 Cal. App. 3d Supp. 32).

Public Intoxication

The offense of public intoxication is complete if the arrestee is intoxicated in a public place and either is unable to exercise care for his or her own safety or for safety of others, or the person interferes with or obstructs or prevents free use of any street, sidewalk, or public way (*People v. Lively*, 10 Cal. App. 4th 1364). In one case, however, a juvenile who was under the influence of a drug in the bedroom of his home in such a condition that he was unable to exercise care for his own safety or that of others, and who came to be in a public place only because his mother had called the police and he was taken there by the police while handcuffed and while apparently resisting, at least to the extent of cursing the officers, did not violate the disorderly conduct statute (*In re David W.*, 116 Cal. App. 3d 689).

Begging

Begging and soliciting for alms does not necessarily involve communication of information or opinion; therefore, approaching individuals for that purpose is not protected by the First Amendment (*People v. Zimmerman*, 19 Cal. Rptr. 2d 486).

13-6 Disturbing a Public Meeting

Penal Code 403—Disturbing an Assembly

Every person who, without authority of law, willfully disturbs or breaks up any assembly or meeting that is not unlawful in its character, other than an assembly or meeting referred to in Section 302 of the Penal Code or Section 18340 of the Elections Code, is guilty of a misdemeanor.

13-7 Trespassing

Penal Code 602—Trespasses Constituting Misdemeanors; Enumeration

Except as provided in Section 602.8, every person who willfully commits a trespass by any of the following acts is guilty of a misdemeanor:

(a) [Standing timber.] Cutting down, destroying, or injuring any kind of wood or timber standing or growing upon the lands of another.
(b) [Carrying away timber.] Carrying away any kind of wood or timber lying on those lands.
(c) [Injury to or severance from freehold.] Maliciously injuring or severing from the freehold of another anything attached to it, or its produce.
(d) [Soil removal.] Digging, taking, or carrying away from any lot situated within the limits of any incorporated city, without the license of the owner or legal occupant, any earth, soil, or stone.
(e) [Soil removal from public property.] Digging, taking, or carrying away from land in any city or town laid down on the map or plan of the city, or otherwise recognized or established as a street, alley, avenue, or park, without the license of the proper authorities, any earth, soil, or stone.
(f) [Highway signs, etc.] Maliciously tearing down, damaging, mutilating, or destroying any sign, signboard, or notice placed upon, or affixed to, any property belonging to the state, or to any city, county, city and county, town or village, or upon any property of any person, by the state or by an automobile association, which sign, signboard, or notice is intended to indicate or designate a road, or a highway, or is intended to direct travelers from one point to another, or relates to fires, fire control, or any other matter involving the protection of the property, or putting up, affixing, fastening, printing, or painting upon any property belonging to the state, or to any city, county,

town, or village, or dedicated to the public, or upon any property of any person, without license from the owner, any notice, advertisement, or designation of, or any name for any commodity, whether for sale or otherwise, or any picture, sign, or device intended to call attention to it.

(g) [Oyster lands.] Entering upon any lands owned by any other person whereon oysters or other shellfish are planted or growing; or injuring, gathering, or carrying away any oysters or other shellfish planted, growing, or on any such lands, whether covered by water or not, without the license of the owner or legal occupant; or destroying or removing, or causing to be removed or destroyed, any stakes, marks, fences, or signs intended to designate the boundaries and limits of any such lands.

(h) [Fences, gates, and signs.] Willfully opening, tearing down, or otherwise destroying any fence on the enclosed land of another, or opening any gate, bar, or fence of another and willfully leaving it open without the written permission of the owner, or maliciously tearing down, mutilating, or destroying any sign, signboard, or other notice forbidding shooting on private property.

(i) [Fires.] Building fires upon any lands owned by another where signs forbidding trespass are displayed at intervals not greater than one mile along the exterior boundaries and at all roads and trails entering the lands, without first having obtained written permission from the owner of the lands or the owner's agent, or the person in lawful possession.

(j) [Purpose to injure.] Entering any lands, whether unenclosed or enclosed by fence, for the purpose of injuring any property or property rights or with the intention of interfering with, obstructing, or injuring any lawful business or occupation carried on by the owner of the land, the owner's agent or by the person in lawful possession.

(k) [Posted lands.] Entering any lands under cultivation or enclosed by fence, belonging to, or occupied by, another, or entering upon uncultivated or unenclosed lands where signs forbidding trespass are displayed at intervals not less than three to the mile along all exterior boundaries and at all roads and trails entering the lands without the written permission of the owner of the land, the owner's agent or of the person in lawful possession, and

   (1) Refusing or failing to leave the lands immediately upon being requested by the owner of the land, the owner's agent, or by the person in lawful possession to leave the lands, or

   (2) Tearing down, mutilating, or destroying any sign, signboard, or notice forbidding trespass or hunting on the lands, or

   (3) Removing, injuring, unlocking, or tampering with any lock on any gate on or leading into the lands, or

   (4) Discharging any firearm

(l) [Occupation.] Entering and occupying real property or structures of any kind without the consent of the owner, the owner's agent, or the person in lawful possession.

(m)[Driving on private land.] Driving any vehicle, as defined in Section 670 of the Vehicle Code, upon real property belonging to, or lawfully occupied by, another and known not to be open to the general public, without the consent of the owner, the owner's agent, or the person in lawful possession. This subdivision shall not apply to any person described in Section 22350 of the Business and Professions Code who is making a lawful service of process.

(n) [Refusal to leave private property.] Refusing or failing to leave land, real property, or structures belonging to or lawfully occupied by another and not open to the general public, upon being requested to leave. . . .

(o) [Closed lands.] Entering upon any lands declared closed to entry as provided in Section 4256 of the Public Resources Code, if the closed areas shall have been posted with notices declaring the closure, at intervals not greater than one mile along the exterior boundaries or along roads and trails passing through the lands.

(p) [Refusal to leave public building.] Refusing or failing to leave a public building of a public agency during those hours of the day or night when the building is regularly closed to the public upon being requested to do so by a regularly employed guard, watchman, or custodian of the public agency owning or maintaining the building or property, if the surrounding circumstances are such as to indicate to a reasonable person that the person has no apparent lawful business to pursue.

(q) [Skiing in closed area.] Knowingly skiing in an area or on a ski trail which is closed to the public and which has signs posted indicating the closure.

(r) [Hotels or motels.] Refusing or failing to leave a hotel or motel, where he or she has obtained accommodations and has refused to pay for those accommodations, upon request of the proprietor or manager. . . .

(s) [Entry on private property by person convicted of violent felony.] Entering upon private property, including contiguous land, real property, or structures thereon belonging to the same owner, whether or not generally open to the public, after having been informed by a peace officer at the request of the owner, the owner's agent, or the person in lawful possession, and upon being informed by the peace officer that he or she is acting at the request of the owner, the owner's agent, or the person in lawful possession, that the property is not open to the particular person; or refusing or failing to leave the property upon being asked to leave the property in the manner provided in this subdivision.

(t) [Airport operations area.] Knowingly entering, by an unauthorized person, upon any airport operations area if the area has been posted with notices restricting access to authorized personnel only and the postings occur not greater than every 150 feet along the exterior boundary.

(u) [Battered women's shelters.] Refusing or failing to leave a battered women's shelter at any time after being requested to leave by a managing authority of the shelter.

13-7a Discussion

Penal Code 602 provides that a person is guilty of trespassing (misdemeanor) who enters and occupies real property or structures without consent from the owner or person in lawful possession. Transient noncontinuous possession is not considered as occupying (*People v. Catalano*, 29 Cal. 3d 1). Although the mere presence on private property may not be a trespass, refusing to leave private property not open to the public after being asked to leave by the owner or by a peace officer at the owner's request is a trespass (*People v. Medrano*, 78 Cal. App. 3d 198).

There is no trespass if the private property is open to the general public, unless the property is being used in a manner not related to the purpose for which it is open to the public (*People v. Lundgren*, 189 Cal. App. 3d 381).

Penal Code 647c—Obstructing Movement on Street or Public Place

Every person who willfully and maliciously obstructs the free movement of any person on any street, sidewalk, or other public place or on or in any place open to the public is guilty of a misdemeanor. Nothing in this section affects the power of a county or a city to regulate conduct upon a street, sidewalk, or other public place or on or in a place open to the public.

13-8 Obstruction of Sidewalk or Street

Penal Code 407 provides, in part, that whenever two or more persons assemble together to do an unlawful act, or do a lawful act in a violent, boisterous, or tumultuous manner, such assembly is an unlawful assembly. This is a specific intent crime, since those assembled must intend to commit an unlawful act, or a lawful act in a violent, boisterous, or tumultuous manner. Violation of the penal section is a misdemeanor.

13-9 Unlawful Assembly

Penal Code 416—Duty of Crowds to Disperse When Ordered; Restitution for Property Damage

(a) If two or more persons assemble for the purpose of disturbing the public peace, or committing any unlawful act, and do not disperse on being desired or commanded so to do by a public officer, the persons so offending are severally guilty of a misdemeanor.
(b) Any person who, as a result of violating subdivision (a), personally causes damage to real or personal property, which is either publicly or privately owned, shall make restitution for the damage he or she caused, including, but not limited to, the costs of cleaning up, repairing, replacing, or restoring the property. Any restitution required to be paid pursuant to this subdivision shall be paid directly to the victim. If the court determines that the defendant is unable to pay restitution, the court shall order the defendant to perform community service, as the court deems appropriate, in lieu of the direct restitution payment.
(c) This section shall not preclude the court from imposing restitution in the form of a penalty assessment pursuant to Section 1464 if the court, in its discretion, deems that additional restitution appropriate.
(d) The burden of proof on the issue of whether any defendant or defendants personally caused any property damage shall rest with the prosecuting agency or claimant. In no event shall the burden of proof on this issue shift to the defendant or any of several defendants to prove that he or she was not responsible for the property damage.

13-10 Disobedience of a Dispersal Order

Penal Code 404 and 406 deal with riots. Section 406 provides that whenever two or more persons, assembled and acting together, make an attempt to advance toward the commission of an act that would be a riot, if actually committed, that the assembly is a rout.

Section 404 provides that any use of force or violence, disturbing the public peace, or any threat to use such force or violence, if accompanied by immediate power of execution, by two or more persons acting together, and without authority of law, is a riot. The group must be acting together with a common intent, and

13-11 Incitement to, or Participation in, a Rout or Riot

there must be at least threats to use force or violence that is apparently available. In addition, the threats or use of force must actually disturb the peace. Public peace is considered disturbed when the actions of the group excite terror, alarm, and consternation in the neighborhood. PC 404.6 prohibits using others to riot or to burn or otherwise to destroy property.

13-12 Public Nuisance

PC 370 defines a *public nuisance* as anything that is injurious to health, or is indecent, or offensive to the senses, or an obstruction to the free use of property that interferes with the comfortable enjoyment of life or property by an entire community or neighborhood, or by any considerable number of persons, or unlawfully obstructs the free passage or customary use of any navigable lake, or river, bay, stream, canal, or basin, or any public park, square, street, or highway.

PC 372 states (in part) that every person who maintains or commits any public nuisance, or who willfully fails to perform any legal duty relating to the removal of a public nuisance, is guilty of a misdemeanor. A nuisance can be an act, condition, thing, or person causing trouble, annoyance, or inconvenience. Before prosecution may be had under PC 372, the accused must be given notice to abate the public nuisance and an opportunity to do so.

13-13 Gaming Violations

Penal Code 330—Gaming Defined; Punishment

Every person who deals, plays, or carries on, opens, or causes to be opened, or who conducts, either as owner or employee, whether for hire or not, any game of faro, monte, roulette, lansquenet, rouge et noire, rondo, tan, fan-tan, seven-and-a-half, twenty-one, hokey-pokey, or any banking or percentage game played with cards, dice, or any device, for money, checks, credit, or other representative of value, and every person who plays or bets at or against any of those prohibited games, is guilty of a misdemeanor, and shall be punishable by a fine not less than one hundred dollars ($100) nor more than one thousand dollars ($1,000), or by imprisonment in the county jail not exceeding six months, or by both the fine and imprisonment.

Penal Code 321—Sale of Tickets, Chances, Shares, or Interest

PUNISHMENT FOR SELLING LOTTERY TICKETS. Every person who sells, gives, or in any manner whatever, furnishes or transfers to or for any other person any ticket, chance, share, or interest, or any paper, certificate, or instrument purporting or understood to be or to represent any ticket, chance, share, or interest in, or depending upon the event of any lottery, is guilty of a misdemeanor.

13-13a Discussion

Every state in the United States, including Nevada, extensively regulates gambling. In California, not all gambling is illegal. The most common illegal forms of gambling include the following:

- Lottery (except the official state lottery). *Lottery* is defined as any scheme for the disposal or distribution of property by chance, among persons who have paid or promised to give any valuable consideration for the chance of obtaining such property or a portion of it, or any interest in such property (PC 326.5). Note: A "football pool" is a lottery, and therefore is illegal. The key phrase is *by chance*. If the winning depends on skill, not chance, it may not be gambling.

- Chain letters. Chain letters and pyramid schemes are a violation of PC 327.
- Bookmaking. Bookmaking is a violation of PC 337(a).
- Operating an unlicensed gaming house is a violation of PC 330.
- Slot machines are a violation of PC 330.1.

PC 337(s) provides that in certain counties with populations in excess of 4 million people, the voters can approve draw poker establishments. The question shall appear on the ballot in substantially the following form:

"Shall draw poker, including lowball poker, be prohibited in ____ County? Yes ____ No ____"

If a majority of electors voting vote affirmatively, draw poker shall be prohibited in the unincorporated territory in the county. The statute is based on the legislative determination that in counties with a large, concentrated population, problems incident to the playing of draw poker are, in part, qualitatively, as well as quantitatively, different from the problems in smaller counties.

Sale, Transportation, and So On, of Gambling Devices

PC 330.8 provides that the sale, transportation, storage, and manufacture of gambling devices, including the acquisition and assembly of essential parts for the devices, is permitted, provided those devices are sold, transported, stored, and manufactured only for subsequent transportation in interstate or foreign commerce when that transportation is not prohibited by any applicable federal law. Those activities may be conducted only by persons who have registered with the United States government pursuant to Chapter 24 (commencing with Section 1171) of Title 15 of the United States Code, as amended. Those gambling devices shall not be displayed to the general public or sold for use in California regardless of where purchased, nor held nor manufactured in violation of any applicable federal law. A violation of this section is a misdemeanor.

Card-Monte, Trick, and Sure-Thing Games

PC 332 provides that every person who by the game of "three card monte," or any other game, device, sleight of hand, pretensions to fortune telling, trick, or other means whatever, by use of cards or other implements or instruments, or while betting on sides or hands of any play or game, fraudulently obtains from another person money or property of any description shall be punished as in case of larceny of property of like value. *Fraudulently obtains* includes, but is not limited to, cheating, including, for example, gaining an unfair advantage for any player in any game through a technique or device not sanctioned by the rules of the game. To establish the value of property under this section, poker chips, tokens, or markers have the monetary value assigned to them by the players in any game.

Antique Slot Machines

PC 330.7 makes it a defense to any prosecution for the possession of slot machines, if the defendant shows that the slot machine is an antique slot machine and was not operated for gambling purposes while in the defendant's possession. For the purposes of this section, the term *antique slot machine* means a slot machine that is over 25 years of age. No slot machine seized from any defendant shall be destroyed or otherwise altered until after a final court determination that such a defense is not applicable. If the defense is applicable, the machine shall be returned pursuant to provisions of law providing for the return of property. It is the stated purpose of PC 330.7 to protect the collection and restoration of antique slot machines not presently utilized for gambling purposes because of their aesthetic interest and importance in California history.

Gaming Houses and Public Nuisances

PC 331 discusses the liability of owners and lessors of gaming houses. That section provides that every person who knowingly permits any of the prohibited games to be played, conducted, or dealt in any house owned or rented by such person, in whole or in part, is guilty of a crime.

Under PC 11225, every building or place used for the purpose of illegal gambling as defined by state law or local ordinance, lewdness, assignation, or prostitution, and every building or place in or upon which acts of illegal gambling as defined by state law or local ordinance, lewdness, assignation, or prostitution, are held or occur, is a nuisance that shall be enjoined, abated, and prevented, and for which damages may be recovered, whether it is a public or private nuisance. Nothing in this subdivision shall be construed to apply the definition of a nuisance to a private residence where illegal gambling is conducted on an intermittent basis and without the purpose of producing profit for the owner or occupier of the premises.

Every building or place used as a bathhouse that as a primary activity encourages or permits conduct that according to the guidelines of the federal Centers for Disease Control can transmit AIDS, including, but not limited to, anal intercourse, oral copulation, or vaginal intercourse, is a nuisance that shall be enjoined, abated, and prevented, and for which damages may be recovered, whether it is a public or private nuisance.

For purposes of this subdivision, a *bathhouse* means a business that, as its primary purpose, provides facilities for a spa, whirlpool, communal bath, sauna, steam bath, mineral bath, mud bath, or facilities for swimming.

Pursuant to PC 11226, whenever there is reason to believe that a nuisance as defined in this article is kept, maintained, or is in existence in any county, the district attorney, in the name of the people of the state of California, shall, or the city attorney of an incorporated city, or any citizen of the state resident within the county, in his or her own name, may maintain an action in equity to abate and prevent the nuisance and to perpetually enjoin the person conducting or maintaining it, and the owner, lessee, or agent of the building, or place, in or upon which the nuisance exists, from directly or indirectly maintaining or permitting it.

Prosecution of Gaming Violations

PC 335 declares that every district attorney, sheriff, or police officer must inform against and diligently prosecute persons whom they have reasonable cause to believe are offenders of gaming violations; every officer refusing or neglecting so to do is guilty of a misdemeanor. Under PC 333, any person duly summoned as a witness for the prosecution, on any proceedings involving gaming violations statutes, who neglects or refuses to attend, as required, is guilty of a misdemeanor.

Destruction of Gambling Devices

According to PC 335(a), in addition to any other remedy provided by law, any peace officer may seize any machine or other device the possession or control of which is penalized by the laws of California that prohibit lotteries or gambling. A notice of intention to destroy the machine or device as provided in this section must be posted in a conspicuous place upon the premises where the machine or device was seized. The machine or device shall be held by the officer for 30 days after the posting, and if no action is commenced to recover the machine or device within that time, the machine or device shall be destroyed. If the machine or device is held by the court, in any such action, to be in violation of such laws, or any of them, it shall be destroyed by an officer immediately after the decision of the court has become final.

The superior court has jurisdiction of any such actions or proceedings commenced to recover the possession of a machine or device or any money seized in connection with it.

Any and all money seized in or in connection with such a machine or device shall, immediately after such machine or device has been destroyed, be paid into the treasury of the city or county where the machine or device was seized, to be deposited in the general fund.

Trick Devices

PC 334 prohibits the use, manufacture, or sale of a hidden device to diminish the chances of a player, or any other fraudulent means of winning at a concession; that is, owning or operating a game of razzle-dazzle. Every person who owns or operates any concession, and who fraudulently obtains money from another by means of any hidden mechanical device or obstruction with the intent to diminish the chance of any patron to win a prize, or by any other fraudulent means, shall be punished as in the case of theft of property of like value. Any person who manufactures or sells any mechanical device or obstruction for a concession that he or she knows or reasonably should know will be fraudulently used to diminish the chance of any patron to win a prize is guilty of a misdemeanor. Any person who owns or operates any game at a fair or carnival of a type known as razzle-dazzle is also guilty of a misdemeanor.

Razzle-dazzle means a series of games of skill or chance in which the player pays money or other valuable consideration in return for each opportunity to make successive attempts to obtain points by the use of dice, darts, marbles, or other implements, and where such points are accumulated in successive games by the player toward a total number of points, determined by the operator, which is required for the player to win a prize or other valuable consideration. *Concession* means any game or concession open to the public and operated for profit in which the patron pays a fee for participating and may receive a prize upon a later happening. Note: This section does not prohibit or preempt more restrictive regulation of any concession at a fair or carnival by any local governmental entity.

Transmitting Gaming Information

PC 337(i) provides that every person who knowingly transmits information about the progress or results of a horse race, or information about wagers, betting odds, changes in betting odds, post or off times, jockey or player changes in any contest or trial, or purported contest or trial, involving humans, beasts, or mechanical apparatus by any means whatsoever including, but not limited to telephone, telegraph, radio, and semaphore when such information is transmitted to or by a person or persons engaged in illegal gambling operations, is punishable by imprisonment in the county jail for a period of not more than one year or in the state prison.

This section does not prohibit a newspaper from printing such results or information as news, or any television or radio station from telecasting or broadcasting such results or information as news. This section also does not jeopardize any common carrier or its agents performing operations within the scope of a public franchise or any gambling operation authorized by law.

Touting

PC 337.1 makes touting a crime. That section provides that any person who knowingly and designedly by false representation attempts to or does persuade, procure, or cause another person to wager on a horse in a race to be run in this state or elsewhere, and upon which money is wagered in this state, and who asks or demands compensation as a reward for information or purported information given in such case, is a tout and is guilty of touting. Any person who is a tout, or who attempts or conspires to commit touting, is guilty of a misdemeanor. For a second offense in California, he or she shall be imprisoned.

Under PC 337.3, any person who in the commission of touting falsely uses the name of any official of the California Horse Racing Board, its inspectors or attaches, or of any official of any race track association, or the names of any owner, trainer, jockey, or other person licensed by the California Horse Racing Board as the source of any information or purported information is guilty of a felony and is punishable by a fine of not more than five thousand dollars ($5,000) or by imprisonment in the state prison, or by both such fine and imprisonment. Under PC 337.4, any person who in the commission of touting obtains more than four hundred dollars ($400) may, in addition to being prosecuted for touting, be prosecuted for the violation of grand theft.

Gambling Ships

PC 11300 states that it is unlawful for any person within California to solicit, entice, induce, persuade, or procure, or to aid in soliciting, enticing, inducing, persuading, or procuring, any person to visit any gambling ship, whether such gambling ship is within or without the jurisdiction of the State. As used in this article, *craft* includes every boat, ship, vessel, craft, barge, hulk, float, or other thing capable of floating.

According to PC 11302, it also is unlawful for any person within California to solicit, entice, induce, persuade, or procure, or to aid in soliciting, enticing, inducing, persuading, or procuring, any person to visit any craft, whether such craft is within or without the jurisdiction of the State, from which craft any person is transported, conveyed, or carried to any gambling ship, whether such gambling ship is within or without the jurisdiction of the State.

In addition, it is also unlawful for any person, firm, association, or corporation to transport, convey, or carry, or to aid in transporting, conveying, or carrying, any person to any gambling ship, whether such gambling ship is within or without the jurisdiction of the State (see PC 11303). Under PC 11305, any boat, ship, vessel, watercraft, barge, airplane, seaplane, or aircraft, hereinafter called "means of conveyance," used to transport, convey, or carry persons in violation of this article is a public nuisance that shall be enjoined, abated, and prevented.

13-14 Unauthorized Entry of Disaster Area

Under PC 409.5, whenever a calamity such as a flood, storm, fire, earthquake, explosion, accident, or other disaster creates a menace to the public health or safety, officers of the Department of the California Highway Patrol, police departments, marshal's office or sheriff's office, any officer or employee of the Department of Forestry and Fire Protection, any officer or employee of the Department of Parks and Recreation designated a peace officer, any officer or employee of the Department of Fish and Game designated a peace officer, and any publicly employed full-time lifeguard or publicly employed full-time marine safety officer while acting in a supervisory position in the performance of his or her official duties may close an area where the menace exists for its duration by means of ropes, markers, or guards to any and all persons not authorized by the lifeguard or officer to enter or remain within the enclosed area. If the calamity creates an immediate menace to the public health, the local health officer may close the area where the menace exists.

The officers may close the immediate area surrounding any emergency field command post or any other command post activated to abate any calamity enumerated in PC 409.5 or any riot or other civil disturbance to any and all unauthorized persons pursuant to the conditions set forth in this section whether or not the field command post or other command post is located near to the actual calamity or riot or other civil disturbance. Any unauthorized person who willfully and knowingly enters an area closed and who willfully remains within the area after receiving notice to evacuate or leave shall be guilty of a misdemeanor. A duly authorized representative of any news service, newspaper, or radio or television station or network may enter the areas closed.

13-15 Bicycles

Vehicle Code 21200 provides that every person riding a bicycle upon a highway has all the rights and is subject to all the provisions applicable to the driver of a vehicle by this division, and including, but not limited to, provisions concerning driving under the influence of alcoholic beverages or drugs.

13-16 Criminal Profiteering

Penal Code 186—Title of Act

This act may be cited as the California Control of Profits of Organized Crime Act.

Penal Code 186.1—Legislative Findings and Declaration

The Legislature hereby finds and declares that an effective means of punishing and deterring criminal activities of organized crime is through the forfeiture of profits acquired and accumulated as a result of such criminal activities. It is the intent of the Legislature that the "California Control of Profits of Organized Crime Act" be used by prosecutors to punish and deter only such activities.

Penal Code 186.2—Criminal Profiteering—Definitions

For purposes of the application of this chapter, the following definitions shall govern:

(a) *Criminal profiteering activity* means any act committed or attempted or any threat made for financial gain or advantage, which act or threat may be charged as a crime under any of the following sections:

  (1) Arson, as defined in Section 451
  (2) Bribery, as defined in Sections 67, 67.5, and 68
  (3) Child pornography or exploitation, as defined in subdivision(b) of Section 311.2, or Section 311.3 or 311.4, which may be prosecuted as a felony
  (4) Felonious assault, as defined in Section 245
  (5) Embezzlement, as defined in Sections 424 and 503
  (6) Extortion, as defined in Section 518
  (7) Forgery, as defined in Section 470
  (8) Gambling, as defined in Sections 337a to 337f, inclusive, and Section 337i, except the activities of a person who participates solely as an individual bettor

(9) Kidnapping, as defined in Section 207

(10) Mayhem, as defined in Section 203

(11) Murder, as defined in Section 187

(12) Pimping and pandering, as defined in Section 266

(13) Receiving stolen property, as defined in Section 496

(14) Robbery, as defined in Section 211

(15) Solicitation of crimes, as defined in Section 653f

(16) Grand theft, as defined in Section 487

(17) Trafficking in controlled substances, as defined in Sections 11351, 11352, and 11353 of the Health and Safety Code

(18) Violation of the laws governing corporate securities, as defined in Section 25541 of the Corporations Code

(19) Any of the offenses contained in Chapter 7.5 (commencing with Section 311) of Title 9, relating to obscene matter, or in Chapter 7.6 (commencing with Section 313) of Title 9, relating to harmful matter which may be prosecuted as a felony [obscenity statutes]

(20) Presentation of a false or fraudulent claim, as defined in Section 550

(21) Money laundering, as defined in Section 186.10

(22) False or fraudulent activities, schemes, or artifices, as described in Section 14107 of the Welfare and Institutions Code

(23) Offenses relating to the counterfeit of a registered mark, as specified in Section 350

(24) Offenses relating to the unauthorized access to computers, computer systems, and computer data, as specified in Section 502

(25) Conspiracy to commit any of the crimes listed above, as defined in Section 182

(26) Engaging in a pattern of criminal gang activity, as defined in subdivision (e) of Section 186.22

(b) *Pattern of criminal profiteering activity* means engaging in at least two incidents of criminal profiteering, as defined by this act, which meet the following requirements:

(1) Have the same or a similar purpose, result, principals, victims, or methods of commission, or are otherwise interrelated by distinguishing characteristics

(2) Are not isolated events

(3) Were committed as a criminal activity of organized crime.

Acts which would constitute a *pattern of criminal profiteering activity* may not be used by a prosecuting agency to seek the remedies provided by this chapter unless the underlying offense occurred after the effective date of this chapter and the prior act occurred within 10 years, excluding any period of imprisonment, of the commission of the underlying offense. A prior act may not be used by a prosecuting agency to seek remedies provided by this chapter if a prosecution for that act resulted in an acquittal.

(c) *Prosecuting agency* means the Attorney General or the district attorney of any county.

(d) *Organized crime* means crime which is of a conspiratorial nature and that is either of an organized nature and which seeks to supply illegal goods and services such as narcotics, prostitution, loan sharking, gambling, and pornography, or that, through planning and coordination of individual efforts, seeks to conduct the illegal activities of arson for profit, hijacking, insurance fraud, smuggling, operating vehicle theft rings, or systematically encumbering the assets of a business for the purpose of defrauding creditors. "Organized crime" also means crime committed by a criminal street gang, as defined in subdivision (f) of Section 186.22. *Organized crime* also means false or fraudulent activities, schemes, or artifices, as described in Section 14107 of the Welfare and Institutions Code.

(e) *Underlying offense* means an offense enumerated in subdivision (a) for which the defendant is being prosecuted.

Penal Code 186.9—Definitions [Money Laundering]

As used in this chapter:

(a) *Conducts* includes, but is not limited to, initiating, concluding, or participating in conducting, initiating, or concluding a transaction.

(b) *Financial institution* means, when located or doing business in this state, any national bank or banking association, state bank or banking association, commercial bank or trust company organized under the laws of the United States or any state, any private bank, industrial savings bank, savings bank or thrift institution, savings and loan association, or building and loan association organized under the laws of the United States or any state, any insured institution as defined in Section 401 of the National Housing Act (12 U.S.C. Sec. 1724(a)), any credit union organized under the laws of the United States or any state, any national banking association or corporation acting under Chapter 6 (commencing with Section 601) of Title 12 of the United States Code, any agency, agent or branch of a foreign bank, any currency dealer or exchange, any person or business engaged primarily in the cashing of checks, any person or business who regularly engages in the issuing, selling, or redeeming of traveler's checks, money orders, or similar instruments, any broker or dealer in securities registered or required to be registered with the Securities and Exchange Commission under the Securities Exchange Act of 1934 or with the Commissioner of Corporations under Part 3 (commencing with Section 25200) of Division 1 of Title 4 of the Corporations Code, any licensed transmitter of funds or other person or business regularly engaged in transmitting funds to a foreign nation for others, any investment banker or investment company, any insurer, any dealer in gold, silver, or platinum bullion or coins, diamonds, emeralds, rubies, or sapphires, any pawnbroker, any telegraph company, any personal property broker, any person or business acting as a real property securities dealer within the meaning of Section 10237 of the Business and Professions Code, whether licensed to do so or not, any person or business acting within the meaning and scope of subdivisions (d) and (e) of Section 10131 and Section 10131.1 of the Business and Professions Code, whether licensed to do so or not, any person or business regularly engaged in gaming within the meaning and scope of Section 330, any person or business regularly engaged in pool selling or bookmaking within the meaning and scope of Section 337a, any person or business regularly engaged in horse racing whether licensed to do so or not under the Business and Professions Code, any person or business engaged in the operation of a gambling ship within the meaning and scope of Section 11317, any person or business engaged in legal gambling or gaming within the meaning and scope of subdivisions (a) and (b) of Section 19802 of the Business and Professions Code, whether registered to do so or not, and any person or business defined as a "bank," "financial agency," or "financial institution" by Section 5312 of Title 31 of the United States Code or Section 103.11 of Title 31 of the Code of Federal Regulations and any successor provisions thereto.

(c) *Transaction* includes the deposit, withdrawal, transfer, bailment, loan, pledge, payment, or exchange of currency, or a monetary instrument, as defined by subdivision (d), or the electronic, wire, magnetic, or manual transfer of funds between accounts by, through, or to, a financial institution as defined by subdivision (b).

(d) *Monetary instrument* means United States currency and coin; the currency, coin, and foreign bank drafts of any foreign country; payment warrants issued by the United States, this state, or any city, county, or city and county of this state or any other political subdivision thereof; any bank check, cashier's check, traveler's check, personal check, money order, stock, investment security, or negotiable instrument in bearer form or otherwise in such form that title thereto passes upon delivery; gold, silver, or platinum bullion or coins; and diamonds, emeralds, rubies, or sapphires. Except for foreign bank drafts and federal, state, county, or city warrants, "monetary instrument" does not include bank checks, cashier's checks, traveler's checks, personal checks, or money orders made payable to the order of a named party which have not been endorsed or which bear restrictive endorsements, and also does not include personal checks which have been endorsed by the named party and deposited by the named party into the named party's account with a financial institution.

(e) *Criminal activity* means a criminal offense punishable under the laws of this state by death or imprisonment in the state prison or from a criminal offense committed in another jurisdiction punishable under the laws of that jurisdiction by death or imprisonment for a term exceeding one year.

(f) *Foreign bank draft* means a bank draft or check issued or made out by a foreign bank, savings and loan, casa de cambio, credit union, currency dealer or exchanger, check cashing business, money transmitter, insurance company, investment or private bank, or any other foreign financial institution that provides similar financial services, on an account in the name of the foreign bank or foreign financial institution held at a bank or other financial institution located in the United States or a territory of the United States.

Penal Code 186.10—Multiple Transactions, Value over $5,000; Intent to Promote Criminal Activity

(a) Any person who conducts or attempts to conduct a transaction or more than one transaction within a 24-hour period involving a monetary instrument or instruments of a total value exceeding five thousand dollars ($5,000) through one or more financial institutions (1) with the intent to promote, manage, establish, carry on, or facilitate the promotion, management, establishment, or carrying on of any criminal activity, or (2) knowing that the monetary instrument represents the proceeds of, or is derived directly or indirectly from the proceeds of, criminal activity, is guilty of the crime of money laundering. In consideration of the constitutional right to counsel afforded by the Sixth Amendment to the United States Constitution and Section 15 of Article I of the California Constitution, when a case involves an attorney who accepts a fee for representing a client in a criminal investigation or proceeding, the prosecution shall additionally be required to prove that the monetary instrument was accepted by the attorney with the intent to disguise or aid in disguising the source of the funds or the nature of the criminal activity.

A violation of this section shall be punished by imprisonment in a county jail for not more than one year or in the state prison, by a fine of not more than two hundred fifty thousand dollars ($250,000) or twice the value of the property transacted, whichever is greater, or by both that imprisonment and fine. However, for a second or subsequent conviction for a violation of this section, the maximum fine that may be imposed is five hundred thousand dollars ($500,000) or five times the value of the property transacted, whichever is greater.

(b) Notwithstanding any other law, for purposes of this section, each individual transaction conducted in excess of five thousand dollars ($5,000), or each series of transactions conducted within a 24-hour period that total in excess of five thousand dollars ($5,000), shall constitute a separate, punishable offense.

(c)

    (1) Any person who is punished under subdivision (a) by imprisonment in the state prison shall also be subject to an additional term of imprisonment in the state prison as follows:

        (A) If the value of the transaction or transactions exceeds fifty thousand dollars ($50,000) but is less than one hundred fifty thousand dollars ($150,000), the court, in addition to and consecutive to the felony punishment otherwise imposed pursuant to this section, shall impose an additional term of imprisonment of one year.

        (B) If the value of the transaction or transactions exceeds one hundred fifty thousand dollars ($150,000) but is less than one million dollars ($1,000,000), the court, in addition to and consecutive to the felony punishment otherwise imposed pursuant to this section, shall impose an additional term of imprisonment of two years.

        (C) If the value of the transaction or transactions exceeds one million dollars ($1,000,000), but is less than two million five hundred thousand dollars ($2,500,000), the court, in addition to and consecutive to the felony punishment otherwise imposed pursuant to this section, shall impose an additional term of imprisonment of three years.

        (D) If the value of the transaction or transactions exceeds two million five hundred thousand dollars ($2,500,000), the court, in addition to and consecutive to the felony punishment otherwise prescribed by this section, shall impose an additional term of imprisonment of four years.

    (2)

        (A) An additional term of imprisonment as provided for in this subdivision shall not be imposed unless the facts of a transaction or transactions, or attempted transaction or transactions, of a value described in paragraph (1), are charged in the accusatory pleading, and are either admitted to by the defendant or are found to be true by the trier of fact.

        (B) An additional term of imprisonment as provided for in this subdivision may be imposed with respect to an accusatory pleading charging multiple violations of this section, regardless of whether any single violation charged in that pleading involves a transaction or attempted transaction of a value covered by paragraph (1), if the violations charged in that pleading arise from a common scheme or plan and the aggregate value of the alleged transactions or attempted transactions is of a value covered by paragraph (1).

All pleadings under this section shall remain subject to the rules of joinder and severance stated in Section 954.

(d) Penal Code 186.22 provides, in part, that any person who actively participates in any criminal street gang with knowledge that its members engage in or have engaged in a pattern of criminal gang activity, and who willfully promotes, furthers, or assists in any felonious criminal conduct by members of that gang, shall be punished by imprisonment in a county jail or by imprisonment for 16 months, or two or three years. If the crime is committed within 1,000 feet of a school, during hours that the school is open for classes or school-related programs or when minors are using the facility that fact shall be a circumstance in aggravation of the crime.

13-16a Discussion

The criminal profiteering or organized crime statutes provide that when selected other penal statutes are violated for financial gain two or more times by organized crime or any person who is engaged in a pattern of criminal profiteering, the offender(s) are guilty of criminal profiteering in addition to the other crimes involved.

Discussion Questions

Discussion Questions

1. What are some of the problems involved in prosecuting public nuisance crimes?
2. Differentiate between a rout and a riot.
3. What constitutes the offense of trespassing under PC 602?
4. What are the three types of disturbing the peace crimes?
5. What constitutes lewd and lascivious conduct?
6. Define *gaming*.
7. What are the purposes behind the criminal profiteering statutes?

Self-Study Quiz

Self-Study Quiz

True/False

1. Unlawfully obstructing a river is not a public nuisance.
2. A rout is an attempted riot.
3. Unlawful assembly is a specific intent crime.
4. To be guilty of trespass, a person must enter and occupy real property or structures.
5. For purposes of disorderly conduct crimes, *solicit* means to strongly urge; to entice or lure, especially into evil; to attempt to seduce; or to accost for an immoral purpose.
6. The evasion of the payment of any fare on a public transportation is a violation of a state penal statute.
7. Disorderly conduct is a felony offense.
8. Prostitution includes the common lewdness of a woman for gain.
9. The offense of public intoxication is complete if the individual is intoxicated in a public place but is still able to exercise care for his or her safety, the safety of others, and is not interfering with or obstructs the free use of any street, sidewalk, and so on.
10. Disturbing a public meeting is a felony.
11. The crime of unlawful assembly is a specific intent crime.
12. *Touting* is not a crime in California.
13. *Criminal profiteering activity* does not require that the act constituting the crime be committed or attempted for financial gain or advantage.
14. A person is guilty of *disturbing the peace* by unlawfully fighting.
15. It is not illegal to own an antique slot machine.

Crimes against the Justice System and Counterfeiting

The real significance of crime is in its being a breach of faith with the community of mankind.

Joseph Conrad, Lord Jim, 1900

14-1 Bribery

Penal Code 67—Bribing Executive Officer

Every person who gives or offers any bribe to any executive officer in this state, with intent to influence him in respect to any act, decision, vote, opinion, or other proceeding as such officer, is punishable by imprisonment in the state prison for two, three, or four years, and is disqualified from holding any office in this state.

Penal Code 67.5—Bribing Ministerial Officer

(a) Every person who gives or offers as a bribe to any ministerial officer, employee, or appointee of the State of California, county or city therein, or political subdivision thereof, any thing the theft of which would be petty theft is guilty of a misdemeanor.

(b) If the theft of the thing given or offered would be grand theft the offense is a felony.

Penal Code 68—Officer Asking or Receiving Bribes

Every executive or ministerial officer, employee, or appointee of the State of California, county or city therein or political subdivision thereof, who asks, receives, or agrees to receive, any bribe, upon any agreement or understanding that his vote, opinion, or action upon any matter then pending, or which may be brought before him in his official capacity, shall be influenced thereby, is punishable by imprisonment in the state prison for two, three, or four years; and, in addition thereto, forfeits his office, and is forever disqualified from holding any office in this state.

Penal Code 69—Resisting or Deterring Officer

Every person who attempts, by means of any threat or violence, to deter or prevent an executive officer from performing any duty imposed upon such officer by law, or who knowingly resists, by the use of force or violence, such officer, in the performance of his duty, is punishable by a fine not exceeding ten thousand dollars ($10,000), or by imprisonment in the state prison, or in a county jail not exceeding one year, or by both such fine and imprisonment.

Penal Code 70—Official Asking or Accepting Gratuity

(a) Every executive or ministerial officer, employee, or appointee of the State of California, or any county or city therein, or any political subdivision thereof, who knowingly asks, receives, or agrees to receive any emolument, gratuity, or reward, or any promise thereof excepting such as may be authorized by law for doing an official act, is guilty of a misdemeanor.

(b) This section does not prohibit deputy registrars of voters from receiving compensation when authorized by local ordinance from any candidate, political committee, or statewide political organization for securing the registration of voters.

(c) Nothing in this section precludes a peace officer . . . from engaging in, or being employed in, casual or part-time employment as a private security guard or patrolman for a public entity while off duty from his or her principal employment and outside his or her regular employment as a peace officer of a state or local agency, and exercising the powers of a peace officer concurrently with that employment, provided that the peace officer is in a police uniform and is subject to reasonable rules and regulations of the agency for which he or she is a peace officer. . . .

(d) Nothing in this section precludes a peace officer . . . from engaging in, or being employed in, casual or part-time employment as a private security guard or patrolman by a private employer while off duty from his or her principal employment and outside his or her regular employment as a peace officer, and exercising the powers of a peace officer concurrently with that employment, provided that all of the following are true:

(1) The peace officer is in his or her police uniform.

(2) The casual or part-time employment as a private security guard or patrolman is approved by the county board of supervisors with jurisdiction over the principal employer or by the board's designee or by the city council with jurisdiction over the principal employer or by the council's designee.

(3) The wearing of uniforms and equipment is approved by the principal employer.

(4) The peace officer is subject to reasonable rules and regulations of the agency for which he or she is a peace officer. . . .

Notwithstanding the above provisions, a peace officer, while off duty from his or her principal employment and outside his or her regular employment as a peace officer of a state or local agency, shall not exercise the powers of a police officer if employed by a private employer as a security guard during a strike, lockout, picketing, or other physical demonstration of a labor dispute at the site of the strike, lockout, picketing, or other physical demonstration of a labor dispute. The issue of whether or not casual or part-time employment as a private security guard or patrolman pursuant to this subdivision is to be approved shall not be a subject for collective bargaining. Any and all civil and criminal liability arising out of the secondary employment of any peace officer pursuant to this subdivision shall be borne by the officer's principal employer. The principal employer may require the secondary employer to enter into an indemnity agreement as a condition of approving casual or part-time employment pursuant to this subdivision.

Penal Code 70.5—Acceptance of Money or Thing of Value by Commissioner or Deputy Commissioner of Civil Marriages

Every commissioner of civil marriages or every deputy commissioner of civil marriages who accepts any money or other thing of value for performing any marriage pursuant to Section 401 of the Family Code, including any money or thing of value voluntarily tendered by the persons about to be married or who have been married by the commissioner of civil marriages or deputy commissioner of civil marriages, other than a fee expressly imposed by law for performance of a marriage, whether the acceptance occurs before or after performance of the marriage and whether or not performance of the marriage is conditioned on the giving of such money or the thing of value by the persons being married, is guilty of a misdemeanor.

It is not a necessary element of the offense described by this section that the acceptance of the money or other thing of value be committed with intent to commit extortion or with other criminal intent. This section does not apply to the request or acceptance by any retired commissioner of civil marriages of a fee for the performance of a marriage. This section is inapplicable to the acceptance of a fee for the performance of a marriage on Saturday, Sunday, or a legal holiday.

14-1a Elements of the Crime of Bribery

The crime of bribery in California is covered in several different laws. Each of the statutes defines the giving, offering, or receiving of a bribe by a specific class of individuals. Generally, the elements of bribery are as follows:

1. The asking, giving, accepting, or offering anything of value or an advantage, or the promise of same
2. To an individual of the class named in one of the specific bribery statutes
3. With the intent to corruptly influence any act, decision, vote, opinion, or other official function or duty of such person

14-1b Discussion

The offense of receiving a bribe is completed with the consent to accept the bribe. There need not be any actual tender, transfer, or showing of money. The offense of giving a bribe is complete when the bribe is delivered to the person intended to be bribed. The crime of receiving a bribe is complete once the defendant asks, receives, or agrees to receive or accept the bribe for an unlawful act of influence. It is not necessary that the person solicited consent to giving a bribe. Accordingly, a person is guilty of receiving a bribe if he or she either asks, agrees to accept, or actually accepts a bribe.

It is not required that the bribe be offered to an official with actual authority as long as the official's act is within the general scope of duties to the person being bribed.

Similar to the crime of bribery is the crime of unauthorized gratuities under PC 70. This crime consists of the asking, receiving, or agreeing to receive any gratuity by a peace officer or other executive or ministerial officer of the state, county, city, or political subdivision for doing an official act.

Other bribery statutes under the Penal Code include:

- PC 85—Giving or offering a bribe to members of the legislature.
- PC 86—Asking for or receiving a bribe by members of the legislature.
- PC 92—Giving or offering a bribe to a judge, juror, referee, arbitrator, or umpire.
- PC 93—Asking for or receiving a bribe by a judge, referee, arbitrator, juror, or umpire.
- PC 95—Corruptly attempting to influence a juror's decision.
- PC 137—Offering or giving a witness a bribe to withhold true or give false testimony.
- PC 137—Receiving or offering to receive a bribe by a witness to withhold true or give false testimony.
- PC 165—Giving or offering a bribe to any member of a council, board of supervisors, or board of trustees.
- PC 337b—Giving or offering a bribe to any participant in any athletic or sporting event.
- PC 653f—Soliciting someone else to offer or accept a bribe.

14-2 Perjury

Penal Code 118—Perjury

(a) Every person who, having taken an oath that he or she will testify, declare, depose, or certify truly before any competent tribunal, officer, or person, in any of the cases in which the oath may by law of the state of California be administered, willfully and contrary to the oath, states as true any material matter which he or she knows to be false, and every person who testifies, declares, deposes, or certifies under penalty of perjury in any of the cases in which the testimony, declarations, depositions, or certification is permitted by law of the state of California under penalty of perjury and willfully states as true any material matter which he or she knows to be false, is guilty of perjury.

This subdivision is applicable whether the statement, or the testimony, declaration, deposition, or certification is made or subscribed within or without the State of California.

(b) No person shall be convicted of perjury where proof of falsity rests solely upon contradiction by testimony of a single person other than the defendant. Proof of falsity may be established by direct or indirect evidence.

Penal Code 118a—False Affidavit

Any person who, in any affidavit taken before any person authorized to administer oaths, swears, affirms, declares, deposes, or certifies that he will testify, declare, depose, or certify before any competent tribunal, officer, or person, in any case then pending or thereafter to be instituted, in any particular manner, or to any particular fact, and in such affidavit willfully and contrary to such oath states as true any material matter which he knows to be false, is guilty of perjury. In any prosecution under this section, the subsequent testimony of such person, in any action involving the matters in such affidavit contained, which is contrary to any of the matters in such affidavit contained, shall be prima facie evidence that the matters in such affidavit were false.

Penal Code 119—Oath Includes Affirmation, etc.

The term *oath,* as used in the last two sections, includes an affirmation and every other mode authorized by law of attesting the truth of that which is stated.

Penal Code 120—Oath of Officer As to Future Performance Not Included

So much of an oath of office as relates to the future performance of official duties is not such an oath as is intended by the two preceding sections (i.e., to support perjury charges).

Penal Code 121—Irregular Administration of Oath Not Perjury Defense

It is no defense to a prosecution for perjury that the oath was administered or taken in an irregular manner, or that the person accused of perjury did not go before, or was not in the presence of, the officer purporting to administer the oath, if such accused caused or procured such officer to certify that the oath had been taken or administered.

Penal Code 122—Competency of Accused Not a Defense

It is no defense to a prosecution for perjury that the accused was not competent to give the testimony, deposition, or certificate of which falsehood is alleged. It is sufficient that he did give such testimony or make such deposition or certificate.

Penal Code 123—Lack of Knowledge of Materiality Not a Defense

It is no defense to a prosecution for perjury that the accused did not know the materiality of the false statement made by him; or that it did not, in fact, affect the proceeding in or for which it was made. It is sufficient that it was material, and might have being used to affect such proceeding.

Penal Code 124—Making of Deposition or Affidavit Complete

The making of a deposition, affidavit, or certificate is deemed to be complete, within the provisions of this chapter, from the time when it is delivered by the accused to any other person, with the intent that it be uttered or published as true.

Penal Code 125—Unqualified Statement Same As False Statement

An unqualified statement of that which one does not know to be true is equivalent to a statement of that which one knows to be false.

Penal Code 126—Perjury, Punishment

Perjury is punishable by imprisonment in the state prison for two, three, or four years.

Penal Code 127—Subornation of Perjury

Every person who willfully procures another person to commit perjury is guilty of subornation of perjury, and is punishable in the same manner as he would be if personally guilty of the perjury so procured.

Penal Code 128—Penalty for Perjury Resulting in Capital Punishment

Every person who, by willful perjury or subornation of perjury procures the conviction and execution of any innocent person, is punishable by death or life imprisonment without possibility of parole. . . .

Penal Code 129—False Statement Purportedly under Oath

Every person who, being required by law to make any return, statement, or report, under oath, willfully makes and delivers any such return, statement, or report, purporting to be under oath, knowing the same to be false in any particular, is guilty of perjury, whether such oath was in fact taken or not.

14-2a Elements

The following are the elements of the crime of perjury:

- Knowingly making a false oral or written statement
- Made either under oath or "under penalty of perjury"
- With respect to a fact which is material
- Before a legal tribunal, proceeding, or person

14-2b Discussion

The testimony is considered as *material* if it could *probably* have influenced the trier of fact. The prosecution need not establish that it did in fact influence the trier of fact. The statement must be made either with knowledge that it was false or an unqualified statement of that which one does not know to be true. An honest mistake does not constitute perjury. Note: The stating under oath that one does not remember a material fact when he or she does in fact remember is perjury. The term *oath* includes affirmation and every other mode authorized by law of attesting the truth of that which is stated.

The fact that the individual making the statement does not know the materiality of the false statement is no defense to the crime of perjury. It is sufficient if the false statement was in fact material. Also note that it is not a defense to perjury that the person making the statement was incompetent to be a witness.

Penal Code 146a—Arrest or Search by Person Impersonating an Officer

(a) Any person who falsely represents himself or herself to be a deputy or clerk in any state department and who, in that assumed character, does any of the following is guilty of a misdemeanor punishable by imprisonment in a county jail not exceeding six months, by a fine not exceeding two thousand five hundred dollars ($2,500), or both the fine and imprisonment:

    (1) Arrests, detains, or threatens to arrest or detain any person
    (2) Otherwise intimidates any person
    (3) Searches any person, building, or other property of any person
    (4) Obtains money, property, or other thing of value

(b) Any person who falsely represents himself or herself to be a public officer, investigator, or inspector in any state department and who, in that assumed character, does any of the following shall be punished by imprisonment in a county jail not exceeding one year, by a fine not exceeding two thousand five hundred dollars ($2,500), or by both that fine and imprisonment, or by imprisonment in the state prison:

    (1) Arrests, detains, or threatens to arrest or detain any person
    (2) Otherwise intimidates any person
    (3) Searches any person, building, or other property of any person
    (4) Obtains money, property, or other thing of value

Vehicle Code 27—Impersonation of CHP Member

Any person who without authority impersonates, or wears the badge of, a member of the California Highway Patrol with intention to deceive anyone is guilty of a misdemeanor.

Penal Code 146b—Simulating Official Inquiries

Every person who, with intent to lead another to believe that a request or demand for information is being made by the state, a county, city, or other governmental entity, when such is not the case, sends to such other person a written or printed form or other communication which reasonably appears to be such request or demand by such governmental entity, is guilty of a misdemeanor.

Public Resources Code 4022—Impersonating a Ranger

(a) The titles of ranger, park ranger, and forest ranger, and derivations thereof, may only be used by persons who are peace officers under Chapter 4.5 (commencing with Section 830) of Title 3 of Part 2 of the Penal Code, employees of the Department of Forestry and Fire Protection, or employees of the Department of Parks and Recreation classified as State Park Ranger (Permanent Intermittent). Any person, other than a peace officer or employee of the Department of Parks and Recreation, as described in this section, or employee of the Department of Forestry and Fire Protection, who willfully wears, exhibits, or uses any authorized badge, insignia, emblem, device, label, title, or card of a ranger, park ranger, forest ranger, or a derivation thereof, to identify the person as a ranger, park ranger, or forest ranger, or who willfully wears, exhibits, or uses any badge, insignia, emblem, device, label, title, or card of a ranger, park ranger, or forest ranger, which so resembles the authorized version that would deceive an ordinary, reasonable person into believing that it is authorized for the use of a ranger, park ranger, or forest ranger, is guilty of an infraction.

14-4 Filing a False Police Report

Penal Code 118.1 makes it a crime for a peace officer to file a false police report. That section provides that if a peace officer knowingly and intentionally files a report with false information regarding the commission or investigation of a crime with the agency that employs him or her, whether or not the statement is certified or otherwise expressly reported as true, that officer is guilty of filing a false report punishable by imprisonment in the county jail for up to one year, or in the state prison for one, two, or three years. This section does not apply to the contents of any statement that the peace officer attributes in the report to any other person.

14-5 Refusal to Join Posse Comitatus

Penal Code 150 provides that every able-bodied person above 18 years of age who neglects or refuses to join the posse comitatus, or power of the county, by neglecting or refusing to aid and assist in taking or arresting any person against whom there may be issued any process, or by neglecting to aid and assist in retaking any person who, after being arrested or confined, may have escaped from arrest or imprisonment, or by neglecting or refusing to aid and assist in preventing any breach of the peace, or the commission of any criminal offense, being thereto lawfully required by any uniformed peace officer, or by any peace officer who identifies himself or herself with a badge or identification card issued by the officer's employing agency, or by any judge, is punishable by fine of not less than fifty dollars ($50) nor more than one thousand dollars($1,000).

PC 723 provides that when a sheriff or other public officer authorized to execute process finds, or has reason to apprehend, that resistance will be made to the execution of the process, the officer may command as many able-bodied inhabitants of the officer's county as he or she may think proper to assist in overcoming the resistance and, if necessary, in seizing, arresting, and confining the persons resisting, and their aiders and abettors. Under the provisions of PC 724, the officer must certify to the court from which the process issued the names of the persons resisting his or her request for assistance, and their aiders and abettors, to the end that they may be proceeded against for their contempt of the court.

14-6 False Information to Police Officer

Penal Code 148.5 makes it a crime for any person to report to any peace officer listed in Section 830.1 or 830.2 (sheriff, deputy sheriff, police officer, California Highway Patrol person, member of California State University Police Departments, game wardens, marshals, fire marshals, district attorney, or deputy district attorney, etc.) that a felony or misdemeanor has been committed, knowing the report to be false, is guilty of a misdemeanor if (1) the false information is given while the peace officer is engaged in the performance of his or her duties as a peace officer and (2) the person providing the false information knows or should have known that the person receiving the information is a peace officer.

Likewise, every person who reports to any employee who is assigned to accept reports from citizens, either directly or by telephone, and who is employed by a state or local agency (law enforcement) that a felony or misdemeanor has been committed, knowing the report to be false, is guilty of a misdemeanor if (1) the false information is given while the employee is engaged in the performance of his or her duties as an agency employee and (2) the person providing the false information knows or should have known that the person receiving the information is an agency employee engaged in the performance of the duties described in PC 148.5.

Every person who makes a report to a grand jury that a felony or misdemeanor has been committed, knowing the report to be false, is guilty of a misdemeanor. PC 148.5 should not be construed as prohibiting or precluding a charge of perjury or contempt for any report made under oath in an investigation or proceeding before a grand jury. The section does not apply to reports made by persons who are required by statute to report known or suspected instances of child abuse, dependent adult abuse, or elder abuse.

Under PC 148.6, every person who files any allegation of misconduct against any peace officer knowing the allegation to be false is guilty of a misdemeanor. Any law enforcement agency accepting an allegation of misconduct against a peace officer shall require the complainant to read and sign the following advisory, all in boldface type:

> **You have the right to make a complaint against a police officer for any improper police conduct. california law requires this agency to have a procedure to investigate citizens' complaints. You have a right to a written description of this procedure. This agency may find after investigation that there is not enough evidence to warrant action on your complaint; even if that is the case, you have the right to make the complaint and have it investigated if you believe an officer behaved improperly. Citizen complaints and any reports or findings relating to complaints must be retained by this agency for at least five years. It is against the law to make a complaint that you know to be false. If you make a complaint against an officer knowing that it is false, you can be prosecuted on a misdemeanor charge.**

I have read and understood the above statement.

_____ Complainant

Every person who files a *civil claim* against a peace officer or a lien against his or her property, knowing the claim or lien to be false and with the intent to harass or dissuade the officer from carrying out his or her official duties, is guilty of a misdemeanor. PC 148.6 applies only to claims pertaining to actions that arise in the course and scope of the peace officer's duties.

14-7 Violation of Court Order

The courts use their contempt powers to enforce their orders. PC 166 provides that any person guilty of any contempt of court, of any of the following kinds, is guilty of a misdemeanor:

(1) Disorderly, contemptuous, or insolent behavior committed during the sitting of any court of justice, in immediate view and presence of the court, and directly tending to interrupt its proceedings or to impair the respect due to its authority.

(2) Behavior as specified in paragraph (1) committed in the presence of any referee, while actually engaged in any trial or hearing, pursuant to the order of any court, or in the presence of any jury while actually sitting for the trial of a cause, or upon any inquest or other proceedings authorized by law.

(3) Any breach of the peace, noise, or other disturbance directly tending to interrupt the proceedings of any court.

(4) Willful disobedience of any process or order lawfully issued by any court.

(5) Resistance willfully offered by any person to the lawful order or process of any court.

(6) The contumacious and unlawful refusal of any person to be sworn as a witness; or, when so sworn, the like refusal to answer any material question.

(7) The publication of a false or grossly inaccurate report of the proceedings of any court.

PC 422.9 and PC 273.6 provide that any willful and knowing violation of a protective or stay away order issued by a court shall be a misdemeanor punishable by a fine of not more than one thousand dollars ($1,000), or by imprisonment in the county jail for not more than six months, or by both the fine and imprisonment. If the person has previously been convicted one or more times of violating a protective order, he or she shall be imprisoned in the county jail for not more than one year. Subject to the discretion of the court, the prosecution shall have the opportunity to present witnesses and relevant evidence at the time of the sentencing of a defendant pursuant to this subdivision.

14-8 Lynching

Penal Code 405a—Lynching Defined

The taking by means of a riot of any person from the lawful custody of any peace officer is a *lynching*.

Penal Code 405b—Lynching, Punishment

Every person who participates in any lynching is punishable by imprisonment in the state prison for two, three, or four years.

Penal Code 4550—Penalties for Rescue or Attempt to Rescue

Every person who rescues or attempts to rescue, or aids another person in rescuing or attempting to rescue any prisoner from any prison, or prison road camp or any jail or county road camp, or from any officer or person having him in lawful custody, is punishable as follows:

1. If such prisoner was in custody upon a conviction of a felony punishable with death: by imprisonment in the state prison for two, three or four years;
2. If such prisoner was in custody otherwise than as specified in subsection 1 hereof: by imprisonment in the state prison, or by imprisonment in the county jail not to exceed one year.

14-9 Intimidation of Victim or Witness

PC 422.9 provides that any person who is guilty of contempt of court by willfully contacting a victim by phone, mail, or directly and who has been previously convicted of a violation of Section 646.9 shall be punished by imprisonment in a county jail for not more than one year, by a fine of five thousand dollars ($5,000), or by both that fine and imprisonment. For the purposes of sentencing under this subdivision, each contact shall constitute a separate violation of this subdivision. The fact that the person who makes contact with a victim is incarcerated is not a defense to this violation.

Under PC 136.1:

(a) Any person who does any of the following is guilty of a misdemeanor:

(1) Knowingly and maliciously prevents or dissuades any witness or victim from attending or giving testimony at any trial, proceeding, or inquiry authorized by law.

(2) Knowingly and maliciously attempts to prevent or dissuade any witness or victim from attending or giving testimony at any trial, proceeding, or inquiry authorized by law.

(b) Except as provided in subdivision (c), every person who attempts to prevent or dissuade another person who has been the victim of a crime or who is witness to a crime from doing any of the following is guilty of a misdemeanor:

(1) Making any report of such victimization to any peace officer or state or local law enforcement officer or probation or parole or correctional officer or prosecuting agency or to any judge.

(2) Causing a complaint, indictment, information, probation or parole violation to be sought and prosecuted, and assisting in the prosecution thereof.

(3) Arresting or causing or seeking the arrest of any person in connection with such victimization.

(c) Every person doing any of the acts described in subdivision (a) or (b) knowingly and maliciously under any one or more of the following circumstances, is guilty of a felony punishable by imprisonment in the state prison for two, three, or four years under any of the following circumstances:

(1) Where the act is accompanied by force or by an express or implied threat of force or violence, upon a witness or victim or any third person or the property of any victim, witness, or any third person.

(2) Where the act is in furtherance of a conspiracy.

(3) Where the act is committed by any person who has been convicted of any violation of this section, any predecessor law hereto or any federal statute or statute of any other state which, if the act prosecuted was committed in this state, would be a violation of this section.

(4) Where the act is committed by any person for pecuniary gain or for any other consideration acting upon the request of any other person. All parties to such a transaction are guilty of a felony.

(d) Every person attempting the commission of any act described in subdivisions (a), (b), and (c) is guilty of the offense attempted without regard to success or failure of such attempt. The fact that no person was injured physically, or in fact intimidated, shall be no defense against any prosecution under this section.

(e) Nothing in this section precludes the imposition of an enhancement for great bodily injury where the injury inflicted is significant or substantial.

(f) The use of force during the commission of any offense described in subdivision (c) shall be considered a circumstance in aggravation of the crime in imposing a term of imprisonment under subdivision (b) of Section 1170.

Penal Code 136.2—Orders by Court

Upon a good cause belief that harm to, or intimidation or dissuasion of, a victim or witness has occurred or is reasonably likely to occur, any court with jurisdiction over a criminal matter may issue orders including, but not limited to, the following:

(a) Any order issued pursuant to Section 6320 of the Family Code.

(b) An order that a defendant shall not violate any provision of Section 136.1.

(c) An order that a person before the court other than a defendant, including, but not limited to, a subpoenaed witness or other person entering the courtroom of the court, shall not violate any provisions of Section 136.1.

(d) An order that any person described in this section shall have no communication whatsoever with any specified witness or any victim, except through an attorney under any reasonable restrictions that the court may impose.

(e) An order calling for a hearing to determine if an order as described in subdivisions (a) to (d), inclusive, should be issued.

(f) An order that a particular law enforcement agency within the jurisdiction of the court provide protection for a victim or a witness, or both, or for immediate family members of a victim or a witness who reside in the same household as the victim or witness or within reasonable proximity of the victim's or witness's household, as determined by the court. The order shall not be made without the consent of the law enforcement agency except for limited and specified periods of time and upon an express finding by the court of a clear and present danger of harm to the victim or witness or immediate family members of the victim or witness.

For purposes of this subdivision, "immediate family members" include the spouse, children, or parents of the victim or witness.

(g) Any order protecting victims of violent crime from contact, with the intent to annoy, harass, threaten, or commit acts of violence, by the defendant. The court or its designee shall transmit orders made under this subdivision to law enforcement personnel within one business day of the issuance of the order, pursuant to subdivision (a) of Section 6380 of the Family Code.

Any order issued by a court pursuant to this subdivision shall be issued on forms adopted by the Judicial Council of California and that have been approved by the Department of Justice pursuant to subdivision (i) of Section 6380 of the Family Code. However, the fact that an order issued by a court pursuant to this section was not issued on forms adopted by the Judicial Council and approved by the Department of Justice shall not, in and of itself, make the order unenforceable.

Any person violating any order made pursuant to subdivisions (a) to (g), inclusive, may be punished for any substantive offense described in Section 136.1, or for a contempt of the court making the order. No finding of contempt shall be a bar to prosecution for a violation of Section 136.1. However, any person so held in contempt shall be entitled to credit for any punishment imposed therein against any sentence imposed upon conviction of an offense described in Section 136.1. Any conviction or acquittal for any substantive offense under Section 136.1 shall be a bar to a subsequent punishment for contempt arising out of the same act.

(h) In all cases where the defendant is charged with a crime of domestic violence, as defined in Section 13700, the court shall consider issuing the above-described orders on its own motion. In order to facilitate this, the court's records of all criminal cases involving domestic violence shall be marked to clearly alert the court to this issue.

(i) The Judicial Council shall adopt forms for orders under this section.

Penal Code 136.5—Carrying a Deadly Weapon to Prevent a Witness from Testifying

Any person who has upon his person a deadly weapon with the intent to use such weapon to commit a violation of Section 136.1 is guilty of an offense punishable by imprisonment in the county jail for not more than one year, or in the state prison.

Penal Code 136.7—Disclosure of Witness or Victim's Name and Address by Persons Imprisoned for Sexual Offense to Initiate Unauthorized Correspondence

Every person imprisoned in a county jail or the state prison who has been convicted of a sexual offense, including, but not limited to, a violation of Section 243.4, 261, 261.5, 262, 264.1, 266, 266a, 266b, 266c, 266f, 285, 286, 288, 288a, or 289, who knowingly reveals the name and address of any witness or victim to that offense to any other prisoner with the intent that the other prisoner will intimidate or harass the witness or victim through the initiation of unauthorized correspondence with the witness or victim, is guilty of a public offense, punishable by imprisonment in the county jail not to exceed one year, or by imprisonment in the state prison.

Nothing in this section shall prevent the interviewing of witnesses.

Penal Code 471—Making False Entries in Records or Returns

14-10 Making False Entries in Records or Returns

Every person who, with intent to defraud another, makes, forges, or alters any entry in any book of records, any instrument purporting to be any record or return specified in the preceding section, is guilty of forgery.

Penal Code 471.5—Falsifying Medical Records

Any person who alters or modifies the medical record of any person, with fraudulent intent, or who, with fraudulent intent, creates any false medical records, is guilty of a misdemeanor.

Penal Code 115—Offering False or Forged Instruments to Be Filed

14-11 Filing Forged Instruments

(a) Every person who knowingly procures or offers any false or forged instrument to be filed, registered, or recorded in any public office within this state, which instrument, if genuine, might be filed, registered, or recorded under any law of this state or of the United States, is guilty of a felony.
(b) Each instrument which is procured or offered to be filed, registered, or recorded in violation of subdivision (a) shall constitute a separate violation of this section.
[Subsections (c) and (d) referring to punishments are omitted.]

Penal Code 115.5—Filing False or Forged Documents or Instruments

(a) Every person who files any false or forged document or instrument with the county recorder which affects title to, places an encumbrance on, or places an interest secured by a mortgage or deed or trust on, real property consisting of a single-family residence containing not more than four dwelling units, with knowledge that the document is false or forged is punishable. . . .
(b) Every person who makes a false sworn statement to a notary public, with knowledge that the statement is false, to induce the notary public to perform an improper notarial act on an instrument or document affecting title to, or placing an encumbrance on, real property containing not more than four dwelling units is guilty of a felony.

14-11a Discussion

The filing or offering for filing or the making of a false sworn statement to a notary public must be "with the knowledge" that the documents or statements are forged or false. There is no requirement, however, to establish an "intent to defraud."

14-12 Altering Certified Copies of Official Records

Penal Code 115.3—Altering Certified Copies of Official Records

Any person who alters a certified copy of an official record, or knowingly furnishes an altered certified copy of an official record, of this state, including the executive, legislative, and judicial branches thereof, or of any city, county, city and county, district, or political subdivision thereof, is guilty of a misdemeanor.

14-12a Discussion

The offense of altering certified copies of official records does not require an "intent to defraud." The mere altering of certified copies is sufficient to constitute the offense.

14-13 Counterfeiting

Penal Code 477—Counterfeiting Coin, Bullion, etc.

Every person who counterfeits any of the species of gold or silver coin current in this state, or any kind of species of gold dust, gold or silver bullion, or bars, lumps, pieces, or nuggets, or who sells, passes, or gives in payment such counterfeit coin, dust, bullion, bars, lumps, pieces, or nuggets, or permits, with intention to defraud any person, knowing the same to be counterfeited, is guilty of counterfeiting.

Penal Code 479—Counterfeit Gold or Silver Coins, etc.

Every person who has in his possession, or receives for any other person, any counterfeit gold or silver coin of the species current in this state, or any counterfeit gold dust, gold or silver bullion or bars, lumps, pieces or nuggets, with the intention to sell, utter, put off or pass the same, or permits, causes or procures the same to be sold, uttered or passed, with intention to defraud any person, knowing the same to be counterfeit, is punishable by imprisonment in the state prison. . . .

Penal Code 480—Possessing or Making Counterfeit Dies or Plates

(a) Every person who makes, or knowingly has in his or her possession any die, plate, or any apparatus, paper, metal, machine, or other thing whatever, made use of in counterfeiting coin current in this state, or in counterfeiting gold dust, gold or silver bars, bullion, lumps, pieces, or nuggets, or in counterfeiting bank notes or bills, is punishable by imprisonment in the state prison for two, three, or four years; and all dies, plates, apparatus, papers, metals, or machines intended for the purpose aforesaid, must be destroyed. . . .

(1) If the counterfeiting apparatus or machine used to violate this section is a computer, computer system, or computer network, the apparatus or machine shall be disposed of pursuant to Section 502.01.

(2) For the purposes of this section, "computer system" and "computer network" have the same meaning as that specified in Section 502. The terms "computer, computer system, or computer network" include any software or data residing on the computer, computer system, or computer network used in a violation of this section.

Counterfeiting of U.S. currency is a federal crime and is subject to prosecution in U.S. District Courts. It is also a state crime, and the states have concurrent power to punish (*In re Dixon*, 41 Cal. 2d 756). By statute, counterfeiting includes more than the making of phony currency. For example, a conviction for the counterfeiting of pari-mutuel tickets was upheld in one case. Note: The intent to defraud is similar to that required for forgery (*People v. Bratis*, 73 Cal. App. 3d 751).

14-13a Discussion

Penal Code 483—Ticket Scalping

14-14 Ticket Scalping

Except as otherwise provided . . . any person . . . that shall sell to another any ticket, pass, scrip, mileage or commutation book, coupon, or other instrument for passage on a common carrier, for the use of any person not entitled to use the same according to the terms of the book or portion thereof from which it was detached, shall be guilty of a misdemeanor.

Unlike forgery or counterfeiting, ticket scalping is a general intent crime. This crime also differs in that there is no requirement to establish an intent to defraud as a necessary element. For example, most sports tickets have restrictions printed on them limiting their transfer or resale. Accordingly, reselling the tickets in violation of the ticket restrictions is an offense under this section.

14-14a Discussion

Practicum

You are a deputy sheriff. One of the local businesses, in an attempt to have more police presence, offers to provide you with a free meal each day, if while on duty and in uniform, you stop by their store and spend at least 15 minutes in the store.

1. Have you committed any crime by agreeing to this arrangement?
2. Has the store owner committed any crime by offering this arrangement?
3. Would it make any difference if instead of a free meal, the store owner offered you money?

Discussion Questions

1. What constitutes bribery?
2. Explain the general elements of the crime of bribery in the state of California.
3. What are the elements of the crime of perjury?
4. Describe the crime of lynching.

5. Does requiring a person to read and sign a statement before accepting an allegation of misconduct against a peace officer tend to make individuals reluctant to file such reports? What could be the purposes of such a requirement?
6. Explain what constitutes counterfeiting.

Self-Study Quiz

Self-Study Quiz

True/False

1. Bribing a ministerial officer is always a felony.
2. The offense of receiving a bribe is complete with the agreement to accept the bribe.
3. t is required that a bribe be offered to an official with actual authority to do the requested act.
4. A person may be convicted of perjury solely upon contradiction by testimony of a trustworthy witness.
5. Regarding perjury crimes, the term *oath* does not include an affirmation.
6. When being tried for perjury, the fact that the defendant was not competent to give the false testimony involved is no defense.
7. To be perjury, the false facts must be material to the proceedings.
8. An unqualified statement of that which one does not know to be true is equivalent to a statement of that which one knows to be false.
9. Subornation to perjury was a common law crime and is not currently a crime in California.
10. It is a felony to impersonate a California Highway Patrol officer.

Weapons Violations

15-1 Drawing, Exhibiting, or Discharging a Firearm

Penal Code 417—Drawing, Exhibiting, or Using Firearm or Deadly Weapon; Self-Defense; Peace Officers

(a)

(1) Every person who, except in self-defense, in the presence of any other person, draws or exhibits any deadly weapon whatsoever, other than a firearm, in a rude, angry, or threatening manner, or who in any manner, unlawfully uses the same in any fight or quarrel is guilty of a misdemeanor. . . .

(2) Every person who, except in self-defense, in the presence of any other person, draws or exhibits any firearm, whether loaded or unloaded, in a rude, angry, or threatening manner, or who in any manner, unlawfully uses the same in any fight or quarrel is guilty of a misdemeanor. . . .

(b) Every person who, except in self-defense, in the presence of any other person, draws or exhibits any loaded firearm in a rude, angry, or threatening manner, or who, in any manner, unlawfully uses any loaded firearm in any fight or quarrel upon the grounds of any day care center . . . shall be punished by imprisonment in the state prison for one, two, or three years, or by imprisonment in a county jail for not less than three months, nor more than one year.

(c) Every person who, in the immediate presence of a peace officer, draws or exhibits any firearm, whether loaded or unloaded, in a rude, angry, or threatening manner, and who knows, or reasonably should know, by the officer's uniformed appearance or other action of identification by the officer, that he or she is a peace officer engaged in the performance of his or her duties, and that peace officer is engaged in the performance of his or her duties is guilty of a felony. . . .

15-1a Discussion

As used to impose criminal liability for exhibiting a firearm in the presence of a peace officer, the requirement for only constructive knowledge, as opposed to actual knowledge, of the peace officer's status does not violate the Eighth and Fourteenth Amendments to the U.S. Constitution; culpability based on "should have known" constructive knowledge standard is not vague or over broad (*People v. Mathews*, 25 Cal. App. 4th 89).

Due process is not violated by the fact that a defendant can be convicted of exhibiting a firearm in presence of a peace officer based on whether he "reasonably should know" that the victim was a peace officer, since there is no constitutional impediment to the enactment of law that requires something less than actual knowledge in the mind of the perpetrator (*People v. Mathews*, 25 Cal. App. 4th 89).

Firearm

In respect to the offense of brandishing a firearm, the word *firearm* includes a pistol, revolver, or rifle, or any other device designed to be used as a weapon from which a projectile may be expelled by the force of any explosion or other form of combustion; an object that meets this definition is a "firearm" even if it is not loaded (*People v. Norton*, 80 Cal. App. 3d Supp. 14).

In one case, the defendant could not be convicted of assault with a firearm and unlawfully exhibiting a firearm in angry manner, where the weapon the defendant used was a pellet gun that operated by use of compressed air, rather than by explosion or other form of combustion. A firearm is an instrument used in propulsion of shot, shell, or bullets by the action of gunpowder exploded within it. The legislature's failure to define firearm in Titles 8 and 11 of the Penal Code, governing crimes against the person and crimes against the public peace, respectively, while expressly including pellet gun in its definition of a firearm to make the sale of a firearm to a minor a misdemeanor, raised strong inference that a firearm is intended to be used for purposes of gun control and minors in a sense different from its common meaning (*In re Jose A.*, 5 Cal. App. 4th 697).

Elements of Offense

In *People v. Chavira* (3 Cal. App. 3d 988), all the elements required for conviction of the crime of displaying a firearm in a rude and boisterous manner were held to be present where the record clearly showed that the weapon was seen by victims, was pointed at them, and was fired. The pointing of the weapon at a person is not a necessary element of the offense of exhibiting a deadly weapon in a rude, angry, or threatening manner (*Garfield v. Peoples Finance & Thrift Co. of Riverside*, 24 Cal. App. 2d 144).

Victim's Awareness

Violation of statute regarding brandishing of weapon, Penal Code 417(a)(2), did not require an awareness on victim's part that gun was being brandished in *People v. McKinzie* (179 Cal. App. 3d 789).

Intent

In *People v. Lipscomb* (17 Cal. App. 4th 564), the defendant charged with assault with a firearm was not entitled to instruction on the lesser-related offense of brandishing a weapon as there was no basis on which jury could have found offense to be less than that charged. In this case, the victim, having heard gun shots, went from his backyard to his garage, intending to close garage door. The defendant ran into garage with gun in hand, pointed it at victim, ordered him into house, and warned him that he "didn't want to have to shoot"; the defendant's statement that he "didn't want to have to shoot" did not demonstrate that he never intended to commit battery and, thus, could not have been guilty of assault.

As regards the offense to brandishing a firearm or deadly weapon, it is not necessary to show that the possessor intended to inflict injury on a victim; once it is shown that the weapon was exhibited in a rude, angry, and threatening manner, the offense is complete and special instructions about the probable future use of the weapon would be irrelevant (*People v. Norton*, 80 Cal. App. 3d Supp. 14).

Defense of Others

This section does not forbid a person from drawing a weapon in a threatening manner in order to defend others (*People v. Kirk*, 192 Cal. App. 3d Supp. 15).

Lesser and Included Offenses

The offense of brandishing a weapon is not a lesser included offense of murder, with or without the use of a firearm, nor of assault with a deadly weapon or assault with intent to commit murder (*People v. Beach*, 147 Cal. App. 3d 612). In one case, drawing or exhibiting a firearm was not a necessarily included offense within the charged offense of assault with a deadly weapon where the pleading charged the assault in a general matter without alleging that a weapon was "drawn or exhibited" in a rude, angry, or threatening manner (*People v. Orr*, 43 Cal. App. 3d 666).

15-2 Firearms in Vehicles

Penal Code 417.3—Drawing or Exhibiting Firearm to Person in Motor Vehicle

Every person who, except in self-defense, in the presence of any other person who is an occupant of a motor vehicle proceeding on a public street or highway, draws or exhibits any firearm, whether loaded or unloaded, in a threatening manner against another person in such a way as to cause a reasonable person apprehension or fear bodily harm is guilty of a felony.

Nothing in this statute shall preclude or prohibit prosecution under any other statute.

Penal Code 374c—Discharging Firearms on a Public Highway

Every person who shoots any firearm from or upon a public road or highway is guilty of a misdemeanor.

15-2a Discussion

PC 417.3 was enacted by the Legislature as a direct result of the "freeway" shootings that started in Southern California and later spread to other parts of the state. It is assumed that the phrase "proceeding on a public street or highway" includes those situations where the motor vehicles are stopped in traffic because of traffic lights or traffic problems. Since the crime is drawing or exhibiting a firearm, the offense may be committed with either a loaded or unloaded weapon.

PC 12034 makes it a misdemeanor to discharge a firearm from a motor vehicle. If the weapon is discharged at another person, the crime is a felony. PC 246, set forth in the next section, 15-3, also provides that any person who maliciously and willfully discharges a firearm at an inhabited dwelling, house, occupied motor vehicle, or inhabited house car is guilty of a felony (wobbler).

15-3 Shooting at an Inhabited Dwelling, etc.

Penal Code 246—Shooting at Inhabited Dwelling House, Occupied Building, Vehicle, or Aircraft, or Inhabited House, Car, or Camper; Punishment

Any person who shall maliciously and willfully discharge a firearm at an inhabited dwelling house, occupied building, occupied motor vehicle, occupied aircraft, inhabited house car . . . or inhabited camper . . . is guilty of a felony, and upon conviction shall be punished by imprisonment in the state prison for three, five, or seven years, or by imprisonment in the county jail for a term of not less than six months and not exceeding one year.

15-3a Discussion

Inhabited Dwelling House

Inhabited means currently being used for dwelling purposes, whether occupied or not. A building is considered inhabited, for the purposes of the crime of discharging a firearm at an inhabited dwelling house, if permanent residents are living there, even if the dwelling is temporarily unoccupied (*People v. White*, 4 Cal. App. 4th 1299).

Occupied Building

An occupied building is a building with any person in it. It is not necessary that the offender know that the building is occupied. In *People v. Adams* (137 Cal. App. 3d 346), shooting into an attached garage was considered a shooting into an "occupied building" within the meaning of PC 246.

Recreational Vehicles

Recreational vehicles, although suitable and used for weekend trips including overnight stays, are not within the meaning or definition of "house" or "building" as used in PC 246 proscribing discharge of firearm into "inhabited dwelling house or occupied building" (*People v. Moreland*, 81 Cal. App. 3d 11).

Shooting Within Dwelling or Building

Firing of a pistol within a dwelling house is not a violation of the crime of discharging a firearm at an inhabited dwelling house (*People v. Stepney*, 120 Cal. App. 3d 1016).

Intent

Discharging a firearm at an occupied motor vehicle is a general intent crime (*People v. Williams*, 102 Cal. App. 3d 1018). Discharging a firearm with a reckless disregard of probable consequences and with the *intent* to cause such consequences is a violation of the prohibition of shooting at an inhabited dwelling house. The shooting must have been done with the intent to hit building for there to be a conviction (*People v. Chavira*, 3 Cal. App. 3d 988).

Felony-Murder

The willful discharge of a firearm at an inhabited dwelling house, considered in the abstract, involves a high probability that death will result and, thus, is an inherently dangerous felony for the purposes of second-degree felony-murder doctrine even though the occupant of the dwelling may be absent at the actual time of shooting, in light of the significant likelihood that occupant may be present at any time (*People v. Hansen*, 9 Cal. 4th 300).

Included Offenses

Assault with a deadly weapon is not a lesser and necessarily included offense of willfully and maliciously discharging a firearm at an occupied vehicle, since the latter offense may be committed without committing the former offense, in that the defendant may commit the latter offense by discharging a firearm into an inhabited but temporarily unoccupied dwelling. For conviction, it is not necessary under the latter offense to prove that the defendant's act came dangerously close to actually physically injuring a person, and the defendant need not necessarily have the present ability to commit violent injury to another to commit the latter offense (*In re Daniel R.*, 20 Cal. App. 4th 239).

15-4 Dangerous Weapons Control Act

Penal Code 12000

This Chapter shall be known and may be cited as *The Dangerous Weapons Control Act.*

Penal Code 12001 Definitions

(a) As used in this title, the terms *pistol, revolver,* and *firearm capable of being concealed upon the person* shall apply to and include any device designed to be used as a weapon, from which is expelled a projectile by the force of any explosion, or other form of combustion, and which has a barrel less than 16 inches in length. These terms also include any device which has a barrel 16 inches or more in length which is designed to be interchanged with a barrel less than 16 inches in length.

(b) As used in this title, *firearm* means any device, designed to be used as a weapon, from which is expelled through a barrel a projectile by the force of any explosion or other form of combustion.

(c) The term *firearm* includes the frame or receiver of the weapon.

(d) The term *firearm* also shall include any rocket, rocket propelled projectile launcher, or similar device containing any explosive or incendiary material whether or not the device is designed for emergency or distress signaling purposes.

(e)

  (1) ... the term *firearm* does not include an unloaded firearm which is defined as an *antique firearm.* ...

  (2) ... the term *firearm* does not include an unloaded firearm that meets both of the following:

    (A) It is not a pistol, revolver, or other firearm capable of being concealed upon the person.

    (B) It is a curio or relic, as defined in Section 178.11 of Title 27 of the Code of Federal Regulations.

(f) Nothing shall prevent a device defined as a *pistol, revolver,* or *firearm capable of being concealed upon the person* from also being found to be a short-barreled shotgun or a short-barreled rifle, as defined in Section 12020.

(g) ... the term *BB device* means any instrument that expels a metallic projectile, such as a BB or a pellet, through the force of air pressure, CO_2 pressure, or spring action, or any spot marker gun.

(h) As used in this title, *wholesaler* means any person who is licensed as a dealer pursuant to Chapter 44 (commencing with Section 921) of Title 18 of the United States Code and the regulations issued pursuant thereto who sells, transfers, or assigns firearms, or parts of firearms, to persons who are licensed as manufacturers, importers, or gunsmiths pursuant to Chapter 44 (commencing with Section 921) of Title 18 of the United States Code, or persons licensed pursuant to Section 12071, and includes persons who receive finished parts of firearms and assemble them into completed or partially completed firearms in furtherance of that purpose.

  Wholesaler shall not include a manufacturer, importer, or gunsmith who is licensed to engage in those activities pursuant to Chapter 44 (commencing with Section 921) of Title 18 of the United States Code or a person licensed pursuant to Section 12071 and the regulations issued pursuant thereto. A wholesaler also does not include those persons dealing exclusively in grips, stocks, and other parts of firearms that are not frames or receivers thereof.

(i) ... *Application to purchase* means either of the following:

  (1) The initial completion of the register by the purchaser, transferee, or person being loaned the firearm as required by subdivision (a) of Section 12076.

  (2) The initial completion of the LEFT by the purchaser, transferee, or person being loaned the firearm as required by subdivision (d) of Section 12084.

(j) For purposes of Section 12023, a firearm shall be deemed to be *loaded* whenever both the firearm and the unexpended ammunition capable of being discharged from the firearm are in the immediate possession of the same person.

(k) For purposes of Sections 12021, 12021.1, 12025, 12070, 12072, 12073, 12078, and 12101 of this code, and Sections 8100, 8101, and 8103 of the Welfare and Institutions Code, notwithstanding the fact that the term *any firearm* may be used in those sections, each firearm or the frame or receiver of the same shall constitute a distinct and separate offense under those sections.

(l) For purposes of Section 12020, a violation of that section as to each firearm, weapon, or device enumerated therein shall constitute a distinct and separate offense.

15-4a General Concepts Regarding Dangerous Weapons

- Except in specified locations, carrying an unconcealed handgun in public is legal.
- Peace officers generally may carry concealed handguns in public.
- A person may carry a concealed handgun in his or her own home or place of business.
- In most cases, the possession of a handgun by a minor is a misdemeanor.
- Felons are generally prohibited from carrying or possessing a handgun.
- Members of the military may carry a concealed weapon when on duty.
- Firearm registration is generally only required when ownership of a firearm is transferred.
- Possession of a handgun in a trunk of an automobile is legal.
- Possession of a short-barreled shotgun is illegal.
- Possession of a concealed rifle in public is legal.
- Carrying a loaded firearm in public is a misdemeanor.
- Carrying a loaded firearm in a vehicle is illegal.
- Possession of armor-piercing handgun ammunition is illegal.
- Possession of a firearm by a drug addict or a felon is illegal.
- Possession of a firearm on school property is illegal.
- Possession of a zip gun, wallet gun, or machine gun is illegal.
- Carrying a switchblade knife with a blade over two inches is illegal.
- Possession of a billy club, shobizue, shiruken, or silencer is a felony.
- Exhibiting a firearm in a threatening manner is illegal.
- Exhibiting any firearm in a rude or angry manner is a misdemeanor.
- Exhibiting an imitation firearm in a threatening manner is a misdemeanor.
- A handgun is a pistol, revolver, or other firearm with a barrel length of less than 16 inches.
- Possession of tear gas for purposes of self-defense is legal.

15-4b Discussion

The intent of the legislature in adopting the *Dangerous Weapons Control Act* was to limit, as far as possible, the use of instruments commonly associated with criminal activity *(People v. Washington,* 237 Cal. App. 2d 59). As one court noted, the Dangerous Weapons Control Act, Stats. 1923, c. 339, was designed to minimize the danger to public safety arising from free access to firearms that can be used for crimes of violence *(People v. Scott,* 24 Cal. 2d 774).

Section 12022.5 sets forth additional punishment where a firearm is used in the commission of certain crimes, is outside the ambit of the statutory definitions under this section of *pistol, revolver,* and *firearm capable of being concealed upon the person,* so that courts are free to interpret Section 12022.5 to achieve its individual objective without regard to the case law defining firearms for the purpose of prohibition involving ex-convicts *(People v. Hayden,* 30 Cal. App. 3d 446).

Firearm

In a trial for the possession of a traditional handgun, the full legal definition of *firearm* provided by model instruction might have confused jury and, thus, the trial court could instead give an alternative instruction that *a firearm* included handgun (*People v. Runnion*, 30 Cal. App. 4th 852). One court, however, noted that instructions in the case were insufficient to enable a jury to properly determine whether the robbery defendant possessed and used a firearm, for sentence enhancement purposes; since the instructions did not apprise jury of the necessity of determining whether the defendant possessed the barrel assembly in addition to the receiver, so as to comply with legislative changes in definition of "firearm," and evidence was conflicting as to what defendant had possessed and used (*People v. Gailord*, 13 Cal. App. 4th 1643).

The court held in *People v. Talkington* (140 Cal. App. 3d 557) that a tightly rolled tube of paper with one end closed with melted plastic, loaded with 30 match heads whose only purpose could have been to propel some kind of missile or other object, was a firearm for the purpose of the crime that prohibits the possession of weapon in a detention facility, notwithstanding the fact that there was no showing that the device would work or could injure someone.

A deadly weapon does not cease to be one by becoming temporarily inefficient (*People v. Williams*, 100 Cal. App. 149). A Taser TF-1 weapon is both a firearm capable of being concealed upon the person and a deadly weapon within the meaning of gun control laws (58 Ops. Atty. Gen. 777, 10-30-75).

Length of Barrel

In one case, information charging the defendants with violation of the statute prohibiting felons to carry firearms capable of being concealed upon person was sufficient to allege that the firearms had barrels of less than 12 inches in length, where the information referred to the statute, the jury was instructed as to the essential elements of offense, and evidence amply showed a violation of the statute (*People v. Israel*, 91 Cal. App. 2d 773).

Antiques

In a prosecution for the violation of Dangerous Weapons Control Act prohibiting possession by one previously convicted of felony of a firearm capable of being concealed on the person, the prosecution is not required to prove that the gun was not an antique pistol or revolver incapable of use as such (*People v. De Falco*, 176 Cal. App. 2d 590). This defense is an affirmative defense, and thus the defense must establish any exception for the weapon.

Local Regulation

A California city does not have the legislative authority to prohibit the possession of operative handguns within the city even if law enforcement officers are excluded from the prohibition (65 Ops. Atty. Gen. 457, 8-3-82).

Penal Code 12001.5—Sawed-Off Shotguns Not Authorized

. . . Nothing shall be construed as authorizing the manufacture, importation into the state, keeping for sale, or giving, lending, or possession of any sawed-off shotgun, as defined in Section 12020.

Penal Code 12002—Law Enforcement Equipment Exempt

[This section permits peace officers to carry wooden clubs, batons, or other authorized equipment. Certified uniformed security guards engaged in any lawful business, also, may carry wooden clubs or batons for purposes of protecting and preserving property or life within the scope of his or her employment.]

Penal Code 12020—Manufacture, Sale, Possession, etc., of Certain Weapons

[This section makes the manufacture, sale, possession, and so on, of the following weapons a felony or misdemeanor]:

1. Cane or wallet gun
2. Any firearm which is not immediately recognizable as a firearm
3. Any ammunition which contains or consists of any flechette dart
4. Any bullet containing or carrying an explosive agent
5. Any ballistic knife
6. Any instrument or weapon of the kind commonly known as a blackjack, slingshot, billy, nunchaku, sandclub, sandbag, or sawed-off shotgun
7. Metal knuckles
8. Any explosive substance, any dirk, or dagger.

Penal Code 12020.5—Advertising Sale of Weapons

[This section makes it unlawful for any person to advertise the sale of any prohibited weapon.]

Penal Code 148—Resisting or Obstructing Public Officer; Removal of Officer's Firearm

[This section makes it a felony for any person to remove or take a firearm from the person of, or immediate presence of, a public officer, during the commission of any offense. Any attempt to remove or take a firearm from a public officer is a misdemeanor. Taking of a weapon other than a firearm from a public officer is also a misdemeanor.]

Penal Code 12026—Possession at Residence or Place of Business

[This section permits an adult to purchase and to possess at his or her residence or place of business a firearm without permit or license.]

Penal Code 12026.1—Transportation in Trunk or Locked Container

[This section makes it legal for an adult to carry a concealed handgun within the locked trunk of a motor vehicle, or in a locked container other than the glove compartment. The handgun may be carried to and from the vehicle while concealed within the locked container.]

Penal Code 12022.5—Additional Punishment for Use of Firearm

[This section provides for an additional term of imprisonment for using a firearm in the commission of a felony. Note: This is a sentence enhancement, and therefore, must be alleged in the complaint, indictment or information and proved if not admitted by the accused.]

15-5 Loaning of Firearms

In 1994, the legislature made significant changes in the Dangerous Weapons Control Act to handle the problems involving the loaning of firearms to minors and others. The *Assembly Daily Journal for the 1993–94 Regular Session,* pages 5638–5640, contained the following letter dated March 8, 1994, from Senator Steve Peace regarding the intent of A.B. 482 (Stats. 1994, c. 23):

> The primary thrust of this bill is to address the possession and supplying to minors of handguns in a manner that attacks the criminal element, particularly gang members, while recognizing the possession and loan of handguns to minors for sporting and similar lawful purposes.
>
> In addition, the bill clarifies the status of firearms loans in California, equalizes the penalty for carrying a concealed pistol, revolver, or other firearm capable of being concealed upon the person on the person or in a vehicle, creates a crime for carrying a 'loaded', as defined, firearm with intent to commit a felony, and addresses various firearms trafficking issues.
>
> Two questions have arisen as to AB 482. The first question relates to the issue of firearms loans. The second question pertains to the law of self-defense as it relates to minors.
>
> As to firearms loans, current law requires that all sales, loans, and transfers of firearms be processed through a state licensed firearms dealer or a local law enforcement agency. However, there is a considerable dispute as to whether dealers can process loans.
>
> There are only two exemptions from the requirement that dealers process loans, and they are contained in Penal Code Section 12078(d) and (h). The burden of proof throughout the weapons area is upon a person to show that he or she is within an exemption (e.g., *People v. Jiminez,* 8 Cal. App. 4th 391). Unless a person falls within exemption, it is probable that loans are prohibited in this state now.
>
> To address the loan issue, AB 482 does the following:
>
> • Expressly states through amendments to numerous code sections that loans of firearms are to be processed by and through dealers and local law enforcement agencies in the same exact manner as sales and transfers.
>
> • Adds an exemption from dealer or law enforcement processing for loan of a long gun to a licensed hunter for processing for use in hunting during the duration of the specific hunting season. (New Penal Code Section 12078(q).)
>
> • Leaves in place verbatim the existing 30-day loan exemption and loan at target range exemption set forth above. As such, those persons who can now avail themselves of the existing exemptions can continue to do so.
>
> • Exempts from the requirements placed on dealers under Penal Code Sections 12071 and 12073 and subdivision (c) of Section 12072(c), the loan of a firearm by a dealer at a target range operated by or that are a part of the dealer's operation for use solely at the range. (See proposed Penal Code Section 12073(b)(7) and proposed Penal Code Section 12078(k)(6).)

- Clarifies through an exemption to Penal Code Section 12073 that delivery by a dealer of an unloaded firearm to a gunsmith for service or repair need not be DROS'd. This conforms Section 12073 to an existing Section 12071 and 12072 (c) and (d) exemption on this issue. (See current Penal Code Section 12078(e) and proposed Penal Code Section 12073(b)(8).)

- Exempts from the ban on sales, loans, and transfers of firearms to minors and from the requirement of dealer processing/law enforcement processing of sales, loans and transfers the various loans and transfers of firearms to minors permitted by this bill. (See proposed Penal Code Section 12078(p).)

The various exemptions in proposed Section 12078(p) for loans and transfers of firearms to minors from dealer processing are necessary as both existing federal and state laws prohibit firearms dealers from physically delivering pistols, revolvers, and other firearms capable of being concealed upon the person to persons under age 21 and any other firearm to a person under age 18.

Under the provisions of existing Penal Code Section 12082, dealers physically take possession of firearms when processing private transactions. As such, unless an exemption from Penal Code Section 12072(d) (dealer processing) exists, these loans and transfers cannot be legally accomplished.

As to the issue of self-defense, a question has arisen as to whether the amendments made to my Assembly Bill 482 to Penal Code Sections 12078 and 12101 in any way changes the law of self defense vis-a-vis the possession of a firearm by a minor, be it a pistol, revolver, rifle or shotgun, for that purpose by a minor.

It is my understanding that both the California Constitution and the California Penal Code contain general provisions pertaining to the rights of any individual to exercise self-defense and the defense of others and that those provisions affect the furnishing to and possession of firearms.

AB 482 is in no way intended to supersede, affect, expand or contract decisional and statutory authority on the possession of firearms by minors in the defense of themselves or others.

I hope that this clarifies legislative intent in this matter.

15-6 Altering Serial Numbers on Firearms

PC 12090 provides that any person who changes, alters, removes, or obliterates the name of the maker, model, manufacturer's number, or other mark of identification, including any distinguishing number or mark assigned by the Department of Justice on any pistol, revolver, or any other firearm, without first having secured written permission from the department to make such change, alteration, or removal shall be punished by imprisonment in the state prison. PC 12091 makes it a crime to possess any pistol or revolver upon which the name of the maker, model, manufacturer's number, or other mark of identification has been changed, altered, removed, or obliterated. It also shall be presumptive evidence that the possessor has changed, altered, removed, or obliterated the same.

Under PC 12092, the Department of Justice, upon request, may assign a distinguishing number or mark of identification to any pistol or revolver whenever it is without a manufacturer's number or other mark of identification or whenever the manufacturer's number or other mark of identification or the distinguishing number or mark assigned by the department has been destroyed or obliterated. PC 12093 states that any person may place or stamp on any pistol, revolver, or other firearm any number or identifying indicium, provided the number or identifying indicium does not change, alter, remove, or obliterate the manufacturer's name, number, model, or other mark of identification. This section does not prohibit restoration by the owner of the name of the maker, model, or of the original manufactor's number or other mark of identification when such restoration is authorized by the department, nor prevent any manufacturer from placing in the ordinary course of business the name of the maker, model, manufacturer's number, or other mark of identification upon a new firearm.

PC 12094 provides that any person with knowledge of any change, alteration, removal, or obliteration described herein, who buys, receives, disposes of, sells, offers for sale, or has in his possession any pistol, revolver, or other firearm that has had the name of the maker, model, or the manufacturer's number of other mark of identification including any distinguishing number or mark assigned by the Department of Justice changed, altered, removed, or obliterated is guilty of a misdemeanor.

15-7 Weapons on School Grounds

Penal Code 626.95 (b) encourages state and local authorities to cause signs to be posted around playgrounds and youth centers that warn against the possession of firearms upon the grounds of or within playgrounds or youth centers. *Playground* means any park or recreational area specifically designed to be used by children that has play equipment installed, including public grounds designed for athletic activities such as baseball, football, soccer, or basketball, or any similar facility located on public or private school grounds, or on city or county parks. *Youth center* means any public or private facility that is used to host recreational or social activities for minors while minors are present.

PC 626.10 makes it a crime for any person, except a duly appointed peace officer as defined in Chapter 4.5 (commencing with Section 830) of Title 3 of Part 2, a full-time paid peace officer of another state or the federal government who is carrying out official duties while in this state, a person summoned by any officer to assist in making arrests or preserving the peace while the person is actually engaged in assisting any officer, or a member of the military forces of this state or the United States who is engaged in the performance of his or her duties, who brings or possesses any dirk, dagger, ice pick, knife having a blade longer than two and a half inches, folding knife with a blade that locks into place, a razor with an unguarded blade, a taser, or a stun gun, as defined in subdivision (a) of Section 244.5, any instrument that expels a metallic projectile such as a BB or a pellet, through the force of air pressure, CO_2 pressure, or spring action, or any spot marker gun, upon the grounds of, or within, any public or private school providing instruction in kindergarten or any of grades 1 to 12, inclusive, is guilty of a public offense, punishable by imprisonment in a county jail not exceeding one year, or by imprisonment in the state prison.

The preceding prohibitions do not apply to any person who brings or possesses a knife having a blade longer than two and a half inches or a razor with an unguarded blade upon the grounds of, or within, a public or private school providing instruction in kindergarten or any of grades 1 to 12, inclusive, or any private university, state university, or community college at the direction of a faculty member of the private university, state university, or community college, or a certificated or classified employee of the school for use in a private university, state university, community college, or school-sponsored activity or class. In addition, any person may bring an instrument that expels a metallic projectile such as a BB or a pellet, through the force of air pressure, CO_2 pressure, or spring action, or any spot marker gun upon the grounds of, or within, a public or private school providing instruction in kindergarten or any of grades 1 to 12, inclusive, if the person has the written permission of the school principal or his or her designee.

Any certificated or classified employee or school peace officer of a public or private school providing instruction in kindergarten or any of grades 1 to 12, inclusive, may seize any prohibited weapons, and any certificated or classified employee or school peace officer of any private university, state university, or community college may seize any of the weapons from the possession of any person upon the grounds of, or within, the school if he or she knows, or has reasonable cause to know, the person is prohibited from bringing or possessing the weapon upon the grounds of, or within, the school. A *dirk* or *dagger* means a knife or other instrument with or without a handguard that is capable of ready use as a stabbing weapon that may inflict great bodily injury or death.

15-8 Mental Patients and Deadly Weapons

WI 8100 provides that a person shall not have in his or her possession or under his or her custody or control, or purchase or receive, or attempt to purchase or receive, any firearms whatsoever or any other deadly weapon, if he or she has been admitted to a facility and is receiving inpatient treatment and, in the opinion of the attending health professional who is primarily responsible for the patient's treatment of a mental disorder, is a danger to self or others, even though the patient has consented to that treatment. A person is not subject to this subdivision once he or she is discharged from the facility.

The individual may petition the superior court of his or her county of residence for an order that he or she may own, possess, have custody or control over, receive, or purchase firearms. At the time the petition is filed, the clerk of the court shall set a hearing date and notify the person, the Department of Justice, and the district attorney. The people of the state of California shall be the respondent in the proceeding and shall be represented by the district attorney. Upon motion of the district attorney, or upon its own motion, the superior court may transfer the petition to the county in which the person resided at the time of the statements, or the county in which the person made the statements.

Under WI 8101, any person who knowingly supplies, sells, gives, or allows possession or control of a deadly weapon to any person described in Section 8100 or 8103 (person receiving treatment for mental problems) is punishable by imprisonment in the state prison, or in a county jail for a period of not exceeding one year, by a fine of not exceeding one thousand dollars ($1,000), or by both the fine and imprisonment. If the deadly weapon is a firearm, the defendant may be punished by imprisonment in the state prison for two, three, or four years.

Whenever a person who has been detained or apprehended for examination of his or her mental condition or who is a person described in Section 8100 or 8103 is found to own, have in his or her possession, or have under his or her control any firearm whatsoever, or any other deadly weapon, the firearm or other deadly weapon shall be confiscated by any law enforcement agency or peace officer, who shall retain custody of the firearm or other deadly weapon.

15-9 Possession of Switchblade

Penal Code 653k—Switchblade Knives

[This section makes it a misdemeanor to have a switchblade knife in the passenger compartment of a vehicle, including the glove compartment. *Switchblade* is defined as a knife having the appearance of a pocket knife, which includes a spring blade knife, snapblade knife, gravity knife, or any other similar type knife with a blade or blades that are two or more inches long and that can be released by a flick of a button, pressure on the handle, flip of the wrist, or other mechanical device.]

15-10 Possession of Firearm by Felon

Penal Code 12021—Convicts, Persons Convicted of Offenses Involving Violent Use of Firearms, and Addicts Prohibited from Possessing Firearms

[This section makes it unlawful for any person who has previously been convicted of a felony under the laws of any state or the federal government to possess any firearm. Prohibition under this section does not apply to those convicted of a felony under federal law unless the offense is similar to a felony in the state of California or the accused served at least 30 days in a federal correctional facility or received a fine of more than $1,000.]

Penal Code 12021.1—Persons Previously Convicted of Violent Offense Prohibited from Possessing Firearms

[This section makes it a felony or misdemeanor for persons previously convicted of a violent offense (26 violent offenses listed in the section) to possess any firearm.]

15-11 Concealed Weapons

Under PC 12025, a person is guilty of carrying a concealed firearm when he or she does any of the following:

(1) Carries concealed within any vehicle which is under his or her control or direction any pistol, revolver, or other firearm capable of being concealed upon the person.
(2) Carries concealed upon his or her person any pistol, revolver, or other firearm capable of being concealed upon the person. Firearms carried openly in belt holsters are not concealed within the meaning of this section.

PC 12026.2 contains miscellaneous exceptions to prohibitions against concealed firearms. The exceptions include:

(1) The possession of a firearm by an authorized participant in a motion picture, television, or video production or entertainment event when the participant lawfully uses the firearm as part of that production or event or while going directly to, or coming directly from, that production or event.
(2) The possession of a firearm in a locked container by a member of any club or organization, organized for the purpose of lawfully collecting and lawfully displaying pistols, revolvers, or other firearms, while the member is at meetings of the clubs or organizations or while going directly to, and coming directly from, those meetings.
(3) The transportation of a firearm by a participant when going directly to, or coming directly from, a recognized safety or hunter safety class, or a recognized sporting event involving that firearm.

(4) The transportation of a firearm by a person when going directly to, or coming directly from, a fixed place of business or private residential property for the purpose of the lawful repair or the lawful transfer, sale, or loan of that firearm.

(5) The transportation of a firearm by a person listed in Section 12026 when going directly from the place where that person lawfully received that firearm to that person's place of residence or place of business or to private property owned or lawfully possessed by that person.

(6) The transportation of a firearm by a person when going directly to, or coming directly from, a gun show, swap meet, or similar event to which the public is invited, for the purpose of displaying that firearm in a lawful manner.

(7) The transportation of a firearm by an authorized employee or agent of a supplier of firearms when going directly to, or coming directly from, a motion picture, television, or video production or entertainment event for the purpose of providing that firearm to an authorized participant to lawfully use as a part of that production or event.

(8) The transportation of a firearm by a person when going directly to, or coming directly from, a target range, which holds a regulatory or business license, for the purposes of practicing shooting at targets with that firearm at that target range.

(9) The transportation of a firearm by a person when going directly to, or coming directly from, a place designated by a person authorized to issue licenses pursuant to Section 12050 when done at the request of the issuing agency so that the issuing agency can determine whether or not a license should be issued to that person to carry that firearm.

(10) The transportation of a firearm by a person when going directly to, or coming directly from, a law enforcement agency for the purpose of a lawful transfer, sale, or loan of that firearm pursuant to Section 12084.

(11) The transportation of a firearm by a person when going directly to, or coming directly from, a lawful camping activity for the purpose of having that firearm available for lawful personal protection while at the lawful campsite. This paragraph shall not be construed to override the statutory authority granted to the Department of Parks and Recreation or any other state or local governmental agencies to promulgate rules and regulations governing the administration of parks and campgrounds.

(12) The transportation of a firearm by a person when going directly to, or coming directly from, a gun show or event, as defined in Section 178.100 of Title 27 of the Code of Federal Regulations, for the purpose of lawfully transferring, selling, or loaning that firearm in accordance with subdivision (d) of Section 12072.

The term *locked container* means a secure container that is fully enclosed and locked by a padlock, key lock, combination lock, or similar locking device. The term "locked container" does not include the utility or glove compartment of a motor vehicle.

PC 12027 also contains exceptions to the prohibition regarding the carrying of concealed weapons. Some of those exceptions follow:

(1) Any peace officer whether active or honorably retired and other duty appointed peace officers who during the course and scope of their employment as peace officers were authorized to, and did, carry firearms, full-time paid peace officers of other states and the federal government who are carrying out official duties while in California, or any person summoned by any of these officers to assist in making arrests or preserving the peace while he or she is actually engaged in assisting that officer. Any peace officer described in this paragraph who has been honorably retired shall be issued an identification certificate by the law enforcement agency from which the officer has retired. The issuing agency may charge a fee necessary to cover any reasonable expenses incurred by the agency in issuing certificates pursuant to this subdivision. The term *honorably retired* includes all peace officers who have qualified for, and have accepted, a service or disability retirement. The term "honorably retired" does not include an officer who has agreed to a service retirement in lieu of termination.

(2) The possession or transportation of unloaded pistols, revolvers, or other firearms capable of being concealed upon the person as merchandise by a person who is engaged in the business of manufacturing, importing, wholesaling, repairing, or dealing in firearms and who is licensed to engage in that business or the authorized representative or authorized agent of that person while engaged in the lawful course of the business.

(3) Members of the Army, Navy, Air Force, Coast Guard, or Marine Corps of the United States, or the National Guard, when on duty, or organizations which are by law authorized to purchase or receive those weapons from the United States or this state.

(4) The carrying of unloaded pistols, revolvers, or other firearms capable of being concealed upon the person by duly authorized military or civil organizations while parading, or the members thereof when going to and from the places of meeting of their respective organizations.

(5) Guards or messengers of common carriers, banks, and other financial institutions while actually employed in and about the shipment, transportation, or delivery of any money, treasure, bullion, bonds, or other thing of value within this state.

(6) Members of any club or organization organized for the purpose of practicing shooting at targets upon established target ranges, whether public or private, while the members are using pistols, revolvers, or other firearms capable of being concealed upon the person upon the target ranges, or transporting these firearms unloaded when going to and from the ranges.

(7) Licensed hunters or fishermen carrying pistols, revolvers, or other firearms capable of being concealed upon the person while engaged in hunting or fishing, or transporting those firearms unloaded when going to or returning from the hunting or fishing expedition.

(8) Transportation of unloaded firearms by a person operating a licensed common carrier or an authorized agent or employee thereof when transported in conformance with applicable federal law.

(9) Upon approval of the sheriff of the county in which they reside, honorably retired federal officers or agents of federal law enforcement agencies, including, but not limited to, the Federal Bureau of Investigation, the Secret Service, the United States Customs Service, the Federal Bureau of Alcohol, Tobacco, and Firearms, the Federal Bureau of Narcotics, the Drug Enforcement Administration, the United States Border Patrol, and officers or agents of the Internal Revenue Service who were authorized to carry weapons while on duty, who were assigned to duty within the state for a period of not less than one year, or who retired from active service in the state.

Retired federal officers or agents shall provide the sheriff with certification from the agency from which they retired certifying their service in the state, the nature of their retirement, and indicating the agency's concurrence that the retired federal officer or agent should be accorded the privilege of carrying a concealed firearm.

Penal Code 12040—Masked during Criminal Possession of Firearm

(a) A person commits criminal possession of a firearm when he or she carries a firearm in a public place or on any public street while masked so as to hide his or her identity.
(b) Criminal possession of a firearm is punishable by imprisonment in the state prison or by imprisonment in a county jail not to exceed one year.
(c) Subdivision (a) shall not apply to the following:

(1) A peace officer who is in the performance of his or her duties.
(2) Full-time paid peace officers of other states and the federal government who are carrying out official duties while in this state.
(3) Any person summoned by any of the officers enumerated in paragraph (1) or (2) to assist in making arrests or preserving the peace while he or she is actually engaged in assisting that officer.
(4) The possession of an unloaded firearm or a firearm loaded with blank ammunition by an authorized participant in, or while rehearsing for, a motion picture, television, video production, entertainment event, entertainment activity, or lawfully organized and conducted activity when the participant lawfully uses the firearm as part of that production, event, or activity.
(5) The possession of a firearm by a licensed hunter while actually engaged in lawful hunting, or while going directly to or returning directly from the hunting expedition.

Penal Code 12050—Police May Issue License to Carry Concealed Weapons

(a)

(1) The sheriff of a county or the chief or other head of a municipal police department of any city or city and county, upon proof that the person applying is of good moral character, that good cause exists for the issuance, and that the person applying is a resident of the county, may issue to that person a license to carry a pistol, revolver, or other firearm capable of being concealed upon the person in either one of the following formats:

(A) A license to carry a concealed pistol, revolver, or other firearm capable of being concealed upon the person.

(B) Where the population of the county is less than 200,000 persons according to the most recent federal decennial census, a license to carry loaded and exposed in that county a pistol, revolver, or other firearm capable of being concealed upon the person.

(2) A license issued pursuant to this section is valid for any period of time not to exceed one year from the date of the license, or in the case of a peace officer appointed pursuant to Section 830.6, three years from the date of the license.

(b) A license may include any reasonable restrictions or conditions which the issuing authority deems warranted, including restrictions as to the time, place, manner, and circumstances under which the person may carry a pistol, revolver, or other firearm capable of being concealed upon the person.

(c) Any restrictions imposed pursuant to subdivision (b) shall be indicated on any license issued.

Penal Code 12020—Manufacture, Importation, Sale, Possession or Carrying Concealed Weapons

[This section makes it a felony (wobbler) to manufacture, import, sell, possess, or carry a concealed or disguised firearm or other deadly weapon. A recent modification to the section included "camouflaging firearm containers" within the prohibition. Concealed weapons include cane guns, wallet guns, sawed-off shotguns, flechette darts, and ballistic knives.]

15-12 Carrying a Loaded Weapon

Penal Code 12031—Loaded Firearms—Carrying in Public Place or in Vehicle

[This section prohibits the carrying of a loaded firearm in public places or in a vehicle.]

15-13 Unsafe Storage of Firearms

Penal Code 12035—Criminal Storage of a Firearm

Any person who keeps any loaded firearm within any premises which is under his or her custody of control where a child under the age of 14 years may gain access to the weapon is guilty of PC 12035.

PC 12800(b) contains legislative findings regarding storage of weapons. Parts of that section are set forth below:

(b) The Legislature further finds and declares as follows:

(1) It has been documented that firearms accidents are one of the leading causes of accidental deaths for children ages 14 years and under. Almost all of the firearms involved in these accidents are pistols, revolvers, or other firearms capable of being concealed upon the person.

(2) On average, one child 18 years of age or under is accidentally killed, and 10 are injured, by a firearm every day across the United States.

(3) Firearm wounds to children who are 16 years of age and under have increased 300 percent in major urban areas since 1986.

(4) In 1987, the last year for which statistics are available, there were 44 accidental firearms deaths among California children 18 years of age and younger.

(5) Although statistics are not kept for injuries resulting from accidental shootings, it is estimated that for every firearms death, there are at least five nonfatal firearms injuries. Using this figure, it is estimated that approximately 220 California children were injured in nonfatal, accidental shootings in 1987.

(6) Research has indicated that easy access in homes to loaded pistols, revolvers, and other firearms capable of being concealed upon the person is a chief contributing factor in unintentional shootings of children. Nearly 8,700,000 youngsters in the United States have access to pistols, revolvers, and other firearms capable of being concealed upon the person.

(7) Educating purchasers and transferees of pistols, revolvers, and other firearms capable of being concealed upon the person, and persons who are loaned pistols, revolvers, or other firearms capable of being concealed upon the person pursuant to Section 12071, 12072, or 12084, would make them more aware of their responsibilities as gun owners and would help to eliminate the ignorance or neglect that leads to children playing with loaded pistols, revolvers, and other firearms capable of being concealed upon the person.

(c) It is, therefore, the intent of the Legislature, in enacting this article, to require in this state that purchasers and transferees of pistols, revolvers, and other firearms capable of being concealed upon the person, and persons who are loaned pistols, revolvers, or other firearms capable of being concealed upon the person pursuant to Section 12071, 12072, or 12084, obtain a basic familiarity with those firearms, including, but not limited to, the safe handling and storage of those firearms, methods for childproofing those firearms, and the responsibilities associated with ownership of those firearms.

(d) It is further the intent of the Legislature, in enacting this article, to establish a program that would help to eliminate the potential for accidental deaths and injuries, particularly those involving children, which are caused by the unsafe handling of pistols, revolvers, and other firearms capable of being concealed upon the person.

15-14 Tear Gas

Penal Code 12402—Tear Gas Weapon Defined

The term *tear gas weapon* as used in this chapter shall apply to and include:

(a) Any shell, cartridge, or bomb capable of being discharged or exploded, when the discharge or explosion will cause or permit the release or emission of tear gases.

(b) Any revolvers, pistols, fountain pen guns, billies, or other form of device, portable or fixed, intended for the projection or release of tear gas except those regularly manufactured and sold for use with firearm ammunition.

Penal Code 12403.7—Possession by Others; Qualifications

(a) Notwithstanding any other law, any person may purchase, possess, or use tear gas and tear gas weapons for the projection or release of tear gas if the tear gas and tear gas weapons are used solely for self-defense purposes, subject to the following requirements:

(1) No person convicted of a felony or any crime involving an assault under the laws of the United States, of the state of California, or any other state, government, or country or convicted of misuse of tear gas under paragraph (8) shall purchase, possess, or use tear gas or tear gas weapons.

(2) No person who is addicted to any narcotic drug shall purchase, possess, or use tear gas or tear gas weapons.

(3) No person shall sell or furnish any tear gas or tear gas weapon to a minor.

(4) No person who is a minor shall purchase, possess, or use tear gas or tear gas weapons.

(5)

  (A) No person shall purchase, possess, or use any tear gas weapon that expels a projectile, or that expels the tear gas by any method other than an aerosol spray, or that contains more than 2.5 ounces net weight of aerosol spray.

  (B) Every tear gas container and tear gas weapon that may be lawfully purchased, possessed, and used pursuant to this section shall have a label that states: "WARNING: The use of this substance or device for any purpose other than self-defense is a crime under the law. The contents are dangerous—use with care."

  (C) After January 1, 1984, every tear gas container and tear gas weapon that may be lawfully purchased, possessed, and used pursuant to this section shall have a label that discloses the date on which the useful life of the tear gas weapon expires.

  (D) Every tear gas container and tear gas weapon that may be lawfully purchased pursuant to this section shall be accompanied at the time of purchase by printed instructions for use.

(6) Effective March 1, 1994, every tear gas container and tear gas weapon that may be lawfully purchased, possessed, and used pursuant to this section be accompanied by an insert including directions for use, first aid information, safety and storage information, and explanation of the legal ramifications of improper use of the tear gas container or tear gas product.

(7) Any person who uses tear gas or tear gas weapons except in self-defense is guilty of a public offense and is punishable by imprisonment in a state prison for 16 months, or two or three years or in a county jail not to exceed one year or by a fine not to exceed one thousand dollars ($1,000), or by both the fine and imprisonment, except that if the use is against a peace officer, as defined in Chapter 4.5 (commencing with Section 830) of Title 3 of Part 2, engaged in the performance of his or her official duties and the person committing the offense knows or reasonably should know that the victim is a peace officer, the offense is punishable by imprisonment in a state prison for 16 months or two or three years or by a fine of one thousand dollars ($1,000), or by both the fine and imprisonment.

Penal Code 12403.8—Possession by Minor; Qualifications

(a) Notwithstanding paragraph (4) of subdivision (a) of Section 12403.7, a minor who has attained the age of 16 years may purchase and possess tear gas or tear gas weapons pursuant to this chapter if he or she is accompanied by a parent or guardian, or has the written consent of his or her parent or guardian.

Penal Code 12420—Tear Gas or Tear Gas Weapon; Sale, Possession or Transportation Prohibited

Any person, firm, or corporation who within this state knowingly sells or offers for sale, possesses, or transports any tear gas or tear gas weapon, except as permitted under the provisions of this chapter, is guilty of a public offense and upon conviction thereof shall be punishable by imprisonment in the county jail for not exceeding one year or by a fine not to exceed two thousand dollars ($2,000), or by both.

Penal Code 12421—Maker's Name and Serial Number

Each tear gas weapon sold, transported, or possessed under the authority of this chapter shall bear the name of the manufacturer and a serial number applied by him.

Penal Code 12422—Alteration of Identification

Any person who changes, alters, removes or obliterates the name of the manufacturer, the serial number or any other mark of identification on any tear gas weapon is guilty of a public offense and, upon conviction, shall be punished by imprisonment in the state prison or by a fine of not more than two thousand dollars ($2,000) or by both.

Possession of any such weapon upon which the same shall have been changed, altered, removed, or obliterated, shall be presumptive evidence that such possessor has changed, altered, removed, or obliterated the same.

Penal Code 12423—Permit to Possess or Transport

The Department of Justice may issue a permit for the possession and transportation of tear gas or tear gas weapons that are not intended or certified for personal self-defense purposes, upon proof that good cause exists for the issuance thereof to the applicant for this permit. The permit may also allow the applicant to install, maintain, and operate a protective system involving the use of tear gas or tear gas weapons in any place which is accurately and completely described in the application for the permit.

Penal Code 635—Manufacture, Sale, and Possession of Eavesdropping Devices; Punishment; Recidivists; Exceptions

15-15 Eavesdropping Equipment

(a) Every person who manufactures, assembles, sells, offers for sale, advertises for sale, possesses, transports, imports, or furnishes to another any device which is primarily or exclusively designed or intended for eavesdropping upon the communication of another, or any device which is primarily or exclusively designed or intended for the unauthorized interception or reception of communications between cellular radio telephones or between a cellular radio telephone and a landline telephone in violation of Section 632.5, or communications between cordless telephones or between a cordless telephone and a landline telephone in violation of Section 632.6, shall be punished by a fine not exceeding two thousand five hundred dollars ($2,500), by imprisonment in the county jail not exceeding one year, or in the state prison, or by both that fine and imprisonment. . . .

(b) This section does not apply to either of the following:

(1) An act otherwise prohibited by this section when performed by any of the following:

(A) A communication utility or an officer, employee or agent thereof for the purpose of construction, maintenance, conduct, or operation of, or otherwise incident to the use of, the services or facilities of the utility.

(B) A state, county, or municipal law enforcement agency or an agency of the federal government.

(C) A person engaged in selling devices specified in subdivision (a) for use by, or resale to, agencies of a foreign government under terms approved by the federal government, communication utilities, state, county, or municipal law enforcement agencies, or agencies of the federal government.

(2) Possession by a subscriber to communication utility service of a device specified in subdivision (a) furnished by the utility pursuant to its tariffs.

15-16 Federal Gun Laws

There are also numerous federal statutes that deal with the possession of dangerous weapons. The first major federal law was the *National Firearms Act of 1934* which regulated the possession of machine guns and short-barreled firearms. Many of the federal statutes overlap state laws. Generally speaking, the federal laws provide for harsher penalties than comparable state laws.

Practicum

Joe is arrested for possession of a shotgun with a short barrel on school property. He claims that the weapon was given to him by another student and was an antique that was intended to be delivered to the school museum. What crimes, if any, is he guilty of?

Discussion Questions

1. Define *firearm*.
2. Why do the statutes allow an adult to possess a firearm without a permit in his or her residence?
3. What constitutes a pistol?
4. Differentiate between the crimes of shooting at an inhabited dwelling and shooting at an occupied building.

5. What was the intent of the legislature in adopting the Dangerous Weapons Control Act?
6. Define *sawed-off shotgun*.
7. When is it illegal to possess tear gas?

Self-Study Quiz

Self-Study Quiz

True/False

1. A deadly weapon can be any object capable of causing death or great bodily injury from the manner in which it is used.
2. The Dangerous Weapons Control Act applies only to persons using illegal weapons.
3. It is a misdemeanor to willfully discharge a firearm at an inhabited dwelling.
4. Discharging a firearm at an occupied motor vehicle is a specific intent crime.
5. The term *firearm* includes an unloaded pistol.
6. A sawed-off shotgun may also be considered as a pistol.
7. A weapon that temporarily does not function properly is no longer considered a dangerous weapon.
8. The crime of exhibiting a firearm in an angry manner requires that the firearm be pointed at someone in an angry manner.
9. California cities may prohibit weapons within their city limits by citizens.
10. The Dangerous Weapons Control Act prohibits the drawing of a weapon in self-defense.
11. It is illegal to loan a weapon to a felon.
12. It is permissible to carry a loaded weapon in an automobile if it is locked in the trunk of the vehicle.
13. A tear gas weapon includes a cartridge that is capable of being discharged or exploded, and when discharged or exploded will cause the emission of tear gas.
14. A person who is addicted to narcotic drugs may possess tear gas for self-protection but not any firearms.
15. Tear gas weapons are required to bear a serial number and the name of the manufacturer.

Regulatory Crimes and Other Misconduct

The duty to disclose knowledge of crime rests upon all citizens.
Justice Robert H. Jackson
Stein v. New York, 346 U.S. 156, 184 (1953)

16-1 Sexually Violent Predators

The California State Legislature has determined that a small but extremely dangerous group of sexually violent predators have diagnosable mental disorders that can be identified while they are incarcerated. These persons are not considered safe to be at large and, if released, present a danger to the health and safety of others in that they are likely to engage in acts of sexual violence. The legislature, before establishing a sexually violent predators commitment process, determined that California needed a civil commitment procedure to allow the state a means to place and treat such persons in a secure mental facility.

16-1a Definitions

WI 6600 states that a *sexually violent predator* means a person who has been convicted of a sexually violent offense against two or more victims for which he or she received a determinate sentence (fixed) and who has a diagnosed mental disorder that makes the person a danger to the health and safety of others in that it is likely that he or she will engage in sexually violent criminal behavior in the future.

Conviction of one or more of the crimes enumerated in WI 6600 shall constitute evidence that may support a court or jury determination that the person is a sexually violent predator, but shall not be the sole basis for the determination. The existence of any prior convictions may be shown with documentary evidence. The details underlying the commission of an offense that led to a prior conviction, including a predatory relationship with the victim, may be shown by documentary evidence, including, but not limited to, preliminary hearing transcripts, trial transcripts, probation and sentencing reports, and evaluations by the State Department of Mental Health. Jurors shall be admonished that they may not find a person a sexually violent predator based on prior offenses absent relevant evidence of a currently diagnosed mental disorder that makes the person a danger to the health and safety of others in that it is likely that he or she will engage in sexually violent criminal behavior.

Sexually violent offense means the following acts when committed by force, violence, duress, menace, or fear of immediate and unlawful bodily injury on the victim or another person, and that are committed on, before, or after the effective date of WI 6600 and result in a conviction or a finding of not guilty by reason of insanity, as provided in subdivision (a): a felony violation of paragraph (2) of subdivision (a) of Section 261 (forcible rape), paragraph (1) of subdivision (a) of Section 262 (forcible spousal rape), Section 264.1 (rape in concert), subdivision (a) or (b) of Section 288 (lewd or lascivious act with a child under age 14), or subdivision (a) of Section 289 of the Penal Code (penetration of genital or anal with foreign object), or sodomy or oral copulation in violation of Section 286 or 288a of the Penal Code.

Diagnosed mental disorder includes a congenital or acquired condition affecting the emotional or volitional capacity that predisposes the person to the commission of criminal sexual acts in a degree constituting the person a menace to the health and safety of others. "Danger to the health and safety of others" does not require proof of a recent overt act while the offender is in custody. *Predatory* means an act is directed toward a stranger, a person of casual acquaintance with whom no substantial relationship exists, or an individual with whom a relationship has been established or promoted for the primary purpose of victimization. *Recent overt act* means any criminal act that manifests a likelihood that the actor may engage in sexually violent predatory criminal behavior.

16-1b Discussion

Under WI 6601, whenever the Director of Corrections determines that an individual who is in custody under the jurisdiction of the Department of Corrections, and who is either serving a determinate prison sentence or whose parole has been revoked, may be a sexually violent predator, the director shall, at least six months prior to that individual's scheduled date for release from prison, refer the person for evaluation in accordance with this section. However, if the inmate was received by the department with less than nine months of his or her sentence to serve, or if the inmate's release date is modified by judicial or administrative action, the director may refer the person for evaluation in accordance with this section at a date that is less than six months prior to the inmate's scheduled release date.

The person shall be screened by the Department of Corrections and the Board of Prison Terms based on whether the person has committed a sexually violent predatory offense and on a review of the person's social, criminal, and institutional history. This screening shall be conducted in accordance with a structured screening instrument developed and updated by the State Department of Mental Health in consultation with the Department of Corrections. If, as a result of this screening, it is determined that the person is likely to be a sexually violent predator, the Department of Corrections shall refer the person to the State Department of Mental Health for a full evaluation of whether the person meets the criteria.

The State Department of Mental Health shall evaluate the person in accordance with a standardized assessment protocol, developed and updated by the State Department of Mental Health, to determine whether the person is a sexually violent predator as defined in this article. The standardized assessment protocol shall require assessment of diagnosable mental disorders, as well as various factors known to be associated with the risk of reoffense among sex offenders. Risk factors to be considered shall include criminal and psychosexual history; type, degree, and duration of sexual deviance; and severity of mental disorder.

The person shall be evaluated by two practicing psychiatrists or psychologists, or one practicing psychiatrist and one practicing psychologist, designated by the director of mental health. If both evaluators concur that the person has a diagnosed mental disorder such that he or she is likely to engage in acts of sexual violence without appropriate treatment and custody, the director of mental health shall forward a request for a petition for commitment under Section 6602 to the county designated in subdivision (i). Copies of the evaluation reports and any other supporting documents shall be made available to the attorney designated by the county pursuant to subdivision (i) who may file a petition for commitment.

If one of the professionals performing the evaluation does not concur that the person meets the criteria, but the other professional concludes that the person meets those criteria, the director of mental health shall arrange for further examination of the person by two independent professionals.

If the State Department of Mental Health determines that the person is a sexually violent predator, the director of mental health shall forward a request for a petition to be filed for commitment. Copies of the evaluation reports and any other supporting documents shall be made available to the attorney designated by the county who may file a petition for commitment in the superior court. If the county's designated counsel concurs with the recommendation, a petition for commitment shall be filed in the superior court of the county in which the person was convicted of the offense for which he or she was committed to the jurisdiction of the Department of Corrections. The petition shall be filed, and the proceedings shall be handled, by either the district attorney or the county counsel of that county. The county board of supervisors shall designate either the district attorney or the county counsel to assume responsibility for proceedings under this article.

A judge of the superior court shall review the petition and shall determine whether there is probable cause to believe that the individual named in the petition is likely to engage in sexually violent predatory criminal behavior upon his or her release. The person named in the petition shall be entitled to assistance of counsel at the probable cause hearing. If the judge determines there is not probable cause, he or she shall dismiss the petition and any person subject to parole shall report to parole. If the judge determines that there is probable cause, the judge shall order that the person remain in custody in a secure facility until a trial is completed and shall order that a trial be conducted to determine whether the person is, by reason of a diagnosed mental disorder, a danger to the health and safety of others in that the person is likely to engage in acts of sexual violence upon his or her release from the jurisdiction of the Department of Corrections or other secure facility.

A person subject to this article shall be entitled to a trial by jury, the assistance of counsel, the right to retain experts or professional persons to perform an examination on his or her behalf, and the right to have access to all relevant medical and psychological records and reports. In the case of a person who is indigent, the court shall appoint counsel to assist him or her, and, upon the person's request, assist the person in obtaining an expert or professional person to perform an examination or participate in the trial on the person's behalf.

A unanimous verdict shall be required in any jury trial. The court or jury shall determine whether, beyond a reasonable doubt, the person is a sexually violent predator. If the court or jury is not satisfied beyond a reasonable doubt that the person is a sexually violent predator, the court shall direct that the person be released at the conclusion of the term for which he or she was initially sentenced, or that the person be unconditionally released at the end of parole, whichever is applicable. If the court or jury determines that the person is a sexually violent predator, the person shall be committed for two years to the custody of the State Department of Mental Health for appropriate treatment and confinement in a secure facility designated by the director of mental health, and the person shall not be kept in actual custody longer than two years unless a subsequent extended commitment is obtained from the court. Time spent on conditional release shall not count toward the two-year term of commitment, unless the person is placed in a locked facility by the conditional release program, in which case the time in a locked facility shall count toward the two-year term of commitment. The facility shall be located on the grounds of an institution under the jurisdiction of the Department of Corrections.

A person found to be a sexually violent predator and committed to the custody of the State Department of Mental Health shall have a current examination of his or her mental condition made at least once every year. The person may retain, or if he or she is indigent and so requests, the court may appoint, a qualified expert or professional person to examine him or her, and the expert or professional person shall have access to all records concerning the person.

16-2 Fish and Game Laws

Fish and Game Code 2005—Lights and Sniperscopes; Exemptions

It is unlawful to use an artificial light to assist in the taking of game birds, game mammals, or game fish, except that this section shall not apply to sport fishing in ocean waters or other waters where night fishing is permitted if the lights are not used on or as part of the fishing tackle, commercial fishing, nor to the taking of mammals. . . .

It is unlawful for any person, or one or more persons, to throw or cast the rays of any spotlight, headlight, or other artificial light on any highway or in any field, woodland, or forest where game mammals, fur-bearing mammals, or nongame mammals are commonly found, or upon any game mammal, fur-bearing mammal, or nongame mammal, while having in his possession or under his control any firearm or weapon with which such mammal could be killed, even though the mammal is not killed, injured, shot at, or otherwise pursued.

It is unlawful to use or possess at any time any infrared or similar light used in connection with an electronic viewing device sometimes designated as a sniper-scope to assist in the taking of birds, mammals, amphibia, or fish.

The provisions of this section shall not apply to the following:

(a) To the use of a hand held flashlight no larger, nor emitting more light, than a two-cell, three-volt flashlight, provided such light is not affixed in any way to a weapon, or to the use of a lamp or lantern which does not cast a directional beam of light.

(b) In the case of headlights of a motor vehicle operated in a usual manner and there is no attempt or intent to locate a game mammal, fur-bearing mammal, or nongame mammal.

(c) To the owner, or his employee, of land devoted to the agricultural industry while on such land, or land controlled by such an owner and in connection with such agricultural industry.

(d) Such other uses as the commission may authorize by regulation.

No person shall be arrested for violation of this section except by a peace officer.

Food and Agriculture Code 2006—Loaded Rifle or Shotgun in Vehicle

It is unlawful to possess a loaded rifle or shotgun in any vehicle or conveyance or its attachments which is standing on or along or is being driven on or along any public highway or other way open to the public.

A rifle or shotgun shall be deemed to be loaded for the purposes of this section when there is an unexpended cartridge or shell in the firing chamber but not when the only cartridges or shells are in the magazine.

The provisions of this section shall not apply to peace officers or members of the armed forces of this State or the United States, while on duty or going to or returning from duty.

Food and Agriculture Code 3002—Shoot Game from Vehicle, Boat, or Plane

It is unlawful to shoot at any game bird or mammal, including a marine mammal . . . from a powerboat, sailboat, motor vehicle, or airplane.

Food and Agriculture Code 3003.5—Pursue, Drive, or Herd Any Bird or Mammal with Motorized Vehicle

It is unlawful to pursue, drive, or herd any bird or mammal with any motorized water, land, or air vehicle, including, but not limited to, a motor vehicle, airplane, powerboat, or snowmobile. . . .

16-3 Welfare Fraud

WI 10980—Aid or Public Assistance; Unlawful Acts; Punishments

(a) Any person who, willfully and knowingly, with the intent to deceive, makes a false statement or representation or knowingly fails to disclose a material fact in order to obtain aid . . . or who, knowing he or she is not entitled thereto, attempts to obtain aid or to continue to receive aid to which he or she is not entitled, or to receive a larger amount than that to which he or she is legally entitled, is guilty of a misdemeanor, punishable by imprisonment in the county jail for a period of not more than six months, a fine of not more than five hundred dollars ($500), or by both such imprisonment and fine.

(b) Any person who knowingly makes more than one application for aid under the provisions of this division with the intent of establishing multiple entitlements for any person for the same period or who makes an application for such aid for a fictitious or nonexistent person or by claiming a false identity for any person is guilty of a felony, punishable by imprisonment in the state prison for a period of 16 months, two years, or three years, a fine of not more than five thousand dollars ($5,000), or by both such imprisonment and fine, or by imprisonment in the county jail for a period of not more than one year, or a fine of not more than one thousand dollars ($1,000), or by both such imprisonment and fine.

(c) Whenever any person has, by means of false statement or representation or by impersonation or other fraudulent device, obtained or retained aid under the provisions of this division for himself or herself or for a child not in fact entitled thereto, the person obtaining such aid shall be punished as follows:

(1) If the total amount of such aid obtained or retained is four hundred dollars ($400) or less, by imprisonment in the county jail for a period of not more than six months, a fine of not more than five hundred dollars ($500), or by both such imprisonment and fine.

(2) If the total amount of such aid obtained or retained is more than four hundred dollars ($400), by imprisonment in the state prison for a period of 16 months, two years, or three years, a fine of not more than five thousand dollars ($5,000), or by both such imprisonment and fine; or by imprisonment in the county jail for a period of not more than one year, or a fine of not more than one thousand dollars ($1,000), or by both such imprisonment and fine.

(d) Any person who knowingly uses, transfers, acquires, or possesses blank authorizations to participate in the federal Food Stamp Program in any manner not authorized by Chapter 10 (commencing with Section 18900) of Part 6 with the intent to defraud is guilty of a felony, punishable by imprisonment in the state prison for a period of 16 months, two years, or three years, a fine of not more than five thousand dollars ($5,000), or by both such imprisonment and fine.

(e) Any person who counterfeits or alters or knowingly uses, transfers, acquires, or possesses counterfeited or altered authorizations to participate in the federal Food Stamp Program or food stamps in any manner not authorized by the Food Stamp Act of 1964 (Public Law 88-525 and all amendments made thereto) or the federal regulations pursuant to the act is guilty of forgery.

(f) Any person who fraudulently appropriates food stamps or authorizations to participate in the federal Food Stamp Program with which he or she has been entrusted pursuant to his or her duties as a public employee is guilty of embezzlement of public funds.

(g) Whoever knowingly uses, transfers, sells, purchases, or possesses food stamps or authorizations to participate in the federal Food Stamp Program in any manner not authorized by Chapter 10 (commencing with Section 18900), of Part 6, or by the federal Food Stamp Act of 1977 (Public Law 95-113 and all amendments made thereto) is; (1) guilty of a misdemeanor if the face value of the food stamps or the authorizations to participate is four hundred dollars ($400) or less, and shall be punished by imprisonment in the county jail for a period of not more than six months, a fine of not more than five hundred dollars ($500), or by both such imprisonment and fine, or (2) guilty of a felony if the face value of the food stamps or the authorizations to participate exceeds four hundred dollars ($400), and shall be punished by imprisonment in the state prison for a period of 16 months, two years, or three years, a fine of not more than five thousand dollars ($5,000), or by both such imprisonment and fine or by imprisonment in the county jail for a period of not more than one year, or a fine of not more than one thousand dollars ($1,000), or by both such imprisonment and fine.

WI 11482—False Representation to Obtain, or Unlawful Receipt or Attempt to Receive Aid

Any person other than a needy child, who willfully and knowingly, with the intent to deceive, makes a false statement or representation or knowingly fails to disclose a material fact to obtain aid, or who, knowing he or she is not entitled thereto, attempts to obtain aid or to continue to receive aid to which he or she is not entitled, or a larger amount than that to which he or she is legally entitled, is guilty of a misdemeanor. . . .

WI 11483—Fraud to Obtain Aid; Restitution

. . . [W]henever any person has, by means of false statement or representation or by impersonation or other fraudulent device, obtained aid for a child not in fact entitled thereto, the person obtaining such aid shall be subject to prosecution. . . .

When the allegation is limited to failure to report not more than two thousand dollars ($2,000) of income or resources, or the failure to report the presence of an additional person or persons in the household, all actions necessary to secure restitution shall be brought against persons in violation of Section 10980. The action for restitution may be satisfied by sending a registered letter requesting restitution to the last address at which the person was receiving public assistance.

Penal Code 439—Procuring Insurance from Unlicensed Company

16-4 Insurance-Related Crimes

Every person who in this State procures, or agrees to procure, any insurance for a resident of this State, from any insurance company not incorporated under the laws of this State, unless such company or its agent has filed the bond required by the laws of this State relating to insurance, is guilty of a misdemeanor.

Penal Code 548—Defrauding Insurer

(a) Every person who willfully injures, destroys, secretes, abandons, or disposes of any property which at the time is insured against loss or damage by theft, or embezzlement, or any casualty with intent to defraud or prejudice the insurer, whether the property is the property or in the possession of such person or any other person, is punishable by imprisonment in the state prison for two, three, or five years and by a fine not exceeding fifty thousand dollars ($50,000). For purposes of this section, "casualty" does not include fire.

(b) Any person who violates subdivision (a) and who has a prior conviction of the offense set forth in that subdivision, in Section 550 of this code, or in former Section 556 or former Section 1871.1 of the Insurance Code, shall receive a two-year enhancement for each prior conviction in addition to the sentence provided under subdivision (a). The existence of any fact which would subject a person to a penalty enhancement shall be alleged in the information or indictment and either admitted by the defendant in open court, or found to be true by the jury trying the issue of guilt or by the court where guilt is established by plea of guilty or *nolo contendere* or by trial by the court sitting without a jury.

Penal Code 549—False Insurance Claim Pending; Solicit, etc., Any Business

Any firm, corporation, partnership, or association, or any person acting in his or her individual capacity, or in his or her capacity as a public or private employee, who solicits, accepts, or refers any business to or from any individual or entity with the knowledge that, or with reckless disregard for whether, the individual or entity for or from whom the solicitation or referral is made, or the individual or entity who is solicited or referred, intends to violate Section 550 of this code or Section 1871.4 of the Insurance Code is guilty of a crime, punishable upon a first conviction by imprisonment in the county jail for not more than one year or by imprisonment in the state prison for 16 months, two years, or three years, or by a fine not exceeding ten thousand dollars ($10,000), or by both that fine and imprisonment. A second or subsequent conviction is punishable by imprisonment in the state prison.

Penal Code 550—False or Fraudulent Claims [Subparagraphs (a) & (b) only]

(a) It is unlawful to do any of the following, or to aid, abet, solicit, or conspire with any person to do any of the following:

   (1) Knowingly present or cause to be presented any false or fraudulent claim for the payment of a loss or injury, including payment of a loss or injury under a contract of insurance.

   (2) Knowingly present multiple claims for the same loss or injury, including presentation of multiple claims to more than one insurer, with an intent to defraud.

   (3) Knowingly cause or participate in a vehicular collision, or any other vehicular accident, for the purpose of presenting any false or fraudulent claim.

   (4) Knowingly present a false or fraudulent claim for the payments of a loss for theft, destruction, damage, or conversion of a motor vehicle, a motor vehicle part, or contents of a motor vehicle.

(5) Knowingly prepare, make, or subscribe any writing, with the intent to present or use it, or to allow it to be presented in support of any false or fraudulent claim.

(6) Knowingly make or cause to be made any false or fraudulent claim for payment of a health care benefit.

(7) Knowingly submit a claim for a health care benefit which was not used by, or on behalf of, the claimant.

(8) Knowingly present multiple claims for payment of the same health care benefit with an intent to defraud.

(9) Knowingly present for payment any undercharges for health care benefits on behalf of a specific claimant unless any known overcharges for health care benefits for that claimant are presented for reconciliation at that same time.

(10) For purposes of paragraphs (6) to (9), inclusive, a claim or a claim for payment of a health care benefit also means a claim or claim for payment submitted by or on the behalf of a provider of any workers' compensation health benefits under the Labor Code.

(b) It is unlawful to do, or to knowingly assist or conspire with any person to do, any of the following:

(1) Present or cause to be presented any written or oral statement as part of, or in support of or opposition to, a claim for payment or other benefit pursuant to an insurance policy, knowing that the statement contains any false or misleading information concerning any material fact.

(2) Prepare or make any written or oral statement that is intended to be presented to any insurer or any insurance claimant in connection with, or in support of or opposition to, any claim or payment or other benefit pursuant to an insurance policy, knowing that the statement contains any false or misleading information concerning any material fact.

(3) Conceal or knowingly fail to disclose the occurrence of an event that affects any person's initial or continued right or entitlement to any insurance benefit or payment, or the amount of any benefit or payment to which the person is entitled.

(4) Prepare or make any written or oral statement, intended to be presented to any insurer or producer for the purpose of obtaining a motor vehicle insurance policy, that the person to be the insured resides or is domiciled in this state when, in fact, that person resides or is domiciled in a state other than this state.

Penal Code 551—Offer of Fee, Commission, etc., to Insurance Agent, Broker, or Adjuster for Repairs Covered by Insurance

(a) It is unlawful for any automotive repair dealer, contractor, or employees or agents thereof to offer to any insurance agent, broker, or adjuster any fee, commission, profit sharing, or other form of direct or indirect consideration for referring an insured to an automotive repair dealer or its employees or agents for vehicle repairs covered under a policyholder's automobile physical damage or automobile collision coverage, or to a contractor or its employees or agents for repairs to or replacement of a structure covered by a residential or commercial insurance policy.

(b) Except in cases in which the amount of the repair or replacement claim has been determined by the insurer and the repair or replacement services are performed in accordance with that determination or in accordance with provided estimates that are accepted by the insurer, it is unlawful for any automotive repair dealer, contractor, or employees or agents thereof to knowingly offer or give any discount intended to offset a deductible required by a policy of insurance covering repairs to or replacement of a motor vehicle or residential or commercial structure. This subdivision does not prohibit an advertisement for repair or replacement services at a discount as long as the amount of the repair or replacement claim has been determined by the insurer and the repair or replacement services are performed in accordance with that determination or in accordance with provided estimates that are accepted by the insurer.

(c) A violation of this section is a public offense. Where the amount at issue exceeds four hundred dollars ($400), the offense is punishable by imprisonment in the state prison for 16 months, or 2 or 3 years, by a fine of not more than ten thousand dollars ($10,000), or by both that imprisonment and fine; or by imprisonment in a county jail not to exceed one year, by a fine of not more than one thousand dollars ($1,000), or by both that imprisonment and fine. In all other cases, the offense is punishable by imprisonment in a county jail not to exceed six months, by a fine of not more than one thousand dollars ($1,000), or by both that imprisonment and fine.

(d) & (e) [omitted]

Penal Code 801.5—Insurance Fraud; Statute of Limitations

Notwithstanding Section 801 or any other provision of law, prosecution for any offense described in subdivision (c) of Section 803 shall be commenced within four years after discovery of the commission of the offense, or within four years after the completion of the offense, whichever is later.

16-5 Driving Offense

Vehicle Code 1656.2—Summary of Financial Responsibility Laws

. . . The Robbins-McAlister Financial Responsibility Act requires every driver to maintain proof of valid automobile liability insurance, bond, cash deposit, or self-insurance which has been approved by the Department of Motor Vehicles.

You must provide proof of financial responsibility after you are cited by a peace officer for a traffic violation. The act requires that you provide the officer with the name of your insurer and the policy identification number. Your insurer will provide written evidence of this number. The back of your vehicle registration form contains a space for writing this information. Failure to prove your financial responsibility can result in fines of up to two hundred forty dollars ($240) and loss of your driver's license. Falsification of proof can result in fines of up to five hundred dollars ($500) or 30 days in jail, or both. Under existing law, if you are involved in an accident that results in damages over five hundred dollars ($500) or in any injury or fatality, you must file a report of the accident with the Department of Motor Vehicles within 10 days of the accident. If you fail to file a report or fail to provide evidence of financial responsibility on the report, your driving privilege will be suspended for one year. Your suspension notice will notify you of the department's action and of your right to a hearing. Your suspension notice will also inform you that if you request a hearing, it must be conducted within 30 days of your written request, and that a decision is to be rendered within 15 days of the conclusion of the hearing.

Vehicle Code 13201—Certain Offenses: Suspension of Driving Privilege

A court may suspend, for not more than six months, the privilege of any person to operate a motor vehicle upon conviction of any of the following offenses:

(a) Failure of the driver of a vehicle involved in an accident to stop or otherwise comply with Section 20002.

(b) Reckless driving proximately causing bodily injury to any person under Section 23104.

(c) Failure of the driver of a vehicle to stop at a railway grade crossing as required by Section 22452.

(d) Evading a peace officer in violation of Section 2800.1 or 2800.2, or in violation of Section 2800.3 if the person's license is not revoked for that violation pursuant to paragraph (3) of subdivision (a) of Section 13351.

(e)

    (1) Knowingly causing or participating in a vehicular collision, or any other vehicular accident, for the purpose of presenting or causing to be presented any false or fraudulent insurance claim.

    (2) In lieu of suspending a person's driving privilege pursuant to paragraph (1), the court may order the privilege to operate a motor vehicle restricted to necessary travel to and from that person's place of employment for not more than six months. If driving a motor vehicle is necessary to perform the duties of the person's employment, the court may restrict the driving privilege to allow driving in that person's scope of employment. Whenever a person's driving privilege is restricted pursuant to this paragraph, the person shall be required to maintain proof of financial responsibility.

Vehicle Code 13201.5—License Suspension: Prostitution Violation Within 1000 Feet of Residence

A court may suspend, for not more than 30 days, the privilege of any person to operate a motor vehicle upon conviction of subdivision (b) of Section 647 of the Penal Code [prostitution] where the violation was committed within 1,000 feet of a private residence and with the use of a vehicle.

Vehicle Code 16000—Accident Report

(a) The driver of every motor vehicle who is in any manner involved in an accident originating from the operation of a motor vehicle on any street or highway or any reportable off-highway accident defined in Section 16000.1 which has resulted in damage to the property of any one person in excess of five hundred dollars ($500) or in bodily injury or in the death of any person shall, within 10 days after the accident, report the accident, either personally or through an insurance agent, broker, or legal representative, on a form approved by the department to the office of the department at Sacramento, subject to the provisions of this chapter. The driver shall identify on the form, by name and current residence address, if available, any person involved in the accident complaining of bodily injury.

(b) A report is not required pursuant to subdivision (a) if the motor vehicle involved in the accident was owned or leased by, or under the direction of, the United States, this state, another state, or a local agency.

(c) If none of the parties involved in an accident has reported that accident to the department within one year following the date of the accident, the department is not required to file the report, and the driver's license suspension requirements of Section 16004 or 16070 do not apply.

Vehicle Code 16000.1—Reportable Off-Highway Accident

(a) For purposes of this division, a *reportable off-highway accident* means an accident which includes all of the following:

(1) Occurs off the street or highway.
(2) Involves a vehicle that is subject to registration under this code.
(3) Results in damages to the property of any one person in excess of five hundred dollars ($500) or in bodily injury or in the death of any person.

(b) A "reportable off-highway accident" does not include any accident which occurs off-highway in which damage occurs only to the property of the driver or owner of the motor vehicle and no bodily injury or death of a person occurs.

Vehicle Code 16003—Driver Incapacity

If any driver is physically incapable of making the report, and is not the owner of the motor vehicle involved in the accident, the owner shall, as soon as he learns of the accident, report the matter in writing to the department.

Vehicle Code 16002—Vehicle of Employer

If the driver at the time of the accident was driving a motor vehicle owned, operated, or leased by the employer of the driver and with the permission of the employer, then the driver shall within five days after the accident report the accident to his employer on a form approved by the employer. Within 10 days after receipt of the report the employer shall transmit a report on a form approved by the department to the office of the department at Sacramento, except that an employer need not transmit such report when the vehicle involved in the accident is owned or operated as described in Section 16051 or 16052, or is owned or operated by any person or corporation who has filed with the department a certificate of an insurance carrier or surety company that there is in effect a policy or bond meeting the requirements of Section 16056 and when such policy or bond is in force with respect to the vehicle at the time of the accident.

16-5c Financial Responsibility Laws

Vehicle Code 16000.7—Uninsured Motor Vehicle

As used in this division an *uninsured motor vehicle* is a motor vehicle for which financial responsibility as provided in Section 16021 was not in effect at the time of the accident.

Vehicle Code 16000.8—Failure to Prove Existence of Financial Responsibility; Fraud by Agent or Broker

(a) Notwithstanding any other provision of this chapter, if the failure of the driver of a motor vehicle involved in an accident to prove the existence of financial responsibility, as required by Section 16020, was due to the fraudulent acts of an insurance agent or broker, the department shall terminate any suspension action taken pursuant to Section 16070, when both of the following conditions are met:

(1) The driver provides documentation from the Department of Insurance that the insurance agent or broker has been found to have committed fraud in the transaction of automobile liability insurance, or provides documentation that criminal charges have been filed against the agent or broker due to fraud or theft related to the sale of automobile liability insurances.

(2) The driver furnishes proof to the department that financial responsibility meeting the requirements of Section 16021 is currently in effect.

(b) It is the intent of the Legislature in enacting this section that individuals who are the victims of insurance fraud not be penalized for violating the financial responsibility laws when that violation was due to the fraudulent acts of others. Persons with documented evidence of fraud involving their insurance coverage, such as where an insurance agent accepted the premium payment for coverage but willfully failed to obtain the coverage and led the customer to believe insurance was in effect, should retain their driving privileges provided they give evidence that valid liability insurance is currently in effect.

Vehicle Code 16050.5—Liability Insurance; Furnish Information

The owner of a vehicle, who has a liability insurance policy with respect to the vehicle, shall, upon request, furnish insurance information to a person who, while operating the vehicle with the owner's permission, is involved in a reportable accident with the insured vehicle, or to the department whenever the department is required to establish whether the permitted driver meets the financial responsibility requirements of Section 16020.

Vehicle Code 16051—Publicly Owned Vehicles

Proof may be established by filing a report indicating that the motor vehicle involved in the accident was owned or leased by or under the direction of the United States, this State, or any political subdivision of this State or municipality thereof.

Vehicle Code 16052—Self-Insurer

Proof may be established if the owner of the motor vehicle involved in the accident was a self-insurer. Any person in whose name more than 25 motor vehicles are registered may qualify as a self-insurer by obtaining a certificate of self-insurance issued by the department as provided in this article.

Vehicle Code 16451—Owner's Policy

An owner's policy of motor vehicle liability insurance shall insure the named insured and any other person using any motor vehicle registered to the named insured with the express or implied permission of the named insured, against loss from the liability imposed by law for damages arising out of ownership, maintenance, or use of the motor vehicle within the continental limits of the United States to the extent and aggregate amount, exclusive of interest and costs, with respect to each motor vehicle, of fifteen thousand dollars ($15,000) for bodily injury to or death of each person as a result of any one accident and, subject to the limit as to one person, the amount of thirty thousand dollars ($30,000) for bodily injury to or death of all persons as a result of any one accident and the amount of five thousand dollars ($5,000) for damage to property of others as a result of any one accident.

Vehicle Code 16452—Operator's Policy

An operator's policy of motor vehicle liability insurance shall insure the person named as insured therein against loss from the liability imposed on that person by law for damages arising out of use by that person of any motor vehicle not owned by that person, and for any subsequently acquired motor vehicle for a period not to exceed 10 days from date of purchase, within the same territorial limits and subject to the same limits of liability as are provided for in an owner's policy of liability insurance.

16-5d Other Driving Regulations

Vehicle Code 16001—Driverless Runaway Vehicle

If the vehicle involved was a driverless runaway vehicle and was parked with the express or implied permission of the registered owner, the registered owner of the vehicle shall be construed to have been the driver of the vehicle for the purposes of this chapter.

Vehicle Code 16004—Mandatory Suspension of License

(a) The department shall suspend the driving privilege of any person who fails, refuses, or neglects to make a report of an accident as required in this chapter.

(b) A suspension taken under this section shall remain in effect until terminated by receipt of the report of the accident or upon receipt of evidence that financial responsibility as provided in Section 16021 is in effect.

(c) The driving privilege shall not be suspended under this section, and, if a suspension has been imposed and is in effect under this section, that suspension shall be terminated, if the driving privilege is suspended under Section 16370 or 16381 as the result of a judgment arising out of the same accident for which the report of the accident is required by this section. The department may suspend or reimpose the suspension of the driving privilege of a person under this section if the suspension under Section 16370 or 16381 is later set aside for a reason other than that the person has satisfied the judgment in full or to the extent provided in Chapter 2 (commencing with Section 16250) and has given proof of financial responsibility as provided in Chapter 3 (commencing with Section 16430).

16-6 Agricultural Crimes

16-6a Theft of Fruits, Nuts, and Vegetables

Food and Agriculture Code 851—Intent to Protect against Theft

It is the intent of this chapter to establish a means of identifying the owner of any fruits, nuts, or vegetables which are the food product of any tree, vine, or plant so as to provide an additional control over thefts of these commodities within the state.

Food and Agriculture Code 861—Proof of Ownership for Lots over 200 Pounds

For lots of over 200 pounds of any fruits, nuts, or vegetables that are the food product of any tree, vine, or plant, or for lots of over 200 pounds of any burl wood from a walnut tree, living or dead, and that are marketed for commercial purposes, all of the following apply:

(a) Every person who sells the commodity shall provide the buyer or transporter with a record of proof of ownership for each lot of the commodity.

(b) Every person who buys the commodity for resale shall obtain from the previous buyer or from the transporter a record of proof of ownership for each lot of the commodity.

(c) Every person who transports for commercial purposes shall possess a record showing proof of ownership for each lot of the commodity during transportation.

Food and Agriculture Code 862—Right to Inspect

Upon probable cause to believe any fruits, nuts, vegetables, or walnut burl regulated pursuant to this chapter is in unlawful possession, proof of ownership shall be made available for inspection upon request of the secretary, the commissioner, or by any peace officer. If the secretary or the commissioner has probable cause to believe that any fruits, nuts, vegetables, or walnut burl regulated pursuant to this chapter is in unlawful possession, he or she may request a peace officer to stop the vehicle pursuant to Section 881 for inspection. The record shall contain the following information:

(a) Name, address, telephone number, and signatures of the seller or the seller's authorized representative.

(b) Name, address, and telephone number of the buyer or consignee if not sold.

(c) Common or generic name and quantity of the commodity involved.

(d) Date of transaction and date of commencement of transportation.

Food and Agriculture Code 863—Proof of Ownership

A bill of lading, bill of sale, certified farmers certificate, data obtainable by electronic transmission which is accessible to a common carrier, or a similar type document shall be considered proof of ownership for purposes of this chapter.

Food and Agriculture Code 864—Falsify Information to Show Proof of Ownership

It is unlawful for any person to knowingly falsify or cause to be falsified any information in a record intended to show proof of ownership.

Food and Agriculture Code 865—Retain Record for 60 Days

A copy of the record shall be retained by the buyer and seller for a period of 60 days after delivery.

Food and Agriculture Code 866—Minimal Requirements for Transportation

This chapter establishes minimal requirements for the transportation and identification of agricultural commodities. A county may, by ordinance, impose additional requirements regarding this transportation and identification.

Food and Agriculture Code 871—Exemptions

This chapter does not apply to the following agricultural commodities:

(a) Commodities transported from the farm or ranch where they are produced to a commercial packing plant within this state for processing or packing.

(b) Commodities transported and accompanied by a valid permit, disposal order, or certificate issued by the director or the commissioner for any reason other than to comply with this chapter.

Food and Agriculture Code 881—Right to Stop

Any peace officer, upon probable cause to believe an agricultural commodity regulated pursuant to this chapter is being unlawfully transported, may stop the vehicle and request proof of ownership of the commodity.

Food and Agriculture Code 882—Seizing of Commodity

Upon reasonable belief that a person is in unlawful possession of a commodity regulated by this chapter, the commodity may be held by the director, the commissioner, or by any peace officer and shall be turned over to the custody of the commissioner. The commissioner may hold the commodity on the premises where it was seized until disposed of according to the requirements of Section 884.

Food and Agriculture Code 883—Ascertaining Ownership, Release to Owner

The director, the commissioner, or a peace officer may investigate to ascertain the ownership of any commodity that has been held pursuant to this chapter. If the lawful owner is located, the commodity shall be released to the owner or his or her agent. The commissioner may require reasonable payment to cover costs incurred in the storing of the commodity, but not to exceed the value of the commodity being held.

Food and Agriculture Code 884—Commissioners Right to Sell at Public Auction

(a) If for any reason the commodity is not released to the rightful owner after being in the custody of the commissioner for 48 hours or, in the case of a highly perishable commodity, any shorter period of time that the commissioner deems necessary, the commissioner may sell the commodity by public auction or by private sale at fair market value to a commercial packer of the commodity. All of the proceeds derived from the sale of the commodity shall be held by the commissioner for a period of not less than six months, during which time the lawful owner of the commodity may submit satisfactory proof of ownership and obtain possession of the proceeds. The commissioner may require the payment by the owner of an amount sufficient to cover the costs incurred for a storage and sale of the commodity, but not to exceed the sale price of the commodity. If, after retention of the proceeds for a period of at least six months, no demand is made or if proof of ownership is not supplied, the commissioner shall deposit the proceeds of the sale of the commodity in the general fund of the county.

(b) If any seized commodity remains unsold after being offered for sale pursuant to this section, the commissioner may donate the commodity to a nonprofit charitable organization.

16-6b Prevention of Introduction or Spread of Pests

Food and Agriculture Code 5341

To prevent the introduction into, or the spread within this state, of pests, the director shall maintain at such places within this state as he deems necessary plant quarantine inspection stations for the purpose of inspecting all conveyances which might carry plants or other things which are, or are liable to be, infested or infected with any pest.

Food and Agriculture Code 5341.5

(a) Every operator of a motor vehicle entering the state with a shipment of any agricultural commodity shall cause the vehicle and the shipment to be inspected, and shall obtain a certificate of inspection, at the plant quarantine inspection station nearest the point of entry into the state.

(b) Failure to obtain the required certificate of inspection shall subject the operator of the vehicle and the registered owner of the vehicle, if a different person or legal entity, to separate civil penalties of not more than one thousand dollars ($1,000) for each violation. In determining the severity of the penalty to be imposed, the court shall consider any prior violations of the same nature within the preceding 24 months, the commodity being transported, and any evidence, including deviation from normal and usual routes, that the operator of the vehicle intentionally avoided inspection.

(c) Inspection shall not be required when the operator of the vehicle would be required to travel a distance of 15 miles or more from normal and usual routes for the particular trip to obtain the required inspection and certification, or when weather conditions or road closures on normal and usual routes prevent travel to the nearest plant quarantine inspection station.

(d) Violation of this section is a separate offense from violation of any other provision of this code and proceedings under this section shall not be deemed to prevent separate proceedings for any other offense.

(e) Proceedings under this section may be brought by the director or, with the director's concurrence, by the district attorney of the county in which the violation occurred. The civil penalty shall be awarded to the agency which brings the enforcement action for use by that agency in enforcing the provisions of this code.

(f) The director may, by regulation or executive order, as the director deems advisable, permit exceptions for certain commodities, areas, and times consistent with the purposes of this division, patterns of local traffic near border areas, and availability of inspection stations.

(g) Persons holding a valid permit to transport cattle pursuant to Section 21067 are exempt from this section.

Food and Agriculture Code 5342

Plant quarantine officers at plant quarantine inspection stations may ascertain the origin, quantity, and kinds of meat and meat products, poultry and poultry products, eggs, and livestock transported into or out of this state through the stations. The operator of any vehicle which is transporting any such commodity into or out of the state through any plant quarantine inspection station shall stop and give this information upon request to a plant quarantine officer at the plant quarantine inspection station. Such request may be by a sign, which is openly displayed at the station, or by any other means which is deemed by the director as effective. The director may accept, on behalf of the state, donations of money from any person to defray the costs of the department under this section. Any such money shall be paid into the State Treasury and credited to the Department of Agriculture Fund. The director may limit expenditures under this section relating to livestock to the amounts so donated for this purpose, and shall limit expenditures under this section relating to poultry and poultry products and eggs to the amounts so donated for this purpose.

Food and Agriculture Code 5343

The director shall cause conspicuous signs to be erected at or near each inspection station which disclose the existence of the station.

Food and Agriculture Code 5344

(a) It is unlawful for the operator of any vehicle to fail to stop the vehicle at an inspection station or to willfully avoid an inspection station. It is also unlawful for the operator to fail to stop either upon demand of a clearly identified plant quarantine officer or upon demand of an officer of the California Highway Patrol, when the officer orders the operator to stop for the purpose of determining whether any quarantine which is established pursuant to any provision of this division is being violated.
(b) Notwithstanding Section 5309, a violation of this section is a misdemeanor and grounds for the vehicle to be stopped for inspection.

Food and Agriculture Code 5345

It is unlawful for any person to operate upon any highway in this state any vehicle which, in violation of Section 5344, was not stopped as required by that section, if the person who is operating such vehicle knows of such violation of Section 5344. The violation of this section continues unless and until one of the following occurs:

(a) A period of 24 hours has elapsed following the violation of Section 5344.
(b) The operator who violated Section 5344 has been apprehended and the vehicle which is involved has been inspected and released from quarantine by any authorized state plant quarantine officer. An operator who is so apprehended does not violate this section by reason of operating the vehicle en route to the closest inspection station immediately following his apprehension for violation of Section 5344, nor does any other person, who operates the vehicle for such purpose, violate this section.

Food and Agriculture Code 5346

(a) It is unlawful for any person to conceal any plant from any plant quarantine officer or to fail to present it or any quarantined article for inspection at the request of such officer.
(b) It is unlawful to move into California any outdoor household article from a federally regulated gypsy moth area unless accompanied by certification that the article has been inspected and does not contain gypsy moth egg masses. The director may adopt regulations to specify the type of certification and inspection required as necessary to carry out this section.

16-6c Garbage Disposal

Food and Agriculture Code 16151—Disposal of Garbage; Exceptions

It is unlawful for any person to throw, discharge, deposit, remove, or carry garbage, or cause, suffer, or procure garbage to be thrown, discharged, deposited, removed, or carried, from any vessel, aircraft, or any other vehicle into any territorial waters, or onto land within the state, except for any of the following:

(a) Immediate burning in incinerators.
(b) Approved treatment or approved disposal under the supervision and pursuant to the regulations of the director.

(c) Delivery to a garbage collector that, for the purpose of accepting garbage, is licensed by the director or by the federal government.

Food and Agriculture Code 16901—Animals on Railroad Tracks

16-6d Animals

It is unlawful for any person to do any of the following:

(a) Lead, drive, or conduct any animal along the track of a railroad, unless the railroad is built within the limits of a public highway or public place.
(b) Permit any animal to be placed within the fences of a railroad for grazing or other purposes if he has the right to prevent it.

Food and Agriculture Code 16902—Animals at Large

A person that owns or controls the possession of any livestock shall not willfully or negligently permit any of the livestock to stray upon, or remain unaccompanied by a person in charge or control of the livestock upon, a public highway, if both sides of the highway are adjoined by property which is separated from the highway by a fence, wall, hedge, sidewalk, curb, lawn, or building.

16-7 Cruelty to Animals

Under PC 597 any person who maliciously and intentionally maims, mutilates, tortures, or wounds a living animal, or maliciously and intentionally kills an animal, is guilty of an offense punishable by imprisonment in the state prison, or by a fine of not more than twenty thousand dollars ($20,000), or by both the fine and imprisonment or, alternatively, by imprisonment in the county jail for not more than one year, or by a fine of not more than twenty thousand dollars ($20,000), or by both the fine and imprisonment. Any person who overdrives, overloads, drives when overloaded, overworks, tortures, torments, deprives of necessary sustenance, drink, or shelter, cruelly beats, mutilates, or cruelly kills any animal, or causes or procures any animal to be so overdriven, overloaded, driven when overloaded, overworked, tortured, tormented, deprived of necessary sustenance, drink, shelter, or to be cruelly beaten, mutilated, or cruelly killed; and whoever, having the charge or custody of any animal, either as owner or otherwise, subjects any animal to needless suffering, or inflicts unnecessary cruelty upon the animal, or in any manner abuses any animal, or fails to provide the animal with proper food, drink, or shelter or protection from the weather, or who drives, rides, or otherwise uses the animal when unfit for labor, is, for every such offense, guilty of a crime punishable as a misdemeanor or as a felony or alternatively punishable as a misdemeanor or a felony and by a fine of not more than twenty thousand dollars ($20,000).

Every person who maliciously and intentionally maims, mutilates, or tortures any mammal, bird, reptile, amphibian, or fish is guilty of an offense punishable by imprisonment in the state prison, or by a fine of not more than twenty thousand dollars ($20,000), or by both the fine and imprisonment, or, alternatively, by imprisonment in the county jail for not more than one year, by a fine of not more than twenty thousand dollars ($20,000), or by both the fine and imprisonment.

Under PC 597.1, every owner, driver, or keeper of any animal who permits the animal to be in any building, enclosure, lane, street, square, or lot of any city, county, city and county, or judicial district without proper care and attention is guilty of a misdemeanor. Any peace officer, humane society officer, or animal control officer shall take possession of the stray or abandoned animal and shall provide care and treatment for the animal until the animal is deemed to be in suitable condition to be returned to the owner. Every sick, disabled, infirm, or crippled animal, except a dog or cat, that is abandoned in any city, county, city and county, or judicial district may be killed by the officer if, after a reasonable search, no owner of the animal can be found. It shall be the duty of all peace officers, humane society officers, and animal control officers to cause the animal to be killed or rehabilitated and placed in a suitable home on information that the animal is stray or abandoned. The officer may likewise take charge of any animal, including a dog or cat, that by reason of lameness, sickness, feebleness, or neglect is unfit for the labor it is performing, or that in any other manner is being cruelly treated, and provide care and treatment for the animal until it is deemed to be in a suitable condition to be returned to the owner.

Any peace officer, humane society officer, or animal control officer shall convey all injured cats and dogs found without their owners in a public place directly to a veterinarian known by the officer to be a veterinarian who ordinarily treats dogs and cats for a determination of whether the animal shall be immediately and humanely destroyed or shall be hospitalized under proper care and given emergency treatment. If the owner does not redeem the animal within the locally prescribed waiting period, the veterinarian may personally perform euthanasia on the animal. If the animal is treated and recovers from its injuries, the veterinarian may keep the animal for purposes of adoption, provided the responsible animal control agency has first been contacted and has refused to take possession of the animal.

16-7a Dog Fighting

PC 597.5 provides that, any person who (1) owns, possesses, keeps, or trains any dog, with the intent that the dog shall be engaged in an exhibition of fighting with another dog; or (2) for amusement or gain, causes any dog to fight with another dog, or causes any dogs to injure each other is guilty of a felony. Any person who is knowingly present, as a spectator, at any place, building, or tenement where preparations are being made for an exhibition of the fighting of dogs, with the intent to be present at those preparations, or is knowingly present at that exhibition or at any other fighting or injuring, is guilty of a misdemeanor.

16-7b Fighting Animals or Birds

Any person who, for amusement or gain, causes any bull, bear, cock, or other animal, not including any dog, to fight with like kind of animal or creature, or causes any such animal, including any dog, to fight with a different kind of animal or creature, or with any human being; or who, for amusement or gain, worries or injures any such bull, bear, cock, dog, or other animal, or causes any such bull, bear, cock, or other animal, not including any dog, to worry or injure each other; and any person who permits the same to be done on any premises under his or her charge or control; and any person who aids, abets, or is present at such fighting or worrying of such animal or creature, as a spectator, is guilty of a misdemeanor (see PC 597[b]).

Under PC 597(c), whoever owns, possesses, keeps, or trains any bird or animal, with the intent that such bird or animal shall be engaged in an exhibition of fighting, or is present at any place, building, or tenement, where preparations are being made for an exhibition of the fighting of birds or animals, with the intent to be present at such exhibition, or is present at such exhibition, is guilty of a misdemeanor. This section does not apply to an exhibition of fighting of a dog with another dog.

Pursuant to PC 597(d), any sheriff, police, or peace officer may enter any place, building, or tenement where there is an exhibition of the fighting of birds or animals, or where preparations are being made for such an exhibition, and, without a warrant, arrest all persons present.

PC 597(i) provides that it is unlawful for anyone to manufacture, buy, sell, barter, exchange, or have in his or her possession any of the implements commonly known as gaffs or slashers, or any other sharp implement designed to be attached in place of the natural spur of a gamecock or other fighting bird. It is also a crime under PC 597(j) for any person to own, possess, or keep any cock with the intent that such cock shall be used or engaged by himself or by his vendee or by any other person in any exhibition of fighting is guilty of a misdemeanor.

PC 597(s) makes it a crime to willfully abandon any domestic dog or cat. PC 597(t) prohibits the keeping of an animal confined in an enclosed area unless it is provided with an adequate exercise area. If the animal is restricted by a leash, rope, or chain, the leash, rope, or chain shall be affixed in such a manner that it will prevent the animal from becoming entangled or injured and permit the animal access to adequate shelter, food, and water. Violation of this section constitutes a misdemeanor. Under PC 598, every person who, within any public cemetery or burying ground, kills, wounds, or traps any bird, or destroys any bird's nest other than swallows' nests, or removes any eggs or young birds from any nest, is guilty of a misdemeanor. It is also a crime under PC 598(a) to kill any dog or cat with the sole intent of selling or giving away the pelt of such animal.

16-7c Killing or Abandoning Animals

Practicum

Does the sexually violent predators' commitment procedures allow the state to punish someone for a crime he or she may commit in the future? Should the state be allowed to commit someone based on the fact that he or she may commit a crime in the future? Explain your answers.

Discussion Questions

1. What is the procedure to have someone committed under the *violent sexual predators commitment procedures?*
2. Why is it unlawful to use lights and sniperscopes to assist in the taking of wild game?
3. What are the elements of the crime of welfare fraud?
4. What constitutes a false or fraudulent insurance claim?
5. Explain the financial responsibility laws pertaining to vehicles.
6. What are some of the offenses for which your driving privileges may be suspended?
7. What types of automobile accidents are required to be reported?

Self-Study Quiz

True/False

1. To be considered as a *sexually violent predator* the person must have been convicted of sexually violent crimes against three or more victims.

2. The commitment process for sexually violent predators does not provide for the right of a jury trial.

3. *Diagnosed mental disorder* refers to congenital and not acquired conditions.

4. Lights may not be used in night fishing.

5. It is unlawful to shoot game birds but not fish from a motor vehicle.

6. Welfare fraud is always a felony in California.

7. It is a crime to present multiple claims for the same loss or injury.

8. Failure to stop at a railway crossing may be grounds to suspend your driving privileges.

9. It is a crime to kill a cat for the purposes of selling its fur.

10. It is a crime to be a spectator at an exhibition of the fighting of dogs.

11. California prohibits the burning of garbage in incinerators.

12. A copy of the record of the purchase of fruits must be retained by the buyer for a period of 90 days.

Chapter 17

Computer Crimes

It ain't no sin if you crack a few laws now and then, just so long as you don't break any.
Mae West
Every Day's a Holiday, 1937

17-1 Introduction

Most crimes committed by the use of a computer are traditional crimes such as larceny and fraud. The computer, like a handgun, is a more efficient tool to use in completing criminal conduct. In most cases, the traditional crimes are more appropriately prosecuted under the other laws relating to theft, invasion of privacy, and so on. Computer technology, however, makes it impractical to prosecute some criminal activities under traditional criminal statutes. For example, in the theft of software data, nothing of substance is "carried away." In *Ward v. California* (3 Computer Law Service. Rep. 206, Cal. Super. Ct. 1972), an employee was charged with grand theft of a computer program. He committed the theft by transmitting electrical impulses over the telephone lines. The court held that the item must be tangible in order for it to be carried away and therefore there was not the theft of an item. Accordingly, new statutes were enacted to regulate misconduct in the use of computers. As of January 1997, computers were mentioned 98 times in the Penal Code. Computer misconduct, in many cases, may now be prosecuted under either traditional criminal statutes or statutes designed to combat computer misconduct.

The Computer Fraud and Abuse Act of 1984 (PL98-473, Title II, Section 2102[a]) was the first federal act to combat computer fraud. The act provides that it is a crime for anyone to use a public telephone system to access, without authority, any computer data processing system. The Act also makes it a crime to access without authorization any data processing system if the data processing system is involved in or used in relationship to interstate commerce.

17-2 Computers As Crime-Fighting Tools

Computers are also useful as crime-fighting tools. For example, PC 13894.8 provides for the use of a "livescan" fingerprint computer system to take the fingerprints of persons arrested for driving under the influence of alcohol or drugs, or both. PC 14201.6 requires that the Department of Justice establish and maintain a publicly accessible computer Internet directory of information relating to the following:

- Persons for whom an arrest warrant has been issued pursuant to an alleged violation of any offense defined as a violent felony
- Critical missing children
- Unsolved homicides

The attorney general determines the extent of information and the priority of cases to be included in the directory. The AG's office shall keep confidential, and not enter into the directory, either of the following:

1. Information regarding any case for which the AG has determined that disclosure pursuant to this section would endanger the safety of a person involved in an investigation or the successful completion of the investigation or a related investigation.
2. Information regarding an arrest warrant for which the issuing magistrate has determined that disclosure pursuant to this section would endanger the safety of a person involved in an investigation or the successful completion of the investigation or a related investigation.

Critical missing child includes, but is not limited to, any case of a missing child for which there is evidence or indications that the child is at risk.

PC 14202.1 provides for the establishment of a violent crime information system to tracking violent offenders. The AG is required to establish and maintain, upon appropriation of funds by the legislature, within the center the Violent Crime

Information System to track and monitor violent offenders and their activities. The Violent Crime Information System uses computer technology to compare unsolved crime scenes and methods of operation information against the file of known violent sexual assault, kidnapping, and homicide offenders (containing over 40,000 violent, kidnapping, and homicide offenders). The system provides local law enforcement agencies with investigative leads to assist in the resolution of violent crimes.

Penal Code 502—Computer Related Crimes

(a) It is the intent of the Legislature in enacting this section to expand the degree of protection afforded to individuals, businesses, and governmental agencies from tampering, interference, damage, and unauthorized access to lawfully created computer data and computer systems. The Legislature finds and declares that the proliferation of computer technology has resulted in a concomitant proliferation of computer crime and other forms of unauthorized access to computers, computer systems, and computer data.
The Legislature further finds and declares that protection of the integrity of all types and forms of lawfully created computers, computer systems, and computer data is vital to the protection of the privacy of individuals as well as to the well-being of financial institutions, business concerns, governmental agencies, and others within this state that lawfully utilize those computers, computer systems, and data.

(b) For the purposes of this section, the following terms have the following meanings:

(1) *Access* means to gain entry to, instruct, or communicate with the logical, arithmetical, or memory function resources of a computer, computer system, or computer network.

(2) *Computer network* means any system which provides communications between one or more computer systems and input/output devices including, but not limited to, display terminals and printers connected by telecommunication facilities.

(3) *Computer program or software* means a set of instructions or statements, and related data, that when executed in actual or modified form, cause a computer, computer system, or computer network to perform specified functions.

(4) *Computer services* includes, but is not limited to, computer time, data processing, or storage functions, or other uses of a computer, computer system, or computer network.

(5) *Computer system* means a device or collection of devices, including support devices and excluding calculators which are not programmable and capable of being used in conjunction with external files, one or more of which contain computer programs, electronic instructions, input data, and output data, that performs functions including, but not limited to, logic, arithmetic, data storage and retrieval, communication, and control.

(6) *Data* means a representation of information, knowledge, facts, concepts, computer software, computer programs, or instructions. Data may be in any form, in storage media, or as stored in the memory of the computer or in transit or presented on a display device.

17-3 Computer-Related Crimes

(7) *Supporting documentation* includes, but is not limited to, all information, in any form, pertaining to the design, construction, classification, implementation, use, or modification of a computer, computer system, computer network, computer program, or computer software, which information is not generally available to the public and is necessary for the operation of a computer, computer system, computer network, computer program, or computer software.

(8) *Injury* means any alteration, deletion, damage, or destruction of a computer system, computer network, computer program, or data caused by the access.

(9) *Victim expenditure* means any expenditure reasonably and necessarily incurred by the owner or lessee to verify that a computer system, computer network, computer program, or data was or was not altered, deleted, damaged, or destroyed by the access.

(10) *Computer contaminant* means any set of computer instructions that are designed to modify, damage, destroy, record, or transmit information within a computer, computer system, or computer network without the intent or permission of the owner of the information. They include, but are not limited to, a group of computer instructions commonly called *viruses* or *worms*, which are self-replicating or self-propagating and are designed to contaminate other computer programs or computer data, consume computer resources, modify, destroy, record, or transmit data, or in some other fashion usurp the normal operation of the computer, computer system, or computer network.

(c) Except as provided in subdivision (h), any person who commits any of the following acts is guilty of a public offense:

(1) Knowingly accesses and without permission alters, damages, deletes, destroys, or otherwise uses any data, computer, computer system, or computer network in order to either (A) devise or execute any scheme or artifice to defraud, deceive, or extort, or (B) wrongfully control or obtain money, property, or data.

(2) Knowingly accesses and without permission takes, copies, or makes use of any data from a computer, computer system, or computer network, or takes or copies any supporting documentation, whether existing or residing internal or external to a computer, computer system, or computer network.

(3) Knowingly and without permission uses or causes to be used computer services.

(4) Knowingly accesses and without permission adds, alters, damages, deletes, or destroys any data, computer software, or computer programs which reside or exist internal or external to a computer, computer system, or computer network.

(5) Knowingly and without permission disrupts or causes the disruption of computer services or denies or causes the denial of computer services to an authorized user of a computer, computer system, or computer network.

(6) Knowingly and without permission provides or assists in providing a means of accessing a computer, computer system, or computer network in violation of this section.

(7) Knowingly and without permission accesses or causes to be accessed any computer, computer system, or computer network.

(8) Knowingly introduces any computer contaminant into any computer, computer system, or computer network.

(d)

(1) Any person who violates any of the provisions of paragraph (1), (2), (4), or (5) of subdivision (c) is punishable by a fine not exceeding ten thousand dollars ($10,000), or by imprisonment in the state prison for 16 months, or two or three years, or by both that fine and imprisonment, or by a fine not exceeding five thousand dollars ($5,000), or by imprisonment in the county jail not exceeding one year, or by both that fine and imprisonment.

(2) Any person who violates paragraph (3) of subdivision (c) is punishable as follows:

(A) For the first violation which does not result in injury, and where the value of the computer services used does not exceed four hundred dollars ($400), by a fine not exceeding five thousand dollars ($5,000), or by imprisonment in the county jail not exceeding one year, or by both that fine and imprisonment.

(B) For any violation which results in a victim expenditure in an amount greater than five thousand dollars ($5,000) or in an injury, or if the value of the computer services used exceeds four hundred dollars ($400), or for any second or subsequent violation, by a fine not exceeding ten thousand dollars ($10,000), or by imprisonment in the state prison for 16 months, or two or three years, or by both that fine and imprisonment, or by a fine not exceeding five thousand dollars ($5,000), or by imprisonment in the county jail not exceeding one year, or by both that fine and imprisonment.

(3) Any person who violates paragraph (6), (7), or (8) of subdivision (c) is punishable as follows:

(A) For a first violation which does not result in injury, an infraction punishable by a fine not exceeding two hundred fifty dollars ($250).

(B) For any violation which results in a victim expenditure in an amount not greater than five thousand dollars ($5,000), or for a second or subsequent violation, by a fine not exceeding five thousand dollars ($5,000), or by imprisonment in the county jail not exceeding one year, or by both that fine and imprisonment.

(C) For any violation which results in a victim expenditure in an amount greater than five thousand dollars ($5,000), by a fine not exceeding ten thousand dollars ($10,000), or by imprisonment in the state prison for 16 months, or two or three years, or by both that fine and imprisonment, or by a fine not exceeding five thousand dollars ($5,000), or by imprisonment in the county jail not exceeding one year, or by both that fine and imprisonment.

(e)

    (1) In addition to any other civil remedy available, the owner or lessee of the computer, computer system, computer network, computer program, or data may bring a civil action against any person convicted under this section for compensatory damages, including any expenditure reasonably and necessarily incurred by the owner or lessee to verify that a computer system, computer network, computer program, or data was or was not altered, damaged, or deleted by the access. For the purposes of actions authorized by this subdivision, the conduct of an unemancipated minor shall be imputed to the parent or legal guardian having control or custody of the minor, pursuant to the provisions of Section 1714.1 of the Civil Code.

    (2) In any action brought pursuant to this subdivision the court may award reasonable attorney's fees to a prevailing party.

    (3) A community college, state university, or academic institution accredited in this state is required to include computer related crimes as a specific violation of college or university student conduct policies and regulations that may subject a student to disciplinary sanctions up to and including dismissal from the academic institution. This paragraph shall not apply to the University of California unless the Board of Regents adopts a resolution to that effect.

(f) This section shall not be construed to preclude the applicability of any other provision of the criminal law of this state which applies or may apply to any transaction, nor shall it make illegal any employee labor relations activities that are within the scope and protection of state or federal labor laws.

(g) Any computer, computer system, computer network, or any software or data, owned by the defendant, which is used during the commission of any public offense described in subdivision (c) or any computer, owned by the defendant, which is used as a repository for the storage of software or data illegally obtained in violation of subdivision (c) shall be subject to forfeiture, as specified in Section 502.01.

(h)

    (1) Subdivision (c) does not apply to any person who accesses his or her employer's computer system, computer network, computer program, or data when acting within the scope of his or her lawful employment.

    (2) Paragraph (3) of subdivision (c) does not apply to any employee who accesses or uses his or her employer's computer system, computer network, computer program, or data when acting outside the scope of his or her lawful employment, so long as the employee's activities do not cause an injury, as defined in paragraph (8) of subdivision (b), to the employer or another, or so long as the value of supplies and computer services, as defined in paragraph (4) of subdivision (b), which are used do not exceed an accumulated total of one hundred dollars ($100).

(i) No activity exempted from prosecution under paragraph (2) of subdivision (h) which incidentally violates paragraph (2), (4), or (7) of subdivision (c) shall be prosecuted under those paragraphs.

(j) For purposes of bringing a civil or a criminal action under this section, a person who causes, by any means, the access of a computer, computer system, or computer network in one jurisdiction from another jurisdiction is deemed to have personally accessed the computer, computer system, or computer network in each jurisdiction.

(k) In determining the terms and conditions applicable to a person convicted of a violation of this section the court shall consider the following:

   (1) The court shall consider prohibitions on access to and use of computers.
   (2) Except as otherwise required by law, the court shall consider alternate sentencing, including community service, if the defendant shows remorse and recognition of the wrongdoing, and an inclination not to repeat the offense.

Penal Code 502.01—Property Used in Computer Crimes; Forfeiture

(a) As used in this section:

   (1) *Property subject to forfeiture* means any property of the defendant that is a computer, computer system, or computer network, and any software or data residing thereon, if the computer, computer system, or computer network was used in committing a violation of subdivision (c) of Section 502 or a violation of Section 502.7 or was used as a repository for the storage of software or data obtained in violation of those provisions. If the defendant is a minor, it also includes property of the parent or guardian of the defendant.
   (2) *Sentencing court* means the court sentencing a person found guilty of violating subdivision (c) of Section 502 or a violation of Section 502.7 or, in the case of a minor found to be a person described in Section 602 of the Welfare and Institutions Code because of a violation of those provisions, the juvenile court.
   (3) *Interest* means any property interest in the property subject to forfeiture.
   (4) Security interest means an interest that is a lien, mortgage, security interest, or interest under a conditional sales contract.
   (5) *Value* has the following meanings:

      (A) When counterfeit items of computer software are manufactured or possessed for sale, the "value" of those items shall be equivalent to the retail price or fair market price of the true items that are counterfeited.
      (B) When counterfeited but unassembled components of computer software packages are recovered, including, but not limited to, counterfeited computer diskettes, instruction manuals, or licensing envelopes, the "value" of those components of computer software packages shall be equivalent to the retail price or fair market price of the number of completed computer software packages that could have been made from those components.

(b) The sentencing court shall, upon petition by the prosecuting attorney, at any time following sentencing, or by agreement of all parties, at the time of sentencing, conduct a hearing to determine whether any property or property interest is subject to forfeiture under this section. At the forfeiture hearing, the prosecuting attorney shall have the burden of establishing, by a preponderance of the evidence, that the property or property interests are subject to forfeiture. The prosecuting attorney may retain seized property that may be subject to forfeiture until the sentencing hearing.

(c) Prior to the commencement of a forfeiture proceeding, the law enforcement agency seizing the property subject to forfeiture shall make an investigation as to any person other than the defendant who may have an interest in it. At least 30 days before the hearing to determine whether the property should be forfeited, the prosecuting agency shall send notice of the hearing to any person who may have an interest in the property that arose before the seizure.

A person claiming an interest in the property shall file a motion for the redemption of that interest at least 10 days before the hearing on forfeiture, and shall send a copy of the motion to the prosecuting agency and to the probation department.

If a motion to redeem an interest has been filed, the sentencing court shall hold a hearing to identify all persons who possess valid interests in the property. No person shall hold a valid interest in the property if, by a preponderance of the evidence, the prosecuting agency shows that the person knew or should have known that the property was being used in violation of subdivision (c) of Section 502 or Section 502.7, and that the person did not take reasonable steps to prevent that use, or if the interest is a security interest, the person knew or should have known at the time that the security interest was created that the property would be used for a violation.

(d) If the sentencing court finds that a person holds a valid interest in the property, the following provisions shall apply:

(1) The court shall determine the value of the property.

(2) The court shall determine the value of each valid interest in the property.

(3) If the value of the property is greater than the value of the interest, the holder of the interest shall be entitled to ownership of the property upon paying the court the difference between the value of the property and the value of the valid interest.

If the holder of the interest declines to pay the amount determined under paragraph (2), the court may order the property sold and designate the prosecutor or any other agency to sell the property. The designated agency shall be entitled to seize the property and the holder of the interest shall forward any documentation underlying the interest, including any ownership certificates for that property, to the designated agency. The designated agency shall sell the property and pay the owner of the interest the proceeds, up to the value of that interest.

(4) If the value of the property is less than the value of the interest, the designated agency shall sell the property and pay the owner of the interest the proceeds, up to the value of that interest.

(e) If the defendant was a minor at the time of the offense, this subdivision shall apply to property subject to forfeiture that is the property of the parent or guardian of the minor.

(1) The prosecuting agency shall notify the parent or guardian of the forfeiture hearing at least 30 days before the date set for the hearing.

(2) The computer shall not be subject to forfeiture if the parent or guardian files a signed statement with the court at least 10 days before the date set for the hearing that the minor shall not have access to any computer owned by the parent or guardian for two years after the date on which the minor is sentenced.

(3) If the minor is convicted of a violation of subdivision (c) of Section 502 or Section 502.7 within two years after the date on which the minor is sentenced, and the violation involves a computer owned by the parent or guardian, the original property subject to forfeiture, and the property involved in the new offense, shall be subject to forfeiture notwithstanding paragraph (2).

(f) If the defendant is found to have the only valid interest in the property subject to forfeiture, it shall be distributed as follows:

(1) First, to the victim, if the victim elects to take the property as full or partial restitution for injury, victim expenditures, or compensatory damages, as defined in paragraph (1) of subdivision (e) of Section 502. If the victim elects to receive the property under this paragraph, the value of the property shall be determined by the court and that amount shall be credited against the restitution owed by the defendant. The victim shall not be penalized for electing not to accept the forfeited property in lieu of full or partial restitution.

(2) Second, at the discretion of the court, to one or more of the following agencies or entities:

(A) The prosecuting agency.
(B) The public entity of which the prosecuting agency is a part.
(C) The public entity whose officers or employees conducted the investigation resulting in forfeiture.
(D) Other state and local public entities, including school districts.
(E) Nonprofit charitable organizations.

(g) If the property is to be sold, the court may designate the prosecuting agency or any other agency to sell the property at auction. The proceeds of the sale shall be distributed by the court as follows:

(1) To the bona fide or innocent purchaser or encumbrancer, conditional sales vendor, or mortgagee of the property up to the amount of his or her interest in the property, if the court orders a distribution to that person.
(2) The balance, if any, to be retained by the court, subject to the provisions for distribution under subdivision (f).

17-4 Theft of Trade Secrets by Use of a Computer

Penal Code 499(c), which involves the theft of trade secrets, was modified in 1996 to include the theft of computer data and related computer programs.

Penal Code 499(c)—Theft of Trade Secrets

(a) [Definitions (1) to (8) omitted. Definitions omitted similar to those set forth in PC 502 in the preceding Section 17-3 .]

(9) *Trade secret* means information, including a formula, pattern, compilation, program, device, method, technique, or process, that:

(A) Derives independent economic value, actual or potential, from not being generally known to the public or to other persons who can obtain economic value from its disclosure or use; and
(B) Is the subject of efforts that are reasonable under the circumstances to maintain its secrecy.

(b) Every person is guilty of theft who, with intent to deprive or withhold the control of a trade secret from its owner, or with an intent to appropriate a trade secret to his or her own use or to the use of another, does any of the following:

(1) Steals, takes, carries away, or uses without authorization, a trade secret.
(2) Fraudulently appropriates any article representing a trade secret entrusted to him or her.
(3) Having unlawfully obtained access to the article, without authority makes or causes to be made a copy of any article representing a trade secret.
(4) Having obtained access to the article through a relationship of trust and confidence, without authority and in breach of the obligations created by that relationship, makes or causes to be made, directly from and in the presence of the article, a copy of any article representing a trade secret.

17-5 Other Computer Crimes

Penal Code 350 deals with counterfeit trademarks. That section also makes it a crime for any person who, without the consent of the registrant, willfully manufactures, intentionally sells, or knowingly possesses for sale at the point of sale any counterfeit computer parts. That section also provides that when counterfeited but unassembled components of computer software packages are recovered, including, but not limited to, counterfeited computer diskettes, instruction manuals, or licensing envelopes, the number of "articles" shall be equivalent to the number of completed computer software packages that could have been made from those components.

PC 311.11, which makes it illegal for any person to knowingly possess or control any matter depicting sexual conduct of a person under the age of 14 years, expressly includes the possession or control of computer hardware, computer software, computer floppy disc, data storage media, CD-ROM, or computer-generated equipment.

PC 311.3 provides that a person is guilty of sexual exploitation of a child if he or she knowingly develops, duplicates, prints, or exchanges any representation of information, data, or image, including, but not limited to, any film, filmstrip, photograph, negative, slide, photocopy, videotape, video laser disc, computer hardware, computer software, computer floppy disc, data storage media, CD-ROM, or computer-generated equipment or any other computer-generated image that contains or incorporates in any manner, any film or filmstrip that depicts a person under the age of 18 years engaged in an act of sexual conduct.

PC 484(j) covers the publishing of computer codes and so on. That section provides that any person who publishes the number or code of an existing, canceled, revoked, expired, or nonexistent access card, personal identification number, computer password, access code, debit card number, bank account number, or the numbering or coding that is employed in the issuance of access cards, with the intent that it be used or with knowledge or reason to believe that it will be used to avoid the payment of any lawful charge, or with intent to defraud or aid another in defrauding, is guilty of a misdemeanor. As used in this section, "publishes" means the communication of information to any one or more persons, either orally, in person, or by telephone, radio, or television, or on a computer network or computer bulletin board, or in a writing of any kind, including without limitation a letter or memorandum, circular or handbill, newspaper or magazine article, or book.

Practicum
Practicum

Wayne copies computer programs and gives them to his friends. What crimes has he committed. Have his friends committed any crimes by accepting and using those copied programs?

Discussion Questions
Discussion Questions

1. Explain how computer crimes generally differ from noncomputer-related crimes.
2. What are some of the practical problems involved in prosecuting traditional crimes that are committed by the use of a computer?
3. What is the legal definition of a computer? Computer program?
4. How have computers assisted in solving crimes?
5. Explain the attorney general's responsibilities in regard to maintaining computer data bases.

Self-Study Quiz
Self-Study Quiz

True/False

1. Few computer-generated crimes are considered traditional crimes.
2. Computer misconduct may, in many cases, be prosecuted as a traditional crime.
3. The governor's office is required by statute to maintain a computer listing of missing children.
4. The attorney general has a duty to disclose information regarding a pending investigation, even if such disclosure would endanger an individual's safety.
5. The phrase "critical missing child" is limited to those cases where the child is missing and there is evidence that the child is at risk.
6. The unauthorized access to a computer database may constitute criminal behavior.
7. A computer network definition is limited to computer terminals and printers that are connected together.
8. *Computer system* means a device or collection of devices, including support devices and calculators, that are not programmable and capable of being used in conjunction with external files, one or more of which contain computer programs, electronic instructions, input data, and output data.
9. *Data* mean a representation of information, knowledge, facts, concepts, computer software, computer programs, or instructions.
10. Data may be in any form—storage media, stored in the memory of the computer, in transit, or presented on a display device.
11. *Computer contaminant* means any set of computer instructions that are designed to modify, damage, destroy, record, or transmit information within a computer, computer system, or computer network without the intent or permission of the owner of the information.
12. A community college, state university, or academic institution accredited in California, including the University of California, is required by statute to include computer-related crimes as a specific violation of college or university student conduct policies and regulations.

Codes Index

396   Codes Index

Subject Index